Resources for Teaching ELEMENTARY SCHOOL Science

NATIONAL SCIENCE RESOURCES CEN

The National Science Resources Center (NSRC)
the National Academy of Sciences and the
Institution to improve the teaching of science in
schools. The NSRC collects and dissemi
about exemplary teaching resources, develops and
nates curriculum materials, and sponsors outreach ac
specifically in the areas of leadership development an
nical assistance, to help school districts develop an
hands-on science programs. The NSRC is located in the
and Industries Building of the Smithsonian Institution
the Capital Gallery Building in Washington, D.C.

NATIONAL ACADEMY OF SCIENCES

The National Academy of Sciences is a private, nonprofit, self-perpetuating society of distinguished scholars engaged in scientific and engineering research, dedicated to the furtherance of science and technology and to their use for the general welfare. Upon the authority of the charter granted to it by the Congress in 1863, the Academy has a mandate that requires it to advise the federal government on scientific and technical matters. Dr. Bruce M. Alberts is president of the National Academy of Sciences.

NATIONAL RESEARCH COUNCIL

The National Research Council was organized by the National Academy of Sciences in 1916 to associate the broad community of science and technology with the Academy's purposes of furthering knowledge and advising the federal government. Functioning in accordance with general policies determined by the Academy, the Council has become the principal operating agency of both the National Academy of Sciences and the National Academy of Engineering in providing services to the government, the public, and the scientific and engineering communities. The Council is administered jointly by both Academies and the Institute of Medicine. Dr. Bruce M. Alberts and Dr. Harold Liebowitz are chairman and vice chairman, respectively, of the National Research Council.

SMITHSONIAN INSTITUTION

The Smithsonian Institution was created by act of Congress in 1846 in accordance with the will of Englishman James Smithson, who in 1826 bequeathed his property to the United States of America, "to found at Washington, under the name of the Smithsonian Institution, an establishment for the increase and diffusion of knowledge among men." The Smithsonian has since evolved into an institution devoted to public education, research, and national service in the arts, sciences, and history. This independent federal establishment is the world's largest museum complex and is responsible for public and scholarly activities, exhibitions, and research projects nationwide and overseas.

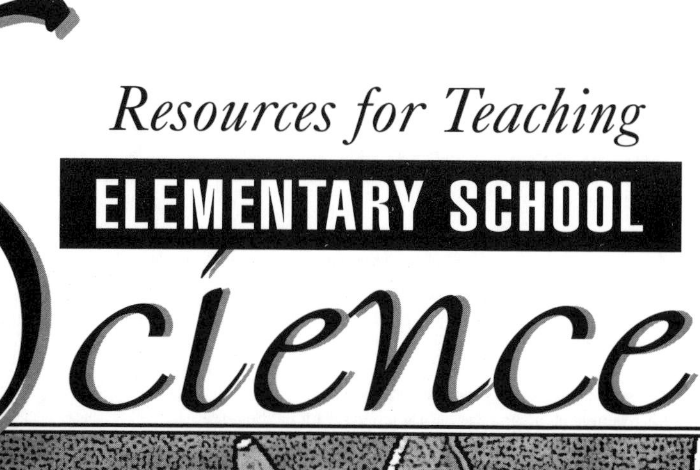

Resources for Teaching Elementary School Science

NATIONAL SCIENCE RESOURCES CENTER
National Academy of Sciences
Smithsonian Institution

NATIONAL ACADEMY PRESS
Washington, D.C. 1996

NATIONAL ACADEMY PRESS • 2101 Constitution Avenue, N.W. • Washington, D.C. 20418

NOTICE: *Resources for Teaching Elementary School Science* is a completely revised and updated edition of its predecessor volume—*Science for Children: Resources for Teachers,* which was developed and produced by the National Science Resources Center and published by the National Academy Press in 1988.

The views expressed in this book are solely those of its contributors and do not necessarily reflect the views of the National Academy of Sciences or the Smithsonian Institution.

Every effort was made to ensure the accuracy of information presented in this volume. The National Science Resources Center makes no representation that the information in this guide is absolutely without error.

Library of Congress Cataloging-in-Publication Data

Resources for teaching elementary school science / National Science Resources Center, National Academy of Sciences, Smithsonian Institution.

p. cm.

Rev. ed. of: Science for children. 1988.

Includes indexes.

ISBN 0-309-05293-9

1. Science—Study and teaching (Elementary)—United States—Bibliography. I. National Science Resources Center (U.S.) II. Science for children.

Z5818.S3R47 1996

[LB1585]

372.3′5044—dc19 —dc20 95-26429

CIP

Printed in the United States of America

National Science Resources Center

Arts and Industries Building, Room 1201
Smithsonian Institution
Washington, D.C. 20560

Douglas Lapp, Executive Director
Charles N. Hardy, Deputy Director for Information Dissemination, Materials Development, and Publications
Sally Goetz Shuler, Deputy Director for Development, External Relations, and Outreach
Evelyn M. Ernst, Information Dissemination Director
Dean Trackman, Publications Director

Project Development Team

Evelyn M. Ernst, Director
Barbara K. Johnson, Research Associate
Terence Proctor, Information Technology Specialist
Dorothy Sawicki, Project Managing Editor
Theodore D. Schultz, Program Officer, Networking
Sharon Seaward, Program Assistant
Rita C. Warpeha, Resource/Database Specialist
Max-Karl Winkler, Cover Illustrations
Jonathan Kronstadt, Writer Consultant
Abigail Porter, Writer Consultant

Cover and photo credits appear on p. 289.

National Academy Press

Sally Stanfield, Editorial Coordination
Francesca Moghari, Cover Design
Liz Clark, Isely &/or Clark Design, Book Design
Linda C. Humphrey, Page Layout

NATIONAL SCIENCE RESOURCES CENTER ADVISORY BOARD

Contents

PART 4. ANCILLARY RESOURCES FOR ELEMENTARY SCIENCE TEACHERS

APPENDIXES

Foreword

In late 1995, the National Research Council completed the development of the *National Science Education Standards,* accomplishing an important task that was first requested by the governors of our nation's 50 states in 1989. Designed to guide the teaching of science in kindergarten through twelfth grade, these *Standards* provide a concrete vision of what is needed to achieve excellence in science education in the United States. The vision in the *Standards* reflects the consensus of the thousands of teachers, scientists, science educators, and other experts across the country who authored and critiqued its successive drafts.

The *Standards* specify the understandings and abilities that all students should achieve by the end of the fourth, eighth, and twelfth grades. They deal with science content, emphasizing that this content can be taught through the use of many different curricula. At the same time, they recognize the importance of carefully designed curriculum units that have been tested by teachers and shown to be effective in promoting student understanding. To help parents, teachers, schools, and school districts select outstanding curricula for the science education of their children, we are now pleased to introduce the publication *Resources for Teaching Elementary School Science.*

Developed by the National Science Resources Center (NSRC), *Resources for Teaching Elementary School Science* is a guide packed with carefully gathered and reviewed information about hands-on, inquiry-based curriculum materials and resources for teaching science in kindergarten through sixth grade. It will help teachers implement the principles contained in the *National Science Education Standards,* because it is based on the same fundamental tenets: the need for active inquiry and the critical importance of teaching for understanding, as science becomes a core activity in every grade—from kindergarten through high school.

The NSRC has made many significant contributions to science education reform since its inception in 1985. In addition to the development of science curriculum materials, the Center has been active in other areas of curriculum reform, including information dissemination, leadership development, and technical assistance to school districts. It plans to develop volumes similar to this one to aid middle school and high school science teaching in the not-too-distant future.

As NSRC's sponsoring organizations, the National Academy of Sciences and the Smithsonian Institution take great pride in the issuance of this publication. Producing a system of science education that prepares all of America's children for a productive and fulfilling life in the twenty-first century will be a lengthy, and sometimes slow and difficult process—for the *National Science Education Standards* constitute a call for a revolution in science education, and such fundamental changes take time. Good hands-on, inquiry-based science curricula are a crucial component of this effort to improve our schools, and we view *Resources for Teaching Elementary School Science* as a landmark book for all those interested in the education of children.

Bruce M. Alberts
President
National Academy of Sciences

I. Michael Heyman
Secretary
Smithsonian Institution

PREFACE

ON BEHALF of the National Science Resources Center (NSRC), I am pleased to introduce readers to this new volume, *Resources for Teaching Elementary School Science*. It replaces *Science for Children: Resources for Teachers* as the NSRC's current guide to hands-on, inquiry-centered elementary school science curriculum materials and resources. Although important changes have been made in this completely updated and revised edition, it retains many important elements of the original, as well as its spirit and purpose—namely, to help elementary school teachers teach science more effectively in their classrooms.

The NSRC produced the first edition of the guide in 1988, and that volume became a valued resource almost immediately. Since 1988, elementary science curriculum materials have proliferated and efforts in science education reform have taken on new intensity, culminating recently in the publication of the landmark *National Science Education Standards* from the National Research Council.

Resources for Teaching Elementary School Science was under development at the same time that work on the *National Science Education Standards* was proceeding, and the NSRC has endeavored to ensure that the new resource guide will be responsive to the recommendations in that historic document. The guide is designed to provide teachers, principals, school district administrators, and others with up-to-date information on curriculum materials that are consonant with the principles advocated in the *Standards*. These principles include an emphasis on student inquiry, teaching for understanding, and the inclusion of science as a core subject in every grade, starting in kindergarten.

We at the NSRC believe that this new edition of *Resources for Teaching Elementary School Science* responds to a critical need in science education today. The sheer volume of science curriculum materials now available can be daunting for individual teachers and for school systems trying to select the most effective materials for their specific needs.

Although there is a broad range of science teaching resources that are available to serve the needs of elementary school teachers, the quality of these published materials varies greatly. Authoritative guidance in evaluating materials is essential to making sound decisions, and the complication of evaluating the science content, together with the hands-on, inquiry-based aspects of materials, requires special expertise. For all these reasons, *Resources for Teaching Elementary School Science* can be a productive and time-saving tool for teachers and school districts, and ultimately, of course, of great benefit to their students.

To select the curriculum materials to be included in this new guide, the NSRC, which is operated jointly by the National Academy of Sciences and the Smithsonian Institution, established an extensive, rigorous review process. This process required the development of criteria by which reviewers could assess instructional materials. The evaluation criteria established by the NSRC for this purpose were informed by the emerging National

Science Education Standards and are consistent with the philosophy and the basic principles articulated in the standards. (These evaluation criteria appear in Appendix B in this volume and can be used independently by teachers and school districts for assessing curriculum materials.)

Among directories and databases of elementary school science curriculum materials, *Resources for Teaching Elementary School Science* is unique for basing its selection of materials on a formal review process. This review was carried out in two phases, involving a panel of teacher reviewers and a panel of scientist reviewers. (The review process is described in the Introduction to the Guide; the reviewers are listed in the Acknowledgments.)

With respect to the structure of the new book, *Resources for Teaching Elementary School Science* retains the major sections and useful indexes of the previous edition. The chapter now called "Museums and Other Places to Visit" has been expanded considerably. The redesign of the interior of the book includes mechanical adjustments to make the information in the guide more accessible to readers. An example is the use of a system of entry numbers for the annotations to help locate them easily.

This new edition lists and annotates materials and resources for kindergarten through sixth grade. Readers may be pleased to note that the NSRC plans to develop guides for middle school and high school in the not-too-distant future.

Inspiration for the 1988 edition of this reference volume can be attributed to Sally Goetz Shuler, NSRC's Deputy Director for Development, External Relations, and Outreach, who recognized the need for such a book almost 10 years ago.

Building on the strengths of the previous edition, Evelyn M. Ernst, NSRC Program Director for Information Dissemination and general editor of *Resources for Teaching Elementary School Science,* joined NSRC to direct this project. Working with her staff and with Chuck Hardy, the NSRC Deputy Director for Information Dissemination, Materials Development, and Publications, she has guided the project through all phases of development—from formulation of the evaluation criteria through panel review to publication.

We would like to thank the NSRC's parent institutions, the National Academy of Sciences and the Smithsonian Institution, for their vision and support in helping NSRC undertake this project. We look forward to hearing from users of the volume as to its effectiveness in meeting their needs, together with any suggestions they may have for its improvement.

DOUGLAS LAPP
Executive Director
National Science Resources Center
January 1996

ACKNOWLEDGMENTS

PRODUCING *Resources for Teaching Elementary School Science* has been an immense undertaking and a rewarding one. It could not have been accomplished without the hard work and dedication of a core group of staff, combined with the efforts of a large number of reviewers, consultants, volunteers, and other professionals.

The National Science Resources Center (NSRC) is grateful to its Advisory Board, whose membership is listed at the beginning of this book, for its continued guidance and direction. Special appreciation is extended to the members of the Executive Committee—Ann Bay, Hubert M. Dyasi, Robert M. Fitch, Lynn Margulis, John A. Moore, and Carlo Parravano—for their helpful comments on the final manuscript.

This edition of the guide was brought to fruition with support from Bayer Foundation, Bristol-Myers Squibb Foundation, Inc., Digital Equipment Corporation, The Dow Chemical Company Foundation, Hewlett-Packard Company, the National Science Foundation, and the U.S. Department of Education. The U.S. Department of Education and the U.S. Department of Defense also provided support for the first edition.

Special thanks go to Evelyn M. Ernst, project director and general editor, and to her staff and to the consultants who participated in the work on the volume. Barbara K. Johnson contributed to the development of the curriculum and teacher reference sections and assisted with the logistics of the second phase of the curriculum materials review process. Theodore Schultz surveyed museums, professional organizations, and other institutions and drafted annotations for these sections of the guide. Rita C. Warpeha, with the assistance of consultants Lorraine Hayes and Russell Smith, cataloged and researched the many materials received for review. Terence Proctor, NSRC information technology specialist, provided technical support. Sharon Seaward assisted staff and provided logistical support during all aspects of the project. Consultants Jonathan Kronstadt and Abigail Porter and NSRC staff member Lynn Miller drafted annotations. Michaela Oldfield assisted with manuscript preparation. Dorothy Sawicki served as developmental and managing editor for the resource guide and drafted overview and introductory material.

The NSRC appreciates the assistance of the many hundreds of organizations and individuals who contributed time and effort to the information-gathering and review stages of the manuscript. Thanks go to reviewers of the final manuscript, Joyce Dutcher, Instructional Specialist in Elementary Science/Health with Fort Bend Independent School District in Sugar Land, Tex.; and to Becky Smith, Elementary Science/Social Sciences Curriculum Materials Editor with Mesa Public Schools in Mesa, Ariz. NSRC also acknowledges with gratitude the technical review of the chapter "Museums and Other Places to Visit" carried out by the Association of Science-Technology Centers under the direction of Bonnie Van Dorn and Ellen Griffee.

And, finally, this guide would not have been possible without the support of the many teachers and scientists who reviewed curriculum materials. Following are lists of their names and affiliations.

TEACHER REVIEW PANEL

SEAN DUFFY
Teacher, Fairfax County Public Schools, Flint Hill Elementary School, Vienna, Va.

ANNETTE EDLER
Science Teacher/Coordinator, Prince Georges County Public Schools, Potomac Landing Elementary School, Fort Washington, Md.

PAMELA I. ELLISON
Teacher, Fairfax County Public Schools, Hayfield Secondary/Intermediate School, Alexandria, Va.

DOREEN L. HALL
Teacher, Montgomery County Public Schools, Brookhaven Elementary School, Rockville, Md.

DARLENE HAZEN
Teacher, Fairfax County Public Schools, Kings Park Elementary School, Springfield, Va.

SUSANNE JERDE
Teacher, Highline School District, Sunnydale Elementary School, Seattle, Wash.

DON JOHNSON
Teacher, Fort Bend Independent School District, Settlers Way Elementary School, Sugar Land, Tex.

DEBRA L. JONES
Science Curriculum Specialist, Fairfax County Public Schools, Fairfax, Va.

SANDRA L. KLEIN
Teacher, Highline School District, Parkside Primary School, Des Moines, Wash.

NANCY MASTERSON
Teacher, Mesa Public Schools, Taft Elementary School, Mesa, Ariz.

PATRICIA MCCLURE
Science Program Specialist, Fairfax County Public Schools, Fairfax, Va.

ANNE MARIE MILNER
Teacher, Fort Bend Independent School District, Barrington Place Elementary, Sugar Land, Tex.

SHIRLEY MITCHELL
Teacher, Arlington Public Schools, Jamestown Elementary School, Arlington, Va.

HELEN C. MURPHY
Teacher, Montgomery County Public Schools, Summit Hall Elementary School, Gaithersburg, Md.

MARY ANN PETERSON
Teacher, Arlington Public Schools, Williamsburg Middle School, Arlington, Va.

DEBRA S. REEDER
Teacher, Fairfax County Public Schools, Clifton Elementary School, Clifton, Va.

KITTY LOU SMITH
Teacher, Fairfax County Public Schools, West Springfield High School, Springfield, Va.

ROGER SPRATT
Teacher Specialist for Health/Science/Mathematics, Mesa Public Schools, Ariz.

LAURIE THOMPSON
Resource Teacher, Project SEED, Pasadena Unified School District, Pasadena, Calif.

MARY COLLEEN THOMPSON
Teacher, Fort Bend Independent School District, Settlers Way Elementary School, Sugar Land, Tex.

MARY T. TSOTSIS
Resource Teacher, Project SEED, Pasadena Unified School District, Pasadena, Calif.

GWENDOLYN M. WILLIAMS
Teacher, Fairfax County Public Schools, Silverbrook Elementary School, Fairfax Station, Va.

EUGENE F. WILSON
Teacher, Clara Barton Center for Children, Cabin John, Md.

SCIENTIST REVIEW PANEL

LENA AUSTIN
Associate Professor, Department of Microbiology, Howard University, Washington, D.C.

EARL BLOCH
Associate Professor, Howard University Medical School, Washington, D.C.

WILLIAM C. BURTON
Geologist, U.S. Geological Survey, Reston, Va.

EARL CALLEN
Professor Emeritus, Department of Physics, American University, Washington, D.C.

IDA CHOW
Assistant Professor, Department of Biology, American University, Washington, D.C.; and Executive Officer, Society for Developmental Biology, Bethesda, Md.

ANNA COBLE
Associate Professor, Department of Physics and Astrophysics, Howard University, Washington, D.C.; and President, Minority Women in Science, Washington, D.C.

ELAINE DAVIS
Assistant Professor, Department of Biology, Howard University, Washington, D.C.

RICHARD DIECCHIO
Associate Professor of Geology, Department of Geography and Earth Systems Science, George Mason University, Fairfax, Va.

LAFAYETTE FREDERICK
Professor (retired), Department of Biology, Howard University, Washington, D.C.

DAVID HERSHEY
Adjunct Faculty Member, Prince Georges County Community College, Hyattsville, Md.

PHILIP B. JOHNSON
Physicist, Loral Corporation, Manassas, Va.

HOWARD KAPLAN
Retired, Department of Biology and Environmental Science, University of the District of Columbia, Washington, D.C.

DONALD KELSO
Associate Professor, Department of Biology, George Mason University, Fairfax, Va.

RAMON LOPEZ
Associate Research Scientist, Department of Astronomy, University of Maryland, College Park, Md.; and Director of Education and Outreach, The American Physical Society, College Park, Md.

IRWIN MANNING
Physicist (retired), Naval Research Laboratory, Bethesda, Md.

EDWARD MAX
Molecular Biologist, Center for Biologic Evaluation and Research, Food and Drug Administration, Bethesda, Md.

GEORGE MUSHRUSH
Professor and Chair, Department of Chemistry, George Mason University, Fairfax, Va.

JOSEPH NEALE
Professor and Chair, Department of Biology, Georgetown University, Washington, D.C.

JOHN POJETA
Geologist, U.S. Geological Survey, Washington, D.C.

LARRY ROCKWOOD
Associate Professor, Department of Biology, George Mason University, Fairfax, Va.

JAY SHAFFER
Professor, Department of Biology, George Mason University, Fairfax, Va.

TOPPER SHUTT
Meteorologist, WUSA TV, Channel 9, Washington, D.C.

GERALDINE TWITTY
Assistant Professor, Department of Biology, Howard University, Washington, D.C.

DAVID WILLIAMS
Adjunct Faculty Member, Department of Chemistry, George Mason University, Fairfax, Va.

NANCY ZELLER
Adjunct Professor, Department of Biology, American University, Washington, D.C.

PART 1

INTRODUCTION TO THE GUIDE

Observing a Bess beetle

Part 1

Few decisions have greater impact on the effectiveness of science teaching in the nation's schools than the process of selecting instructional materials. This selection determines to a large extent what will or will not be taught to children; it establishes the basis of teachers' professional growth opportunities in science instruction; and it accounts for major budget outlays for school systems.

Yet it is difficult for entire school districts, let alone individual classroom teachers, to find the time and resources to research the ever-growing volume of available curriculum materials, to assess them for scientific content and processes, and to arrive at the combination of materials suitable for their needs. Schools and teachers need authoritative information that addresses the educational and scientific aspects of teaching elementary school science to help make their selections.

In response to this need, the National Science Resources Center (NSRC), sponsored jointly by the National Academy of Sciences and the Smithsonian Institution, has produced *Resources for Teaching Elementary School Science*—an annotated guide to hands-on, inquiry-centered curriculum materials and sources of information and assistance for teaching elementary school science. This new volume is a completely revised and updated edition of the NSRC's best-selling resource guide, *Science for Children: Resources for Teachers.* The new edition focuses on curriculum materials published between 1985 and 1995 for kindergarten through sixth grade and on sources of information relevant to teaching science in the same grades.

The goal of the National Science Resources Center in developing *Resources for Teaching Elementary School Science* is to help teachers teach science more effectively. Thus, the NSRC has brought together in one source a list of carefully reviewed and selected materials and resources. These curriculum materials and other resources support inquiry-based science teaching that fosters understanding of science concepts through hands-on student investigations. Teachers, principals, administrators in schools and school districts, science curriculum specialists, parents, and those involved in systemic reform of science education will find the guide a rich source of current information.

The materials and resources listed can be used to improve an existing program or to design a complete curriculum. It should be emphasized, however, that the guide is not a recipe for an elementary school science program.

Contents of the Guide

Following is a brief description of the contents and organization of the volume. It contains four parts:

- **Part 1:** Introduction to the Guide
- **Part 2:** Elementary School Science Curriculum Materials
- **Part 3:** Teacher's References
- **Part 4:** Ancillary Resources for Elementary Science Teachers

Part 2 contains about 350 individual entries that list and annotate curriculum materials. (The process by which these materials were selected is described below, in the section on "NSRC's Curriculum Evaluation Criteria and Review Process.") The overview in part 2 is followed by four chapters: chapter 1, "Life Science"; chapter 2, "Earth Science"; chapter 3, "Physical Science"; and chapter 4, "Multidisciplinary and Applied Science."

The annotations in these chapters are subdivided in the following categories: Core Materials, Supplementary Materials, and Science Activity Books. (The categories are defined in the part 2 overview.)

Chapter 5, "Curriculum Projects Past and Present," completes part 2, with information on major funded projects in hands-on elementary science over the years dating back to the late 1960s and early 1970s.

Part 3, "Teacher's References," has an overview and three short chapters of annotations: chapter 6, "Books on Teaching Science"; chapter 7, "Science Book Lists and Resource Guides"; and chapter 8, "Periodicals." Chapter 6 is an annotated list of about 50 volumes that provide background information and a broad range of pedagogical resources for good science teaching. Chapter 7 annotates about 25 directories and guides, including guides to science trade books for children and to materials and other resources. Chapter 8 annotates about 35 periodicals, including some magazines for children. The periodicals in the chapter were selected for their excellence as instructional tools, for the high quality of their articles and stories on scientific topics, for their appeal to children, and for their adaptability to classroom use.

Part 4 of the guide—"Ancillary Resources for Elementary Science Teachers"—contains two chapters that focus on facilities, associations, and federal and other organizations that have programs, services, and materials relevant to some aspect of hands-on, inquiry-based elementary school science education. The resources included in chapters 9 and 10 can significantly enhance the effectiveness of science education efforts.

Chapter 9, "Museums and Other Places to Visit," identifies almost 600 facilities—for example, museums, zoos, science and technology centers, and children's museums—to which elementary science teachers can take their classes for hands-on science experiences beyond the classroom. Annotations are provided for about half of those institutions—those considered to be making a significant effort to help teachers teach science more effectively.

Chapter 10, "Professional Associations and U.S. Government Organizations," presents annotated entries for about 120 institutions with a wide range of scientific, educational, and professional missions. The purpose of the chapter is to guide teachers to private and public sources of information, materials, and services that support elementary school science both directly and indirectly, and to identify science education facilities and relevant programs administered by U.S. government organizations.

Finally, the appendixes in the volume include a list of "Publishers and Suppliers" (appendix A) for curriculum materials and other publications annotated in the guide. Appendix B discusses and reproduces the NSRC evaluation criteria formulated for use in the review of curriculum materials.

Multiple indexes are provided to help readers access information quickly and efficiently.

NSRC's Curriculum Evaluation Criteria and Review Process

Consistent with the NSRC's philosophy of science teaching and with the recently published *National Science Education Standards* of the National Research Council, the materials included in this guide are hands-on and inquiry-centered. Briefly described, such materials provide opportunities for children to learn through direct observation and experimentation; they engage students in experiences not simply to confirm the "right" answer but to investigate the nature of things and to arrive at explanations that are scientifically correct and satisfying to children; they offer students opportunities to experiment productively, to ask questions and find their own answers, and to develop patience, persistence, and confidence in their ability to tackle and solve real problems.

To produce evaluation criteria for identifying the most effective print instructional materials available, the NSRC drew upon three primary sources:

- the experience of teachers, superintendents, principals, and science curriculum coordinators across the United States;
- the quality standards identified by the NSRC for evaluating units of science instruction in its ongoing review of science curriculum materials under the auspices of the National Academy of Sciences and the Smithsonian Institution; and
- the National Science Education Standards, which were under development at the same time as this resource guide.

The evaluation criteria that NSRC developed were applied in the structured review of curriculum materials. The criteria consist of two sets of questions. The first focuses on pedagogical issues, the second on science issues.

The pedagogical criteria elaborate on the following key questions: (1) Do the materials address the important goals of elementary science teaching and learning? (2) Are inquiry and activity the basis of the learning experiences? (3) Are the topic of the unit and the modes of instruction developmentally appropriate? Additional issues related to presentation and format and to hands-on science materials are then considered.

The set of criteria on science issues expands upon the key questions of whether the science content is accurate, up to date, and effectively presented. It then focuses on aspects of the way science is presented in the materials—for example, whether the writing style is interesting and engaging while respecting scientific language.

The NSRC evaluation criteria are reprinted in appendix B, "NSRC Evaluation Criteria for Curriculum Materials." Teachers, curriculum specialists, curriculum developers, principals, superintendents, and those involved in various aspects of science education reform may find the criteria not only instructive, but useful as an actual review instrument when the need arises to consider the strengths and weaknesses of particular curriculum materials.

The review process developed by the NSRC for the selection of curriculum materials consisted of two phases:

- **PHASE I:** Teams of experienced teachers and science curriculum specialists reviewed materials for pedagogical appropriateness. Each document received a minimum of two independent reviews. Volumes not recommended in this phase received no further consideration.

Phase I review teams consisted of teachers and science curriculum specialists experienced and knowledgeable in the teaching of elementary school science. Most members of the teams were lead science teachers or master teachers who had taught in school districts with effective science programs. Their backgrounds included participation in numerous science curriculum development activities; they had training and experience teaching children with different learning styles and abilities, and had taught student populations representing diverse cultural and ethnic backgrounds.

Phase I teams included individuals with experience and training in cooperative learning, assessment strategies, the integration of curriculum, and the use of modern technology. Reviewers had experience with a variety of instructional materials for elementary school science programs and were able to use the NSRC evalution criteria effectively to identify differences and to recognize strengths and weaknesses in curriculum materials.

- **PHASE II:** Scientists reviewed the materials recommended in Phase I to determine if their science content is accurate, current, and presented effectively.

Phase II review teams consisted of scientists with expertise in one of four areas—life science, earth science, physical science, and applied science or technology. Every effort was made to match each scientist reviewer with curriculum materials relevant to his or her area of expertise.

The members of the scientist review teams were teaching professors, working scientists, and others with an understanding of precollege science education. Their involvement with precollege students and science took various forms—for example, in judging science fairs, making classroom presentations about science concepts and careers in science, and sharing their science expertise with classroom teachers. Many of the panel members had experience teaching science at undergraduate and graduate levels; some had taught science courses to future teachers.

Materials that passed review by both the teacher and the scientist review panels are annotated in part 2 of the guide. It should be noted that not every individual entry in the guide necessarily meets all the criteria. The NSRC evaluation criteria were designed as a standard to be met, as the ideal level of quality to be sought, and as a working tool that can help inform science curriculum as it is developed. The criteria represent goals—but reachable goals. The curriculum materials included in this guide have accomplished the overall objective of meeting these goals, thereby enhancing the teaching of science through hands-on, inquiry-centered, pedagogically and scientifically sound learning experiences.

The curriculum materials are not ranked or rated here for several reasons. They have all achieved the general objectives set by the criteria. Their inclusion indicates that teachers and scientists have judged them to be effective materials. Beyond that, each item is unique and accomplishes these objectives in its own individual fashion. Ultimately, it is up to teachers and schools to select the particular materials that best fit their needs. Thus, ranking could be misleading—what might be considered exceedingly useful in one classroom might be less so elsewhere because of different needs and circumstances. The full array of materials presented for consideration is meant to offer diversity so that teachers and schools can select what best suits their own needs.

No judgment should be inferred about any elementary science programs, materials, or sources of assistance not included. The guide presents a selected, not an exhaustive, listing of elementary school science curriculum materials.

What Is Not Included in the Guide

Several kinds of teaching resources are not reviewed in *Resources for Teaching Elementary School Science.* Computer software for elementary science, audiovisual materials, science trade books, and elementary science textbooks are not included.

Many excellent science software and audiovisual products exist, can play an important role in the science classroom, and can be integrated with print materials and kits to enrich science teaching. The guide does not undertake to review the vast array of available software programs and audiovisual materials, such as films, videotapes, filmstrips, slides, posters, videodisks, multimedia programs, and so forth. It concentrates instead on print curriculum materials, although some of these also have a software or audiovisual component.

For current information on software and audiovisual products, readers are referred to a software directory and a variety of periodicals and resource guides that feature reviews of audiovisual and computer software materials. (See chapter 7, “Science Book Lists and Resource Guides” and chapter 8, “Periodicals.”)

Resources for Teaching Elementary School Science also does not attempt to review the vast number of science trade books available to enrich children’s knowledge and understanding. Many teachers use such books as an integral part of their science curriculum, and the NSRC urges teachers to supplement hands-on activities in the classroom with extensive reading. For sources of current information on science trade books, readers are referred to chapters 7 and 8.

And, finally, elementary science textbooks, which typically include few opportunities for meaningful hands-on experiences, are not included. Although textbooks are at times used successfully as supplements to inquiry-based science programs, the NSRC believes that an elementary science program should not be centered on the use of a textbook alone. Science is a process and a way of thinking. Both aspects require active participation by the individual learner. Students need to be able to carry out scientific investigations using a wide variety of concrete materials, set up their own experiments, change variables systematically, make accurate observations and measurements, and record and graph data.

Getting Started

Readers with differing experience in the teaching of elementary school science will no doubt use this volume. The National Science Resources Center encourages those wanting to get under way with hands-on inquiry-centered science teaching as well as those experienced in this style of teaching to explore the wide array of materials and resources described here.

Research has shown that most children learn science better and sharpen their problem-solving skills most effectively through hands-on instruction. To teachers who are just getting started with this approach, the NSRC recommends that they begin by introducing hands-on units one at a time into their science classes in order to become more comfortable with this style of teaching. Time and again, that experience has encouraged teachers to expand their hands-on teaching, for they see their students learning science in a way that engages them and offers lasting educational benefits.

Children take natural delight in "doing" science. The National Science Resources Center offers *Resources for Teaching Elementary School Science* in the hope that it will encourage more and more teachers to teach hands-on science and that it will help them to do so successfully.

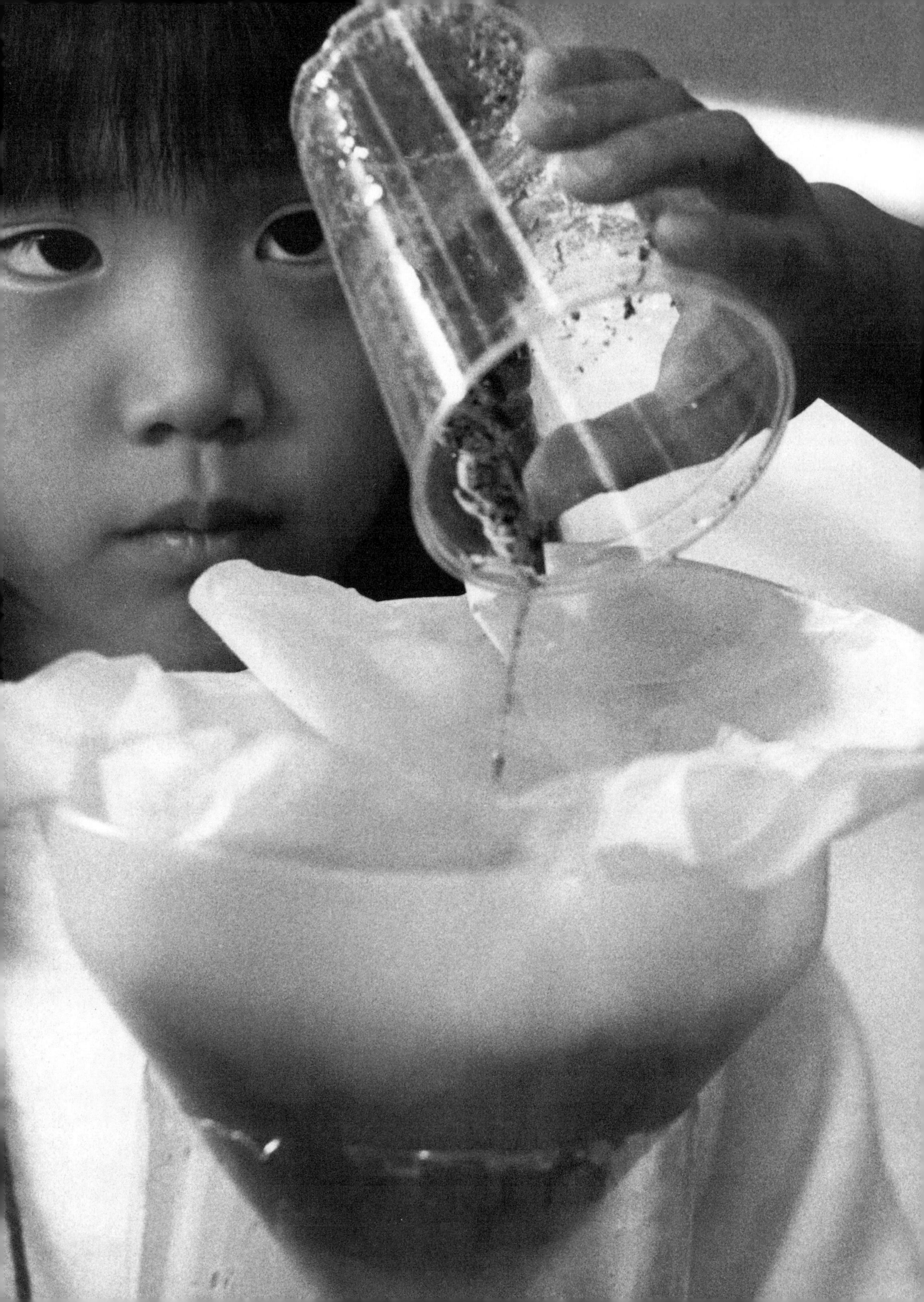

Filtering a solution

PART 2

ELEMENTARY SCHOOL SCIENCE CURRICULUM MATERIALS

Part 2 Overview

Part 2, "Elementary School Science Curriculum Materials," focuses on the subject and the setting that together define the National Science Resources Center's mission—improving the teaching of science in the classroom. The chapters in this part of the book provide annotations to an extensive selection of currently available print curriculum materials produced between 1985 and 1995 for teaching hands-on, inquiry-based science in elementary school, grades kindergarten through six.

As described in the "Introduction to the Guide," an extensive review process involving educators and scientists was the mechanism for selecting the more than 350 individual titles annotated in chapters 1 through 4. These materials are presented by subject area:

- Chapter 1, "Life Science," includes materials on plants, animals, ecology, general biology, and human biology.
- Chapter 2, "Earth Science," includes materials relating to geology, geography, weather, and astronomy.
- Chapter 3, "Physical Science," includes materials on such topics as light and color, sound, electricity, heat, energy, magnetism, density, forces and motion, and equilibrium.
- Chapter 4, "Multidisciplinary and Applied Science," includes materials that relate to several scientific disciplines, integrate scientific disciplines, or focus on the application of scientific processes; interdisciplinary materials are included.

Some curriculum materials concentrate on two or more subject areas. An example would be a unit on the environment that focuses on both life and earth sciences. The annotation for such a unit would appear in chapter 1 if the life science component was emphasized most; it would appear in chapter 2 if greater emphasis was on the earth science component; and it would appear in chapter 4 if the components were emphasized equally, or presented in an integrated format. In other words, the placement of an annotation in a particular chapter in this guide simply attempts to reflect the emphasis in the unit itself. To locate annotations, readers can refer to the various indexes in the guide, including the index of topics in the curriculum materials and the index of scientific areas and categories of the curriculum materials, by grade level.

The Organization of Materials in Chapters 1-4

The annotations in the curriculum chapters are placed in categories that can be identified as three major levels of materials in teaching hands-on, inquiry-based elementary school science:

- **Core Materials**
- **Supplementary Materials**
- **Science Activity Books**

This grouping allows readers organized and easy access to the full array of materials presented in each scientific area. Descriptions of what constitutes "core," "supplementary," and "science activity books" for the purposes of this volume are as follows:

- **Core materials** are substantial enough to form the foundation of an effective elementary school science curriculum. They (1) focus on concept development and understanding; (2) allow students to study a subject in depth over an extended period of time—typically 6 to 8 weeks, depending upon the grade level; (3) are grade-level specific (that is, they were developed for science classes in one, or at most two, specific grade levels); and (4) include a variety of assessment activities that are aligned with the goals of hands-on, inquiry-based science teaching and learning as an integral part of the module.
- **Supplementary materials** are activity-centered units judged to be supportive of inquiry-based science teaching that fosters understanding of science concepts through hands-on student investigations. Although these materials provide support and enrichment, they do not have the depth or focus of core units.
- **Science activity books** offer excellent hands-on science activities for children. Such books provide practical ideas for facilitating science learning but are often too broad in scope or too specific in focus to serve as the foundation of an elementary science program. These materials can be used, however, as supplements to existing curriculum or as independent investigations to enhance children's experience of science.

Placing the materials in categories implies no judgment as to the quality, merit, or desirability of any particular title. All of the materials annotated here are considered to be effective teaching materials.

The Annotations

- **Titles arranged alphabetically and by entry numbers.** The annotations in chapters 1 through 4 are arranged alphabetically by title in each category. In addition, each annotation has a two-part entry number. (The chapter number is given before the period; the number after the period locates the entry within that chapter. For example, the first entry number in chapter 1 is 1.1; the second entry in chapter 2 is 2.2, and so on.) The entry numbers within each curriculum chapter run consecutively through Core Materials, Supplementary Materials, and Science Activity Books. The guide's indexes locate each title by its entry number.
- **"Nuts and bolts"** boxes. Each entry in chapters 1 through 4 includes an annotation, together with bibliographic and ordering information. "Nuts and bolts" details about the bibliographic and ordering information are presented in boxes throughout these chapters. The boxes include lists of spelled-out acronyms of series titles.
- **Bibliographic information.** The bibliographic information is based on the actual volumes reviewed. Some titles may have been revised or updated since materials were submitted for review. Therefore, when readers inquire about a particular title, they may find that a more recent version is available.
- **Grade-level recommendation.** At the beginning of each annotation is the grade level recommended by teacher reviewers during the review process. The recommendation reflects the reviewers' judgment of the levels for which the activities would be most appropriate and successful. In some instances, the grade differs slightly from the publisher's advertised level.
- **Description of the curriculum material.** The curriculum annotations themselves were written specifically to provide information and assistance to those involved in teaching classes and designing programs in elementary school science. These descriptions focus on what students will learn through the module or activity book. Each annotation describes the organization of the piece of curriculum material and the support it provides for teachers.
- **Unit structure and time required for completion.** Information is also given about the structure of a unit and the length of time needed to complete it—for example, the number of lessons or class sessions, the suggested length of lessons, or the overall time required. Such information is taken directly from the unit or activity book itself, although not all units or books state this information consistently.
- **Specific features of units.** For reasons of time and space, the annotations do not attempt to mention every aspect of every module or activity book. For example, they may or may not comment on specifics such as students working in teams or groups unless this is a special focus of the piece. But they do attempt to provide readers with an overall sense of each unit or activity book and to mention specially helpful or unexpected features.

- **Major elements of core materials.** For core materials, the last paragraph of the annotations lists the major elements of the teacher's guides. Readers are referred to the NSRC Evaluation Criteria in appendix B for additional details of what core materials are expected to include.

Curriculum Projects Described in Chapter 5

Chapter 5, "Curriculum Projects Past and Present," completes part 2 of the guide. It presents information on some major funded projects in hands-on elementary science dating back to the 1960s and early 1970s. The chapter provides project descriptions and lists of titles produced by these projects, including projects with publications annotated in this volume. In addition to its value for general readers, the information in chapter 5 may be of particular interest to developers of elementary science curriculum materials.

CHAPTER 1

LIFE SCIENCE

LIFE SCIENCE—CORE MATERIALS

1.1 Animal Studies. STC. Field-test ed. Washington, D.C.: National Science Resources Center, 1995.

Grade: 4 In *Animal Studies,* students explore the relationship between three animals and their respective habitats. The animals are a dwarf African frog, a fiddler crab, and a land snail. Working in small groups, students create a classroom habitat for each organism. They observe how the animals interact with living and nonliving elements in their habitats. Using information from the animal logs they compile, students compare and contrast the animals' structural and behavioral characteristics, which permit the animals to survive and reproduce in their own environments. Becoming familiar with some of the ways animal behaviorists study animals, students record their observations, make drawings, read about actual research studies, research their own questions, and report their findings.

Animal Studies is a 16-lesson unit that requires 8 weeks to complete. The teacher's guide includes a unit overview, the 16 lesson plans, an annotated bibliography of additional resources, and information on maintaining live materials. A student activity book with simple instructions and illustrations accompanies the unit.

The module includes science background information, detailed instructions on planning for and conducting each activity, an extensive assessment component, and extensions for integration and enrichment. Materials are available in a kit.

Prices: Teacher's Guide, $14.95. Student Activity Book, $3.50. Unit, $349.95. ***Publisher/supplier:*** Carolina Biological Supply. ***Materials:*** Available locally, from commercial suppliers, or in unit.

1.2 Animals Two by Two. FOSS. (Developed by Lawrence Hall of Science, Berkeley, Calif.) Chicago, Ill.: Encyclopaedia Britannica Educational Corp., 1993.

Grade: K *Animals Two by Two* provides kindergartners with opportunities to compare four pairs of common land and water animals—guppies and goldfish, land snails and water snails, pillbugs and sowbugs, and small earthworms and large night crawlers. In each of 4 activities, students first observe and care for one animal. Then they are introduced to another animal similar to the first but with differences in structure and behavior. Students compare the structures and behaviors of the two organisms. In a fifth activity, which is optional, students set up a classroom incubator to hatch fertile chicken eggs. The animals are maintained in classroom aquariums and terrariums and are investigated by small groups of students "working alone together" in cooperative learning clusters.

Dissecting an owl pellet

About the Annotations in "Life Science—Core Materials"

Entry Numbers
Curriculum materials are arranged alphabetically by title in each category (Core Materials, Supplementary Materials, and Science Activity Books) in chapters 1 through 4 of this guide. In addition, each annotation has a two-part entry number. For each entry number, the chapter number is given before the period; the number after the period locates the entry within that chapter.

For example, the first entry number in chapter 1 is 1.1; the second entry in chapter 2 is 2.2, and so on.

The entry numbers within each curriculum chapter run consecutively through Core Materials, Supplementary Materials, and Science Activity Books.

Order of Bibliographic Information
Following is the arrangement of the facts of publication in the annotations in this section:

- **Title of publication.**
- **Series title**, or series acronym if commonly used.
- **Authors** (either individual names or organizational author).
- Name and location of **developer** (in parentheses), if different from publisher.
- **Place of publication, publisher, and date of publication.**

Series Acronyms
Following are **acronyms of series titles** in "Life Science—Core Materials." (Series titles that are spelled out are not included in this list.)

FOSS Full Option Science System
SCIS 3 Science Curriculum Improvement Study
STC Science and Technology for Children

Price and Acquisition Information
Ordering information is presented in a block immediately below the annotation. Included are the following:

- **Prices** of teacher's guides, activity books, and kits or units.
- The name of a principal **publisher/supplier** (not necessarily the sole source) for the items listed in the price category. (The address and phone and fax numbers for each publisher and supplier appear in appendix A, "Publishers and Suppliers.")
- An indication of the various sources from which one might obtain the required **materials.**

Organized in 5 activities, *Animals Two by Two* requires about 20 class sessions to complete. The teacher's guide includes a module overview, the 5 individual activity folios, duplication masters (in English and Spanish) for student sheets, and an annotated bibliography.

The module includes science background information, detailed instructions on planning for and conducting each activity, an extensive assessment component, and extensions for integration and enrichment. Materials are available in a kit.

Prices: Teacher's Guide (ISBN 0-7826-1154-0), $101. Complete module, $305. ***Publisher/supplier:*** Encyclopaedia Britannica Educational Corp. ***Materials:*** Available locally, from commercial suppliers, or in module.

1.3 Bones and Skeletons. Insights. Newton, Mass.: Education Development Center, 1994.

Grades: 4, 5 *Bones and Skeletons* opens with a challenge to students to investigate a mystery object—an owl pellet. During the unit, students explore major human and animal bone groups, teeth, joints, and skeletons. The classification of animals as herbivores, carnivores, and omnivores is introduced, and students consider how the structures of living things reflect their adaptation to the environment. They learn about various bone structures and their functions in different animals, and find out how bones, muscles, tendons, ligaments, and joints work together to produce movement. With this knowledge they can reconstruct the skeletons in their owl pellets, identify the animals, and describe their appearance and behaviors.

The unit's 15 Learning Experiences require a minimum of 21 class sessions over a period of 6 to 8 weeks. The teacher's guide includes an overview, the 15 Learning Experiences, reproducible masters for student sheets, and annotated lists of suggested readings and audiovisual materials.

This module includes science background information, detailed instructions on planning for and conducting each activity, an extensive assessment component, and extensions for integration and enrichment. Materials are available in a kit.

Prices: Teacher's Guide (ISBN 0-89292-174-9), $65. Materials kit, $220. (Prices differ in California, Nevada, and Indiana.) ***Publisher/ supplier:*** Optical Data. ***Materials:*** Available locally, from commercial suppliers, or in kit.

1.4 Communities. SCIS 3. Robert C. Knott and Herbert D. Thier. Hudson, N.H.: Delta Education, 1992.

Grade: 5 In *Communities,* students investigate the interactions of producers, consumers, and decomposers in an ecological community. Through a sequence of experiments and investigations, they learn that seeds produce plants exactly like the ones they came from. Students find out that seeds contain stored food for the plant embryo's early development and growth and that after this stored food is consumed, plants make their food through the process of photosynthesis. Students set up terrariums containing a variety of plants and animals, and observe the feeding behavior of plant-eaters and animal-eaters. The death of terrarium organisms provides opportunities to explore the role of decomposers. Students apply the concept of community as they play a card game depicting the feeding relationships in their terrariums, the transfer of food energy from one organism to another, and the recycling of raw materials. The unit ends with students describing a food web in which humans are the central focus.

Communities is organized in 5 sections consisting of a total of 10 chapters, requiring 16 weeks to complete. The teacher's guide includes an introduction to the unit, lesson plans for each of the 5 sections, a glossary, and blackline masters for a student journal.

This module includes science background information, detailed instructions on planning for and conducting each activity, an extensive assessment component, and extensions for integration and enrichment. Materials are available in a kit.

Prices: Teacher's Guide (ISBN 0-87504-940-0), $39.50. Kit, $640.00. ***Publisher/supplier:*** Delta Education. ***Materials:*** Available locally, from commercial suppliers, or in kit.

1.5 Ecosystems. SCIS 3. Robert C. Knott and Herbert D. Thier. Hudson, N.H.: Delta Education, 1993.

Grade: 6 *Ecosystems* introduces students to physical and biological aspects of ecosystems in the world around them. The unit begins with students constructing aquarium-terrarium systems. They discover evidence of the water cycle as they observe evaporation and condensation in this system and in other experimental setups. Activities include the use of snails, ladybugs, aphids, daphnia, guppies, hornwort, and algae. Students use bromthymol blue (an indicator) to explore the role of plants and animals in the oxygen-carbon dioxide cycle, and they learn about the food-mineral cycle and investigate various aspects of the water cycle and water pollution. Diagrams of the three cycles illustrate the exchange and cycling of materials in an ecosystem. Students also study photographs of natural ecosystems, data cards listing features of ecosystems, and maps showing the locations of seven different ecosystems in the United States and Canada.

Ecosystems is organized in 5 sections consisting of a total of 22 chapters, requiring 17 weeks to complete. The teacher's guide includes an introduction to the unit, lesson plans for each of the 5 sections, a glossary, and blackline masters for a student journal.

The module includes science background information, detailed instructions on planning for and conducting each activity, an extensive assessment component, and extensions for integration and enrichment. Materials are available in a kit.

Prices: Teacher's Guide (ISBN 0-87504-942-7), $39.50. Kit, $680.00. ***Publisher/supplier:*** Delta Education. ***Materials:*** Available locally, from commercial suppliers, or in kit.

1.6 Environments. FOSS. (Developed by Lawrence Hall of Science, Berkeley, Calif.) Chicago, Ill.: Encyclopaedia Britannica Educational Corp., 1993.

Grades: 5, 6 *Environments* introduces students to several basic concepts of environmental biology. Structured investigations in both terrestrial and aquatic systems develop the concepts of environmental factor, tolerance, environmental preference, and environmental range. In this unit, students observe interactions in a terrarium; investigate the environmental preferences of isopods and beetles; determine the water tolerance of seeds and plants; monitor environmental factors in freshwater aquariums; and investigate the salt tolerance of plants and brine shrimp eggs.

Environments consists of 6 activities and requires 8 weeks to complete. The teacher's guide includes a module overview, the 6 individual activity folios, duplication masters (in English and Spanish) for student sheets, and an annotated bibliography.

The module includes science background information, detailed instructions on planning for and conducting each activity, an extensive assessment component, and extensions for integration and enrichment. Materials are available in a kit.

Prices: Teacher's Guide (ISBN 0-7826-0070-0), $101. Complete module, $399. ***Publisher/supplier:*** Encyclopaedia Britannica Educational Corp. ***Materials:*** Available locally, from commercial suppliers, or in module.

1.7 Environments. SCIS 3. Robert C. Knott and Herbert D. Thier. Hudson, N.H.: Delta Education, 1992.

Grade: 4 *Environments* focuses students' attention on the conditions that surround an organism and that are necessary for its survival. Concepts explored in the unit include biotic and abiotic environmental factors, adaptation, precipitation, evaporation, controlled experiment, range, optimum conditions, response, and variation. Living organisms—hermit crabs, beetles, and isopods—are the focus of the students' investigations. Among the activities in the unit, students have a contest to grow the tallest plant through manipulation of the plants' environment. Other activities include field trips to observe changes in organisms and in the environment, student-designed experiments to see how environmental factors can influence organisms, and the planning of a "perfect" environment for one or several organisms. During the activities, students observe, and collect, record, and interpret data in their own journals. Throughout, the focus is on relationships and on cause and effect.

Environments is organized in 5 sections, divided into 18 chapters, requiring about 17 weeks to complete. The teacher's guide includes an introduction to the unit, lesson plans for each of the 5 sections, a glossary, and blackline masters for a student journal.

This module includes science background information, detailed instructions on planning for and conducting each activity, an extensive assessment component, and extensions for integration and enrichment. Materials are available in a kit.

Prices: Teacher's Guide (ISBN 0-87504-938-9), $39.50. Kit, $680.00. ***Publisher/supplier:*** Delta Education. ***Materials:*** Available locally, from commercial suppliers, or in kit.

1.8 Experiments with Plants. STC. (Developed by National Science Resources Center, Washington, D.C.) Burlington, N.C.: Carolina Biological Supply Co., 1992.

Grade: 6 In *Experiments with Plants,* students learn how to design and conduct controlled experiments by using the 40-day life cycle of a *Brassica* plant as a vehicle for experimentation. They learn about the variables that affect plant growth and reproduction as they design and set up an experiment to manipulate an isolated variable. Students then plant seeds according to their experiment plans; they determine the effects of their experiments on the plants' life cycle through data collection, measurement, observation, and recording. After observing the entire life cycle, they communicate the results of their experiments. The unit concludes with two sets of experiments involving germination, geotropism, and phototropism. Some prior study of plants and plant life cycles is helpful, but not essential, for students in *Experiments with Plants.*

This is a 15-lesson unit that requires 8 weeks to complete. The teacher's guide includes a unit overview, the 15 lesson plans, an annotated bibliography of additional resources, and information on maintaining live materials. A student activity book with simple instructions and illustrations accompanies the unit.

The module includes science background information, detailed instructions on planning for and conducting each activity, an extensive assessment component, and extensions for integration and enrichment. Materials are available in a kit.

Prices: Teacher's Guide, $14.95. Student Activity Book, $3.50. Unit, $279.95. ***Publisher/supplier:*** Carolina Biological Supply. ***Materials:*** Available locally, from commercial suppliers, or in unit.

1.9 Food and Nutrition. FOSS. (Developed by Lawrence Hall of Science, Berkeley, Calif.) Chicago, Ill.: Encyclopaedia Britannica Educational Corp., 1993.

Grades: 5, 6 The unit *Food and Nutrition* helps students understand what food is, what its chemical components are, and how several nutrient groups contribute to making food healthful. Students test foods for their acid content, as well as for their vitamin C, fat, and sugar content. Next they learn how to read nutritional information on package labels, how to calculate the caloric content of foods, and how to use their own knowledge and the nutritional information from the packaging lists of product ingredients to plan and evaluate lunch menus. Activities involve students in measuring and comparing, observing, and analyzing.

Food and Nutrition consists of 4 activities, requiring about 10 sessions of 45 to 60 minutes each over a 7-week period. The teacher's guide includes a module overview, the 4 individual activity folios, duplication masters (in English and Spanish) for student sheets, and an annotated bibliography.

The module includes science background information, detailed instructions on planning for and conducting each activity, an extensive assessment component, and extensions for integration and enrichment. Materials are available in a kit.

Prices: Teacher's Guide (ISBN 0-7826-0093-X), $101. Complete module, $429. ***Publisher/supplier:*** Encyclopaedia Britannica Educational Corp. ***Materials:*** Available locally, from commercial suppliers, or in module.

1.10 Growing Things. Insights. Newton, Mass.: Education Development Center, 1994.

Grades: 2, 3 In *Growing Things,* children learn how plants grow, what functions different parts of plants perform, and how various factors influence plant growth. The module begins with a field trip that gives students the opportunity to observe, describe, record information about, and compare plants in their school neighborhood. Later, students in small groups perform classroom activities that focus their attention on the growth and development of plants from seeds to seedlings to small plants. They observe and draw germinating seeds, and they plant bean seeds and chart the growth and development of their bean plants. Students design and conduct experiments to explore factors, such as light, moisture, and space, that affect plant growth. They set up an exhibit of their work to share with the school community. Students make observations, notes, and drawings and discuss their findings with the class.

The unit's 16 well-organized Learning Experiences can be done in a minimum of 21 sessions over a period of 6 to 8 weeks. The module includes an overview, the 16 Learning Experiences, reproducible masters for student sheets, and annotated lists of suggested readings and audiovisual materials.

The module includes science background information, detailed instructions on planning for and conducting each activity, an extensive assessment component, and extensions for integration and enrichment. Materials are available in a kit.

Prices: Teacher's Guide (ISBN 0-89292-169-2), $65. Materials kit, $247. (Prices differ in California, Nevada, and Indiana.) ***Publisher/supplier:*** Optical Data. ***Materials:*** Available locally, from commercial suppliers, or in kit.

1.11 Habitats. Insights. Newton, Mass.: Education Development Center, 1994.

Grades: 2, 3 In *Habitats,* students explore what living things need in order to survive, and they look at how these needs are met. They examine the school and neighborhood as a habitat for human beings, then select a small area for close examination, mapping its potential as a microhabitat for the small organisms living there. Students investigate the effects physical conditions have on the kinds and numbers of organisms in a habitat. They identify structures and behaviors that help creatures adapt to the environment they live in. Student-constructed terrariums serve as temporary microhabitats for the small organisms students collect, observe, and later release. Language development is an integral part of the module, and mathematics skills (such as classifying and measuring) are used in the context of the science study.

Habitats consists of 9 Learning Experiences, requiring about 16 class sessions, or about 6 to 8 weeks, to complete. The teacher's guide includes an overview, the 9 Learning Experiences, reproducible masters for student sheets, and annotated lists of suggested readings and audiovisual materials.

This module includes science background information, detailed instructions on planning for and conducting each activity, an extensive assessment component, and extensions for integration and enrichment. Materials are available in a kit.

Prices: Teacher's Guide (ISBN 0-89292-170-6), $65. Materials kit, $241. (Prices differ in California, Nevada, and Indiana.) ***Publisher/supplier:*** Optical Data. ***Materials:*** Available locally, from commercial suppliers, or in kit.

1.12 Human Body. FOSS. (Developed by Lawrence Hall of Science, Berkeley, Calif.) Chicago, Ill.: Encyclopaedia Britannica Educational Corp., 1993.

Grades: 3, 4 In the *Human Body* module, students discover how bones, joints, and muscles work together. They learn about the variety of sizes and forms of human bones and the role of the skeleton in the support, protection, and movement of the body. They find out how muscles are arranged across joints to move bones and learn about the functions of tendons and ligaments. During the unit, students assemble a 19-piece articulated model skeleton. They build a model leg and foot with simulated muscles and tendons, construct a model thumb with tendons and ligaments, and compare human skeletal joints to analogous mechanical structures. In the final activity, they work with a falling-cup device to investigate response time.

The Human Body consists of 4 activities, which require about 10 class sessions to complete. The teacher's guide includes a module overview, the 4 individual activity folios, duplication masters (in English and Spanish) for student sheets, and an annotated bibliography.

This module includes science background information, detailed instructions on planning for and conducting each activity, an extensive assessment component, and extensions for integration and enrichment. Materials are available in a kit.

Prices: Teacher's Guide (ISBN 0-7826-0046-8), $101. Complete module, $335. ***Publisher/supplier:*** Encyclopaedia Britannica Educational Corp. ***Materials:*** Available locally, from commercial suppliers, or in module.

1.13 Human Body Systems. Insights. Newton, Mass.: Education Development Center, 1994.

Grade: 6 *Human Body Systems* is designed to convey to students basic concepts about how three systems—the human circulatory, digestive, and respiratory systems—work together. As students explore these systems, beginning with the cell and the vital role it plays as a basic component of the body, they develop a sense of the size, location, and function of some of their internal organs. Students are introduced to the ideas that the individual parts of the body are all part of one larger system and that these parts work together to take in food, process it for energy, and get rid of waste. Students engage in a variety of activities that demonstrate how the three systems work interdependently to provide the cells in the body with the nutrients and energy they need.

Human Body Systems consists of 13 Learning Experiences, requiring a minimum of 24 class sessions. The teacher's guide includes an overview, the 13 Learning Experiences, reproducible masters for student sheets, and annotated lists of suggested readings and audiovisual materials.

This module includes science background information, detailed instructions on planning for and conducting each activity, an extensive assessment component, and extensions for integration and enrichment. Materials are available in a kit.

Prices: Teacher's Guide (ISBN 0-89292-179-X), $65. Materials kit, $441. (Prices differ in California, Nevada, and Indiana.) ***Publisher/supplier:*** Optical Data. ***Materials:*** Available locally, from commercial suppliers, or in kit.

1.14 Insects. FOSS. (Developed by Lawrence Hall of Science, Berkeley, Calif.) Chicago, Ill.: Encyclopaedia Britannica Educational Corp., 1993.

Grades: 1, 2 The *Insects* module introduces young students to the life sequences and diversity of forms of insects—mealworms, waxworms, milkweed bugs, butterflies, crickets, and ants. A new insect is introduced in each activity. Students care for the insects over the course of the unit. They observe and compare insect structures and behaviors in different stages of the life cycle, witnessing complete and simple insect metamorphosis. They discuss and record their findings and pose questions for resolution. Suggestions for obtaining and disposing of insects are given.

Insects consists of 6 activities that require about 12 weeks to complete. The teacher's guide includes a module overview, the 6 individual activity folios, duplication masters (in English and Spanish) for student sheets, and an annotated bibliography.

This module includes science background information, detailed instructions on planning for and conducting each activity, an extensive assessment component, and extensions for integration and enrichment. Materials are available in a kit.

Prices: Teacher's Guide (ISBN 0-7826-1156-7), $101. Complete module, $440. ***Publisher/supplier:*** Encyclopaedia Britannica Educational Corp. ***Materials:*** Available locally, from commercial suppliers, or in module.

1.15 The Life Cycle of Butterflies. STC. (Developed by National Science Resources Center, Washington, D.C.) Burlington, N.C.: Carolina Biological Supply Co., 1992.

Grade: 2 In *The Life Cycle of Butterflies,* children learn about the life cycle of the Painted Lady by observing this butterfly's month-long metamorphosis from a small caterpillar to an adult butterfly. Students learn about the caterpillar's basic needs for air, water, food, and shelter. They watch caterpillars crawl, hang upside down, spin silk, eat, grow, molt, and turn into chrysalises. Students then observe and learn about the adult butterfly when it emerges, and, finally, they observe the butterflies as they lay eggs and die, completing their life cycle. The children compare the Painted Lady's life cycle with the life cycles of other living creatures. Throughout the unit, students develop observational and recording skills. Well-designed activity sheets provide opportunities for them to record their observations, drawings, and ideas.

The Life Cycle of Butterflies is a 15-lesson unit that requires 6 weeks to complete. The teacher's guide includes a unit overview, the 15 lesson plans, instructions for making simple butterfly cages, information about raising a second generation of butterflies, and an annotated bibliography. A consumable notebook for students (available in English and Spanish) accompanies the unit.

This module includes science background information, detailed instructions on planning for and conducting each activity, an extensive assessment component, and extensions for integration and enrichment. Materials are available in a kit.

Prices: Teacher's Guide, $14.95. Consumable Student Notebook, $2.00. Unit, $124.95. ***Publisher/supplier:*** Carolina Biological Supply. ***Materials:*** Available locally, from commercial suppliers, or in unit.

1.16 Life Cycles. SCIS 3. Robert C. Knott and Herbert D. Thier. Hudson, N.H.: Delta Education, 1992.

Grade: 2 *Life Cycles* focuses students' attention on the lives of representative plants and animals and on their patterns of development and growth as the organisms live through their life cycles. Students first observe plants growing from seeds into seedlings into mature, seed-producing plants. As the unit progresses, students discover that although some seeds and eggs appear to be very much alike, they become vastly different as they mature. Through extensive activities with the life cycles of frogs, crickets, fruit flies, moths, mealworms, and butterflies, students increase their understanding of the concepts of development and growth in animals.

Life Cycles is organized in 4 sections, with 16 lessons, and requires approximately 17 weeks to complete. The teacher's guide includes an introduction to the unit, lesson plans for each of the 4 sections, a glossary, and blackline masters for a student journal.

The module includes science background information, detailed instructions on planning for and conducting each activity, an extensive assessment component, and extensions for integration and enrichment. Materials are available in a kit.

Prices: Teacher's Guide (ISBN 0-87504-934-6), $39.50. Kit, $670.00. ***Publisher/supplier:*** Delta Education. ***Materials:*** Available locally, from commercial suppliers, or in kit.

1.17 Living Things. Insights. Newton, Mass.: Education Development Center, 1994.

Grades: K, 1 *Living Things* is a study of the local environment. Through the module's Learning Experiences, children learn to observe changes in plants and animals over time and to understand what these living things need for survival and growth. They compare the shapes of trees and leaves. They observe changes in a tree and investigate the plants and animals living in and around the tree. Students build terrariums using plants and small animals collected locally. (The animals are later released.) In the classroom they plant bean seeds and take care of them as the bean seeds grow into seedlings.

Living Things consists of 14 Learning Experiences, which require about 22 class sessions to complete. The teacher's guide includes an overview, the 14 Learning Experiences, reproducible masters for student sheets, and annotated lists of suggested readings and audiovisual materials.

This module includes science background information, detailed instructions on planning for and conducting each activity, an extensive assessment component, and extensions for integration and enrichment. Materials are available in a kit.

Prices: Teacher's Guide (ISBN 0-89292-166-8), $65. Materials kit, $259. (Prices differ in California, Nevada, and Indiana.) ***Publisher/supplier:*** Optical Data. ***Materials:*** Available locally, from commercial suppliers, or in kit.

1.18 Microworlds. STC. (Developed by National Science Resources Center, Washington, D.C.) Burlington, N.C.: Carolina Biological Supply Co., 1991.

Grade: 5 *Microworlds* develops students' observational skills and allows them to become adept at using hand lenses, microscopes, slides, and related apparatus to view living and nonliving specimens. Students make close observations of common objects with hand lenses and learn about different lenses and how they work. They use a microscope to observe inanimate objects such as hair and magazine photographs. Students explore the concept of field of view, prepare different types of slides, and examine the cells of an onion. Then they use their new expertise to view microscopic living organisms under magnification. Throughout the unit they record their observations by writing and drawing.

Microworlds is a 16-lesson unit that requires 8 weeks to complete. The teacher's guide includes a unit overview, the 16 lesson plans, and an annotated bibliography of additional resources. A student activity book with simple instructions and illustrations accompanies the unit. The appendixes include a supplementary drawing lesson and tips on caring for live cultures.

The module includes science background information, detailed instructions on planning for and conducting each activity, an extensive assessment component, and extensions for integration and enrichment. Materials are available in a kit.

Prices: Teacher's Guide, $14.95. Student Activity Book, $3.50. Unit, $404.95. ***Publisher/supplier:*** Carolina Biological Supply. ***Materials:*** Available locally, from commercial suppliers, or in unit.

1.19 Myself and Others. Insights. Newton, Mass.: Education Development Center, 1994.

Grades: K, 1 Students explore the similarities and differences between themselves and their classmates in *Myself and Others.* Through such activities as drawing full-body outlines and observing and discussing height, hand size and shape, skin color, and other physical characteristics, students learn that although there are similarities among all children, each child is unique. Students organize their observations as they measure, compare, and classify. They record their observations on graphs, charts, and murals. At the end of the module, they learn about concepts such as growth and development by looking into their own past, present, and future. The module helps children develop a positive approach to differences as they gain greater awareness and understanding of their own physical characteristics and those of their classmates.

Myself and Others consists of 13 Learning Experiences, which require about 20 class sessions to complete. The teacher's guide includes an overview, the 13 Learning Experiences, reproducible masters for student sheets, and annotated lists of suggested readings and audiovisual materials.

This module includes science background information, detailed instructions on planning for and conducting each activity, an extensive assessment component, and extensions for integration and enrichment. Materials are available in a kit.

Prices: Teacher's Guide (ISBN 0-89292-167-6), $65. Materials kit, $350. (Prices differ in California, Nevada, and Indiana.) ***Publisher/supplier:*** Optical Data. ***Materials:*** Available locally, from commercial suppliers, or in kit.

1.20 New Plants. FOSS. (Developed by Lawrence Hall of Science, Berkeley, Calif.) Chicago, Ill.: Encyclopaedia Britannica Educational Corp., 1993.

Grades: 1, 2 This module engages students' interest in a process familiar in daily life—the growing of new plants. Students learn about the structures of flowering plants and discover various ways to propagate new plants from mature plants. They grow plants from seed using rapid-cycling *Brassica* and observe the complete life cycle of this plant in about 5 weeks. Students plant a miniature weedy lawn of rye grass (monocots) and alfalfa (dicots) and compare the impact of "mowing" on each plant. They grow and monitor the growth of new plants from cuttings, bulbs, and roots.

New Plants consists of 4 activities, which require 10 weeks to complete. The teacher's guide includes a module overview, the 4 individual activity folios, duplication masters (in English and Spanish) for student sheets, and an annotated bibliography.

This module includes science background information, detailed instructions on planning for and conducting each activity, an extensive assessment component, and extensions for integration and enrichment. Materials are available in a kit.

Prices: Teacher's Guide (ISBN 0-7826-1150-8), $101. Complete module, $485. ***Publisher/supplier:*** Encyclopaedia Britannica Educational Corp. ***Materials:*** Available locally, from commercial suppliers, or in module.

1.21 Organisms. SCIS 3. Robert C. Knott and Herbert D. Thier. Hudson, N.H.: Delta Education, 1992.

Grade: 1 Through a series of activities and experiments, *Organisms* provides young students with basic information about living things. Children are introduced to the concept of habitat, and they observe environmental changes affecting life within various habitats. They plant seeds, observe their development, and experiment to determine how external conditions such as water and light affect seed germination and plant growth. Students set up aquariums with a variety of plants and animals; observe the interaction of the aquarium organisms; and discuss natural events that occur, such as feeding, birth, growth, and death. Then they explore the schoolyard or local neighborhood for plants and animals in their natural habitats. Students are introduced to the concept of a food chain as they investigate algal growth in the aquarium, introduce *Daphnia* culture that eat the algae, and then observe guppies eating daphnia. Students start their own *Daphnia* culture, monitor changes in population size, and infer that the changes are due to death and birth. Through experiments and other observations, students learn that detritus comes from dead plants and animals as well as from animal waste.

Organisms is organized in 6 sections, with 17 lessons, and requires approximately 17 weeks to complete. The teacher's guide includes an introduction to the unit, lesson plans for each of the sections, a glossary, and blackline masters for a student journal.

This module includes science background information, detailed instructions on planning for and conducting each activity, an extensive assessment component, and extensions for integration and enrichment. Materials are available in a kit.

Prices: Teacher's Guide (ISBN 0-87504-932-X), $39.50. Kit, $490.00. ***Publisher/supplier:*** Delta Education. ***Materials:*** Available locally, from commercial suppliers, or in kit.

1.22 Organisms. STC. Field-test ed. Washington, D.C.: National Science Resources Center, 1993.

Grade: 1 In *Organisms,* students explore the similarities and differences between plants and animals. They develop an understanding of what plants and animals need so they can live, and begin to understand that organisms grow and change over time. During the unit, students create and observe a terrarium woodland habitat containing pine seedlings, pillow moss, pillbugs, and Bess beetles, and set up and observe an aquarium freshwater habitat containing *Elodea* and *Cabomba* plants, ramshorn snails, and guppies. Students use Venn diagrams to make comparisons between plants and animals. Throughout the unit they discuss, draw, and write about what they observe. Students are encouraged to extend what they have learned about what organisms need to what humans need to live and grow.

Organisms is a 16-lesson unit that requires 8 weeks to complete. The teacher's guide includes a unit overview, the 16 lesson plans, and an annotated bibliography of additional resources. A student activity book with simple instructions and illustrations accompanies the unit. The appendixes include tips on maintaining live materials and suggestions for discussing birth and death.

This module includes science background information, detailed instructions on planning for and conducting each activity, an extensive assessment component, and extensions for integration and enrichment. Materials are available in a kit.

Prices: Teacher's Guide, $14.95. Consumable Student Notebook, $2.00. Unit, $349.95. ***Publisher/supplier:*** Carolina Biological Supply. ***Materials:*** Available locally, through commercial suppliers, or in unit.

1.23 Plant Growth and Development. STC. (Developed by National Science Resources Center, Washington, D.C.) Burlington, N.C.: Carolina Biological Supply Co., 1991.

Grade: 3 In *Plant Growth and Development,* students observe the complete life cycle of a fast-growing *Brassica* plant. They learn that the cycle includes germination, growth, the development of specialized body parts, and even death, with the promise of new life in the seed. Students examine and plant seeds. Then they thin and transplant young plants, observe the emergence of leaves and buds, cross-pollinate plants using dead bees, and harvest seeds. They make frequent observations of their plants and record their observations both in writing and with scientific drawings. Students quantify their observations by taking measurements and recording them on growth graphs.

Plant Growth and Development is a 16-lesson unit that requires 8 weeks to complete.The teacher's guide includes a unit overview, the 16 lesson plans, and an annotated bibliography of additional resources. A student activity book with simple instructions and illustrations accompanies the unit. The appendixes include a lesson on graphing and blackline masters for graph paper.

The module includes science background information, detailed instructions on planning for and conducting each activity, an extensive assessment component, and extensions for integration and enrichment. Materials are available in a kit.

Prices: Teacher's Guide, $14.95. Student Activity Book, $3.50. Unit, $279.95. ***Publisher/supplier:*** Carolina Biological Supply. ***Materials:*** Available locally, through commercial suppliers, or in unit.

1.24 Populations. SCIS 3. Robert C. Knott and Herbert D. Thier. Hudson, N.H.: Delta Education, 1992.

Grade: 3 In *Populations,* students learn about the dynamics of plant and animal populations by observing them interacting in student-made aquariums and terrariums. The populations of plants and animals that students investigate are aphids, daphnia, chameleons, crickets, snails, damselfly nymphs, duckweed, hornwort, and algae. Students see isolated populations of daphnia and aphids increase and decrease, and they learn to relate these changes to reproduction and death. The concept of biotic potential is also explored. By observing the interactions of plant and animal populations, students gain an understanding of food relationships and of the interrelationships between populations. The unit emphasizes the interaction and interdependency of all living things. During the activities students have the opportunity to observe, experiment, report findings, analyze results, and explore events and processes they do not understand.

Populations is organized in 5 sections consisting of a total of 19 lessons, requiring 14 to 16 weeks to complete. The teacher's guide includes an introduction to the unit, lesson plans for each of the 5 sections, a glossary, and blackline masters for a student journal.

The module includes science background information, detailed instructions on planning for and conducting each activity, an extensive assessment component, and extensions for integration and enrichment. Materials are available in a kit.

Prices: Teacher's Guide (ISBN 0-87504-936-2), $39.50. Kit, $590.00. ***Publisher/supplier:*** Delta Education. ***Materials:*** Available locally, from commercial suppliers, or in kit.

1.25 The Senses. Insights. Newton, Mass.: Education Development Center, 1994.

Grades: K, 1 *The Senses* provides a variety of experiences that help children become more aware of their senses and more accustomed to using them as tools for observing and describing the world around them. The module features activities such as the following: using the senses to describe "mystery" objects hidden inside bags and boxes; taking outdoor walks and using texture and sound to describe objects encountered along the way; and engaging in a sense-based examination of popcorn from kernel to fully cooked snack. The activities offer ongoing opportunities for children to discuss and record their observations and to compare, sort, and classify objects by various properties.

The Senses consists of 13 Learning Experiences, which require about 16 class sessions to complete. The teacher's guide includes an overview, the 13 Learning Experiences, reproducible masters for student sheets, and annotated lists of suggested readings and audiovisual materials.

This module includes science background information, detailed instructions on planning for and conducting each activity, an extensive assessment component, and extensions for integration and enrichment. Materials are available in a kit.

Prices: Teacher's Guide (ISBN 0-89292-168-4), $65. Materials kit, $181. (Prices differ in California, Nevada, and Indiana.) ***Publisher/ supplier:*** Optical Data. ***Materials:*** Available locally, from commercial suppliers, or in kit.

1.26 Structures of Life. FOSS. (Developed by Lawrence Hall of Science, Berkeley, Calif.) Chicago, Ill.: Encyclopaedia Britannica Educational Corp., 1993.

Grade: 3, 4 Fruit seeds, bean plants, and crayfish provide the building blocks for learning in *Structures of Life,* which introduces students to basic concepts related to similarities and differences among organisms. As students observe, compare, and care for a selection of organisms, they learn to identify properties and characteristics of plants and animals in order to group and sort them. They also investigate some animal behaviors. Activities in the unit include observing and comparing seeds in foods people eat, setting up "seed sprouters" for germinating seeds, planting the seedlings in a liquid nutrient solution, and monitoring the growth of plants in this hydroponic garden through a complete life cycle. Finally, students observe the structure of crayfish and investigate this animal's behavior in an artificial habitat they set up.

Structures of Life consists of 5 activities that require about 10 weeks to complete. The teacher's guide includes a module overview, the 5 individual activity folios, duplication masters (in English and Spanish) for student sheets, and an annotated bibliography.

This module includes science background information, detailed instructions on planning for and conducting each activity, an extensive assessment component, and extensions for integration and enrichment. Materials are available in a kit.

Prices: Teacher's Guide (ISBN 0-7826-0022-0), $101. Complete module, $309. ***Publisher/supplier:*** Encyclopaedia Britannica Educational Corp. ***Materials:*** Available locally, from commercial suppliers, or in module.

1.27 Trees. FOSS. (Developed by Lawrence Hall of Science, Berkeley, Calif.) Chicago, Ill.: Encyclopaedia Britannica Educational Corp., 1993.

Grade: K In *Trees,* young students care for their own classroom tree and discover what a tree needs so that it can grow. Eventually they transplant the classroom tree outdoors. Trees contains 2 umbrella activities—Fall Trees (consisting of 7 parts requiring about 7 class sessions to complete) and Leaves (with 6 parts requiring 6 to 9 class sessions). Fall Trees is introduced through a story about a class that has its own containerized tree. Students discuss what a tree needs to grow. They identify the parts of a tree, observe trees outdoors, and then use card games and puzzles to reinforce what they have learned. In the Leaves activity, students collect various kinds of leaves, compare their shapes and sizes, and make leaf scrapbooks.

The teacher's guide includes a module overview, the 2 individual activity folios, duplication masters (in English and Spanish) for student sheets, and an annotated bibliography.

Students use a variety of real and representational materials; the latter are included in the Teacher's Guide, which also includes poems and songs about trees and leaves in both English and Spanish.

This module includes science background information, detailed instructions on planning for and conducting each activity, an extensive assessment component, and extensions for integration and enrichment. Materials are available in a kit.

Prices: Teacher's Guide (ISBN 0-7826-1138-9), $101. Complete module, $339. ***Publisher/supplier:*** Encyclopaedia Britannica Educational Corp. ***Materials:*** Available locally, from commercial suppliers, or in module.

LIFE SCIENCE—SUPPLEMENTARY MATERIALS

1.28 Adaptations. REEP. Philadelphia, Pa.: Schuylkill Center for Environmental Education, 1991.

Grade: 3 *Adaptations,* an environmental education unit, introduces students to the idea that all plants and animals have certain traits or characteristics (adaptations) that help them survive and reproduce. Students first consider adaptations in humans and the relationship between adaptations and basic life functions. Next they examine adaptations in several plants and animals. The focus of the unit then shifts to the idea that plants and animals survive and reproduce because they have adapted to a particular habitat. Students look briefly at the theory of natural selection before considering what happens if conditions change so rapidly that groups of plants and animals are unable to adapt. Activities include students examining their own thumbs as an adaptation; hiding paper beetles to demonstrate how camouflage helps animals avoid predators; examining seeds to identify adaptations for protection and dispersal; and role-playing animals in a habitat that is suddenly reduced in size. In a final lesson, students identify actions, such as conservation measures, that people can take on behalf of the environment.

Adaptations contains an introduction that includes background information and a lesson summary. The unit contains 10 lessons that stand alone but are designed to be taught in sequence. Each lesson has from 1 to 3 activities of 40 to 60 minutes each.

Price: $20. ***Publisher/supplier:*** Schuylkill Center for Environmental Education. ***Materials:*** Available locally, or from commercial suppliers.

1.29 Alive: What Living Things Are. Scholastic Science Place. (Developed in cooperation with Maryland Science Center, Baltimore, Md.) New York, N.Y.: Scholastic, 1993.

Grade: K In *Alive: What Living Things Are,* children explore the characteristics and diversity of living things. The unit's lessons are grouped in 3 subconcepts: (1) living things have characteristics that can be observed and described; (2) living things have observable life cycles; and (3) nonliving things can have some, but not all, of the characteristics of living things. During the unit, kindergartners take a nature walk and make collages, murals, and puppets as they learn to distinguish between living and nonliving things. The children act out their ideas of plants and animals in a game of charades. They make clay and paper models of animals as they explore animal characteristics. They sort seeds according to their characteristics, and plant seeds and test the effect of various moisture levels on plant growth.

Alive: What Living Things Are consists of 12 lessons requiring 30 minutes each. The conceptual goals of the unit are presented in the lesson-by-lesson story line in the teacher's guide. Each lesson also includes background information; a complete lesson plan, including suggestions for assessing performance and integrating the curriculum; and a list of the print, video, and software support materials required for the lesson.

Prices: Teacher's Guide (ISBN 0-590-26196-7), $17.25. Complete unit, $315.00. Consumables kit, $58.00. ***Publisher/supplier:*** Scholastic. ***Materials:*** Available locally, from commercial suppliers, or in unit.

1.30 Amazing Mammals, Part I. NatureScope. Washington, D.C.: National Wildlife Federation, 1988.

Grades: K-6+ *Amazing Mammals, Part I,* introduces students to the characteristics, biology, and behavior of mammals, and to ways in which humans and other mammals affect one another's lives. Students use observations, games, large-motor activities, creative writing, and crafts as they learn to distinguish mammals from other vertebrate classes and investigate the importance of nonhuman mammals to humans. The chapters in this module usually begin with primary activities and end with intermediate or advanced activities.

Each chapter includes background information, activities, and student activity sheets. The 20 activities in this teacher's guide can be taught independently or as a unit. They are easily integrated into other curricula. A craft section and an appendix of other resources are included.

Price: $7.95 (ISBN 0-945051-29-8). ***Publisher/supplier:*** National Wildlife Federation. ***Materials:*** Available locally.

1.31 Amazing Mammals, Part II. NatureScope. Washington, D.C.: National Wildlife Federation, 1989.

Grades: 1-6+ *Amazing Mammals, Part II,* is an interdisciplinary investigation of the specific characteristics of mammalian groups. Through games, art, and music, students investigate the unique adaptations of primates, rodents, marine mammals, bats, hoofed mammals, and carnivorous and insectivorous mammals.

Each chapter includes detailed background information, activities, and student activity sheets. The 24 activities in this teacher's guide can

ABOUT THE ANNOTATIONS IN "LIFE SCIENCE—SUPPLEMENTARY MATERIALS"

Entry Numbers
Curriculum materials are arranged alphabetically by title in each category (Core Materials, Supplementary Materials, and Science Activity Books) in chapters 1 through 4 of this guide. In addition, each annotation has a two-part entry number. For each entry number, the chapter number is given before the period; the number after the period locates the entry within that chapter.

For example, the first entry number in chapter 1 is 1.1; the second entry in chapter 2 is 2.2, and so on.

The entry numbers within each curriculum chapter run consecutively through Core Materials, Supplementary Materials, and Science Activity Books.

Order of Bibliographic Information
Following is the arrangement of the facts of publication in the annotations in this section:

- **Title of publication.**
- **Series title**, or series acronym if commonly used.
- **Authors** (either individual names or organizational author).
- Name and location of **developer** (in parentheses), if different from publisher.
- **Place of publication, publisher, and date of publication.**

Series Acronyms
Following are **acronyms of series titles** in "Life Science—Supplementary Materials." (Series titles that are spelled out are not included in this list.)

DSM	Delta Science Module
GEMS	Great Explorations in Math and Science
GEMS/PEACHES	Great Explorations in Math and Science/Preschool Explorations for Adults, Children, and Educators in Science
LEAP	Learning about Ecology, Animals, and Plants
REEP	Regional Environmental Education Program
STAR	Science Technology and Reading

Price and Acquisition Information
Ordering information is presented in a block immediately below the annotation. Included are the following:

- **Prices** of teacher's guides, activity books, and kits or units.
- The name of a principal **publisher/supplier** (not necessarily the sole source) for the items listed in the price category. (The address and phone and fax numbers for each publisher and supplier appear in appendix A, "Publishers and Suppliers.")
- An indication of the various sources from which one might obtain the required **materials.**

be taught independently or as a unit. They are easily integrated into other curricula. An appendix of other resources is included. *Amazing Mammals, Part II* contains a limited number of assessment strategies.

Price: $7.95 (ISBN 0-945051-30-1). ***Publisher/supplier:*** National Wildlife Federation. ***Materials:*** Available locally.

1.32 Animal Defenses. GEMS. Jean Echols. Berkeley, Calif.: Lawrence Hall of Science, 1987.

Grades: PreK, K In *Animal Defenses,* children explore the defensive structures and behaviors of dinosaurs and of contemporary animals. Students first supply a paper cutout of a defenseless animal with physical defense mechanisms. Then they dramatize a meeting of their imaginary animals with a *Tyrannosaurus rex.* Successive activities focus on the physical characteristics and defense behaviors of dogs, cats, turtles, lizards, and other animals. Written primarily for use with preschoolers and kindergartners, this guide also contains extensions and modifications for grades 1 and 2.

The highly visual activities in the unit require 2 class sessions. The first set of activities requires 45 minutes; the second, 20 minutes. The lesson plan for each session includes an overview, a suggested time frame, a list of materials, ideas for preparation, and directions for the activity. Patterns for cutouts are included.

Price: $8.50. ***Publisher/supplier:*** LHS GEMS. ***Materials:*** Available locally, or from commercial suppliers.

1.33 Animals in Action. GEMS. Katharine Barrett. Berkeley, Calif.: Lawrence Hall of Science, 1986.

Grades: 6+ In *Animals in Action,* students investigate animal behavior by observing live animals. They first observe and describe the behavior of young animals—for example, gerbils, hamsters, guinea pigs, or chicks—enclosed in a large classroom corral. They then introduce stimulus objects, such as food or shelter, and observe how each animal responds. On the basis of information in *Animals in Action,* students discuss the humane treatment of animals. Teams of students then design, conduct, and evaluate their own animal-behavior experiments, using small organisms such as crayfish, isopods, crickets, or garden snails. Findings are discussed at a simulated scientific convention.

Background information, easy-to-follow lesson plans for each of the 5 sessions, requiring 45 minutes each, and a small-animal resource guide are included in this unit.

Price: $10. ***Publisher/supplier:*** LHS GEMS. ***Materials:*** Available locally, or from commercial suppliers.

1.34 Behavior of Mealworms. DSM. Hudson, N.H.: Delta Education, 1988.

Grades: 4-6 In *Behavior of Mealworms,* students investigate the behavior and physical characteristics of mealworms. After learning about the proper care and handling of these creatures, students observe and record data on mealworms' movement, food-getting behavior, response to stimuli, and behavior in a maze. In a final activity, students plan and conduct a controlled experiment.

Behavior of Mealworms includes a brief module overview, a section on evaluation, a glossary, and blackline masters. The 8 activities take about 3 to 4 weeks (about 12 class sessions) to complete. The 1- and 2-page activities provide background information, teaching suggestions, and a list of the materials needed.

Prices: Teacher's Guide (ISBN 0-87504-715-7), $9.95. Kit, $175.00. ***Publisher/supplier:*** Delta Education. ***Materials:*** Available locally, from commercial suppliers, or in kit.

1.35 Biodiversity: Understanding the Variety of Life. Scholastic Science Place. (Developed in cooperation with Liberty Science Center, Jersey City, N.J.) New York, N.Y.: Scholastic, 1995.

Grades: 6+ Through the activities in *Biodiversity,* students learn that people make choices that affect the survival of their own and other species. The lessons are grouped in three subconcepts: (1) scientists use various methods to measure earth's biodiversity; (2) the variety of species and habitats changes with time; and (3) knowledge of biodiversity helps people make decisions about the environment. In this unit, students use a transect to take a sample of species in the school yard and discover the variety of species present. They observe soil-dwelling species and organisms in a harsh habitat as they explore how conditions in habitats affect diversity. Students classify unknown organisms to discover some problems involved in measuring biodiversity. They examine fossils to learn about extinct species. In other activities, students make a model of competition and explore how competition affects biodiversity. They investigate the effects of catastrophes, overpopulation, and pollution on a habitat.

Biodiversity: Understanding the Variety of Life is a 17-lesson unit consisting of 23 class sessions, typically 40 to 55 minutes in duration. The conceptual goals of the unit are presented in the lesson-by-lesson story line in the teacher's guide. Each lesson also includes background information; a complete lesson plan, including suggestions for assessing performance and integrating the curriculum; and a list of the print, video, and software support materials required for the lesson.

Prices: Teacher's Guide (ISBN 0-590-27779-0), $27. Student Book (ISBN 0-590-27778-2), $10. Complete unit, $450. Consumables kit, $48. ***Publisher/supplier:*** Scholastic. ***Materials:*** Available locally, from commercial suppliers, or in unit.

1.36 Birds, Birds, Birds. NatureScope. Washington, D.C.: National Wildlife Federation, 1989.

Grades: K-6+ Each of the 5 chapters in *Birds, Birds, Birds* deals with a broad theme such as habitats and migration. In this unit, students explore the biological and behavioral characteristics of birds through observations, games, and simulations integrating language arts, history, creative writing, geography, mathematics, social studies, and art.

Each chapter includes background information, activities, and student activity sheets. The 23 activities in this teacher's guide can be taught independently or as a unit. They are easily integrated into other curricula. An appendix includes questions and answers about birds, a glossary, and a list of sources of additional information about birds.

Price: $7.95. ***Publisher/supplier:*** National Wildlife Federation. ***Materials:*** Available locally.

1.37 Body Systems: How Your Body Parts Work Together. Scholastic Science Place. (Developed in cooperation with Thames Science Center, New London, Conn.) New York, N.Y.: Scholastic, 1993.

Grade: 1 Through the simple activities in *Body Systems,* children learn that the human body has parts and systems that work together. The lessons are grouped in two subconcepts: (1) the human body has systems that allow the whole body to move; and (2) the human body has systems that help the whole body obtain and use food, water, and air. Students trace one anothers' body outlines to make life-size cutouts of their body shapes. They use paper models to explore how muscles move the bones at joints. Other activities include students comparing the behavior of voluntary and involuntary muscles through simple kinesthetic activities, blowing into a paper bag to determine how much air their lungs can hold, and designing an obstacle course that involves the use of all their body systems.

Body Systems: How Your Body Parts Work Together consists of 17 class sessions requiring 25 to 45 minutes each. The conceptual goals of the unit are presented in the lesson-by-lesson story line in the teacher's guide. Each lesson also includes background information; a complete lesson plan, including suggestions for assessing performance and integrating the curriculum; and a list of the print, video, and software support materials required for the lesson.

Prices: Teacher's Guide (ISBN 0-590-26205-X), $20.70. Student Book (ISBN 0-590-26137-1), $6.50. Complete unit, $375.00. Consumables kit, $55.00. ***Publisher/supplier:*** Scholastic. ***Materials:*** Available locally, from commercial suppliers, or in unit.

1.38 Butterflies and Moths. DSM. Hudson, N.H.: Delta Education, 1988.

Grades: 2, 3 In *Butterflies and Moths,* students observe the growth and development of butterflies through their life-cycle stages as larvae, pupae, and adults to the eventual laying of eggs to complete one butterfly life cycle. After an activity on caring for caterpillars and butterflies, the activities focus on the various stages of development and on physical characteristics and food needs, as well as on feeding and egg-laying behaviors.

Butterflies and Moths includes a brief module overview, a section on evaluation, a glossary, and blackline masters. The 11 activities take about 6 weeks (about 12 class sessions plus some daily observations) to complete. The 1- and 2-page activities provide background information, teaching suggestions, and a list of the materials needed.

Prices: Teacher's Guide (ISBN 0-87504-714-9), $9.95. Kit, $133.00. ***Publisher/supplier:*** Delta Education. ***Materials:*** Available locally, from commercial suppliers or in kit.

1.39 Buzzing a Hive. GEMS. Jean C. Echols. Berkeley, Calif.: Lawrence Hall of Science, 1987.

Grades: PreK, K-3 In *Buzzing a Hive,* children discover the complex social behavior, communication, and hive environment of the honeybee. They explore the basic structure of a honeybee's body and learn how bees adapt to the larger world. Students participate in a series of art and drama activities, such as dramatizing life in a beehive, performing bee dances, role-playing the pollen-gathering process, and creating a mural. Although this unit is primarily for students in grades 1-3, it includes suggested modifications for use with preschool and kindergarten children. No live bees are required for any of the activities.

The plan for each of the 6 lessons (requiring 9 sessions of 20 to 60 minutes each) contains an overview, a suggested time frame, a list of materials, ideas for preparation, directions for the activity, and extensions. Background information for teachers is in a separate section at the end of the guide.

Price: $12.50. ***Publisher/supplier:*** LHS GEMS. ***Materials:*** Available locally, or from commercial suppliers.

1.40 Change Over Time: How Populations and Species Change. Scholastic Science Place. (Developed in cooperation with Denver Museum of Natural History, Denver, Colo.) New York, N.Y.: Scholastic, 1995.

Grade: 5 In *Change Over Time: How Populations and Species Change,* students acquire information about how living organisms have evolved and about how evolution is studied. The unit's lessons are grouped in three subconcepts: (1) fossils provide evidence that many species which once inhabited the earth have become extinct; (2) changes in the environment and human intervention can result in changes in the characteristics of a population, and those changes are passed on to succeeding generations; and (3) variation and natural selection have resulted in the evolution of new species. During the unit students make a model of a fossil, investigate two methods for dating fossils, evaluate several theories about the extinction of the dinosaur, and play a game to simulate how natural selection may affect the survival of a population.

Change Over Time: How Populations and Species Change is a 17-lesson unit consisting of 23 sessions of 40 to 50 minutes each. The conceptual goals of the unit are presented in the lesson-by-lesson story line in the teacher's guide. Each lesson also includes background information; a complete lesson plan, including suggestions for assessing performance and integrating the curriculum; and a list of the print, video, and software support materials required for the lesson.

Prices: Teacher's Guide (ISBN 0-590-27707-3), $27. Student Book (ISBN 0-590-27706-5), $10. Complete unit, $450. Consumables kit, $92. ***Publisher/supplier:*** Scholastic. ***Materials:*** Available locally, from commercial suppliers, or in unit.

1.41 Classifying Living Things: How Organisms Are Related. Scholastic Science Place. (Developed in cooperation with Indianapolis Zoo, Indianapolis, Ind.) New York, N.Y.: Scholastic, 1995.

Grade: 3 A sense of order about the plant and animal kingdoms emerges in *Classifying Living Things.* The unit's lessons are arranged in three subconcepts: (1) living organisms can be grouped in five large kingdoms; (2) large groups of living things can be classified into smaller and smaller groups, with each smaller group sharing more characteristics; and (3) the smallest classification group is a species. Sample activities include the following: organizing a school store to practice putting similar items together; observing fungi and photographs of monerans and protists and comparing them with plants and animals; observing crickets and generalizing about how animals are different from plants; growing seedlings to explore plant characteristics; classifying arthropods in four groups; making models of insect mouthparts; comparing human thumbprints to study how members of the same species vary; and making a model classification system for organisms in a grassland ecosystem.

Classifying Living Things: How Organisms Are Related consists of 17 class sessions of 30 to 50 minutes each. The conceptual goals of the unit are presented in the lesson-by-lesson story line in the teacher's guide. Each lesson also includes background information; a complete lesson plan, including suggestions for assessing performance and integrating the curriculum; and a list of the print, video, and software support materials required for the lesson.

Prices: Teacher's Guide (ISBN 0-590-27611-5), $20.70. Student Book (ISBN 0-590-27610-7), $6.50. Complete unit, $375.00. Consumables kit, $70.00. ***Publisher/supplier:*** Scholastic. ***Materials:*** Available locally, from commercial suppliers, or in unit.

1.42 Classroom Plants. DSM. Hudson, N.H.: Delta Education, 1988.

Grades: 2, 3 In *Classroom Plants,* students plant, grow, and care for plants under a variety of conditions. They first observe and compare various seeds and then plant seeds in soil and in water. Then they investigate the needs of plants, observe different types of roots, grow new plants from plant parts, examine leaves and flowers, and grow flowering plants. Instructions on the care of plants in the classroom are provided.

Classroom Plants includes 9 activities requiring 30 to 40 minutes each, plus daily observation time, but the activities are designed to be staggered over the course of a school year. The unit includes a brief module overview, a section on evaluation, a glossary, and blackline masters. The 1- and 2-page activities provide background information, teaching suggestions, and a list of materials needed.

Prices: Teacher's Guide (ISBN 0-87504-713-0), $9.95. Kit, $133.00. ***Publisher/supplier:*** Delta Education. ***Materials:*** Available locally, from commercial suppliers, or in kit.

1.43 Communities. Prepared by Museum To Go Resource Center. Philadelphia, Pa.: Franklin Institute, 1989.

Grades: 4-6 *Communities* follows the flow of energy through a natural community. Students study seeds, green plants, animals, and decomposers, focusing on the role each plays during the transfer of energy in a food chain. Students identify the parts of a seed and then, by germinating and planting lima bean, corn, and peanut seeds, they discover how each part contributes to plant growth. Students construct a terrarium to explore how plants live in communities. They construct simple models of a leaf and molecules to investigate photosynthesis. They identify producers, consumers, and decomposers and describe the roles of each. Then they set up a food chain relay to describe the interdependence of members of a particular food chain.

Each activity in *Communities* features a teacher's page that provides an overview of the lesson. Reproducible student pages include a materials list and instructions for setting up and conducting the activity, including diagrams, recording sheets, and summary questions.

Price: Complete kit, $145. ***Publisher/supplier:*** Science Kit and Boreal Laboratories. ***Materials:*** Available locally, from commercial suppliers, or in kit.

1.44 Communities. REEP. Philadelphia, Pa.: Schuylkill Center for Environmental Education, 1991.

Grade: 2 *Communities,* an environmental education unit, introduces students to the idea of a "natural community"—what it is, how it compares with the "human community," how humans affect the natural community, and how they can reduce their negative effects on the natural community. Activities include the following: students work a food chain puzzle; they draw maps of their own habitats; they collect plants and animals for a classroom aquarium; they role-play predators and prey; and they assess noise, litter, erosion and other examples of the effects of human actions on the natural community surrounding their school.

Communities contains an introduction that includes background information and a lesson summary. The unit contains 10 lessons, which stand alone but are designed to be taught in sequence. Each lesson has from 1 to 3 activities. One to 3 class periods are required for each activity.

Price: $20. ***Publisher/supplier:*** Schuylkill Center for Environmental Education. ***Materials:*** Available locally, or from commercial suppliers.

1.45 Communities. REEP. Philadelphia, Pa.: Schuylkill Center for Environmental Education, 1991.

Grade: 6 In *Communities,* an environmental education unit, students examine several interactions between the living (biotic) and nonliving (abiotic) components of the environment and identify some environmental problems resulting from human activities in ecosystems. Activities in the unit include the following: students draw a mural of their community; they use plant and animal cutouts to construct food chains and webs; they role-play predator and prey; they build a mini-ecosystem—a terrarium; they collect and compare data on abiotic factors at the school site; they research and report on the impact of a particular human action on ecosystems; and they write letters to local officials about a land use issue they have researched.

Communities contains an introduction that includes background information and a lesson summary. The unit consists of 10 lessons that stand alone but are designed to be taught in sequence. Each lesson has from 1 to 3 activities. Activities typically require 30 to 60 minutes to complete.

Price: $20. ***Publisher/supplier:*** Schuylkill Center for Environmental Education. ***Materials:*** Available locally, or from commercial suppliers.

1.46 Cycles. REEP. Philadelphia, Pa.: Schuylkill Center for Environmental Education, 1991.

Grade: 5 *Cycles,* an environmental education unit, introduces students to the finite and cyclic nature of minerals, air, and water, which are essential for all life. Students discover the importance of minerals, air, and water as the nonliving building blocks of living tissue. They examine certain conservation actions that they can undertake, specifically, water conservation strategies. The unit includes the following activities: students identify the nonliving essentials of life as they plan an imaginary journey into space; they use pictures to trace the movement of nutrients through several food chains of varying length; they observe how colored water moves up the stem of a plant to its leaves; they visit a wastewater treatment plant; and they monitor their family's water usage over a 24-hour period.

Cycles contains an introduction that includes background information and a lesson summary. The unit contains 10 lessons, which stand alone but are designed to be taught in sequence. Each lesson has from 1 to 3 activities. Activities typically require 1 to 2 class periods.

Price: $20. ***Publisher/supplier:*** Schuylkill Center for Environmental Education. ***Materials:*** Available locally, or from commercial suppliers.

1.47 Earthworms. GEMS. Robert C. Knott, Kimi Hosoume, and Lincoln Bergman. Reprinted with revisions. Berkeley, Calif.: Lawrence Hall of Science, 1991.

Grades: 5-6+ The 3 lessons in *Earthworms* provide students an opportunity to develop science process skills while learning about the responses of earthworms to temperature, wetness, and soil compaction. In the first lesson, students observe how the worms move and turn themselves over and how the organism's skin looks and feels. Then students practice locating and counting the pulse rates of earthworms. In the second and third lessons, they measure the pulse rate of earthworms at different temperatures and graph the results. In discussing why earthworms respond as they do, students learn about cold-blooded animals.

Each lesson in *Earthworms* includes a materials list, preparation steps, and directions for activities and discussion. The guide also includes background information, summary outlines for each lesson, reproducible data sheets, and suggestions for related reading.

Price: $8.50 (ISBN 0-912511-19-2). ***Publisher/supplier:*** LHS GEMS. ***Materials:*** Available locally, or from commercial suppliers.

1.48 Eco-Inquiry: A Guide to Ecological Learning Experiences for the Upper Elementary/Middle Grades. Kathleen Hogan, Institute of Ecosystem Studies. Dubuque, Iowa: Kendall/Hunt Publishing Co., 1994.

Grades: 5-6+ Learning practical ecology from a local perspective is the focus of *Eco-Inquiry.* This guide offers 3 modules, each with a different ecological challenge for students. In module 1, students fulfill a request from a local community to survey what is living on a plot of land. They construct a food web from the study site and write environmental impact statements to trace how one change in the site could affect the entire food web. In module 2, students explore decomposition and construct a classroom decomposition chamber. In module 3, they explore nutrient recycling, doing research to test the effects of compost tea on radish growth. The modules can stand alone or can be used in sequence at one or several grade levels.

Each module contains from 7 to 10 well-developed lessons and requires from 4 to 7 weeks for completion. (Module 1 takes 4 to 5 weeks; module 2 takes 4 to 5 weeks; and module 3 takes 6 to 7 weeks.) The guide offers numerous tips on how best to use the modules. It includes a variety of assessment strategies.

Price: $36.95 (ISBN 0-8403-9584-1). ***Publisher/supplier:*** Kendall/Hunt. ***Materials:*** Available locally, or from commercial suppliers.

1.49 Endangered Species: Wild and Rare. NatureScope. Washington, D.C.: National Wildlife Federation, 1989.

Grades: K-6 *Endangered Species: Wild and Rare* includes background information and activities that focus on the process of extinction and the role of humans in the destruction or conservation of plants and animals and their habitats. Students participate in classroom and playground activities that integrate science with social studies, mathematics, language arts, drama, music, and art as they learn about habitat destruction, wildlife trade, pollution, and other factors that put species in danger. The chapters in this module usually begin with primary activities and end with intermediate or advanced activities.

Endangered Species: Wild and Rare contains 17 lessons organized in 4 chapters; a fifth chapter provides art and craft ideas. Teachers may choose single activities or teach each chapter as a unit. Copycat pages supplement the activities and include ready-to-copy games, puzzles, and worksheets.

Price: $7.95 (ISBN 0-945051-37-9). ***Publisher/supplier:*** National Wildlife Federation. ***Materials:*** Available locally.

1.50 Exploring With Wisconsin Fast Plants. 1990 draft. Paul H. Williams, Richard P. Green, and Coe M. Williams. Madison, Wisc.: University of Wisconsin, 1989.

Grades: 3-6+ Learning about plant growth and development is the focus in *Exploring With Wisconsin Fast Plants.* Wisconsin Fast Plants (specially bred members of the cabbage and mustard families) have a life cycle of 35 to 40 days and can be grown in the classroom under continuous fluorescent light. The book is organized in 5 sections, which contain (1) basic information for teachers using Fast Plants for the first time, including illustrated growing instructions, tips, troubleshooting suggestions, and ideas for subsequent investigations; (2) explorations pertaining to events and stages of the *Brassica* life cycle; (3) additional explorations in plant physiology and ecology; (4) extensions, stories, modeling ideas, and games; and (5) supplementary materials for teachers. Process skills are embedded throughout the unit. Students are encouraged to generate many of the experimentation ideas.

In *Exploring With Wisconsin Fast Plants,* each experiment follows a science exploration flowchart and includes teaching concepts, background information, and step-by-step illustrated instructions.

Price: $15. ***Publisher/supplier:*** Carolina Biological Supply Co. ***Materials:*** Available locally, or from commercial suppliers.

1.51 The Five Senses. REEP. Philadelphia, Pa.: Schuylkill Center for Environmental Education, 1991.

Grade: K *The Five Senses* attempts to foster positive attitudes about the environment by providing opportunities for children to experience the world of nature through a sharpened set of "tools," their five senses. Activities progress from a focus on using each of the five senses individually to using the senses in concert to appreciate the environment. The unit includes the following activities: students try to identify foods while they are blindfolded; they try to recreate the sound of a rainstorm; they search for objects with opposite textures; they use their senses to find some familiar objects outdoors; they pick up trash on the school grounds; and they make a bird feeder from an egg carton.

The Five Senses contains an introduction that includes background information and a lesson summary. The unit contains 10 lessons that stand alone but are designed to be taught in sequence. Each lesson has from 1 to 3 activities.

Price: $20. ***Publisher/supplier:*** Schuylkill Center for Environmental Education. ***Materials:*** Available locally, or from commercial suppliers.

1.52 Food Chains and Webs. DSM. Hudson, N.H.: Delta Education, 1989.

Grades: 4, 5 In *Food Chains and Webs,* students observe the dynamic interaction of the members of a food chain. They first plant rye grass in various mediums and then perform a controlled experiment on plant growth. The activities then move up the food chain as students learn about crickets, which eat the rye grass, and chameleons, which eat the crickets. Another activity focuses on earthworms as examples of decomposers. Students dissect owl pellets and add the resulting information to what has now become a food web.

Food Chains and Webs is a module with 10 activities, requiring 12 sessions of 40 minutes each. The unit includes a brief module overview, a section on evaluation, a glossary, and blackline masters. The 1- and 2-page activities provide teaching strategies and a list of the materials needed.

Prices: Teacher's Guide (ISBN 0-87504-757-2), $9.95. Kit, $265.00. ***Publisher/supplier:*** Delta Education. ***Materials:*** Available locally, from commercial suppliers, or in kit.

1.53 From Seed to Plant. DSM. Hudson, N.H.: Delta Education, 1988.

Grades: K-2 In the module *From Seed to Plant,* children classify seeds by properties. They plant seeds in a class garden, observe and record the development of the seeds and plants, learn about factors that affect plant growth, and identify basic plant parts. The module closes with an activity focusing on the proper care of plants, teaching students to appreciate plants as living things. Hints on how to get plants to thrive in dry, cold classrooms are provided.

From Seed to Plant consists of 9 activities requiring about 12 class sessions over a period of 8 to 10 weeks. It includes a brief module overview, a section on evaluation, a glossary, and blackline masters. The 1- and 2-page activities provide teaching strategies and a list of materials needed.

Prices: Teacher's Guide (ISBN 0-87504-711-4), $9.95. Kit, $105.00. ***Publisher/supplier:*** Delta Education. ***Materials:*** Available locally, from commercial suppliers, or in kit.

1.54 Fungi—Small Wonders. DSM. Hudson, N.H.: Delta Education, 1994.

Grades: 4, 5 *Fungi—Small Wonders* introduces students to the world of fungi. The activities in the unit include the following: students identify the structures of seed plants and discuss their functions; they compare and contrast the parts of mushrooms and bread mold with the parts of a seed plant; they compare the growth rate of two yeast populations, one supplied with food and one without; they collect and interpret data gathered on mold growth; they experiment to determine the effect of temperature on yeast budding; they test for the production of carbon dioxide during yeast fermentation; and they make pretzel dough as an example of how yeast is used.

Fungi—Small Wonders includes 12 activities which require about 22 class sessions to complete. The teacher's guide includes a module overview, a list of objectives for each activity, a planning schedule, background information, and preparation and materials management strategies. A complete lesson plan is provided for each lesson.

Prices: Teacher's Guide (ISBN 0-87504-109-4), $24.95. Kit, $209. ***Publisher/supplier:*** Delta Education. ***Materials:*** Available locally, from commercial suppliers, or in kit.

1.55 Growing Up. Prepared by Museum To Go Resource Center. Philadelphia, Pa.: Franklin Institute, 1990.

Grades: 3-5 Life cycles are explored in *Growing Up*. During the unit students see the various life cycle stages as they occur. In a sequence of 6 activities, they observe the life cycle of a squash plant, recording its growth and identifying its parts; they discover that living things grow from eggs as they observe brine shrimp hatching; students observe the transformation from caterpillar to chrysalis to butterfly, observing and recording growth and changes throughout the life cycle; and they classify animals as to whether or not they require parental support for survival.

Each activity in *Growing Up* features a teacher's page that provides an overview of the lesson. Reproducible student pages include a materials list and instructions for setting up and conducting the activity, including diagrams, recording sheets, and questions. The guide also includes a glossary, student and teacher references, reproducible masters of student worksheets, and a section on butterflies.

Prices: Complete kit, $255.00. Consumables kit, $82.50. ***Publisher/supplier:*** Science Kit and Boreal Laboratories. ***Materials:*** Available locally, from commercial suppliers, or in kit.

1.56 GrowLab: A Complete Guide to Gardening in the Classroom. Eve Pranis and Jack Hale. Burlington, Vt.: National Gardening Association, 1988.

Grades: K-6 This gardening resource book, which can be used to support a variety of curriculum units on plants, is designed to help the classroom teacher plan, plant, and maintain an indoor garden to support a variety of hands-on plant activities for grades K-6. It provides complete instructions for setting up and cultivating an indoor garden, maintaining a healthy environment, tackling pests and other problems, caring for and maintaining equipment, and building support for classroom gardening in the school and community. The guide provides suggestions, including activities, lessons, and experiments, for integrating gardening into all areas of the curriculum.

Appendixes in *GrowLab: A Complete Guide to Gardening in the Classroom* offer a wide range of useful information, including an indoor gardening "Grower's Guide," reproducible worksheets, supply information, plans for building a GrowLab, and an annotated reference section.

Prices: Teacher's Guide (ISBN 0-915873-31-1), $19.95. Complete starter kit, $99.00. ***Publisher/supplier:*** National Gardening Association. ***Materials:*** Available locally, from commercial suppliers, or in kit.

1.57 GrowLab: Activities for Growing Minds. Eve Pranis and Jack Hale. Burlington, Vt.: National Gardening Association, 1990.

Grades: K-6 *GrowLab: Activities for Growing Minds* contains dozens of ideas and activities relating to plants, gardening, and the diversity of life. This curriculum guide to indoor classroom gardening has 4 chapters. Each presents background information and sections of activities representing a number of key life science concepts. Students learn about the basics of growth from seed to plant and about what makes plants thrive and grow. They observe plant life cycles and discover the structures and processes involved in plant reproduction. They explore plant variations and the ways plants adapt to survive particular environmental conditions. They discover the interdependency of earth's living things.

Each activity in *GrowLab: Activities for Growing Minds* includes step-by-step instructions, a targeted grade-level range, a list showing time and materials required, background information, steps for preparation, and suggestions for cross-curricular activities.

Prices: Teacher's Guide (ISBN 0-915873-32-X), $24.95. Complete starter kit, $99.00. ***Publisher/supplier:*** National Gardening Association. ***Materials:*** Available locally, from commercial suppliers, or in kit.

1.58 Habitats. Prepared by Museum To Go Resource Center. Philadelphia, Pa.: Franklin Institute, 1989.

Grades: 4, 5 In *Habitats,* students investigate the environmental factors that influence the survival of an organism in its habitat. Through a series of 8 hands-on activities, they explore the effect of factors such as light, temperature, and moisture on various organisms. Students construct terrariums to observe the effect of these factors on plant growth. They demonstrate the effects of light and moisture on the germination of lima bean seeds and the growth of mold on crackers. They try to influence a corn plant to grow upside down. Then they experiment to determine how changes in temperature and light affect the movement of ladybugs, they investigate how roots grow in different habitats, and they design and construct a model plant based on specific environmental requirements.

Each activity in *Habitats* features a teacher's page that provides an overview of the lesson. Reproducible student pages include a materials list and instructions for setting up and conducting the activity, including diagrams, recording sheets, and questions. The guide also includes a glossary, reproducible masters of student data sheets, and student and teacher references.

Prices: Complete kit, $215. Consumables kit, $85. ***Publisher/ supplier:*** Science Kit and Boreal Laboratories. ***Materials:*** Available locally, from commercial suppliers, or in kit.

1.59 Hands On Elementary School Science: Life Science. Linda Poore. South Pasadena, Calif.: Linda Poore, 1994.

Grades: K-6 *Hands On Elementary School Science: Life Science* consists of 6 separate life science units—organisms, life cycles, aquatic habitats, terrariums, classification of plants and animals, and the human body. Among the activities in these units, students raise mealworms, silkworms, fruit flies, tadpoles, toads, and plants to observe patterns of growth and development. They build aquariums and terrariums in order to observe interactions within habitats and communities. They investigate interactions among the digestive, circulatory, respiratory, nervous, excretory, muscular, and skeletal systems in the human body. Each unit has a central theme, such as energy, interactions and systems, evolution, and patterns of change. Within units, activities are generally sequenced from easier to more complex.

The *Hands On Elementary School Science: Life Science* lesson plans include science background information, suggestions for integrating science with other subject areas, detailed explanations of the experiments, and questions to stimulate student thinking. The reproducible student data sheets are in English and Spanish.

Prices: Activity binder, $130.00 (complete set of six units). Individual unit, $35.00. Kits for individual units: from $138.50 to $272.00. ***Publisher/supplier:*** Linda Poore. ***Materials:*** Available locally, from commercial suppliers, or in kit from Delta Education.

1.60 Hide a Butterfly. GEMS. Jean C. Echols. Berkeley, Calif.: Lawrence Hall of Science, 1986.

Grades: PreK, K-2 In *Hide a Butterfly,* children learn about protective coloration and the behavior of birds and butterflies as they discover how animals and insects adapt to their environments. Students make a mural of a blossoming meadow, create butterfly and bird puppets, and perform a play in which a butterfly escapes the notice of a bird by blending in to the colors of the flowers. Special instructions for using this unit with younger preschool children and with children in grades 1, 2, and 3 are included.

Hide a Butterfly includes 3 sessions of 20 to 60 minutes each. The plan for each session contains an overview, background information, a list of materials, step-by-step directions for preparation and for setting up the classroom, procedures for conducting the activity, and extensions.

Price: $8.50. ***Publisher/supplier:*** LHS GEMS. ***Materials:*** Available locally, or from commercial suppliers.

1.61 Incredible Insects. NatureScope. Washington, D.C.: National Wildlife Federation, 1989.

Grades: K-6 *Incredible Insects* provides background information and activity ideas for an interdisciplinary introduction to the biology and behavior of insects. Through simulations, games, classroom experiments, and outdoor activities, students investigate a variety of topics such as insect classification, metamorphosis, insect habitats and microhabitats, insect adaptations, and insect interactions with humans. Activities are suitable for use in kindergarten to the intermediate grades; they integrate science with language arts, mathematics, social studies, physical education, and art.

Incredible Insects contains 29 lessons organized in 5 chapters; a sixth chapter provides art and craft ideas. Teachers may choose single activities or teach each chapter as a unit. Copycat pages supplement the activities and include ready-to-copy games, puzzles, and worksheets. An appendix includes ideas for making insect traps and nets and suggestions for attracting insects.

Price: $7.95 (ISBN 0-945051-39-5). ***Publisher/supplier:*** National Wildlife Federation. ***Materials:*** Available locally.

1.62 Incredible Insects Discovery Pac. NatureScope. Washington, D.C.: National Wildlife Federation, 1988.

Grades: K-6 The *Incredible Insects Discovery Pac* contains a set of 15 insect photo cards, a collection of stories from *Ranger Rick*, and a variety of activities that supplement the lessons in NatureScope's *Incredible Insects*. The *Discovery Pac* includes activities such as the following: children engage in community investigations; they visit discovery stations to learn about various species; they study insect adaptations; and they read fiction or biographical stories about insects and the people who interact with them.

Price: $10.95. ***Publisher/supplier:*** National Wildlife Federation. ***Materials:*** Available locally.

1.63 Ladybugs. GEMS/PEACHES. Jean C. Echols. Berkeley, Calif.: Lawrence Hall of Science, 1993.

Grades: PreK, K, 1 Role-playing ladybugs in this unit, students pretend to save orange trees, fly away, and eat aphids, among many other experiences. Children in preschool through first grade learn about the ladybug's life cycle, body structure, and defensive behavior. They make paper ladybugs, observe ladybugs in flight, discover ladybugs' favorite foods, and learn that ladybugs help plants by eating tiny insects that damage plants. The module offers numerous ideas for cross-curricular activities in art and drama.

Ladybugs consists of 5 activities (about 13 class sessions). Each lesson includes a materials list, preparation steps, and directions for activities and discussions. The guide also includes summary outlines of each activity, background information, reproducible illustrations, and suggestions for related reading.

Price: $12.50 (ISBN 0-912511-86-9). ***Publisher/supplier:*** LHS GEMS/ PEACHES. ***Materials:*** Available locally, or from commercial suppliers.

1.64 LEAP, Learning About Ecology, Animals, and Plants. Project LEAP. Ithaca, N.Y.: Cornell University, Department of Education, 1995.

Grade: 1 *LEAP,* Grade 1, the second guide in this K-6 series on plants, animals, and ecology, includes 4 sequential units. Each is based on a central concept (living versus nonliving, seeds, people's use of plants, and life cycles). Each unit contains background information and 7 to 9 activities. The activities are of 3 types—introductory, focus, and summary. Examples include planting seeds and pebbles to distinguish living from nonliving things, dissecting seeds to identify their parts and functions, making pretzels from wheat seeds, and recording growth and change in mealworms as they pass through the stages of their life cycle. The activities in these units can be used in conjunction with other science curricula and other subjects, including reading, writing, art, and mathematics.

A concept map is provided for each unit to show key concepts and their relationships. An activity typically includes an overview, a statement of the time required, a materials list, procedures, and "high jumps."

Price: $50. ***Publisher/supplier:*** Cornell University, Instructional Materials Service. ***Materials:*** Available locally, or from commercial suppliers.

1.65 Let's Hear It For Herps! NatureScope. Washington, D.C.: National Wildlife Federation, 1987.

Grades: K-6 *Let's Hear It For Herps!* uses an interdisciplinary approach to the study of reptiles and amphibians, their characteristics, life cycles, and interactions with humans. Students engage in experiments, games, and simulations that introduce them to the variety of these animals and their adaptations for survival. Students investigate the history of reptiles and amphibians and explore scenarios for the future, including what might happen to these animals because of predation, overhunting, and habitat destruction. The chapters in this module usually begin with primary activities and end with intermediate or advanced activities.

Let's Hear It For Herps! contains 20 lessons organized in 4 chapters; a fifth chapter provides art and craft ideas. Teachers may choose single activities or teach each chapter as a unit. Copycat pages supplement the activities and include ready-to-copy games, puzzles, and worksheets.

Price: $7.95 (ISBN 0-945051-42-5). ***Publisher/supplier:*** National Wildlife Federation. ***Materials:*** Available locally.

1.66 Life Processes: How a Living Thing Stays Alive. Scholastic Science Place. (Developed in cooperation with St. Louis Science Center, St. Louis, Mo.) New York, N.Y.: Scholastic, 1995.

Grade: 4 In *Life Processes: How a Living Thing Stays Alive,* students acquire information about the different processes needed for living things to survive. The unit's lessons are grouped in 3 subconcepts: (1) organisms must take in and use materials and get rid of wastes; (2) organisms must grow and respond to changes in their environment; and (3) for a species to continue, some of its organisms must reproduce. Examples of lessons in this unit include the following: students compare seedlings grown with light and without light; they observe the behavior of sowbugs; and they play a species survival game.

Life Processes: How a Living Thing Stays Alive is a 17-lesson unit consisting of 23 class sessions of 30 to 55 minutes each. The conceptual goals of the unit are presented in the lesson-by-lesson story line in the teacher's guide. Each lesson also includes background information; a complete lesson plan, including suggestions for assessing performance and integrating the curriculum; and a list of the print, video, and software support materials required for the lesson.

Prices: Teacher's Guide (ISBN 0-590-27659-X), $27. Student Book (ISBN 0-590-27658-1), $10. Complete unit, $450. Consumables kit, $125. ***Publisher/supplier:*** Scholastic. ***Materials:*** Available locally, from commercial suppliers, or in unit.

1.67 Living Things: How Plants and Animals Work. Scholastic Science Place. (Developed in cooperation with Science Place, Dallas, Tex.) New York, N.Y.: Scholastic, 1993.

Grade: 1 *Living Things: How Plants and Animals Work* focuses on the many different ways life in nature is sustained. The lessons in this unit are grouped in 3 subconcepts: (1) plants and animals are living things that meet their differing basic needs in different ways; (2) the structures of different kinds of plants vary to help meet their individual needs; and (3) different kinds of animals also have different structures that help them meet their needs. Activities in the unit include the following: taking a nature walk to observe similarities and differences between plants and animals; planting "mystery" seeds; examining the roots of "mystery" plants to learn how stems take food from the soil; discovering that plants need light by observing them bend toward their source of light; and investigating how the different parts of animals' bodies help them obtain food, eat, breathe, move, and survive.

Living Things: How Plants and Animals Work is a 17-lesson unit typically requiring 30- to 45-minute sessions. The conceptual goals of the unit are presented in the lesson-by-lesson story line in the teacher's guide. Each lesson also includes background information; a complete lesson plan, including suggestions for assessing performance and integrating the curriculum; and a list of the print, video, and software support materials required for the lesson.

Prices: Teacher's Guide (ISBN 0-590-26202-5), $20.70. Student Book (ISBN 0-590-26134-7), $6.50. Complete unit, $375.00. Consumables kit, $67.00. ***Publisher/supplier:*** Scholastic. ***Materials:*** Available locally, from commercial suppliers, or in unit.

1.68 Mapping Animal Movements. GEMS. Katharine Barrett. Berkeley, Calif.: Lawrence Hall of Science, 1987.

Grades: 5-6+ In *Mapping Animal Movements,* students carry out hands-on experiences with animals and learn research techniques used by field biologists to study animal behavior. Students practice a sampling system, using the classroom as a habitat. They use this skill to observe, track, map, graph, and identify patterns in the movements of a variety of animals, such as crickets and hamsters. Students first observe the animals in an empty container; adding food and shelter to the container, students compare the animals' movements before and after their environment changes.

Mapping Animal Movements includes easy-to-follow lesson plans for each of the 4 activities (requiring 30 to 45 minutes each), suggestions for the care and handling of animals, and reproducible student data sheets. Each lesson plan includes an overview, background information, a list of materials, and detailed instructions for preparation and for conducting the activity.

Price: $10. ***Publisher/supplier:*** LHS GEMS. ***Materials:*** Available locally, or from commercial suppliers.

1.69 Mapping Fish Habitats. GEMS. Katharine Barrett and Cary I. Sneider. Berkeley, Calif.: Lawrence Hall of Science, 1987.

Grades: 6+ In *Mapping Fish Habitats,* students discover that fish have behavioral differences that provide clues about what various fish need to survive and how they interact with each other and their environment. Students set up a fish tank, map fish movements using systematic sampling methods, identify the home range, and then plan and conduct experiments to determine the effects of an environmental change on the home ranges of the fish.

Mapping Fish Habitats includes useful information about setting up an aquarium and interesting facts about fish, as well as specific lesson plans for each of the 4 activities in this unit. Each activity requires a 30- to 45-minute session plus time for daily observations. An overview, a list of materials, and step-by-step instructions for preparing and conducting the lesson are included for each activity.

Price: $10. ***Publisher/supplier:*** LHS GEMS. ***Materials:*** Available locally, or from commercial suppliers.

1.70 Organisms and Environments: How Living Things Interact. Scholastic Science Place. (Developed in cooperation with Cincinnati Museum of Natural History, Cincinnati, Ohio.) New York, N.Y.: Scholastic, 1995.

Grade: 4 The lessons in this unit, *Organisms and Environments: How Living Things Interact,* are grouped in 3 subconcepts: (1) an ecosystem is made up of living things that interact with each other and with nonliving things; (2) ecosystems supply living things with the energy and materials they need for survival; and (3) ecosystems can change naturally and they can change as a result of the activities of humans. Examples of lessons in this unit include students making models of 4 types of ecosystems and investigating their similarities; comparing water absorption in various types of soil; observing the effects of withholding light from an ecosystem; and examining pictures to observe how ecosystems change over time.

Organisms and Environments: How Living Things Interact is a 17-lesson unit consisting of 23 class sessions typically 30 to 45 minutes in duration. The conceptual goals of the unit are presented in the lesson-by-lesson story line in the teacher's guide. Each lesson also includes background information; a complete lesson plan, including suggestions for assessing performance and integrating the curriculum; and a list of the print, video, and software support materials required for the lesson.

Prices: Teacher's Guide (ISBN 0-590-27683-2), $27. Student Book (ISBN 0-590-27682-4), $10. Complete unit, $450. Consumables kit, $125. ***Publisher/supplier:*** Scholastic. ***Materials:*** Available locally, from commercial suppliers, or in unit.

1.71 Penguins and Their Young. GEMS/PEACHES. Jean C. Echols. Berkeley, Calif.: Lawrence Hall of Science, 1995.

Grades: PreK, K, 1 In *Penguins and Their Young,* an activity-based unit for preschoolers, kindergartners, and first-graders, children play with floating ice, penguins made of cork, and toy fish as they learn about the icy environment of the emperor penguin. They use life-size drawings as they discover that penguins are birds and compare them with other birds. During the unit young students watch a drama about parental care in penguins, role-play parent penguins, play a "hungry-penguins" game to learn about penguins' diets, and set up simple ice investigations.

Penguins and Their Young is organized into 4 activities, requiring a maximum of 14 class sessions. A life-sized penguin poster and reproducible masters of cutouts and student activity sheets are included in the teacher's guide, as well as background information, suggestions for additional resources, literature connections, and summary outlines of all activities.

Price: $15 (ISBN 0-912511-92-3). ***Publisher/supplier:*** LHS GEMS. ***Materials:*** Available locally.

1.72 Pillbug Project: A Guide to Investigation. Robin Burnett. Washington, D.C.: National Science Teachers Association, 1992.

Grades: 3-6 The *Pillbug Project* guides students through 10 days in the life of a pillbug. The activities on the 10 days are as follows: (1) Students collect pillbugs on or near the school grounds and place them in a pillbug hideaway. (2) They observe pillbug characteristics and behavior. (3-5) After reading a story about Patricia Pillbug, they set up observation stations to determine where pillbugs are and then conduct pillbug races. (6) Students retrieve their pillbugs from their outdoor stations and share their findings with the class in a pillbug symposium. (7) Students are encouraged to look at life from a pillbug's perspective and to ask and answer questions about things that are fundamental to a pillbug's life. (8) Students are challenged to question the validity of their experimental results to date. (9) Students choose their own experiments. (10) They gather and present all of their data at a symposium of pillbug experts—themselves.

Each of the 10 lessons in the *Pillbug Project* includes a teacher's note, a materials list, teacher's narrative, and procedures for the experiment. The guide's introduction includes facts about pillbugs and tips on conducting and evaluating the project.

Price: $16.50 (ISBN 0-87355-109-5). ***Publisher/supplier:*** National Science Teachers Association. ***Materials:*** Available locally.

1.73 Plant and Animal Life Cycles. DSM. Hudson, N.H.: Delta Education, 1988.

Grades: 3-5 In *Plant and Animal Life Cycles,* students work with pea plants and fruit flies as they learn about plant and animal life cycles. After focusing on the differences between living, dead, and nonliving things, students plant and germinate seeds and record their observations at each step in the cycle. Observing and comparing the growth and development of their plants and then planting second-generation pea seeds, students see a complete life cycle of the plant. Next they observe fruit fly cultures, following the flies through the larval and pupal stages to adulthood. Biotic potential is introduced to students through experiments with an ear of corn. The module ends with experiments showing what happens when organisms die and decompose.

Plant and Animal Life Cycles consists of 11 activities, requiring 11 class sessions of 30 to 40 minutes each, plus daily observations. It includes a brief module overview, a section on evaluation, a glossary, and blackline masters. The 1- and 2-page activities list materials needed and provide teaching suggestions.

Prices: Teacher's Guide (ISBN 0-87504-716-5), $9.95. Kit, $169.00. ***Publisher/supplier:*** Delta Education. ***Materials:*** Available locally, from commercial suppliers, or in kit.

1.74 Plant and Animal Populations. DSM. Hudson, N.H.: Delta Education, 1989.

Grades: 2, 3 The *Plant and Animal Populations* module introduces students to the concepts of population dynamics as they build environments for ants, ladybugs, algae, and other organisms. Students set up terrariums and aquariums to observe ways in which plants and animals are adapted to water and land habitats. They see social interaction among animals as they observe ants. In other activities they observe and record changes in species populations over time, learning about factors such as dispersal, interaction, and population control. Watching populations increase and decrease, students learn about reproduction, death, and overcrowding. They create their own population game and learn that some animals are better adapted to their habitat than others are and so are more likely to survive.

Plant and Animal Populations has 10 activities and takes from 6 to 8 weeks to complete. It includes a brief module overview, a section on evaluation, a glossary, and blackline masters. The 1- and 2-page activities provide teaching suggestions and a list of materials needed.

Prices: Teacher's Guide (ISBN 0-87504-760-2), $9.95. Kit, $275.00. ***Publisher/supplier:*** Delta Education. ***Materials:*** Available locally, from commercial suppliers, or in kit.

1.75 Plants and Animals. REEP. Philadelphia, Pa.: Schuylkill Center for Environmental Education, 1991.

Grade: 1 *Plants and Animals,* an environmental education unit, introduces children to plants, animals, their habitats, and the need to preserve habitats. Activities begin with an overview of the characteristics of living and nonliving things and of the features that distinguish plants from animals. Students then examine the concepts of habitat and habitat destruction. The unit includes the following activities: students search for examples of living and nonliving things on the school grounds; they experiment with the needs of a growing plant for light and water; they play a game that depicts the impact of human actions on the habitats of grizzly bears; and they perform a drama about a possible cause of the extinction of dinosaurs.

Plants and Animals contains an introduction that includes background information and a lesson summary. The unit contains 10 lessons that stand alone but are designed to be taught in sequence. Each lesson has from 1 to 3 activities.

Price: $20. ***Publisher/supplier:*** Schuylkill Center for Environmental Education. ***Materials:*** Available locally, or from commercial suppliers.

1.76 Pond Life. DSM. Hudson, N.H.: Delta Education, 1994.

Grades: 4-6 In *Pond Life,* students visit a pond and investigate water, plant, and animal life. In the classroom, students set up and maintain aquariums containing organisms typically found in a freshwater pond and compare this aquarium ecosystem to the pond ecosystem. Students observe and describe macro- and microscopic organisms in their aquarium ecosystem. They make a hay infusion, comparing the organisms in it with those found in their aquariums. Finally, they examine the food chains that exist in a pond, looking at the relationships between producers and consumers.

Pond Life consists of 12 activities which require about 20 class sessions. The teacher's guide includes a module overview, a list of objectives for each activity, a planning schedule, background information, and preparation and materials management strategies. A complete lesson plan is provided for each lesson.

Prices: Teacher's Guide (ISBN 0-87504-121-3), $24.95. Kit, $220.50. ***Publisher/supplier:*** Delta Education. ***Materials:*** Available locally, from commercial suppliers, or in kit.

1.77 Rain Forests: Tropical Treasures. NatureScope. Washington, D.C.: National Wildlife Federation, 1989.

Grades: K-6+ In *Rain Forests: Tropical Treasures,* students learn about the problems associated with deforestation in the rain forests, about the diversity of life forms in these forests, and about the ways people depend on tropical resources. Classroom and outdoor activities include experiments, stories, games, discussions, and simulations that integrate science with language arts, art, music, social studies, and geography. The chapters in the module usually begin with activities for primary grades and end with advanced activities for upper grades.

Rain Forests: Tropical Treasures contains 17 lessons organized in 4 chapters; a fifth chapter provides art and craft ideas. Teachers may select single activities or teach each chapter as a unit. An appendix provides a list of rain forest exhibits around the United States. Copycat pages supplement the activities and include ready-to-copy maps, puzzles, coloring pages, and worksheets.

Price: $7.95 (ISBN 0-945051-41-7). ***Publisher/supplier:*** National Wildlife Federation. ***Materials:*** Available locally.

1.78 Small Things and Microscopes. DSM. Eileen Terrill. Hudson, N.H.: Delta Education, 1994.

Grades: 4-6 Students' perspectives widen as they learn about magnification in *Small Things and Microscopes.* Students use magnifiers as tools for drawing and creating tiny objects. They learn to identify and adjust the various parts of a microscope, prepare wet mounts, stain specimens, measure microscopic differences in hair and thread widths, compare the structures of various plant and animal cells, use depression slides to observe living organisms, and culture bacteria and monitor their population growth.

Small Things and Microscopes consists of 13 lessons, which require about 18 class sessions to complete. The teacher's guide includes a module overview, a list of objectives for each activity, a planning schedule, background information, and preparation and materials management strategies. A complete lesson plan is provided for each lesson.

Prices: Teacher's Guide (ISBN 0-87504-152-3), $24.95. Kit, $230.00. ***Publisher/supplier:*** Delta Education. ***Materials:*** Available locally, from commercial suppliers, or in kit.

1.79 STAR Ecology Lab. STAR. Washington, D.C.: Reading Is Fundamental, 1993.

Grades: 4-6 In *STAR Ecology Lab,* students become residents of a mythical town—Anytown—whose residents must decide what to do with a large tract of undeveloped land, known as Lakeland. Through a series of hands-on activities, students conduct experiments and gather data to help them decide what to do with the land. Students represent various interest groups—conservationists, recreation advocates, developers, business-growth advocates, and so on—at a town meeting. Then they vote on the plans offered. Students draw up a site plan using the school grounds as the plot of land to be developed. They test air quality and soil permeability and percolation rate, learn about water filtration, conduct a population study and a recreation survey, and use mathematics to interpret employment data for Anytown.

The *STAR Ecology Lab* includes ideas for cross-curricular integration, from writing an "eco haiku" to making a relief map of Lakeland. It also includes a list of resources, including books, computer software, and audiovisual materials.

Prices: Teacher's Guide, $21.90. Mentor's Guide, $3.90. ***Publisher/supplier:*** Kendall/Hunt. ***Materials:*** Available locally.

1.80 STAR Sports Lab. STAR. Washington, D.C.: Reading Is Fundamental, 1993.

Grades: 4-6 *STAR Sports Lab* uses the popularity of sports to teach students various scientific aspects of sports and fitness. The learning module begins with a story about students participating in a city-sponsored sports clinic and concludes with the class designing and manning a sports clinic at their school. Students conduct an experiment on the relative bounciness of balls; they experiment to determine how simple exercise affects the heart rate; they test and learn the importance of an athlete's reaction speed by trying to catch a ruler as it drops; and they design a helmet to protect an egg during a fall off a wall.

The guide includes numerous suggestions for cross-curricular activities. For example, students practice sportscasting and look for examples of good sportswriting. They use their mathematical skills to calculate how many calories are burned from participating in various sports. They compile a booklet of jump-rope jingles. The guide includes a list of resources, including books, computer software, and audiovisual materials.

Prices: Teacher's Guide, $21.90. Mentor's Guide, $3.90. ***Publisher/supplier:*** Kendall/Hunt. ***Materials:*** Available locally.

1.81 Staying Well: How You Can Take Care of Your Body. Scholastic Science Place. (Developed in cooperation with Science Museums of Charlotte, Charlotte, N.C.) New York, N.Y.: Scholastic, 1993.

Grade: 2 In *Staying Well: How You Can Take Care of Your Body,* students explore various body systems and learn that the body is a special mechanism that needs proper care to stay healthy. The unit's lessons are grouped in 2 subconcepts: (1) the human body requires nutrition, exercise, and rest in order to function properly; and (2) a person makes decisions that affect how well his or her body functions. Examples of lessons in this unit include students making a food clock to record how many times a day their body needs food, testing food samples for starch, making up a dance exercise, and making a feel-good poster.

Staying Well: How You Can Take Care of Your Body is a 17-lesson unit typically requiring 35- to 45-minute class sessions. The conceptual goals of the unit are presented in the lesson-by-lesson story line in the teacher's guide. Each lesson also includes background information; a complete lesson plan, including suggestions for assessing performance and integrating the curriculum; and a list of the print, video, and software support materials required for the lesson.

Prices: Teacher's Guide (ISBN 0-590-26211-4), $20.70. Student Book (ISBN 0-590-26143-6), $6.50. Complete unit, $375.00. Consumables kit, $31.00. ***Publisher/supplier:*** Scholastic. ***Materials:*** Available locally, from commercial suppliers, or in unit.

1.82 Support Systems: How Bones and Muscles Work Together. Scholastic Science Place. (Developed in cooperation with Fort Worth Museum of Science and History, Fort Worth, Tex.) New York, N.Y.: Scholastic, 1995.

Grade: 3 How we stand, bend, and lift are among the questions students learn to answer in *Support Systems: How Bones and Muscles Work Together.* The lessons in this unit are grouped in 3 subconcepts: (1) bones, cartilage, and ligaments form a skeletal system that supports and protects the body; (2) muscles connected to bones by tendons move the bones; and (3) a person makes decisions that affect the health of his or her body's support systems. Students examine bones to observe their structure, study X-rays to explore how bone and cartilage change as people grow, examine how joints between bones enable them to move, examine food labels to find out what foods are best for bones and muscles, and build robots that simulate human movements.

Support Systems: How Bones and Muscles Work Together is a 17-lesson unit requiring 30- to 40-minute class sessions. The conceptual goals of the unit are presented in the lesson-by-lesson story line in the teacher's guide. Each lesson also includes background information; a complete lesson plan, including suggestions for assessing performance and integrating the curriculum; and a list of the print, video, and software support materials required for the lesson.

Prices: Teacher's Guide (ISBN 0-590-27619-0), $20.70. Student Book (ISBN 0-590-27618-2), $6.50. Complete unit, $375.00. Consumables kit, $64.00. ***Publisher/supplier:*** Scholastic. ***Materials:*** Available locally, from commercial suppliers, or in unit.

1.83 Terrarium Habitats. GEMS. Kimi Hosoume and Jacqueline Barber. Berkeley, Calif.: Lawrence Hall of Science, 1994.

Grades: K-6 In *Terrarium Habitats,* students watch nature's processes unfold in their own classroom. Working in teams, they carefully observe and describe the characteristics of a sample of garden soil. Each team then builds a miniforest terrarium habitat. Easily obtained animals such as earthworms and pillbugs are observed and then placed in the terrarium. Students monitor activity in the terrariums daily and record their observations in a journal. In the final activity they have an opportunity to explore interactions within their terrarium habitats as they choose and add other animals, plants, and food items. Modifications are suggested for grades K-2.

Each of the 5 activities (requiring 45 to 60 minutes each) in *Terrarium Habitats* includes a materials list, preparation steps, and directions for activities and discussions. The guide also includes extensive background information, summary outlines of each lesson, reproducible blackline masters, and suggestions for related reading and other resources.

Price: $12.50 (ISBN 0-912511-85-0). ***Publisher/supplier:*** LHS GEMS. ***Materials:*** Available locally, or from commercial suppliers.

1.84 Transport Systems: How Your Body Changes and Uses Food, Water, and Air. Scholastic Science Place. (Developed in cooperation with Staten Island Children's Museum, Staten Island, N.Y.) New York, N.Y.: Scholastic, 1995.

Grade: 5 In *Transport Systems,* students acquire information about the transport systems of the human body. The unit's lessons are grouped in three subconcepts: (1) the digestive system and the respiratory system supply the circulatory system with certain materials that the body needs; (2) the circulatory system carries materials from the digestive and respiratory systems to and from all the body's cells; and (3) a person makes decisions that affect the health of his or her body's transport systems. Examples of lessons in this unit include students making models of their stomachs, mouths, and lungs; measuring their pulse rate; writing a balanced eating plan; and designing a transport game.

Transport Systems: How Your Body Changes and Uses Food, Water, and Air is a 17-lesson unit requiring 23 40- to 55-minute class sessions. The conceptual goals of the unit are presented in the lesson-by-lesson story line in the teacher's guide. Each lesson also includes background information; a complete lesson plan, including suggestions for assessing performance and integrating the curriculum; and a list of the print, video, and software support materials required for the lesson.

Prices: Teacher's Guide (ISBN 0-590-27715-04), $27. Student Book (ISBN 0-590-27714-6), $10. Complete unit, $450. Consumables kit, $96. ***Publisher/supplier:*** Scholastic. ***Materials:*** Available locally, from commercial suppliers, or in unit.

1.85 Tree Homes. GEMS/PEACHES. Jean C. Echols. Berkeley, Calif.: Lawrence Hall of Science, 1993.

Grades: PreK, K, 1 *Tree Homes* is designed to stimulate children's interest in trees and the animals that live in tree homes. Information on the dependence of many animals on tree holes for warm, safe homes is woven into the structured activities, as is the concept of measurement (of tree-hole sizes and shapes). In the first lesson, students observe and learn about a living tree and make their own child-sized cardboard trees. Next they learn about bears, through a combination of drama, role-playing, and sorting activities. After exploring the many ways animals keep warm, students learn about the lives and habits of raccoons and owls. Finally, they discover that bears, raccoons, and owls move out of their tree-hole homes and that other animals move in.

Each of the 6 lessons in *Tree Homes* includes a materials list, preparation steps, and directions for activities and discussion. The guide also includes background information, summary outlines of each lesson, reproducible illustrations, and suggestions for related reading.

Price: $12.50 (ISBN 0-912511-87-8). ***Publisher/supplier:*** LHS GEMS. ***Materials:*** Available locally, or from commercial suppliers.

1.86 Trees Are Terrific! NatureScope. Washington, D.C.: National Wildlife Federation, 1989.

Grades: K-6+ *Trees Are Terrific!* includes background information and activities for an interdisciplinary introduction to the biology of trees and forest ecology. Through observations, experiments, games, and simulations, students from kindergarten through the intermediate grades investigate the characteristics of trees, their growth and reproduction, and their influence on human life.

Trees Are Terrific! contains 24 lessons organized in 5 chapters; a sixth chapter provides art and craft ideas. Teachers may select single activities or teach each chapter as a unit. Copycat pages supplement the activities and include ready-to-copy puzzles, coloring pages, and worksheets.

Price: $7.95. ***Publisher/supplier:*** National Wildlife Federation. ***Materials:*** Available locally, or from commercial suppliers.

1.87 The Underground Connection: A Prekindergarten Science Unit. Rockville, Md.: Montgomery County Public Schools, Division of Academic Programs, Office of Instruction and Program Development, 1992.

Grades: PreK, K *The Underground Connection* involves young children in hands-on, multisensory activities as they explore the world of growing plants. The children work at an exploration center. The activities focus on seeds, soil, and planting. Examples of the activities include finding seeds in fruits, going on an outdoor seed hunt, germinating seeds, examining soil samples, creating a worm habitat, and planting bulbs in the schoolyard. Art, mathematics, music, language arts, and health and safety extension ideas are incorporated in the activities. Icons in the guide indicate special characteristics of activities, such as group participation, multicultural material, and seasonality.

Underground Connection includes appendixes on the curriculum areas supported by each section, multicultural perspectives, tips on planting an outdoor garden, a time frame/calendar for activities, a list of resource materials, and a sample letter to parents.

Prices: Teacher's Guide, $25. Complete kit, $270. Consumables kit, $44. ***Publisher/supplier:*** Montgomery County Public Schools. ***Materials:*** Available locally, from commercial suppliers, or in kit from SEMPCO.

1.88 Wading into Wetlands. NatureScope. Washington, D.C.: National Wildlife Federation, 1989.

Grades: K-6 *Wading into Wetlands* includes background information and activities for an interdisciplinary introduction to the ecology of wetlands, including salt marshes and mangrove swamps, and freshwater swamps, marshes, and bogs. Students participate in classroom and field experiences, observing flora and fauna. They engage in experiments, games, writing, art, and mathematical activities that demonstrate the unique characteristics of wetlands and their importance to wildlife and humans. Chapters usually begin with primary activities and end with intermediate or advanced activities.

Wading into Wetlands contains 20 lessons organized in 4 chapters; a fifth chapter provides art and craft ideas. Teachers may choose single activities or teach each chapter as a unit. Copycat pages supplement the activities and include ready-to-copy games, puzzles, and worksheets.

Price: $7.95. ***Publisher/supplier:*** National Wildlife Federation. ***Materials:*** Available locally, or from commercial suppliers.

1.89 You and Your Body. DSM. Hudson, N.H.: Delta Education, 1994.

Grades: 5, 6 In *You and Your Body,* students investigate several organ systems of the human body as well as foods and nutrition. Activities include students constructing models of an arm and a leg to simulate the role of muscles and joints in movement, and measuring their own reaction times, pulse rate, and lung capacity. They observe and discuss the properties of skin and teeth. They test a variety of foods to determine the relative protein and fat content. Students investigate their senses of smell, touch, hearing, and sight.

You and Your Body includes 14 activities, which require about 17 class sessions. The teacher's guide includes a module overview, a list of objectives for each activity, a planning schedule, background information, and preparation and materials management strategies. A complete lesson plan is provided for each lesson.

Prices: Teacher's Guide (ISBN 0-87504-105-1), $24.95. Kit, $259.00. ***Publisher/supplier:*** Delta Education. ***Materials:*** Available locally, from commercial suppliers, or in kit.

LIFE SCIENCE—SCIENCE ACTIVITY BOOKS

ABOUT THE ANNOTATIONS IN "LIFE SCIENCE—SCIENCE ACTIVITY BOOKS"

Entry Numbers

Curriculum materials are arranged alphabetically by title in each category (Core Materials, Supplementary Materials, and Science Activity Books) in chapters 1 through 4 of this guide. In addition, each annotation has a two-part entry number. For each entry number, the chapter number is given before the period; the number after the period locates the entry within that chapter.

For example, the first entry number in chapter 1 is 1.1; the second entry in chapter 2 is 2.2, and so on.

The entry numbers within each curriculum chapter run consecutively through Core Materials, Supplementary Materials, and Science Activity Books.

Order of Bibliographic Information

Following is the arrangement of the facts of publication in the annotations in this section:

- **Title of publication.**
- **Series title,** or series acronym if commonly used.
- **Authors** (either individual names or organizational author).
- Name and location of **developer** (in parentheses), if different from publisher.
- **Place of publication, publisher, and date of publication.**

Series Acronym

Following is the **acronym of one series title** in "Life Science—Science Activity Books." (Series titles that are spelled out are not included in this list.)

AIMS Activities Integrating Mathematics and Science

Price and Acquisition Information

Ordering information is presented in a block immediately below the annotation. Included are the following:

- **Prices** of teacher's guides, activity books, and kits or units.
- The name of a principal **publisher/supplier** (not necessarily the sole source) for the items listed in the price category. (The address and phone and fax numbers for each publisher and supplier appear in appendix A, "Publishers and Suppliers.")
- An indication of the various sources from which one might obtain the required **materials.**

1.90 All About Penguins. San Diego, Calif.: Sea World, 1992.

Grades: 4-6+ In *All About Penguins,* students discover where penguins live, what they eat, what animals try to eat them, how penguins have adapted to their various environments, how they reproduce, and how human actions affect the prospects of penguins for survival. Students investigate the insulative qualities of penguin blubber and feathers. They test their own jumping abilities against those of a rockhopper penguin attempting to avoid a predator. They make posters about public awareness of environmental threats to penguins.

Included in this 15-page teacher's guide are illustrations of the 17 species of penguins and information about their size, geographical distribution, prey, predators, and population. The guide also provides an illustration of a penguin food chain; a world map of penguin species distribution; sections on conservation and Antarctica; and a bibliography.

Price: $5. ***Publisher/supplier:*** Sea World of California. ***Materials:*** Available locally.

1.91 All About Sea Turtles. San Diego, Calif.: Sea World, 1992.

Grades: K-6+ Through the series of interdisciplinary activities in *All About Sea Turtles,* students learn about these creatures and become more aware of endangered species. Activities include the following: students play a listening game using vocabulary words relating to sea turtles; they learn about the body parts of sea turtles by constructing a sea turtle puppet; they take on the role of sea turtle hatchlings to show how they are disoriented by bright lights; they run a relay race to learn about sea turtles' diet and the effects of pollution on it; they learn about sea turtle predators by reciting riddles; and they develop an advertising campaign to educate the public about the plight of sea turtles.

This 23-page teacher's guide includes illustrations and brief information about 6 species of sea turtles, a sea turtle fact sheet, 12 activities, and suggestions for further reading. Each activity includes a suggested grade level, objectives, a list of materials needed, and directions.

Price: $5. ***Publisher/supplier:*** Sea World of California. ***Materials:*** Available locally.

1.92 Bottle Biology. Paul H. Williams. Dubuque, Iowa: Kendall/Hunt Publishing Co., 1993.

Grades: 1-6+ *Bottle Biology* offers creative ways to teach science concepts and process skills using the ubiquitous 2-liter plastic soda bottle. Students build, fill, observe, and explore the bottle, which acts as a decomposition column, a fermentation chamber, a sedimentation bottle, a soil column, a fruit fly trap and breeder, a predator-prey column, a TerrAqua column, and an ecocolumn. Detailed instructions and illustrations, activities, and teaching tips are included. There are suggested activities and experiments for each type of column. Examples of activities include making pH indicators, building a terrarium to house carnivorous plants, building a tropical rainforest ecocolumn, and constructing a bottle microscope. Instructions on using empty film cans in experiments on germination, gravitropism, and phototropism are also included.

Each of *Bottle Biology*'s 10 chapters features background information. An annotated bibliography is included.

Price: $15.95 (ISBN 0-8403-8601-X). ***Publisher/supplier:*** Kendall/Hunt. ***Materials:*** Available locally.

1.93 The Budding Botanist: Investigations with Plants. AIMS. Evalyn Hoover, Howard Larimer, Sheryl Mercier, and Michael Walsh. Fresno, Calif.: AIMS Education Foundation, 1993.

Grades: 3-6 *The Budding Botanist* presents 30 activities concerned with the investigation of seed plants. Mathematics and science skills are tested, and other disciplines are integrated, as students investigate the following topic areas: seeds, seed structure, seed germination, seed dispersal, functions of plant parts, photosynthesis, seed and fruit development, and the structure of cells. Sample activities include comparing seeds by their physical characteristics, dissecting seeds, germinating seeds, using natural materials to make pictures of trees, and making models of plant cells.

Worksheets accompany the hands-on activities in *The Budding Botanist*, and each lesson includes an introductory statement; lists of mathematics skills, science processes, and materials; key questions, background information, management suggestions, procedures, discussion questions, extension ideas, and curriculum correlations.

Price: $14.95 (ISBN 1-881431-40-1). ***Publisher/supplier:*** AIMS Education Foundation. ***Materials:*** Available locally.

1.94 Bugwise. Pamela M. Hickman. A publication of the Federation of Ontario Naturalists. Toronto, Ontario, Canada: Kids Can Press, 1990.

Grades: 4-6 Dozens of inventive activities highlight *Bugwise*, an introduction to insects and spiders. The activity book is organized in 6 sections: (1) Aquatic Insects, (2) Insects in Winter, (3) Investigating Insects, (4) Some Insects Up Close, (5) Insect Survival, and (6) Insect Impostors. Some suggested activities include making waterscopes to observe aquatic insects, collecting and dissecting galls to observe insects in winter, looking for "life on a leaf," constructing ant palaces, and catching and releasing flying insects and spiders. Dozens of nuggets of information about insects and their behaviors are included, as well as helpful tips on using commonly available materials to collect, house, and observe insects.

The plentiful illustrations are a notable feature of *Bugwise*. The technical illustrations are of good quality; the nontechnical illustrations are lively and expressive.

Price: $9.57 (ISBN 0-921103-91-3). ***Publisher/supplier:*** Addison-Wesley. ***Materials:*** Available locally.

1.95 Butterflies Abound! A Whole Language Resource Guide for K-4. Seddon Kelly Beaty and Irene Fountas. Menlo Park, Calif.: Addison-Wesley Publishing Co., 1993.

Grades: K-4 Based on a whole language philosophy, *Butterflies Abound!* offers a broad range of suggestions for interdisciplinary activities and experiences to enrich a core unit on butterflies or moths. In addition to completing scientific activities such as examining butterfly wings, students perform plays and skits on butterfly life cycles, and even follow simple recipes to create caterpillar and butterfly snacks for an end-of-unit celebration. The science section of this resource guide is organized in 5 key concepts: (1) insects, (2) metamorphosis and anatomy, (3) basic needs and behaviors, (4) protective behaviors, and (5) variety and classifications. These concepts can be explored in any order, and several concepts may be explored simultaneously. Related learning experiences in the other subject area sections are cross-referenced in the science sections.

Each concept section in *Butterflies Abound!* includes sample questions, extensive background information, and suggestions for a wide variety of learning experiences. The guide then offers butterfly-related sections on language arts, mathematics, social studies, art, drama, music, cooking, and physical activities.

Price: $26.85 (ISBN 0-201-45504-8). ***Publisher/supplier:*** Addison-Wesley. ***Materials:*** Available locally.

1.96 Critters. AIMS. Fresno, Calif.: AIMS Education Foundation, 1989.

Grades: K-6 *Critters* takes a look at the habits and habitats of a wide variety of crawling, swimming, and walking members of the animal kingdom. This book is filled with varied activities. For example, students make insects out of clay and pipe cleaners, race snails to determine whether big snails or small snails travel faster, and test the temperature preferences of isopods. Mathematics and science skills are tested and other disciplines are integrated as students investigate the following topics: insects and spiders, mealworms, earthworms, snails, silkworms, isopods, aquatic creatures, adaptations and camouflage, and food chains.

Worksheets with lively illustrations accompany the activities. Each lesson in *Critters* includes an introductory statement; lists of mathematics skills, science processes, and materials; key questions, background information, management suggestions, procedures, discussion questions, extension ideas, and curriculum connections.

Price: $16.95 (ISBN 1-881431-23-1). ***Publisher/supplier:*** AIMS Education Foundation. ***Materials:*** Available locally.

1.97 Gentle Giants of the Sea. Paul Kastner, Joan Kastner, and Jessica A. Porter. 2nd ed. Friday Harbor, Wash.: The Whale Museum, 1986.

Grades: K-6 In *Gentle Giants of the Sea,* students learn about whales—the largest creatures on earth—through reading selections and multidisciplinary activities. They also learn about the delicate balance of the earth's ecosystem and how all living things are interrelated. In a series of 14 well-planned lessons, students explore the size, characteristics, and main body parts of whales. They discover how whales eat, breathe, make sounds, and use echolocation. Students learn about the whale's social structure, reproduction, and behavior. They acquire an understanding of the complexity of life in the ocean and develop an awareness of and concern for the interaction of whales and people. Activities include discussions, research projects, art projects, puppet shows, classification exercises, card games, collages, and creative writing.

Each lesson contains student text (lesson information written at a grade-4 to -6 reading level), objectives, teacher's notes, sources of more information, and a materials list and descriptions of lesson activities. A glossary, coloring pages, and a bibliography are also provided.

Price: $15.95 (ISBN 0-933331-25-8). ***Publisher/supplier:*** The Whale Museum. ***Materials:*** Available locally.

1.98 Habitats. Pamela Hickman. A Publication of the Federation of Ontario Naturalists. Toronto, Ontario, Canada: Kids Can Press, 1993.

Grades: 3-6+ The activities in *Habitats,* a colorful resource book, are designed to encourage students to take a closer look at nature as they create temporary minihabitats. Most of the habitats can be made either in a 1-gallon jar or in an aquarium. Students view the growth, natural changes, life cycles, and special adaptations of plants and animals. Sample activities include observing life in a rotting log, building a wormery, and planting a miniforest. Activities are designed to promote environmental awareness and respect for living things.

Each activity in *Habitats* includes a short introduction, a list of materials, step-by-step illustrated instructions, tips on what to look for in observing a particular type of habitat, habitat watch, and a feature called The Big Picture.

Price: $9.57 (ISBN 1-55074-066-0). ***Publisher/supplier:*** Addison-Wesley. ***Materials:*** Available locally.

1.99 Hands On Biology Activities for Elementary Schools. Fundamentals of Science. Nancy Coggins Lynch. Annapolis, Md.: Alpha Publishing Co., 1990.

Grades: 4-6 *Hands On Biology Activities for Elementary Schools* offers 50 activities on concepts ranging from osmosis to depth perception to recycling. Examples of activities include determining the amount of vitamin C in various juices; using carrots and celery to learn how to make a cross-section; comparing the germination rates of various seeds; using limewater to test for carbon dioxide in one's breath; and examining cheek cells with a microscope. Activities encourage the use of basic experimental design components.

Each activity is preceded by a teacher's section featuring a list of goals, safety notes, and steps for preparation, and hints. Each activity provides student safety notes, a short vocabulary list, an introduction, a materials list, step-by-step procedures, a section on recording results and observations, conclusions, and suggestions for further study. Reproducible masters for student data sheets must be purchased separately.

Price: Teacher's Guide, $44.95. ***Publisher/supplier:*** Alpha. ***Materials:*** Available locally.

1.100 Insects and Other Crawlers. Windows on Elementary Science. Joan Westley. Mountain View, Calif.: Creative Publications, 1988.

Grades: K-2 In the *Insects and Other Crawlers* unit, children investigate beetles, ants, ladybugs, butterflies, moths, and grasshoppers. They discover how these creatures move, eat, and adapt to their environments. Students make homes for the bugs; they examine spiderwebs, wasps' nests, ant farms, and beehives; they listen to insect sounds; and they observe and compare camouflage, symmetry, and many other aspects of insects and other crawlers. Activities are sequenced by increasing levels of difficulty, but do not have to be used in order.

Each of the 28 activities in *Insects and Other Crawlers* lists a learning objective, process skills, materials needed, questions for discussion, directions for the exploration, and extensions.

Prices: Teacher's Guide (ISBN 0-88488-706-05), $13.75. Complete kit, $250.00. ***Publisher/supplier:*** Creative Publications. ***Materials:*** Available locally, from commercial suppliers, or in kit.

1.101 Just Outside the Door. Kaleidoscope. East Lansing, Mich.: 4-H Youth Programs, Cooperative Extension Service, Michigan State University, 1991.

Grades: K-3 *Just Outside the Door* uses a variety of activities to help young learners explore the world around them. Although designed for 4-H clubs, this leader's guide can be easily adapted to the classroom. Besides offering scientific experiments, it includes activities with songs, poems, drama, arts and crafts, card and movement games, stories, and field trips. Examples of the activities include comparing heat absorption of clothing of different colors, imitating the motion of caterpillars, examining seeds and identifying their parts, and comparing how fast ice in different locations melts. In addition to 3 sections on insects (identification, an insect safari, and insect growth and development), the guide features sections exploring the basic characteristics of fruits, seeds, water, and birds.

Each section of *Just Outside the Door* includes a statement of overall purpose, the suggested teaching sequence, information about what children need to know to carry out the activities, instructions, suggestions of fun things to do, and a mini-poster to take home.

Price: $2.60. ***Publisher/supplier:*** Michigan State University Bulletin Office. ***Materials:*** Available locally, or from commercial suppliers.

1.102 Leaf and Seed Matching Game. Nature Education Kits. Newton, Kans.: Young Naturalist Co., 1992.

Grades: K-3 In *Leaf and Seed Matching Game,* young students develop science process skills while using real specimens of leaves and seeds that are included in this inexpensive kit. The kit includes 20 leaf specimens and 20 seed specimens, and offers 8 games in which students match, play detective, classify, count and measure, collect leaves and seeds, observe shapes and pictures of leaves and seeds, and focus on how seeds travel.

For each game, the teacher's guide includes purpose, procedure, questions for students to answer, and follow-up activities. Directions are included for 3 levels of games (preschool, intermediate, and advanced). The kit functions as a nature display when not being used as a game.

Price: Kit, $25.95. ***Publisher/supplier:*** Young Naturalist. ***Materials:*** Available locally, from commercial suppliers, or in kit.

1.103 Life in the Desert. Primary Science Resource Guide. Ilene L. Follman. St. Louis, Mo.: Milliken Publishing Co., 1992.

Grades: K-3 Students explore the incredible variety of life in the desert in this unit, which offers 4 colorful posters, reproducible worksheets, and illustrated activities that help bring the desert into the classroom. Students explore where deserts exist, what deserts in different places have in common and how they differ, and how living things survive in and adapt to a desert environment. Activities are grouped in 3 sections: (1) The Desert: Where Is It? What Is It?; (2) Desert Plants: Amazing Adaptations; and (3) Desert Animals: Advantageous Adaptations. Examples of activities include taking a guided imagery walk in the desert, creating sand dunes, demonstrating how the leaves of desert plants lose less water than those of nondesert plants, planting a desert landscape, and obtaining and caring for a desert pet.

Life in the Desert includes information for teachers and parents, information on getting started with the activities, a bibliography, and instructions on how to use the 4 posters.

Price: $7.95 (ISBN 1-55863-364-2). ***Publisher/supplier:*** Milliken. ***Materials:*** Available locally.

1.104 The National Arbor Day Foundation's Discovery Curriculum. Nebraska City, Nebr.: National Arbor Day Foundation, no date.

Grades: 4-6 Promoting wise environmental stewardship is the primary goal of the *National Arbor Day Foundation's Discovery Curriculum.* The activities in this unit encourage 3 levels of environmental learning: (1) initial awareness and understanding, focusing on plant mechanics, food webs, habitats, adaptations, and biomagnification; (2) expanding the knowledge base, focusing on environment mapping, ecosystems, organisms, populations, and communities; and (3) translating awareness and knowledge into action, focusing on value-based decision making, issue investigation and resolution, and the importance of individual action in activities such as recycling and water usage. Examples of activities include constructing a food pyramid that must support all of its members, playing a version of freeze tag that explores predator-prey relationships, and writing a personal code of environmental ethics.

This guide also includes a resource section, suggested questions for individual or small group investigations, and a bibliography.

Price: $19.95. ***Publisher/supplier:*** National Arbor Day Foundation. ***Materials:*** Available locally, or from commercial suppliers.

1.105 Nature Kit: From Seeds to Sprouts! Santa Barbara, Calif.: Santa Barbara Botanic Garden and the Santa Barbara County Education Office, 1992.

Grades: K-4 *Nature Kit: From Seeds to Sprouts* is a resource guide to activities in 3 sections that focus on (1) plant life cycles, seed anatomy, and development; (2) seed dispersal; and (3) germination and conditions that affect seed and plant growth. Each section features several activities. Examples of the activities, which are copiously illustrated, include testing the effects of sunlight on seeds and seedlings; writing a short story from the perspective of a dispersing seed; and attempting to germinate fresh, frozen, and dried ears of corn to determine which condition is most favorable to successful germination.

Each activity in the *Nature Kit* provides a complete lesson plan, including reproducible masters for student data sheets in English and Spanish.

Price: Kit, $19.95. ***Publisher/supplier:*** Santa Barbara Botanic Garden. ***Materials:*** Available locally, or from commercial suppliers.

1.106 Naturewatch: Exploring Nature With Your Children. Adrienne Katz. Reading, Mass.: Addison-Wesley Publishing Co., 1986.

Grades: 1-6 Increasing children's awareness of the natural world is the goal of *Naturewatch: Exploring Nature With Your Children.* Written for both adults (primarily parents) and children, this book contains a variety of nature activities with simple instructions and illustrations. The numerous activities include students testing how leaves repel water, propagating plants in various ways, growing strawberries in an earthenware pot, making a caterpillar cage, making a drinking machine for birds, making bark rubbings, tracking animal footprints, pressing flowers, and making herbal talcum powder. The book also presents nontoxic ways of controlling pests and provides lists of poisonous plants, annuals, plants suited to window box gardening, and flowers suited for drying.

Price: $9.57 (ISBN 0-201-10457-1). ***Publisher/supplier:*** Addison-Wesley. ***Materials:*** Available locally, or from commercial suppliers.

1.107 Plantwise. Pamela M. Hickman. A publication of the Federation of Ontario Naturalists. Toronto, Ontario, Canada: Kids Can Press, 1991.

Grades: 4-6 *Plantwise* contains extensive information about many types of plants and offers a wide variety of plant-related activities. Through reading selections, students learn about seeds, leaves, flowers, roots, trees, bark, cones, ferns, mosses, grasses, killer plants, aquatic and desert plants, molds, fungi, and rotters (the small creatures that recycle wood by breaking it down). Among the activities, students grow plants from roots, investigate geotropism, collect leaves and make "leaf skeletons," dissect a flower, search for fern spores, learn how to make maple syrup, plant a moss garden, and dye clothes with natural dyes from plants. The concluding section of the book includes information about the uses of plants and tells us why plants are so important to the environment. Suggestions for what students can do to help save plants from becoming endangered or extinct are given.

Prices: Paperback (ISBN 1-55074-044-X), $8.95. Hardcover (ISBN 1-55074-001-6), $16.95. ***Publisher/supplier:*** University of Toronto Press. ***Materials:*** Available locally, or from commercial suppliers.

1.108 Primarily Plants. AIMS. Evalyn Hoover and Sheryl Mercier. Fresno, Calif.: AIMS Education Foundation, 1990.

Grades: K-3 The 26 activities in *Primarily Plants* range from making "baggie" gardens to going on leaf safaris. Mathematics and science skills are tested as students carry out these hands-on activities and do the worksheets that accompany them. Activities cover the following topic areas: seeds, spores, plant growth, plant parts, seed dispersal, bulbs, cuttings, plant needs (for soil, sunlight, water, and air), and why people need plants.

Each lesson in *Primarily Plants* includes a brief introductory statement, a list of mathematics skills and science processes used in the activities, a materials list, key questions addressed in the activities, background information, management suggestions, procedures, discussion questions, and extension activities.

Price: $14.95 (ISBN 1-881431-24-X). ***Publisher/supplier:*** AIMS Education Foundation. ***Materials:*** Available locally.

1.109 Project WILD Activity Guide. 2nd ed. Bethesda, Md.: Project WILD, 1992.

Grades: K-6+ *Project WILD Activity Guide* is part of an interdisciplinary conservation and environmental education program. The guide's 113 activities are organized in 7 sections: (1) Awareness and Appreciation; (2) Diversity of Wildlife Values; (3) Ecological Principles; (4) Management and Conservation; (5) People, Culture and Wildlife; (6) Trends, Issues and Consequences; and (7) Responsible Human Actions. Examples of the activities include identifying similarities and differences in the basic needs of ants and humans; forming an interconnected circle of students to demonstrate the components of a habitat; observing camouflage techniques in live animals; and recommending changes that could benefit wildlife.

A glossary, a conceptual framework, and a guide to the ecosystem concept are included among the guide's 23 appendixes. Activities are cross-referenced by skills used, length of activity, subject, and grade level. Although this guide is written for teachers of grades K-12, the majority of its activities are most appropriate for grades 4 and above.

Price: Attendance at Project WILD workshop. ***Publisher/supplier:*** Project WILD. ***Materials:*** Available locally, or from commercial suppliers.

1.110 Project WILD Aquatic Education Activity Guide. 2nd ed. Bethesda, Md.: Project WILD, 1992.

Grades: K-6+ *Project WILD Aquatic Education Activity Guide* is part of an interdisciplinary conservation and environmental education program. The guide's 40 activities are organized in 7 sections: (1) Awareness and Appreciation; (2) Diversity of Wildlife Values; (3) Ecological Principles; (4) Management and Conservation; (5) Culture and Wildlife; (6) Trends, Issues and Consequences; and (7) Responsible Human Actions. Examples of the activities include calculating the volume of water on the planet, drawing life-size replicas of whales on school grounds, simulating the effects of the changing technology of fishing on fish populations, and producing a newspaper on a variety of issues concerning aquatic wildlife.

A glossary, a conceptual framework, and a guide to the ecosystem concept are included among the guide's 26 appendixes. Activities are cross-referenced by skills used, length of activity, subject, and grade level. Although this guide is written for teachers of grades K-12, the majority of its activities are most appropriate for grades 4 and above.

Price: Attendance at Project WILD Workshop. ***Publisher/supplier:*** Project WILD. ***Materials:*** Available locally, or from commercial suppliers.

1.111 The Schoolyard Environment. Primary Science Resource Guide. Ilene L. Follman. St. Louis, Mo.: Milliken Publishing Co., 1992.

Grades: K-3 *The Schoolyard Environment* provides a host of activities to help children learn about soil, plants, animals, adaptations, growth, and cycles of change. Studying the schoolyard environment, students discover similarities, differences, and interactions among living things, learn about relationships between living and nonliving things, and about the relationship of humans to the environment. Groups of students examine a 1-foot-square plot of land and record their observations. They plant seeds and monitor plant growth, compare soils, dig for earthworms, adopt a tree for study, and collect and house insects. They survey an area for animal tracks, birds, litter, and shadows.

This teacher's guide includes reproducible masters for student data sheets, a bibliography, and 4 posters that are used to stimulate discussion.

Price: $7.95 (ISBN 1-55863-362-6). ***Publisher/supplier:*** Milliken. ***Materials:*** Available locally.

1.112 Seeds and Weeds. Windows on Elementary Science. Joan Westley. Mountain View, Calif.: Creative Publications, 1988.

Grades: K-2 In *Seeds and Weeds,* children examine and compare many types of seeds. They investigate seeds in their own environment and explore the various ways seeds travel and plant themselves. Students plant seeds and watch the changes that occur during seed germination and plant growth. They count, sort, grind, cook, taste, and dissect seeds, and use them to make musical instruments. Activities are sequenced by increasing levels of difficulty but do not have to be used in order.

Each of the 28 activities in *Seeds and Weeds* lists a learning objective, process skills, materials needed, questions for discussion, directions for the exploration, and extensions.

Prices: Teacher's Guide (ISBN 0-88488-710-3), $13.75. Complete kit, $250.00. ***Publisher/supplier:*** Creative Publications. ***Materials:*** Available locally, from commercial suppliers, or in kit.

1.113 **Western Creeks and Ponds. Family Science Adventure Kit.** Tustin, Calif.: Acorn Naturalists, 1991.

Grades: 3-6 Whirligig beetles, water striders, and plankton are among the creatures of interest in *Western Creeks and Ponds,* an activity kit that centers its explorations on the banks of a freshwater creek or pond. The small, reusable kit contains 6 activity cards, 3 petri dishes, a dip net, a mini-plant-press, a plankton syringe, a combination binoculars/compass, and a field guide to common pond life. The activity cards feature background information on one side and instructions for activities on the other. Sample activities include observing the behavior of whirligig beetles and water striders; experimenting with surface tension; examining leaves for the presence of insect larvae; and studying the body structures of various species of water nymphs.

Price: Kit, $22.95. ***Publisher/supplier:*** Acorn Naturalists. ***Materials:*** Available locally, from commercial suppliers, or in kit.

1.114 **Wetlands.** Pamela Hickman. A Publication of the Federation of Ontario Naturalists. Toronto, Ontario, Canada: Kids Can Press, 1993.

Grades: 3-6 Through simple reading selections, experiments, and projects, *Wetlands* introduces students to the varied animal and plant life in a wetland—the place where land and water meet. Students examine wetland mud and peat for small creatures. They investigate the important natural absorption and filtration ability of wetland soils and discover how wetland roots help stop erosion. Students observe the growth of phytoplankton (algae) and zooplankton (tiny floating animals), make plaster casts of animal tracks, and draw a map of a red-winged blackbird's territory. They grow duckweed in different solutions, create mushroom spore prints, and set up an aquarium. Students learn about the habits and life cycles of a variety of wetland wildlife (including ducks, reptiles, frogs, toads, leeches, snails, bats, muskrats, and beavers). The activity book concludes with a simple board game that explains why wetlands are endangered habitats and what can be done to protect them.

Price: $9.95 (ISBN 1-55074-126-8). ***Publisher/supplier:*** University of Toronto Press. ***Materials:*** Available locally, or from commercial suppliers.

1.115 **What Do Plants Need to Grow.** Pamela Emery. Sacramento, Calif.: California Foundation for Agriculture in the Classroom, 1993.

Grades: 2-4 Integrating agriculture into the science curriculum is the goal of *What Do Plants Need to Grow.* Through a series of experiments and activities, students learn that plants are living things that require water, air, light, and nutrients. They examine relationships between plants and other living and nonliving things. Examples of activities include dissecting seeds, examining plants to learn their basic parts, testing the relative growth of plants exposed to different amounts of fertilizer, and observing root systems of radish plants to understand the importance of root hairs.

Each of 13 lessons in the guide includes a statement of purpose, concepts covered, a list of materials, time requirements, background information, and procedures. Most lessons include variations and extension ideas. The book also includes answers to commonly asked questions, lists of additional resources and references, and a glossary.

Price: $6.50. ***Publisher/supplier:*** California Foundation for Agriculture in the Classroom. ***Materials:*** Available locally.

CHAPTER 2

EARTH SCIENCE

EARTH SCIENCE—CORE MATERIALS

2.1 Air and Weather. FOSS. (Developed by Lawrence Hall of Science, Berkeley, Calif.) Chicago, Ill.: Encyclopaedia Britannica Educational Corp., 1993.

Grades: 1, 2 In *Air and Weather,* students monitor the weather, explore the properties of air, and construct devices that use moving air to function. Students monitor temperature, rainfall, wind, and clouds; they use a thermometer, a rain gauge, an anemometer, and a cloud window. They record their observations in a student weather journal and on a class weather calendar. They organize and graph class weather data collected over a period of 4 weeks. Students explore properties of air using plastic syringes and tubes; they find that air takes up space and builds up pressure when compressed. They construct parachutes, propellers, balloon rockets, gliders, pinwheels, streamers, wind socks, kites, and whirligigs to investigate the interaction of objects with moving air.

Air and Weather consists of 4 activities, requiring 8 to 10 weeks to complete. The teacher's guide includes a module overview, 4 individual activity folios, duplication masters (in English and Spanish) for student sheets, and an annotated bibliography.

The module includes science background information, detailed instructions on planning for and conducting each activity, an extensive assessment component, and extensions for integration and enrichment. Materials are available in a kit.

Prices: Teacher's Guide (ISBN 0-7826-1152-4), $101. Complete module, $495. ***Publisher/supplier:*** Encyclopaedia Britannica Educational Corp. ***Materials:*** Available locally, from commercial suppliers, or in module.

2.2 Earth Materials. FOSS. (Developed by Lawrence Hall of Science, Berkeley, Calif.) Chicago, Ill.: Encyclopaedia Britannica Educational Corp., 1993.

Grades: 3, 4 *Earth Materials* includes 4 sequential activities on observable characteristics of solid materials from the earth—namely, rocks and minerals. Students are involved in activities that challenge them to observe, compare, put together, take apart, and organize as they investigate simulated and real rocks. The activities include taking apart homemade rocks to investigate their composition; exploring the properties of four minerals (calcite, quartz, gypsum, and fluorite) and then seriating the minerals according to hardness; testing four rock samples (granite, limestone, marble, and sandstone) for the presence of calcite; sorting rocks and minerals; and identifying the minerals present in pink granite.

The 4 activities in *Earth Materials* require 7 weeks (about 12 class ses-

Identifying a rock sample

About the Annotations in "Earth Science—Core Materials"

Entry Numbers
Curriculum materials are arranged alphabetically by title in each category (Core Materials, Supplementary Materials, and Science Activity Books) in chapters 1 through 4 of this guide. In addition, each annotation has a two-part entry number. For each entry number, the chapter number is given before the period; the number after the period locates the entry within that chapter.

For example, the first entry number in chapter 1 is 1.1; the second entry in chapter 2 is 2.2, and so on.

The entry numbers within each curriculum chapter run consecutively through Core Materials, Supplementary Materials, and Science Activity Books.

Order of Bibliographic Information
Following is the arrangement of the facts of publication in the annotations in this section:

- **Title of publication.**
- **Series title,** or series acronym if commonly used.
- **Authors** (either individual names or organizational author).
- Name and location of **developer** (in parentheses), if different from publisher.
- **Place of publication, publisher, and date of publication.**

Series Acronyms
Following are **acronyms of series titles** in "Earth Science—Core Materials." (Series titles that are spelled out are not included in this list.)

FOSS Full Option Science System
STC Science and Technology for Children

Price and Acquision Information
Ordering information is presented in a block immediately below the annotation. Included are the following:

- **Prices** of teacher's guides, activity books, and kits or units.
- The name of a principal **publisher/supplier** (not necessarily the sole source) for the items listed in the price category. (The address and phone and fax numbers for each publisher and supplier appear in appendix A, "Publishers and Suppliers.")
- An indication of the various sources from which one might obtain the required **materials.**

sions) to complete. The teacher's guide includes a module overview, the 4 individual activity folios, duplication masters (in English and Spanish) for student sheets, and an annotated bibliography.

This module includes science background information, detailed instructions on planning for and conducting each activity, an extensive assessment component, and extensions for integration and enrichment. Materials are available in a kit.

Prices: Teacher's Guide (ISBN 0-7826-0016-6), $101. Complete module: $319. ***Publisher/supplier:*** Encyclopaedia Britannica Educational Corp. ***Materials:*** Available locally, from commercial suppliers, or in module.

2.3 **Ecosystems. STC.** Field-test ed. Washington, D.C.: National Science Resources Center, 1992.

Grade: 5 In *Ecosystems,* students learn about the interdependence of organisms and the natural environment by using 2-liter soda bottles to set up, observe, and experiment with two miniature ecosystems—an aquarium and a terrarium. After studying the two separate ecosystems, students connect them and observe the ecocolumn, noting any changes that may indicate an imbalance in the system. They read about aquatic and terrestrial organisms—plants, algae, fungi, bacteria, and animals—and pollution. They study habitat changes and conduct experiments simulating the effects of acid rain, road salt, and fertilizer. As a final activity, students in small groups investigate a real ecosystem in danger—the Chesapeake Bay. They read about the problems of the bay, analyze the situation from several points of view, propose possible solutions, and begin to grapple with the trade-offs involved in various solutions.

Ecosystems is a 16-lesson unit that requires 8 weeks to complete.The teacher's guide includes a unit overview, the 16 lesson plans, an annotated bibliography of additional resources, and information on maintaining live materials. A student activity book with simple instructions and illustrations accompanies the unit.

The module includes science background information, detailed instructions on planning for and conducting each activity, an extensive assessment component, and extensions for integration and enrichment. Materials are available in a kit.

Prices: Teacher's Guide, $14.95. Student Activity Book, $3.50. Unit, $349.95. ***Publisher/supplier:*** Carolina Biological Supply. ***Materials:*** Available locally, from commercial suppliers, or in unit.

2.4 Landforms. FOSS. (Developed by Lawrence Hall of Science, Berkeley, Calif.) Chicago, Ill.: Encyclopaedia Britannica Educational Corp., 1993.

Grades: 5, 6 The *Landforms* module consists of 5 activities that introduce students to concepts of physical geography and mapping. Students first create a three-dimensional model of their school site and transfer information about the locations of landforms and structures in their model to a grid. This allows them to relate physical structures to representations on maps. They use stream tables to simulate the creation of landforms. Students then construct a three-dimensional foam model of an actual mountain, Mount Shasta; then they create a topographic map of the mountain and compare it to a topographic map of the same mountain from the U.S. Geological Survey.

Landforms contains 5 multipart activities, requiring 18 class sessions over a 10-week period to complete. The teacher's guide includes a module overview, the 5 individual activity folios, duplication masters (in English and Spanish) for student sheets, and an annotated bibliography.

This module includes science background information, detailed instructions on planning for and conducting each activity, an extensive assessment component, and extensions for integration and enrichment. Materials are available in a kit.

Prices: Teacher's Guide (ISBN 0-7826-0065-4), $101. Complete module, $599. ***Publisher/supplier:*** Encyclopaedia Britannica Educational Corp. ***Materials:*** Available locally, from commercial suppliers, or in module.

2.5 Measurement. FOSS. (Developed by Lawrence Hall of Science, Berkeley, Calif.) Chicago, Ill.: Encyclopaedia Britannica Educational Corp., 1993.

Grades: 3, 4 This module introduces students to metric measurement. They work in collaborative groups of four to learn the standard units used to measure length (meter), weight (gram), fluid volume (liter), and temperature (degree Celsius); they use appropriate tools to make measurements. Among the activities, students make and use meter tapes to measure objects and to make body comparisons. They use a balance and weights to weigh common objects and to investigate the water absorbency of a sponge. They use beakers, syringes, and graduated cylinders to measure the capacity of several containers. They use thermometers to measure and monitor temperatures, such as the rate of cooling of water when ice is added. Each activity concludes with applications of students' new knowledge and skills that give them experience and familiarity with the metric system.

Measurement contains 4 multipart activities, requiring from 12 to 15 class sessions to complete. The teacher's guide includes a module overview, the 4 individual activity folios, duplication masters (in English and Spanish) for student sheets, and an annotated bibliography.

The module includes science background information, detailed instructions on planning for and conducting each activity, an extensive assessment component, and extensions for integration and enrichment. Materials are available in a kit.

Price: Teacher's Guide (ISBN 0-7826-0005-0), $101. Complete module, $599. ***Publisher/supplier:*** Encyclopaedia Britannica Educational Corp. ***Materials:*** Available locally, from commercial suppliers, or in module.

2.6 Measuring Time. STC. (Developed by National Science Resources Center, Washington, D.C.) Burlington, N.C.: Carolina Biological Supply Co., 1994.

Grade: 6 In *Measuring Time,* students explore timekeeping first by observing the natural cycles of the sun and moon and then by building and investigating mechanical devices designed to measure time. Activities include recording the length and position of shadows at different times of day, devising a calendar, and predicting and observing the phases of the moon. In other activities, students construct and experiment with sinking water clocks and pendulums, build and adjust a working clock escapement, and make a 1-minute timer. Throughout the unit, students are encouraged to develop an appreciation of advances over the centuries in measuring time. They record ideas, questions, and descriptions of their work in notebooks; they organize and report results in charts, tables, and graphs; and they discuss and analyze their experiences in small groups and with the class.

Measuring Time is a 16-lesson module requiring 8 weeks to complete. The teacher's guide includes a unit overview, the 16 lesson plans, and an annotated bibliography. A student activity book with simple instructions and illustrations accompanies the unit.

This module includes science background information, detailed instructions on planning for and conducting each activity, an extensive assessment component, and extensions for integration and enrichment. Materials are available in a kit.

Prices: Teacher's Guide, $14.95. Student Activity Book, $3.50. Unit, $399.95. ***Publisher/supplier:*** Carolina Biological Supply. ***Materials:*** Available locally, from commercial suppliers, or in unit.

2.7 Pebbles, Sand, and Silt. FOSS. (Developed by Lawrence Hall of Science, Berkeley, Calif.) Chicago, Ill.: Encyclopaedia Britannica Educational Corp., 1993.

Grades: 1, 2 In *Pebbles, Sand, and Silt,* students develop skills such as observing, comparing, organizing, seriating, and inferring as they explore the properties of rocks and soil and the use of these substances in everyday life. They investigate several types of rocks (basalt, scoria, and tuff) and learn about their properties. Then they use a series of screens with different mesh sizes to separate a river rock mixture consisting of earth materials of different sizes. After learning how earth materials are used to construct objects, students put together and take apart different types of soil.

Pebbles, Sand, and Silt contains 4 multipart activities, requiring about 25 class sessions to complete. The teacher's guide includes a module overview, the 4 individual activity folios, duplication masters (in English and Spanish) for student sheets, and an annotated bibliography.

The module includes science background information, detailed instructions on planning for and conducting each activity, an extensive assessment component, and extensions for integration and enrichment. Materials are available in a kit.

Price: Teacher's Guide (ISBN 0-7826-1144-3), $101. Complete module, $465. ***Publisher/supplier:*** Encyclopaedia Britannica Educational Corp. ***Materials:*** Available locally, from commercial suppliers, or in module.

2.8 Reading the Environment. Insights. Newton, Mass.: Education Development Center, 1994.

Grades: 4, 5 In *Reading the Environment,* students search for, categorize, interpret, and analyze evidence which shows that changes in their environment are taking place or have taken place in the past. In the first half of the module, students examine and categorize changes in themselves, in their classroom, and in the schoolyard. They designate two small outdoor plots that they examine over time for evidence of change. They use drawings, rubbings, and words to record their observations on a large Class Change Chart and learn to make connections between cause and effect. In the second half of the module, students expand their concept of change over time to a geologic scale. They create and use several extended time lines, examine and sort rocks, learn about the formation and disintegration of rocks, and carry out weathering and erosion experiments. They also explore the formation of fossils and the kind of evidence fossils can provide about changes that took place long ago.

Reading the Environment is a 6-to-8 week module that can be completed in a minimum of 22 to 24 sessions. The teacher's guide includes a unit overview, 17 Learning Experiences, reproducible masters for student sheets, and annotated lists of additional resources to use with the module.

The module includes science background information, detailed instructions on planning for and conducting each activity, an extensive assessment component, and extensions for integration and enrichment. Materials are available in a kit.

Prices: Teacher's Guide (ISBN 0-89292-177-3), $65. Materials kit, $324. (Prices differ in California, Nevada, and Indiana.) ***Publisher/supplier:*** Optical Data Corp. ***Materials:*** Available locally, from commercial suppliers, or in kit.

2.9 Rocks and Minerals. STC. Field-test ed. Washington, D.C.: National Science Resources Center, 1994.

Grade: 3 In *Rocks and Minerals,* students investigate common rocks and the predominant minerals found in them. After sorting and describing rocks by various physical features, they read about how rocks are formed and how they change as a result of heat or pressure. Students perform a series of physical and chemical field tests that geologists use to identify properties of minerals, and they construct mineral profile sheets to use in making a "minerals field guide." Students combine information from another field guide with the knowledge and skills they have acquired to identify 12 minerals by name and to identify 3 mystery minerals. Finally, they learn about uses for rocks and minerals such as basalt, granite, quartz, and fluorite.

Rocks and Minerals is a 16-lesson module requiring 8 weeks to complete. The teacher's guide includes a unit overview, the 16 lesson plans, an annotated bibliography, and blackline masters of student record sheets and mineral identification cards. A student activity book with simple instructions and illustrations accompanies the unit.

This module includes science background information, detailed instructions on planning for and conducting each activity, an extensive assessment component, and extensions for integration and enrichment. Materials are available in a kit.

Prices: Teacher's Guide, $14.95. Student Activity Book, $3.50. Unit, $563.00. ***Publisher/supplier:*** Carolina Biological Supply. ***Materials:*** Available locally, from commercial suppliers, or in unit.

2.10 **Soils. STC.** (Developed by National Science Resources Center, Washington, D.C.) Burlington, N.C.: Carolina Biological Supply Co., 1995.

Grade: 2 In the *Soils* module, students use standard techniques of soil science to investigate basic soil components and their properties. They examine soil samples with a hand lens, make soil smears, and investigate the plasticity of moist soils. Students mix soil components (sand, clay, and humus) with water and observe the immediate and long-term results of shaking the mixtures. They explore the porosity and water retention of soils. Students then apply and interpret these same tests to characterize an unfamiliar soil mixture. The unit includes a 5-week composting experiment, as well as planting experiments with different types of soil. In a final activity, students plan and carry out investigations of local soil.

Soils is a 16-lesson module requiring 8 weeks to complete. The teacher's guide includes a unit overview, the 16 lesson plans, an annotated bibliography, blackline masters for student record sheets, and tips on using redworms in the classroom. An optional consumable notebook for students, *My Soils Book,* includes most of the record sheets and the three reading selections used in this unit.

This module includes science background information, detailed instructions on planning for and conducting each activity, an extensive assessment component, and extensions for integration and enrichment. Materials are available in a kit.

Prices: Teacher's Guide, $14.95. Consumable Student Notebook, $2.00. Unit, $349.95. ***Publisher/ supplier:*** Carolina Biological Supply. ***Materials:*** Available locally, from commercial suppliers, or in unit.

2.11 **Solar Energy. FOSS.** (Developed by Lawrence Hall of Science, Berkeley, Calif.) Chicago, Ill.: Encyclopaedia Britannica Educational Corp., 1993.

Grades: 5, 6 This module features 4 multipart activities focused on related aspects of solar energy and culminating in its use in solar homes. Students chart changes in the size and position of shadows as the relative position of the sun changes. They investigate temperature changes in equal amounts of water, sand, dry soil, and wet soil when the sun shines on them; they relate the temperature differences to the properties of the materials. Students then conduct controlled experiments to test the effect of three variables on the collection of solar energy by solar water heaters. (The variables are the color of the solar collector, its being covered or uncovered, and its surface area.) Finally, students assemble model solar homes, looking for the most efficient way to heat them. Throughout the unit students organize data on charts and graphs to establish relationships between variables.

Solar Energy contains 4 multipart activities, requiring about 12 class sessions to complete. The teacher's guide includes a module overview, the 4 individual activity folios, duplication masters (in English and Spanish) for student sheets, and an annotated bibliography.

The module includes science background information, detailed instructions on planning for and conducting each activity, an extensive assessment component, and extensions for integration and enrichment. Materials are available in a kit.

Prices: Teacher's Guide (ISBN 0-7826-0087-5), $101. Complete module, $415. ***Publisher/supplier:*** Encyclopaedia Britannica Educational Corp. ***Materials:*** Available locally, from commercial suppliers, or in module.

2.12 **There Is No Away. Insights.** Newton, Mass.: Education Development Center, 1994.

Grade: 6 *There Is No Away* introduces students to the subjects of waste production, disposal, and control, and focuses on solid waste disposal and water pollution. The first half of the module develops students' awareness of the amount and variety of trash people generate. Students collect and analyze a day's waste (collected on the school premises) and explore the schoolyard for manufactured and natural waste materials. Students then design and set up controlled experiments to find out what happens to organic and inorganic waste in a sanitary landfill. They examine how the soil in, around, and under a landfill can influence the quality of groundwater. In the second half of the module, they design and construct a model sanitary landfill, investigate the steps involved in purifying water, and develop ideas for alternative packaging and recycling.

There Is No Away is organized in 16 Learning Experiences that can be done in a minimum of 27 sessions over about 6 to 8 weeks. The teacher's guide includes a unit overview, the 16 Learning Experiences, reproducible masters for student sheets, and annotated lists of additional resources to use with the module.

The module includes science background information, detailed instructions on planning for and conducting each activity, an extensive assessment component, and extensions for integration and enrichment. Materials are available in a kit.

Prices: Teacher's Guide (ISBN 0-89292-181-1), $65. Materials kit, $285. (Prices differ in California, Nevada, and Indiana.) ***Publisher/ supplier:*** Optical Data. ***Materials:*** Available locally, from commercial suppliers, or in kit.

2.13 Water. FOSS. (Developed by Lawrence Hall of Science, Berkeley, Calif.) Chicago, Ill.: Encyclopaedia Britannica Educational Corp., 1993.

Grades: 3, 4 In this module consisting of 4 multipart activities, students explore water in all its forms: they investigate surface tension, freezing, expansion, density, evaporation, condensation, water quality, and natural processes of water recycling. Students first explore the properties of water, its behavior on different surfaces, how to change its surface tension, and how gravity affects the rate of flow down an inclined plane. Students then observe the properties of water as it is heated, cooled, and frozen; they experiment with evaporation and condensation; and they test various samples of water for the presence of dissolved calcium and magnesium (that is, they test water hardness) and see what happens when water runs over earth materials.

The 4 multipart activities in *Water* require 19 or 20 class sessions to complete. The teacher's guide includes a module overview, 4 individual activity folios, duplication masters (in English and Spanish) for student sheets, and an annotated bibliography.

The module includes science background information, detailed instructions on planning for and conducting each activity, an extensive assessment component, and extensions for integration and enrichment. Materials are available in a kit.

Prices: Teacher's Guide (ISBN 0-7826-0440-9), $101. Complete module, $469. ***Publisher/supplier:*** Encyclopaedia Britannica Educational Corp. ***Materials:*** Available locally, from commercial suppliers, or in module.

2.14 Weather. STC. (Developed by National Science Resources Center, Washington, D.C.) Burlington, N.C.: Carolina Biological Supply Co., 1995.

Grade: 1 The unit *Weather* introduces children to 4 important features of weather: wind, temperature, cloud cover, and precipitation. Young students gather information about the weather with their senses and with simple weather instruments. They learn to read a Fahrenheit thermometer; they construct and interpret a wind scale to estimate the speed of wind; they make a rain gauge to collect and measure rainfall; and they observe clouds and categorize them in 3 basic groups. Throughout the unit children use a class weather calendar, along with other charts and graphs, to record and interpret data about the weather. Students conduct an experiment to investigate the effect colors can have on thermometer readings, and they relate their findings to the color of clothing they might choose to wear in specific types of weather. They also experiment with ways that different types of fabric respond to water, drawing conclusions about which fabric would keep them driest on a rainy day.

Weather consists of 16 lessons requiring 8 weeks to complete. The teacher's guide includes a unit overview, the 16 lesson plans, an annotated bibliography, and supplementary information on the development of the Fahrenheit and Celsius scales. An appendix with the Celsius version of all record sheets is also included. An optional consumable student notebook (available in English and Spanish) includes all the record sheets and student instructions contained in the teacher's guide.

This module includes science background information, detailed instructions on planning for and conducting each activity, an extensive assessment component, and extensions for integration and enrichment. Materials are available in a kit.

Prices: Teacher's Guide (ISBN 0-89278-713-9), $14.95. Consumable Student Notebook (ISBN 0-89278-714-7), $2.00. Unit, $379.95. ***Publisher/supplier:*** Carolina Biological Supply. ***Materials:*** Available locally, from commercial suppliers, or in unit.

EARTH SCIENCE—SUPPLEMENTARY MATERIALS

2.15 Air. **DSM.** Hudson, N.H.: Delta Education, 1989.

Grades: 2-4 The module *Air* introduces students to the basic properties of air and how it behaves. During the unit, students observe that air takes up space, that it has volume and can be moved and divided, that it expands when heated and contracts when cooled, and that it exerts pressure on other substances. Hands-on activities in the unit include constructing parachutes to discover the effects of air resistance; building wind gauges to measure wind speed; and making and flying paper airplanes to test students' knowledge of air movement, pressure, and resistance.

This module includes an overview, a glossary, evaluation activities, and reproducible masters for student worksheets. The 9 activities of *Air* require 12 class sessions to complete. Each activity includes a vocabulary list, a list of materials needed, preparation steps, teaching suggestions, and reinforcement activities.

Prices: Teacher's Guide (ISBN 0-87504-752-1), $9.95. Kit, $217.00. ***Publisher/supplier:*** Delta Education. ***Materials:*** Available locally, from commercial suppliers, or in kit.

2.16 **Air, Sun and Water: How Weather Works. Scholastic Science Place.** (Developed in cooperation with Franklin Institute, Philadelphia, Pa.) New York, N.Y.: Scholastic, 1993.

Grade: 1 In *Air, Sun and Water,* children learn about these components of weather, which they discover can be observed and measured. The unit's lessons are grouped in 3 subconcepts: (1) weather is composed of the conditions of the surrounding air; (2) the sun heats the air, which moves, changes direction, and moves

ABOUT THE ANNOTATIONS IN "EARTH SCIENCE—SUPPLEMENTARY MATERIALS"

Entry Numbers

Curriculum materials are arranged alphabetically by title in each category (Core Materials, Supplementary Materials, and Science Activity Books) in chapters 1 through 4 of this guide. In addition, each annotation has a two-part entry number. For each entry number, the chapter number is given before the period; the number after the period locates the entry within that chapter.

For example, the first entry number in chapter 1 is 1.1; the second entry in chapter 2 is 2.2, and so on.

The entry numbers within each curriculum chapter run consecutively through Core Materials, Supplementary Materials, and Science Activity Books.

Order of Bibliographic Information

Following is the arrangement of the facts of publication in the annotations in this section:

- **Title** of publication.
- **Series title,** or series acronym if commonly used.
- **Authors** (either individual names or organizational author).
- Name and location of **developer** (in parentheses), if different from publisher.
- **Place of publication, publisher, and date of publication.**

Series Acronyms

Following are **acronyms of series titles** in "Earth Science—Supplementary Materials." (Series titles that are spelled out are not included in this list.)

DSM Delta Science Module
GEMS Great Explorations in Math and Science
STAR Science Technology and Reading

Price and Acquisition Information

Ordering information is presented in a block immediately below the annotation. Included are the following:

- **Prices** of teacher's guides, activity books, and kits or units.
- The name of a principal **publisher/supplier** (not necessarily the sole source) for the items listed in the price category. (The address and phone and fax numbers for each publisher and supplier appear in appendix A, "Publishers and Suppliers.")
- An indication of the various sources from which one might obtain the required **materials.**

other things; and (3) the sun heats water and makes it move through the water cycle. Lessons in this unit include students reading books and taking a video field trip to explore weather, recording weather observations, observing and comparing different rates of evaporation, and discussing climate patterns.

Air, Sun and Water consists of 17 lessons of 35 to 40 minutes each. The conceptual goals of the unit are presented in the lesson-by-lesson story line in the teacher's guide. Each lesson also includes background information; a complete lesson plan, including suggestions for assessing performance and integrating the curriculum; and a list of the print, video, and software support materials required for the lesson.

Prices: Teacher's Guide (ISBN 0-590-26203-3), $20.70. Student Book (ISBN 0-590-26135-5), $6.50. Complete unit, $375.00. Consumables kit, $62.00. ***Publisher/supplier:*** Scholastic. ***Materials:*** Available locally, from commercial suppliers, or in unit.

2.17 Convection: A Current Event. GEMS. Alan Gould. Berkeley, Calif.: Lawrence Hall of Science, 1988.

Grades: 6+ Students explore the physical phenomenon of convection and generalize their findings to understand wind patterns in *Convection: A Current Event.* The teacher's guide introduces the concept of convection and then offers 3 sessions: Observing Convection in Water, Getting the Whole Picture, and Convection and Wind. In the first session, students use food coloring to trace convection currents in water. In the second session, they apply their knowledge to guide an imaginary submarine through ocean currents generated near a hot volcanic vent. In the third session, the teacher presents 3 demonstrations to show that convection occurs in gases as well as in liquids, and students apply what they have learned to explain house heating and to predict wind patterns.

Each session in *Convection: A Current Event* is illustrated, requires 30 to 60 minutes, and includes detailed instructions for planning and conducting the activities. Reproducible masters of student worksheets are included.

Price: $10. ***Publisher/supplier:*** LHS GEMS. ***Materials:*** Available locally, or from commercial suppliers.

2.18 Digging into Dinosaurs. NatureScope. Washington, D.C.: National Wildlife Federation, 1989.

Grades: K-5 *Digging into Dinosaurs* uses activities involving games, songs, stories, drawings, and drama to introduce students and teachers to these extinct animals and the world in which they lived. Fossil evidence forms the basis for information provided by the guide. In classroom and playground lessons that integrate science with mathematics, language arts, social studies, art, music, and physical education, students from kindergarten to the intermediate grades learn the comparative sizes of dinosaurs, how they were named, and what their lives might have been like.

Digging into Dinosaurs contains 20 lessons organized in 5 chapters; a sixth chapter provides art and craft ideas. Teachers may choose single activities or teach each chapter as a unit. Copycat pages supplement the activities and provide games, puzzles, and worksheets.

Price: $7.95. ***Publisher/supplier:*** National Wildlife Federation. ***Materials:*** Available locally.

2.19 Dinosaur Classification. DSM. Hudson, N.H.: Delta Education, 1989.

Grades: 3-5 *Dinosaur Classification* introduces students to methods of studying prehistoric animals. They first create a timeline on the history of the earth and place drawings of dinosaurs and other organisms on it. During the unit, students examine the role of bones and footprints as fossil evidence. They collect and graph data showing the relationship between the length of stride and height and then apply these findings to estimate the height of dinosaurs. Students compare the relative sizes of dinosaurs, use data to hypothesize about dinosaur habitats and behaviors, and devise and use their own dinosaur classification system.

Dinosaur Classification contains 4 activities, requiring 12 class sessions. Each activity includes a vocabulary list, a list of materials needed, preparation steps, teaching suggestions, and reinforcement activities. Reproducible masters for student worksheets are provided in the teacher's guide.

Prices: Teacher's Guide (ISBN 0-87504-754-8), $9.95. Kit, $170.00. ***Publisher/supplier:*** Delta Education. ***Materials:*** Available locally, from commercial suppliers, or in kit.

2.20 Earth, Moon, and Stars. GEMS. Cary I. Sneider. Reprinted with revisions. Berkeley, Calif.: Lawrence Hall of Science, 1989.

Grades: 5-6+ In *Earth, Moon, and Stars,* students investigate the following: ancient models of the universe, the earth's shape, gravity, the moon and its phases, star clocks, and star maps. They compare four ancient models of the earth to learn how each one explained common events seen daily in the sky. They use a questionnaire to launch a discussion about the shape of the earth and gravity. Students investigate the phases of the moon and use a model to explain the moon's monthly cycle of phases. They use star clocks and star maps.

Earth, Moon, and Stars contains 6 activities requiring a total of 16 sessions (10 to 90 minutes each). The guide includes background information, a suggested time frame, a list of materials, ideas for preparation, step-by-step directions, and reproducible student worksheets.

Price: $10. ***Publisher/supplier:*** LHS GEMS. ***Materials:*** Available locally, or from commercial suppliers.

2.21 Earth Movements. DSM. Hudson, N.H.: Delta Education, 1988.

Grades: 3-5 In *Earth Movements,* which focuses on the earth's tectonic plates and convection currents, students develop a general understanding of the dynamics of earth movements. Through modeling, they investigate the consequences of plate movement—seafloor spreading, mountain building, volcanism, and earthquakes. They construct and erupt model volcanoes and explore reasons for earthquakes.

Earth Movements contains 10 activities, requiring 12 sessions of 30 minutes each to complete. Each activity includes a vocabulary list, a list of materials needed, preparation steps, teaching suggestions, and reinforcement activities. The teacher's guide includes reproducible masters for student worksheets.

Prices: Teacher's Guide (ISBN 0-87504-755-6), $9.95. Kit, $179.00. ***Publisher/supplier:*** Delta Education. ***Materials:*** Available locally, from commercial suppliers, or in kit.

2.22 Erosion. DSM. Hudson, N.H.: Delta Education, 1994.

Grades: 5-6+ In *Erosion,* students investigate how wind, glaciers, and especially water cause erosion of the earth's surfaces and how the effects of erosion can be reduced. Students construct a stream table to test the effects of several variables on the process of erosion. The variables include vegetation, slope, water volume, and type of material being eroded. They compare the erosion and deposition characteristics of several types of earth materials; they simulate the erosive effect of wave action along a shoreline; and they test the effects of wind on sand before and after building a model windbreak.

A detailed lesson is provided for each of the 12 activities, which require approximately 15 class sessions. The teacher's guide includes an overview, a list of objectives for each activity, a planning schedule, background information, and preparation and materials management strategies.

Prices: Teacher's Guide (ISBN 0-87504-117-5), $24.95. Kit, $270.00. ***Publisher/supplier:*** Delta Education. ***Materials:*** Available locally, from commercial suppliers, or in kit.

2.23 Geology: The Active Earth. NatureScope. Washington, D.C.: National Wildlife Federation, 1988.

Grades: K-5 *Geology: The Active Earth* is an interdisciplinary investigation of the nature of the earth. Students explore what the earth is made of, how old it is, how it was formed, and how it continues to be formed. Classroom and outdoor activities, including simple investigations, stories, discussions, modeling, and creative writing, focus on rocks and minerals, landforms, fossil records, the structure of the earth, and earth movements such as quakes and volcanoes. The unit's activities, suitable for use in kindergarten to the intermediate grades, integrate science with geography, mathematics, language arts, and art.

Geology: The Active Earth contains 18 lessons organized in 5 chapters. Teachers may choose single activities or teach each chapter as a unit. Copycat pages supplement the activities and include ready-to-copy maps, games, puzzles, and worksheets.

Price: $7.95. ***Publisher/supplier:*** National Wildlife Federation. ***Materials:*** Available locally.

2.24 How Landforms Change: Exploring Earth's Crust. Scholastic Science Place. (Developed in cooperation with Brooklyn Children's Museum, Brooklyn, N.Y.) New York, N.Y.: Scholastic, 1995.

Grade: 5 In *How Landforms Change: Exploring Earth's Crust,* students learn that as structures of the earth's crust break down, new structures form. The unit's lessons are grouped in 3 subconcepts: (1) the outermost of earth's 3 layers is the crust, where all landforms are found; (2) movement within the earth's crust builds and changes landforms; and (3) physical and chemical weathering change landforms. Activities in this unit include collecting and examining various rock samples, making a model of the earth's crustal plates and simulating a plate collision, and building a seismograph. Other activities include observing the way plants affect the earth and designing a probe to explore the planets in another solar system.

How Landforms Change: Exploring Earth's Crust is a 17-lesson unit. The conceptual goals of the unit are presented in the lesson-by-lesson story line in the teacher's guide. Each lesson also includes background information; a complete lesson plan, including suggestions for assessing performance and integrating the curriculum; and a list of the print, video, and software support materials required for the lesson.

Prices: Teacher's Guide (ISBN 0-590-27722-7), $27. Student Book, $10. Complete unit, $450. Consumables kit, $76. ***Publisher/supplier:*** Scholastic. ***Materials:*** Available locally, from commercial suppliers, or in unit.

2.25 The Moons of Jupiter. GEMS. Debra Sutter, Cary Sneider, Alan Gould, and others. Berkeley, Calif.: Lawrence Hall of Science, 1993.

Grades: 4-6+ In this unit, students learn about the exciting world of planets and space exploration by studying Jupiter and its moons. During the unit's 5 activities, students track Jupiter's moons, investigate the creation of craters, create a scale model of the Jupiter system using their schoolyard, go on a tour of the Jupiter system as viewed by the *Voyager* spacecraft, and design and build model space stations. Students are introduced to the work of Galileo and other early astronomers. They have the opportunity to observe photographs of Jupiter and its moons and to discuss and record information; they compare the moons' features with other, more familiar things; and they venture possible ideas, explanations, or conclusions based on what they have seen. In all of the activities, students create and use models of various kinds.

The Moons of Jupiter requires about 5 to 7 sessions of 40 to 50 minutes each. This thorough guide contains summary outlines, background information, detailed lesson plans, literature connections, activity sheets, and suggestions for additional resources. A set of 23 slides is included with the teacher's guide.

Price: $28 (ISBN 0-912511-84-2). ***Publisher/supplier:*** LHS GEMS. ***Materials:*** Available locally, or from commercial suppliers.

2.26 River Cutters. GEMS. Jefferey Kaufmann, Robert C. Knott, and Lincoln Bergman. Reprinted with revisions. Berkeley, Calif.: Lawrence Hall of Science, 1992.

Grades: 6+ *River Cutters* gives students a sense of events in a river system over time. The unit includes not only earth science and ecology but social studies. Concepts of erosion, pollution, toxic waste, and human manipulation of rivers are introduced. Students first create their own model rivers, observing and recording information about them. During the first 4 sessions of the unit, they acquire geological terminology and begin to understand rivers as dynamic, ever-changing systems. During 3 optional sessions, students have the opportunity to explore the relationship between the angle of the river models and the events that occur in the developing river, experimenting with dams and modeling problems in toxic waste disposal. Students develop skills such as designing models, experimenting, recording data, communicating, and decision making. It is important that diatomaceous earth be used and that teachers make a few trial runs with the river model prior to the class session.

The first 4 sessions in *River Cutters* require 30 to 45 minutes each; the 3 optional sessions require 45 to 60 minutes each. Each session's lesson plan includes an overview, a materials list, and detailed instructions (including diagrams) for preparing and for conducting the activity. Background information and a reproducible master of the student data sheet are included.

Price: $10 (ISBN 0-912511-67-2). ***Publisher/supplier:*** LHS GEMS. ***Materials:*** Available locally, or from commercial suppliers.

2.27 Rocks and Minerals. DSM. Hudson, N.H.: Delta Education, 1994.

Grades: 5, 6 In this module students investigate the properties and uses of rocks and minerals and are introduced to some of the methods geologists use to gather data about the materials that make up the earth. Students describe minerals in terms of properties such as luster, hardness, and streak color. They apply their knowledge in inferring some of the mineral constituents of rocks. During the unit, students develop a list of how different rocks and minerals have been used by humans through time. They construct three-dimensional models of crystals, grow crystals, and take a geological field trip to gather and interpret data on rocks and minerals.

Rocks and Minerals includes an overview, a list of objectives for each activity, a planning schedule, background information, and preparation and materials management strategies. A detailed lesson plan is provided for each of the 12 activities, which require 20 class sessions of 30 to 50 minutes each.

Prices: Teacher's Guide (ISBN 0-87504-101-9), $24.95. Kit, $259.00. ***Publisher/supplier:*** Delta Education. ***Materials:*** Available locally, from commercial suppliers, or in kit.

2.28 Rocks and Soil: How Weather and Other Forces Change the Earth. Scholastic Science Place. (Developed in cooperation with Cranbrook Institute of Science, Bloomfield Hills, Mich.) New York, N.Y.: Scholastic, 1993.

Grade: 2 Students learn that the earth is changing in *Rocks and Soil.* The unit's lessons are grouped in 3 subconcepts: (1) products form as the earth changes, (2) certain processes and forces cause the earth to change, and (3) the earth changes over a long period of time. Lessons include students observing the characteristics of rocks, demonstrating how rocks form in water, constructing a model to simulate an earthquake, comparing soil samples, and building an erosion model.

Rocks and Soil is a 17-lesson unit. The conceptual goals of the unit are presented in the lesson-by-lesson story line in the teacher's guide. Each lesson also includes background information; a complete lesson plan, including suggestions for assessing performance and integrating the curriculum; and a list of the print, video, and software support materials required for the lesson.

Prices: Teacher's Guide (ISBN 0-590-26209-2), $20.70. Student Book (ISBN 0-590-26141-X), $6.50. Complete unit, $375.00. Consumables kit, $71.00. ***Publisher/supplier:*** Scholastic. ***Materials:*** Available locally, from commercial suppliers, or in unit.

2.29 Soil. DSM. Hudson, N.H.: Delta Education, 1989.

Grades: 2-4 In the module *Soil,* students discover how soil is formed, examine soil components and compare types of soil, investigate soil erosion and pollution, and begin to understand the importance of soil to plants and animals. Activities in the unit include students observing earthworms and discovering their role in cultivating soil, collecting and examining soil samples, and simulating erosion of soil by wind and water.

Soil consists of 10 activities requiring 12 class sessions of 30 minutes each to complete. A detailed lesson plan is provided for each activity. Reproducible masters of student data sheets are included.

Prices: Teacher's Guide (ISBN 0-87504-761-0), $9.95. Kit, $210.00. ***Publisher/supplier:*** Delta Education. ***Materials:*** Available locally, from commercial suppliers, or in kit.

2.30 Solar System. DSM. Hudson, N.H.: Delta Education, 1988.

Grades: 4-6 In *Solar System,* students build graphic and physical models to help them determine the relative sizes of the sun and the planets in the solar system and the distances between them. Activities use one scale for the relative sizes of the sun and the planets and another scale to model the relative distances in the solar system. Students also use models to interpret data about moon phases and solar and lunar eclipses.

Solar System is a 10-activity module requiring about 12 class sessions of 40 minutes each. The unit includes a brief module overview, a section on evaluation, a glossary, and blackline masters. The 2-page activities provide teaching strategies and a list of materials needed.

Prices: Teacher's Guide (ISBN 0-87504-763-7), $9.95. Kit, $249.00. ***Publisher/supplier:*** Delta Education. ***Materials:*** Available locally, from commercial suppliers, or in kit.

2.31 The Solar System: How the Sun, Moon, and Planets Move. Scholastic Science Place. (Developed in cooperation with Rochester Museum and Science Center, Rochester, N.Y.) New York, N.Y.: Scholastic, 1995.

Grade: 5 In *The Solar System: How the Sun, Moon, and Planets Move,* students learn that our solar system and the bodies that make it up are in constant motion. The unit's lessons are grouped in 3 subconcepts: (1) our solar system includes the sun and the objects that move around it; (2) the relative motions of the sun, earth, and earth's moon result in changes on earth; and (3) earth's position within the solar system helps make the planet uniquely able to support life as we know it. Examples of lessons in this unit include making a sundial to observe how the sun's changing position relates to our sense of time; using a ball and string to model the movement of a planet around the sun and to demonstrate how gravity holds the solar system together; using a model to observe how sunlight and the moon's orbit create the lunar phases; and comparing conditions on various planets.

The Solar System is a 17-lesson unit requiring 30- to 45-minute class sessions. The conceptual goals of the unit are presented in the lesson-by-lesson story line in the teacher's guide. Each lesson also includes background information; a complete lesson plan, including suggestions for assessing performance and integrating the curriculum; and a list of the print, video, and software support materials required for the lesson.

Prices: Teacher's Guide (ISBN 0-590-27627-1), $20.70. Student Book (ISBN 0-590-27626-3), $6.50. Complete unit, $ 375.00. ***Publisher/supplier:*** Scholastic. ***Materials:*** Available locally, from commercial suppliers, or in unit.

2.32 STAR Geology Lab. STAR. Washington, D.C.: Reading Is Fundamental, 1993.

Grades: 4-6 In *STAR Geology Lab,* a story about the discovery of a geode by a character in a fictional classroom provides a backdrop and source of background information for a series of geology lab explorations. Students first conduct a rock-hunting expedition around the schoolyard. To identify the rocks, they test them for the presence of carbonates and conduct a streak (color) test. They learn how sedimentary rocks are formed by making artificial sandstone. To simulate core sampling—a technique used by scientists to study the geological history of an area—students make multilayered sandwiches and use straws to extract a "core sample." Students use clay models of folding rock layers to show how movement in the earth's crust creates mountains. They use large blocks of ice to simulate glacial action and its effect on land. Finally, students make molds and casts to simulate the process of fossilization. Students examine the format and features of nature guides as a model for writing their own geology field guides. Examples of interdisciplinary activities include developing recipes for a geological cookbook, creating sand paintings, and role-playing specialists in geology-related fields.

The guide provides a list of resources including books, computer software, and audiovisual materials.

Prices: Teacher's Guide, $21.90. Mentor's Guide, $3.90. ***Publisher/ supplier:*** Kendall/Hunt. ***Materials:*** Available locally.

2.33 Sunshine and Shadows. DSM. Hudson, N.H.: Delta Education, 1988.

Grades: K, 1 *Sunshine and Shadows* introduces students to some of the characteristics of light as they record the shape and movement of shadows. They learn to observe, describe, manipulate, and identify shadows. Using the sun, lamps, and flashlights as light sources, children learn that the shape, size, and location of a shadow depend on the position of the light source relative to the object that casts the shadow.

Sunshine and Shadows contains 8 activities, which require 12 sessions of 15 to 35 minutes to complete. Each activity includes a vocabulary list, a list of materials needed, preparation steps, teaching suggestions, and reinforcement activities. Reproducible masters of student worksheets are provided.

Prices: Teacher's Guide (ISBN 0-87504-719-X), $9.95. Kit, $185.00. ***Publisher/supplier:*** Delta Education. ***Materials:*** Available locally, from commercial suppliers, or in kit.

2.34 The Universe: Exploring Stars, Constellations, and Galaxies. Scholastic Science Place. (Developed in cooperation with Houston Museum of Natural Science, Houston, Tex.) New York, N.Y.: Scholastic, 1995.

Grades: 6+ In *The Universe: Exploring Stars, Constellations, and Galaxies,* students learn that the stars and other bodies that make up the universe are constantly changing. The unit's lessons are grouped in 3 subconcepts: (1) stars can be studied from earth using direct and indirect evidence; (2) stars have predictable life cycles and exist in groups; and (3) the universe is constantly expanding. Students use a sampling technique to discover how it is possible to estimate the number of stars in the sky. They observe why constellations change position over a year, investigate how parallax is used to measure the distance from earth to the stars, and build a model to show how the universe is expanding.

The Universe is a 17-lesson unit requiring about 22 class sessions of 45 minutes each. The conceptual goals of the unit are presented in the lesson-by-lesson story line in the teacher's guide. Each lesson also includes background information; a complete lesson plan, including suggestions for assessing performance and integrating the curriculum; and a list of the print, video, and software support materials required for the lesson.

Prices: Teacher's Guide (ISBN 0-590-27771-5), $27. Student Book (ISBN 0-590-27770-7), $10. Complete unit, $450. Consumables kit, $70. ***Publisher/supplier:*** Scholastic. ***Materials:*** Available locally, from commercial suppliers, or in unit.

2.35 Using Land: How People Change the Structures of Land. Scholastic Science Place. (Developed in cooperation with Science Center of Connecticut, West Hartford, Conn.) New York, N.Y.: Scholastic, 1995.

Grade: 3 In *Using Land: How People Change the Structures of Land,* students learn that land is a natural resource that is changed by natural processes and by human activities. The unit's lessons are grouped in 3 subconcepts: (1) weathering, erosion, and deposition break down landforms and build new ones; (2) humans have increased the rates of weathering and erosion by using the land; and (3) people can use land in ways that minimize damage and can partially repair damage already done. Lessons in this unit include students testing the effects of acid on a rock and making inferences about weathering from their own observations; modeling how rain moves weathered material down mountains and carves water channels; making a model of a delta to observe how the deposition of eroded material builds new landforms; and planning and building a model of a community designed to use land wisely.

Using Land: How People Change the Structures of Land is a 17-lesson unit. The conceptual goals are presented in the lesson-by-lesson story line in the teacher's guide. Each lesson also includes background information; a complete lesson plan, including suggestions for assessing performance and integrating the curriculum; and a list of the print, video, and software support materials required for the lesson.

Prices: Teacher's Guide (ISBN 0-590-27635-2), $20.70. Student Book (ISBN 0-590-27634-4), $6.50. Complete unit, $375.00. Consumables kit, $72.00. ***Publisher/supplier:*** Scholastic. ***Materials:*** Available locally, from commercial suppliers, or in unit.

2.36 Using Water: How You Use and Change Water. Scholastic Science Place. (Developed in cooperation with Orlando Science Center, Orlando, Fla.) New York, N.Y.: Scholastic 1993.

Grade: 2 In *Using Water: How You Use and Change Water,* students learn that water is a natural resource that people use and change in various ways. The unit's lessons are grouped in 3 subconcepts: (1) water is found in various forms in the environment; (2) water is a basic necessity of life and a resource for many human activities; and (3) most human activities affect water quality. Lessons in this unit include students making a solar still to see how salt water can become freshwater, keeping a water-use diary, building a model of a water tunnel, making a model of a septic tank to see how wastewater is removed from homes, and testing the effectiveness of water filters.

Using Water is a 17-lesson unit, requiring 35- to 50-minute class sessions. The conceptual goals of the unit are presented in the lesson-by-lesson story line in the teacher's guide. Each lesson also includes background information; a complete lesson plan, including suggestions for assessing performance and integrating the curriculum; and a list of the print, video, and software support materials required for the lesson.

Prices: Teacher's Guide (ISBN 0-590-26212-2), $20.70. Student Book (ISBN 0-590-26144-4), $6.50. Complete unit, $375.00. Consumables kit, $71.00. ***Publisher/supplier:*** Scholastic. ***Materials:*** Available locally, from commercial suppliers, or in unit.

2.37 Water Cycle. DSM. Hudson, N.H.: Delta Education, 1989.

Grades: 4, 5 Students learn about the water cycle from clouds to sea level in the 7 activities of this unit. They build models to simulate evaporation, condensation, and precipitation, observing and describing the continuous recycling of water. Students look at evaporation in the classroom and then in an outdoor puddle. Collecting water released from the leaves of plants through the process of transpiration, they focus on how plants give off water vapor. Students design and build a water cycle chamber to observe evaporation and condensation in a closed system.

Each of the 12 class sessions (requiring 40 minutes each) includes a vocabulary list, a list of materials needed, preparation steps, teaching suggestions, and reinforcement activities.

Prices: Teacher's Guide (ISBN 0-87504-764-5), $9.95. Kit, $218.00. ***Publisher/supplier:*** Delta Education. ***Materials:*** Available locally, from commercial suppliers, or in kit.

2.38 Weather Forecasting. DSM. Hudson, N.H.: Delta Education, 1995.

Grades: 5, 6 In *Weather Forecasting,* students make weather observations and collect weather-related data and information that they display on a weather station they construct. Students explore how collecting data on temperature, rainfall, and wind helps them forecast the weather. Through participation in the activities in this unit, students are able to relate barometric pressure readings to weather conditions. They learn to code weather information and to plot weather fronts and discover the usefulness of tracking areas of similar air pressure and temperature on a weather map. Students learn the conditions necessary for clouds to form, and begin to associate specific types of clouds with specific types of weather conditions.

Weather Forecasting includes 12 activities that require about 14 class sessions to complete. The teacher's guide includes a module overview, a list of objectives for each activity, a planning schedule, background information, and preparation and materials management strategies. A complete lesson plan is provided for each lesson.

Prices: Teacher's Guide (ISBN 0-87504-123-X), $24.95. Kit, $240.00. ***Publisher/supplier:*** Delta Education. ***Materials:*** Available locally, from commercial suppliers, or in kit.

2.39 Wild About Weather. NatureScope. Washington, D.C.: National Wildlife Federation, 1989.

Grades: K-4 *Wild About Weather* provides background information and activity ideas for an interdisciplinary introduction to the causes, kinds, and impact of weather. Students from kindergarten to intermediate grades engage in experiments, games, and simulations as they investigate how weather phenomena happen, how weather affects the earth and its inhabitants, and how meteorologists predict the weather.

Wild About Weather includes 27 lessons organized in 5 chapters; a sixth chapter provides art and craft ideas. Teachers may choose single activities or teach each chapter as a unit. Copycat pages supplement the activities and provide maps, games, puzzles, and worksheets.

Price: $7.95 (ISBN 0-945051-45-X). ***Publisher/supplier:*** National Wildlife Federation. ***Materials:*** Available locally.

EARTH SCIENCE—SCIENCE ACTIVITY BOOKS

ABOUT THE ANNOTATIONS IN "EARTH SCIENCE—SCIENCE ACTIVITY BOOKS"

Entry Numbers
Curriculum materials are arranged alphabetically by title in each category (Core Materials, Supplementary Materials, and Science Activity Books in chapters 1 through 4 of this guide. In addition, each annotation has a two-part entry number. For each entry number, the chapter number is given before the period; the number after the period locates the entry within that chapter.

For example, the first entry number in chapter 1 is 1.1; the second entry in chapter 2 is 2.2, and so on.

The entry numbers within each curriculum chapter run consecutively through Core Materials, Supplementary Materials, and Science Activity Books.

Order of Bibliographic Information
Following is the arrangement of the facts of publication in the annotations in this section:

- **Title of publication.**
- **Series title,** or series acronym if commonly used.
- **Authors** (either individual names or organizational author).
- Name and location of **developer** (in parentheses), if different from publisher.
- **Place of publication, publisher, and date of publication.**

Series Acronyms
Following are **acronyms of series titles** in "Earth Science—Science Activity Books." (Series titles that are spelled out are not included in this list.)

AIMS Activities Integrating Mathematics and Science
CESI Council for Elementary Science International
NSTA/FEMA National Science Teachers Association/Federal Emergency Management Agency

Price and Acquisition Information
Ordering information is presented in a block immediately below the annotation. Included are the following:

- **Prices** of teacher's guides, activity books, and kits or units.
- The name of a principal **publisher/supplier** (not necessarily the sole source) for the items listed in the price category. (The address and phone and fax numbers for each publisher and supplier appear in appendix A, "Publishers and Suppliers.")
- An indication of the various sources from which one might obtain the required **materials.**

2.40 Adventures With Rocks and Minerals: Geology Experiments for Young People. Adventures with Science. Lloyd H. Barrow. Hillside, N.J.: Enslow Publishers, 1991.

Grades: 4, 5 *Adventures With Rocks and Minerals: Geology Experiments for Young People* is a collection of 30 questions and experiments designed to demonstrate the properties of rocks and minerals and their relation to environmental concerns such as erosion, earthquakes, acid rain, and water pollution. Activities for home or school include the following: using a nail file to determine the relative hardness of minerals, growing crystals, using a milk carton filled with soil to test how slope affects soil erosion, and using white vinegar and radish seeds to explore effects of acid rain on plants.

Each activity in this guide includes a materials list, procedure, observation questions, a discussion, and suggestions of other investigations.

Price: $16.95 (ISBN 0-89490-263-6). ***Publisher/supplier:*** Enslow. ***Materials:*** Available locally, or from commercial suppliers.

2.41 Air and Water. Prepared by Museum To Go Resource Center. Philadelphia, Pa.: Franklin Institute, 1988.

Grades: 2-4 During the 6 activities in *Air and Water,* students answer some fundamental scientific questions. They explore the following topics: (1) what air is and how we know it is there, (2) how air and water are important to living things, (3) how water is like other liquids, (4) how we know what will sink and what will float, (5) how salt water affects plant growth, and (6) how air can be used to do work. Activities include students making pinwheels, comparing the germination of wet and dry seeds both with and without air, comparing the properties of water and Kool-Aid, experimenting to determine the effects of freshwater and salt water on the growth of bean seeds, and demonstrating which objects will float in water.

Each activity in *Air and Water* features a teacher's page and several student pages, which include instructions for setting up and conducting the activity, questions, diagrams, and data sheets.

Prices: Complete kit, $199.00. Consumables kit, $82.50. ***Publisher/ supplier:*** Science Kit and Boreal Laboratories. ***Materials:*** Available locally, from commercial suppliers, or in kit.

2.42 The Amateur Meteorologist: Explorations and Investigations. Amateur Science Series. H. Michael Mogil and Barbara G. Levine. New York, N.Y.: Franklin Watts, 1993.

Grades: 4-6+ In the activities of *The Amateur Meteorologist: Explorations and Investigations,* students build their own weather instruments from readily available materials. Other investigations in this activity and resource book on weather observing and forecasting introduce skills needed to identify clouds, to read weather maps, to calculate dew point and relative humidity, and to determine windchill and degree-days. Useful background information is also included on the water cycle, cloud formation, sun and seasons, pressure and wind, and stormy weather. This beginners guide to meteorology features numerous photographs and charts.

Price: $19 (ISBN 0-531-11045-1). ***Publisher/supplier:*** Franklin Watts. ***Materials:*** Available locally, or from commercial suppliers.

2.43 Blue Planet. Carolyn E. Schmidt. Washington, D.C.: National Air and Space Museum, Office of Education, 1990.

Grades: 5-6+ Looking at earth from space provides students with a unique perspective in *Blue Planet,* an activity book designed to be used in conjunction with the IMAX film of the same name, produced by the Smithsonian Institution's National Air and Space Museum. The information, activities, and resources in the book cover many environmental and earth science topics, from earthquakes to groundwater filtration to solar heating. This varied selection offers teachers of students in grades 3-12 a wide range of resources from which to choose. Many of the activities are designed to develop students' observational skills, especially with regard to the changing nature of the earth's environment. The guide lists 40 locations where *Blue Planet* can be seen.

Price: Free to educators in response to request on school letterhead. ***Publisher/supplier:*** National Air and Space Museum. ***Materials:*** Available locally, or from commercial suppliers.

2.44 Earthquakes: A Teacher's Package for K-6. NSTA/FEMA Earthquake Curriculum. National Science Teachers Association. Washington, D.C.: U.S. Government Printing Office, 1993.

Grades: K-6 *Earthquakes: A Teacher's Package for K-6* offers a cross-curricular approach to the study of these events. Copiously illustrated, this teacher's manual contains dozens of activities under 6 unit headings: (1) Defining an Earthquake, (2) Why and Where Earthquakes Occur, (3) Physical Results of Earthquakes, (4) Measuring Earthquakes, (5) Recognizing Earthquakes, and (6) Earthquake Safety and Survival. The units are intended to be used in order. Activities include using a hard-boiled egg to simulate the layers of the earth, constructing models of three types of faults, simulating an earthquake using wooden sticks and coffee grounds, and practicing proper reactions to an earthquake.

Each of the first 5 units in *Earthquakes* includes background information, lessons, and activities for each of 3 grade levels: K-2, 3-4, and 5-6, as well as master pages that may be reproduced for transparencies, handouts, and worksheets.

Prices: Single copy free to educators when requested from FEMA on school letterhead; $17.95 through National Science Teachers Association. ***Publisher/supplier:*** Federal Emergency Management Agency. ***Materials:*** Available locally, or from commercial suppliers.

2.45 Earth, Sun and Moon: Just Passing Time. Prepared by Museum To Go Resource Center. Philadelphia, Pa.: Franklin Institute, 1988.

Grades: 5-6+ *Earth, Sun and Moon: Just Passing Time* examines the positions of the earth, sun, and moon in relation to one another. The unit's 8 activities also focus on the natural movements of the earth and moon relative to the sun and to each other and investigate how our concept of time corresponds to these movements. Activities include students using a model of the earth and a flashlight to simulate the earth's rotation and resulting daylight and darkness. They simulate circular and elliptical orbits as well as the earth revolving around the sun. Students make a moon phase calendar and construct a model of the three bodies to demonstrate their relative positions and to show the difference between rotation and revolution.

Each activity in the unit features a teacher's page and several student pages, which include instructions for setting up and conducting the activity, questions, diagrams, and student data sheets.

Prices: Complete kit, $225.00. Consumables kit, $78.00. ***Publisher/ supplier:*** Science Kit and Boreal Laboratories. ***Materials:*** Materials available locally, from commercial suppliers, or in kit.

2.46 Exploring Space: Using Seymour Simon's Astronomy Books in the Classroom. Barbara Bourne and Wendy Saul. New York, N.Y.: Morrow Junior Books, 1994.

Grades: 5, 6 *Exploring Space: Using Seymour Simon's Astronomy Books in the Classroom* contains about 50 space-related activities that build on information in astronomy books by Seymour Simon and other prominent authors of children's nonfiction books. Each activity has a different theme, such as magnetic storms on the sun, black holes, or developing a space quiz. In addition to experiments, this guide for teachers and parents proposes topics for writing assignments and discussions and suggests titles for further reading. Teachers are encouraged to select from among the activities and to encourage their students to amend and refine them. Striking, full-color photographs and useful diagrams appear throughout the guide.

Price: $9.95 (ISBN 0-688-12723-1). ***Publisher/supplier:*** Morrow Junior Books. ***Materials:*** Available locally, or from commercial suppliers.

2.47 Finding Your Way: Navigation Activities from the Exploratorium. Peter Weiss and the staff of the Exploratorium. San Francisco, Calif.: The Exploratorium, 1992.

Grades: 4-6+ Inspired by an exhibit at the Exploratorium museum in San Francisco celebrating "the amazing human ability to get from here to there," *Finding Your Way* contains sections on finding north, making maps, and orienting oneself on the planet. Activities include the following: students use a dial watch and the sun to find true north and then make and use a magnetic compass to find magnetic north; they make a clinometer to measure the height of an object, then use a "shrinking tower" scale to determine how far away the object is; they measure and map a hill in three dimensions; they use the North Star and a clinometer to measure latitude; and they use a north-south line and a time-zone table to determine longitude.

Each activity includes an objective, a materials list, instructions, and an explanation that provides scientific, technological, and historical context. The book offers helpful illustrations and clear, easy-to-follow directions.

Price: $5.95 (ISBN 0-943451-35-3). ***Publisher/supplier:*** The Exploratorium. ***Materials:*** Available locally, or from commercial suppliers.

2.48 Franklin's Forecaster. Prepared by Museum To Go Resource Center. Philadelphia, Pa.: Franklin Institute, 1990.

Grades: K-2 Students learn about weather in *Franklin's Forecaster,* a unit featuring activities conducted with Benjamin Franklin as the focal point. Activities relate to portions of a book entitled *The Many Lives of Benjamin Franklin.* Students record daily weather conditions, compare and construct models of different kinds of clouds, and draw conclusions about the kinds of weather each brings. They construct a "Franklin Flyer" and a "Franklin Floater" to demonstrate that air moves objects. They learn to use a thermometer and to distinguish between different temperatures without a thermometer.

Each activity in *Franklin's Forecaster* features a teacher's page and several student pages, which provide instructions for setting up and conducting the activity, questions, diagrams, and student data sheets.

Prices: Complete kit, $235. Consumables kit, $60. ***Publisher/ supplier:*** Science Kit and Boreal Laboratories. ***Materials:*** Available locally, from commercial suppliers, or in kit.

2.49 Geothermal Energy. Marilyn Nemzer and Deborah Page. Tiburon, Calif.: Geothermal Education Office, 1994.

Grades: 5-6+ *Geothermal Energy,* designed for use with students in grades 4 to 8, describes geothermal energy in the context of the world's energy needs. The information and activities in this well-illustrated guide involve students in an in-depth study of geothermal energy, including its geology, history, and many uses. Science activities are integrated with mathematics, social studies, and language arts. Teachers are encouraged to choose the lessons and activities most appropriate for their students' needs. The activities in the 6 sections of this unit include, for example, demonstrating the effects of burning fuels using mirrors and various heat sources, using swirling colored water to show how hot mantle rock moves in convection currents, testing the effects of heat on evaporation, producing electric current in a magnet, and making a model geothermal steam engine.

Each section in *Geothermal Energy* includes a section "For the Teacher"; activities include an introduction, a materials list, and step-by-step directions.

Price: $12. ***Publisher/supplier:*** Geothermal Education Office. ***Materials:*** Available locally, or from commercial suppliers.

2.50 The Great Ocean Rescue. Watertown, Mass.: Tom Snyder Productions, 1993.

Grades: 5-6+ *The Great Ocean Rescue* is a videodisc package designed to engage students in learning about the ocean and related topics in earth science, environmental science, and life science through a cooperative learning experience. The activity (requiring 4 to 12 class periods) consists of 4 rescue missions that take students to trouble spots in the ocean. Students view a videodisc description of the mission, then break into small groups, with each student in the group adopting the role of a different scientist, such as a geologist, marine biologist, oceanographer, or environmental scientist, to analyze the information. Each group reports its recommendations to the class, and the class decides the trouble spot location. Small groups reconvene to come up with possible solutions to the problem and the class then decides on the best solution.

The videodisc includes a library of short movies that complement and extend the rescue activity. Reproducible masters of student worksheets and a poster-sized map of the ocean floor are included.

Prices: Classroom kit, $349.95. Software for Mac or Windows (optional), $49.95. ***Publisher/supplier:*** Tom Snyder Productions. ***Materials:*** Available in kit.

2.51 The Great Solar System Rescue. Cambridge, Mass.: Tom Snyder Productions, 1992.

Grades: 4-6+ In *The Great Solar System Rescue,* a videodisc-based simulation set in the year 2210, four probes are lost in space and the class must rescue them. Students analyze data in order to find the best way of rescuing the probes. They view a videodisc description of the mission, then break into small groups, with each student assuming the role of a specific scientist, such as an astronomer, meteorologist, geologist, or space historian, to analyze the information. Each group reports its recommendations to the class and the class decides where to travel. When the probe is located, the small groups reconvene to develop rescue plans, and the class again decides on the best plan.

The videodiscs include a library of short movies and stills that complement and extend the rescue activity.

Prices: Classroom kit, $349.95. Software for Mac or Windows (optional), $49.95. ***Publisher/supplier:*** Tom Snyder Productions. ***Materials:*** Available in kit.

2.52 Hands on Elementary School Science: Earth Science. Linda Poore. South Pasadena, Calif.: Linda Poore, 1994.

Grades: K-6 The 51 activities in *Hands on Elementary School Science: Earth Science* are organized in 6 thematic units—(1) Rocks and Soil; (2) Weather; (3) Rocks, Erosion, and Weathering; (4) Space; (5) Earth Resources; and (6) Oceans. Activities in these units include the following: (1) students observe and compare rocks and experiment with different soils; (2) they experiment with wind, rain, dew, frost, fog, and smog; (3) students identify rocks by testing for properties and experiment to discover how erosion and weathering change the earth; (4) they experiment to discover causes of eclipses, orbits, moon phases, the greenhouse effect, and the effects of gravity and zero gravity; (5) they experiment with fossils, minerals, soil, land, water, and air; and (6) they experiment with salinity, oil spills, beach erosion due to wave action, causes of currents, desalination, and tides.

Reproducible masters of student worksheets are included in English and Spanish.

Prices: Activity binder, $130.00 (complete set of 6 units with school license). Individual unit, $35.00. Kits for individual units: from $186.70 to $299.30. ***Publisher/supplier:*** Linda Poore. ***Materials:*** Available locally, from commercial suppliers, or in kit from Delta Education.

2.53 Investigating Science with Dinosaurs. Craig A. Munsart. Englewood, Colo.: Teacher Ideas Press/ Libraries Unlimited, 1993.

Grades: 4-6+ *Investigating Science with Dinosaurs* contains activities and information to help students explore what is known about dinosaurs, ranging from topics such as their warmbloodedness to their digestion and "architecture." Activities in the guide help students examine the geographical and geological principles that form the basis of our understanding of the Age of Dinosaurs and the world these creatures inhabited. Students discover the importance of interpreting evidence, chart the relationships among different dinosaurs, and they locate inaccuracies about dinosaurs in books. They assemble full-size drawings of a dinosaur skeleton, translate the Latin and Greek roots of dinosaur names, make models that simulate dinosaur ligaments, create and interpret animals' tracks, and make paper-bag headpieces with eye holes to simulate dinosaur vision.

The appendixes include a summary chart of activities, information about fossils and geologic time, and a pronunciation guide to extinct animals. A bibliography and glossary are included.

Price: $23 (ISBN 1-56308-008-7). ***Publisher/supplier:*** Teacher Ideas Press. ***Materials:*** Available locally, or from commercial suppliers.

2.54 Our Sea of Clouds: An Introduction to Cloud and Sky Watching. H. Michael Mogil, Allan E. Eustis, and Barbara G. Levine. Rockville, Md.: How the Weatherworks, 1992.

Grades: 4-6 *Our Sea of Clouds: An Introduction to Cloud and Sky Watching* is designed to offer teachers a broad perspective on clouds and sky and on the historical background of cloud observing. The 50 multidisciplinary activities, which incorporate mathematics, geography, art, and language arts, offer students opportunities to experiment, predict, observe, classify, and hypothesize about cloud and sky phenomena. The guide is organized in 6 sections that focus on (1) an introduction to sky observation, (2) collecting and interpreting data about sky phenomena, (3) forecasting and climatology, (4) experimenting with clouds, (5) how weather affects our moods and feelings, and (6) weather-related optical phenomena. Examples of activities include students recording sky data on a monthly weather calendar, creating their own cloud maps from the newspaper's weather page, creating clouds in a bottle, and discussing visibility. Some activities stand alone and others are designed to be used in sequence.

Our Sea of Clouds includes a teacher's guide, a videotape featuring time-lapse and still cloud photography, and 3 full-color cloud charts. Each section includes objectives, a materials list, and instructions for each activity. The guide includes a bibliography, a glossary, and selected readings.

Prices: Teacher's Guide, $14.95. Complete unit, $89.95. ***Publisher/supplier:*** How the Weatherworks. ***Materials:*** Available locally.

2.55 Out of the Rock: Integrated Learning Activities for Students. National Energy Foundation. Salt Lake City, Utah: National Energy Foundation, 1994.

Grades: K-6+ *Out of the Rock* is a mineral resource education guide for teachers that focuses on topics such as mining, geology, the environment, and economics. It includes an introduction, background information, a conceptual framework, sections dealing with careers, tools of the trade, large-group activities, and additional resources. The 4 sections of integrated learning activities are the central component of the guide. Activities include students participating in a "mining day" celebration, inventing a new device or product that uses minerals or items made from minerals, creating stories about the lifestyles of the early miners, learning the characteristics of rocks and minerals, and using mining vocabulary in a game situation.

It is recommended in *Out of the Rock* that each activity be preceded by a reminder of safety procedures, because some of the activities are potentially hazardous due to the use of chemicals, flammable substances, and/or heat.

Price: $25. ***Publisher/supplier:*** National Energy Foundation. ***Materials:*** Available locally, or from commercial suppliers.

2.56 Out of This World. AIMS. Mary Lind, Pam Knecht, Bill Dodge, and others. Rev. ed. Fresno, Calif.: AIMS Education Foundation, 1994.

Grades: 5-6+ In *Out of This World,* students learn about the planets and their relationships by using tables, planetary facts, Venn diagrams, and drawings of the planets. Students determine the relative sizes of the planets and the distances between them in order to construct a model solar system. They compute travel time to the moon and other planets to determine their own ages after imaginary excursions. They compute gravity factors and compare travel time around the equator of each of the planets. *Out of This World* was revised in 1994 to reflect newly acquired information from space research.

Each of the 20 investigations in this guide has a specific lesson plan, including a list of materials, background information, procedures, discussion questions, reproducible student worksheets, and extensions.

Price: $14.95 (ISBN 1-881431-43-6). ***Publisher/supplier:*** AIMS Education Foundation. ***Materials:*** Available locally.

2.57 Rocks, Sand, and Soil. Windows on Elementary Science. Joan Westley. Sunnyvale, Calif.: Creative Publications, 1988.

Grades: PreK, K-2 In *Rocks, Sand, and Soil,* children sort and classify rocks by texture, weight, color, and hardness. They examine soil to determine its components; make sand from rocks; create sand paintings; construct sand timers; and compare soil samples, soil drainage, and plant growth in different soils. Activities in the guide are sequenced by increasing levels of difficulty but do not have to be used in order. Most activities require one class period.

Each of the 28 activities in *Rocks, Sand, and Soil* includes a learning objective, process skills, materials needed, suggested questions for discussions, directions for the exploration, and extensions.

Prices: Teacher's Guide (ISBN 0-88488-707-3), $13.75. Kit, $250.00. ***Publisher/supplier:*** Creative Publications. ***Materials:*** Available locally, from commercial suppliers, or in kit.

2.58 The Story of Drinking Water. 3rd ed. John Dale, Pattianne Corsentino, and Roxanne Brickell. Denver, Colo.: American Water Works Association, 1992.

Grades: 4-6+ *The Story of Drinking Water* attempts to build an appreciation and understanding of the importance of a safe and reliable water supply. The teacher's guide features 19 activities that address a variety of topics ranging from what students know about water, to water treatment, to cycles, supply, use, and conservation. Activities include students making models of the hydrologic cycle, constructing miniature wells to explore the concept of an aquifer, studying chlorine's use as a disinfectant, and investigating the dynamics of water pressure. Many of the activities integrate other curriculum areas—for example, geography in studying water distribution, social studies in creating a solution to the problem of wasted water, and mathematics in learning the concept of 1 part per million.

The teacher's guide is designed to accompany a student booklet by the same title, and is available in English, Spanish, French, and metric.

Price: $7 (ISBN 0-89867-608-8). ***Publisher/supplier:*** American Water Works Association. ***Materials:*** Available locally.

2.59 Water, Stones, and Fossil Bones. CESI Sourcebook VI. Washington, D.C.: National Science Teachers Association and Council for Elementary Science International (CESI), 1991.

Grades: K-6+ *Water, Stones, and Fossil Bones* offers 51 well-illustrated earth science activities from dozens of authors. Activities are grouped within the topics of space, land, water, air, and the earth's past. Activities include making a scale model of the solar system, using Play-Doh to simulate layers of sedimentary rock, creating miniature landfills in a plastic cup, building a solar collector, and making a fossil cast.

Each activity includes background information, a short description of the concepts or skills developed, questions to initiate discussion, step-by-step procedures, and suggestions for further investigation.

Price: $16.50 (ISBN 0-87355-101-X). ***Publisher/supplier:*** Council for Elementary Science International. ***Materials:*** Available locally, or from commercial suppliers.

2.60 Weather and Climate. Step-by-Step Science Series. Toni Albert. Greensboro, N.C.: Carson-Dellosa Publishing Co., 1995.

Grades: 4-6 *Weather and Climate* is a collection of activities designed to introduce students to the elements of weather and climate and the impact they have on daily life. The 37 activities are grouped in 5 sections: (1) introducing weather, (2) elements of weather, (3) meteorology, (4) climate, and (5) man's effect on weather. Activities include making a chart of the layers of the atmosphere, making a windsock to determine wind direction, observing and recording information about clouds, testing the air for particle pollution, and keeping a weather notebook. Students also research topics in books, newspapers, and encyclopedias.

Each activity in *Weather and Climate* includes a statement of purpose, background information, a list of materials, and step-by-step instructions.

Price: $5.95. ***Publisher/supplier:*** Carson-Dellosa. ***Materials:*** Available locally.

2.61 The Weather Kit. Boston, Mass.: Museum of Science, 1992.

Grades: 4-6 *The Weather Kit,* a multidisciplinary curriculum kit from the Museum of Science in Boston, may be used for an intensive study of weather over a 5-week period or as a source of individual weather-related activities. Students collect and measure raindrops; make clouds in bottles; detect air currents inside the school; and measure humidity, temperature, wind speed, and direction with homemade and professional equipment. Activities are grouped in 5 sections: (1) introduction to weather, (2) the sun and thermal energy, (3) air and the atmosphere, (4) water, and (5) weather.

Each activity in *The Weather Kit* includes a statement of purpose, background information, a materials list, and procedures. Some include discussion questions and ideas for further exploration. Instructions on how to access a free on-line weather service are included.

Price: Rental for 5 weeks: $105, plus $7 shipping. ***Publisher/supplier:*** Museum of Science. ***Materials:*** Available locally, from commercial suppliers, or in kit.

CHAPTER 3

PHYSICAL SCIENCE

PHYSICAL SCIENCE—CORE MATERIALS

3.1 Balance and Motion. FOSS. (Developed by Lawrence Hall of Science, Berkeley, Calif.) Chicago, Ill.: Encyclopaedia Britannica Educational Corp., 1993.

Grades: 1, 2 In *Balance and Motion,* children discover how objects balance, spin, and roll. They explore balance, counterbalance, and stability by using counterweights to balance cardboard shapes and to make a pencil stand on its point. They apply their understanding of balance and stability by making mobiles. Students investigate spinning—rotational motion—by constructing tops, zoomers, and twirlers. They explore rolling motion by rolling objects down slopes; constructing and experimenting with wheel-and-axle systems; observing the way paper cups roll, then exploring ways to make them roll straight and weighting them to see how their rolling changes. In a final activity, students make one long runway through which a marble can roll nonstop.

The 3 activity folios in *Balance and Motion* require a minimum of 13 class sessions to complete. The teacher's guide includes a module overview, the 3 individual activity folios, duplication masters (in English and Spanish) for student sheets, and an annotated bibliography.

The module includes science background information, detailed instructions on planning for and conducting each activity, an extensive assessment component, and extensions for integration and enrichment. Materials are available in a kit.

Prices: Teacher's Guide (ISBN 0-7826-1142-7), $101. Complete module, $339. ***Publisher/supplier:*** Encyclopaedia Britannica Educational Corp. ***Materials:*** Available locally, from commercial suppliers, or in module.

3.2 Balancing and Weighing. STC. Field-test ed. Washington, D.C.: National Science Resources Center, 1993.

Grade: 2 *Balancing and Weighing* presents activities that help young students explore the relationship between balance and weight. Working in groups of two to four, children manipulate objects, use a beam balance, and build mobiles to explore balance. They use an equal-arm balance to compare objects and then place them in serial order according to weight. They learn through experimentation that weighing is simply the process of balancing an object against a certain number of other units. Children apply what they have learned about balancing and weighing to explore the relationships among density, weight, and volume by working with cupfuls of food. In a final activity, they use equal-arm balances to find out which of five

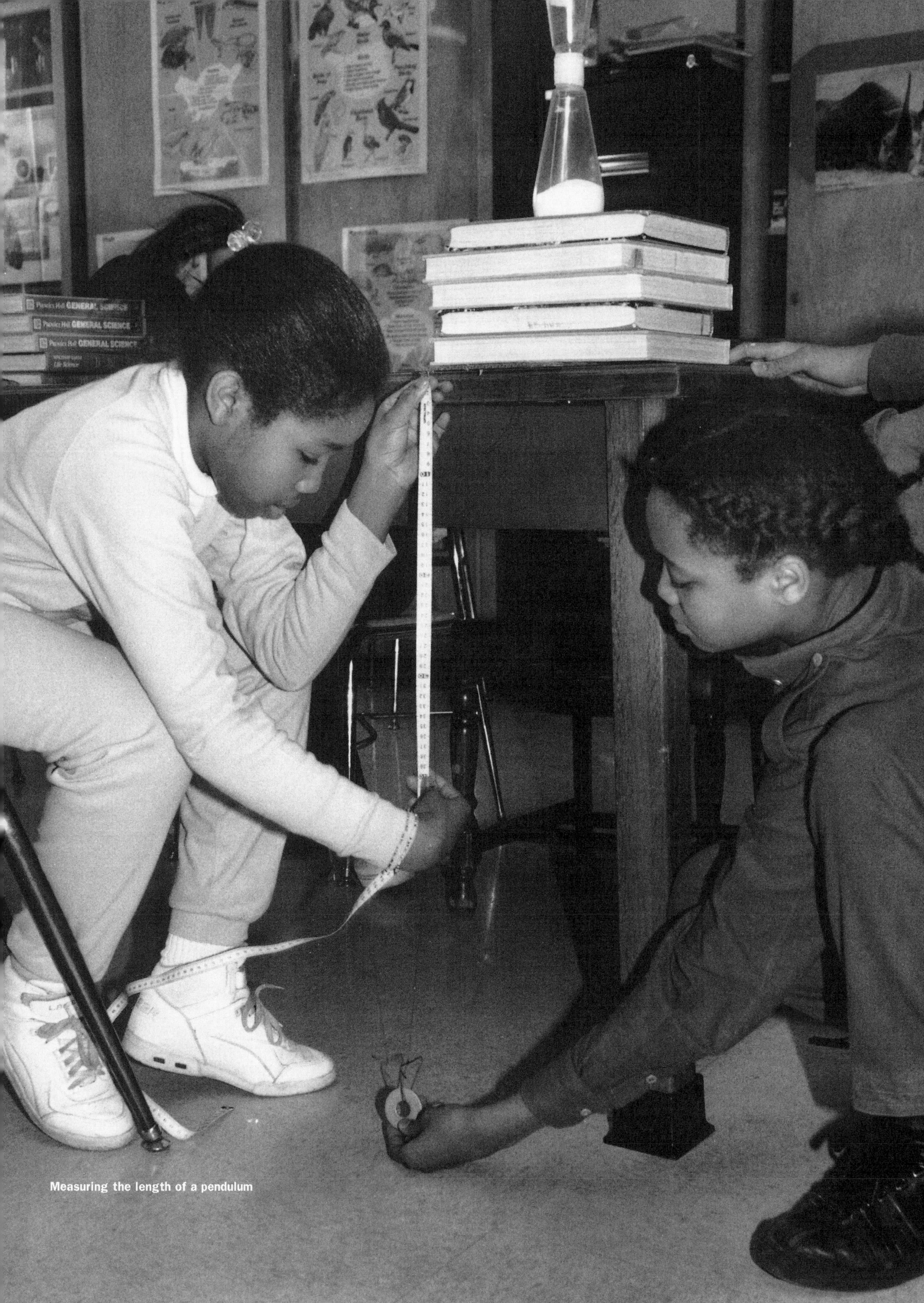

Measuring the length of a pendulum

ABOUT THE ANNOTATIONS IN "PHYSICAL SCIENCE—CORE MATERIALS"

Entry Numbers
Curriculum materials are arranged alphabetically by title in each category (Core Materials, Supplementary Materials, and Science Activity Books) in chapters 1 through 4 of this guide. In addition, each annotation has a two-part entry number. For each entry number, the chapter number is given before the period; the number after the period locates the entry within that chapter.

For example, the first entry number in chapter 1 is 1.1; the second entry in chapter 2 is 2.2, and so on.

The entry numbers within each curriculum chapter run consecutively through Core Materials, Supplementary Materials, and Science Activity Books.

Order of Bibliographic Information
Following is the arrangement of the facts of publication in the annotations in this section:

- **Title of publication.**
- **Series title**, or series acronym if commonly used.
- **Authors** (either individual names or organizational author).
- Name and location of developer (in parentheses), if different from publisher.
- **Place of publication, publisher, and date of publication.**

Series Acronyms
Following are **acronyms of series titles** in "Physical Science—Core Materials." (Series titles that are spelled out are not included in this list.)

FOSS Full Option Science System
SCIS 3 Science Curriculum Improvement Study
STC Science and Technology for Children

Price and Acquisition Information
Ordering information is presented in a block immediately below the annotation. Included are the following:

- **Prices** of teacher's guides, activity books, and kits or units.
- The name of a principal **publisher/supplier** (not necessarily the sole source) for the items listed in the price category. (The address and phone and fax numbers for each publisher and supplier appear in appendix A, "Publishers and Suppliers.")
- An indication of the various sources from which one might obtain the required **materials.**

containers holds a certain number of marbles. Throughout the unit children gather and organize data in graphs and tables and make weight comparisons.

Balancing and Weighing is a 16-lesson unit requiring 8 weeks to complete. The teacher's guide includes a unit overview, the 16 lesson plans, reproducible masters for teacher's record charts of student progress, and an annotated bibliography. An optional consumable notebook for students accompanies the unit.

The module includes science background information, detailed instructions on planning for and conducting each activity, an extensive assessment component, and extensions for integration and enrichment. Materials are available in a kit.

Prices: Teacher's Guide, $14.95. Consumable Student Notebook, $2.00. Unit, $399.95. ***Publisher/supplier:*** Carolina Biological Supply. ***Materials:*** Available locally, from commercial suppliers, or in unit.

3.3 Balls and Ramps. Insights. Newton, Mass.: Education Development Center, 1994.

Grades: K, 1 In *Balls and Ramps,* children learn about the properties and characteristics of balls and the things that affect the way balls move. Working in both small and large groups, students investigate the bounciness of balls of different size, weight, and composition; the effects of shape, size, weight, and smoothness on how a ball rolls; the relationship between the height of the starting point and the energy of a ball when it leaves a ramp; and the effect of the weight and size of a ball on how quickly it reaches the bottom of a ramp and how far it goes. Concepts such as gravity, friction, inertia, and momentum are discovered by students during these activities, although teachers are advised not to introduce these terms to young students.

Balls and Ramps consists of 14 Learning Experiences, requiring about 20 class sessions over 6 to 8 weeks. The teacher's guide includes a unit overview, the 14 Learning Experiences, reproducible masters for student sheets, and annotated lists of additional resources to use with the module.

The module includes science background information, detailed instructions on planning for and conducting each activity, an extensive assessment component, and extensions for integration and enrichment. Materials are available in a kit.

Prices: Teacher's Guide (ISBN 0-89292-165-X), $65. Materials kit, $298. (Prices differ in California, Nevada, and Indiana.) ***Publisher/supplier:*** Optical Data. ***Materials:*** Available locally, from commercial suppliers, or in kit.

3.4 Changes of State. Insights. Newton, Mass.: Education Development Center, 1994.

Grades: 4, 5 In *Changes of State,* students learn that water is a form of matter that can exist as a solid, liquid, or gas, and they discover the factors that cause changes in the state of water. Working both individually and in small groups, students investigate the factors that influence how fast ice melts, and they explore evaporation, condensation, and freezing. An optional activity on sublimation and condensation to a solid is included. Students learn that changes of state are physical and that they can be reversed by adding or taking away heat energy. In a final activity that can serve as a performance assessment, students create small terrariums for watching and recording the water cycle. As ice melts they record the temperature of water and graph the data. They also design and conduct experiments that explore how heat and surface area affect speed of evaporation. Throughout the module students conduct and record their own observations with charts and drawings and in notebooks. They are encouraged to explore how changes of state affect their lives. Students are not expected to understand their observations on a molecular level.

Changes of State consists of 15 Learning Experiences, requiring a total of at least 20 sessions, or about 6 to 8 weeks to complete. The teacher's guide includes a unit overview, the 15 Learning Experiences, reproducible masters for student sheets, and annotated lists of additional resources to use with the module.

The module includes science background information, detailed instructions on planning for and conducting each activity, an extensive assessment component, and extensions for integration and enrichment. Materials are available in a kit.

Prices: Teacher's Guide (ISBN 0-89292-175-7), $65. Materials kit, $324. (Prices differ in California, Nevada, and Indiana.) ***Publisher/supplier:*** Optical Data. ***Materials:*** Available locally, from commercial suppliers, or in kit.

3.5 Chemical Tests. STC. (Developed by National Science Resources Center, Washington, D.C.) Burlington, N.C.: Carolina Biological Supply Co., 1994.

Grade: 3 In *Chemical Tests,* students perform a series of physical and chemical tests to identify five "mystery" solids (sugar, alum, talc, baking soda, and cornstarch). At the same time they explore some concepts basic to general chemistry: they investigate physical and chemical properties and how to describe them, and they explore physical and chemical changes that occur when different solids and liquids are mixed together or separated. As a result, students are introduced to solubility, filtration, evaporation, crystallization, acids, bases, and neutral substances. From experimentation and observation, which are emphasized throughout the unit, students have the opportunity to learn basic safety and laboratory skills. They record, question, analyze, and draw conclusions from test results. The student activity book includes simple instructions, reading selections, and ideas for exploring topics further.

Chemical Tests is a 16-lesson unit that requires 6 to 8 weeks to complete. The teacher's guide includes a unit overview, the 16 lesson plans, an annotated bibliography, and instructions for making test solutions and a materials management poster.

The module includes science background information, detailed instructions on planning for and conducting each activity, an extensive assessment component, and extensions for integration and enrichment. Materials are available in a kit.

Prices: Teacher's Guide, $14.95. Student Activity Book, $3.50. Unit, $349.95. ***Publisher/supplier:*** Carolina Biological Supply. ***Materials:*** Available locally, from commercial suppliers, or in unit.

3.6 **Circuits and Pathways. Insights.** Newton, Mass.: Education Development Center, 1994.

Grades: 4, 5 In *Circuits and Pathways,* students learn about electricity and how it works by exploring its properties in simple circuits. In the first half of the module, they explore ways to wire a motor to a battery to make the motor spin in different directions; they light a bulb in different ways, using only a battery, a bulb, and a wire; they observe the inner structure of a bulb and trace the pathway the electric current follows through the bulb; and they discover what materials conduct or do not conduct electricity. In the second half of the module, students explore and create series and parallel circuits, construct bulb-brightness meters, make switches, investigate electric resistance, and build fuses to determine how they function in a circuit. In a culminating activity, students use what they have learned to design mystery boxes.

Circuits and Pathways consists of 15 Learning Experiences, requiring a total of at least 20 sessions, or about 6 to 8 weeks to complete. The teacher's guide includes a unit overview, the 15 Learning Experiences, reproducible masters for student sheets, and annotated lists of additional resources to use with the module.

The module includes science background information, detailed instructions on planning for and conducting each activity, an extensive assessment component, and extensions for integration and enrichment. Materials are available in a kit.

Prices: Teacher's Guide (ISBN 0-89292-176-5), $65. Materials kit, $428. (Prices differ in California, Nevada, and Indiana.) ***Publisher/supplier:*** Optical Data. ***Materials:*** Available locally, from commercial suppliers, or in kit.

3.7 **Electric Circuits. STC.** (Developed by National Science Resources Center, Washington, D.C.) Burlington, N.C.: Carolina Biological Supply Co., 1991.

Grade: 4 *Electric Circuits* introduces students to the basic properties of electricity as they construct and test electric circuits using wires, light bulbs, and cells (batteries). Working in teams of two to four, students explore different kinds of circuits and switches, learn about conductors and insulators, construct circuit testers, light bulbs and then a flashlight, and discover the properties of diodes. For the final activity, students apply what they have learned to wire a cardboard box house, lighting each room. Throughout this unit, students also collect, record, and interpret data and learn to use the data and observations to predict results of additional experiments.

Electric Circuits is a 16-lesson unit that requires 6 to 8 weeks to complete. The teacher's guide includes a unit overview; the 16 lesson plans; an annotated bibliography; and illustrated instructions on using a wire stripper, removing the base from a light bulb, and making circuit boxes. A student activity book with simple illustrations and instructions accompanies the unit.

The module includes science background information, detailed instructions on planning for and conducting each activity, an extensive assessment component, and extensions for integration and enrichment. Materials are available in a kit.

Prices: Teacher's Guide, $14.95. Student Activity Book, $3.50. Unit, $349.95. ***Publisher/supplier:*** Carolina Biological Supply. ***Materials:*** Available locally, from commercial suppliers, or in unit.

3.8 **Energy Sources. SCIS 3.** Herbert D. Thier and Robert C. Knott. Hudson, N.H.: Delta Education, 1992.

Grade: 5 *Energy Sources* provides students with opportunities to learn about the energy transfers that accompany the interaction of matter in solid, liquid, and gaseous forms. Students explore multiple energy transfers as they conduct controlled experiments with rotoplanes (propeller-driven rotating platforms); observe the transfer of energy from warm water to cold water; conduct experiments in which they melt and preserve ice; focus on motion as evidence of energy transfer by working with spheres that roll down ramps and collide with a moving target; and explore the use of sunlight as an energy source. Throughout the unit students measure and record distances and temperatures, display their data in histograms and on line graphs, and use their measurements to make quantitative comparisons.

Energy Systems is organized in 5 sections consisting of a total of 20 chapters. The teacher's guide includes an introduction to the unit, lesson plans for each of the 5 sections, a glossary, and blackline masters for a student journal.

The module includes science background information, detailed instructions on planning for and conducting each activity, an extensive assessment component, and extensions for integration and enrichment. Materials are available in a kit.

Prices: Teacher's Guide (ISBN 0-87504-939-7), $39.50. Kit, $760.00. ***Publisher/supplier:*** Delta Education. ***Materials:*** Available locally, from commercial suppliers, or in kit.

3.9 Fabrics. FOSS. (Developed by Lawrence Hall of Science, Berkeley, Calif.) Chicago, Ill.: Encyclopaedia Britannica Educational Corp., 1993.

Grade: K The *Fabrics* module uses a familiar product to teach scientific concepts and themes to young learners. In this unit, children observe and describe the different properties of fabrics. They compare fabrics to discover how they are alike and different, and they observe interactions of fabric with water and other substances. Students take fabric apart into threads to see how it was made. They make a fabric by weaving yarn, try to remove various stains from fabrics, and dye fabrics. The unit is designed for "working alone together"—that is, for students grouped in clusters of 4 to 10, with each student using his or her own materials in close proximity to others. Although written for kindergarten, the activities and materials may also be suitable for first grade.

Fabrics consists of 2 activities requiring a minimum of 11 class sessions. The teacher's guide includes a module overview, the 2 individual activity folios, an annotated bibliography, and instruction cards for adults assisting with the learning centers.

The module includes science background information, detailed instructions on planning for and conducting each activity, an extensive assessment component, and extensions for integration and enrichment. Materials are available in a kit.

Prices: Teacher's Guide (ISBN 0-7826-1158-3), $101. Complete module, $395. ***Publisher/supplier:*** Encyclopaedia Britannica Educational Corp. ***Materials:*** Available locally, from commercial suppliers, or in module.

3.10 Floating and Sinking. STC. Field-test ed. Washington, D.C.: National Science Resources Center, 1992.

Grade: 5 *Floating and Sinking* introduces students to the phenomenon of buoyancy through a series of investigations with freshwater and salt water. Students first make and test predictions about which objects will float or sink. Then they consider the variables involved. After calibrating a spring scale for weighing objects, students begin isolating and testing the effect of these variables on an object's buoyancy. To investigate the effects of size and weight, students design, build, and test boats made from clay and aluminum foil, measure the weight of objects in and out of water, measure the weight of equal volumes of freshwater and salt water, and measure buoyant force by pulling objects under water. In the final activity, students apply what they have learned to predict whether a mystery cylinder will float or sink. Throughout the unit, students make and test predictions, record observations and test results, and construct charts and graphs to facilitate data analysis.

Floating and Sinking is a 16-lesson unit that requires 6 to 8 weeks to complete. The teacher's guide includes a unit overview, the 16 lesson plans, an annotated bibliography, reproducible masters, and instructions on repairing the spring scale. The student activity book that accompanies this unit provides helpful illustrations and directions for completing activities.

The module includes science background information, detailed instructions on planning for and conducting each activity, an extensive assessment component, and extensions for integration and enrichment. Materials are available in a kit.

Prices: Teacher's Guide, $14.95. Student Activity Book, $3.50. Unit, $399.95. ***Publisher/supplier:*** Carolina Biological Supply. ***Materials:*** Available locally, from commercial suppliers, or in unit.

3.11 Food Chemistry. STC. (Developed by National Science Resources Center, Washington, D.C.) Burlington, N.C.: Carolina Biological Supply Co., 1994.

Grade: 5 In *Food Chemistry,* students investigate the basic nutrients in foods they eat. They conduct a series of physical and chemical tests to discover which nutrients—starches, glucose, fats, and proteins—are in common foods. They learn about the role nutrients play in human growth and development, read about the importance of vitamins and other nutrients, and examine food labels for nutritional information. In a final activity, students apply testing techniques they learn in the unit to analyze the nutritional components of a marshmallow. Throughout the unit, students gather, organize, and interpret data. By comparing results from tests, they learn the important concept that chemical tests are not always clearly positive or negative.

Food Chemistry is a 16-lesson unit requiring 6 to 8 weeks to complete. The teacher's guide includes a unit overview, the 16 lesson plans, an annotated bibliography, reproducible masters, and instructions for making test solutions and papers. The student activity book that accompanies this unit provides helpful illustrations and directions for completing activities.

The module includes science background information, detailed instructions on planning for and conducting each activity, an extensive assessment component, and extensions for integration and enrichment. Materials are available in a kit.

Prices: Teacher's Guide, $14.95. Student Activity Book, $3.50. Unit, $349.95. ***Publisher/supplier:*** Carolina Biological Supply. ***Materials:*** Available locally, from commercial suppliers, or in unit.

3.12 Levers and Pulleys. FOSS. (Developed by Lawrence Hall of Science, Berkeley, Calif.) Chicago, Ill.: Encyclopaedia Britannica Educational Corp., 1993.

Grades: 5, 6 In *Levers and Pulleys,* students discover that these two types of simple machines are important in their daily lives. They are first introduced to the parts of a lever. Then they construct their own Class 1 levers and experiment to determine the relationship between load and effort for maximum advantage. Subsequently, they explore Class 2 and Class 3 levers, determine the advantage gained by using each, and look at common tools that are applications of each class. Students apply their knowledge of load, effort, and advantage to assemble and investigate four different one- and two-pulley systems. They discover the mechanical advantages and disadvantages of each system. Throughout the unit, students work in pairs or in small groups to construct their own simple machines; conduct their own experiments; and gather, record, and interpret their own data.

Levers and Pulleys consists of 4 activities, requiring a total of 16 class sessions of about 45 minutes each. The teacher's guide includes a module overview, the 4 individual activity folios, duplication masters (in both English and Spanish) for student sheets, and an annotated bibliography.

The module includes science background information, detailed instructions on planning for and conducting each activity, an extensive assessment component, and extensions for integration and enrichment. Materials are available in a kit.

Prices: Teacher's Guide (ISBN 0-7826-0059-X), $101. Complete module, $539. ***Publisher/supplier:*** Encyclopaedia Britannica Educational Corp. ***Materials:*** Available locally, from commercial suppliers, or in module.

3.13 Lifting Heavy Things. Insights. Newton, Mass.: Education Development Center, 1994.

Grades: 2, 3 In *Lifting Heavy Things,* students discover that the lever, inclined plane, and pulley are simple machines that help people lift heavy things and make work easier. They experiment with miniature levers of different lengths to explore how a lever works, then apply what they have learned to real tools that are levers. Students look for inclined planes in their neighborhood and experiment with miniature inclined planes of different lengths. They discover how pulleys work by constructing one-, two-, and three-pulley systems in the classroom. Applying what they have learned, students design a construction site that uses only human power and simple machines. In the final activity, they go on a scavenger hunt for tools or machines that make work easier.

Lifting Heavy Things consists of 9 Learning Experiences, requiring a total of at least 15 class sessions, or about 6 to 8 weeks to complete. The teacher's guide includes a unit overview, the 9 Learning Experiences, reproducible masters for student sheets, and annotated lists of additional resources to use with the module.

The module includes science background information, detailed instructions on planning for and conducting each activity, an extensive assessment component, and extensions for integration and enrichment. Materials are available in a kit.

Prices: Teacher's Guide (ISBN 0-89292-171-4), $65. Materials kit, $259. (Prices differ in California, Nevada, and Indiana.) ***Publisher/supplier:*** Optical Data. ***Materials:*** Available locally, from commercial suppliers, or in kit.

3.14 Liquids. Insights. Newton, Mass.: Education Development Center, 1994.

Grades: 2, 3 In this module, students explore the unique characteristics of liquids. They investigate how liquids behave with other liquids and how solids and liquids interact with each other. Students explore the physical characteristics of water, oil, and corn syrup and use their findings about the similarities and differences among these and other liquids to create a definition of "all liquids." Then they experiment to determine how liquids behave when they are mixed with one another and how liquids and solids interact with each other. Students investigate the ways various objects behave in each of the three liquids. They identify some characteristics, such as density and shape, that determine whether an object will float or sink in water, and they perform experiments to make "sinkers" float. In a final activity, students apply the concepts they have learned and the skills they have developed as they design and build a boat, a bath toy, or a game that involves liquids.

Liquids consists of 12 Learning Experiences, requiring a minimum of 20 class sessions, or about 6 to 8 weeks to complete. The teacher's guide includes a unit overview, the 12 Learning Experiences, reproducible masters for student sheets, and annotated lists of additional resources to use with the module.

The module includes science background information, detailed instructions on planning for and conducting each activity, an extensive assessment component, and extensions for integration and enrichment. Materials are available in a kit.

Prices: Teacher's Guide (ISBN 0-89292-172-2), $65. Materials kit, $389. (Prices differ in California, Nevada, and Indiana.) ***Publisher/supplier:*** Optical Data. ***Materials:*** Available locally, from commercial suppliers, or in kit.

3.15 Magnetism and Electricity. FOSS. (Developed by Lawrence Hall of Science, Berkeley, Calif.) Chicago, Ill.: Encyclopaedia Britannica Educational Corp., 1993.

Grades: 3, 4 *Electricity and Magnetism* consists of 4 multipart activities designed to allow students to discover the properties of permanent magnets, the flow of electricity in circuits and the characteristics of conductor and insulator, and the relationship between electricity and magnetism. Students measure the force of attraction between magnets, construct an electrical circuit, and build electromagnets of different strengths. Finally, they apply what they have learned as they wire a telegraph. Assessment devices, which include hands-on, pictorial, and reflective-question assessment, are included in a separate section of the teacher's guide. Each activity allows for links to other disciplines and for further study.

Electricity and Magnetism consists of 4 activities, requiring 6 to 8 weeks to complete. The teacher's guide includes a module overview, the 4 individual activity folios, duplication masters (in both English and Spanish) for student sheets, and an annotated bibliography.

The module includes science background information, detailed instructions on planning for and conducting each activity, an extensive assessment component, and extensions for integration and enrichment. Materials are available in a kit.

Prices: Teacher's Guide (ISBN 0-7826-0034-4), $101. Complete module, $559. ***Publisher/supplier:*** Encyclopaedia Britannica Educational Corp. ***Materials:*** Available locally, from commercial suppliers, or in module.

3.16 Magnets and Motors. STC. (Developed by National Science Resources Center, Washington, D.C.) Burlington, N.C.: Carolina Biological Supply Co., 1991.

Grade: 6 In *Magnets and Motors,* students are introduced to electromagnetism and electromagnetic motors. They experiment with magnets, make a compass, and observe and investigate magnetism's connection with electricity. They develop an understanding of how a motor works, and they experiment with three different electric motors, including two that they make. During the unit, students apply previous learning to make and test hypotheses and learn how to design and conduct controlled experiments. Students use activity sheets and a science journal to record their questions, ideas, observations, and results of experiments.

Magnets and Motors is a 16-lesson unit that requires 6 to 8 weeks to complete. The teacher's guide includes a unit overview, the 16 lesson plans, an annotated bibliography, and reproducible masters. A well-organized student activity book provides instructions for carrying out the activities. Appendixes include background information and instructions for setting up a classroom learning center.

The module includes science background information, detailed instructions on planning for and conducting each activity, an extensive assessment component, and extensions for integration and enrichment. Materials are available in a kit.

Prices: Teacher's Guide, $14.95. Student Activity Book, $3.50. Unit, $404.95. ***Publisher/supplier:*** Carolina Biological Supply. ***Materials:*** Available locally, from commercial suppliers, or in unit.

3.17 Material Objects. SCIS 3. Herbert D. Thier and Robert C. Knott. Hudson, N.H.: Delta Education, 1992.

Grade: 1 In *Material Objects,* young students are introduced to the concept of matter as they investigate the properties of solids, liquids, and gases. Children first sort and group objects by properties such as shape, size, and texture, and then they categorize objects according to the materials of which they are made, such as metal, wood, and plastic. Students apply the concept of material by comparing soil and rock samples. The woods and metals are later classified into subgroups. Students are introduced to the concept of serial ordering as they arrange wooden dowels according to length and thickness. By comparing wood pieces, wood shavings, and wood dust, they observe that an object's shape and appearance can change while the material it is made of remains the same. Students sort liquids by property and then mix liquids and describe the properties of the resulting mixture. They are introduced to floating and sinking. By comparing air-filled balloons with helium-filled balloons, they are introduced to the gaseous phase of matter and to the idea that gases (like solids and liquids) have properties.

Material Objects is organized in 5 sections consisting of a total of 20 chapters requiring about 29 class sessions. The teacher's guide includes an introduction to the unit, lesson plans for each of the sections, a glossary, and blackline masters for a student journal.

The module includes science background information, detailed instructions on planning for and conducting each activity, an extensive assessment component, and extensions for integration and enrichment. Materials are available in a kit.

Prices: Teacher's Guide (ISBN 0-87504-931-1), $39.50. Kit, $650.00. ***Publisher/supplier:*** Delta Education. ***Materials:*** Available locally, from commercial suppliers, or in kit.

3.18 **Mixtures and Solutions. FOSS.** (Developed by Lawrence Hall of Science, Berkeley, Calif.) Chicago, Ill.: Encyclopaedia Britannica Educational Corp., 1993.

Grades: 5, 6 *Mixtures and Solutions* introduces students to some concepts of basic chemistry—mixture, solution, concentration, saturation, and chemical reaction. Activities include separating mixtures using the techniques of sifting, dissolving, filtering, and evaporating. Other activities involve making saturated solutions of salt and citric acid and then comparing the solubility of these two substances in water; determining the relative concentration of salt solutions; and observing chemical reactions that result in the formation of a gas and a precipitate and then applying the techniques of filtering and evaporation to separate some of the reaction products.

Mixtures and Solutions consists of 4 activities, requiring a total of 13 class sessions, or about 7 weeks, to complete. The teacher's guide includes a module overview, the 4 individual activity folios, duplication masters (in both English and Spanish) for student sheets, and an annotated bibliography.

The module includes science background information, detailed instructions on planning for and conducting each activity, an extensive assessment component, and extensions for integration and enrichment. Materials are available in a kit.

Prices: Teacher's Guide (ISBN 0-7826-0081-6), $101. Complete module, $469. ***Publisher/supplier:*** Encyclopaedia Britannica Educational Corp. ***Materials:*** Available locally, from commercial suppliers, or in module.

3.19 **Mysterious Powder. Insights.** Newton, Mass.: Education Development Center, 1994.

Grades: 4, 5 In *Mysterious Powder,* students discover how scientists investigate and learn about unknown substances. The module emphasizes problem solving and the use of the scientific process as a way of understanding the natural world. By investigating a simulated environmental event (the mysterious appearance of a white powder in a school yard), students learn that substances possess characteristic physical and chemical properties and that knowledge of these properties can be used to solve problems. To solve the mystery, students use their senses (sight, touch, and smell) to explore six unknown white powders, all common household items, that might have covered the school yard. They analyze the six powders using four liquids (water, alcohol, oil, and vinegar) and three indicators (iodine, phenolphthalein, and phenol red). A Neighborhood Map reveals possible sources of the mysterious powder. At the end of the module, using information they have gathered and organized, students are able to identify the mystery powder. They write an environmental report to the school board about what the powder is, whether it is dangerous, and where it could have come from.

Mysterious Powder consists of 13 Learning Experiences, requiring 16 to 20 class sessions to complete. The teacher's guide includes a unit overview, the 13 Learning Experiences, reproducible masters for student sheets, and annotated lists of additional resources to use with the module.

The module includes science background information, detailed instructions on planning for and conducting each activity, an extensive assessment component, and extensions for integration and enrichment. Materials are available in a kit.

Prices: Teacher's Guide (ISBN 0-89292-178-1), $65. Materials kit, $332. (Prices differ in California, Nevada, and Indiana.) ***Publisher/supplier:*** Optical Data. ***Materials:*** Available locally, from commercial suppliers, or in kit.

3.20 **Paper. FOSS.** (Developed by Lawrence Hall of Science, Berkeley, Calif.) Chicago, Ill.: Encyclopaedia Britannica Educational Corp., 1993.

Grade: K In the module *Paper,* kindergartners examine the properties of paper, explore the different ways it can be folded and fastened together to make various objects, observe how paper interacts with water, and investigate ways paper can be recycled. Activities include comparing samples of several different kinds of paper, going on a paper hunt, and making paper collages. Students use crayons, pencils, and markers to determine what makes paper suitable for writing and drawing. They fold paper into envelopes and boxes, and they make a piece of recycled paper.

Paper consists of 3 activities, requiring about 15 class sessions of 20 to 30 minutes each. The teacher's guide includes a module overview, the 3 individual activity folios, duplication masters (in both English and Spanish) for student sheets, and an annotated bibliography.

The module includes science background information, detailed instructions on planning for and conducting each activity, an extensive assessment component, and extensions for integration and enrichment. Materials are available in a kit.

Prices: Teacher's Guide (ISBN 0-7826-1148-6), $101. Complete module, $345. ***Publisher/supplier:*** Encyclopaedia Britannica Educational Corp. ***Materials:*** Available locally, from commercial suppliers, or in module.

3.21 Physics of Sound. FOSS. (Developed by Lawrence Hall of Science, Berkeley, Calif.) Chicago, Ill.: Encyclopaedia Britannica Educational Corp., 1993.

Grades: 3, 4 In *Physics of Sound,* students employ skills of listening, investigating, observing, comparing, recording, and organizing to learn about the characteristics of sound. First they test their ability to discriminate between sounds made by objects when they are dropped. Then they compare how sound travels through water, solids, and air from a source to a receiver. They construct "musical" instruments to investigate variables that affect pitch—the length of vibrating objects, the tension of vibrating strings, and the rate at which sound sources vibrate. They adjust the instrument to change the pitch, make the sound travel farther, or make the sound louder.

Physics of Sound consists of 4 activities, requiring about 8 to 10 class sessions of 45 to 50 minutes each. The teacher's guide includes a module overview, the 4 individual activity folios, duplication masters (in both English and Spanish) for student sheets, and an annotated bibliography.

The module includes science background information, detailed instructions on planning for and conducting each activity, an extensive assessment component, and extensions for integration and enrichment. Materials are available in a kit.

Prices: Teacher's Guide (ISBN 0-7826-0011-5), $101. Complete module, $419. ***Publisher/supplier:*** Encyclopaedia Britannica Educational Corp. ***Materials:*** Available locally, from commercial suppliers, or in module.

3.22 Relative Position and Motion. SCIS 3. Herbert D. Thier and Robert C. Knott. Hudson, N.H.: Delta Education, 1993.

Grade: 4 *Relative Position and Motion* is an interdisciplinary unit that focuses on space and time relationships. Activities include making and flying paper airplanes to investigate how variables such as an airplane's weight and the setting of its wing flaps affect its flight; using reference objects to describe the relative position of objects; and examining motion, the direction in which objects move, and the speed with which objects move, through a variety of examples. Students use rectangular coordinates to describe the relative position of pegs on a pegboard and then apply this technique to locate places on a grid map of Washington, D.C. They use polar coordinates to solve a puzzle using a polar grid; they use a specially designed model to simulate the positions and motions of the earth, sun, and moon; and they examine the causes of night and day, the seasons, eclipses, and phases of the moon.

Relative Position and Motion is organized in 6 sections consisting of a total of 20 chapters requiring about 40 class sessions to complete. The teacher's guide includes an introduction to the unit, lesson plans for each of the sections, a glossary, and blackline masters for a student journal.

The module includes science background information, detailed instructions on planning for and conducting each activity, an extensive assessment component, and extensions for integration and enrichment. Materials are available in a kit.

Prices: Teacher's Guide (ISBN 0-87504-937-0), $39.50. Kit, $685.00. ***Publisher/supplier:*** Delta Education. ***Materials:*** Available locally, from commercial suppliers, or in kit.

3.23 Scientific Theories. SCIS 3. Robert C. Knott and Herbert D. Thier. Hudson, N.H.: Delta Education, 1993.

Grade: 6 In this unit, students are introduced to the meaning of scientific theories through the study of electric circuits, magnets, light, and earthquakes. They have the opportunity to develop and test their own theories to explain their observations. The activities include students comparing interaction at a distance (between magnets) with touching interaction (electric circuits); exploring the periodic motion of pendulums; and testing their hypotheses concerning their investigation of electric circuit puzzles and a mystery box. Students use prisms and filters to develop their first detailed scientific theory—a theory of colored light; they devise a magnetic field theory to explain magnetic interaction at a distance; and they develop an electricity theory to describe and explain the transfer of electrical energy from a battery to energy receivers in a closed electric circuit. Students use lenses and mirrors to formulate a ray theory of light, and they develop theories to explain the causes and effects of earthquakes.

Scientific Theories is organized in 7 sections consisting of a total of 25 chapters requiring about 45 class sessions to complete. The teacher's guide includes an introduction to the unit, lesson plans for each of the sections, a glossary, and blackline masters for a student journal.

The module includes science background information, detailed instructions on planning for and conducting each activity, an extensive assessment component, and extensions for integration and enrichment. Materials are available in a kit.

Prices: Teacher's Guide (ISBN 0-87504-941-9), $39.50. Kit: $715.00. ***Publisher/supplier:*** Delta Education. ***Materials:*** Available locally, from commercial suppliers, or in kit.

3.24 Solids and Liquids. FOSS. (Developed by Lawrence Hall of Science, Berkeley, Calif.) Chicago, Ill.: Encyclopaedia Britannica Educational Corp., 1993.

Grades: 1, 2 *Solids and Liquids* engages students in 4 multiphase activities that allow them to develop science process skills while learning the properties and characteristics of solids and liquids. Students first observe, describe, and sort pieces of wood, metal, plastic, and other solid materials according to their properties. Then they use the materials and their new knowledge to construct towers, bridges, and tunnels. They work with beans, rice, and cornmeal to find out how solids behave when the pieces are small. They pour the solids from container to container and separate a mixture of them using screens of different sizes. Next, students investigate the properties of seven different liquids and play games to reinforce vocabulary associated with liquids. In the final set of activities, students mix familiar solids with water, observe the mixtures, and then describe and graph the changes. They also observe what happens when the liquids examined earlier are mixed with water. In the last activity of the set, students investigate to determine if toothpaste is a solid or a liquid.

Solids and Liquids consists of 4 activities, requiring about 19 class sessions of 20 to 45 minutes each. The teacher's guide includes a module overview, the 4 individual activity folios, duplication masters (in both English and Spanish) for student sheets, and an annotated bibliography.

The module includes science background information, detailed instructions on planning for and conducting each activity, an extensive assessment component, and extensions for integration and enrichment. Materials are available in a kit.

Prices: Teacher's Guide (ISBN 0-7826-1140-0), $101. Complete module, $575. ***Publisher/supplier:*** Encyclopaedia Britannica Educational Corp. ***Materials:*** Available locally, from commercial suppliers, or in module.

3.25 Sound. Insights. Newton, Mass.: Education Development Center, 1994.

Grades: 2, 3 The module *Sound* begins by having students identify sounds from a tape recording and closes with a classroom recital of students' songs played on instruments they made from lengths of wood, flowerpots and string, or dried beans and a can. During the unit, students investigate some of the main characteristics of sound, including pitch, volume, and quality. Activities include constructing a kazoo to demonstrate that sounds are caused by vibrations; exploring the relationship between pitch and tension using rubber bands, pegboards, and golf tees; and comparing the sounds generated by different-sized washers hanging from strings to determine the relationship between pitch and the size of the vibrating object. Students also build their own "telephones" and explore which materials work best and which variables affect sound transmission.

Sound consists of 14 Learning Experiences, requiring about 24 class sessions to complete. The teacher's guide includes a unit overview, the 14 Learning Experiences, reproducible masters for student sheets, and annotated lists of additional resources to use with the module.

The module includes science background information, detailed instructions on planning for and conducting each activity, an extensive assessment component, and extensions for integration and enrichment. Materials are available in a kit.

Prices: Teacher's Guide (ISBN 0-89292-173-0), $65. Materials kit, $299. (Prices differ in California, Nevada, and Indiana.) ***Publisher/supplier:*** Optical Data. ***Materials:*** Available locally, from commercial suppliers, or in kit.

3.26 Sounds. STC. Field-test ed. Washington, D.C.: National Science Resources Center, 1991.

Grade: 3 In this unit on *Sounds,* students investigate the causes and characteristics of sound and explore how people can hear sounds better. They investigate the characteristics of sound by experimenting with a variety of simple devices. They observe that vibrations produce sounds; they investigate how sound travels through different materials; they explore how humans produce sounds; and they discover the effect of the length of the sound-producing material on the pitch of the sound and the effect of tension on pitch. They demonstrate these concepts by making simple sound-producing devices. Students then expand their investigations of pitch to include both length and tension and apply what they learned to building a string instrument. Students build a model eardrum, read about how the ear is constructed, and learn how to protect their ears from damage.

Sounds is a 16-lesson unit, requiring 6 to 8 weeks to complete. The teacher's guide includes a unit overview, the 16 lesson plans, an annotated bibliography, and reproducible masters. A well-organized student activity book provides instructions for carrying out the activities. Appendixes include information on coping with hearing impairments.

The module includes science background information, detailed instructions on planning for and conducting each activity, an extensive assessment component, and extensions for integration and enrichment. Materials are available in a kit.

Prices: Teacher's Guide (ISBN 0-89278-695-7, California revision), $14.95. Student Activity Book, $3.50. Unit, $421.00. ***Publisher/supplier:*** Carolina Biological Supply. ***Materials:*** Available locally, from commercial suppliers, or in unit.

3.27 Structures. Insights. Newton, Mass.: Education Development Center, 1994.

Grade: 6 Students develop an understanding of some of the basic principles of structures in this unit. The concepts covered include live load (the weight of a structure's own materials) and dead load (added weight), tension and compression, and the relationship of materials and shape to structure and strength. Students first look at structures in their school neighborhood and record the variety of sizes, shapes, materials, and functions they find. Then they explore how these characteristics affect a structure's ability to remain standing. Students learn to build standing structures using straws and paper clips, index cards, and other materials. Next they explore how dead load and live load affect the stability of their straw structures. In the process they learn that the arrangement of beams, columns, and diagonal supports in a framework is important in helping make the structure strong enough to support loads. Students work primarily in groups of four. They have many opportunities for drawing and recording information.

Structures consists of 13 Learning Experiences, requiring at least 24 class sessions, or about 6 to 8 weeks, to complete. The teacher's guide includes a unit overview, the 13 Learning Experiences, reproducible masters for student sheets, and annotated lists of additional resources to use with the module.

The module includes science background information, detailed instructions on planning for and conducting each activity, an extensive assessment component, and extensions for integration and enrichment. Materials are available in a kit.

Prices: Teacher's Guide (ISBN 0-89292-180-3), $65. Materials kit, $259. (Prices differ in California, Nevada, and Indiana.) ***Publisher/supplier:*** Optical Data. ***Materials:*** Available locally, from commercial suppliers, or in unit.

3.28 Subsystems and Variables. SCIS 3. Herbert D. Thier and Robert C. Knott. Hudson, N.H.: Delta Education, 1992.

Grade: 3 In *Subsystems and Variables,* students learn to identify and define variables in specific systems or subsystems of interacting objects. Within a defined subsystem (i.e., a grouping of objects smaller than the entire system of interest at that time), they investigate variables through controlled experiments. Students apply the concept of subsystems to their investigations of electric circuits, temperature-sensitive cards, solutions and nonsolutions, water and ice, solid and liquid butyl stearate, sound-producing sticks, playground equipment, whirly birds, and the earth as a system. In this unit, complex ideas are introduced through concrete and engaging activities. Students measure temperatures, use the processes of filtration and evaporation, and learn to construct and interpret histograms and line graphs to determine trends in collected data.

Subsystems and Variables is organized in 6 sections consisting of a total of 22 chapters requiring about 37 class sessions to complete. The teacher's guide includes an introduction to the unit, lesson plans for each of the sections, a glossary, and blackline masters for a student journal.

The module includes science background information, detailed instructions on planning for and conducting each activity, an extensive assessment component, and extensions for integration and enrichment. Materials are available in a kit.

Prices: Teacher's Guide (ISBN 0-87504-935-4), $39.50. Kit, $710.00. ***Publisher/supplier:*** Delta Education. ***Materials:*** Available locally, from commercial suppliers, or in kit.

3.29 Wood. FOSS. (Developed by Lawrence Hall of Science, Berkeley, Calif.) Chicago, Ill.: Encyclopaedia Britannica Educational Corp., 1993.

Grade: K *Wood,* a curriculum module for kindergartners on the properties and uses of wood, consists of 2 multiphase activities. In the first activity, Properties of Wood, students observe and compare five types of wood (pine, plywood, redwood, particleboard, and basswood). Then they go on a wood hunt, experiment with how wood and water interact, and use rubber bands and paper clips to sink equivalent samples of different types of wood. They organize their results by constructing a bar graph with the paper clips. In the second activity, Woodworking, students sand basswood; compare sawdust and wood shavings; make particleboard from sawdust; make sandwich wood (plywood) by gluing together thin pieces of wood; nail pieces of wood together; stain wood; and make wood sculptures using wood, glue, and nails. The children work in small cooperative groups. The module uses a learning center approach for the activities.

The 2 activities in *Wood* require about 12 class sessions of about 20 to 30 minutes each. The teacher's guide includes a module overview, the 2 individual activity folios, duplication masters (in both English and Spanish) for student sheets, and an annotated bibliography.

The module includes science background information, detailed instructions on planning for and conducting each activity, an extensive assessment component, and extensions for integration and enrichment. Materials are available in a kit.

Prices: Teacher's Guide (ISBN 0-7826-1146-X), $101. Complete module, $355. ***Publisher/supplier:*** Encyclopaedia Britannica Educational Corp. ***Materials:*** Available locally, from commercial suppliers, or in module.

PHYSICAL SCIENCE—SUPPLEMENTARY MATERIALS

ABOUT THE ANNOTATIONS IN "PHYSICAL SCIENCE—SUPPLEMENTARY MATERIALS"

Entry Numbers

Curriculum materials are arranged alphabetically by title in each category (Core Materials, Supplementary Materials, and Science Activity Books) in chapters 1 through 4 of this guide. In addition, each annotation has a two-part entry number. For each entry number, the chapter number is given before the period; the number after the period locates the entry within that chapter.

For example, the first entry number in chapter 1 is 1.1; the second entry in chapter 2 is 2.2, and so on.

The entry numbers within each curriculum chapter run consecutively through Core, Supplementary, and Science Activity Books.

Order of Bibliographic Information

Following is the arrangement of the facts of publication in the annotations in this section:

- **Title of publication.**
- **Series title,** or series acronym if commonly used.
- **Authors** (either individual names or organizational author).
- Name and location of **developer** (in parentheses), if different from publisher.
- **Place of publication, publisher, and date of publication.**

Series Acronyms

Following are **acronyms of series titles** in "Physical Science—Supplementary Materials." (Series titles that are spelled out are not included in this list.)

DSM Delta Science Module
GEMS Great Explorations in Math and Science
STAR Science Technology and Reading

Price and Acquisition Information

Ordering information is presented in a block immediately below the annotation. Included are the following:

- **Prices** of teacher's guides, activity books, and kits or units.
- The name of a principal **publisher/supplier** (not necessarily the sole source) for the items listed in the price category. (The address and phone and fax numbers for each publisher and supplier appear in appendix A, "Publishers and Suppliers.")
- An indication of the various sources from which one might obtain the required **materials.**

3.30 Bubble Festival. GEMS. Jacqueline Barber and Carolyn Willard. Berkeley, Calif.: Lawrence Hall of Science, 1992.

Grades: 5-6+ In *Bubble Festival,* students participate in a variety of bubble activities in a learning station format. The unit's classroom tabletop activities provide open-ended explorations in an informal, student-centered setting. The guide includes flexible suggestions to help teachers maximize the effectiveness of learning stations and to help them present the challenges of each station, manage classroom logistics, explore scientific content in greater depth, and provide literature and writing extensions. "Activity Task Cards for Volunteers" explain the learning goals of each activity, suggest additional questions to ask students, and explain how to maintain stations so they are safe and ready for successive groups. Blackline masters of signs for the learning stations are included for each activity.

Bubble Festival includes 12 tabletop activities, with detailed instructions on how to set them up.

Price: $12.50 (ISBN 0-912511-80-X).
Publisher/supplier: LHS GEMS.
Materials: Available locally, or from commercial suppliers.

3.31 Bubble-ology. GEMS. Jacqueline Barber. Reprinted with revisions. Berkeley, Calif.: Lawrence Hall of Science, 1987.

Grades: 5-6+ In *Bubble-ology,* students use bubbles to investigate light and color, aerodynamics, chemical composition, surface tension, and technology. During this unit, they create an ideal bubble-blowing instrument, determine which brand of dishwashing liquid will make the biggest bubble, test the effect of different amounts of glycerin on the size of bubbles, apply Bernoulli's principle to keep a bubble aloft, and use color to predict bubble survival.

Bubble-ology consists of 6 activities requiring 8 to 10 class sessions of 45 to 60 minutes each. The module includes a brief introduction, a materials list, detailed instructions for preparing and conducting the lesson, and extension ideas. Useful summary outlines and reproducible student worksheets are included.

Price: $8.50. ***Publisher/supplier:*** LHS GEMS. ***Materials:*** Available locally, or from commercial suppliers.

3.32 Color Analyzers. GEMS. Cary I. Sneider, Alan Gould, and Cheryl Hawthorne. Reprinted with revisions. Berkeley, Calif.: Lawrence Hall of Science, 1991.

Grades: 5-6+ In *Color Analyzers,* students investigate light and color while experimenting with diffraction gratings and color filters. The unit's activities include using diffraction gratings to look at light sources and using colored light filters to decipher and invent secret messages. These activities draw students into investigations of light and color and help them discover why different objects appear to be different colors. Activities to provide additional experiences with light perception are suggested.

Color Analyzers includes 4 sessions of 30 to 60 minutes each. The lesson plan for each session includes an overview, a list of materials, blackline masters of student worksheets, and complete instructions for planning and conducting the activity. A class set of diffraction gratings and color filters is included with the teacher's guide.

Price: $15 (ISBN 0-912511-14-1). ***Publisher/supplier:*** LHS GEMS. ***Materials:*** Available locally, or from commercial suppliers.

3.33 Color and Light. DSM. The National Learning Center. Hudson, N.H.: Delta Education, 1994.

Grades: 5, 6 In *Color and Light,* students investigate the relationships between pigments, color filters, and the light that strikes them. Students mix samples of water containing different colors of pigments (food coloring) and observe the new colors that form. Then they separate a mixture of these pigments using the process of paper chromatography. Students investigate the effects of passing white light through different combinations of color filters and compare this process with that of mixing pigments. Color filters and flashlights are used to create colored beams of light as students compare additive color mixing with subtrative color mixing. In other activities, they observe what happens when colored light shines on different-colored objects; they discover how primary colors can be used to produce detailed, full-color images; they observe the effect of color filters on sight; they create the illusion of three-dimensional objects on a flat piece of paper; and they discover what causes an afterimage to form.

Color and Light includes 13 activities, which require about 16 class sessions, typically 40 minutes in length. The teacher's guide includes a module overview, a list of objectives for each activity, a planning schedule, background information, and preparation and materials management strategies. A complete lesson plan is provided for each lesson.

Prices: Teacher's Guide (ISBN 0-87504-113-2), $24.95. Kit, $275.00. ***Publisher/supplier:*** Delta Education. ***Materials:*** Available locally, from commercial suppliers, or in kit.

3.34 Discovering Density. GEMS. Marion E. Buelger. Berkeley, Calif.: Lawrence Hall of Science, 1988.

Grades: 6+ In *Discovering Density,* students learn about the concept of density through 4 hands-on activities using liquids. In the first activity, students layer colored "mystery liquids" of different densities in a drinking straw and discover that some liquids float on top of others. They experiment with colored salt solutions and discover that water containing different amounts of salt also forms layers. Drawing on these two experiments, students learn to define density and to distinguish weight from density. In the third and fourth activities, they create their own mixtures of liquids of different densities using "secret formulas." They predict how the liquids will layer and then test their predictions. Directions for the activities are clear and concise.

Discovering Density requires 4 sessions of 25 to 50 minutes each. The lessons include helpful suggestions for group work, discussion, and classroom management.

Price: $10. ***Publisher/supplier:*** LHS GEMS. ***Materials:*** Available locally, or from commercial suppliers.

3.35 Electrical Circuits. DSM. Hudson, N.H.: Delta Education, 1988.

Grades: 3-5 *Electrical Circuits* features a series of activities during which students identify the parts of a circuit; construct series and parallel circuits; and make a circuit tester, a bulb, and a fuse. They also classify materials as conductors and nonconductors and predict the relative electrical resistance of various wires.

Electrical Circuits consists of 12 activities, requiring 13 class sessions of 40 minutes each. Each activity includes a vocabulary list, a list of materials needed, preparation steps, teaching suggestions and reinforcement activities. Reproducible masters of student worksheets are included.

Prices: Teacher's Guide (ISBN 0-87504-745-9), $9.95. Kit, $231.00. ***Publisher/supplier:*** Delta Education. ***Materials:*** Available locally, from commercial suppliers, or in kit.

3.36 Electromagnetism. DSM. Hudson, N.H.: Delta Education, 1994.

Grades: 4-6 In this unit, students learn the principles of electromagnetism and some of the relationships between magnets and circuits. They first review the properties of magnetism, and then build an electromagnet and experiment to determine which variables affect the strength of the electromagnet. Students apply their knowledge of electric current, magnetism, and electromagnets to construct a buzzer, model motors, and a working telegraph. They observe how a changing magnetic field can produce an electric current.

Electromagnetism consists of 12 activities, requiring 15 class sessions of 40 to 60 minutes each. The teacher's guide includes an overview, a list of objectives for each activity, a planning schedule, background information, and preparation and materials management strategies, as well as a complete lesson plan for each activity.

Prices: Teacher's Guide (ISBN 0-87504-130-5), $24.95. Kit, $325.00. ***Publisher/supplier:*** Delta Education. ***Materials:*** Available locally, from commercial suppliers, or in kit.

3.37 Energy: How You Use Different Forms of Energy. Scholastic Science Place. (Developed in cooperation with Fernbank Museum of Natural History, Atlanta, Ga.) New York, N.Y.: Scholastic, 1993.

Grade: 2 In this unit, students learn that energy exists in different forms. The lessons are grouped within 3 subconcepts: (1) light, heat, sound, and electricity are different forms of energy; (2) energy moves and changes matter; and (3) there are renewable and nonrenewable sources of energy. For explorations in this unit, students tape colored paper to a window to demonstrate that light can change objects. They create hand-shadow shows to learn how light moves. They compare what happens to tea bags in cold and hot water to learn how heat energy changes things. Students learn to control sound waves by making a musical instrument out of a plastic straw. They use wire and a battery to light a bulb, and they produce a television show to discuss ways people can conserve energy.

Energy: How You Use Different Forms of Energy is a 17-lesson unit typically requiring 35- to 45-minute sessions. The conceptual goals are presented in the lesson-by-lesson story line in the teacher's guide. Each lesson also includes background information; a complete lesson plan, including suggestions for assessing performance and integrating the curriculum; and a list of the print, video, and software support materials required for the lesson.

Prices: Teacher's Guide (ISBN 0-590-26210-6), $20.70. Student Book (ISBN 0-590-26142-8), $6.50. Complete unit, $375.00. Consumables kit, $50.00. ***Publisher/supplier:*** Scholastic. ***Materials:*** Available locally, from commercial suppliers, or in unit.

3.38 Investigating Water. DSM. Hudson, N.H.: Delta Education, 1988.

Grades: K-1 In *Investigating Water,* students explore water and discover some of its properties and forms. They use their senses to experiment with melting and evaporating water; with motion, boats, and buoys; and with the capacity of containers. Students make bubble machines, create secondary colors by mixing food coloring and water, and use various materials to make sounds with water. They use a variety of tools as they mix, pour, measure, and change water.

Investigating Water consists of 9 activities of 30 minutes each, requiring about 3 weeks to complete. Each activity includes a vocabulary list, a list of materials needed, preparation steps, teaching suggestions, and reinforcement activities.

Prices: Teacher's Guide, $49.95. Kit, $173.00. ***Publisher/supplier:*** Delta Education. ***Materials:*** Available locally, from commercial suppliers, or in kit.

3.39 Involving Dissolving. GEMS. Leigh Agler. Reprinted with revisions. Berkeley, Calif.: Lawrence Hall of Science, 1991.

Grades: K-3 In *Involving Dissolving,* making substances "disappear" and then reappear helps children understand the concepts of dissolving, evaporation, and crystallization. Students conduct experiments in which substances such as gelatin, salt, and eggshell calcium (calcium carbonate) dissolve and then are "brought back"—helping them grasp the difficult concept that these substances do not really "disappear" when they dissolve, but remain in liquid in another form. As students compare rates at which various substances dissolve and conduct related experiments, they develop process skills such as observing, comparing, describing, recording, and predicting.

Involving Dissolving includes 4 activities requiring 4 to 6 sessions of 15 to 50 minutes each, plus daily observation for 1 to 2 weeks. The plan for each activity includes an overview, a materials list, and complete instructions. Extension ideas and suggestions for modifying the lessons for kindergarten students are provided.

Price: $8.50 (ISBN 0-912511-50-8).
Publisher/supplier: LHS GEMS.
Materials: Available locally, or from commercial suppliers.

3.40 Length and Capacity. DSM. Hudson, N.H.: Delta Education, 1988.

Grades: 1-3 In *Length and Capacity,* students use common classroom materials to learn the concepts length, height, width, and capacity, which are basic to the study of science and mathematics. Students learn to compare the length, height, and width of various objects using nonstandard and standard units of measure. Using sand, water, and various containers, they explore the concept of capacity, and then learn about units of capacity.

Length and Capacity consists of 10 activities of 30 minutes each, which can be conducted over a period of 3 to 4 weeks. Each activity includes a vocabulary list, a list of materials needed, preparation steps, teaching suggestions, and reinforcement activities.

Prices: Teacher's Guide (ISBN 0-87504-741-6), $9.95. Kit, $210.00.
Publisher/supplier: Delta Education.
Materials: Available locally, or from commercial suppliers.

3.41 Lenses and Mirrors. DSM. The National Learning Center. Hudson, N.H.: Delta Education, 1994.

Grades: 5, 6 In *Lenses and Mirrors,* students investigate the refraction and reflection of light by lenses and mirrors as they come to understand how light can be manipulated to help us see things. Students learn how light rays behave when they strike a reflective surface. They discover the connection between the location of an object and the apparent location of its reflection. They find out why light rays passing through a very small hole produce an inverted image. Students apply what they have learned about light reflection to direct light through a maze of mirrors. They investigate the reflection patterns produced by various types and combinations of mirrors, and examine the refraction of light through different types of lenses. Finally, they use what they have learned about vision and lenses to explain how eyeglasses correct eyesight.

Lenses and Mirrors includes 12 activities, which require about 15 class sessions, typically 40 to 45 minutes in length. The teacher's guide includes a module overview, a list of objectives for each activity, a planning schedule, background information, and preparation and materials management strategies. A complete lesson plan is provided for each lesson.

Prices: Teacher's Guide (ISBN 0-87504-115-9), $24.95. Kit, $350.00.
Publisher/supplier: Delta Education.
Materials: Available locally, from commercial suppliers, or in kit.

3.42 Liquid Explorations. GEMS. Leigh Agler. Reprinted with revisions. Berkeley, Calif.: Lawrence Hall of Science, 1991.

Grades: 1-3 In *Liquid Explorations,* a series of 5 activities, children explore the properties of liquids. They play a liquid-classification game in which they examine various liquids and describe the qualities that make one different from another. They observe how food coloring moves through different liquids and discover that some liquids mix while others do not, as they create a secret salad dressing and an "ocean in a bottle." Through these activities, students identify the properties of liquids and note changes that occur when other substances are added to them.

Liquid Explorations includes 5 activities requiring 5 or more class sessions. The lesson plans for each activity present helpful hints for hands-on science in the classroom, a letter to parents, and reproducible student worksheets.

Price: $8.50 (ISBN 0-912511-51-6).
Publisher/supplier: LHS GEMS.
Materials: Available locally, or from commercial suppliers.

3.43 Looking at Liquids. DSM. Hudson, N.H.: Delta Education, 1988.

Grades: 3-5 In *Looking at Liquids,* students explore the behavior of common liquids. They observe, measure, and investigate liquids as they learn about viscosity and cohesion. They compare the reaction of drops of various liquids to several surfaces. They use an equal-arm balance to discover that equal volumes of different liquids do not weigh the same. They measure how fast water evaporates from a wet paper towel and experiment with floating paper clips to demonstrate surface tension. Students alter the surface tension of liquids with soap and alcohol and measure the surface tension of several liquids. They take measurements and record data as they complete the activities.

Looking at Liquids consists of 9 activities that require 3 to 4 weeks to complete. Each activity includes a vocabulary list, a list of materials needed, preparation steps, teaching suggestions, and reinforcement activities. Reproducible masters of student worksheets are included.

Prices: Teacher's Guide (ISBN 0-87504-744-0), $9.95. Kit, $231.00. ***Publisher/supplier:*** Delta Education. ***Materials:*** Available locally, from commercial suppliers, or in kit.

3.44 Motion: How Moving Objects Interact. Scholastic Science Place. (Developed in cooperation with Science Museum of Minnesota, St. Paul, Minn.) New York, N.Y.: Scholastic, 1995.

Grade: 4 In *Motion: How Moving Objects Interact,* students learn that an object's motion is a change in its position over time. The unit's lessons are grouped in 3 subconcepts: (1) forms of motion include straight-line, zigzag, and circular motions; (2) an object's motion only changes if the object is pushed or pulled, and every push or pull is opposed by a push or pull in the opposite direction; and (3) machines can change the size or direction of a push or pull. Activities in this unit include the following: students observe, describe, and make generalizations about moving objects; they investigate forces that affect an object's motion, such as the pushing and pulling action of walking; they make a cardboard wheel to observe how it produces motion; and they use inclined planes and pulley systems to move objects. In a culminating activity, students are challenged to design and make a model of a lifting machine.

Motion is a 17-lesson unit, requiring 24 sessions of 35 to 45 minutes each to complete. The conceptual goals of the unit are presented in the lesson-by-lesson story line in the teacher's guide. Each lesson also includes background information; a complete lesson plan, including suggestions for assessing performance and integrating the curriculum; and a list of the print, video, and software support materials required for the lesson.

Prices: Teacher's Guide (ISBN 0-590-27691-3), $27. Student Book (ISBN 0-590-27690-5), $10. Complete kit, $450. Consumables kit, $52. ***Publisher/supplier:*** Scholastic. ***Materials:*** Available locally, from commercial suppliers, or in unit.

3.45 Of Cabbages and Chemistry. GEMS. Jacqueline Barber. Reprinted with revisions. Berkeley, Calif.: Lawrence Hall of Science, 1991.

Grades: 4-6+ In the module *Of Cabbages and Chemistry,* students discover acids and bases and some of their properties by conducting experiments with red cabbage juice (a natural indicator) and common household liquids. In the first of 4 activities, students mix cabbage juice with various household liquids, then classify the liquids into groups according to the colors of the resulting mixtures. Next they share and compare their results in a classroom "scientific convention"; relate their classifications to the terms "acid," "base," and "neutral"; and then discover through hands-on experimentation that acids and bases are not discrete categories but points along a continuum. In the third and fourth activities, students in grade 6 and above investigate the concepts of concentration and neutralization and apply what they have learned by testing a variety of new liquids and household products.

Of Cabbages and Chemistry includes 4 activities, requiring 4 to 8 sessions of 30 to 50 minutes each. The guide contains appropriate science background information, detailed lesson plans, reproducible masters of student data sheets, and ideas for extensions.

Price: $10 (ISBN 0-912511-63-X). ***Publisher/supplier:*** LHS GEMS. ***Materials:*** Available locally, or from commercial suppliers.

3.46 Oobleck: What Scientists Do. GEMS. Cary I. Sneider. Berkeley, Calif.: Lawrence Hall of Science, 1988.

Grades: 4-6+ In this unit, students investigate an unknown substance called Oobleck, describe its physical properties, experiment to identify its unique characteristics, and hold a scientific convention to discuss the similarities and differences among their findings. Students then design a spacecraft that would be able to land and take off again on an ocean of Oobleck. They compare the scientific methods they employed with those of real scientists.

The format for the 4 lessons (requiring 5 or 6 class sessions of 20 to 45 minutes each) includes a list of materials, suggestions for preparation, and directions for the activity.

Price: $8.50. ***Publisher/supplier:*** LHS GEMS. ***Materials:*** Available locally, or from commercial suppliers.

3.47 Simple Machines. DSM. Hudson, N.H.: Delta Education, 1994.

Grades: 5-6+ By the end of this module, students will have constructed and/or used six *Simple Machines* and will understand how these machines are used to perform a variety of important tasks. During the unit they construct a lever and investigate mechanical advantage, they investigate the transfer of force between the axles and the wheels of a model tractor, they experiment with friction and traction (moving friction), and they examine the structure of a gear and observe how force that is applied to a driving gear is transferred to a driven gear. In other activities, students observe how a pulley redirects applied force, discover how an inclined plane can be used to reduce the amount of force needed to do a given amount of work, and observe how wedges and screws make work easier.

Simple Machines consists of 12 lessons, requiring 12 class sessions of

40 to 50 minutes each. The teacher's guide includes a module overview, a list of objectives for each activity, a planning schedule, background information, and preparation and materials management strategies. A complete lesson plan is provided for each activity. An assessment activity and reproducible masters of student data sheets are also included.

Prices: Teacher's Guide (ISBN 0-87504-119-1), $24.95. Kit, $260.00. ***Publisher/supplier:*** Delta Education. ***Materials:*** Available locally, from commercial suppliers, or in kit.

3.48 Sink or Float. DSM. Hudson, N.H.: Delta Education, 1988.

Grades: 2, 3 In *Sink or Float,* students investigate the concept of buoyancy and principles governing the behavior of boats. Working in pairs, they build a variety of floating vessels. Students first predict the buoyancy of pieces of clay formed in various shapes as they learn how shape influences buoyancy. Then they experiment with a variety of materials and designs to identify variables affecting the load capacities of floating vessels. The module culminates in a cargo contest in which students construct boats designed for maximum capacity.

Sink or Float consists of 7 activities that require about 3 weeks to complete. Each activity includes a vocabulary list, a list of materials needed, preparation steps, teaching suggestions, and reinforcement activities. Reproducible masters for student worksheets are included.

Prices: Teacher's Guide (ISBN 0-87504-742-4), $9.95. Kit, $121.00. ***Publisher/supplier:*** Delta Education. ***Materials:*** Available locally, from commercial suppliers, or in kit.

3.49 Solids, Liquids, and Gases: States of Matter and How They Change. Scholastic Science Place. (Developed in cooperation with New York Hall of Science, Corona, N.Y.) New York, N.Y.: Scholastic, 1993.

Grade: 1 In *Solids, Liquids, and Gases,* students learn that matter changes in a variety of ways. The unit's lessons are grouped in 3 subconcepts: (1) matter has properties by which it can be observed and described; (2) properties of matter, such as shape, color, and state, can change; and (3) changes in matter require adding or taking away energy. Examples of activities in this unit include the following: students listen to a story about what scientists do; they take a video trip that introduces them to solids, liquids, and gases; they compare the way liquids and solids behave; they observe what happens when different types of liquids are mixed together; and they melt ice to observe that matter changes form with the help of energy.

Solids, Liquids, and Gases has 17 lessons (typically 20 to 40 minutes in duration). The conceptual goals of the unit are presented in the lesson-by-lesson story line in the teacher's guide. Each lesson also includes background information; a complete lesson plan, including suggestions for assessing performance and integrating the curriculum; and a list of the print, video, and software support materials required for the lesson.

Prices: Teacher's Guide (ISBN 0-590-26204-1), $20.70. Student Book (ISBN 0-590-26136-3), $6.50. Complete kit, $375.00. Consumables kit, $59.00. ***Publisher/supplier:*** Scholastic. ***Materials:*** Available locally, from commercial suppliers, or in unit.

3.50 Sound. DSM. Hudson, N.H.: Delta Education, 1988.

Grades: 2-4 *Sound* introduces students to the concept of sound and what causes it. The unit opens with an activity called Sound Detectives, in which students try to identify objects by the sounds the objects produce. Students develop an operational definition of volume, compare how sound travels through air and through a solid, and manipulate variables to determine which ones can alter the pitch of a sound.

Sound consists of 10 activities, requiring 12 class sessions to complete. Each activity includes a vocabulary list, a list of materials needed, preparation steps, teaching suggestions, and reinforcement activities.

Prices: Teacher's Guide (ISBN 0-87504-747-5), $9.95. Kit, $147.00. ***Publisher/supplier:*** Delta Education. ***Materials:*** Available locally, from commercial suppliers, or in kit.

3.51 STAR Flight Lab. STAR. Washington, D.C.: Reading Is Fundamental, 1995.

Grades: 5-6+ *STAR Flight Lab* introduces activities on the science of flight with a collection of historical anecdotes tracing the development of flight science and technology. Students experiment with kites, parachutes, airfoils, gliders, and balloon rockets to understand 4 forces acting on an aircraft in flight—lift, drag, thrust, and gravity. They measure altitude, wind speed, rate of descent, and flight distance. Information, procedures, and test data are recorded in student flight logs. Examples of cross-curricular activities include analyzing the elements of science fiction stories; constructing a flight history timeline; calculating and comparing flight times for airplanes throughout history; and drawing a scene as viewed from a hot air balloon.

STAR Flight Lab provides a list of resources, including books, computer software, and audiovisual materials.

Prices: Teacher's Guide, $21.90. Mentor's Guide, $3.90. ***Publisher/supplier:*** Kendall/Hunt. ***Materials:*** Available locally, or from commercial suppliers.

3.52 **STAR Inventor's Lab. STAR.** Washington, D.C.: Reading Is Fundamental, 1994.

Grades: 3-6 The story of Lewis Latimer, an African-American inventor who was a colleague of Thomas Edison, provides the context for a series of investigations using electrical circuitry in *STAR Inventor's Lab.* As apprentices, students construct simple electric circuits and an electromagnet. As journeymen they apply their skills and knowledge to build a model cottage with electrical sources, an electromagnetic crane, or an electronic quiz game. As inventors they are challenged to create an invention or a prototype of an invention. The unit includes additional activities to tie the inventor's lab to reading, social studies, art, and mathematics, including learning more about inventors by reading about their lives and careers, wiring a dollhouse, and building a better book bag.

STAR Inventor's Lab provides a list of resources, including books, computer software, and audiovisual materials.

Prices: Teacher's Guide, $21.50. Mentor's Guide, $3.90. ***Publisher/supplier:*** Kendall/Hunt. ***Materials:*** Available locally, or from commercial suppliers.

3.53 **States of Matter. DSM.** Hudson, N.H.: Delta Education, 1988.

Grades: 2-4 In *States of Matter,* students discover the effects of temperature on changes in states of matter. They predict and then measure the time required to melt an ice cube and infer variables that affect the rate of melting. Then they design and conduct experiments to increase the rate of melting and construct insulated containers to prevent ice from melting. Through simple experiments, students learn that not all substances change state at the same rate and that different substances have different freezing points.

States of Matter consists of 7 activities. Each activity includes a vocabulary list, a list of materials needed, preparation steps, teaching suggestions, and reinforcement activities.

Prices: Teacher's Guide, $9.95. Kit, $169.00. ***Publisher/supplier:*** Delta Education. ***Materials:*** Available locally, from commercial suppliers, or in kit.

PHYSICAL SCIENCE—SCIENCE ACTIVITY BOOKS

3.54 Adventures in Science and Mathematics: Integrated Activities for Young Children. Julie G. Whitney and Linda J. Sheffield. New Rochelle, N.Y.: Cuisenaire Company of America, 1991.

Grade: 2 In *Adventures in Science and Mathematics,* students use the scientific method to investigate a variety of concepts, primarily in the physical sciences. In the first of the 5 units in this guide, they develop their observational skills by identifying and comparing the characteristics of a variety of rocks. In the second and third units, they explore the relationship between force, energy, and motion through simple experiments using blocks, balloon rockets, pendulums, pulleys, and balls. In the fourth unit, students study motion in fluids by investigating the behavior of waves, testing the viscosity of various fluids, and simulating soil erosion. Students learn about light in the fifth unit by experimenting with mirrors, prisms, and screens. Every activity is designed to follow the same basic process: experiment and observe, discuss, hypothesize, test hypotheses, discuss results, and explore further.

Each of the 5 units in *Adventures in Science and Mathematics* begins with an overview and background information about each activity in that unit. The 22 activities can be done in small groups or in pairs, in combination with class discussion.

Price: $9.95 (ISBN 0-938587-18-8). ***Publisher/supplier:*** Cuisenaire Company of America. ***Materials:*** Available locally.

ABOUT THE ANNOTATIONS IN "PHYSICAL SCIENCE—SCIENCE ACTIVITY BOOKS"

Entry Numbers

Curriculum materials are arranged alphabetically by title in each category (Core Materials, Supplementary Materials, and Science Activity Books) in chapters 1 through 4 of this guide. In addition, each annotation has a two-part entry number. For each entry number, the chapter number is given before the period; the number after the period locates the entry within that chapter.

For example, the first entry number in chapter 1 is 1.1; the second entry in chapter 2 is 2.2, and so on.

The entry numbers within each curriculum chapter run consecutively through Core, Supplementary, and Science Activity Books.

Order of Bibliographic Information

Following is the arrangement of the facts of publication in the annotations in this section:

- **Title** of publication.
- **Series title,** or series acronym if commonly used.
- **Authors** (either individual names or organizational author).
- Name and location of **developer** (in parentheses), if different from publisher.
- **Place of publication, publisher, and date of publication.**

Series Acronyms

Following are acronyms of series titles in "Physical Science—Science Activity Books." (Series titles that are spelled out are not included in this list.)

AIMS Activities Integrating Mathematics and Science
CESI Council for Elementary Science International
GEMS Great Explorations in Math and Science

Price and Acquisition Information

Ordering information is presented in a block immediately below the annotation. Included are the following:

- **Prices** of teacher's guides, activity books, and kits or units.
- The name of a principal **publisher/supplier** (not necessarily the sole source) for the items listed in the price category. (The address and phone and fax numbers for each publisher and supplier appear in appendix A, "Publishers and Suppliers.")
- An indication of the various sources from which one might obtain the required **materials.**

3.55 Animal Sounds. Mary Marcussen. San Francisco, Calif.: California Academy of Sciences, 1991.

Grades: 3-5 *Animal Sounds* fills the classroom with sounds made by frogs, crickets, whales, mosquitoes, songbirds, and penguins. The teacher's guide, with 19 activities, is accompanied by a cassette tape of various animal sounds narrated by scientists who explain what animal is making the sound, how the sound is physically produced, and how the animal uses sound to communicate. The teacher's guide is divided in 5 sections. Activities in the first 3 sections provide a basic understanding of the physical principles of sound. In the fourth section, students then use their understanding of how sound works to explore the human ear and the human voice-producing mechanism and compare them with those of other animals. The final section explores ways in which animals use sound for communication and ways in which humans use sound in technology. Activities include students making voice prints, comparing how sound travels through different materials, and demonstrating how echoes are produced.

The activities in *Animal Sounds* include an introduction, a materials list, procedure, things to think about, and extension ideas.

Price: $12.95 (ISBN 9-940228-31-9). ***Publisher/supplier:*** California Academy of Sciences. ***Materials:*** Available locally.

3.56 BUZ: A Hands-on Electrical Energy Education Program. Delmarva Power Energy Education Program. Wilmington, Del.: Delmarva Power, 1989.

Grades: 4-6 The nuts and bolts of electricity and its use are explored in *BUZ: A Hands-on Electrical Energy Education Program.* Through the activities in this guide, students investigate simple circuits, examine electricity as a form of energy, test conductors and insulators, make circuit diagrams, discover how electricity is generated and delivered, and learn to use electricity safely and wisely. Activities include predicting whether or not a bulb will glow in given circuits before testing the circuits, using balloons to investigate static electricity, and classifying items as electrical conductors or as insulators. In other activities, students distinguish between safe and unsafe electrical environments and chart the kilowatt usage of various appliances.

Each lesson includes background information and several activities. Reproducible worksheets and a set of transparency masters accompany the teacher's guide.

Price: Teacher's Guide comes with a BUZ teacher training workshop. ***Publisher/supplier:*** Delmarva Power. ***Materials:*** Available locally, from commercial suppliers, or in kit from Delmarva Power.

3.57 Circles: Shapes in Math, Science and Nature. Catherine Sheldrick Ross. Toronto, Ontario, Canada: Kids Can Press, 1992.

Grades: 5-6+ From superdomes to sunflowers, *Circles: Shapes in Math, Science and Nature* takes in just about every round thing that children may be able to think of. This activity book has 9 topic areas: amazing circles, living in circles, far-out circles, spheres, discs, cylinders, cones, spirals, and be a circle. Students learn to measure the circumference, radius, and diameter of a circle. They fold circles to make other shapes; interlock circles to make petal patterns; and make ellipses, domes, sundials, pinwheel disks, castle towers, cone hats, and other round objects. Historical material focuses on Stonehenge, the circular cities of Europe in the fifteenth and sixteenth centuries, and many other topics.

Price: Canadian $12.95 (ISBN 1-55074-064-4). ***Publisher/supplier:*** University of Toronto Press. ***Materials:*** Available locally.

3.58 Crime Lab Chemistry. GEMS. Jacqueline Barber. Reprinted with revisions. Berkeley, Calif.: Lawrence Hall of Science, 1989.

Grades: 4-6+ In *Crime Lab Chemistry,* students play the part of crime lab chemists to solve a mystery. They discover which of several black pens was used to write a ransom note. This guide capitalizes on students' enthusiasm for solving mysteries to develop such skills as analyzing data and making inferences. Students use the process of paper chromatography to separate the pigments contained in the ink on the ransom note. This same technique is then used to analyze the ink in several pens. Students compare the chromatograms to determine which pen was used to write the note.

Crime Lab Chemistry requires 2 class sessions of 35 to 45 minutes each. The teacher's guide includes an introduction, detailed information on time and materials needed and on steps in advance preparation, as well as suggestions for other mysteries to be solved, and summary outlines for both sessions.

Price: $8.50. ***Publisher/supplier:*** LHS GEMS. ***Materials:*** Available locally, or from commercial suppliers.

3.59 Cycling Back to Nature With Biodegradable Polymers. Robert L. Horton, Joe E. Heimlich, and James R. Hollyer. Chevy Chase, Md.: National 4-H Council, 1994.

Grades: 6+ *Cycling Back to Nature With Biodegradable Polymers* is a source book of activities addressing the environmental influence of natural products, manufactured products, and by-products of the earth's natural cycles. The guide's 9 chapters focus on (1) earth's four natural cycles; (2) interaction between producers, consumers, and decomposers within natural cycles; (3) the production of plastic; (4) the presence of plastics in the environment; (5) biodegradable polymers as an important breakthrough; (6) composting as nature's way of recycling; (7) the need to recycle traditional plastics; (8) the range of possibilities for packaging with biodegradable polymers; and (9) increasing public awareness. Activities in the unit include experimenting with the effects of yeast on food decomposition, taking inventory of the plastic items in the packaging of students' lunches, and experimenting with water-soluble biodegradable polymers. Lessons may be used independently of each other or in sequence.

Appendixes in the unit include an earth cycle bio sheet, instructions for making a compost pile, plastic labeling information, a packaging scavenger hunt, and a letterwriting tip sheet.

Price: $9. ***Publisher/supplier:*** National 4-H Supply Service. ***Materials:*** Available locally, or from commercial suppliers.

3.60 Electrical Connections. AIMS. Maureen Allen, Diane Bredt, Judy Calderwood, and others. Fresno, Calif.: AIMS Education Foundation, 1991.

Grades: 4-6+ *Electrical Connections* is a collection of activities in which mathematics and science skills are tested and other disciplines are integrated. Students investigate the following topic areas: static electricity, electric circuits, switches, circuit breakers, conductors, insulators, electromagnetism, galvanometers, and chemical and electrical energy. Among the many activities in the guide, students experiment with static electricity, construct a circuit quiz board, and make a galvanometer to detect small amounts of electrical current.

Electrical Connections provides worksheets with lively illustrations for its 26 activities, each of which has a complete lesson plan.

Price: Teacher's Guide (ISBN 1-881431-28-2), $14.95. ***Publisher/supplier:*** AIMS Education Foundation. ***Materials:*** Available locally, or from commercial suppliers.

3.61 Explorabook: A Kid's Science Museum in a Book. John Cassidy. Palo Alto, Calif.: Klutz Press, 1991.

Grades: 3-6 Complete with its own magnet, two pouches of agar, and plastic shields that bend light waves, *Explorabook: A Kid's Science Museum in a Book* offers more than 50 activities designed to help students extend their thinking, research, and problem-solving skills. The activities are grouped in 7 sections: (1) magnetism, (2) bending light waves, (3) bacterial stories, (4) light wave craziness, (5) homemade science, (6) bouncing light rays, and (7) optical illusions. Activities include constructing an antigravity machine, making food for bacteria, and following a mirror maze. Except for the section on homemade science, each section contains the special tools needed for the activities.

Prices: $18.95 (ISBN 1-878257-14-5). ***Publisher/supplier:*** Klutz Press. ***Materials:*** Most materials needed are included in book. Any others needed are available locally.

3.62 Exploratorium Science Snackbook: Teacher Created Versions of Exploratorium Exhibits. Exploratorium Teacher Institute. San Francisco, Calif.: The Exploratorium, 1991.

Grades: 3-6+ *Exploratorium Science Snackbook* offers teachers the opportunity to create exhibits from a unique science museum in their own classroom. This resource book offers 107 "Snacks" from the Exploratorium in San Francisco. Each Snack contains instructions for building a classroom version of a particular Exploratorium exhibit. Examples include suspending a ball in a stream of air, using mirrors to make multiple images, making a portable cloud in a bottle, using polarized light to make a stained glass window without glass, and creating a simple electric motor. A Snack can be used as a demonstration, as a lab, or as an interactive exhibit for student use.

Each "recipe" in the *Snackbook* includes instructions, advice, and helpful hints and is accompanied by photographs and line drawings. Icons identify the main concepts associated with each Snack.

Price: $29.95 (ISBN 0-943451-25-6). ***Publisher/supplier:*** The Exploratorium. ***Materials:*** Available locally, from commercial suppliers, or from suppliers listed in "Materials" section of *Snackbook*.

3.63 Flight Power: Practical Science Activities for Grades 4-6. Power of Science. Grant Phillips. Mount Waverley, Victoria, Australia: Dellasta, 1991.

Grades: 4-6 The easy-to-follow activities in *Flight Power* introduce students to various aspects of flight. Using everyday materials and working individually or in groups, students construct and explore simple aerofoils, gliders, helicopters, hot-air balloons, parachutes, boomerangs, balloon rockets, and a vinegar rocket launcher.

Each of the 8 activities in *Flight Power* includes an explanation of how the construction works, together with reproducible investigation sheets for recording information and observations. Also included are challenge sheets and problem pages that encourage critical thinking and creativity.

Price: $10.95 (ISBN 0-947138-87-0). ***Publisher/supplier:*** Mondo. ***Materials:*** Available locally.

3.64 Flights of Imagination: An Introduction to Aerodynamics. Wayne Hosking. Rev. ed. Washington, D.C.: National Science Teachers Association, 1990.

Grades: 5-6+ *Flights of Imagination* provides instructions for activities using student-constructed kites, gliders, and airfoils to investigate fundamental principles of aerodynamics. Students explore questions such as how the wind makes a kite rise; why some kites require a tail; how a dihedral adds stability; and what effect different materials have on a kite's durability, construction time, and flight performance. The more quantitative investigations on topics such as aspect ratio, weight-to-area factor, wind speed and lift, and angle of elevation are more appropriate for secondary school students but may be of interest to teachers who wish to improve their background knowledge.

Flights of Imagination consists of 18 activities. Appendixes on when, where, and how to fly a kite are included, along with a safety code, glossary, and resource list.

Price: $10.50 (ISBN 0-87355-067-6). ***Publisher/supplier:*** National Science Teachers Association. ***Materials:*** Available locally, or from commercial suppliers.

3.65 Gears. Enfield, Conn.: LEGO Dacta, 1993.

Grades: 4-6 This booklet contains information about gears, simple hands-on gear activities, and appropriate diagrams and illustrations. It is designed to be used with the LEGO DACTA Gear Set, which uses the popular LEGO construction blocks to teach about gears. Students first learn the definition of a gear. Then they build models that will gear up (increase speed) and gear down (increase force). They arrange gears so they turn in the same direction, in opposite directions, or at 90-degree angles to each other. They discover that how fast or how slowly one gear makes another turn depends on the number of teeth on the gear. Students are challenged to design and build a spinning sign and a moving target.

Each activity in *Gears* states the main idea involved and provides illustrated instructions, additional information, and extension ideas. The guide lists the process and critical thinking skills involved in the activities.

Prices: Teacher's Guide (ISBN 0-914831-82-8), $5. Gear Classroom Pack, $175. Individual Gear Set, $15. ***Publisher/supplier:*** LEGO Dacta. ***Materials:*** Available from LEGO Dacta.

3.66 Idea Factory's Whodunits: Mysteries for Science Class Detectives. Marilyn Blackmer and Sandi Schlichting. Riverview, Fla.: Idea Factory, 1991.

Grades: 2-4 *Idea Factory's Whodunits: Mysteries for Science Class Detectives* is a collection of "mysteries" and problems occurring at home, at school, and on the playground that can be solved with a little science knowledge. Each mystery includes a short story followed by the question to be investigated. One mystery is included for each of the following topics: fingerprinting, mirror images, chromatography, magnetism, capillary action, the characteristics of matter, conductors and nonconductors of electricity, physical properties and chemical changes, colors, body proportions, properties of air, crystals, inertia, and density. Each lesson can stand alone or can be used as part of an on-going unit.

The book's introduction offers teachers suggestions for grouping students, approaches to problem-solving, brainstorming tips and rules, and a section on science safety. Each lesson includes objectives, background information, a list of materials, brainstorming ideas, procedure, extension activities, and appropriate student data sheets.

Price: $10.95. ***Publisher/supplier:*** Idea Factory. ***Materials:*** Available locally.

3.67 In the Air. Science Spirals. Julie Fitzpatrick. London, England: Evans Brothers, 1991.

Grades: 2-4 *In the Air* is a little book filled with student-directed activities on the subject of air. Aided by simple instructions, easily obtained materials, and colorful illustrations, students make flying tails, bags-on-a-stick, parachutes, and kites. They test the effects of altering the shape and weight of materials on the speed with which they fall through the air. They make and test the flights of paper gliders of various sizes and weights, and they use balloons to simulate the effects of a jet engine. A master materials list is included.

Price: $13.95 (ISBN 0-237-60207-5). ***Publisher/supplier:*** Trafalgar Square. ***Materials:*** Available locally.

3.68 It's a Gas. Margaret Griffin and Ruth Griffin. Toronto, Ontario, Canada: Kids Can Press, 1993.

Grades: 4-6+ *It's a Gas* contains simple activities and brief reading selections from which students learn about the properties and behavior of gases; about how gases differ from liquids and solids; and about gases in our bodies, gases used for lighting, heating, and refrigeration, and gases in the earth's atmosphere. Students conduct experiments to discover that some gases weigh more than others. They learn about the expansion of gases in bread and cake dough during baking. They build a model greenhouse to see what a good heat-trap a greenhouse can be and to understand how greenhouse gases trap heat in a similar way. These activities require common materials such as vinegar, sodium bicarbonate, rice, plants, and plastic bottles.

Price: US$9.95 (ISBN 1-55074-120-9). ***Publisher/supplier:*** University of Toronto Press. ***Materials:*** Available locally.

3.69 Kids' Kitchen Chemistry. Anne Lawes. Mount Waverley, Victoria, Australia: Dellasta, 1993.

Grades: 3-6 In *Kids' Kitchen Chemistry,* the characters Sally and Pete make their own kitchen chemistry set and proceed to learn about basic principles of chemistry with materials found around the house. Soap-powered boats, ice cream spiders, and fantasy-colored fountains are just a few of the products that come from the 20 experiments in this book. Activities include making a working model of a soda-acid fire extinguisher, growing crystals from a salt solution, using detergent to change surface tension, and separating colored chemicals using a simple chromatography column.

Kids' Kitchen Chemistry features 20 activities. Each activity includes a stated goal, lists of equipment and chemicals needed, step-by-step instructions, a place to record results, and postexperiment comments.

Price: $14.50 (ISBN 1-875627-16-2). ***Publisher/supplier:*** Mondo. ***Materials:*** Available locally.

3.70 Kitchen Chemistry. Step-by-Step Science Series. John B. Bath and Sally C. Mayberry. Greensboro, N.C.: Carson-Dellosa Publishing Co., 1994.

Grades: 4-6 *Kitchen Chemistry* is a collection of 39 activities designed to introduce students to solutions, mixtures, acids and bases, and chemical reactions using readily available, inexpensive materials. Activities include demonstrating that particles of water move faster when heated, making a suspension, making invisible ink, testing for acids and bases using a red cabbage indicator, and making a soap-powered boat.

Each activity in *Kitchen Chemistry* includes background information (where appropriate), a problem statement, a list of materials, procedure, expected results, and critical thinking questions.

Price: $5.95 (ISBN 4-4222-1137-6). ***Publisher/supplier:*** Carson-Dellosa. ***Materials:*** Available locally.

3.71 Levers. Enfield, Conn.: LEGO Dacta, 1993.

Grades: 5, 6 This booklet contains information about levers, simple hands-on lever activities, and appropriate diagrams and illustrations. It is designed to be used with the LEGO DACTA Lever Set, which uses the popular LEGO construction blocks to explore the three classes of levers. Students first learn the definition of a lever. Then they construct working models of first-, second-, and third-class levers and build models of devices that incorporate them. Students are challenged to design and build two devices: one that can pick up a weighted brick while being operated with one hand, and another that can be raised and lowered and locked into a raised and lowered position.

Each activity in *Levers* states the main idea involved and provides illustrated instructions, additional information, and extension ideas. The guide lists the process and critical thinking skills involved in the activities.

Prices: Teacher's Guide (ISBN 0-914831-83-6), $5. Lever Classroom Pack, $175. Individual Lever Set, $15. ***Publisher/supplier:*** LEGO Dacta. ***Materials:*** Available from LEGO Dacta.

3.72 Light. Investigate and Discover Series. Robert Gardner. New York, N.Y.: Julian Messner/Simon & Schuster, 1991.

Grades: 5-6+ Many of the investigations and features in *Light* are related to exhibits at the Science Museum at the Franklin Institute in Philadelphia. Each chapter features science background information and as many as 7 investigations. Through the experiments and activities in this guide, students explore the shadows cast by objects in bright light and try to explain the shadows' shapes and sizes. They investigate how light is reflected, how images are formed, and where those images are. They produce pinhole images, experiment with refraction of light, and examine and attempt to explain the behavior of colored light and colored objects. In a final activity, students are introduced to the wave and particle models as explanations of the properties of light.

Each chapter features extensive science background information and up to 7 investigations, including experiments with step-by-step instructions and less-structured activities that encourage students to explore on their own, at home or at school.

Price: $9.95 (ISBN 0-671-69042-6). ***Publisher/supplier:*** Silver Burdett Ginn. ***Materials:*** Available locally.

3.73 Light, Color, and Shadows. Windows on Elementary Science. Joan Westley. Sunnyvale, Calif.: Creative Publications, 1988.

Grades: PreK, K-2 In *Light, Color, and Shadows,* children use mirrors, prisms, colored cellophane, and stained glass, and play shadow tag to investigate light and shadows. Students observe how much light passes through objects, order colors from lightest to darkest, make rainbows, see how a mirror reflects light, and play shadow games. The 28 activities are sequenced by increasing level of difficulty, but it is not essential to use them in order.

Each 2-page activity in *Light, Color, and Shadows* has a summary statement describing the investigation, a list of the skills and necessary materials, and directions on how to set up for instruction. Also included are sections on getting started, guiding children's actions, and stretching their thinking.

Prices: Teacher's Guide (ISBN 0-88488-709-X), $13.75. Complete kit, $250.00. ***Publisher/supplier:*** Creative Publications. ***Materials:*** Available locally, from commercial suppliers, or in kit.

3.74 Machine Shop. AIMS. Donna Battcher, Sheldon Erickson, Karen Martini, and others. Fresno, Calif.: AIMS Education Foundation, 1993.

Grades: 5-6+ Journal entries about the uses of various simple machines and the forces that affect them provide a story line for the activities in *Machine Shop,* an activity book on the mechanics of physics in which mathematics and science skills are tested and other disciplines are integrated. Students investigate the following topic areas: simple machines; friction; inclined planes; levers and leverage; force, energy, and energy conservation; wheels and belts; gears and tooth ratios; wheel and axle systems; and pulleys, wedges, and mechanical advantage. Activities include students using a seesaw to explore the properties of effort, resistance, and torque; constructing and testing a high-performance catapult; and determining the mechanical advantage for different nuts and bolts.

Machine Shop provides reproducible student worksheets, including data charts, tables, and graphs. A complete lesson plan is included for each of the 23 activities.

Price: Teacher's Guide (ISBN 1-881431-39-8), $14.95. ***Publisher/supplier:*** AIMS Education Foundation. ***Materials:*** Available locally, or from commercial suppliers.

3.75 Machines at Work. Project Science. Alan Ward. New York, N.Y.: Franklin Watts, 1993.

Grades: 3-5 The simple activities and projects in this 32-page book provide an introduction to machines. *Machines at Work* focuses on levers, pulleys, ramps and screws, cranks, compound machines, work, force, and friction. Each section has a brief introduction followed by several activities, each of which includes an illustration, a materials list, and directions for performing the activity. A glossary is included.

Price: $16.80 (ISBN 0-531-14243-4). ***Publisher/supplier:*** Franklin Watts. ***Materials:*** Available locally.

3.76 Marble Mania. Prepared by Museum To Go Resource Center. Philadelphia, Pa.: Franklin Institute, 1989.

Grades: 3-5 *Marble Mania* uses marbles to introduce students to the concept of systems and subsystems. In 8 activities, students develop an awareness of the interdependence of subsystems through observation of interacting objects. Activities include designing and building a marble maze, observing and discussing the effect that changing one part of the maze has on the whole system, then redesigning and enlarging the maze so that the original maze is a subsystem of the new maze. Students make predictions based on observations of patterns and compare predictions with actual data. They use a variety of procedures to separate a system into its subsystems.

Each activity in *Marble Mania* features a teacher's page with an overview of the lesson. Reproducible student pages include a materials list and instructions for setting up and conducting the activity, including questions, diagrams, and recording sheets.

Prices: Complete kit, $255. Consumables kit, $50. ***Publisher/supplier:*** Science Kit and Boreal Laboratories. ***Materials:*** Available locally, from commercial suppliers, or in kit.

3.77 Mechanical Power: Practical Science Activities for Grades 4-6. Power of Science. Phillipa Beeson. Mount Waverley, Victoria, Australia: Dellasta, 1992.

Grades: 4-6 Students investigate pulleys, levers, gears, wheel-and-axle systems, inclined planes, and flywheels in *Mechanical Power.* This book is a collection of activities about the mechanics of machines and tools. Students compare the lifting power of single and double pulley systems; they experiment with levers to find the best position to apply effort; they demonstrate how wheel-and-axle systems reduce friction; and they design and build a machine that either fulfills an entirely new function or improves upon an existing machine. Reproducible student worksheets are included.

Price: $14.95 (ISBN 0-947138-90-0). ***Publisher/supplier:*** Mondo. ***Materials:*** Available locally, or from commercial suppliers.

3.78 Mirrors. Science Spirals. Reprinted with revisions. Julie Fitzpatrick. London, England: Evans Brothers, 1991.

Grades: 1-3 *Mirrors* is a colorful little book of mirror-related activities. Students use mirrors to explore the changing effect of reflections and to investigate some of the uses of mirrors. They use mirrors to make symmetrical patterns, practice "mirror writing," construct a simple kaleidoscope, and compare images produced in concave and convex mirrors. Plastic or double-sided unbreakable mirrors are recommended. The book provides easy-to-follow instructions, color drawings, and diagrams for these student-directed activities.

Price: $13.95 (ISBN 0-237-60209-1). ***Publisher/supplier:*** Trafalgar Square. ***Materials:*** Available locally.

3.79 Mirrors: Finding Out About the Properties of Light. A Boston Children's Museum Activity Book. Bernie Zubrowski. New York, N.Y.: Beech Tree Books (Morrow), 1992.

Grades: 4, 5 Students explore mirrors of every type from every angle in *Mirrors: Finding Out About the Properties of Light.* Activities are organized in 3 sections—plane mirrors, transparent mirrors, and curved mirrors—and are designed to be used in sequence. Examples include students lining up two mirrors to see hundreds of reflections, playing "hide and seek" using four mirrors, using a flashlight and mirrors to create a "monster maze," shining flashlights on plastic sheets to create ghostly images, using mirrors to create optical illusions, and making funny faces in flexible plastic sheets.

The lessons in *Mirrors* include diagrams, illustrations, and background information. Six activities use a game format.

Price: $6.95 (ISBN 0-688-10591-2). ***Publisher/supplier:*** William Morrow. ***Materials:*** Available locally, or from commercial suppliers.

3.80 Mystery Festival. GEMS. Kevin Beals and Carolyn Willard. Berkeley, Calif.: Lawrence Hall of Science, 1994.

Grades: 2-6+ *Mystery Festival* contains instructions for organizing 2 make-believe crime scenes, or "mysteries," in a classroom. Student-detectives subsequently observe, investigate, and attempt to solve the mysteries. The mystery "Who Borrowed Mr. Bear?" is for younger students (grades 1-3), and the mystery "Who Killed Felix?" for older students (grades 4-8). Working in teams, students gather evidence at the crime scene and then conduct hands-on forensic tests, such as a thread test, fingerprint comparisons, chromatography, pH tests, and powder tests at activity stations. Students learn to distinguish between evidence and inference. They develop their critical thinking and problem-solving skills. Preparation for the 2 mysteries is substantial when using the unit for the first time.

Mystery Festival provides detailed information and planning instructions, and includes suggestions for pre-teaching games and for the use of parent volunteers.

Price: $20 (ISBN 0-912511-89-3). ***Publisher/supplier:*** LHS GEMS. ***Materials:*** Available locally, or from commercial suppliers.

3.81 Physical Science Activities for Elementary and Middle School. CESI Sourcebook V. 2nd ed. Mark R. Malone. Washington, D.C.: Council for Elementary Science International (CESI), 1994.

Grades: 1-6 *Physical Science Activities for Elementary and Middle School,* a sourcebook of physical science activities, contains materials developed for teachers by teachers who have tested them with their own students. Topics include sound, light and color, electricity, forces and motion, simple machines, heat, matter, chemistry, and space. Activities include making a cardboard tube kazoo to investigate sound, making paper dolls dance because of static electricity, predicting the velocity of a rolling ball by observing its motion along a rail, using shadows to tell time, and learning about bonding by making slime.

The lesson plan for each of the 119 activities in this guide includes the following components: a short description of the concepts and/or skills developed by the activity; a list of materials and equipment needed; suggestions for planning, organizing, and implementing the activities; ideas for extending the lesson; and a list of references.

Price: $19. ***Publisher/supplier:*** CESI. ***Materials:*** Available locally, or from commercial suppliers.

3.82 Popping With Power. AIMS. Carol Bland, Helen Crossley, Susan Dixon, and others. Rev. ed. Fresno, Calif.: AIMS Education Foundation, 1994.

Grades: 3, 4 *Popping with Power* includes investigations on a variety of energy-related topics, such as simple machines, heat conservation, and electricity. Students operate simple machines, investigate the relationship between pendulum length and frequency, discover why some balls bounce higher than others, design a wind-powered vehicle, and observe the effect of color on heat retention. They determine which materials carry the strongest electical charge, which home appliances use the most electricity, and how the force of wind affects a suspension bridge. While many of the activities in this revised edition are in their original form, some have been updated and rewritten in a new format and others are new.

Popping with Power provides reproducible student worksheets, including data charts, tables, and graphs. A complete lesson plan is included for each of the 24 activities.

Price: Teacher's Guide (ISBN 1-881431-51-7), $14.95. ***Publisher/ supplier:*** AIMS Education Foundation. ***Materials:*** Available locally, or from commercial suppliers.

3.83 Pulleys. Enfield, Conn.: LEGO Dacta, 1993.

Grades: 5, 6 This booklet contains information about pulleys, simple pulley activities, and appropriate diagrams and illustrations. It is designed to be used with the LEGO DACTA Pulley Set, which uses the popular LEGO construction blocks. Students first learn the definition of a pulley. Then they arrange pulleys to investigate the direction of rotation of the driver and the follower and to find out how the turning ratio of one pulley to another is determined by the size of the pulleys. Students are challenged to design and build two devices: a conveyor-belt system that uses a belt drive to carry packages, and a boat mover that winches a boat onto the shore.

Each activity in *Pulleys* states the main idea involved and provides illustrated instructions, additional information, and extension ideas. The guide lists the process and critical thinking skills involved in the activities.

Prices: Teacher's Guide (ISBN 0-914831-84-4), $5. Pulley Classroom Pack, $175. Individual Pulley Set, $15. ***Publisher/supplier:*** LEGO Dacta. ***Materials:*** Available from LEGO Dacta.

3.84 Science Express. An Ontario Science Centre Book. Carol Gold. Toronto, Ontario, Canada: Kids Can Press, 1991.

Grades: 3-6 *Science Express* contains 36 simple experiments that can be performed at home or in the classroom. Each experiment focuses on one scientific principle or phenomenon. Examples include racing soup cans, making paper from broccoli, testing the effects of sound vibrations on a lit candle, and making an air cannon. Each activity includes a materials list and step-by-step instructions, as well as an explanation of the scientific principle or phenomenon involved.

Price: $8.61 (ISBN 1-55074-017-2). ***Publisher/supplier:*** Addison-Wesley. ***Materials:*** Available locally.

3.85 Soap Films and Bubbles. AIMS. Ann Wiebe. Fresno, Calif.: AIMS Education Foundation, 1990.

Grades: 4-6+ Students learn about molecules, surface tension, light waves, air pressure, and patterns by experimenting with soap film in *Soap Films and Bubbles.* In a series of introductory activities, students first explore the effects of wet and dry surfaces on bubbles. They discover that all free-floating bubbles are spherical in shape, and they explore various combinations of bubbles and the structures and patterns they form. Students construct models of water and soap molecules as they investigate surface tension and the chemistry of soap film. In advanced activities, students take a quantitative look at geometric shapes; they discover the mathematical relationship between the size of two equal rings and the distance soap film will stretch between them (catenary curves). They experiment to determine the minimum distances between given numbers of points (Steiner's problem). They find a formula relating the parts of polyhedrons.

Soap Films and Bubbles provides reproducible student worksheets, including data charts, tables, and graphs. A complete lesson plan is included for each of the 21 activities.

Price: Teacher's Guide (ISBN 1-881431-25-8), $14.95. ***Publisher/ supplier:*** AIMS Education Foundation. ***Materials:*** Available locally, or from commercial suppliers.

3.86 Sound Science. Etta Kaner. Toronto, Ontario, Canada: Kids Can Press, 1991.

Grades: 3-6+ Lively illustrations, easy-to-follow instructions, and jokes, games, and challenges are among the features of the activity book *Sound Science.* The book is divided in sections focusing on the human ear, how sound travels, how sound is used, musical instruments, and devices for sending sound over long distances. Examples of activities include making a wailing bowl, playing sound charades, making and playing a one-stringed instrument, and reinventing the phonograph. Experiments use simple, everyday items; many activities could be conducted independently by students.

Each activity in *Sound Science* features a short introduction, a materials list, step-by-step instructions, a brief explanation, and short items of interest on subjects such as hearing-ear dogs and sound in outer space.

Price: $9.57 (ISBN 1-55074-054-7). ***Publisher/supplier:*** Addison-Wesley. ***Materials:*** Available locally.

3.87 Teaching Elementary Science With Toys. CESI Sourcebook VII. Columbus, Ohio: ERIC Clearinghouse for Science, Mathematics, and Environmental Education; and Washington, D.C.: Council for Elementary Science International (CESI), 1993.

Grades: K-6 *Teaching Elementary Science With Toys: CESI Sourcebook VII* is a sourcebook of activities and strategies for using toys to teach science concepts and to develop science process skills. Toys are used in these activities and strategies to help students focus on natural phenomena, to provoke imagination, and to promote scientific thinking. Students use toys that fly, roll, bounce, float, store and release energy, and change colors as they explore concepts of motion, force, energy, heat, sound, light, magnetism, and electricity. Some activities concentrate more on concept development and others more on science process. Examples include exploring the concept of vibration using buttons and string, making a rubber ball from natural latex, predicting the results of a game of pin the tail on the donkey, observing the difference in flight distance of a Frisbee and an Aerobie, and classifying toys in a catalog.

Each of the 29 lesson plans in this sourcebook has background information, step-by-step procedures, and ideas for further challenges.

Price: $19. ***Publisher/supplier:*** CESI. ***Materials:*** Available locally, or from commercial suppliers.

3.88 Towers and Bridges. Science Spirals. Julie Fitzpatrick. Reprinted with revisions. London, England: Evans Brothers, 1991.

Grades: 2, 3 *Towers and Bridges* is a colorful little book of student-directed activities that emphasizes constructing models that work. Students experience some of the engineering problems to be solved in any construction as they build simple towers and investigate their stability, test the relative strength of two brick walls, investigate various types of supports and beams, and design and build models of arch and suspension bridges. The book provides easy-to-follow instructions, color drawings, and diagrams.

Price: $13.95 (ISBN 0-237-60213-X). ***Publisher/supplier:*** Trafalgar Square. ***Materials:*** Available locally.

3.89 Water and Ice. Windows on Elementary Science. Joan Westley. Sunnyvale, Calif.: Creative Publications, 1988.

Grades: PreK, K-2 In *Water and Ice,* children explore mixing, dissolving, absorbing, melting, evaporating, and freezing water. Students compare how sand and salt mix with water; they explore the soaking capacity of materials, construct boats that float, and find ways to keep ice from melting, among the many activities in the guide. The 28 investigations are sequenced by increasing level of difficulty but do not need to be completed in order.

Each 2-page activity in *Water and Ice* has a summary statement describing the investigation, a list of the skills and necessary materials, and directions on how to set up for instruction. Also included are sections on getting started, guiding children's actions, and stretching their thinking.

Prices: Teacher's Guide (ISBN 0-88488-708-1), $13.75. Complete kit, $250.00. ***Publisher/supplier:*** Creative Publications. ***Materials:*** Available locally, from commercial suppliers, or in kit.

3.90 Wheels. Science Spirals. Julie Fitzpatrick. Reprinted with revisions. London, England: Evans Brothers, 1991.

Grades: 1-3 *Wheels* is a small, colorful activity book for young learners. It takes children through the design process of making models with moving parts and encourages them to find ways to adapt their models. Students discover which shapes slide and which roll. They investigate wheel-and-axle systems; experiment with friction, including ways of increasing or decreasing friction; and explore the movement of pulley wheels and gear wheels. The book provides easy-to-follow instructions, color drawings, and diagrams for these student-directed activities.

Price: $13.95 (ISBN 0-237-60214-8). ***Publisher/supplier:*** Trafalgar Square. ***Materials:*** Available locally.

3.91 Wizard's Lab. GEMS/Exhibit Guides. Cary Sneider and Alan Gould. Reprinted with revisions. Berkeley, Calif.: Lawrence Hall of Science, 1992.

Grades: K-6+ *Wizard's Lab* provides 10 interactive exhibits that can be used in a variety of settings—for example, at a science center, at a classroom learning station, in a discovery room, or on family science night. The wide spectrum of stimulating activities in physical science offered in this guide includes the spinning platform, solar cells and light polarizers, resonant pendula, magnets, lenses, the "human battery," the oscilloscope and sound, and the harmonograph. Most of the exhibits utilize common materials and equipment available from most hardware, electronics, or variety stores and lumberyards. The skills developed include observing, analyzing, and finding patterns.

Wizard's Lab provides background information recorded on cards with cartoon wizard figures that briefly explains the principles behind each exhibit. Detailed and illustrated instructions for constructing each exhibit are included in the teacher's guide.

Price: $20 (ISBN 0-912511-71-0). ***Publisher/supplier:*** LHS GEMS. ***Materials:*** Available locally, or from commercial suppliers.

CHAPTER 4

Multidisciplinary and Applied Science

MULTIDISCIPLINARY AND APPLIED SCIENCE—CORE MATERIALS

4.1 Beginnings. SCIS 3. Herbert D. Thier and Robert C. Knott. Hudson, N.H.: Delta Education, 1992.

Grade: K *Beginnings,* a year-long module, introduces kindergartners to a variety of basic scientific concepts and process skills. The major topics of the module's 10 sections, which may be taught in any order, are (1) Life on Land, (2) Color, (3) Shape, (4) Texture, (5) Odor, (6) Life in Water, (7) Sound, (8) Size, (9) Quantity, and (10) Position. The activities develop process skills such as observing, classifying, communicating, comparing, counting, describing, and ordering. Among the activities, children observe plants and animals in terrariums and aquariums; they identify, compare, and sort objects and organisms by color, shape, size, and texture; they describe odors and sounds; they compare quantities; and they describe the relative position of objects.

The 10 sections in *Beginnings* contain 56 chapters. The teacher's guide includes an introduction to the unit, lesson plans for each section, and a glossary.

The module includes science background information, detailed instructions on planning for and conducting each activity, an extensive assessment component, and extensions for integration and enrichment. Materials are available in a kit.

Prices: Teacher's Guide (ISBN 0-87504-930-3), $39.50. Kit, $565.00. ***Publisher/supplier:*** Delta Education. ***Materials:*** Available locally, from commercial suppliers, or in kit.

4.2 Ideas and Inventions. FOSS. (Developed by Lawrence Hall of Science, Berkeley, Calif.) Chicago, Ill.: Encyclopaedia Britannica Educational Corp., 1992.

Grades: 3, 4 *Ideas and Inventions* consists of 4 activities that promote student inventiveness. Each activity provides science content while introducing a conventional technique for revealing the unseen. Students use the techniques from the structured part of the activities—crayon rubbing, chromatography, carbon printing, and mirror imagery—to invent something or to produce games, puzzles, artwork, and other creations. Divergent thinking and creativity are encouraged.

The 4 activities in *Ideas and Inventions* require a total of at least 10 class sessions. The teacher's guide includes a module overview, the 4 activity folios, duplication

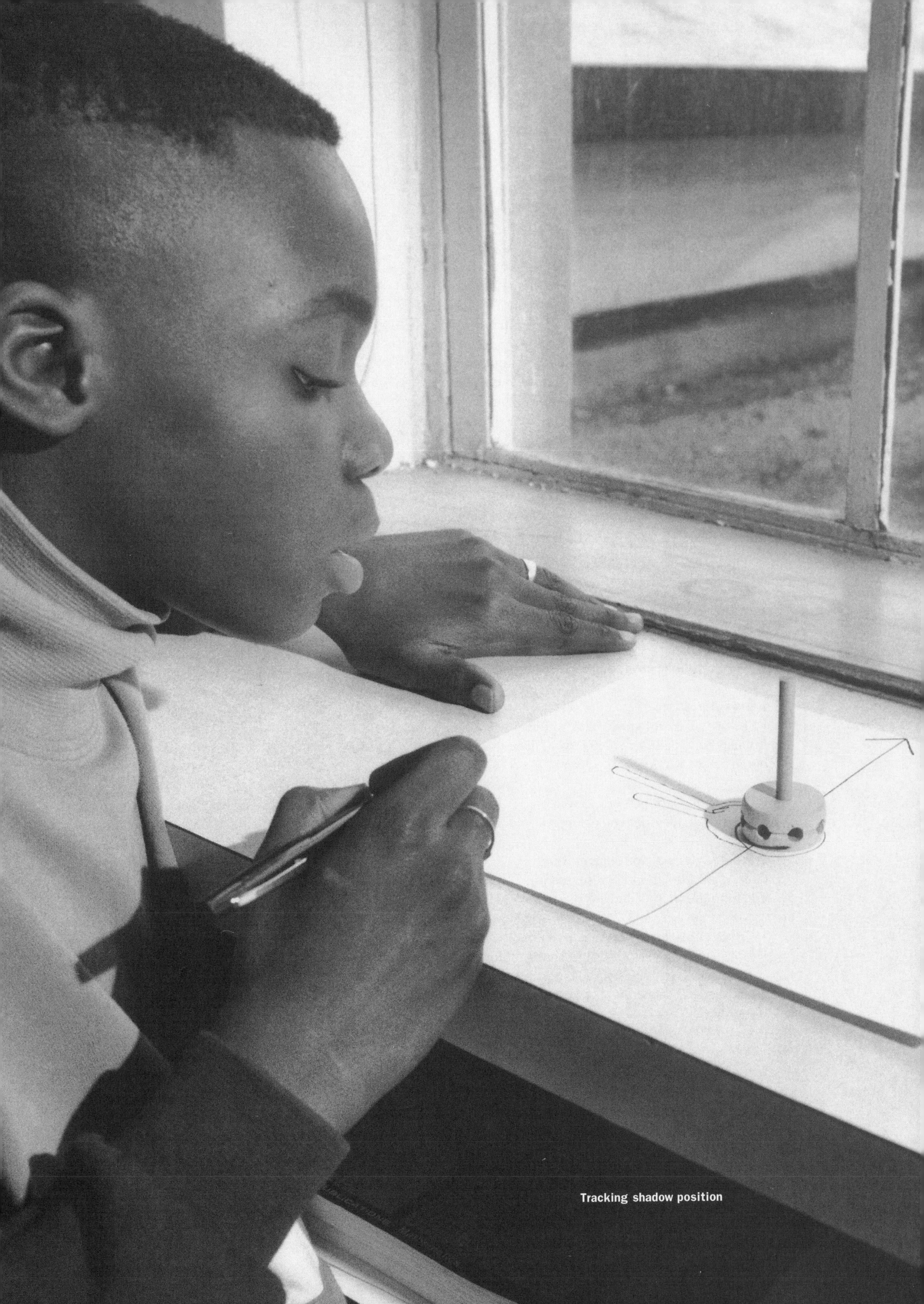

Tracking shadow position

About the Annotations in "Multidisciplinary and Applied Science—Core Materials"

Entry Numbers

Curriculum materials are arranged alphabetically by title in each category (Core Materials, Supplementary Materials, and Science Activity Books) in chapters 1 through 4 of this guide. In addition, each annotation has a two-part entry number. For each entry number, the chapter number is given before the period; the number after the period locates the entry within that chapter.

For example, the first entry number in chapter 1 is 1.1; the second entry in chapter 2 is 2.2, and so on.

The entry numbers within each curriculum chapter run consecutively through Core Materials, Supplementary Materials, and Science Activity Books.

Order of Bibliographic Information

Following is the arrangement of the facts of publication in the annotations in this section:

- **Title of publication.**
- **Series title**, or series acronym if commonly used.
- **Authors** (either individual names or organizational author).
- Name and location of **developer** (in parentheses), if different from publisher.
- **Place of publication, publisher, and date of publication.**

Series Acronyms

Following are **acronyms of series titles** in "Multidisciplinary and Applied Science—Core Materials." (Series titles that are spelled out are not included in this list.)

FOSS Full Option Science System
SCIS 3 Science Curriculum Improvement Study

Price and Acquisition Information

Ordering information is presented in a block immediately below the annotation. Included are the following:

- **Prices** of teacher's guides, activity books, and kits or units.
- The name of a principal **publisher/supplier** (not necessarily the sole source) for the items listed in the price category. (The address and phone and fax numbers for each publisher and supplier appear in appendix A, "Publishers and Suppliers.")
- An indication of the various sources from which one might obtain the required **materials.**

masters (in English and Spanish) for student sheets, and an annotated bibliography.

This module includes science background information, detailed instructions on planning for and conducting each activity, an extensive assessment component, and extensions for integration and enrichment. Materials are available in a kit.

Prices: Teacher's Guide (ISBN 0-7826-0028-X), $101. Complete module, $279. ***Publisher/supplier:*** Encyclopaedia Britannica Educational Corp. ***Materials:*** Available locally, from commercial suppliers, or in module.

4.3 Interaction and Systems. SCIS 3. Herbert D. Thier and Robert C. Knott. Hudson, N.H.: Delta Education, 1992.

Grade: 2 *Interaction and Systems* is a comprehensive, half-year program of physical science and earth science during which students investigate evidence of interaction in a variety of systems. For example, in physical science they investigate batteries interacting with bulbs, and magnets interacting with paper clips and other metallic objects. The systems concept is applied to the earth sciences as students observe and describe the interaction between land and water. Students gain practical experience with the mathematical concepts of ratio and proportion as they experiment with gear and pulley systems. They interpret dissolving, color change, precipitation, and evaporation as evidence of interaction. Through activities with static electricity, magnets, and compasses they investigate interactions between objects that are not in contact. Throughout this unit, students have the opportunity to observe and collect data, experiment, hypothesize, interpret findings, discuss results, and make predictions.

Interaction and Systems has 7 sections consisting of a total of 21 chapters. The teacher's guide includes an introduction to the unit, lesson plans for each section, a glossary, and blackline masters for a student journal.

This module includes science background information, detailed instructions on planning for and conducting each activity, an extensive assessment component, and extensions for integration and enrichment. Materials are available in a kit.

Prices: Teacher's Guide (ISBN 0-87504-933-8), $39.50. Kit, $650.00. ***Publisher/supplier:*** Delta Education. ***Materials:*** Available locally, from commercial suppliers, or in kit.

4.4 Models and Designs. FOSS. (Developed by Lawrence Hall of Science, Berkeley, Calif.) Chicago, Ill.: Encyclopaedia Britannica Educational Corp., 1992.

Grades: 5, 6 The *Models and Designs* module provides students with experiences that develop the concept of a scientific model and engage them in the processes of design and construction. Students work in cooperative groups to create solutions to a variety of real-world problems as they consider the relationship of structure to function. They use their senses to investigate sealed black boxes, and then they develop conceptual models of the boxes' contents and construct physical models to test their ideas. Students engineer a model that replicates the behavior of another model—a fanciful device called a hum dinger. They construct a self-propelled cart of their own design and modify the cart to perform specific tricks.

The *Models and Designs* module consists of 4 activities, requiring about 12 class sessions to complete. The teacher's guide includes a module overview, the 4 individual activity folios, duplication masters (in English and Spanish) for student sheets, and an annotated bibliography.

This module includes science background information, detailed instructions on planning for and conducting each activity, an extensive assessment component, and extensions for integration and enrichment. Materials are available in a kit.

Prices: Teacher's Guide (ISBN 0-7826-0075-1), $101. Complete module, $495. ***Publisher/supplier:*** Encyclopaedia Britannica Educational Corp. ***Materials:*** Available locally, from commercial suppliers, or in module.

4.5 Variables. FOSS. (Developed by Lawrence Hall of Science, Berkeley, Calif.) Chicago, Ill.: Encyclopaedia Britannica Educational Corp., 1993.

Grades: 5, 6 In *Variables,* students investigate the concept "variable" as they design and conduct their own experiments with pendulums, airplanes, boats, and catapults. They systematically investigate weight, release position, and length of pendulums to find out which of these variables affects the number of swings completed in a given period of time. They make paper boats of various heights and determine how many pennies each boat can hold before sinking. They build windup airplanes to fly along a string, and then they control variables such as the number of times the propeller is wound, the weight of the plane, and the slope of the string in measuring how far the planes will fly. They catapult objects of various sizes and weights to investigate the variables that contribute to the highest and longest flips.

Variables consists of 4 major activities, requiring a total of about 20 class sessions. The teacher's guide includes a module overview, the 4 activity folios, duplication masters (in English and Spanish) for the student sheets, and an annotated bibliography.

This module includes science background information, detailed instructions on planning for and conducting each activity, an extensive assessment component, and extensions for integration and enrichment. Materials are available in a kit.

Prices: Teacher's Guide (ISBN 0-7826-0052-2), $101. Complete module, $319. ***Publisher/supplier:*** Encyclopaedia Britannica Educational Corp. ***Materials:*** Available locally, from commercial suppliers, or in module.

MULTIDISCIPLINARY AND APPLIED SCIENCE—SUPPLEMENTARY MATERIALS

ABOUT THE ANNOTATIONS IN "MULTIDISCIPLINARY AND APPLIED SCIENCE— SUPPLEMENTARY MATERIALS"

Entry Numbers

Curriculum materials are arranged alphabetically by title in each category (Core Materials, Supplementary Materials, and Science Activity Books) in chapters 1 through 4 of this guide. In addition, each annotation has a two-part entry number. For each entry number, the chapter number is given before the period; the number after the period locates the entry within that chapter.

For example, the first entry number in chapter 1 is 1.1; the second entry in chapter 2 is 2.2, and so on.

The entry numbers within each curriculum chapter run consecutively through Core Materials, Supplementary Materials, and Science Activity Books.

Order of Bibliographic Information

Following is the arrangement of the facts of publication in the annotations in this section:

- **Title of publication.**
- **Series title,** or series acronym if commonly used.
- **Authors** (either individual names or organizational author).
- Name and location of **developer** (in parentheses), if different from publisher.
- **Place of publication, publisher, and date of publication.**

Series Acronyms

Following are acronyms of series titles in "Multidisciplinary and Applied Science—Supplementary Materials." (Series titles that are spelled out are not included in this list.)

DSM Delta Science Module
GEMS Great Explorations in Math and Science
REEP Regional Environmental Education Program
STAR Science Technology and Reading

Price and Acquisition Information

Ordering information is presented in a block immediately below the annotation. Included are the following:

- **Prices** of teacher's guides, activity books, and kits or units.
- The name of a principal **publisher/supplier** (not necessarily the sole source) for the items listed in the price category. (The address and phone and fax numbers for each publisher and supplier appear in Appendix A, "Publishers and Suppliers.")
- An indication of the various sources from which one might obtain the required **materials.**

4.6 Acid Rain. GEMS. Colin Hocking, Jacqueline Barber, and Jan Coonrod. Berkeley, Calif.: Lawrence Hall of Science, 1990.

Grades: 6+ A unit on an important environmental issue, *Acid Rain* fosters scientific inquiry and critical thinking skills through varied activity formats. Students develop a working knowledge of the pH scale by measuring the pH of everyday solutions; they make "fake lakes" and determine how the pH changes after an acid rainstorm; and they investigate the effect of buffering to reduce the acidity of lakes. In other activities, students conduct a plant-growth experiment to determine the effect of various dilutions of acid on seed germination; they present a play focusing on the effects of acid rain on aquatic life; they play a "startling statements" game; and they hold a town meeting to discuss possible solutions to the problem of acid rain. The unit provides students with much information on acid rain, encourages them to analyze complex environmental issues, and illustrates interrelationships of science, technology, and society.

The teacher's guide includes background information on acid rain and detailed instructions for conducting each of the 8 sessions, which require 50 minutes each.

Price: $15 (ISBN 0-912511-74-5).
Publisher/supplier: LHS GEMS.
Materials: Available locally, or from commercial suppliers.

4.7 Build It! Festival. GEMS. Philip Gonsalves and Jaine Kopp. Berkeley, Calif.: Lawrence Hall of Science, 1995.

Grades: K-6 Originally designed as a large-group festival presentation by the Lawrence Hall of Science, *Build It! Festival* is adapted to the individual classroom in this teacher's guide. Working in pairs or small groups at learning stations, students connect geometry to the real-world experience of building various structures. A preliminary activity involves free exploration with the manipulatives used in *Build It!* Then, in an introductory activity, students design and build structures using pattern blocks. In the next 8 activities, they construct three-dimensional shapes using two-dimensional paper shapes; they create two- and three-dimensional shapes out of newspaper dowels; they construct three-dimensional structures using snap-together geometric shapes; they explore bilateral symmetry as they make designs with pattern blocks; they figure out patterns and continue them; and they make tessellations and tangrams.

Each activity features an overview, a list of materials needed, instructions for preparing and presenting the activity, extension ideas, and reproducible masters for all patterns used in the unit. Some activities offer two options—one for younger and one for older students. The guide also includes a glossary, a list of resource books and literature connections, sources for the materials used in the book, and a section on how to make *Build It!* a schoolwide event.

Price: $20 (ISBN 0-912511-88-5). ***Publisher/supplier:*** LHS GEMS. ***Materials:*** Available locally, or from commercial suppliers.

4.8 Change Around Us. Life Lab Science. Seattle, Wash.: Videodiscovery, 1992.

Grade: 2 In *Change Around Us,* children build an outdoor or indoor garden to use as a laboratory for a year. They explore patterns of change in the natural world and learn that resources change as they are used, recycled, or depleted. Investigations are organized in 8 units: (1) Sensing Changes, (2) Investigating Plants, (3) Investigating Water, (4) Investigating Air, (5) Investigating Food, (6) Investigating Food Chains, (7) Investigating Resources, and (8) Conserving Resources. Activities include students working in small groups to create imaginary insects, devising an experiment to test an assumption about plant needs, predicting what will happen to ice cubes placed in various locations, tracing food items to their sources, and making and maintaining a compost pile. Each unit integrates earth, life, and physical science concepts.

The 8 units in *Change Around Us* include 54 activities, typically 30 to 60 minutes long. For each unit, the teacher's guide provides a planning calendar, an activity chart with a summary of each activity, and a book list. Each lesson plan includes background information, a list of the materials required, step-by-step instructions for preparing for and conducting the activity, suggestions for review and reinforcement, and extension ideas. A student lab book is available in both English and Spanish. A garden log, videodisc, music tape, and tool kit are also available to supplement the teacher's guide.

Prices: Teacher's Guide (ISBN 1-56307-200-9), $80. Student Lab Book (ISBN 1-56307-174-6), $9. Life Lab Package, $575. Complete Life Lab Science Kit, $375. ***Publisher/supplier:*** Videodiscovery. ***Materials:*** Available locally, from commercial suppliers, or in kit from Let's Get Growing.

4.9 Change Over Time. Life Lab Science. Seattle, Wash.: Videodiscovery, 1994.

Grade: 5 In *Change Over Time,* students build an outdoor or indoor garden to use as a laboratory for a year. They discover that living things have characteristics that enable them to survive and that these characteristics change over time in response to changes in the earth and its atmosphere. The investigations are organized in 8 individual modules: (1) Changes, (2) Adaptations, (3) Energy and Change, (4) Seasonal Change, (5) Weather and Climate Changes, (6) Soil Changes, (7) Growing Together, and (8) Change Over Time. Activities include students investigating physical and chemical changes, exploring how living things survive in their habitats, experimenting with different kinds of insulation, and making a model of the earth's orbit. In other activities they compile data about climate, observe how earthworms affect soil, dissect flowers and identify the parts, and create a garden timeline. Each module integrates earth, life, and physical science concepts.

Change Over Time has 8 modules, each including 6 to 8 activities of 30 to 90 minutes. The modules may be used in sequence or organized according to an existing curriculum. Each module contains a teacher's resource section and a student lab book. The teacher's resource section provides complete information for setting up and conducting the lessons. It includes a summary of each activity, a unit planner, a list of recommended literature, and an assessment checklist. The student lab book (available in English and Spanish) provides space for students to write notes, draw field sketches, and record data and observations. It also includes pre- and post-assessment lab sheets, a unit calendar, and a student newsletter.

Prices: Teacher's Resource Books (complete set) (ISBN 1-56307-199-1), $265. Life Lab package, $300. Science garden kit (complete), $375. ***Publisher/supplier:*** Videodiscovery. ***Materials:*** Available locally, from commercial suppliers, or in kit from Let's Get Growing.

4.10 Connections. Life Lab Science. Seattle, Wash.: Videodiscovery, 1994.

Grade: 4 In *Connections,* students build an outdoor or indoor garden that they use as a laboratory for a year. They discover that organisms, the environment, and the interactions between the two are linked together in an ecosystem. They learn how a system sustains itself over time. *Connections* has 8 individual modules: (1) Interactions, (2) Habitats, (3) Water Interactions, (4) Nutrient Interactions, (5) Light Interactions, (6) Food Webs, (7) Ecosystems, and (8) Sustainable Systems. Activities include the following: students observe interactions in a microhabitat; they experiment with variables affecting plant growth; they create and monitor open and closed terrariums; they analyze compost to understand factors influencing decomposition; and they explore the effects of light on plants and animals. In other activities, students investigate toxins in food chains, create dioramas of ecosystems, and create a sustainable garden plan. Each module integrates earth, life, and physical science concepts.

Each of the 8 modules in *Connections* has 8 to 9 activities, requiring 30 to 60 minutes each. The modules may be used in sequence or organized according to an existing curriculum. Each module contains a teacher's resource section and a student lab book. The teacher's resource section provides complete information for setting up and conducting the lessons. It includes a summary of each activity, a unit planner, a book list, an endangered species project section, and an assessment checklist. The student lab book (available in English and Spanish) provides space for students to write notes, draw field sketches, and record data and observations. It also includes pre- and post-assessment lab sheets, a unit calendar, and a student newsletter.

Prices: Teacher's Resource Books (complete set) (ISBN 1-56307-198-3), $265. Life Lab package, $300. Science garden kit (complete), $375. ***Publisher/supplier:*** Videodiscovery. ***Materials:*** Available locally, from commercial suppliers, or in kit from Let's Get Growing.

4.11 Discovering Deserts. NatureScope. Washington, D.C.: National Wildlife Federation, 1989.

Grades: 3-6 The interdisciplinary activities in *Discovering Deserts* introduce students to the ecology of arid lands. Through games, songs, stories, drawings, and drama, students explore the following topics: what a desert is, how deserts form, and the different types of deserts; the ways in which plants and animals have adapted to harsh desert conditions; plant and animal relationships in desert communities; and the ways in which people are changing desert habitats.

Discovering Deserts has 5 chapters (each on a broad theme), a craft section, and an appendix. Teachers may choose from the 23 activities or teach each chapter as a unit. Copycat pages supplement the activities and provide games, puzzles, and worksheets.

Price: $7.95 (ISBN 0-945051-34-4). ***Publisher/supplier:*** National Wildlife Federation. ***Materials:*** Available locally, or from commercial suppliers.

4.12 Diving into Oceans. NatureScope. Washington, D.C.: National Wildlife Federation, 1989.

Grades: K-6 *Diving into Oceans* introduces students to the physical properties of the sea, the variety of habitats from deep ocean floor to intertidal zone, the variety of plants and animals that live in these habitats, and the interactions between people and the marine environment. Students conduct simulation experiments with saltwater; they play food web and symbiosis games; and they engage in many other activities that integrate art, language arts, mathematics, and social science with study of the ocean.

Diving into Oceans has 4 chapters (each on a broad theme), a craft section, and an appendix. Teachers may choose single activities from among the 19 provided, or they can teach each chapter as a unit. Copycat pages supplement the activities and provide games, puzzles, and worksheets.

Price: $7.95 (ISBN 0-945051-36-0). ***Publisher/supplier:*** National Wildlife Federation. ***Materials:*** Available locally, or from commercial suppliers.

4.13 Earth Is Home. Life Lab Science. Seattle, Wash.: Videodiscovery, 1992.

Grade: 1 In *Earth Is Home,* students build an indoor or outdoor garden to use as a laboratory throughout the year. Investigations are organized in 7 units: (1) Sensing Our World, (2) Exploring Soil, (3) Observing Earth's Cycles, (4) Investigating Weather, (5) Exploring Plant Life, (6) Exploring Animal Life, and (7) Investigating Garden Homes. Each unit integrates earth, life, and physical science concepts.

The 7 units have a total of 59 activities, typically 20 to 40 minutes long. For each unit the teacher's guide provides a unit planning calendar, an activity chart with a summary of each activity, and a book list. Each lesson plan includes background information, a list of the materials required, step-by-step instructions on preparing for and conducting the activity, suggestions for review and reinforcement, and extension ideas. A student lab book is available in English and Spanish. A garden log, videodisc, music tape, and tool kit are available to supplement the teacher's guide.

Prices: Teacher's Resource Book (ISBN 1-56307-170-3), $80. Student Lab Book (ISBN 1-56307-169-X), $9. Complete Life Lab Science Kit, $375. ***Publisher/supplier:*** Videodiscovery. ***Materials:*** Available locally, from commercial suppliers, or in kit from Let's Get Growing.

4.14 Energy, Grade 4. REEP. Philadelphia, Pa.: The Schuylkill Center for Environmental Education, 1991.

Grade: 4 *Energy,* an environmental education unit, introduces students to energy, its various forms, the need for energy to "fuel" both living organisms and machines, and the impact of human actions on nonrenewable energy sources. Activities include the following: students identify the various forms that energy can take; they role-play the main components of the process of photosynthesis; and they test for the presence of starch in leaves. Students also construct models of food chains, dramatize the steps in making coal, and learn to read an electric meter.

The introduction to *Energy* includes background information and a lesson summary. The unit has 10 lessons that stand alone but are designed to be taught in sequence. Each lesson has from 1 to 3 activities.

Price: $20. ***Publisher/supplier:*** Schuylkill Center for Environmental Education. ***Materials:*** Available locally, or from commercial suppliers.

4.15 Great Explorations. Life Lab Science. Seattle, Wash.: Videodiscovery, 1992.

Grade: K In *Great Explorations,* kindergartners build an outdoor or indoor garden to use as a laboratory for a year as they utilize their senses to learn about the world around them. The investigations are organized in 6 units: (1) Exploring Our Senses, (2) Exploring Water, (3) Exploring Soil, (4) Exploring Plants, (5) Exploring Garden Animals, and (6) Garden Celebrations. Through the activities, students make discoveries about soil, water, plants, and animals. They use sifters, funnels, and measuring cups to explore the properties of soils; they search the garden for scented objects; they find and investigate earthworms to discover their habits and how they react to stimuli; and they germinate seeds to learn that seeds become sprouts. The scientific concepts that children study—such as life cycles, weather, decomposition, and habitats—are observed from real life. Each unit integrates earth, life, and physical science concepts.

The 6 units in *Great Explorations* consist of a total of 69 activities, typically 30 minutes in length. For each unit the teacher's guide provides a unit planning calendar, an activity chart with a summary of each activity, and a book list. Each lesson plan includes background information, a list of the materials required, step-by-step instructions for preparing for and conducting the activity, suggestions for review and reinforcement, and extension ideas. Some activities in each unit are conducted at a free-exploration station. A garden log, videodisc, music tape, and tool kit are available to supplement the teacher's guide.

Prices: Teacher's Guide (ISBN 1-56307-163-0), $80. Life Lab Package (ISBN 1-56307-163-0), $430. Complete Life Lab Science Kit, $375. ***Publisher/supplier:*** Videodiscovery. ***Materials:*** Available locally, from commercial suppliers, or in kit from Let's Get Growing.

4.16 The Growing Classroom: Garden-Based Science. Roberta Jaffe and Gary Appel. New York, N.Y.: Addison-Wesley Publishing Co., 1990.

Grades: 3-6 *The Growing Classroom* is a sourcebook with 13 units of activities for teachers interested in developing a garden-based science program. The book provides general information about the Life Lab program and explains why the garden provides an important, exciting context for learning science. Information on starting a school garden and incorporating it into the classroom is presented. There are suggestions for adapting the Life Lab program to specific needs and resources, management techniques, and ideas for cultivating community support. The activities relate to specific concepts and topics such as "The Living Earth," "Cycles and Changes," "Climate," and "Nutrients."

The Growing Classroom includes blackline masters, equipment designs and planting guides, a scope and sequence chart, and a complete materials list for each unit.

Price: $36.32 (ISBN 0-201-21539-X). ***Distributor:*** Addison-Wesley. ***Materials:*** Available locally, or from commercial suppliers.

4.17 Hot Water and Warm Homes From Sunlight. GEMS. Alan Gould. Berkeley, Calif.: Lawrence Hall of Science, 1986.

Grades: 5-6+ In *Hot Water and Warm Homes From Sunlight,* students perform experiments with model houses and water heating to investigate solar power. An activity on the experimental design and results of a plant-growth study introduces students to the concept and essential elements of a controlled experiment. Students then build model houses to determine how windows affect passive solar heating of the house. They use aluminum pie pans as model water heaters to investigate the effect of clear covers on water-heating efficiency.

Each of the 5 lesson plans (requiring a total of 5 or 6 class sessions of 45 minutes each) includes an overview, a list of materials, suggestions for preparation, directions for the activity, and extensions. Reproducible masters of patterns and student data sheets are included in the teacher's guide.

Price: $10. ***Publisher/supplier:*** LHS GEMS. ***Materials:*** Available locally, or from commercial suppliers.

4.18 How People Get Food: How People Produce, Change, and Move Food. Scholastic Science Place. (Developed in cooperation with Children's Museum of Indianapolis, Indianapolis, Ind.) New York, N.Y.: Scholastic, 1993.

Grade: 2 Food production, preservation, and distribution are among the topics explored in *How People Get Food.* The lessons are grouped in 3 subconcepts: (1) as the human population grows, more food must be produced to feed more people; (2) inventions to solve food problems have caused new problems that people are working to solve; and (3) food must be safely moved from places where it is produced to places where it is bought. Activities include students freezing orange slices to demonstrate the effect of cold on crops, experimenting with hydroponic farming on a small scale, preserving fruit, and researching how their favorite foods get to them.

How People Get Food has 14 lessons. The conceptual goals of the unit are presented in the lesson-by-lesson story line in the teacher's guide. Each lesson has background information; a complete lesson plan, including suggestions for assessing performance and integrating the curriculum; and a list of the print, video, and software support materials required.

Prices: Teacher's Guide (ISBN 0-590-26145-2), $20.70. Student Book, $6.50. Complete unit, $375.00. Consumables kit, $29.00. ***Publisher/supplier:*** Scholastic. ***Materials:*** Available locally, from commercial suppliers, or in unit.

4.19 How People Invent: How Problems and Solutions Change Over Time. Scholastic Science Place. (Developed in cooperation with Children's Museum of Memphis, Memphis, Tenn.) New York, N.Y.: Scholastic, 1995.

Grade: 5 In *How People Invent,* students explore invention from the brainstorming process to the development of a working model. The lessons are grouped in 3 subconcepts: (1) people use problem-solving methods to invent new processes and devices, (2) new inventions and new applications of existing inventions are developed by observing and thinking about everyday occurrences, and (3) inventors use models to make and test new inventions and to minimize the dangers of untested technologies. Activities include developing and testing hypotheses about the relative speed of falling objects and using trial and error to solve problems involving the load capacity of aluminum foil boats. Students also make scale drawings and then use the drawings to construct a model of a building that could withstand an earthquake. They make model gliders and refine them into model airplanes before exploring jet propulsion.

How People Invent is a 17-lesson unit. The conceptual goals of the unit are presented in the lesson-by-lesson story line in the teacher's guide. Each lesson also includes background information; a complete lesson plan, including suggestions for assessing performance and integrating the curriculum; and a list of the print, video, and software support materials required.

Prices: Teacher's Guide (ISBN 0-590-27747-2), $27. Student Book, $10. Complete unit, $450. Consumables kit, $76. ***Publisher/supplier:*** Scholastic. ***Materials:*** Available locally, from commercial suppliers, or in unit.

4.20 How Things Work. Life Lab Science. Seattle, Wash.: Videodiscovery, 1992.

Grades: 2, 3 In *How Things Work,* students build an indoor or outdoor garden to use as a laboratory throughout the year. They investigate structures in the natural world and discover how the smaller parts contribute to the way the whole structure works. Investigations are organized in 8 units: (1) Sensory Explorations, (2) Seeds, (3) Soil, (4) Weather and Climate, (5) Tools, (6) Plants, (7) Garden Animals, and (8) Habitats. Activities include students working in small groups as they make detailed observations about a plant, comparing seeds that "hitchhike" on fur with those that disperse in other ways, and performing a simple experiment to explore the capacity of various soils to hold water. In other activities, they record measurements from a weather station, explore how garden tools work as levers, compare the roots of watered and unwatered plants, and map animal movements on sand. Each unit integrates earth, life, and physical science concepts.

The 8 units consist of a total of 59 activities, typically 30 to 45 minutes long. For each unit the teacher's guide provides a planning calendar, an activity chart with a summary of each activity, and a book list. Each lesson plan provides background information, a list of the materials required, step-by-step instructions for preparing for and conducting the activity, suggestions for review and reinforcement, and extension ideas. A student lab book is available in both English and Spanish. A garden log, videodisc, music tape, and tool kit are available to supplement the teacher's guide.

Prices: Teacher's Guide (ISBN 1-56307-205-X), $80. Student Lab Book (ISBN 1-56307-204-1), $9. Life Lab Package, $575. Complete Life Lab Science Kit, $375. ***Publisher/ supplier:*** Videodiscovery. ***Materials:*** Available locally, from commercial suppliers, or in kits from Let's Get Growing.

4.21 Key Stage 1, Reception Teacher's File. New Horizons Science 5-16. Cambridge, England: Cambridge University Press, 1991.

Grade: K *Key Stage 1, Reception Teacher's File,* designed to meet British national curriculum standards, provides a range of ideas to give a science aspect to any theme, topic, or area of study in the kindergarten classroom. This teacher's guide is organized into 3 parts. Part 1 describes the use of interactive displays (that is, learning centers) in science activities. Part 2 provides ideas for science activities in 5 areas of "play"—domestic, water, sand, clay, and construction. In part 2, students experiment with objects that float and sink, compare the characteristics of wet and dry sand, and build a wall from toy bricks and test its strength. Part 3 includes science activities organized in 5 themes: living things and their environment, weather, materials, energy and forces, and ourselves. In part 3, students sort, weigh, and cook vegetables; test materials to see if they are waterproof; measure the capacity of a number of different bags; play with toy vehicles that move heavy loads; play a pairing game; and much more.

The teacher's guide for *Key Stage 1, Reception Teacher's File,* includes numerous photographs and provides complete instructions for each activity. It features 2 appendixes—on multicultural aspects of science education and on construction kits—and several reproducible masters. A set of 5 student workbooks corresponding to the 5 themes presented in part 3 are available.

Price: $53.30 (ISBN 0-521-39794-4). ***Publisher/supplier:*** Cambridge University Press. ***Materials:*** Available locally, or from commercial suppliers.

4.22 Key Stage 1, Y1-2, Teacher's File. New Horizons Science 5-16. Cambridge, England: Cambridge University Press, 1991.

Grades: 1, 2 *Key Stage 1, Y1-2, Teacher's File,* provides an introduction to New Horizons: Science 5-16, a curriculum designed to meet British national curriculum standards at key stage 1. The volume contains essential information about the development and design of the project and about the 22 modules to be used throughout Y1 and Y2 (year 1 and year 2) of the curriculum. This teacher's guide includes 10 of these modules. They focus on the following topics: weather, similarities and differences among humans, physical and chemical characteristics of materials, electricity, pushing and pulling forces, everyday waste products, and health and human safety. Each module contains (1) a plan of the module, (2) a summary of which statements of attainment are covered in the module and where they can be assessed, (3) a "thinking ahead" list of resources that may need to be organized in advance, (4) notes on presenting the module, (5) 5 activities with ideas for extensions, and (6) an exploration. Each module is self-contained and offers a series of scientific learning experiences that can be easily integrated in topics and themes common to primary classes. Several modules may be linked to provide a longer period of study.

Key Stage 1, Y1-2, Teacher's File, includes 10 modules. Copymasters, games, pupils' storybooks, and flip book pictures accompany the modules.

Price: $157 (ISBN 0-521-39795-2). ***Publisher/supplier:*** Cambridge University Press. ***Materials:*** Available locally, or from commercial suppliers.

4.23 Once Upon a GEMS Guide: Connecting Young People's Literature to Great Explorations in Math and Science. GEMS/Handbooks. Berkeley, Calif.: Lawrence Hall of Science, 1993.

Grades: Teacher Resource The *Once Upon a GEMS Guide* is an annotated bibliography of selected titles of young people's literature. The 3 major sections are (1) GEMS Guides, (2) Math Strands, and (3) Science Themes. The first section makes literature connections for 40 GEMS teacher's guides and provides a synopsis of the activities, including the concepts, skills, and themes addressed in each guide. The second section makes literature connections and provides definitions for 8 mathematics strands. The third section makes literature connections and provides definitions for 10 major themes in science. In each section, literary selections are listed alphabetically by title, with an estimated age range and an annotation. Many of the books consider ways that issues related to multicultural diversity, equality, and gender are involved in science and mathematics education.

Price: $24 (ISBN 0-912511-78-8). ***Publisher/supplier:*** LHS GEMS. ***Materials:*** Available locally, or from commercial suppliers.

4.24 Paper Towel Testing. GEMS. Cary I. Sneider and Jacqueline Barber. Berkeley, Calif.: Lawrence Hall of Science, 1987.

Grades: 5-6+ In *Paper Towel Testing,* students design and conduct scientific tests to compare the qualities of several brands of paper towels. Teams of students plan and conduct controlled experiments to determine which brand is most absorbent and which has the greatest wet strength. They discuss their results and plan and conduct follow-up experiments. Results are averaged and compared. After calculating the unit cost of each brand of paper towel, students reexamine their findings and discuss which brand is the best buy.

The guide includes detailed instructions for conducting each extension idea and provides summary outlines of the 4 sessions, which require 30 to 35 minutes each. Reproducible masters of student data sheets are included.

Price: $8.50. ***Publisher/supplier:*** LHS GEMS. ***Materials:*** Available locally, or from commercial suppliers.

4.25 Pollution. DSM. Hudson, N.H.: Delta Education, 1994.

Grades: 5, 6 This module introduces students to the concept of pollution. They explore solid waste disposal, air pollution, water pollution, and noise pollution. Activities include the following: students determine the average volume of paper waste that their classmates generate on a daily basis; they recycle old newspaper; they collect particles from the air and then determine their concentration level and infer their source; they construct a simple water filtration system; they test the pH of water samples; and they take a sound survey in their school.

Pollution includes 12 activities that require about 22 class sessions, typically 30 to 45 minutes long. The teacher's guide includes a module overview, a list of objectives for each activity, a planning schedule, background information, and preparation and materials management strategies. A complete lesson plan is provided for each lesson.

Prices: Teacher's Guide (ISBN 0-87504-107-8), $24.95. Kit, $245.00. ***Publisher/supplier:*** Delta Education. ***Materials:*** Available locally, from commercial suppliers, or in kit.

4.26 Science and Technology by Design: 1. Colin Webb. Sydney, Australia: Harcourt Brace Jovanovich, 1992.

Grades: 3, 4 The activities in *Science and Technology by Design: 1* involve investigating, designing, making, and using technology. The more than 100 activities are organized in 11 units. Among these activities, students investigate how things balance, distinguish between living and nonliving things, and explore the properties of water. They make a variety of things that demonstrate their understanding of heat as a form of energy, they explore light and vision, and they investigate the properties of materials and how they can be changed. Other activities include making and calibrating timing devices, designing constructions that explore the properties of air and wind, designing and making sound devices, and using constructions to investigate a number of mechanical principles.

Science and Technology by Design: 1 provides an introduction to each unit. The 2-page activities consist of a reproducible student page that presents the challenge and provides notes for the teacher that explain the scientific concept involved, along with ideas to stimulate discussion.

Price: Aust. $49.95 (ISBN 0-7295-2849-9). ***Publisher/supplier:*** Harcourt Brace, Australia. ***Materials:*** Available locally, or from commercial suppliers.

4.27 Science and Technology by Design: 2. Colin Webb. Sydney, Australia: Harcourt Brace Jovanovich, 1992.

Grades: 4-6 The activities in *Science and Technology by Design: 2* involve investigating, designing, making, and using technology. The nearly 100 activities are organized in 8 units. Students (1) design and make a variety of simple machines; (2) explore ideas about health, diet, and the need for exercise and sleep, and look at the five senses; (3) explore the properties and shapes of materials as they build various structures; (4) design, investigate, and solve problems using fibers; (5) develop an understanding of the nature of energy, methods of storing energy, uses of energy, and the effect different types of energy have on some materials; (6) investigate flying models, different types of animals that fly, how air can be used to do work, and how to make instruments that can measure the movement of air; (7) investigate playground animals and plants; and (8) consider how animals and people communicate.

Science and Technology by Design: 2 provides an introduction for each unit. The 2-page activities consist of a reproducible student page that presents the challenge, and provides notes for the teacher explaining the scientific concept involved, along with ideas to stimulate discussion.

Price: Aust. $49.50 (ISBN 0-7295-2851-0). ***Publisher/supplier:*** Harcourt Brace, Australia. ***Materials:*** Available locally, or from commercial suppliers.

4.28 Science and Technology by Design: 3. Colin Webb. Sydney, Australia: Harcourt Brace Jovanovich, 1992.

Grades: 4, 5 The activities in *Science and Technology by Design: 3* involve investigating, designing, making, and using technology. The nearly 100 activities are organized in 10 units. Students (1) design and calibrate simple measuring instruments; (2) use the activity of microorganisms in practical ways such as making bread, cottage cheese, and yogurt; (3) investigate structures built by animals, by various civilizations, and by contemporary society; (4) investigate space; (5) explore concepts related to the muscular and skeletal systems, body movement, circulation, respiration, diet, reactions, and learning; (6) investigate the use of levers, wheels, gears, and pulleys performing design tasks; (7) investigate the various forms of energy and the ways people use energy in their homes, for transport, and as food; (8) look at a variety of testing procedures, such as market research surveys; (9) investigate things that are used for entertainment; and (10) examine aspects of packaging.

Science and Technology by Design: 3 provides an introduction for each unit. The 2-page activities consist of a reproducible student page that presents the challenge, and provides notes for the teacher explaining the scientific concept involved, along with ideas to stimulate discussion.

Price: Aust. $49.95 (ISBN 0-7295-2854-5). ***Publisher/supplier:*** Harcourt Brace, Australia. ***Materials:*** Available locally, or from commercial suppliers.

4.29 STAR Mystery Lab. STAR. Washington, D.C.: Reading Is Fundamental, 1994.

Grades: 3, 4 Students use the scientific method to solve a mystery in *STAR Mystery Lab.* A story narrative sets the scene for a series of investigations. Students use the techniques of fingerprinting and paper chromatography to identify a mysterious classroom intruder. Students sharpen their observation skills as they examine common objects, describe their properties, and provide an eyewitness account of an unexpected event they observe. They investigate the popular genre of mysteries, or detective fiction, to discover connections between detective work and problem solving in the science lab, the crime lab, and mystery reading.

STAR Mystery Lab includes ideas for cross-curricular integration, such as organizing a news team to "cover the case" and plotting a fictional mystery. It also includes a list of resources, including books, computer software, and audiovisual materials.

Prices: Teacher's Guide, $21.90. Mentor's Guide, $3.90. ***Publisher/supplier:*** Kendall/Hunt. ***Materials:*** Available locally, or from commercial suppliers.

4.30 Vitamin C Testing. GEMS. Jacqueline Barber. Reprinted with revisions. Berkeley, Calif.: Lawrence Hall of Science, 1990.

Grades: 4-6+ *Vitamin C Testing* offers an introduction to chemistry and nutrition by providing students with the materials and techniques needed to test the vitamin C content in common juices. Students learn to use the chemical technique titration. They compare the vitamin C content of different juices and graph the results. For more advanced study students examine the effects of heat and freezing (or other treatment) on vitamin C content. The skills developed in this unit include performing chemistry lab techniques, experimenting, analyzing data, and graphing and drawing conclusions. Summary outlines help the teacher guide students through the activities. All materials are available in local stores except for the indicator chemical (indophenol) and plastic vials, which can be ordered from a scientific supply company.

The lesson plan for each of the 4 sessions of 45 minutes each includes an overview, a materials list, and detailed instructions for preparing for and conducting the activity. The guide includes reproducible masters of student data sheets.

Price: $8.50 (ISBN 0-912511-70-2). ***Publisher/supplier:*** LHS GEMS. ***Materials:*** Available locally, or from commercial suppliers.

4.31 The Voyage of the Mimi: Ecosystems With Island Survivors. Bank Street College Project in Science and Mathematics. Scotts Valley, Calif.: Wings for Learning, 1992.

Grades: 5-6+ *Ecosystems With Island Survivors,* a learning module derived from *The Voyage of the Mimi* video series, introduces students to the essential elements of ecosystems and the relationships among these systems. Food chains and food webs are emphasized. The software, which is an integral part of this unit, features a game called "Island Survivors," a 2-part program in which students select 8 species—4 that live on land and 4 that live in a pond—to inhabit an island ecosystem. Students can change the population levels of the species and manipulate other variables to test their effects on the ecosystem. The goal is to keep the species alive for a year without destroying the island ecosystem.

This curriculum module features 3 components: a student guide, teacher's guide, and software. The student guide is a book of readings and activities about ecosystems; it contains a description of the software, as well as instructions for using it. The teacher's guide contains discussion questions and activity ideas for the topics covered in the student guide, as well as reproducible masters, extension activities, and lesson plans for using the software and worksheets.

Prices: Teacher's Guide, $20.00. Student Guide, $3.95. Complete module, Macintosh/Windows, $99.00; Apple, $79.00. ***Publisher/supplier:*** Sunburst Communications. ***Materials:*** Available locally, from commercial suppliers, or from distributor.

4.32 The Voyage of the Mimi: Language Arts Resource Guide. Bank Street College Project in Science and Mathematics. Laurie Weisman. Scotts Valley, Calif.: Wings for Learning, 1990.

Grades: Teacher Resource *The Voyage of the Mimi: Language Arts Resource Guide* is a guide to using *The Voyage of the Mimi* video series in language arts lessons. Activities take a variety of forms, such as public speaking, drama, prose, poetry, mapping, writing, and music. They include, for example, writing character descriptions of the *Mimi's* crew members; keeping a journal of the voyage; discussing how bird songs compare with whale songs; preparing a series of newscasts based on the events of the voyage; and looking analytically at the impact of audiovisual techniques used in the video series.

For each of the 26 video segments in the series, the guide includes a plot summary, discussion questions, several diverse language arts activities, and suggested resources for further investigation. The guide also includes a nautical glossary, a bibliography, and reproducible fact sheets on topics from whaling and Native American culture to "salty yarns."

Price: $39. ***Publisher/supplier:*** Sunburst Communications. ***Materials:*** Available locally, from commercial suppliers, or from distributor.

4.33 The Voyage of the Mimi: Maps and Navigation with Navigation Computer Activities. Bank Street College Project in Science and Mathematics. New York, N.Y.: Holt, Rinehart and Winston, 1985.

Grades: 5-6+ *Maps and Navigation* is a learning module derived from the content of *The Voyage of the Mimi* video series. Activities relate to the navigation skills and instruments seen in various video segments of the series. Students learn the concepts, skills, and tools that help navigators find their way at sea, then apply those skills in computer-based activities. They learn the fundamentals of navigation to find buried treasure, avoid a hurricane, and pinpoint their ship's location. The culminating activity is a navigation simulation in which students apply map skills and mathematical concepts to find a fishing trawler that has accidentally caught a humpback whale in its net.

The module consists of a teacher's guide, a student guide, and 4 software games.

Prices: Teacher's Guide for Apple (ISBN 0-03-000974-X), $20.00. Student Guide, $3.95. Complete package, Macintosh/Windows, $99.00; Apple, $79.00. ***Publisher/supplier:*** Sunburst Communications. ***Materials:*** Available locally, from commercial suppliers, or from distributor.

4.34 The Voyage of the Mimi: Overview Guide. Bank Street College Project in Science and Mathematics. Pleasantville, N.Y.: Sunburst/Wings for Learning, 1985.

Grades: 5-6+ *The Voyage of the Mimi: Overview Guide* provides lessons and activities for each segment of *The Voyage of the Mimi* video series. The series consists of 26 segments—13 dramatic episodes, each followed by a documentary-style expedition that takes students to aquariums, museums, and other places where people are doing scientific work related to whales, sailing ships, and oceans. The *Overview Guide* shows how the various components of the unit are linked. This guide includes a lesson plan for each segment of the video series. Each lesson plan has questions for class discussion, activities and opportunities for making connections with other components of *The Voyage of the Mimi* materials or other aspects of this curriculum. The guide includes 25 pages of background information on whales, blackline masters for use with student activities, and a metric/English-measurement conversion chart.

Prices: $30. ***Publisher/supplier:*** Sunburst Communications. ***Materials:*** Available locally, from commercial suppliers, or from distributor.

4.35 The Voyage of the Mimi: The Book. Bank Street College Project in Science and Mathematics. Scotts Valley, Calif.: Wings for Learning, 1985.

Grades: 5-6+ *The Voyage of the Mimi: The Book* is the student guide for *The Voyage of the Mimi* curriculum. Through the video series, computer navigation activities, learning modules, and other components, students are taken on a voyage to study humpback whales in the Gulf of Maine. Along the way they study such science topics as electricity, sound, animal classification, and ecology. Students identify individual humpback whales by their fluke pattern; they learn how information is gathered from the ocean floor; they learn to construct a solar still to convert seawater into fresh water; they analyze patterns of whale sounds; and they learn how to estimate a whale population.

The student guide contains 13 sections, each including a narrative episode of the story; an account from an aquarium, museum, or other place where people are doing scientific work about whales, sailing ships, or the ocean; and one or more activities. The book has color photographs and illustrations and a glossary of reference terms. This guide must be used in conjunction with *The Voyage of the Mimi* video series and teacher's guides.

Price: $9.95 (ISBN 1-55826-149-4). ***Publisher/supplier:*** Sunburst Communications. ***Materials:*** Available locally.

4.36 The Voyage of the Mimi: Whales and Their Environments. Bank Street College Project in Science and Mathematics. Theodore Ducas and Sara Ann Friedman. New York, N.Y.: Holt, Rinehart and Winston, 1985.

Grades: 5-6+ *Whales and Their Environments,* a learning module derived from *The Voyage of the Mimi* video series, is about the environments of whales and people. An integral part of this module is The Bank Street Laboratory, a combination of software and hardware that allows students to collect, store, display, and analyze information about 3 physical phenomena—heat and temperature, sound, and light. Students examine the effects of these phenomena on the lives and environment of humans and whales. The activities are designed to explore the properties of the phenomena through a variety of measurement and display formats. Examples of activities include comparing temperature scales, testing insulators, measuring heat loss, exploring the loudness of sound, investigating the frequency of sound, measuring the speed of sound, investigating light intensity and distance from the source, scattering light, and measuring reflection.

Each activity includes the materials needed, steps for procedure, and background information. The Bank Street Laboratory consists of an interface board and 6 sensors, which measure temperature, loudness and pitch of sounds, and the intensity of light.

Prices: Teacher's Guide, $20.00. Student Guide, $3.95. Complete module, Macintosh/Windows, $495.00; Apple, $390.00. ***Publisher/supplier:*** Sunburst Communications. ***Materials:*** Available locally, from commercial suppliers, or from distributor.

MULTIDISCIPLINARY AND APPLIED SCIENCE—SCIENCE ACTIVITY BOOKS

ABOUT THE ANNOTATIONS IN "MULTIDISCIPLINARY AND APPLIED SCIENCE—SCIENCE ACTIVITY BOOKS"

Entry Numbers

Curriculum materials are arranged alphabetically by title in each category (Core Materials, Supplementary Materials, and Science Activity Books) in chapters 1 through 4 of this guide. In addition, each annotation has a two-part entry number. For each entry number, the chapter number is given before the period; the number after the period locates the entry within that chapter.

For example, the first entry number in chapter 1 is 1.1; the second entry in chapter 2 is 2.2, and so on.

The entry numbers within each curriculum chapter run consecutively through Core Materials, Supplementary Materials, and Science Activity Books.

Order of Bibliographic Information

Following is the arrangement of the facts of publication in the annotations in this section:

- **Title of publication.**
- **Series title**, or series acronym if commonly used.
- **Authors** (either individual names or organizational author).
- Name and location of **developer** (in parentheses), if different from publisher.
- **Place of publication, publisher, and date of publication.**

Series Acronyms

Following are **acronyms of series titles** in "Multidisciplinary and Applied Science—Science Activity Books." (Series titles that are spelled out are not included in this list.)

AIMS Activities Integrating Mathematics and Science
CEPUP Chemical Education for Public Understanding Program
CESI Council for Elementary Science International
ESE Exciting Science and Engineering
GEMS Great Explorations in Math and Science

Price and Acquisition Information

Ordering information is presented in a block immediately below the annotation. Included are the following:

- **Prices** of teacher's guides, activity books, and kits or units.
- The name of a principal **publisher/supplier** (not necessarily the sole source) for the items listed in the price category. (The address and phone and fax numbers for each publisher and supplier appear in appendix A, "Publishers and Suppliers.")
- An indication of the various sources from which one might obtain the required **materials.**

4.37 The Art and Science Connection: Hands-on Activities for Intermediate Students. Kimberley Trolley. Menlo Park, Calif.: Addison-Wesley Publishing Co., 1994.

Grades: 4-6 *The Art and Science Connection* for intermediate students is a sourcebook of creative art activities that integrate art and science concepts and processes. The 30 lessons are organized around 3 conceptual themes of science—structure, interactions, and energy. Activities include drawing, painting, sculpture, bas-relief, printmaking, collage, graphic arts, textiles, and mixed media.

Each lesson includes an overview, student objectives, a list of materials, step-by-step teaching instructions, extension ideas, and suggested resources. Blackline masters for activity sheets, tips for classroom management and working with art and science materials, safety precautions, and a glossary are included.

Price: $19.96 (ISBN 0-201-45545-5). ***Publisher/supplier:*** Addison-Wesley. ***Materials:*** Available locally, or from commercial suppliers.

4.38 The Art and Science Connection: Hands-On Activities for Primary Students. Kimberley Trolley. Menlo Park, Calif.: Addison-Wesley Publishing Co., 1993.

Grades: K-2 *The Art and Science Connection* for primary students is a sourcebook of creative art activities that integrate art and science concepts and processes. The 30 lessons are organized around 3 conceptual themes of science—structure, interactions, and energy. Activities include drawing, painting, sculpture, bas-relief, printmaking, collage, graphic arts, and mixed media.

Each lesson includes an overview, student objectives, a list of materials, step-by-step teaching instructions, extension ideas, and suggested resources. Blackline masters for activity sheets and tips for classroom management are also included.

Price: $19.96 (ISBN 0-201-45544-7). ***Publisher/supplier:*** Addison-Wesley. ***Materials:*** Available locally, or from commercial suppliers.

4.39 Beyond the Classroom: Exploration of Schoolground and Backyard. Charles E. Roth, Cleti Cervoni, Thomas Wellnitz, and Elizabeth Arms. Rev. ed. Lincoln, Mass.: Massachusetts Audubon Society, 1991.

Grades: K-6+ *Beyond the Classroom* uses the school's immediate surroundings as a convenient, familiar natural laboratory. Activities in earth science focus on weather, sky phenomena, erosion and deposition, snow studies, and the water cycle. Life science activities concentrate on animal behavior, plant distribution, plant life cycles, and plant and animal adaptations. Physical science activities include those on simple machines, insulation, energy at work, and materials characteristics.

This volume provides a complete lesson plan for each of its 33 activities. *Beyond the Classroom* was originally entitled *Schoolground Science: Activities for Elementary and Middle Schools.*

Price: $9.95. ***Publisher/supplier:*** Massachusetts Audubon Society. ***Materials:*** Available locally, or from commercial suppliers.

4.40 Chemicals, Health, Environment, and Me (CHEM). CEPUP. Berkeley, Calif.: Lawrence Hall of Science, 1991.

Grades: 5-6+ *Chemicals, Health, Environment, and Me* is a series of 10 units on the nature of chemicals and how they interact with the environment. Students learn to collect, process, and analyze information and to use scientific evidence as a basis for life-style-oriented decisions. The units can be used in any order. They focus on (1) the physical and chemical properties of common substances; (2) food additives; (3) sugar and sugar additives; (4) the threshold of toxicity; (5) smoking and health; (6) qualitative tests used to identify chemicals in highway spills; (7) the identification and disposal of potentially hazardous chemicals; (8) waste disposal and reduction; (9) the carbon cycle; and (10) the contribution of carbon dioxide to the "greenhouse effect."

The *Chemicals, Health, Environment, and Me* program consists of a printed teacher's guide and a complete materials and equipment kit. Each unit contains one or more basic activities as well as ideas for expanding the topic. Each activity has a complete lesson plan and focuses on a single concept. Reproducible blackline masters of student activity sheets are included.

Prices: Teacher's Guide, $24.99. Kit, $125.99. ***Publisher/supplier:*** Sargent-Welch Scientific Co. ***Materials:*** Available locally, from commercial suppliers, or in kit.

4.41 Conserve and Renew: An Energy Education Activity Package for Grades 4-6. Leeann Tourtillot. Rohnert Park, Calif.: The Regional School Energy Extension Project, Energy Center, Sonoma State University, 1990.

Grades: 4-6 *Conserve and Renew* is a collection of energy-education activities on conservation and renewable energy resources. Activities may be used as a unit, or individually, to complement existing curricula. The guide is divided in 6 sections, which focus on (1) what energy is, (2) renewable energy sources, (3) how they are used, (4) energy conservation, (5) recycling, and (6) ethical issues involved in solving energy-related problems. Activities include growing seedlings under varied light conditions and observing their relative growth; analyzing the energy flow and resources used in everyday products; creating strategies for recycling; and role-playing members of the United Nations to debate how to distribute the world's energy resources.

Each section of *Conserve and Renew* has from 3 to 5 investigative activities and several "paper and pencil" activities. Each investigation includes a complete lesson plan. The guide provides a glossary and an annotated bibliography.

Price: $12. ***Publisher/supplier:*** SSU Academic Foundation. ***Materials:*** Available locally, or from commercial suppliers.

4.42 Constructions. Windows on Elementary Science. Joan Westley. Sunnyvale, Calif.: Creative Publications, 1988.

Grades: PreK, K-2 In *Constructions,* students make walls, ramps, bridges, towers, teeter-totters, and wheeled vehicles as they investigate the physics of force, motion, and equilibrium. They classify building materials by strength, weight, and other properties; they observe objects moving down slopes; they investigate chain reactions; and they build a pulley elevator. The 28 activities are sequenced by increasing level of difficulty but do not need to be done in order.

Each 2-page activity has a summary statement describing the investigation, a list of the skills and necessary materials, and directions on how to set up for instruction. Also included are sections on getting started, guiding children's actions, and stretching their thinking.

Prices: Teacher's Guide (ISBN 0-88488-711-1), $13.75. Complete kit, $250.00. ***Publisher/supplier:*** Creative Publications. ***Materials:*** Available locally, from commercial suppliers, or in kit.

4.43 Cooperative Learning—Science: Activities, Experiments and Games. Esther Weiner. New York, N.Y.: Scholastic Professional Books, 1992.

Grades: 3-5 *Cooperative Learning—Science* brings students together in cooperative working groups and integrates science with other curriculum areas. Expository writing skills are emphasized as students write hypotheses and complete observations and conclusions for experiments ranging from physics to food webs. Activities include using Jello to discover that warmer molecules move more quickly than cooler ones do; using chromatography to discover the chemicals present in a leaf; going on an arthropod hunt; and creating a domino derby to test energy transfer within a system.

Cooperative Learning—Science offers an extensive introduction to combining hands-on science activities with cooperative learning. Included are teaching techniques for cooperative learning, suggestions for division of labor, assessing academic skills, and dealing with shy or uncooperative students. The book offers 20 activities of about 30 to 50 minutes each. Except for the games, each activity includes a statement of the science concepts involved, background information, a section on cooperative group management, a list of materials needed, suggestions for getting started, step-by-step procedures, ideas for integrating science with other curriculum areas, and reproducible data sheets.

Price: $12.95 (ISBN 0-590-49240-3). ***Publisher/supplier:*** Scholastic Professional Books. ***Materials:*** Available locally, or from commercial suppliers.

4.44 Discovery Science: Explorations for the Early Years. David A. Winnett, Robert A. Williams, Elizabeth A. Sherwood, and Robert E. Rockwell. Menlo Park, Calif.: Addison-Wesley Publishing Co., 1994.

Grades: K, 1 *Discovery Science: Explorations for the Early Years* offers more than 100 activities in 4 topic areas—magnets, rocks and soil, animals, and plants. In each of these units, the activities are sequenced to build the science process skills of observing, classifying, organizing, and communicating. Activities include measuring the relative strength of magnets; making soil from sand, clay, and humus; comparing the breathing mechanisms of various animals; and photographing plants over time to explore the growth cycle.

Each unit in *Discovery Science* includes an introduction with background information, ideas for free discovery, and storytelling activities; a complete lesson plan for each activity; checkpoint activities for assessing student progress; and activities for providing additional stimulation. Lesson plans include suggestions for integrating other areas of the curriculum. The guide also includes guidelines and suggestions for setting up a discovery center, creating charts and journals, and involving families.

Price: $33.63 (ISBN 0-201-29063-4). ***Publisher/supplier:*** Addison-Wesley. ***Materials:*** Available locally, or from commercial suppliers.

4.45 The Energy Sourcebook: Elementary Unit. Pat Barnett, Judy Bowman, Nancy Causey, and others. Knoxville, Tenn.: Tennessee Valley Authority, 1992.

Grades: 3-6 In *The Energy Sourcebook: Elementary Unit,* students learn to define energy and characterize its forms. They investigate the nature, conduction, generation, and use of electrical energy and examine solar energy and energy from wind, water, and wood. Students learn about the environmental effects of producing and using energy, and they identify applications of energy-saving techniques and why they are important. Various resource-use topics pertinent to the Tennessee Valley region are examined. Activities include making an energy bulletin board, hunting for examples of unsafe electricity use, constructing a simple solar air heater, and listing major causes of and ways to reduce air pollution. In other activities, students compare average monthly electricity usage and match energy-using devices and activities to their appropriate eras.

The Energy Sourcebook provides a complete lesson plan for each of its 47 activities. Some activities include reproducible masters for transparencies and student worksheets. A set of fact sheets provides teachers with information on energy topics.

Price: $35. ***Publisher/supplier:*** Tennessee Valley Authority. ***Materials:*** Available locally, or from commercial suppliers.

4.46 Environmental Education Activity Guide: Pre K-8. Project Learning Tree. Washington, D.C.: American Forest Foundation, 1993.

Grades: K-6 Project Learning Tree's *Environmental Education Activity Guide: Pre K-8* provides activities for investigating environmental issues and encourages students to make informed, responsible decisions. The guide has 5 major themes: (1) diversity, (2) interrelationships, (3) systems, (4) structure and scale, and (5) patterns of change. Each theme has activities in the following areas: environment, resource management and technology, and society and culture. The activities integrate the themes within science, language arts, social studies, art, music, and physical education. Among the activities, for example, students become habitat pen pals and write to each other from the perspective of organisms living in a habitat; they examine rotting logs to learn about decomposition, as well as microhabitats and communities; they role-play managers of a piece of public forest; they learn how land-use decisions and legislation affect wetlands; and they examine the pros and cons of various packaging strategies.

The *Environmental Education Activity Guide* provides a complete lesson plan for each of its nearly 100 activities. The guide also features a glossary and appendixes, including teaching suggestions for controversial issues, multicultural education, working with exceptional students, and teaching outdoors.

Price: Free to teachers who attend a workshop in their own state. ***Publisher/supplier:*** American Forest Foundation. ***Materials:*** Available locally, or from commercial suppliers.

4.47 Exploring Ocean Ecosystems: Curriculum Guide. Zoobooks. San Diego, Calif.: Wildlife Education, 1994.

Grades: 5-6+ This guide tells the story of an ocean ecosystem and how humans interact with it. The module consists of 10 lessons grouped in 3 units—(1) Ocean Ecosystems, (2) Animal Adaptations, and (3) Humans and the Ocean Ecosystems. Students explore the living and nonliving components of an ecosystem by setting up an aquarium or terrarium or by exploring a local mini-ecosystem. Structural and behavioral adaptations are demonstrated and investigated through simulations, games, and classroom projects. In the final unit, students participate in simulations of city council meetings and TV news shows as they examine interactions between humans and ocean ecosystems.

The *Exploring Ocean Ecosystems* module includes a curriculum guide; 8 Zoobooks *titles—Sharks, Whales, Seals and Sea Lions, Seabirds, Dolphins and Porpoises, Sea Otters, Penguins,* and *Turtles;* a teaching strategies supplement; and reproducible student activity sheets.

Prices: Complete Classroom Set, $94.00. Basic Set with one copy each of Curriculum Guide (ISBN 0-937934-93-3), Supplement (ISBN 0-937934-94-1), and magazines, $59.75. Set with Curriculum Guide and Supplement, $39.95. ***Publisher/supplier:*** Wildlife Education. ***Materials:*** Available locally, or from commercial suppliers.

4.48 Farmer McGregor's Greenhouse. ESE. Heslington, York, UK: Chemical Industry Education Centre, and BP International, 1990.

Grades: 4-6 *Farmer McGregor's Greenhouse* gives students the opportunity to design, build, and test a model greenhouse. They first discuss the uses of greenhouses and the types of plants that are commonly grown in them. Students explore factors involved in greenhouse design, and then they design and build a scale model using straws or balsa wood and plastic wrap. They test methods of strengthening the structure to withstand potential storms, and they measure temperature inside the greenhouse and consider ways of controlling the temperature. Finally, students test the effectiveness of their greenhouse by germinating seeds and growing plants in it; they monitor plant growth over several weeks. The unit is designed to be planned and executed by a teacher and an engineer working together.

Farmer McGregor's Greenhouse includes an overview, activity outlines, a summary for the engineer, and reproducible masters for transparencies and student worksheets.

Price: US$8 (ISBN 0-86165-203-7). ***Publisher/supplier:*** Chemical Industry Education Centre. ***Materials:*** Available locally, or from commercial suppliers.

4.49 Fingerprinting. GEMS. Jeremy J. Ahouse. Reprinted with revisions. Berkeley, Calif.: Lawrence Hall of Science, 1989.

Grades: 4-6+ Students explore the similarities and variations of fingerprints in *Fingerprinting.* They take their own fingerprints, devise a scheme for classifying fingerprints, and apply their classification skills to solve a crime. In session 1 students use pencils, paper, and tape to take their fingerprints. In session 2 they group 10 different fingerprints according to the way they look. Students are then introduced to the standard arch-loop-whorl system of fingerprint classification. In the final session, they apply their knowledge of fingerprints to determine which of 5 suspects robbed a safe. The mystery scenario, "Who Robbed the Safe?" includes plot and character sketches. Examples of extension activities include fingerprint art, an introduction to genetics, and role-playing news reporters covering the crime scene.

Fingerprinting includes 3 or 4 sessions of 30 to 60 minutes each. The lesson plan for each session includes an overview, a list of materials, blackline masters of student worksheets, and complete instructions for planning and conducting the activity.

Price: $8.50. ***Publisher/supplier:*** LHS GEMS. ***Materials:*** Available locally, or from commercial suppliers.

4.50 Hands-On Environmental Science Activities. Eugene Kutscher. Annapolis, Md.: Alpha Publishing Co., 1991.

Grades: 5-6+ *Hands-On Environmental Science Activities* offers 40 activities organized in 8 sections: (1) Ecology, (2) Energy, (3) Conservation and the Earth's Resources, (4) Human and Animal Populations, (5) Pollution, (6) Making a Difference, (7) Politics and Economics, and (8) Games for Concerned Citizens. Activities include building a model of a fossil fuel generator, monitoring personal consumption of fresh water, and investigating methods of treating oil spills. In other activities, students simulate the greenhouse effect, observe how crowding affects the behavior of insects, and participate in an exercise about a social dilemma.

A teacher's guide is included with each activity in *Hands-On Environmental Science Activities.* The guide includes the activity's goal, a list of student objectives, suggestions for a prelab discussion, instructions for the investigation, a short vocabulary list, and a list of additional resources and suggestions for further study. Reproducible masters for student data sheets must be purchased separately.

Prices: Teacher's Guide (ISBN 1-56506-000-8), $44.95. Student version, $44.95. ***Publisher/supplier:*** Alpha. ***Materials:*** Available locally, or from commercial suppliers.

4.51 Helping Your Child Learn Science. Nancy Paulu and Margery Martin. Washington, D.C.: U.S. Department of Education, Office of Educational Research and Improvement, 1991.

Grades: K-5 Parents take center stage in *Helping Your Child Learn Science,* an activity book that brings the classroom into the home and community. The activities in the guide focus on such scientific phenomena as inertia, surface tension, buoyancy, and photosynthesis. Examples of activities include demonstrating capillary action using celery stalks and food coloring; searching the neighborhood for bugs and identifying them; making an adhesive material; and testing the effects of temperature and light on mold. The book's introduction includes tips for parents on teaching science to their children and has a section on the basics of science.

Each of the 16 activities includes a short introduction, a materials list, step-by-step instructions, and an information box explaining the scientific concept being addressed. The book includes a section on science activities in the community, tips on how parents can get involved with their children's school science program, and a list of science books and magazines.

Price: $3.25. ***Publisher/supplier:*** U.S. Government Printing Office. ***Materials:*** Available locally, or from commercial suppliers.

4.52 How Sport Works. An Ontario Science Centre Book. Toronto, Ontario, Canada: Kids Can Press, 1988.

Grades: 5, 6 *How Sport Works* is a book of fact-filled articles and science experiments that touch on everything from how baseballs curve to how your brain and body type affect your performance. The book presents facts about muscles, the origin of the racer's crouch, animal athletics, proper warm-up techniques, how dimples affect the flight of golf balls, and other sports/scientific concepts. Activities include students learning about vibration and transfer of energy by determining the sweet spot on a baseball bat; measuring their lung capacity and leaping ability; testing their ability to recognize and respond to patterns like hockey players do; and testing principles of aerodynamics using Frisbees.

How Sport Works features more than 50 activities and articles.

Price: $5.95 (ISBN 1-921103-56-5). ***Publisher/supplier:*** Addison-Wesley. ***Materials:*** Available locally, or from commercial suppliers.

4.53 Idea Factory's Super Science Sourcebook II. Sandi Schlichting and Marilyn Blackmer. Riverview, Fla.: Idea Factory, 1989.

Grades: 1-6 The activities and lessons in *Idea Factory's Super Science Sourcebook II* are in 6 sections: (1) Earth Science, (2) Life Science, (3) Physical Science, (4) Science in the Library, (5) Great Graphing, and (6) Science Trivia. The sections on earth, life, and physical science have 5 or 6 subtopics, with several activities for each subtopic. Activities in these 3 sections include making a wave machine, simulating the ecolocation behavior of bats, and constructing an electrical circuit tester. The section on Science in the Library identifies numerous examples of children's fiction that may be used as a stimulus for science activities. The graphing section contains several graphing activities with blank graph forms. Science Trivia focuses on motivating students to use reference materials and resources.

Idea Factory's Super Science Sourcebook II contains approximately 75 activities in the sections on earth, life, and physical science. Each activity includes an objective, a list of materials, and instructions. Some activities include background information. An index is included.

Price: $19.95. ***Publisher/supplier:*** Idea Factory. ***Materials:*** Available locally, or from commercial suppliers.

4.54 The Inventive Thinking Curriculum Project. Project XL, U.S. Patent and Trademark Office. Washington, D.C.: U.S. Patent and Trademark Office, 1990.

Grades: 1-6+ *The Inventive Thinking Curriculum Project* encourages students to develop their creative potential and synthesize and apply knowledge and skills by creating an invention or innovation to solve a problem. The introduction to this teacher's guide includes 3 models for teaching thinking skills. It presents 12 activities: (1) Introducing Inventive Thinking, (2) Practicing the Creative Part of Inventive Thinking, (3) Practicing Inventive Thinking with the Class, (4) Developing an Invention Idea, (5) Brainstorming for Creative Solutions, (6) Practicing the Critical Parts of Inventive Thinking, (7) Completing the Invention, (8) Naming the Invention, (9) Optional Marketing Activities, (10) Parent Involvement, (11) Young Inventors' Day, and (12) Enrichment—Stories about Great Thinkers and Inventors and Problem-Solving Competitions.

The Inventive Thinking Curriculum Project is designed to be used across all disciplines and grade levels. Copymasters are included.

Price: Free of charge. ***Publisher/supplier:*** U.S. Patent and Trademark Office. ***Materials:*** Available locally, or from commercial suppliers.

4.55 Investigating Your Environment: The MINI Edition. Ogden, Utah: U.S. Forest Service, Intermountain Region, 1994.

Grades: 4-6+ *Investigating Your Environment: The MINI Edition,* a multidisciplinary approach to environmental science activities, contains the 11 most popular chapters from the original 21-chapter version of the volume. The first chapter, on developing an environmental investigation, offers teachers suggestions with respect to developing instructional objectives, question sequences, and lesson plans, among other topics. The remaining chapters focus on forests, interpreting the environment, investigating an environmental issue, land use simulation, natural resources in an urban environment, plant relationships, schoolyard activities, soil, water, and wildlife.

Each chapter includes an introduction, a sketch of its activities, suggestions for combining the activities, a section on curriculum relationships, and fully developed lesson plans, including reproducible planning and data sheets.

Price: Free of charge to educators in response to request on school letterhead. ***Publisher/supplier:*** U.S. Forest Service, Intermountain Region. ***Materials:*** Available locally.

4.56 The Jumbo Book of Science: 136 of the Best Experiments From the Ontario Science Centre. Carol Gold. Ontario Science Centre Books. Toronto, Canada: Kids Can Press, 1994.

Grades: 4-6+ *The Jumbo Book of Science* contains 136 activities and experiments that demonstrate simple scientific phenomena using inexpensive, easy-to-find materials. The activities in this book originally appeared in *Scienceworks, Foodworks,* and *How Sport Works.* They cover topics from how helmets protect one's head to how one becomes a footprint detective. Activities include examining fingerprints under a microscope; using static electricity to pick up pieces of paper and attract water and ping-pong balls; making a solar water cleaner; and building a periscope to see around corners.

The 1- and 2-page activities include lively illustrations, background information, fascinating facts, and step-by-step instructions.

Price: US$10 (ISBN 1-55074-197-7). ***Publisher/supplier:*** University of Toronto Press. ***Materials:*** Available locally, or from commercial suppliers.

4.57 Literature-Based Science Activities: An Integrated Approach. Audrey Brainard and Denise H. Wrubel. New York, N.Y.: Scholastic Professional Books, 1993.

Grades: K-3 *Literature-Based Science Activities* links children's books with science concepts. It highlights children's books that can be used to introduce, extend, or enrich the science content for each of 20 topics: shadows, sound, simple machines, time, seeds and plants, trees, apples, seasons, air, weather, eyes-noses-feet, minibeasts, animal homes, birds, whales, dinosaurs, taking care of our world, reduce-reuse-recycle, the Milky Way Galaxy, and inside and outside planet earth. The section for each topic includes a short synopsis of and activities correlated to each highlighted book, as well as background information, a list of other literature tie-ins, relevant pre- and post-reading activities, suggestions for field trips and invited guests, and reproducible student worksheets. The topic of time, for example, highlights *The Grouchy Ladybug,* by Eric Carle. In the activities related to this book, students measure and compare the length of time required to do certain tasks, measure the size of some of the animals Grouchy Ladybug encounters, find items in the class that are about the same size, and write a class story.

Price: $12.95 (ISBN 0-590-49200-4). ***Publisher/supplier:*** Scholastic Professional Books. ***Materials:*** Available locally.

4.58 Nonpoint Source Pollution Prevention: Grades K-2. Environmental Resource Guides. (Developed by Tennessee Valley Authority, Environmental Education Section.) Pittsburgh, Pa.: Air and Waste Management Association, 1993.

Grades: See this annotation for recommended grade levels. Defining, finding, and preventing or cleaning up nonpoint-source water pollution is the focus of this guide. Its 8 activities and 10 fact sheets provide basic information on the relationships between land use and water quality. It includes activities on agricultural, mining, forestry, and urban sources of pollution. Activities focus on the 4 main types of water pollutants—sediment, nutrients, bacteria, and toxics. Students learn to describe and understand what a water cycle is; they simulate situations where runoff would occur; they observe how pollutants affect water over time; and they observe how groundwater can be polluted by fertilizers, animal wastes, and chemicals. Although the guide identifies the activities as appropriate for grades K through 2, reviewers found them more appropriate for grades 3 and 4.

A complete lesson plan is provided for each activity, including reproducible masters for transparencies and student worksheets. The guide contains an extensive glossary.

Prices: $30. ($20 for A&WMA members). ***Publisher/supplier:*** Air and Waste Management Association (A&WMA). ***Materials:*** Available locally, or from commercial suppliers.

4.59 Nonpoint Source Pollution Prevention: Grades 3-5. Environmental Resource Guides. (Developed by Tennessee Valley Authority, Environmental Education Section.) Pittsburgh, Pa.: Air and Waste Management Association, 1993.

Grades: See this annotation for recommended grade levels. *Nonpoint Source Pollution Prevention* focuses on raising awareness of what has become the largest source of water pollution in the United States—nonpoint-source pollution. The guide's 15 activities and 10 fact sheets provide basic information on the relationships between land use and water quality. It includes activities on agricultural, mining, forest, and urban sources of pollution. Activities focus on the 4 main types of water pollutants—sediment, nutrients, bacteria, and toxics. Students identify water pollutants in a simulated pond; they observe algae growth caused by excess fertilizer use; they trace the movement of water in underground storm sewer systems; and they construct and observe a model landfill. Although the guide identifies the activities as appropriate for grades 3 through 5, reviewers found them more appropriate for grades 4 through 6.

A complete lesson plan is provided for each activity, including reproducible masters for transparencies and student worksheets. It also contains an extensive glossary.

Prices: $30. ($20 for A&WMA members). ***Publisher/supplier:*** Air and Waste Management Association (A&WMA). ***Materials:*** Available locally, or from commercial suppliers.

4.60 Our Wonderful World: Solutions for Math + Science. AIMS. Fresno, Calif.: AIMS Education Foundation, 1986.

Grades: 5-6+ The activities in *Our Wonderful World: Solutions for Math + Science* focus on understanding the natural environment. Investigations are organized in 6 topic areas—air, water, transpiration, soil, plants, and animals/insects. Students are involved in activities such as analyzing the volume of snow, comparing habitats, classifying soils and categorizing leaves by their characteristics, exploring natural selection and camouflage, and testing clothes as insulators. Many of the activities are more appropriately done outdoors.

Our Wonderful World provides reproducible student worksheets, including data charts, tables, and graphs. A complete lesson plan is included for each of the 19 activities.

Price: Teacher's Guide, $14.95. ***Publisher/supplier:*** AIMS Education Foundation. ***Materials:*** Available locally, or from commercial suppliers.

4.61 Overhead and Underfoot. AIMS. Carol Bland, Barry Courtney, Susan Dixon, and others. Rev. ed. Fresno, Calif.: AIMS Education Foundation, 1994.

Grades: 3, 4 The activities in *Overhead and Underfoot* focus on weather and the natural environment. Activities are organized in 4 categories—weather, plants and animals, pollution, and soils and rocks. Examples include the following: students determine how shadows change during the day; they measure wind speed and direction using an anemometer and a wind vane; they measure air pressure and relate readings to weather; and they discover that insects move at a great speed relative to their size. In other activities, they investigate the importance of an animal's coloring in relation to its survival; they identify air pollutants; they classify rocks according to properties; and they explore the components of different soil samples.

Overhead and Underfoot provides reproducible student worksheets, including data charts, tables, and graphs. A complete lesson plan is included for each of the 20 activities.

Price: Teacher's Guide (ISBN 1-881431-52-5), $14.95. ***Publisher/supplier:*** AIMS Education Foundation. ***Materials:*** Available locally, or from commercial suppliers.

4.62 Science and Literature Together: Thirty Elementary Science Units Highlighting the Best in Contemporary Children's Literature. (Developed by Don Nelson, Don Powers, Nancy Chu, and LaVonne Sanborn, Western Illinois University.) Macomb, Ill.: Western Illinois University, 1993.

Grades: K-6 *Science and Literature Together* consists of 30 science modules that highlight contemporary children's literature. This teacher's guide is organized in 6 subject areas—life science, physical science, earth science, health science, environmental science, and the nature of science. Each section includes from 2 to 8 instructional modules. Each module suggests a children's book to read—for example, *Bartholomew and the Oobleck,* by Dr. Seuss, or *Everybody Needs a Rock,* by Byrd Baylor—and provides a synopsis of that book and includes several related activities. Activities include making a butterfly house, making plaster fossils, playing shadow-tag, and adopting a tree to observe and care for during the school year.

The 30 modules in *Science and Literature Together* include a book synopsis, science background information, a list of the materials needed, procedures for conducting the activities, ideas for integrating the children's book, extension ideas, suggestions for curriculum integration, and a list of additional books and curriculum resources.

Price: $15. ***Publisher/supplier:*** Curriculum Publications Clearinghouse. ***Materials:*** Available locally, or from commercial suppliers.

4.63 Science at Play: Fun Ideas for 5 to 8 year Olds. Jenny Feely. Victoria, Australia: Dellasta, 1990.

Grades: 2, 3 *Science at Play* is divided into 8 sections—air, bubbles, heat, light, magnets, mixtures, snails, and water. Each includes from 4 to 9 activities, such as using warm air from a lightbulb to move a spiral of paper, predicting how long a bubble will last, and seeing how changes in temperature affect the size of a balloon. In other activities, students create rainbows by shining sunlight through a glass of water, magnetize nails, test liquids to determine which do and do not mix, watch snails eat, and discover what makes objects float and sink. The sections of the guide may be used as complete units over several weeks, or activities may be used independently.

Each activity in *Science at Play* includes a list of equipment needed and step-by-step instructions. Most include reproducible student worksheets.

Price: $10.95 (ISBN 0-947138-47-1). ***Publisher/supplier:*** Mondo. ***Materials:*** Available locally, or from commercial suppliers.

4.64 Science Comes Alive with Reading Rainbow. Reading Rainbow. Lincoln, Nebr.: Great Plains National (GPN), 1995.

Grades: K-6 *Science Comes Alive with Reading Rainbow* is a teacher's guide designed to supplement the *Reading Rainbow* science programs. *Reading Rainbow* is an educational television series that features a book in each episode; all programs are available on videocassettes. The teacher's guide provides specific activities to use in the days before and after showing each science program. The activities provide opportunities for students to explore the science elements of the program themes and encourage reading for discovery. Examples of activities for the program on the book entitled *The Salamander Room,* by Anne Mazer, include creating animal dioramas, using food samples to attract insects, taking a tree-focused nature trip, and using an old bed sheet under an overhanging branch of a tree or bush to collect small animals. Twenty science programs are featured. A science activity is also included for each of 9 other programs that include a science segment.

Price: $5. ***Publisher/supplier:*** GPN. ***Materials:*** Available locally, or from commercial suppliers.

4.65 Science for Me: Individual Recipes for Young Children. A Good Apple Science Activity Book. Linda Diebert. Carthage, Ill.: Good Apple, 1991.

Grades: K-2 *Science for Me* is an activity book for young children. It features step-by-step instructions for experiments on crystals, seeds, magnets, bubbles, water, and color. Students turn metal objects into temporary magnets, discover why bubbles pop, experiment with surface tension, and observe that colors can be mixed together to form other colors. Each set of activity cards is cut out of the book and used in sequence by students working at learning centers or stations. The cards are printed on heavy stock but can be laminated for extra durability.

Each of 15 activities in *Science for Me* includes a stated objective, teacher's notes, a list of supplies needed, and appropriate "recipe" cards.

Price: $11.99 (ISBN 0-86653-597-7). ***Publisher/supplier:*** Good Apple. ***Materials:*** Available locally, or from commercial suppliers.

4.66 Science in Your Backyard. Robert Gardner and David Webster. New York, N.Y.: Julian Messner/Simon & Schuster, 1987.

Grades: 4-6 *Science in Your Backyard* encourages students to use their backyards, parks, and playgrounds as sites for scientific investigations about animals, plants, weather, light, astronomy, and physics. Examples of activities include collecting insects, preserving leaves, growing trees from seeds, making weather instruments, making a pinhole camera, mapping the sun's path, and investigating friction by sliding down a slide wearing different fabrics and materials. Teachers may wish to supplement the life science activities in this book with a lesson on the proper care and handling of living organisms.

Science in Your Backyard is organized in 8 sections, each of which includes a short introduction followed by a series of activities.

Price: $11.95 (ISBN 0-671-55565-0). ***Publisher/supplier:*** Silver Burdett Ginn. ***Materials:*** Available locally, or from commercial suppliers.

4.67 Science Is. . . Susan V. Bosak. 2nd ed. Richmond Hill, Ontario, and Markham, Ontario, Canada: Scholastic Canada and The Communication Project, 1991.

Grades: 1-6+ *Science Is. . .* is a comprehensive collection of activities, experiments, and projects organized by type of activity, subject area, and topic. The 3 types of activities are as follows: (1) Quickies are short activities that require few or no materials and may be done on the spur of the moment. These may be used to introduce basic concepts in a subject area. (2) Make Time activities require a little planning, some readily available and inexpensive materials, and at least 30 minutes to complete. These activities often deal with key subject area concepts in depth. (3) One Leads to Another—activities within a subject area that build upon one another, emphasize a key theme for the subject area, or result in a completed project, and require some planning. Within each type, activities are organized in 10 subject areas: discovering science, matter and energy, humans, the environment, rocks, plants, living creatures, weather, the heavens, and applying science. In addition to the 10 subject areas, activities are organized into 40 topics; topics interrelate activities within and between subject areas. A master chart shows where items on the 40 topics can be found in the 10 subject areas.

Science Is. . . includes more than 450 experiments, projects, games, puzzles, and stories. Each activity includes a two-line introduction, a materials list, and procedures, as well as appropriate background information and other fact-filled boxes. This sourcebook also includes a section for teachers on how to use the book, an extensive list of resources, and an index.

Price: $29.95 (ISBN 0-590-74070-9). ***Publisher/supplier:*** Scholastic Canada. ***Materials:*** Available locally, or from commercial suppliers.

4.68 Science on a Shoestring. Herb Strongin. 2nd ed., by Kara Strongin and Gloria Strongin. Menlo Park, Calif.: Addison-Wesley Publishing Co., 1991.

Grades: K-6+ This second edition of *Science on a Shoestring* includes 62 investigations grouped under 3 themes—matter, change, and energy. Students investigate how matter behaves, interacts, and how it can change; they become aware of the changes occurring in themselves and in their environment; and they increase their awareness of the effects of gravity, magnetism, electricity, sound, and light upon them and their environment. Most investigations may be introduced without regard to sequence, although a few are sequential.

Each lesson in *Science on a Shoestring* includes a suggested grade level; a list of the materials required to complete the activity (all inexpensive and easily obtainable); a short vocabulary list; a brief overview of the activity, including an explanation of the concepts involved; and step-by-step procedures for conducting the activity. Most lessons also include ideas for home investigations, and questions for discussion and/or evaluation. A master list of materials is included.

Prices: Teacher's Guide (ISBN 0-201-25760-2), $18. Basic Kit, $149. Intermediate Kit, $110. ***Publisher/supplier:*** Learning Spectrum. ***Materials:*** Available locally, from commercial suppliers, or in kit.

4.69 Science Process Skills: Assessing Hands-On Student Performance. Karen L. Ostlund. Menlo Park, Calif.: Addison-Wesley Publishing Co., 1992.

Grades: 1-6 *Science Process Skills* is a collection of activities designed to serve as process-skill assessments at 6 levels of difficulty. Each appraisal is designed to give teachers information about a student's knowledge of and ability to use a particular process skill. Activities may be used to assess students' progress throughout the year, after a specific unit of instruction, or as a year-end evaluation. Examples of activities at various levels include the following: matching buttons, classifying small stones, describing apples from the inside out, predicting how many paper clips a magnet will pick up, using a balance and gram weights to weigh various objects, recording and charting the number of seeds inside green beans, classifying various screws and bolts, investigating which of four different kinds of balls bounce the highest, hypothesizing about how long it will take various objects to fall through liquid, estimating the number of words in a book, and making models to show how air particles move as air is heated and cooled. Blackline masters for recording answers are included.

Price: $14.36 (ISBN 0-201-29092-8). ***Publisher/supplier:*** Addison-Wesley. ***Materials:*** Available locally, or from commercial suppliers.

4.70 Shapes, Loops and Images. GEMS/Exhibit Guides. Susan Jagoda, David Buller, Larry Malone, and Cary Sneider. Berkeley, Calif.: Lawrence Hall of Science, 1987.

Grades: K-6+ Students construct interactive exhibits in *Shapes, Loops and Images,* a GEMS exhibit guide. The module offers 10 exhibits in 4 groups: (1) Tessellations (arrangements of one or more shapes that create a repeating pattern with no overlaps or spaces in between), (2) Giant Pole Puzzles, (3) Single-Mirror Exhibits, and (4) Multi-Mirror Exhibits. The activities are designed to help students develop such skills as observing, comparing, matching, finding patterns, analyzing, relating, visualizing, predicting, experimenting, and inferring. Activities include students testing polygonal shapes to determine which ones tessellate as single shapes, creating their own tessellation shapes, and observing how one tessellating shape can form many different designs. In other activities, students separate rope loops of 3-foot-tall pole puzzles, trace simple shapes while only seeing their hands in a mirror, discover the axes of symmetry of complex forms, and use a three-mirror arrangement to create a kaleidoscope.

The guide features detailed instructions with illustrations for constructing all exhibits and reproducible masters needed for specific exhibits.

Price: $20 (ISBN 0-912511-68-0). ***Publisher/supplier:*** LHS GEMS. ***Materials:*** Available locally, or from commercial suppliers.

4.71 Solar Energy. Alice Moseby. Victoria, Australia: Dellasta, 1993.

Grades: K-4 *Solar Energy* is a small book that includes activities and games as well as text explanations about the sun and solar energy. Its sections focus on the life cycle of a star, tracking the sun, the heat of the sun, the sun as the source of energy for the chain of life, energy-efficient housing, insulation, and solar heaters. Activities include students testing the effect of color on heat absorption, role-playing water molecules, designing solar heaters and energy-efficient houses, and testing the insulating character of various materials.

Price: $14.50 (ISBN 1-875627-32-4). ***Publisher/supplier:*** Mondo. ***Materials:*** Available locally, or from commercial suppliers.

4.72 Sunshine Science: Primary Science and Technology Activities, Years K-7. Osborne Park, Western Australia: Science Teachers' Association of Western Australia, 1992.

Grades: K-6+ *Sunshine Science,* a resource book of activities, focuses on the solar aspects of energy, plants, and animals. A product of the Solar Energy Education Project at Curtin University of Technology in Western Australia, *Sunshine Science* uses its activities to develop 3 concepts: (1) the sun is a source of energy, (2) sunshine is essential for plant growth, and (3) sunshine is essential for animal life. Process skills are emphasized as students carry out the following activities: they investigate the rate at which flowers wither, explore the relationship between the position of the sun and time of day, classify seeds according to their optimum planting period, and collect and interpret data on the water drinking habits of animals. In other activities, students design, construct, and calibrate a thermometer; monitor the activity of lizards under varying temperatures; and use a magnifying glass to concentrate the sun's radiation (close supervision is required).

The activities in *Sunshine Science* are organized according to grade level, with 6 or 7 activities provided for each. The guide includes an introduction and a complete lesson plan for each of its 53 activities, and reproducible masters of charts, data tables, and graphing worksheets.

Price: Aust. $30 (ISBN 0-949820-18-6). ***Publisher/supplier:*** Science Teachers' Association of Western Australia. ***Materials:*** Available locally, or from commercial suppliers.

4.73 Super Science Activities: Favorite Lessons from Master Teachers. Rob Beattie, Diane Bredt, Jean Lyford, and others. Palo Alto, Calif.: Dale Seymour Publications, 1988.

Grades: 5-6+ *Super Science Activities* includes lessons in the physical, earth, and life sciences from the repertoires of eight science teachers. Topics include plate tectonics, earthquakes, genetics, ecology, electricity, and chromatography. Examples of activities include the following: students invent a seismograph, use chromatography to identify the author of a mystery note, build a working battery, and create a balanced ecosystem in an aquarium.

Super Science Activities contains 6 units, each with 3 to 5 lessons and a bibliography. Each lesson has background information, vocabulary, a list of materials, classroom management suggestions, step-by-step procedures, and enrichment activities.

Price: $16.95 (ISBN 0-86651-445-7). ***Publisher/supplier:*** Dale Seymour Publications. ***Materials:*** Available locally, or from commercial suppliers.

4.74 The Tapwater Tour. LaMotte Co. Chestertown, Md.: LaMotte Co., 1989.

Grades: 4-6+ Students perform a water analysis in *The Tapwater Tour,* which is a test kit and "minicurriculum" for exploring drinking water. The unit is designed to be teacher-directed, but it has hands-on activities throughout. Students determine the pH of various solutions; they test water samples for the presence of chlorine, iron, and copper; and they use a soap solution to determine the "hardness" of water samples. They also summarize results in a water quality report. Chemical test tablets and plastic bags required for the activities accompany the teacher's guide.

Prices: Complete kit, $44.00. Replacement kit, $33.35. ***Publisher/supplier:*** LaMotte. ***Materials:*** Available locally, from commercial suppliers, or in kit.

4.75 3-2-1 Classroom Contact. Produced by Children's Television Workshop. Lincoln, Nebr.: Great Plains National (GPN), 1991.

Grades: 4-6 *The 3-2-1-Classroom Contact* teacher's guide is designed to accompany the television science series by the same name, which is available via on-air broadcasts and pre-recorded videocassettes. Each 15-minute program in the series explores a single topic in earth science, life science, physical science, or scientific investigation.

For each program, the guide provides background information, a program synopsis, 2 lessons (each 40 minutes long), blackline masters of student data sheets, and suggestions for extending the lessons into other curricular areas. The first of these 2 lessons for each program provides a framework for viewing and discussion and includes a before-viewing demonstration or class discussion, suggestions to help direct students' viewing, and an after-viewing activity. The second lesson is a hands-on activity to enhance student understanding of scientific principles addressed in the program.

Prices: Teacher's Guide, $12. Video programs, $15 each. Complete set of 30 video programs, $360. ***Publisher/supplier:*** GPN. ***Materials:*** Available locally, or from commercial suppliers.

4.76 Through the Rainbow—Children, Science, and Literature. CESI Sourcebook VIII. Washington, D.C.: Council for Elementary Science International (CESI), 1995.

Grades: K-6 *Through the Rainbow—Children, Science, and Literature* is designed to be used as a framework for a literature-based approach to elementary science instruction. This sourcebook contains 45 activities to link science concepts with children's literature. Topics range from tornados to butterflies to fossils. For example, during an activity entitled "You're Bugging Me," students observe the life cycle of butterflies from egg to adult and monitor the activity in a cricket colony; students compare the two types of insects as they grow and develop. During this activity, Eric Carle's *The Very Hungry Caterpillar* and *The Very Quiet Cricket* are used to initiate discussion and related activities.

Each topic presented in *Through the Rainbow* includes a focus (which summarizes and explains the core science concepts and skills developed in the activities), questions to motivate and stimulate learning, an outline of the key steps in performing the activities, assessment options, additional challenges for students, and suggestions for related literature titles.

Price: $16.50. ***Publisher/supplier:*** CESI. ***Materials:*** Available locally, or from commercial suppliers.

4.77 Tons of Scientifically Provocative and Socially Acceptable Things to Do With Balloons under the Guise of Teaching Science. Glenn McGlathery and Larry Malone. Englewood, Colo.: Teacher Ideas Press/Libraries Unlimited, 1991.

Grades: K-6+ *Tons of . . . Things to Do With Balloons . . .* is a collection of activities that use the ever-popular balloon to teach a variety of science concepts in 83 activities. The activities are organized in 9 topic areas: (1) air pressure, (2) chemical reactions, (3) density, (4) gravity and momentum, (5) membranes, (6) propulsion, (7) sound, (8) static electricity, and (9) models and miscellany. Examples of the activities include using differences in air pressure to put a water balloon into a bottle; inflating a balloon using Alka-Seltzer tablets; challenging students to inflate one balloon inside another balloon; pouring pungent liquids into balloons to demonstrate semipermeable membranes; and making multistage balloon rockets.

The guide presents a short history of balloons and a few tips on buying, storing, and inflating them. Each topic area begins with a mini-essay on the concept involved in its activities. Each activity includes a list of materials, advance preparation, instructions for the activity, and a brief explanation of the science concepts and principles involved.

Price: $18 (ISBN 0-87287-783-3). ***Publisher/supplier:*** Teacher Ideas Press. ***Materials:*** Available locally, or from commercial suppliers.

4.78 Tracks: Language-Conscious Primary Science. Kay Freer and Mitch O'Toole. Melbourne, Australia: Cambridge University Press, 1990.

Grades: K-3 *Tracks: Language-Conscious Primary Science* uses real-world scientific explorations as a tool for developing language skills in young learners. Activities are presented in 6 sections on the topics (1) animal traces, (2) color and shade, (3) animal survival and habitats, (4) sound, (5) movement and forces, and (6) physical and chemical change. Examples of activities include hunting for animal traces; exploring mirror images and reflective surfaces; classifying animals on the basis of similarities and differences; investigating the transmission of sound through materials; and determining how loads can be moved with rollers, wheels, and ramps.

Each of 6 sections in *Tracks* features 4 units, and each unit contains 4 to 10 activities. The guide has a total of 174 activities. Each activity includes an objective, a materials list, and steps for procedure and follow-up. Some of the activities are completed outdoors. The teacher's guide also includes unit overviews, background information, resource sheets, and reproducible masters for student worksheets.

Price: Aust. $39.95 (ISBN 0-521-34904-4). ***Publisher/supplier:*** Cambridge University Press. ***Materials:*** Available locally, or from commercial suppliers.

4.79 25 Science Mini-Books. Esther B. Weiner. New York, N.Y.: Scholastic Professional Books, 1994.

Grades: PreK, K-3 *25 Science Mini-Books* is actually 25 books in 1. Each page is designed to be removed from the activity book and folded into a 6- to 8-page mini-book on a topic or concept in life, earth, or physical science. A description of the concept involved and several suggested mini-activities are included for each mini-book. Examples of the activities include students making a model of the earth's mantle and crust; using water and a plastic bag to make a mini-water-cycle; and bird watching to observe beaks and claws.

This volume includes directions on how to reproduce, fold, and cut the mini-books. It provides suggestions on how to use the books both with pre-reading children and with children older than the suggested grade levels.

Price: $8.95 (ISBN 0-590-49507-0). ***Publisher/supplier:*** Scholastic Professional Books. ***Materials:*** Available locally.

4.80 200 Gooey, Slippery, Slimy, Weird and Fun Experiments. Janice Pratt VanCleave. New York, N.Y.: John Wiley & Sons, 1993.

Grades: 3-6 *200 Gooey, Slippery, Slimy, Weird and Fun Experiments* is a collection of simple demonstrations, activities, and projects that explain basic science principles in the fields of astronomy, biology, chemistry, earth science, and physics. The activities include the following: students demonstrate why a satellite remains in orbit, determine the age of a fish, test materials for the presence of starch, demonstrate how the composition of the earth affects its motion, and use a vibrating string to produce a sound. The activities require inexpensive, common materials, and can be performed at home or in the classroom.

Each experiment in this guide includes a statement of purpose, a materials list, step-by-step instructions, a statement of expected results, and brief explanation.

Price: $12.95 (ISBN 0-471-57921-1). ***Publisher/supplier:*** Wiley. ***Materials:*** Available locally, or from commercial suppliers.

4.81 Waste Away: A Curriculum on Solid Waste. Woodstock, Vt.: Vermont Institute of Natural Science, 1989.

Grades: 5-6+ In *Waste Away* students learn about the problems associated with solid waste disposal. They are encouraged to reduce, reuse, and recycle materials. The 4 lessons define our society's waste problem, investigate its underlying causes, explore the role of waste in our lives, and suggest solutions to waste generation. Classroom activities include discussion groups, pantomime, a puppet show, a slide show, trash- and product-sorting exercises, games, paper recycling, composting, songs, schoolyard trash hunts, puzzles, and role-playing.

Each lesson in *Waste Away* includes background information, detailed instructions for activities, and extensive follow-up activities for the classroom, school, community, or home. Appendixes provide a pre-/postunit survey, information on organizing a "trash festival," ideas for setting up a school recycling program, and a reproducible family booklet of information and activities.

Price: $18.95 (ISBN 0-9617627-2-1). ***Publisher/supplier:*** Whitman Distribution Center. ***Materials:*** Available locally, or from commercial suppliers.

4.82 Waste in Place: Elementary Curriculum Guide. Stamford, Conn.: Keep America Beautiful, 1993.

Grades: 1-6 *Waste in Place* takes an interdisciplinary approach to developing environmental awareness in students. Its activities—several for each grade level—focus on litter prevention and solid waste management. For example, students collect and smash beverage cans to demonstrate preparation for recycling; design and use a "reuse box" for potential waste materials; and "plant" waste items in soil and compare their differing rates of decomposition. In other activities they write songs to encourage people to keep their communities clean, rank litter items from "most harmful" to "least harmful" and discuss their reasoning, compete in a "trash trivia" game, and discuss resource recovery as a solid waste management option. Activities are grouped by grade level, but the guide provides master lists grouped by solid waste concept (litter prevention, reduce, reuse, recycle, compost, recover, hazardous waste, and bury) and by subject area (science, social studies, language arts, mathematics, and art/music).

Waste in Place includes an introduction, background information, a complete lesson plan for each of the 35 activities, a glossary of solid waste terms, implementation recommendations, and an overview of solid waste disposal alternatives.

Price: $35. ***Publisher/supplier:*** Keep America Beautiful. ***Materials:*** Available locally, or from commercial suppliers.

4.83 Wind-Aid. ESE. Heslington, York, UK: Chemical Industry Education Centre, and BP International, 1990.

Grades: 3-5 Designing a windmill to lift water from a well is the ultimate goal of *Wind-Aid,* a science and engineering activity. The unit begins with students constructing a simple toy windmill. Students then receive a (fictitious) letter from a school in Swaziland asking for ideas on how to design and build a machine to lift water from a nearby well. Following a discussion of the limited technology and resources available, students make and test a model windmill. They refine the model by changing one or more design features and investigating changes in performance. Finally, they put their recommendations in the form of a design report for the school in Swaziland. The unit is designed to be planned and executed by an engineer and a teacher working together.

Wind-Aid includes an overview, activity outlines, a summary for the engineer, and reproducible masters for transparencies and student worksheets.

Price: US$8 (ISBN 0-86165-203-7). ***Publisher/supplier:*** Chemical Industry Education Centre. ***Materials:*** Available locally, or from commercial suppliers.

CHAPTER 5

Curriculum Projects Past and Present

This chapter presents background information on "Curriculum Projects Past and Present"—that is, it provides project descriptions and lists of titles produced by some major funded projects in hands-on elementary school science. The National Science Foundation (NSF) supported several such programs in the late 1960s and early 1970s, as did other agencies and organizations. These notable projects are listed, together with some of the more recent projects of the 1980s and 1990s.

Some of the earlier materials listed in this chapter are still commercially available in their original or revised form. Trial editions of some of the NSF-supported materials are available on *Science Helper K-8* (*see* 7.27), a CD-ROM produced by the Knowledge Utilization Project in Science (*see* 5.7).

Materials produced by several of the current projects are annotated in this guide. Readers can locate them through the indexes in the volume.

In addition to its value for general readers, the information included here may be of particular interest to curriculum developers. For information about the availability of any of the titles listed in this chapter, readers may wish to contact the developer at the address or phone or fax number provided in the project annotation.

5.1 Activities Integrating Mathematics and Science (AIMS), AIMS Education Foundation, P.O. Box 8120, Fresno, CA 93747-8120
(209) 255-4094; Fax: (209) 255-6396

AIMS conducts research, provides national leadership training and local workshops and seminars, and publishes elementary and intermediate integrated curriculum materials (K-9) that have been written and tested by teachers. AIMS publications provide activities in a flexible format. The AIMS materials for the elementary grades, listed below, are an outgrowth of a National Science Foundation project, under the auspices of Fresno Pacific College.

Bats Incredible (Grades 2-4)
The Budding Botanist (Grades 3-6)
Critters (Grades K-6)
Down to Earth (Grades 5-9)
Electrical Connections (Grades 4-9)
Fall into Math and Science (Grades K-1)
Finding Your Bearings (Grades 4-9)
Floaters and Sinkers (Grades 5-9)
From Head to Toe (Grades 5-9)
Fun with Foods (Grades 5-9)
Glide into Winter with Math and Science (Grades K-1)
Hardhatting in a Geo-World (Grades 3-4)
Jawbreakers and Heart Thumpers (Grades 3-4)
Machine Shop (Grades 5-9)
Magnificent Microworld Adventures (Grades 4-9)
Math + Science, A Solution (Grades 5-9)
Mostly Magnets (Grades 2-8)
Off the Wall Science: A Poster Series Revisited (Grades 3-9)
Our Wonderful World (Grades 5-9)
Out of This World (Grades 5-9)
Overhead and Underfoot (Grades 3-4)
Pieces and Patterns, A Patchwork in Math and Science (Grades 5-9)

Studying a miniecosystem

Popping with Power (Grades 3-4)
Primarily Bears (Grades K-6)
Primarily Physics (Grades K-3)
Primarily Plants (Grades K-3)
Seasoning Math and Science: Fall and Winter (Grade 2)
Seasoning Math and Science: Spring and Summer (Grade 2)
Sense-able Science (Grades K-1)
The Sky's the Limit! (Grades 5-9)
Soap Films and Bubbles (Grades 4-9)
Spring into Math and Science (Grades K-1)
Through the Eyes of the Explorers: Minds-on Math and Mapping (Grades 5-9)
Water Precious Water (Grades 2-6)

5.2 Conceptually Oriented Program in Elementary Science (COPES), New York University, New York, NY

Inactive. Materials are now available on *Science Helper K-8* (*see* 7.27).

COPES is a general elementary science program (K-6) published in the early 1970s that focuses on 5 major conceptual schemes: (1) structural units of the universe, (2) interaction and change, (3) conservation of energy, (4) degradation of energy, and (5) a statistical view of nature. Relationships between lessons in the units are based on these themes rather than on familiar subject strands. COPES was funded by the National Science Foundation. Its materials are these:

Teacher's Guide for Kindergarten/Grade One
Teacher's Guide for Grade Two
Teacher's Guide for Grade Three
Teacher's Guide for Grade Four
Teacher's Guide for Grade Five
Teacher's Guide for Grade Six
Teacher's Guide for a Conservation of Energy Sequence

5.3 Elementary Science Study (ESS), Education Development Center, 55 Chapel St., Newton, MA 02160 (617) 969-7100; Fax: (617) 965-6325

Inactive. Some trial editions are available on *Science Helper K-8* (*see* 7.27). Trial and commercial editions are available from the ERIC Clearinghouse for Science, Mathematics, and Environmental Education (*see* 10.41). Some commercial or revised editions are available from Delta Education (*see* appendix A).

ESS was begun in the 1960s as a curriculum improvement project of the Education Development Center. The original ESS curriculum materials consisted of 56 hands-on units that could be used either as the core of, or as a supplement to, a general elementary science program. Trial editions were extensively revised for commercial publication on the basis of large-scale classroom teaching. In both trial and commercial editions, children experiment with objects and concepts, defining their own questions and setting their own goals. Teachers and children are encouraged to work with materials in their own way. The project was funded by the National Science Foundation, and the commercial editions were originally published by McGraw-Hill. In the following list of ESS titles, those with an asterisk (*) are currently available in a revised edition from Delta Education (*see* appendix A):

Animal Activity (Grades 4-6)
Animals in the Classroom (Grades 1-3)
**Attribute Games and Problems* (Grades K-9)
**Balloons and Gases* (Grades 5-8)
**Batteries and Bulbs* (Grades 4-6)
Batteries and Bulbs II (Grades 4-8)
**Behavior of Mealworms* (Grades 4-8)
Bones (Grades 1-5)
**Brine Shrimp* (Grades 1-4)
Budding Twigs (Grades 4-6)
Butterflies (Grades K-5)
Changes (Grades 1-4)
**Clay Boats* (Grades 3-6)
**Colored Solutions* (Grades 3-8)
Crayfish (Grades 4-6)
Daytime Astronomy (Grades 4-8)
**Drops, Streams, and Containers* (Grades 3-5)
**Earthworms* (Grades 4-6)
**Eggs & Tadpoles* (Grades K-6)
**Gases and "Airs"* (Grades 5-8)
Geo Blocks (Grades K-4)
**Growing Seeds* (Grades K-3)
**Heating and Cooling* (Grades 6-8)
**Ice Cubes* (Grades 3-5)
**Kitchen Physics* (Grades 5-8)
The Life of Beans and Peas (Grades 1-4)
Light and Shadows (Grades K-3)
**Mapping* (Grades 5-7)
**Match and Measure* (Grades K-2)
**Microgardening, An Introduction to the World of Mold* (Grades 4-6)
Mirror Cards (Grades K-6)
**Mobiles* (Grades K-4)
Mosquitoes: A Resource Book for the Classroom (Grades 4-8)
The Musical Instrument Recipe Book (Grades K-5)
**Mystery Powders* (Grades 3-4)
**Optics* (Grades 4-6)
**Pattern Blocks* (Grades K-6)
**Peas and Particles* (Grades 4-6)
**Pendulums* (Grades 4-6)
Pond Water (Grades 3-6)
**Primary Balancing* (Grades K-4)
Printing (Grades K-6)
**Rocks and Charts* (Grades 3-6)
Sand (Grades K-3)
**Senior Balancing* (Grades 4-8)
**Sink or Float* (Grades 1-7)
**Small Things: An Introduction to the Microscopic World* (Grades 4-6)
**Spinning Tables* (Grades 1-3)
Starting from Seeds (Grades 1-6)
**Stream Tables* (Grades 4-6)
**Structures* (Grades 2-6)
**Tangrams* (Grades K-8)
Tracks (Grades 3-6)
**Water Flow* (Grades 5-6)
Where Is the Moon? (Grades 3-7)
**Whistles and Strings* (Grades 3-6)

5.4 Full Option Science System (FOSS), FOSS Program, Lawrence Hall of Science, University of California, Berkeley, CA 94720
(510) 642-8941; Fax: (510) 642-1055

The FOSS program is designed to engage students in actively constructing scientific concepts through multisensory, hands-on laboratory activities. This K-6 curriculum consists of 27 modules: 5 kindergarten modules organized under topics in the life and physical sciences; 6 modules for grades 1 and 2 organized under topics in the life, physical, and earth sciences; 16 modules for grades 3-6 organized under topics in the life, physical, and earth sciences, and in scientific reasoning and technology. Students in grades 1 and 2 explore 3 modules per year, and each class in grades 3-6 uses 4 modules per year. A multimedia component is available; it is marketed as the Britannica Science System. Development of the FOSS program was funded by the National Science Foundation. The FOSS modules are as follows:

Air and Weather (Grades 1, 2)
Animals Two by Two (Grade K)
Balance and Motion (Grades 1, 2)
Earth Materials (Grades 3, 4)
Environments (Grades 5, 6)
Fabric (Grade K)
Food and Nutrition (Grades 5, 6)
Human Body (Grades 3, 4)
Ideas and Inventions (Grades 3, 4)
Insects (Grades 1, 2)
Landforms (Grades 5, 6)
Levers and Pulleys (Grades 5, 6)
Magnetism and Electricity (Grades 3, 4)
Measurement (Grades 3, 4)
Mixtures and Solutions (Grades 5, 6)
Models and Designs (Grades 5, 6)
New Plants (Grades 1, 2)
Paper (Grade K)
Pebbles, Sand, and Silt (Grades 1, 2)
Physics of Sound (Grades 3, 4)
Solar Energy (Grades 5, 6)
Solids and Liquids (Grades 1, 2)
Structures of Life (Grades 3, 4)
Trees (Grade K)
Variables (Grades 5, 6)
Water (Grades 3, 4)
Wood (Grade K)

5.5 Great Explorations in Math and Science (GEMS), Lawrence Hall of Science, University of California, Berkeley, CA 94720-5220
(510) 642-7771; Fax: (510) 643-0309

GEMS materials consist of teacher's guides, assembly presenter's guides, and exhibit guides, and range in appeal from preschool through high school. These publications integrate mathematics with life, earth, and physical sciences, fostering a "guided discovery" approach to learning. Materials are easily accessible, and lessons are written for teachers with little training in mathematics or science. Funding for the program has been provided by the A. W. Mellon Foundation and the Carnegie Corporation of New York. Following are the titles of GEMS guides for the elementary grades:

Acid Rain (Grades 6-10)
Animal Defenses (Grades PreK, K)
Animals in Action (Grades 5-9)
Bubble Festival: A Guide to Presenting Bubble Activities in a Learning Station Format (Grades K-6)
Bubble-ology (Grades 5-9)
Build It! Festival (Grades K-6)
Buzzing a Hive (Grades Pre-K, K-3)
Chemical Reactions (Grades 6-10)
Color Analyzers (Grades 5-9)
Convection: A Current Event (Grades 6-9)
Crime Lab Chemistry (Grades 4-8)
Discovering Density (Grades 6-10)
Earth, Moon, and Stars (Grades 5-9)
Earthworms (Grades 6-10)
Experimenting with Model Rockets (Grades 6-10)
Fingerprinting (Grades 4-8)
Frog Math: Predict, Ponder, Play (Grades K-3)
Group Solutions: Cooperative Logic Activities (Grades K-4)
Height-O-Meters (Grades 6-10)
Hide a Butterfly (Grades PreK, K-3)
Hot Water and Warm Homes from Sunlight (Grades 4-8)
In All Probability (Grades 4-6)
Investigating Artifacts: Making Masks, Creating Myths, Exploring Middens (Grades K-6)
Involving Dissolving (Grades 1-3)
Ladybugs (Grades PreK, K, 1)
Liquid Explorations (Grades K-3)
The "Magic" of Electricity (Grades 3-6)
Mapping Animal Movements (Grades 5-9)
Mapping Fish Habitats (Grades 6-10)
Moons of Jupiter (Grades 4-9)
More Than Magnifiers (Grades 6-9)
Mystery Festival (Grades 2-8)
Of Cabbages and Chemistry (Grades 4-8)
Oobleck: What Scientists Do (Grades 4-8)
Paper Towel Testing (Grades 5-8)
Penguins and Their Young (Grades PreK, K, 1)
QUADICE (Grades 4-8)
River Cutters (Grades 6-9)
Shapes, Loops, and Images (Grades K-12)
Solids, Liquids, and Gases (Grades 3-6)
Terrarium Habitats (Grades K-6)
Tree Homes (Grades PreK, K-1)
Vitamin C Testing (Grades 4-8)
The Wizard's Lab (Grades K-12)

5.6 Improving Urban Elementary Science (Insights), Education Development Center, 55 Chapel St., Newton, MA 02160
(617) 969-7100; (800) 225-4276;
Fax: (617) 965-6325

Between 1987 and 1992, the Improving Urban Elementary Science project produced the Insights curriculum, which consists of 17 modules, each requiring 6 to 8 weeks to complete, for grades K-6. Topics reflect a balance of life, physical, and earth sciences, and integrate science with the rest of the curriculum, particularly with language arts and mathematics. Insights units are designed to enhance critical thinking, communication, and problem-solving skills. The activities support cultural, racial, and linguistic diversity. Funding was provided by the National Science Foundation. Following are the Insights titles:

Balls and Ramps (Grades K, 1)
Bones and Skeletons (Grades 4, 5)
Changes of State (Grades 4, 5)
Circuits and Pathways (Grades 4, 5)
Growing Things (Grades 2, 3)
Habitats (Grades 2, 3)
Human Body Systems (Grade 6)
Lifting Heavy Things (Grades 2, 3)
Liquids (Grades 2, 3)
Living Things (Grades K, 1)
Myself and Others (Grades K, 1)
The Mysterious Powder (Grades 4, 5)
Reading the Environment (Grades 4, 5)
The Senses (Grades K, 1)
Sound (Grades 2, 3)
Structures (Grade 6)
There Is No Away (Grade 6)

5.7 Knowledge Utilization Project in Science (KUPS), Room 302 Norman Hall, University of Florida, Gainesville, FL 32611
(904) 392-0761; Fax: (904) 392-9193

KUPS has produced a CD-ROM database entitled *Science Helper K-8* (see 7.27), which contains plans for 919 elementary science and mathematics lessons and 2,000 activities, compiled from 7 elementary science curriculum projects funded by the National Science Foundation during the 1960s, 1970s, and 1980s. Information is indexed by program, grade level, subject, process skill, keyword, and content theme. *Science Helper K-8* contains pre-publication book editions; these lessons sometimes contain up to 30 percent more material than the commercial versions. The *Science Helper* can operate on either the PC or the Macintosh platform. Funding was provided by the Carnegie Corporation of New York. Following are the projects whose materials it includes:

COPES	*Conceptually Oriented Program for Elementary Science*
ESS	*Elementary Science Study (partial)*
ESSP	*Elementary School Science Project (Astronomy)*
MINNEMAST	*Minnesota Mathematics and Science Teaching Project*
SAPA	*Science—A Process Approach*
SCIS	*Science Curriculum Improvement Study*
USMES	*Unified Science and Mathematics for Elementary Schools (partial)*

5.8 Learning about Ecology, Animals, and Plants (Project LEAP), Cornell Instructional Materials Service, Department of Education, Cornell University, 420 Kennedy Hall, Ithaca, NY 14853
(607) 255-9252; Fax (607) 255-7905

LEAP is a conceptually oriented life science program for grades K-6. Concepts are sequential; they build toward the central principle that all life on earth depends on the existence of green plants. There are 4 units for each grade level; each unit addresses a particular set of concepts and principles. A sample concept map is included in each unit except that for kindergarten. Development was supported in part by the National Science Foundation. Following are the titles of LEAP units, by grade level, and in sequence:

Kindergarten:	*Growing* *Using Our Senses* *Kinds of Plants and Animals* *One Life: A Person, A Tree*
Grade One:	*What's Alive?* *Seeds* *People Use Plants* *Life Cycles*
Grade Two:	*Alike and Different: Classification of Living Things* *What Plants Need* *Making It Through the Winter: Plants* *Making It Through the Winter: Animals*
Grade Three:	*Linking Chains and Weaving Webs* *Communities* *Plants in Action* *Seasons and the Sun's Energy*
Grade Four:	*Adaptations* *Species* *Flower Power* *From Pieces to Plants*
Grade Five:	*Energy for Green Plants* *Materials Cycle* *Populations and Competition* *Ecosystems: Everything Is Connected*
Grade Six:	*Releasing Energy: Respiration* *Storing Energy* *Species Change* *A Green Future*

5.9 The Life Lab Science Program, 1156 High St., Santa Cruz, CA 95064
(408) 459-2001; Fax: (408) 459-3483

Life Lab Science is a K-5 program of life, earth, and physical science activities in which learning takes place in the context of an indoor or outdoor garden. The program integrates conceptual learning and practical applications to demonstrate to students how science relates to everyday life. A variety of learning experiences are derived from this work, including some that relate to ecology, ethical issues, and decision making. A teacher resource book is provided for each level at grades K-3, with separate student activity books for grades 1-3. Grades 4 and 5 use a modular format, with 8 units for each grade. Funding has been provided by the National Science Foundation and the U.S. Department of Education. Following are the titles of the Life Lab Science Program:

Change Around Us (Grade 2)
Change Over Time (Grade 5)
Connections (Grade 4)
Earth Is Home (Grade 1)
Great Explorations (Grade K)
The Growing Classroom (Grades K-5)
How Things Work (Grade 3)

5.10 National Geographic Kids Network, Technical Education Research Centers (TERC), 2067 Massachusetts Ave., Cambridge, MA 02140
(617) 547-0430; Fax: (617) 349-3535

The National Geographic Kids Network is a telecommunications-based curriculum begun in 1985. The elementary curriculum series consists of 7 units that focus on exploring students' questions about socially significant scientific topics. Each unit combines classroom activities, telecommunication exchanges, and software tools to enhance students' investigations and understanding of unit topics. Students in grades 4-6 collect, discuss, share, and analyze their data with other students around the world. The project is currently designing units that extend the ideas of the elementary series into a middle grades curriculum. Funding has been provided by the National Science Foundation. Titles in the National Geographic Kids Network are as follows:

Acid Rain (Grades 4-6)
Hello! (Grades 4-6)
The Solar System (Grades 4-6)
Too Much Trash? (Grades 4-6)
Weather in Action (Grades 4-6)
What Are We Eating? (Grades 4-6)
What's in Our Water? (Grades 4-6)

5.11 Outdoor Biology Instructional Strategies (OBIS), Lawrence Hall of Science, University of California, Berkeley, CA 94720
(510) 642-1016; Fax: (510) 642-1055

OBIS revolves around ecosystems as students investigate the ecological relationships of living organisms and their physical environment. Activities are conducted in outdoor settings. They employ a variety of strategies, such as games, simulations, craft activities, role playing, experiments, and data analysis. OBIS consists of 97 separate activities that are grouped in 27 modules. There is some duplication of activities among the modules. Activities were written for use with 8- to 15-year-olds. The project was funded by the National Science Foundation. The titles of OBIS modules are as follows:

Adaptations
Animal Behavior
Aquatic Animal Behavior
Backyard
Bio-Crafts
Breakwaters and Bays
Campsite
Child's Play
Desert
Forest
For Eight- to Eleven-Year-Olds
For Large Groups
For Small Groups and Families
Games and Simulations
Human Impact
Lawns and Fields
Neighborhood Woods
Nighttime
OBIS Sampler
Outdoor Study Techniques
Pavement and Parks
Ponds and Lakes
Schoolyard
Seashore
Streams and Rivers
Trail
Wintertime

5.12 Science 5/13, Schools Council, School of Education, University of Bristol, Bristol, England

Inactive. A complete set of this series is maintained at: Teacher's Laboratory, P.O. Box 6480, Brattleboro, VT 05302-6480
(802) 254-3457; Fax: (802) 254-5233

Science 5/13 was a British project jointly sponsored by the Schools Council, the Nuffield Foundation, and the Scottish Education Department. The purpose of the project was to show teachers how to help children between the ages of 5 and 13 learn science through first-hand experience using a variety of methods. This general science series fosters development of content knowledge and science process skills through independent, hands-on investigations of familiar materials. Science 5/13 was first published in Great Britain in the early 1970s by Macdonald and Company. Following are the titles from the Science 5/13 project:

Change: Stages 1 and 2, and Background (Grades 3-7)
Change: Stage 3 (Grades 7-12)
Children and Plastics: Stages 1 and 2, and Background (Grades 4-7)
Coloured Things: Stages 1 and 2 (Grades K-5)
Early Experiences (Grades K-2)
Holes, Gaps and Cavities (Grades 2-5)
Like and Unlike: Stages 1, 2, and 3 (Grades K-7)
Metals: Background Information (Grades 6-8)
Metals: Stages 1 and 2 (Grades 6-8)
Minibeasts: Stages 1 and 2 (Grades K-7)
Ourselves: Stages 1 and 2 (Grades K-4)
Science from Toys: Stages 1 and 2, and Background (Grades K-7)
Science, Models, and Toys: Stage 3 (Grades 7-9)
Structures and Forces: Stages 1 and 2 (Grades 3-6)
Structures and Forces: Stage 3 (Grades 6-8)
Time: Stages 1 and 2, and Background (Grades K-6)
Trees: Stages 1 and 2 (Grades K-7)
Using the Environment:
1: Early Explorations (Grades K-4)
2: Investigations, Parts 1 and 2 (Grades 3-7)
3: Tackling Problems, Parts 1 and 2 (Grades 6-9)
4: Ways and Means (Grades K-9)
With Objectives in Mind (Grades K-9)
Working with Wood: Background Information (Grades 3-6)
Working with Wood: Stages 1 and 2 (Grades 3-6)

5.13 Science Activities for the Visually Impaired/Science Enrichment for Learners with Physical Handicaps (SAVI/SELPH), Center for Multisensory Learning, Lawrence Hall of Science, University of California, Berkeley, CA 94720-5200
(510) 642-8941; Fax: (510) 642-1055

SAVI/SELPH, published in the late 1970s and early 1980s, consists of 9 modules designed for special-education students in grades 4-7. The activities enable all children to participate successfully in multisensory investigations of the life, earth, and physical sciences, increasing their understanding of science concepts and enhancing their science process skills. The modules work well in a variety of settings and can be directed by teachers with little science background. Funding has been provided by the U.S. Office of Education. Materials are available from the Lawrence Hall of Science. Following are the titles produced by SAVI/SELPH:

Communication (Grades 4-7)
Environmental Energy (Grades 4-7)
Environments (Grades 4-7)
Kitchen Interactions (Grades 4-7)
Magnetism and Electricity (Grades 4-7)
Measurement (Grades 4-7)
Mixtures and Solutions (Grades 4-7)
Scientific Reasoning (Grades 4-7)
Structures of Life (Grades 4-7)

5.14 Science and Technology for Children (STC), National Science Resources Center, Arts and Industries Building, Room 1201, Smithsonian Institution, Washington, DC 20560
(202) 357-2555; Fax: (202) 786-2028

The Science and Technology for Children program consists of a series of 24 inquiry-centered curriculum units for grades 1 through 6, with 4 units at each grade level. Students learn about topics in the life, earth, and physical sciences. The technological applications of science and the interactions among science, technology, and society are addressed throughout the program. Units encourage participatory learning and the integration of science with mathematics, language arts, social studies, and art. Development of scientific reasoning skills is emphasized. Funding was provided by the John D. and Catherine T. MacArthur Foundation and the National Science Foundation. The titles produced by the STC project are as follows:

Animal Studies (Grade 4)
Balancing and Weighing (Grade 2)
Changes (Grade 2)
Chemical Tests (Grade 3)
Comparing and Measuring (Grade 1)
Ecosystems (Grade 5)
Electric Circuits (Grade 4)
Experiments with Plants (Grade 6)
Floating and Sinking (Grade 5)
Food Chemistry (Grade 5)
Land and Water (Grade 4)
The Life Cycle of Butterflies (Grade 2)
Magnets and Motors (Grade 6)
Measuring Time (Grade 6)
Microworlds (Grade 5)
Motion and Design (Grade 4)
Organisms (Grade 1)
Plant Growth and Development (Grade 3)
Rocks and Minerals (Grade 3)
Soils (Grade 2)
Solids and Liquids (Grade 1)
Sound (Grade 3)
Technology of Paper (Grade 6)
Weather (Grade 1)

5.15 Science—A Process Approach (SAPA/SAPA II), American Association for the Advancement of Science, Washington, DC 20005
(202) 326-6400

Inactive. Original SAPA materials are available on *Science Helper K-8* (*see* 7.27). SAPA II revisions are available from Delta Education (*see* appendix A).

SAPA and SAPA II are general science programs that focus heavily on processes of science rather than on concepts. In both the first and the second versions, activities form a sequential K-6 modular program in which mastery of specific skills is predicated upon the accumulation of experience. Funded by the National Science Foundation, SAPA was published in the 1960s by the Xerox Education Division. It consists of 7 parts, each containing activity modules appropriate to a particular grade. The SAPA II folio version was originally published in the 1970s by Ginn and Company. Its revised edition contains 105 modules. Following are the 7 parts published for SAPA and the distribution by grade of the 105 SAPA II modules:

SAPA
Part A (Grades K-2)
Part B (Grades 1-3)
Part C (Grades 2-4)
Part D (Grades 3-5)
Part E (Grades 4-6)
Part F (Grades 5-7)
Part G (Grades 6-8)

SAPA II
Level K: Modules 1-15
Level 1: Modules 16-30
Level 2: Modules 31-45
Level 3: Modules 46-60
Level 4: Modules 61-75
Level 5: Modules 76-90
Level 6: Modules 91-105

5.16 Science Curriculum Improvement Study (SCIS/SCIS II/SCIIS/SCIS 3), Lawrence Hall of Science, University of California, Berkeley, CA 94720
(510) 642-8718; Fax: (510) 642-1055

In all stages of its existence, SCIS has focused on the concepts and processes of science for grades K-6. Investigations build from the exploration of materials, through the interpretation of information, to the application of knowledge and skills to new situations. The project was funded by the National Science Foundation in the late 1960s. Both its first and third versions were published by Rand McNally. The second version, SCIS II, was distributed by American Science and Engineering. SCIS 3, developed by Delta Education and two members of the original SCIS team, consists of 13 units: a kindergarten unit and 2 sequences of 6 units each in physical-earth science and life-environmental science for grades 1-6. Following are the titles produced in the 4 SCIS versions:

SCIS
Beginnings (Grades K-1)
Communities (Grade 5)
Ecosystems (Grade 6)
Energy Sources (Grade 5)
Environments (Grade 4)
Interaction and Systems (Grade 2)
Life Cycles (Grade 2)
Material Objects (Grade 1)
Models: Electric and Magnetic Interactions (Grade 6)
Organisms (Grade 1)
Populations (Grade 3)
Relative Position and Motion (Grade 4)
Subsystems and Variables (Grade 3)

SCIS II
Communities (Grade 5)
Ecosystems (Grade 6)
Energy Sources (Grade 5)
Environments (Grade 4)
Interaction and Systems (Grade 2)
Life Cycles (Grade 2)
Material Objects (Grade 1)
Measurement, Motion and Change (Grade 4)
Modeling Systems (Grade 6)
Organisms (Grade 1)
Populations (Grade 3)
Subsystems and Variables (Grade 3)

SCIIS/85
Beginnings (Grades K-1)
Communities (Grade 5)
Ecosystems (Grade 6)
Energy Sources (Grade 5)
Environments (Grade 4)
Interaction and Systems (Grade 2)
Life Cycles (Grade 2)
Material Objects (Grade 1)
Scientific Theories (Grade 6)
Organisms (Grade 1)
Populations (Grade 3)
Relative Position and Motion (Grade 4)
Subsystems and Variables (Grade 3)

SCIS 3
Beginnings (Grade K)
Communities (Grade 5)
Ecosystems (Grade 6)
Energy Sources (Grade 5)
Environments (Grade 4)
Interaction and Systems (Grade 2)
Life Cycles (Grade 2)
Material Objects (Grade 1)
Organisms (Grade 1)
Populations (Grade 3)
Relative Position and Motion (Grade 4)
Scientific Theories (Grade 6)
Subsystems and Variables (Grade 3)

5.17 Unified Science and Mathematics for Elementary Schools (USMES), Education Development Center, 55 Chapel St., Newton, MA 02160
(617) 969-7100; Fax: (617) 965-6325

Inactive. Some original materials have been reissued on *Science Helper K-8* (*see* 7.27); all are available from the ERIC Clearinghouse for Science, Mathematics, and Environmental Education (*see* 10.41).

USMES is a series of 23 guides published in the early 1970s for use in grades K through 8. The units focus on long-range investigations of real and practical problems geared to the local environment. Each unit consists of an opening challenge out of which students create their own investigations, honing their problem-solving skills and acquiring an understanding of major concepts. The USMES project includes activity cards and background papers, as well as the guides. Funding was provided by the National Science Foundation. The USMES units are as follows:

Advertising (Grades 4-8)
Bicycle Transportation (Grades 4-8)
Burglar Alarm Design (Grades 3-8)
Classroom Design (Grades 1-8)
Classroom Management (Grades 1-6)
Consumer Research-Product Testing (Grades 1-8)
Describing People (Grades 1-8)
Designing for Human Proportions (Grades 3-8)
Dice Design (Grades 1-8)
Electromagnet Device Design (Grades 3-8)
Growing Plants (Grades 2-6)
Lunch Lines (Grades 1-8)
Manufacturing (Grades 4-8)
Orientation (Grades 2-8)
Pedestrian Crossings (Grades 2-6)
Play Area Design and Use (Grades 1-8)
School Zoo (Grades K-7)
Soft Drink Design (Grades 1-8)
Traffic Flow (Grades 1-8)
USMES Design Lab Manual (Grades K-8)
The USMES Guide (Grades K-8)
Ways to Learn/Teach (Grades 2-8)
Weather Predictions (Grades 2-8)

PART 3

TEACHER'S REFERENCES

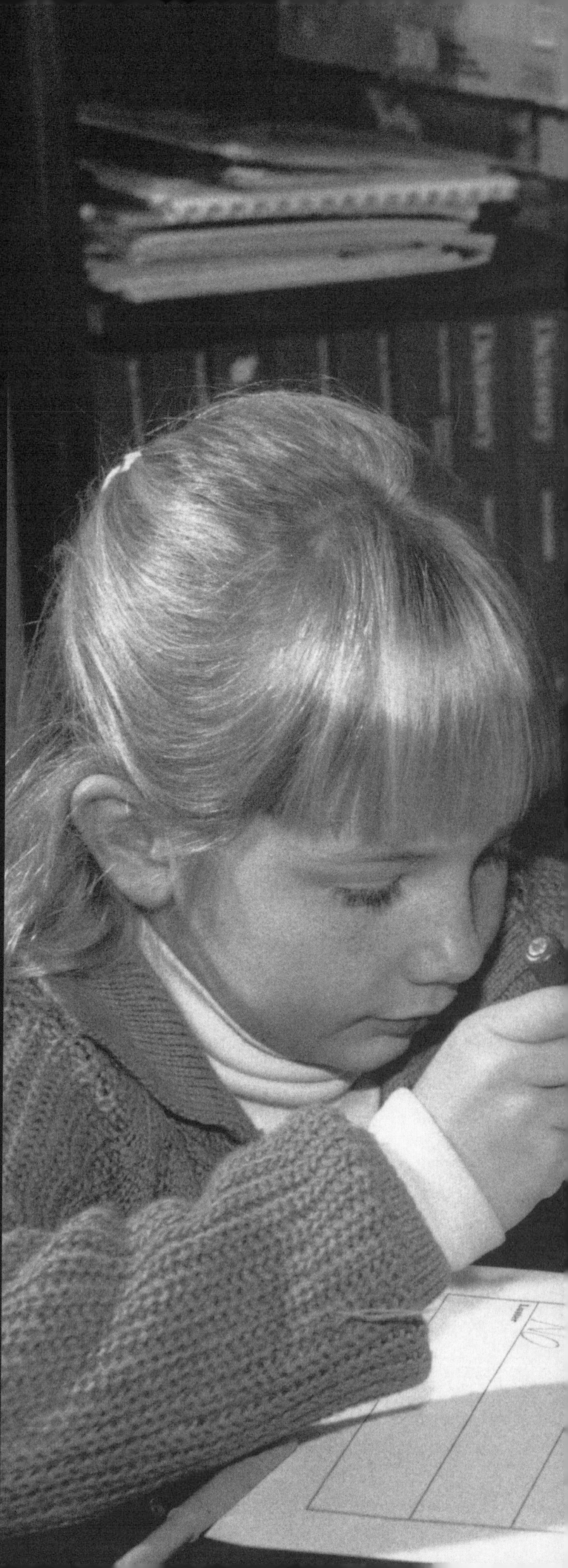

Observing a mineral sample

Part 3 Overview

Part 3, "Teacher's References," consists of annotated lists of reference books and periodicals to which the elementary classroom teacher can turn for assistance in teaching hands-on, inquiry-centered science. The lists are as follows: "Books on Teaching Science," chapter 6; "Science Book Lists and Resource Guides," chapter 7; and "Periodicals," chapter 8.

Chapter 6, "Books on Teaching Science," includes more than 50 titles that offer guidance in learning theory and pedagogical techniques. The reference materials listed in this chapter vary from 30-page monographs to 700-page volumes. The topics covered include, for example:

- the theory and practice of activity-based, inquiry-centered science learning and teaching;
- classroom-tested ideas for planning, organizing, managing, and assessing an integrated guided-discovery program for science classes;
- current issues surrounding the assessment component of science teaching;
- indoor and outdoor activities that encourage the practice of basic science skills such as measuring, observing, and collecting and analyzing data;
- activities that involve an interdisciplinary approach to science teaching and learning;
- information on keeping small animals in the classroom; and
- challenges such as the special learning needs of high-ability learners or the needs of students with disabilities in the science classroom.

Chapter 7, "Science Book Lists and Resource Guides," focuses on about 25 authoritative directories and guides. These reference works provide teachers with reviews and recommendations of books and materials, as well as information on how to select and obtain them. Among the annotated directories in the chapter are—

- bibliographies and reviews of publications and films for students, including lists of trade books highly recommended to satisfy the interests and academic needs of students in science and mathematics;
- guides to science equipment and material resources;
- guides to resources in electronic formats, including a comprehensive directory of computer software for preschool through college; and
- directories of key personnel at organizations such as educational research centers and state and federal agencies of interest to those in elementary school science.

A final category of reference materials is presented in chapter 8, "Periodicals," which annotates 35 magazines for teachers and students. The periodicals were chosen for their excellence as instructional tools, for the quality of their articles and stories on scientific topics, for their appeal to children, and for their adaptability to classroom use. They offer current information in the sciences, ideas and activities for science teaching, and engaging reading matter for students. The annotations indicate the grade level for which each title is recommended. The periodicals listed in chapter 8 include—

- a monthly magazine recommended for use in grades 6 and above that provides articles in a wide range of scientific fields and helps teachers translate the information into classroom projects and curriculum ideas;
- a K-8 resource with articles written by teachers, presenting creative ideas and activities;
- a magazine for grades 3-8 that explores nature, science, and technology through short nonfiction articles with lively, colorful photographs and drawings; and
- a monthly subject index to children's magazines for elementary and middle school students.

Chapters 6 through 8 are not exhaustive. Teachers are encouraged to keep their eyes open for new or other publications for their own lists of references. The absence of any volume or periodical from these lists is not intended as a comment on its quality or usefulness.

Insofar as possible, the current edition of a publication is annotated in part 3. However, later editions of some volumes, particularly annual or biannual directories, may have appeared after the text of *Resources for Teaching Elementary School Science* was completed.

Ordering Information

Prices for the books and periodicals in chapters 6 through 8 are given with the annotations. Costs of shipping and handling are not included. The addresses and phone and fax numbers for publishers of these materials are in appendix A, "Publishers and Suppliers."

Every effort was made to provide accurate, up-to-date ordering information, but readers may also wish to consult annually updated directories, such as *NSTA Science Education Suppliers* (see 7.21), or standard reference directories such as *Books in Print* at their local libraries or bookstores.

Likewise, because prices and availability may change, readers should check the prices of publications or supplies listed before placing an order. In some cases, discounts or special rates may be available to schools and educators.

CHAPTER 6

Books on Teaching Science

6.1 George E. Hein and Sabra Price. **Active Assessment for Active Science: A Guide for Elementary School Teachers.** Portsmouth, N.H.: Heinemann, 1994. 155 pp.

Price: $18.00 (ISBN 0-435-08361-9)

Active Assessment for Active Science is designed for teachers who develop their own assessments for hands-on science. This guide combines practical discussion with well-written theoretical information on the rationale for active assessments. It includes chapters on different forms of assessment, on managing assessment in the classroom, on scoring, on looking for evidence of learning in written student work, on ways that national curriculum developers grapple with and formulate assessments, and on the relationship between assessments and educational values. Rather than providing a system for assessment, the book advocates the development of active assessments that fit a particular teaching style, curriculum, and school climate. Numerous classroom examples of assessments and student work are given.

6.2 David C. Kramer. **Animals in the Classroom: Selection, Care, and Observations.** Menlo Park, Calif.: Addison-Wesley, 1989. 234 pp.

Price: $23.96 (ISBN 0-201-20679-X)

Animals in the Classroom: Selection, Care, and Observations is for elementary and middle school teachers interested in keeping small animals such as earthworms, praying mantises, frogs, and hamsters in the classroom. The book focuses on 28 individual creatures that represent various levels of the animal kingdom, from worms through mammals. A section on each animal combines text and illustrations to describe where and how the animal lives in nature, how to obtain it, and how to care for it with classroom-tested techniques. The book encourages teachers to stimulate student curiosity and interest in learning about animals. It helps teachers select appropriate animals and care for them humanely, and supplies background information to help answer students' questions and provide meaningful learning experiences with the animals. Suggestions for student observations and activities are given.

6.3 Senta A. Raizen, Joan B. Baron, Audrey B. Champagne, and others. **Assessment in Elementary School Science Education.** Washington, D.C.: National Center for Improving Science Education, 1989. 149 pp.

Price: $18.00

This report is one of three that served as the basis of the plan for a national program of science education for American elementary school children (*see* 6.20). The plan was developed by the National Center for

Discussing and analyzing data

ORDERING INFORMATION FOR PUBLICATIONS IN CHAPTER 6

The prices given for books and other publications in chapter 6 do not include the costs of shipping and handling. Before placing an order, readers are advised to contact the publishers of these items for current ordering information, including shipping charges. In some cases, discounts or special rates may be available to schools and educators.

Publishers' names are cited in the bibliographic data of the annotations. Their addresses and phone and fax numbers are listed in appendix A, "Publishers and Suppliers."

Improving Science Education. This volume discusses the assessment component of the plan in depth. It proposes reforms to make both teacher-controlled and externally mandated assessments support excellence in elementary science programs. According to the report, alternatives to traditional testing need to be an explicit part of assessing student achievement and progress in science. The chapters discuss issues in assessment such as testing what matters, the uses of assessment, what and how to assess, the assessment of program features, and improving assessments.

6.4 American Association for the Advancement of Science (AAAS). **Barrier-Free in Brief: Laboratories and Classrooms in Science and Engineering.** Washington, D.C.: AAAS, 1991. 36 pp.

Price: Free of charge (ISBN 0-87168-421-6)

Barrier-Free in Brief was prepared by the American Association for the Advancement of Science's Project on Science, Technology, and Disability. The booklet is a guide for university research laboratories, but it addresses meeting the needs of students with disabilities in the science classroom in any educational institution. A barrier-free classroom is defined as being fully accessible to people with disabilities. The booklet offers specific suggestions about organizing a barrier-free classroom and teaching students with disabilities. It presents related material such as a building access checklist and a list of organizations to contact for information on helping students with particular disabilities.

6.5 American Association for the Advancement of Science (AAAS). **Benchmarks for Science Literacy.** New York, N.Y.: Oxford University Press, 1993. 418 pp.

Price: $21.95 (ISBN 0-19-508986-3); with companion disk, $35.00

Benchmarks for Science Literacy on Disk [text and companion software version]

Price: $24.95; with book, $35.00

Created in close consultation with teachers, administrators, and scientists, *Benchmarks for Science Literacy* and its companion *Benchmarks for Science Literacy on Disk* suggest guidelines for what all students should know and be able to do in science and mathematics by the end of specific grade levels. *Benchmarks* is part of the Project 2061 initiative of the American Association for the Advancement of Science (AAAS). The volume outlines ways of achieving the standards for science literacy recommended in the 1989 AAAS publication *Science for All Americans.* Rather than being a proposed curriculum or a plan for one, *Benchmarks* is a compendium of specific goals that educators and policymakers can use to build new curricula. The software version allows users to browse, assemble, and print benchmarks in various formats, examine conceptual strands, use cross-reference features to identify conceptual connections, and brainstorm activities to address random sets of benchmarks from one grade span.

6.6 Carolyn H. Hampton, Carol D. Hampton, David C. Kramer, and others. **Classroom Creature Culture: Algae to Anoles.** Rev. ed. Arlington, Va.: National Science Teachers Association, 1994. 96 pp.

Price: $12.95 (ISBN 0-87355-120-6)

Classroom Creature Culture is a collection of 43 articles published in the journals of the National Science Teachers Association. The articles suggest ways of collecting, caring for, and investigating plants and small animals in the elementary school classroom. The plants and animals featured are easily obtainable. They range from simple organisms such as duckweed and daphnia to more complicated organisms such as newts, tree frogs, and snakes. Designed expressly for classroom conditions, the methods and techniques described require the least time and fewest resources possible. Plentiful ideas for classroom activities accompany each article. The activities encourage the practice of basic science skills such as measuring, observing, and collecting and analyzing data. Other activities focus on behavioral, morphological, and ecological changes. This publication is an updated version of an anthology published in 1986.

6.7 Robert C. Barkman. **Coaching Science Stars: Pep Talk and Play Book for Real-World Problem Solving.** Tucson, Ariz.: Zephyr Press, 1991. 162 pp.

Price: $19.00 (ISBN 0-913705-60-8)

Coaching Science Stars advocates the adoption of "pep talk"—a pedagogy typically used on the playing field, in the studio, or on stage—for teaching science in the classroom. The meaning and method of such pep talks are first described. Five basic teaching rules are enunciated: (1) create a need to know, (2) challenge students to know, (3) show how to know, (4) apply know-how, and (5) know how to inspire cooperation. The book then describes creative activities that can be done in groups with pep talk pedagogy. The activities have few resource requirements. They allow students to learn the way scientists do: by recognizing patterns, asking the right questions, making predictions with confidence, and doing experiments. The book gives teachers the tools for creating their own science curriculum based on the pep talk model.

6.8 Peter C. Gega. **Concepts and Experiences in Elementary School Science.** 2nd ed. New York, N.Y.: Macmillan Publishing Company, 1994. 511 pp.

Price: $45.00 (ISBN 0-02-341331-X)

Concepts and Experiences in Elementary School Science is a science experience sourcebook for teachers of children ages 5 to 12. It provides basic background information on topics in 12 science areas and presents directions for scores of related activities that enable children to learn science concepts and investigative skills. The many subject areas explored in the activities include light energy and color, plant and animal life, magnetic interactions, simple machines, sound energy, weather, and the human body. Many of the activities offer open-ended problems and topics for students and teachers to explore together. Each section of the book contains a list of books for both younger and older children to encourage further exploration. Brief appendixes suggest publications useful for teaching science and guidelines for caring for animals in the classroom.

6.9 Joyce VanTassel-Baska, Jane M. Bailey, Shelagh Gallagher, and Megan Fettig. **A Conceptual Overview of Science Education for High Ability Learners.** Williamsburg, Va.: College of William and Mary, Center for Gifted Education, 1993. 29 pp.

Price: $5.00

A Conceptual Overview of Science Education for High Ability Learners draws on recent national science education reports and on a review of the special learning needs of gifted learners. The paper outlines and discusses 6 major goals that should be considered when creating science curriculum for high-ability learners in grades K-8. These goals include (1) the development of broad scientific concepts, (2) scientific inquiry skills, (3) a knowledge base in specific science areas, (4) interdisciplinary connections, (5) problem-based learning approaches, and (6) scientific habits of mind. The paper addresses the importance of appropriate curriculum for encouraging girls and minorities to continue studying mathematics and science and the need for any curriculum to be flexible and responsive to change.

6.10 Alfred De Vito. **Creative Wellsprings for Science Teaching.** 2nd ed. West Lafayette, Ind.: Creative Ventures, 1989. 348 pp.

Price: $18.95 (ISBN 0-942034-06-6)

This light-hearted but useful book stresses methods for creative teaching to improve the quality of science education for children. *Creative Wellsprings for Science Teaching* presents three approaches to teaching science—morphological, process, and ideation-generation—and outlines classroom activities that enhance each approach. The book addresses the following topics: educating the gifted in science; science instruction and its enhancement through provocative question asking; the skill of model building; and peripheral enhancements to use in the classroom, such as discrepant events, puzzlers, problems, and tenacious "think abouts." *Creative Wellsprings* emphasizes ways that teachers can expand basic classroom activities into multiple activities and experiments that stimulate thinking and foster a challenging atmosphere.

6.11 Sally Stenhouse Kneidel. **Creepy Crawlies and the Scientific Method: Over 100 Hands-on Science Experiments for Children.** Golden, Colo.: Fulcrum Publishing, 1993. 224 pp.

Price: $15.95 (ISBN 1-55591-118-8)

Creepy Crawlies and the Scientific Method contains 114 experiments, mostly behavioral, with animals that are commonly found in nature. This resource book has 5 sections, with 16 chapters. The first section explains the scientific method as it applies to the experiments in the book. Then it discusses attracting and maintaining "critters." The remaining sections focus on creatures found in and under logs, creatures that live or start life in the water, terrestrial predators, and insect reproduction. Each chapter first describes the animals (mostly insects) and concludes with experiments. Each experiment follows a 5-step procedure involving a question, a hypothesis, methods, results, and conclusions. The book includes reproducible masters for student data sheets. The materials required are available locally or from commercial suppliers.

6.12 Wynne Harlen and Sheila Jelly. **Developing Science in the Primary Classroom.** Portsmouth, N.H.: Heinemann Educational Books, 1990. 71 pp.

Price: $14.00 (ISBN 0-435-08305-8)

This teacher-development book offers guidelines and practical suggestions for creating enjoyable opportunities for children to acquire scientific skills, attitudes, and concepts in the classroom. Designed for teachers who may lack confidence for teaching science, the book discusses how to start, structure, and manage classroom activities on any topic; how to evaluate the success of activities; and how to overcome difficult aspects of a teacher's role during activities (such as handling children's questions). It addresses getting and developing ideas for children's activities, fitting science into an existing curriculum, recognizing and encouraging children's development, and giving attention to concepts and content as well as to process skills. Helpful summary charts and examples reinforce major points and ideas throughout the book.

6.13 Ellen Doris. **Doing What Scientists Do: Children Learn to Investigate Their World.** Portsmouth, N.H.: Heinemann Educational Books, 1991. 194 pp.

Price: $19.50 (ISBN 0-435-08309-0)

Doing What Scientists Do is a practical book that presents an approach to teaching discovery science which helps develop the active interest of elementary school children in the world around them. Designed for teachers and administrators, the book discusses the basics of how children learn, how to inspire curiosity and help satisfy it, how to organize classroom space and materials, how to strike a balance between structure and freedom in the classroom, and how to manage the classroom in a way that encourages focus and interest. The book's many examples of actual classroom work and dialogue illuminate certain principles. Methods are provided for individualizing science learning for children with special needs; helpful suggestions are given for evaluation, grading, and conducting successful field trips. An excellent annotated bibliography includes suggestions for classroom reference books, field guides, films and videos, books that integrate science with literature and art, and teacher's reference books.

6.14 Glenn O. Blough and Julius Schwartz. **Elementary School Science and How to Teach It.** 8th ed. Fort Worth, Tex.: Holt, Rinehart, and Winston, 1990. 664 pp.

Price: $41.00 (ISBN 0-03-011559-0)

The first 5 chapters of *Elementary School Science and How to Teach It* look at (1) objectives and current trends in elementary school science, (2) various theories of child development and how they can help educators plan what and how to teach, (3) issues in science curricula and teaching methods, (4) processes of scientific investigation, and (5) the organization of a science program for all students. The second part of the book has 15 parallel "A" and "B" chapters that offer suggested content and methods for teaching specific concepts in 3 major scientific areas: the earth and the universe, living things, and matter and energy. Emphasis is on activities that encourage the hands-on participation of children of all ages in a science program; science as it relates to people and everyday problems is also emphasized. Each chapter on teaching includes practical ideas for preparation and a list of resources.

6.15 Susan Loucks-Horsley, Roxanne Kapitan, Maura D. Carlson, and others. **Elementary School Science for the '90s.** Alexandria, Va.: Association for Supervision and Curriculum Development, 1990. 166 pp.

Price: $13.95 (ISBN 0-87120-176-3)

Elementary School Science for the '90s, a collaborative book from the National Center for Improving Science Education, outlines ways for educators to ensure that good science learning is an important part of all children's educational experience. Synthesized from research and reports, the book offers a series of 13 recommendations for educators and administrators. It addresses questions about science curriculum, instruction, assessment, and teacher development and support. For each recommendation the authors discuss what is known about the topic from research, literature, and practical experience; what action can be taken; what roles can be played by local and state science leaders; what resources, materials, and exemplary programs exist; and key references. Appendixes list basic science education references and contact information for the resources, models, and exemplary programs described. Examples, checklists, and suggestions are given to prompt readers' ideas and motivation.

6.16 Ann C. Howe and Linda Jones. **Engaging Children in Science.** New York, N.Y.: Macmillan Publishing Company, 1993. 406 pp.

Price: $38.80 (ISBN 0-675-21186-7)

Engaging Children in Science is a guide to an activity-based course in methods of science teaching based on the constructivist approach. It describes how children learn science and suggests how certain teaching strategies capitalize on the way they learn best. Introductory chapters discuss the modern view of science, the theoretical foundations of constructivism, and how current research can be applied to science teaching. The book then discusses the use of science processes as the basis for teaching science concepts to children, different methods of planning and presenting lessons (such as direct instruction, guided discovery, and group and individual investigations), the integration of science with other subjects, evaluation of instruction, and reflective teaching. An extended case study follows the interaction between an experienced teacher and a teacher in training as they discuss the challenges of implementing strategies in a real classroom. *Engaging Children in Science* includes lessons plans, unit plans, and reference to resources for teaching.

6.17 Charles R. Barman. **An Expanded View of the Learning Cycle: New Ideas About an Effective Teaching Strategy.** Council for Elementary Science International (CESI) Monograph and Occasional Paper Series #4. N.P.: CESI, 1990. 37 pp.

Price: $4.00

This monograph introduces its discussion of the learning cycle—a widely used teaching strategy developed for an elementary science program in the 1970s—by providing background information on Jean Piaget's theory of cognitive development, on which the learning cycle was modeled. *An Expanded View of the Learning Cycle* then describes how components of the learning cycle are compatible with other prominent theories of learning—the constructivist view and sociologically and neurologically oriented theories—as well as with current educational themes such as cooperative learning. The appendixes present several learning cycle lessons that illustrate the flexibility of this teaching strategy.

6.18 National Center for Improving Science Education. **The Future of Science in the Elementary Schools: Educating Prospective Teachers.** Senta A. Raizen and Arie M. Michelsohn, eds. San Francisco, Calif.: Jossey-Bass Publishers, 1994. 182 pp.

Price: $27.95 (ISBN 1-55542-624-7)

The Future of Science in Elementary Schools results from a collaborative effort of the National Center for Improving Science Education and a panel of experts convened to study the improvement of preservice science education for elementary school teachers. With a research-based approach to science and learning, the volume offers a new vision for preparing prospective elementary science teachers to be creative facilitators of learning through investigation of the real world instead of people who merely pass on knowledge developed and conceived by others. The authors describe a 3-part interchangeable model for preparing teachers in science, and outline the basics of what prospective teachers need to learn in science and science-pedagogy courses, including fundamental underlying concepts, habits of mind, and effective instructional strategies. Vignettes illustrate the contrast between different approaches to teaching science and the vision needed to reform it.

6.19 National Environmental Education and Training Foundation. **Getting Started: A Guide to Bringing Environmental Education into Your Classroom.** David Bones, ed. Ann Arbor, Mich.: National Consortium for Environmental Education and Training, 1994. 138 pp.

Price: $9.95 (ISBN 1-884782-00-0)

This volume is a collection of real stories about teachers in grades K-12 who started environmental programs in their classrooms. *Getting Started* contains brief, helpful suggestions, resources, and ideas on bringing environmental education into the classroom. The first section provides a brief overview of the scope, history, and value of environmental education. The second offers suggestions for instructional materials, funding, workshops, courses, and in-service opportunities in environmental education. The third section includes information on networking with other environmental educators; securing grants; managing a growing environmental project; and locating awards, scholarships, and stipends. Rather than outlining a comprehensive program, the guide offers stories and information to inspire teachers and help them creatively find resources to meet their own unique needs.

6.20 National Center for Improving Science Education. **Getting Started in Science: A Blueprint for Elementary School Science Education.** 3rd ed. Washington, D.C.: National Center for Improving Science Education, 1989. 61 pp.

Price: $8.40

This report from the National Center for Improving Science Education (NCISE), which is funded by the U.S. Department of Education's Office of Educational Research and Improvement, advocates a hands-on, inquiry-based, constructivist approach to science. The report synthesizes information from 3 other NCISE reports—on curriculum and instruction (*see* 6.15), on assessment (*see* 6.3), and on teacher development and support (*see* 6.18). The "Blueprint" in the report's subtitle is the NCISE plan, based on those 3 reports, for an elementary (K-6) school education system that will serve the needs of American students for education in science and technology well into the next century. In support of its plan, the report presents recommendations directed to the federal government, state and local governments, and policymaking bodies such as national education associations and science-based organizations. Specific recommendations for science education specialists, administrators, teachers, and parents are to be provided by NCISE in a series of implementation guides.

6.21 Paul F. Brandwein and A. Harry Passow, eds. **Gifted Young in Science: Potential Through Performance.** Washington, D.C.: National Science Teachers Association, 1988. 422 pp.

Price: $10.00 (ISBN 0-87355-076-5)

Gifted Young in Science presents 34 essays that probe the phenomenon of talent in science, exploring ways that educators can foster science talent in all children. The authors include natural and physical scientists, psychologists, historians, scholars of curriculum and instruction, teachers of teachers, and writers. The subjects they address include the nature of creativity and giftedness; recognizing and nurturing multiple talents; designing schools, programs, and practices that channel children's interest in science from a young age; and the nature and craft of teaching. The book focuses on creating environments and conditions that evoke and nurture the potential of all students. It includes discussions of the importance of open classrooms and a variety of inquiry modes, the role of science centers, and specialized schools. In a separate section, 9 outstanding scientists, scholars, and teachers reflect on the events or people that led them to their life's work. An annotated bibliography highlights books useful for developing programs and practices for the gifted.

6.22 Maria Sosa, Estrella M. Triana, and Valerie L. Worthington, eds. **Great Explorations: Discovering Science in the Library.** Washington, D.C.: American Association for the Advancement of Science, 1994. 177 pp.

Price: $14.95 (ISBN 0-87168-537-X)

Great Explorations is a product of the American Association for the Advancement of Science's Science Library Institute, a 5-month project that brought together 28 school and public librarians from the Washington, D.C., area to discuss what librarians can do to bring about science, mathematics, and education reform. Based on presentations at the institute, the book contains articles on components of current science education reform; guidelines for developing media programs, selecting science resources, and creating interdisciplinary and hands-on activities in the library; teaching science in a multicultural context; technology in the library; the importance of librarians in disseminating new materials, practices, and techniques; fund-raising opportunities for libraries; and the benefits of partnerships between public and school librarians. Guidelines for conducting a similar institute in other communities are provided.

6.23 Arthur A. Carin. **Guided Discovery Activities for Elementary School Science.** 3rd ed. New York, N.Y.: Macmillan Publishing Company, 1993. 268 pp.

Price: $26.60 (ISBN 0-02-319383-2)

Guided Discovery Activities for Elementary School Science contains simple hands-on science activities to develop children's creative problem-solving skills, awareness of the marvels of the universe, and appreciation for how science and scientists work. Rather than being a curriculum, the activities are a resource for facilitating children's own construction of science and technology concepts. The activities involve a wide range of topics—the environment, ecology, human anatomy and physiology, and health and nutrition. They can be done in any order. Directions, illustrations, useful questions, and references are provided for each activity. *Guided Discovery Activities* emphasizes cooperative learning, but the activities can also be teacher-directed or conducted by individual students. A special series of guided discovery activities for students with special needs is included.

6.24 David L. Haury and Peter Rillero. **Hands-On Approaches to Science Teaching: Questions and Answers from the Field and Research.** Ohio State University, Columbus, June 30, 1992. Distributed by ERIC Clearinghouse for Science, Mathematics, and Environmental Education, Columbus, Ohio, 1992. 32 pp.

Price: $5.25

This brief document uses a question-and-answer format to pose and respond to 10 basic questions often asked by teachers about hands-on science teaching and learning. The questions include, for example: What is hands-on learning? How can practicing teachers gain experience with hands-on methods? How is hands-on learning evaluated? Each question is answered from three perspectives. The first and second responses are provided, respectively, by individual teachers and curriculum developers, identified by name. Following their comments, "Notes from the literature" provide another rich source of information in the form of brief responses to each question from the research literature. Full citations to all references are provided.

6.25 Peter C. Gega. **How to Teach Elementary School Science.** 2nd ed. New York, N.Y.: Macmillan Publishing Company, 1994. 244 pp.

Price: $30.00 (ISBN 0-02-341333-6)

This book explains and shows how to teach science to children in grades K-6. It first reviews the importance of elementary science education and then introduces a broad cluster of teaching skills through step-by-step descriptions and the use of real-life examples. The chapters and exercises should enable teachers to decide what science is basic, useful, and learnable for children; recognize and understand how children learn; use closed-ended and open-ended teaching activities; locate and use a variety of resources; arrange and manage learning centers; and organize and assess science teaching. The first of 5 appendixes presents a sampler of science activities and open-ended investigations to show the kinds of concrete experiences children need in order to learn science. Other appendixes include information about publications, science supply sources, and child development stages. This complete volume is also contained in Part I of the companion book *Science in Elementary Education* (7th ed.) (*see* 6.44).

6.26 Elizabeth Meng and Rodney L. Doran. **Improving Instruction and Learning Through Evaluation: Elementary School Science.** Columbus, Ohio: ERIC Clearinghouse for Science, Mathematics, and Environmental Education, 1993. 182 pp.

Price: $16.75

Improving Instruction and Learning Through Evaluation is designed to help teachers and supervisors expand and improve their assessment efforts. The book addresses different reasons for assessing science learning and discusses the kinds of information that can be gathered. Methods of collecting information, such as written tests, practical tests, observations, and interviews, are presented. The advantages and disadvantages of different methods are considered, and, finally, there is discussion of how to use the information gathered in light of the original purpose. Many examples of assessment items that have been used with science programs are included. The book also gives tips on how to develop assessment instruments.

6.27 Rosemary Althouse. **Investigating Science with Young Children.** New York, N.Y.: Teachers College Press, 1988. 200 pp.

Price: $18.95 (ISBN 0-8077-2912-4)

Teaching science using an open-ended process approach can be an exciting adventure for both teachers and children. With this approach there is neither a predetermined sequence of events for children nor a specific set of directions for the teacher. *Investigating Science with Young Children* outlines 85 activities that teachers can use in guiding 3-, 4-, and 5-year-olds in fruitful, open-ended exploration. The first part of the book presents a theoretical explanation of the benefits of the process approach and the role of the science teacher. The second part describes the activities. For each activity there is a list of materials, suggestions for getting started, and questions and comments teachers can use to guide children as an activity progresses. The activities include such things as exploring water, mixing colors, experimenting with balance, and investigating sand. They can be done in any order.

6.28 Michael J. Caduto and Joseph Bruchac. **Keepers of Life: Discovering Plants Through Native American Stories and Earth Activities for Children.** Golden, Colo.: Fulcrum Publishing, 1994. 265 pp.

Price: $22.95 (ISBN 1-55591-186-2)

This book, about learning to understand, live with, and care for plants, draws on Native American history and culture and uses an interdisciplinary approach. Eighteen carefully selected Native North American stories are combined with imaginative hands-on activities to promote children's understanding of, appreciation for, empathy with, and stewardship of plants. The indoor and outdoor activities in the 15 chapters cover a wide range of concepts: botany; plant ecology; environmental and stewardship issues that are important to plants; and the natural history of North American plants and plantlike organisms. Children are introduced to the greenhouse effect, global warming, ozone depletion, acid rain, endangered species, and extinction. Each chapter includes extensive background information, suggested discussion questions, and extensions. The book emphasizes the complex and interconnected nature of all living things. An index of activities arranged by subject describes the specific lessons taught by each activity. A teacher's guide is available; it lists books, guides to environmental and outdoor education, and interdisciplinary studies.

6.29 Michael J. Caduto and Joseph Bruchac. **Keepers of the Animals: Native American Stories and Wildlife Activities for Children.** Golden, Colo.: Fulcrum Publishing, 1991. 266 pp.

Price: $22.95 (ISBN 1-55591-088-2)

This volume is about learning to understand, live with, and care for animals. Combining 24 carefully selected Native American animal stories with interdisciplinary activities, it guides children through a study of the concepts and topics of wildlife ecology; issues in environmental stewardship; issues that are particularly important to animals; and the natural history and habitat of North American animals, from mollusk to mammal. The activities are designed to provoke curiosity and facilitate discovery of animals and their environments. They involve children in creative arts, theater, reading, writing, listening, science, social studies, mathematics, and sensory awareness. Each chapter includes extensive science background information, discussion questions, and extensions. An index of activities arranged by subject describes the specific lessons taught by each activity. A companion teacher's guide that discusses the nature of Native North American stories and cultures is available. That volume provides lists of books for further reading and suggests guides to environmental and outdoor education.

6.30 Michael J. Caduto and Joseph Bruchac. **Keepers of the Earth: Native American Stories and Environmental Activities for Children.** Golden, Colo.: Fulcrum Publishing, 1989. 209 pp.

Price: $22.95 (ISBN 1-55591-027-0)

This book features a collection of North American Indian stories and related hands-on environmental activities designed to inspire children and to help them feel that they are a part of their surroundings. The emphasis is on an interdisciplinary approach to teaching about the earth and Native American cultures. A wide range of topics is explored: for example, trees, the seasons, soil, water, weather, pollination, life, and death. Each chapter opens with a story, followed by background science information, directions for related indoor and outdoor activities, suggested discussion questions, and extensions. The activities focus on sensory awareness and on understanding and caring for the earth and its inhabitants. An index of activities arranged by subject describes the specific lessons taught by the activities. A teacher's guide is available. It discusses the nature of Indian myths and the cultures from which the stories in *Keepers of the Earth* originated.

6.31 Francis X. Sutman, Virginia French Allen, and Francis Shoemaker. **Learning English Through Science: A Guide to Collaboration for Science Teachers, English Teachers, and Teachers of English as a Second Language.** Washington, D.C.: National Science Teachers Association, 1986. 43 pp.

Price: $4.00 (ISBN 0-87355-061-7)

Addressing the difficulties that multilingual students face in trying to learn science, this booklet offers approaches and advice that facilitate the learning of both the English language and various fields of science. Gathered from research and teaching experience, general strategies are presented for teaching classes that include limited-English-proficient (LEP) students. Also presented are specific methods for preparing LEP students to read science materials, hands-on activities that are particularly effective for teaching science concepts to LEP students, and 3 detailed examples of science lessons that teach both science content and English. The book presents a model for developing and conducting lessons that stress hands-on activities for multilingual students.

6.32 Rosalind Charlesworth and Karen K. Lind. **Math and Science for Young Children.** Albany, N.Y.: Delmar, 1990. 664 pp.

Price: $26.95 (ISBN 0-8273-3402-8)

Math and Science for Young Children offers information to help teachers create developmentally appropriate and integrated mathematics and science curriculum for preschool and primary children. The book suggests activities in a sequence designed to support young children's construction of the concepts and skills essential to a basic understanding of mathematics and science. The activities are organized chronologically by student age. Emphasis is placed on enriching three types of learning opportunities: naturalistic, informal, and structured. A developmentally appropriate and individualized approach to assessment is stressed. Appendixes include a series of developmentally appropriate assessment tasks, a list of children's books with mathematics and science concepts, and finger plays and songs.

6.33 DeAnna Banks Beane. **Mathematics and Science: Critical Filters for the Future of Minority Students.** Washington, D.C.: The Mid-Atlantic Equity Center, The American University, 1988. 62 pp.

Price: $3.25

The goal of *Mathematics and Science: Critical Filters* is to provide information helpful for creating equity-based elementary school science instruction. The resource manual reviews the important role of the school principal in effecting change. It describes factors influencing the underrepresentation of minorities in advanced mathematics and science courses and details the components of successful strategies and programs for addressing underrepresentation. The manual provides materials for curriculum assessment and planning, such as data collection forms and checklists, and offers an annotated list of resources.

6.34 National Research Council. **National Science Education Standards.** Washington, D.C.: National Academy Press, 1995. 300 pp.

Price: $19.95 (ISBN 0-309-05326-9)

In an effort to guide the science education system in the United States, this document offers a vision of what it means to be scientifically literate and describes what students nationwide should know and be able to do in science as a result of their learning experiences. The volume is the result of a 3-year effort that involved contributions from thousands of teachers, parents, scientists, and others. The standards address what students should be able to do and understand at different grade levels, exemplary practices of science teaching and teacher training, criteria for assessing and analyzing learning, the nature and design of the school and district science program, and the support and resources needed to provide all students with the opportunity to learn science. The standards suggested in this document reflect the principles that learning science should be an inquiry-based process, that science in schools should reflect the intellectual trends of contemporary science, and that all Americans have a role in science education reform.

6.35 DeAnna Banks Beane. **Opening Up the Mathematics and Science Filters: Our Schools Did It, So Can Yours!** Chevy Chase, Md.: Mid-Atlantic Center, Mid-Atlantic Equity Consortium, 1992. 104 pp.

Price: $3.25

Opening Up the Mathematics and Science Filters tells the story of the Mid-Atlantic Equity Center's successful 4-year project to increase the participation and performance of African-American and Hispanic students in elementary school mathematics and science. The project brought together 3 school districts and demonstrated that urban and suburban school districts can pool resources, expertise, and expectations to form powerful problem-solving entities. It showed that teachers and counselors can be empowered as reformers for school instructional and student support programs and that school-based intervention in mathematics and science can improve the participation and performance of minority and other students. The guide includes detailed information on the successful project's components and structure, first-hand accounts of project participants, a 9-step guide to implementing a similar program, reflections on things project organizers might have done differently, a list of consultants, and a program checklist.

6.36 Jos Elstgeest, Wynne Harlen, Sheila Jelly, and others. **Primary Science . . . Taking the Plunge: How to Teach Primary Science More Effectively.** Portsmouth, N.H.: Heinemann Educational Books, 1985. 116 pp.

Price: $18.50 (ISBN 0-435-57350-0)

The current emphasis on scientific process skills and attitudes increases the importance of what teachers do and say as classroom activities are carried out. *Primary Science* offers practical advice for increasing the effectiveness of the teacher's role in science activities. The book's 8 chapters deal with many aspects of teaching that often cause concern: making a start, handling difficult questions, encouraging children to write things down, helping them raise questions and observe carefully, planning investigations, and taking into account children's own ideas. The book's many suggestions are based on research into the teaching and learning of science. Simple, real-life anecdotes and examples illustrate the authors' points. Each chapter includes a short outline, a detailed summary, and a list of specific guidelines for practice.

6.37 Robert A. Dean, Melanie Messer Dean, Jack A. Gerlovich, and Vivian Spiglanin. **Safety in the Elementary Science Classroom.** 2nd ed. Washington, D.C.: National Science Teachers Association, 1993. 22 pp.

Price: $5.95 (ISBN 0-87355-117-6)

Safety in the Elementary Science Classroom gives teachers engaged in science activities basic directions and suggestions on how to provide a safe environment for their students. The guide is easy to use and concise. It covers the following areas in detail: In Case of an Accident, Animals in the Classroom, Plants in the Classroom, Eye Protection, First Aid, Field Trips, Fire Prevention and Control, Storage and Labeling, Safe Use of Equipment and Materials, and Safety Checklist. The suggestions are minimum safeguards and should be used with appropriate standards, regulations, state requirements, and federal codes. The guide is printed on a flip chart for posting in the classroom.

6.38 Johanna Scott, ed. **Science and Language Links: Classroom Implications.** Portsmouth, N.H.: Heinemann, 1993. 91 pp.

Price: $14.50 (ISBN 0-435-08338-4)

This brief volume examines the role of language in science learning and the ways science can be used to develop children's language abilities. It discusses theoretical issues in the context of the classroom and offers numerous concrete examples of involving children actively in science and language learning. The book's 7 chapters, all by individual authors who are teachers or teacher educators, are presented in 3 sections: (1) Science and Talking, (2) Science and Writing, and (3) Science and Reading. Chapter topics include reflective questions, hands-on science as an ideal choice for learning a second language, and ways of writing science. The volume originated in Australia. It includes many references to Australian and British source material.

6.39 Rodger W. Bybee, C. Edward Buchwald, Sally Crissman, and others. **Science and Technology Education for the Elementary Years: Frameworks for Curriculum and Instruction.** Washington, D.C.: The National Center for Improving Science Education, 1989. 132 pp.

Price: $14.40

Science and Technology Education for the Elementary Years is a policy statement on science education in elementary schools synthesized by a study panel from findings, recommendations, and perspectives of studies and reports. Emphasizing the importance of developing children's basic attitudes and understanding of science and technology from an early age, this report presents suggestions for educators forming curricular and instructional frameworks. In terms of a curricular framework, the report advocates hands-on activities that relate to the students' world, the development of scientific and technological concepts and skills within a personal and social context, and the study of a few concepts in depth. Regarding an instructional framework, the report recommends a 4-stage constructivist approach to learning, with students building their concepts and skills through a variety of experiences. It also identifies 9 major concepts that should be at the core of an elementary science program, and discusses goals, rationale, and the importance of the educational environment. Appendixes list several exemplary science education programs.

6.40 Eleanor Duckworth, Jack Easley, David Hawkins, and Androula Henriques. **Science Education: A Minds-On Approach for the Elementary Years.** Hillsdale, N.J.: Lawrence Erlbaum Associates, 1990. 191 pp.

Price: $39.95 (ISBN 0-8058-0543-5)

In this volume, 4 authors from different professional backgrounds discuss elementary science education from their respective vantage points. They present approaches to teaching strongly influenced by Piaget that they developed and then put into practice and evaluated. Their results are shared with readers. The authors encourage teachers to be researchers in their own classrooms, investigating phenomena with their students and learning with them. The book illustrates how elementary science can and needs to begin with explorations of events in the everyday world so that students learn how to investigate scientifically to form the basis for later learning of science concepts.

6.41 National Science Teachers Association (NSTA). **Science for All Cultures: A Collection of Articles from NSTA's Journals.** Arlington, Va.: NSTA, 1993. 64 pp.

Price: $16.50 (ISBN 0-87355-122-2)

This booklet presents 14 previously published articles that together provide a basic understanding of multicultural science education, its implications for teacher education and for individual and national well-being, and suggestions for using such an approach as part of teachers' instructional process. The articles include discussions of the underrepresentation of women, African-Americans, Native Americans, and Hispanic people and the significant but unnoted contributions of other cultures to scientific advancement.

6.42 Edward Victor and Richard D. Kellough. **Science for the Elementary School.** 7th ed. New York, N.Y.: Macmillan Publishing Company, 1993. 863 pp.

Price: $67.00 (ISBN 0-02-422901-6)

Science for the Elementary School serves two major purposes: (1) it offers methods and strategies for teaching elementary science, and (2) it provides an overview of science content in clear outline form. More than 750 science activities for the classroom are included. A completely reorganized and rewritten Part I focuses on the developmental elements of teaching. Detailed discussions are presented on the history of science education, goals of elementary school science, the knowledge and skills needed to teach science effectively, characteristics of elementary school children and their intellectual development, teacher behaviors that facilitate student learning in a variety of settings, ways of planning curriculum and lessons, assessments and reporting student achievement, and the importance of continuing and evaluating teachers' professional development. The book emphasizes how teachers can help children gain skills, experiences, and knowledge. Guidelines are included on the use of different aids and media, and information is given about where to obtain classroom materials and resources.

6.43 Marvin Druger, ed. **Science for the Fun of It: A Guide to Informal Science Education.** Washington, D.C.: National Science Teachers Association, 1988. 141 pp.

Price: $11.00 (ISBN 0-87355-074-9)

Science for the Fun of It is a collection of articles highlighting some of the many science learning opportunities that exist outside the classroom. Such resources include zoos, museums, television programs, magazines and books, and a variety of creative programs and projects. Written by people who are involved with informal science education, the articles are designed to help readers become more aware of these resources, of their educational benefits, and of how they can be used effectively. Checklists of helpful hints for using the resources are included. Besides information on the positive aspects of the resources it features, the book gives background information on cognitive psychology, science learning, and audience research for informal learning.

6.44 Peter C. Gega. **Science in Elementary Education.** 7th ed. New York, N.Y.: Macmillan Publishing Company, 1994. 713 pp.

Price: $61.00 (ISBN 0-02-341302-6)

This two-part book, *Science in Elementary Education,* combines practical methods, background information, and activities for teaching science to children. Part I discusses the importance of elementary science education and introduces a broad cluster of teaching skills through step-by-step descriptions and the use of real-life examples. The chapters help teachers decide what science is fundamental, useful, and learnable for children; recognize and understand how children learn; use closed-ended and open-ended teaching activities; locate and use a variety of resources; arrange and manage learning centers; and organize and assess science teaching. (Part I is also published as a separate book under the title *How to Teach Elementary School Science; see* 6.25). Part II contains 12 chapters of subject matter background in different areas, with hundreds of related hands-on activities and investigations to use with children. The activities and investigations use readily obtainable materials and allow children both to learn concepts and procedures and to explore open-ended problems and topics.

6.45 Mike Watts. **The Science of Problem-Solving: A Practical Guide for Science Teachers.** Portsmouth, N.H.: Heinemann, 1991. 160 pp.

Price: $18.50 (ISBN 0-435-08314-7)

Problem solving has been promoted as a way of making education in schools more relevant to students' everyday lives. This book is a practical guide and background reader for teachers in middle and secondary schools. It examines the multiplicity of approaches to problem solving in science and technology and considers the skills, processes, and methods involved. The book explores the background and language of problem solving and discusses the skills, processes, and methods involved. It addresses factors that affect learning in individuals and groups as they solve problems; the transfer and ownership of learning; and managing and incorporating into a curriculum open-ended problem solving where there are multiple solutions. Many examples of problems included in the book are for teachers to use with students. An appendix contains "additional problems."

6.46 Carol M. Butzow and John W. Butzow. **Science Through Children's Literature: An Integrated Approach.** Englewood, Colo.: Teacher Ideas Press/ Libraries Unlimited, 1989. 240 pp.

Price: $24.50 (ISBN 0-87287-667-5)

Science Through Children's Literature: An Integrated Approach explains how children's fiction that is well-selected and conceptually and factually correct can be used to teach elementary science. Although the method is most easily applied with picture books for grades K-3, it can be used in higher grades with short chapters or excerpts from longer sources. The first part of the volume discusses the developmental needs of young children and shows how well-chosen fiction can help them understand and remember scientific concepts. It presents criteria for judging books for possible classroom use and suggests appropriate activities to accompany their use. It suggests ways to work with media specialists in selecting materials, and outlines a sample unit to show how a classic children's book can be the basis for science instruction in the classroom. The second part of *Science Through Children's Literature* lists classroom activities based on 33 popular children's books that cover life science, earth and space science, and physical science.

6.47 Wendy Saul, Jeanne Reardon, Anne Schmidt, and others. **Science Workshop: A Whole Language Approach.** Portsmouth, N.H.: Heinemann, 1993. 158 pp.

Price: $17.50 (ISBN 0-435-08336-8)

Science Workshop: A Whole Language Approach borrows some of the ideas and methods developed in the reading-and-writing workshop approach to teaching and applies them to science instruction. Focusing on a discussion of 3 characteristics of whole language classrooms—authenticity, autonomy, and community—a group of education professionals share their first-hand experiences at promoting student involvement in science using the workshop model. The book includes a theoretical overview of the science workshop; practical advice on getting started, arranging materials, and setting up a classroom; and an excellent resource guide with suggestions for materials and sources of information on a number of science topics.

6.48 Amy Bain, Janet S. Richer, Janet A. Weckman, and Margaret Redman. **Solomon Resource Guide: Science. Vols. 1 and 2.** Cincinnati, Ohio: Solomon Publishing, 1993. Vol. 1: 443 pp. Vol. 2: 485 pp.

Price: $170.00

Developed for teachers who wish to teach without using textbooks, *Solomon Resource Guide* offers references and ideas for creating more than 40 thematic K-8 science education units that utilize hands-on activities and children's literature. The guide contains lists of books, coded by reading ability, that can used to teach one or several topics. It offers descriptions of fiction and nonfiction children's books that relate to basic themes and can be used to stimulate curiosity or language development. It provides simple activities and experiments that use everyday household items, and creative writing and arts activities appropriate for a variety of ability levels. Key concepts that can be used to prepare lessons plans for different grade levels (primary, intermediate, upper) and sample tests are included. Volume 1 is for units on weather, the solar system, plants, animals, energy, and machines. Volume 2 is for units on the earth, habitats, the human body, matter, and ecology.

6.49 Joseph Abruscato. **Teaching Children Science.** 3rd ed. Boston, Mass.: Allyn and Bacon, 1992. 428 pp.

Price: $54.00 (ISBN 0-205-13650-8)

Teaching Children Science, a book for preservice and in-service teachers, offers a broad review of elementary school science and ways of teaching it. The first 8 chapters explore theoretical and practical aspects of planning for learning. Topics include child development goals; discovery learning and science process skills; how to plan for units, daily lessons, and assessments; teaching strategies, textbooks, and classroom management techniques for discovery learning; integrating science with other subjects; and working with children with special needs. The second part of the book provides basic background in science content and concepts for lessons in the life, physical, and earth sciences, together with related discovery activities and demonstrations.

6.50 Arthur A. Carin. **Teaching Modern Science.** 6th ed. New York, N.Y.: Macmillan Publishing Company, 1993. 380 pp.

Price: $44.00 (ISBN 0-02-319381-6)

Teaching Modern Science is designed to introduce novice teachers to the specialized content and teaching strategies for teaching science and technology effectively. Although the book describes several approaches to teaching and learning, it emphasizes a minds-on/hands-on activity-based approach. Practical, classroom-tested ideas are presented on planning, organizing, managing, and assessing an integrated guided-discovery, teaching/learning program for grades K-8. The book includes step-by-step guidelines for creating lessons and suggestions for weaving science and technology themes into activities that are relevant to children's everyday lives. Appendixes list sources for science supplies, equipment, and materials; food requirements for various classroom animals; basic steps for creating a successful learning center; a sample chart for problem solving; and directions for constructing storage areas and homes for living things.

6.51 Helen Ross Russell. **Ten-Minute Field Trips: A Teacher's Guide to Using the Schoolgrounds for Environmental Studies.** 2nd ed. Washington, D.C.: National Science Teachers Association, 1990. 163 pp.

Price: $16.95 (ISBN 0-87355-098-6)

This imaginative book suggests field trips that are short and close-to-school (or home) and hands-on activities that can initiate or enhance classroom learning about the environment. The wide range of engaging investigative experiences—which do not require elaborate equipment or vast knowledge about natural history—involve teachers and children in learning about the world by observing, thinking, and doing. Topics include animals, weather and weather prediction, seasonal changes, building materials, rocks, soil formation, water and its effects, and recycling and natural decomposition. Each general topic is introduced with brief background information. Related introductory (or follow-up) classroom activities and preparations are then presented. Many tips are provided on how to motivate young people to invest time and creative energy in exploring how nature works.

6.52 Wendy Saul and Sybille A. Jagusch, eds. **Vital Connections: Children, Science and Books.** Portsmouth, N.H.: Heinemann, 1992. 165 pp.

Price: $14.95 (ISBN 0-435-08332-5)

Vital Connections is a collection of 15 papers from a symposium sponsored by the Children's Literature Center of the Library of Congress. The theme of the volume is the role of science trade books in helping children realize the pleasures, potential, and limits of science. Representing the views of authors, editors, reviewers, and specialists in children's literature and science, the papers consider a variety of topics: what role science books should play in the lives of children, how children learn science, when science books should be introduced, who decides what children should know, why some topics are prevalent in science books, how science authors approach their work, and what is entailed in selecting and editing science books. The editors note that the volume offers few definitive answers and promotes no conclusive account of ways to write, evaluate, or use juvenile science literature. Instead, it outlines important issues and offers thoughtful discussion.

CHAPTER 7

Science Book Lists and Resource Guides

7.1 ASTC/CIMUSET Directory and Statistics 1995. Washington, D.C.: Association of Science-Technology Centers, 1995. 180 pp.

Price: $35.00 (ISBN 0-944040-39-X)

This directory lists the addresses, phone and fax numbers, e-mail addresses, and names of key staff members at more than 400 institutions. Included are science-technology centers, nature centers, aquariums, planetariums, space theaters, and natural history museums, children's museums, and other multidisciplinary museums. The organizations listed in the directory belong to ASTC (the Association of Science-Technology Centers) or to CIMUSET (the International Committee of Science and Technology Museums, a branch of the International Council of Museums). The statistics in the volume provide information about more than 200 of these institutions. The directory is updated annually.

7.2 John T. Gillespie and Corinne J. Maden, eds. **Best Books for Children: Preschool Through Grade 6.** 5th ed. New Providence, N.J.: R. R. Bowker, 1994. 1,411 pp.

Price: $58.00 (ISBN 0-8352-3455-X)

Best Books for Children lists and provides evaluative comments on approximately 17,140 books highly recommended to fit the reading interests and academic needs of children. The comments are gathered from a number of review sources. The volume lists titles on a broad range of topics and includes an extensive section on the sciences. *Best Books for Children* is organized by topic and indexed by author, illustrator, title, and subject/grade level.

7.3 Margaret N. Coughlan, ed. **Books for Children: A List of Noteworthy Books Published in the United States During 1994.** No. 11. Washington, D.C.: Library of Congress, 1995. 19 pp.

Price: $1.00 (Available from Superintendent of Documents, U.S. Government Printing Office)

Books for Children is a small booklet produced annually by the Children's Literature Center of the Library of Congress. It is an annotated bibliography of some 100 noteworthy titles published the previous year. The books annotated are on wide-ranging topics, including adventure, natural history, and science themes. Entries are loosely arranged by age group and alphabetized by title. Each entry includes a one- or two-sentence description of the book and bibliographic information.

Investigating rocks and minerals

ORDERING INFORMATION FOR PUBLICATIONS IN CHAPTER 7

The prices given for books and other publications in chapter 7 do not include the costs of shipping and handling. Before placing an order, readers are advised to contact the publishers of these references for current ordering information, including shipping charges. In some cases, discounts or special rates may be available to schools and educators.

Publishers' names are cited in the bibliographic data of the annotations. Their addresses and phone and fax numbers are listed in appendix A, "Publishers and Suppliers."

7.4 Gary A. Dunn. **Buggy Books: A Guide to Juvenile and Popular Books on Insects and Their Relatives.** Special Publication No. 3. Lansing, Mich.: Young Entomologists' Society, 1990. 120 pp.

Price: $6.95

Buggy Books lists 736 nonfiction spider and insect books published since 1900 that are appropriate for young people. The guide has 2 sections: (1) books on noninsect arthropods (crustaceans, harvestmen, spiders, mites, ticks, and scorpions) and (2) books on insects. Each section contains an alphabetical listing of titles, as well as subject, author, and age-appropriateness indexes. The subject indexes include headings that could be helpful to teachers—for example, activities, experiments, crafts, photography of insects, and insect ecology.

7.5 Eisenhower National Clearinghouse for Mathematics and Science Education. **Earth Day in the Classroom: Mathematics and Science Materials and Resources for Teachers.** ENC Focus Issue 2. Columbus, Ohio: Eisenhower National Clearinghouse, 1995. 26 pp.

Price: Free of charge.

This issue of *ENC Focus* offers a sampling of high-quality educational materials and other resources that can be used to highlight environmental issues in the classroom or incorporated into teaching about Earth Day. Each entry includes a description of a particular resource or title, a suggested grade level, and a listing of related materials, including those from the same series or items that are of the same resource type, such as videos and software. Because environmental science covers so many subtopics, a wide cross-section of materials in different media or formats is represented. A select bibliography, information on Earth Day Internet resources, and a list of relevant federal groups and agencies are also included.

7.6 Will Snyder and the 1994 National 4-H Energy Education Review Team. **Educating Young People About Energy for Environmental Stewardship: A Guide to Resources for Curriculum Development with an Emphasis on Youth-led, Community-based Learning.** Chevy Chase, Md.: National 4-H Council, Environmental Stewardship Program, 1994. 47 pp.

Price: $5.00

Educating Young People About Energy for Environmental Stewardship is a resource guide for educators who wish to develop energy and environmental curricula and programs. The booklet includes descriptions of important criteria for choosing or evaluating such curricula; general and age-specific suggestions for developing programs and program formats; an annotated list of materials and resource organizations that focus on environmental and energy issues; information on accessing the 4-H electronic Energy Education Resources Database; and an overview chart of resources or organizations for teaching, learning, and program planning.

7.7 Educators Guide to Free Science Materials. 36th ed. Randolph, Wis.: Educators Progress Service, 1995. 259 pp.

Price: $27.95 (ISBN 0-87708-279-0)

The *Educators Guide to Free Science Materials* is an annual annotated listing of selected free, mixed-media science materials. It is designed to provide an up-to-date means of identifying materials currently available. This 36th edition classifies and provides complete information on the titles, sources, availability, and content of 225 films, 21 film strips, 5 sets of slides, 1 audiotape, 772 videotapes, and 374 printed items. The book is divided in sections by media format and is organized by subject within each section. Entries are indexed by title and subject. The guide's source and availability index provides the names and addresses of organizations from which materials may be obtained.

7.8 Patti K. Sinclair. **E For Environment: An Annotated Bibliography of Children's Books with Environmental Themes.** New Providence, N.J.: R. R. Bowker, 1992. 292 pp.

Price: $42.00 (ISBN 0-8352-3028-7)

E for Environment is an annotated guide to 517 children's books with environmental themes. Selections cover a wide range of subjects and are organized in 5 major areas: fostering positive attitudes about the environment, ecology, environmental issues, people and nature, and learning activities. Titles include fiction and nonfiction books for children from preschool to age 14; a handful of titles for adults who work with children are included. An appendix of environmental classics and titles that reflect environmental issues and "ecophilosophy" is provided. Entries are indexed by author, title, and subject.

7.9 National Energy Information Center. **Energy Education Resources: Kindergarten Through 12th Grade.** Washington, D.C.: National Energy Information Center, U.S. Department of Energy, 1995. 86 pp.

Price: Free of charge.

Energy Education Resources, published annually by the U.S. Department of Energy, lists organizations that provide free or low-cost energy-related educational materials to students and educators. The organizations represented range from non-profit educational organizations to utilities, trade associations, publishers, and federal agencies. Each entry includes a short description of the organization, its address, and notes on relevant energy materials. Entries are broadly indexed by subject.

7.10 Richard J. Wilke, ed. **Environmental Education Teacher Resource Handbook: A Practical Guide for K-12 Environmental Education.** Millwood, N.Y.: Kraus International Publications, 1993. 448 pp.

Price: $19.95 (ISBN 0-527-20812-4)

This resource guide provides information on the historical background of environmental education curriculum and presents current, comprehensive information on useful publications, standards, and special materials for implementing a K-12 environmental education program. Topics covered in the first half of the book include creating or revising an environmental education program or curriculum, funding curriculum projects, developing assessment programs, and conducting special projects. Later chapters include an annotated bibliography of children's trade books (organized by subject), addresses and information on publishers and producers of curriculum materials, and an index of recently published reviews of environmental education software, videos, and curriculum guides.

7.11 Eisenhower National Clearinghouse for Mathematics and Science Education. **Equity in the Classroom: Mathematics and Science Materials and Resources for Elementary Teachers.** ENC Focus Issue 1. Columbus, Ohio: Eisenhower National Clearinghouse, 1994. 26 pp.

Price: Free of charge.

This issue of *ENC Focus* highlights a selection of materials and resources that can be useful in assuring that gender, minority status, disabilities, and facility with the English language do not become barriers to the full participation of students in science and mathematics instruction at the elementary level. The 18 titles described in the booklet represent a variety of learning formats and grade levels, and include activity books, CD-ROM titles, and kits. For each title, indicators of usefulness or other evaluative information are noted when available. If the materials were developed in accord with national or state curriculum standards, the particular standards are indicated. A list of selected readings on equity and an overview of organizations concerned with equity in mathematics and science education are provided.

7.12 The Museum of Science and Industry, Chicago, Ill. **Every Teacher's Science Booklist: An Annotated Bibliography of Science Literature for Children.** Bernice Richter and Pamela Nelson, eds. New York, N.Y.: Scholastic Professional Books, 1994. 182 pp.

Price: $18.95 (ISBN 0-590-49381-7)

Every Teacher's Science Booklist presents short reviews of 890 science book titles published since 1990. It is designed to serve as an aid in selecting quality children's science books, planning classroom activities, and conducting science project research. Each review includes a description, the intended grade level, and a rating of the book's overall usefulness. Appendixes list adult resource books, science magazines for children, teacher resource magazines, and general interest science magazines, and provide a directory of publishers. Entries are indexed by author, title, subject, and grade level.

7.13 Wendy Saul. **Find It! Science.** McHenry, Ill.: Follett Software Co., 1995.

Price: $189.00 ($50.00 for each additional disc)

This multimedia CD-ROM is designed to guide teachers, media specialists, and children in selecting appropriate literature to support science education in grades K-8. Featuring a user-friendly, playful interface for elementary and middle school learners, the application contains textual annotations and images of book covers for approximately 2,500 current books. The books were chosen from award-winning lists and recommendations made by librarians and science teachers nationwide. Reviews from journals are included for each book. Minimum hardware and software requirements for using this guide are a 68020 Macintosh with at least 4 MB of RAM, a hard drive with at least 4 to 5 MB of free space, a CD-ROM drive, System 6.0.7, and QuickTimes 1.5.

7.14 Eisenhower National Clearinghouse for Mathematics and Science Education. **Guidebook to Excellence 1994: A Directory of Federal Resources for Mathematics and Science Education Improvement. National Directory.** Columbus, Ohio: Eisenhower National Clearinghouse, 1994. 182 pp.

Price: $18.00 (ISBN 0-16-043142-5)

This book is a directory of federal offices, programs, and facilities concerned with education in mathematics and science in grades K-12. It contains background information on 16 federal departments and agencies, descriptive information about federal offices and programs for mathematics and science education at the national and regional levels, and state-by-state contacts for many of these resources. Although the book does not list all federally funded education programs, it provides contacts for additional information. Regional editions are available for 1994 and 1995.

7.15 Barbara Walthall, ed. **IDEAAAS: Sourcebook for Science, Mathematics and Technology Education.** Washington, D.C.: American Association for the Advancement of Science; Armonk, N.Y.: The Learning Team, 1995. 235 pp.

Price: $24.95 (ISBN 0-87168-545-0) (Available from The Learning Team)

IDEAAAS is a reference work designed to foster communication, connections, and ideas among individuals involved in science, mathematics, and technology education. Included are the following: three detailed guides that can help locate sources of approximately 10,000 activities, materials, and programs within 80 different categories and 7 disciplines; a state-by-state listing of information about resources in each state; a section that details organizations with a national constituency; and a publications and media section. Scientific professional societies, state science societies, state science academies, state and federal agencies, community-based organizations, zoos, planetariums, nature centers, and many other informal or formal places of science are listed. Two indexes are provided: an organization index and a name index of project directors, education directors, curators, or those responsible for science, mathematics, or technology education for each organization listed.

7.16 Donna F. Berlin. **Integrating Science and Mathematics in Teaching and Learning: A Bibliography.** Columbus, Ohio: ERIC Clearinghouse for Science, Mathematics, and Environmental Education, 1991. 54 pp.

Price: $5.50.

Current literature related to reform in science and mathematics education endorses the integration of science and mathematics teaching and learning as a means of improving achievement and attitudes within both disciplines. This bibliography identifies and categorizes literature related to such integration. It is intended for classroom teachers, teacher educators, curriculum specialists, and researchers. The bibliography has 5 sections: (1) Curriculum, (2) Instruction, (3) Research, (4) Curriculum—Instruction, and (5) Curriculum—Evaluation. The fourth and fifth sections classify curriculum programs that include instructional activities and evaluation of curriculum programs. Although the bibliography contains 555 citations, this listing is not meant to be exhaustive and will be updated periodically.

7.17 Carol M. Butzow and John W. Butzow. **Intermediate Science Through Children's Literature: Over Land and Sea.** Englewood, Colo.: Teacher Ideas Press, 1994. 193 pp.

Price: $23.00 (ISBN 0-87287-946-1)

Intermediate Science Through Children's Literature contains ideas and directions for earth and environmental science activities that can be linked to 14 popular children's novels, such as *Julie of the Wolves,* by Jean Craighead George; *The Cay,* by Theodore Taylor; and *Island of the Blue Dolphins,* by Scott O'Dell. The hands-on activities, which can be done in any order or can stand alone, include field trips, simple craft projects, library research, and collateral reading and writing. The first half of the guide combines novels with activities about land: students learn about the American prairie, tornadoes, weather, the Arctic, woods, the Rocky Mountains, and fossils. The second half of the guide connects books and activities that draw upon the environment of the sea: students learn about coral reefs, tropical lagoons, coastal islands, the ocean, wetlands, and whales.

7.18 The Latest and Best of TESS: The Educational Software Selector. 1993 ed. Hampton Bays, N.Y.: Educational Products Information Exchange (EPIE) Institute, 1993. 217 pp.

Price: $14.95 (ISBN 0-916087-16-6)

This 1993 directory is an annotated listing of essential information on 1,350 educational software programs that were among the most recently released Macintosh and MS-DOS programs and/or among the most highly rated by 50 respected software review sources. Organized by curriculum areas, the detailed entries include a program description, review citations, and software requirements. Subjects covered by the science-oriented programs include anatomy and physiology, astronomy, biology, chemistry, earth science, ecology and the environment, geology, meteorology, natural history, and physics. Addresses for software suppliers are provided. (Note: Interested readers should contact the publisher for information on the 1995 CD-ROM version of TESS, which has information on more than 17,000 programs.)

7.19 Isabel Schon. **"Libros de Ciencias en Español."** (A selection of recent science trade books in Spanish.) *Science & Children,* Vol. 32, No. 6 (March 1995): 30-32.

(Available from National Science Teachers Association.)

"Libros de Ciencias en Español" is a short bibliography, published in the National Science Teachers Association journal *Science & Children,* annotating recent science trade books in Spanish. (The annotations are in English.) The books are grouped by subject and within each section are arranged alphabetically by title. The following subject areas are represented: animals, conservation, encyclopedic series, nature, and physical science. A list of U.S. dealers of books in Spanish for children is provided.

7.20 Beverly Taylor Sher. **Notes From a Scientist: Resources and Activities for Gifted Children: Some Suggestions for Parents.** National Science Curriculum Project for High Ability Learners K-8. Williamsburg, Va.: College of William and Mary, Center for Gifted Education, 1993. 11 pp.

Price: $5.00

This brief publication contains thoughtful advice, ideas, and resources for parents and teachers who wish to enrich children's understanding and appreciation of science. It offers recommendations on selecting books, television and radio shows, and toys, and discusses the importance of adult mentors, scientific hobbies, role models, and field trips. The unique need for activities that nurture the development of girls' innate scientific abilities is noted. The emphasis in *Notes From a Scientist* is on creating extracurricular science opportunities that are fun and interesting.

7.21 National Science Teachers Association. **NSTA Science Education Suppliers 1995.** Arlington, Va.: National Science Teachers Association, 1995. 127 pp.

Price: $5.00

NSTA Science Education Suppliers is published annually in conjunction with the January or February issues of *Science & Children, The Science Teacher, Science Scope,* and the *Journal of College Science Teaching.* This yearly publication includes lists of suppliers and school science laboratory equipment; lists of firms producing computer hardware and software; manufacturers and distributors of audiovisual materials and other media; and textbook, resource materials, and trade book publishers.

7.22 Only the Best: The Annual Guide to the Highest-Rated Educational Software and Multimedia 1994-1995. Alexandria, Va.: Association for Supervision and Curriculum Development (ASCD), Education and Technology Resources Center. 1995. 185 pp.

Price: $25.00

Only the Best is an annual review guide of highly rated educational software and multimedia programs, compiled from the findings of top national software and multimedia evaluators. Although the book reviews software programs on a wide variety of topics, science and social studies programs predominate. Each entry includes a program description, cost, grade level, hardware requirements, a list of magazine reviews, and user tips. The guide, which is organized by subject area, also includes a list of titles useful for students or teachers in special education and a directory of software publishers. This title is also available in electronic formats.

7.23 **"Outstanding Science Trade Books for Children for 1995."** *Science & Children,* Vol. 32, No. 6 (March 1995). 6 pp.

Price: $2.00 for a single copy of the 6-page reprint. (Available from Children's Book Council.)

"Outstanding Science Trade Books for Children for 1995" (published in the National Science Teachers Association journal *Science & Children*) is an annotated bibliography of approximately 50 children's science trade books published in 1994. The books, intended primarily for prekindergarten to eighth-grade students, were evaluated by a book review panel appointed by the National Science Teachers Association and the Children's Book Council. Selection for inclusion was based on a book's accuracy of information, readability, and format and illustrations. The books are grouped by subject and within each section are arranged alphabetically by title. The following subject areas are represented in this edition: archaeology, anthropology, and paleontology; biography; earth science; environment and ecology; fiction; life science; physical science; and technology and engineering.

7.24 Maria Sosa and Shirley M. Malcom, eds. ***Science Books & Films'* Best Books for Children 1988-91.** Washington, D.C.: American Association for the Advancement of Science, 1992. 300 pp.

Price: $14.95 (ISBN 0-8058-1879-0) (Available from Lawrence Erlbaum Associates.)

Science Books & Films' Best Books for Children 1988-91 is a guide to recommended children's books and resource materials gathered from reviews published previously in *Science Books & Films,* the review journal of the American Association for the Advancement of Science. Subjects covered include the life and physical sciences, mathematics, engineering and technology, medicine, the social and behavioral sciences, and science/language arts connections. Some sections also contain a separate listing of hands-on science books. Entries are arranged alphabetically within broad subject areas, which are then further subdivided into smaller topics. The guide is indexed by author and title.

7.25 **Science Curriculum Resource Handbook: A Practical Guide for K-12 Science Curriculum.** Millwood, N.Y.: Kraus International Publications, 1992. 384 pp.

Price: $29.95 (ISBN 0-527-20806-X) (Available from Corwin Press.)

This resource book provides basic information on the background of science curriculum design. It presents current information on trends in science teaching and curriculum development in grades K-12 and includes a step-by-step guide to creating or revising curriculum, information on grants for program development, exemplary science curriculum guides, comparisons of state requirements, and sources of ideas and materials for special projects. Rather than prescribing any particular form of curriculum, the handbook gives a sense of the available options and is a practical reference for curriculum developers, teachers, and administrators. It includes an annotated source list for materials, publishers, and project ideas and an index to reviews of science textbooks, videos, software, and support materials.

7.26 Wendy Saul and Alan R. Newman. **Science Fare.** New York, N.Y.: HarperCollins, 1986. 296 pp.

Price: $20.00 (ISBN 0-06-091218-9)

Science Fare suggests approaches to science education that are positive and enjoyable and that engage the natural curiosity and interest of children. The book recommends toys, books, and equipment that enhance any curriculum already in place. In general, *Science Fare* aids adults in providing children with resources that will help them understand and question their world. Practical advice is offered for purchasing science kits, tools, and written materials. This guide and catalog is an excellent sourcebook.

7.27 Mary Budd Rowe. **Science Helper K-8: Version 3.0.** Armonk, N.Y.: The Learning Team, 1993.

Price: $195.00

Science Helper is a compact disc (CD-ROM) produced by the Knowledge Utilization Project in Science (*see* 5.7). It contains plans for 919 elementary science and mathematics lessons and 2,000 activities, compiled from 7 elementary science curriculum projects funded by the National Science Foundation during the 1960s, 1970s, and 1980s. Lessons are included from the following projects: Conceptually Oriented Program in Elementary Science (COPES), Elementary Science Study (ESS), Elementary School Science Project (Astronomy) (ESSP), Minnesota Mathematics and Science Teaching Project (MINNEMAST), Science: A Process Approach (SAPA), Science Curriculum Improvement Study (SCIS), and Unified Science and Mathematics for Elementary Schools (USMES) (*see* chapter 5, "Curriculum Projects Past and

Present," in this guide). Lesson plans or activities can be located on the CD-ROM using the following criteria (alone or in combination): grade level, subject, process skills, keywords, content themes, and programs. Each lesson plan has a detailed abstract that can be viewed on the screen, printed out, and used to find other, related lessons. Background information on each lesson is available, including an introduction, a listing of responsible authors, and the book's original table of contents. All lessons can be printed and copied as often as needed. *Science Helper* can operate on either the PC or the Macintosh platform.

7.28 Smithsonian Resource Guide for Teachers 1995/96. Washington, D.C.: Office of Elementary and Secondary Education, Smithsonian Institution, 1995. 73 pp.

Price: $5.00

The *Smithsonian Resource Guide for Teachers 1995/96* is an annotated listing of educational materials and resources available from the Smithsonian Institution. Science materials are included in the following subject areas: anthropology/human life, astronomy/space sciences, botany/plant life, general science/ecology, geology/minerals/paleontology, and zoology/animal life. Materials are grouped by subject, and within each section are arranged alphabetically by title. The booklet lists catalogs, visitor guides, periodicals, and information on electronic (computer) access to the Smithsonian.

CHAPTER 8

PERIODICALS

8.1 The American Biology Teacher

Grade: Teacher resource *The American Biology Teacher* presents nonfiction articles that report on the results of research on teaching alternatives; discuss the social and ethical implications of biology; provide specific how-to suggestions for laboratory, field activities, or interdisciplinary programs; and present imaginative views of the future and suggestions for coping with changes. The articles, by science educators, are accompanied by statistical graphs and tables and are fully referenced. Each issue includes a software review (which gives a general description of the software's purpose and information on ease of operation), and several reviews of recent books on biology. The magazine provides background reading for elementary teachers.

Issues/price: 8 per year; $48.00 per year for National Association of Biology Teachers members; $60.00 per year for nonmembers. ***Publisher:*** National Association of Biology Teachers.

8.2 Art to Zoo

Grade: Teachers of grades 3-6+ *Art to Zoo* brings exhibit-based lessons and activities from the Smithsonian Institution to science, social studies, and art teachers. Each issue focuses on one theme and contains a step-by-step lesson plan outlining background information, lesson objectives, materials used, and subject covered. Also included are an English/Spanish "pull-out" page (which can be duplicated for student use) of questions and activities and a list of resources for further information. *Art to Zoo* features black and white photographs and illustrations. The publication is dedicated to promoting the use of community resources among students and teachers nationally.

Issues/price: 4 per year; free of charge. ***Publisher:*** Smithsonian Institution, Office of Elementary and Secondary Education.

8.3 Chem Matters

Grade: Teacher resource *Chem Matters* is a magazine written for high school students that is also a useful source for keeping elementary school teachers up to date on recent chemical advances. Nonfiction articles covering such issues as nicotine patches, biodegradable bags, insect arsenals, and the chemistry of ink help relate chemistry to everyday life. Each issue contains puzzles, cartoons, and descriptions of real-life mysteries solved through chemistry. The *Chem Matters Classroom Guide* for teachers offers additional facts and background information for each article, as well as high-school-level chemistry demonstrations, laboratory experiments, and questions for students to answer.

Issues/price: 4 per year; $7.75 per year. *Chem Matters Classroom Guide:* 4 per year; $3.00 per year; no additional charge with subscriptions of 5 or more copies of *Chem Matters.* ***Publisher:*** American Chemical Society.

Reading for information

ORDERING INFORMATION FOR PERIODICALS IN CHAPTER 8

To obtain the most current ordering information, readers should contact the publishers of the periodicals in chapter 8 directly. In some cases, discounts or special rates may be available to schools and educators.

The name of the publisher for each periodical is given immediately after its annotation. Publishers' addresses and phone and fax numbers are listed in appendix A, "Publishers and Suppliers."

8.4 Chickadee

Grade: Students, preschool-grade 4 (ages 3-9) *Chickadee* magazine introduces young children to the world of nature and science. Each issue focuses on a key subject and includes brief, easy-to-read articles with minimal text accompanied by colorful photographs and lively illustrations. In addition, there are stories for reading aloud, games, hands-on experiments, posters, puzzles, and cartoons.

Issues/price: 10 per year; $14.95 per year. ***Publisher:*** Owl Communications.

8.5 Children's Magazine Guide

Grade: Students, grades 5-6+; teachers *Children's Magazine Guide* is a monthly subject index to children's magazines created for elementary and middle school students. Indexing 42 popular children's magazines, it directs users to specific articles on topics such as science, sports, current events, and popular culture. In addition, it indexes 9 major magazines and journals for teachers. The guide helps children find the science articles they need and is a useful tool for developing students' research skills. Every entry in this guide includes the name of the article, author, magazine, issue date, and page numbers.

Issues/price: 9 per year; $48.00 per year. ***Publisher:*** R. R. Bowker.

8.6 Connect

Grade: Teachers of grades K-6+ *Connect* is a bimonthly newsletter published throughout the school year. It offers practical articles, written by teachers, to support hands-on learning, problem solving, and multidisciplinary approaches to the teaching of science and mathematics. Each 20-page issue focuses on a key theme, such as investigating water, wetlands, energy, or variation and classification, and includes photographs and illustrations. Regular features include science and technology news (that is, current news stories chosen because of the teaching opportunities they offer) and resource reviews (theme-related items selected for their high quality and immediate usefulness).

Issues/price: 5 per year; $20.00 per year. ***Publisher:*** Teachers' Laboratory.

8.7 Discover

Grade: Students, grades 6+; teachers *Discover* magazine provides detailed, informative articles on biology, chemistry, computer science, earth science, engineering, environmental science, mathematics, physical science, physics, space science, and technology. Each issue contains sections on breakthroughs in science, technology, and medicine, as well as a "Vital Signs" section written by medical professionals to capture the human side of medicine, a "Science Classics" cartoon section, and suggestions for further reading.

Each issue has a teaching guide to help translate information in the articles into classroom projects, curriculum ideas, and research activities. The teaching guide offers suggestions for using the magazine in different curriculum areas, vocabulary words of interest, and a reproducible quiz.

Issues/price: 12 per year; $17.49 per year ($14.55 for school year only). ***Publisher:*** Discover Science Program.

8.8 Dolphin Log

Grade: Students, grades 2-6+ Each issue of *Dolphin Log* presents a variety of nonfiction articles on science, natural history, marine biology, ecology, and the environment as they relate to the global water system. The articles have colorful and instructive photographs. Features cover such subjects as sharks, making recycled paper, survivors of ancient seas, and the comeback of the California grey whale. Regular features include "Nature News," "Did You Know?" (interesting and fun facts), "Creature Feature" (a focused exploration of one animal), and the "Cousteau Adventure" cartoon series. The magazine has games, puzzles, and hands-on activities for children.

Issues/price: 6 per year; $15.00 per year. ***Publisher:*** Cousteau Society.

8.9 Electronic Learning

Grade: Teacher resource Educational technology, industry news, and conference and research reports are regularly featured subjects in *Electronic Learning,* a magazine on technology and school change. This periodical offers in-depth reviews of hardware and software. One major section provides articles on "Curriculum and Instruction." Another section, "Technology," focuses on evaluation and selection of software and on new and emerging technologies. An "Update" section provides a listing of new products available to educators, including software, hardware, books, CD-ROMs, and videodiscs.

Issues/price: 8 per year; $23.95 per year. ***Publisher:*** Scholastic.

8.10 Instructor

Grade: Teacher resource *Instructor* addresses all areas of elementary school curriculum and instruction. In addition to sections such as "Ready to Write" and "Math in Action," the magazine offers articles about child development and behavior, practical strategies for working with parents, and effective new teaching methods. It provides features and columns written by teachers, and ready-to-use hands-on activities. Each issue includes a hands-on science column or article and, once a year (in March), science is highlighted.

Issues/price: 8 per year; $19.95 per year. ***Publisher:*** Scholastic.

8.11 International Wildlife

Grade: Students, grades 6+; teachers *International Wildlife* features in-depth nonfiction articles exploring wildlife topics from around the world and global environmental issues. A representative sampling from an issue might include articles on the Fennec fox in the Algerian Sahara, disappearing forests in Canada, the earth's top 10 environmental problems, the Bahama Parrot, and the diversity of life in Borneo's Mount Kinabalu. Articles are accompanied by excellent photographs. This magazine is a useful tool for both teacher and student research on nature worldwide and is a natural supplement to the classroom library.

Issues/price: 6 per year; $16.00 per year. ***Publisher:*** National Wildlife Federation.

8.12 Kid City

Grade: Students, grades 1-5 *Kid City* (formerly, *Electric Company*) helps make learning enjoyable for students from 6 to 10 years old. The magazine features short articles on science, history, and social studies, and has lively, colorful photographs and drawings. Examples of science topics covered include flying squirrels, the senses, kangaroos, and how animals defend themselves naturally. Each issue includes stories, games, and puzzles to challenge students, as well as fiction, poetry, and art by children. Regular features include "Kid City News" (interesting news bits about children, towns, and schools across the country), "True But Strange" (facts from science and history), and children's reviews of new books, toys, games, tapes, and videos.

Issues/price: 10 per year; $16.97 per year. ***Publisher:*** Children's Television Workshop.

8.13 Kids Discover

Grade: Students, grades 1-6+ *Kids Discover* helps children explore the wonder of the world around them. Each issue focuses on a key theme, such as oceans, rain forests, fire, weather, light, volcanoes, or space. Easy-to-read text is accompanied by excellent color photographs and illustrations. The magazine poses challenging questions to children, and includes puzzles, additional resources for children and teachers on the issue's theme, and instructions for related hands-on activities.

Issues/price: 10 per year; $19.95 per year. ***Publisher:*** Kids Discover.

8.14 Learning

Grade: Teachers of grades K-6+ *Learning* presents creative ideas across the curriculum as well as activities for teachers. Most issues focus on a key theme, such as rain forests, multiculturalism, or the White House bicentennial. In preparation for Earth Day on April 22, the March issue each year focuses on a key science theme. All articles are written by teachers for teachers. Subjects of the features include teaching techniques (for example, creative conflict resolution or motivating underachievers), teaching success stories, activity ideas, tips and time savers, a teacher-to-teacher reader exchange, and an activity book focusing on a particular subject.

Issues/price: 9 per year; $20.00 per year. ***Publisher:*** Learning.

8.15 Learning and Leading with Technology

Grade: Teacher resource This journal for technology-using educators, formerly entitled *The Computing Teacher,* presents information on all aspects of precollege educational technology. It offers articles in subject areas such as application software, computer literacy, hypermedia/multimedia, and telecommunications/distance learning. Two major sections of the journal are "Technology in the Curriculum" (with articles on applications in various curriculum areas including science) and "Educational Policy and Leadership." Columns of particular interest to elementary science teachers are "Software Reviews," "Mining the Internet," and "Multimedia Sandbox."

Issues/price: 8 per year; $55.00 per year for International Society for Technology in Education members; $61.00 per year for nonmembers. ***Publisher:*** International Society for Technology in Education.

8.16 National Geographic World

Grade: Students, grades 3-6+; teachers
A goal of *National Geographic World* is to instill curiosity about the world in young readers and to encourage geographic awareness. Each issue offers five or six nonfiction articles on science, geography, the environment, natural history, sports, and achievements of young people and adults. Articles are accompanied by excellent color photographs and illustrations, and children's art and writing are often included. The magazine features puzzles, maps, games, posters, hands-on projects, and contests to spark interest and encourage interactivity. *National Geographic World* is a useful teaching aid for a variety of curriculum goals.

Issues/price: 12 per year; $14.95 per year. ***Publisher:*** National Geographic Society.

8.17 National Wildlife

Grade: Students, grades 6+; teachers
National Wildlife features in-depth nonfiction articles about nature, wildlife, and important environmental trends and issues. A representative sampling from an issue might include articles on dolphins, Superfund, recycling for the birds, beavers, Alaskan grizzlies, and the effects of flooding in the Midwest. Articles are accompanied by excellent photographs. This magazine is a useful tool for both teacher and student research on nature. It is a natural supplement to the classroom library.

Issues/price: 6 per year; $16.00 per year. ***Publisher:*** National Wildlife Federation.

8.18 NOVA Teacher's Guide

Grade: Students, grades 6+; teachers
NOVA Teacher's Guide, published in conjunction with the Public Broadcasting System (PBS) series of *NOVA* educational science programs, helps teachers use the *NOVA* series with their classes. The guide includes 1-page lesson plans for many of the programs. Each lesson identifies a teaching focus and gives a brief program overview. The lesson plans suggest activities and discussions to conduct before and after viewing the *NOVA* programs. A reproducible student activity page accompanies each lesson to help students develop useful critical thinking skills.

NOVAzine, a magazine for students, comes in the teacher's guide. The student magazine contains nonfiction articles, interviews with notable people, puzzles, quizzes, and maps that relate to the PBS series being broadcast as the magazine is published. All or part of *NOVAzine* may be photocopied and distributed to students.

Issues/price: 2 per year; free of charge. ***Publisher:*** WGBH Boston.

8.19 Odyssey

Grade: Students, grades 4-6+ *Odyssey* presents nonfiction information related to astronomy. Each issue focuses on a main theme, such as technology from the space program, the moon, or superstition and science. Regular features include "Activity to Discover" (suggestions for do-it-yourself activities related to the issue's featured topic), "Backyard Observations" (tips on astronomical occurrences children can watch for the month), "Future Forum" (children's written thoughts on a proposed subject of interest), and "Ask Ely" (a question-and-answer column). *Odyssey* features excellent color photographs and illustrations.

Issues/price: 10 per year; $24.95 per year. ***Publisher:*** Cobblestone.

8.20 Owl

Grade: Students, grades 3-6 *Owl* magazine helps children explore nature and science. Each issue focuses on a key topic such as wolves, goats, the Arctic, or island life. The magazine includes short, readable nonfiction articles, folk tales, puzzles and games, posters, cartoon adventures, and hands-on activities, all accompanied by colorful photographs.

Issues/price: 10 per year; $14.95 per year. ***Publisher:*** Owl Communications.

8.21 Ranger Rick

Grade: Students, grades 1-6 *Ranger Rick* helps children learn about animals and their habitats, about how to help endangered species, and about what other young people are doing to protect the environment. Each issue contains readable nonfiction text with excellent color photographs and drawings. Regular features include fictional stories about wildlife, "Dear Ranger Rick" (letters to the editor from children), puzzles, hands-on activities, and jokes and riddles.

Issues/price: 12 per year; $15.00 per year. ***Publisher:*** National Wildlife Federation.

8.22 Science Activities

Grade: Teachers of grades 1-6+ *Science Activities* is a source of experiments, explorations, and projects for the classroom science teacher. Written by science educators, each issue contains a cross-section of activities for all ages, from the young child to the advanced high school student. Each issue focuses on a key theme, such as exploring the earth inside and out, natural science activities indoors and out, and ecology at the mall and in the classroom. A sampling of topics from *Science Activities* includes fun with fungi, science through drama, discovering wildlife, and electrical conductivity. Regular features include news notes, computer news, book reviews, and information about new products available to the classroom teacher.

Issues/price: 4 per year; $58.00 per year for institutions; $32.00 per year for individuals; single-copy price, $14.50. ***Publisher:*** Heldref Publications.

8.23 Science & Children

Grade: Teachers of grades PreK, K-6+ *Science & Children* is a journal on teaching elementary school science. It contains articles by educators for educators on how to teach specific science activities (such as experiments with worms and fun-filled physics), as well as on more general aspects of science teaching (such as how to improve children's observational skills and reasoning abilities). Each article concludes with a list of topic-related resources. Regular features include "In the News" (science news items from around the country), "Teaching Teachers" (practical teaching methods for preservice and in-service teachers), and reviews of newly available print and software resources.

Issues/price: 8 per year; $52.00 per year, including National Science Teachers Association membership. ***Publisher:*** National Science Teachers Association.

8.24 Science Books & Films

Grade: Teachers of grades PreK, K-6+ *Science Books & Films* is written for librarians, media specialists, curriculum supervisors, science teachers, and others responsible for recommending or purchasing science materials. It provides critical reviews of the scientific accuracy and presentation of print, audiovisual, and electronic resources intended for use in science, technology, and mathematics education. Reviews include descriptions of the merits and demerits of a book or film and any accompanying supplements; the content, technical quality, and instructional value; the audience(s) for which the material is most appropriate and why; and how the material could be used for collateral reading or viewing, reference, or classroom use. Each issue includes a feature article, reviews by young readers, audiovisual notes about educational or professional materials and programs, an index of books and films, and a selection of the reviewers' favorite titles from that issue.

Issues/price: 9 per year; $40.00 per year. ***Publisher:*** American Association for the Advancement of Science.

8.25 Scienceland

Grade: Students, grades K-3 *Scienceland* nurtures scientific thinking in young children. Each volume focuses on a main theme, such as pill bugs, robots, or the Space Shuttle. Large, easy-to-read text accompanies excellent photographs and enjoyable drawings. Articles challenge children by asking questions and offering "Can you do this?" suggestions for activities. They help build reading skills with pull-out vocabulary words and definitions. Accompanying each volume of *Scienceland* is a teacher's guide, including an introduction to that volume's subject matter, objectives for each reading and activity, questions designed to focus children's thinking, and suggestions for additional activities.

Issues/price: 8 per year; $19.95 per year for regular edition (lighter paper stock); $42.00 per year for deluxe edition (heavier paper stock); $15.00 per year for teacher's manuals. ***Publisher:*** Scienceland.

8.26 Science News

Grade: Teachers of grades 6+ Though written primarily for scientists and university professors, *Science News* can be used by teachers at all levels to stay abreast of the latest developments in science, engineering, medicine, and mathematics. Each issue contains a lengthy article on a current subject of interest, such as the human genome, biodiversity, and erosion, as well as brief news items on such topics as biomedicine, chemistry, space science, and the environment.

Issues/price: Published weekly; $44.50 per year. ***Publisher:*** Science Service.

8.27 Science Scope

Grade: Teachers of grades 6+ Each issue of *Science Scope* presents nonfiction articles by science educators on the life, physical, and earth sciences and on science and society. The magazine provides science teachers with ideas for creative, well-designed, and safe hands-on activities and demonstrations. Each issue features "scoops" (news items on recent scientific discoveries or investigations); information on helpful science resources; short, practical, how-to tips on lessons and teaching methods; and a colorful science poster relating to a key article in the issue.

Issues/price: 8 per year; $52.00 per year, including National Science Teachers Association membership. ***Publisher:*** National Science Teachers Association.

8.28 The Science Teacher

Grade: Teacher resource *The Science Teacher* provides nonfiction articles by science educators on innovations in science teaching, current developments in science, and classroom projects and experiments. Each issue contains brief news items on recent scientific discoveries, an idea bank of hands-on activities, and reviews of books and software relevant to teaching science. Though targeted for junior and senior high school teachers, librarians, principals, and supervisors, this magazine is a useful source of background information for elementary science teachers.

Issues/price: 9 per year; $52.00 per year, including National Science Teachers Association membership. ***Publisher:*** National Science Teachers Association.

8.29 Science Weekly

Grade: Students, grades K-6+ Each issue of *Science Weekly* focuses on a single current science topic, such as volcanoes, wind power, or maps, and presents information on that topic from seven different reading levels. For each reading level, regular features include a vocabulary list, a weekly hands-on lab, a weekly problem-solving exercise, and a "writing for science" exercise. Accompanying each issue are teachers' notes (also keyed to specific reading levels) covering background information, questions and activities, and further suggestions for curriculum involvement.

Issues/price: 16 per year; $9.95 per year per student for subscriptions of 19 or fewer; $4.95 per year per student for subscriptions of 20 or more. ***Publisher:*** Science Weekly.

8.30 SuperScience Blue

Grade: Students, grades 4-6 *SuperScience Blue* provides science material that fits into all areas of the curriculum and helps students see the science connections around them. Containing in-depth nonfiction articles and related hands-on activities, each issue explores one key topic, such as hurricanes, endangered animals, or the physics and chemistry of construction. Accompanying each issue (at additional cost) is a teacher's guide, *SuperScience Blue Teacher,* outlining article topics, related curriculum areas, relevant process skills, learning objectives, general background, suggestions on introducing subject matter, questions for discussion, and lab tips. A resource section cites related books for teachers and children. Regular features of *SuperScience Blue* include an "Ask the Experts" question-and-answer column, a "We Dare You" problem-solving challenge, and a colorful, instructive, foldout poster relating to the issue topic.

Issues/price: 8 per year; $6.95 per year for magazine only; $27.80 per year for magazine and teacher's guide. ***Publisher:*** Scholastic.

8.31 SuperScience Red

Grade: Students, grades 1-3 *SuperScience Red* provides science material that fits into all areas of the curriculum and helps students see the science connections around them. Containing brief, easy-to-read nonfiction articles and related hands-on activities, each issue explores a key topic, such as magnets, trees, or foods and health. Accompanying each issue (at additional cost) are teaching notes outlining article topics, related cross-curricular objectives, tips on management, assessment, background, and extension ideas. A resource section cites related books for teachers and children. Regular features include a "Mystery" question to challenge children, science news, a math lab activity, and a colorful foldout poster relating to the issue topic.

Issues/price: 6 per year; $4.95 per year for magazine only; $25.00 per year for magazine and teacher's guide. ***Publisher:*** Scholastic.

8.32 3-2-1 Contact

Grade: Students, grades 3-6+ *3-2-1 Contact* explores nature, science, and technology through short nonfiction articles accompanied by lively, colorful photographs and drawings. Examples of topics covered include animal-tracking satellites, the world of snowboarders, peculiar pets, and a journey through a rain forest. Each issue also provides games, puzzles, contests, and suggestions for hands-on activities. Regular features include "News Blasts" (brief items about enjoyable or exciting science stories), interesting questions and answers, reviews of video and computer games, "Future File" (interesting scientific developments coming our way), and "Basic Training" (a set of hands-on computer instructions challenging children to solve a particular problem).

Issues/price: 10 per year; $17.97 per year. ***Publisher:*** Children's Television Workshop.

8.33 WonderScience

Grade: Students, grades 6+; teachers *WonderScience* provides enjoyable physical science activities for children and adults to do together. Each issue focuses on a key topic, such as optical illusions, weather measurements, the physics of music, or physics on the playground. Several hands-on activities related to the key topic are outlined. Each activity is accompanied by a list of the materials needed and step-by-step instructions for parents or teachers and children to follow. A letter to parents and teachers offers background science information and helpful hints about each activity.

Issues/price: 8 per year; $9.50 per year. ***Publisher:*** American Chemical Society.

8.34 Your Big Backyard

Grade: Students, grades PreK, K, 1 *Your Big Backyard* introduces children to the world of nature and helps them realize what people can do to protect the environment. The magazine combines colorful close-up photographs and illustrations with simple text. Regular features include read-to-me stories, poems, photos of baby animals, riddles, hands-on activities, and games. Each issue includes a letter to parents with supplemental information and questions to ask children about the articles involved. Teachers may want to refer to *Your Big Backyard* for ideas on outdoor activities, a science corner, and nature crafts. Animal and wildlife photographs provide useful material for class bulletin boards.

Issues/price: 12 per year; $14.00 per year. ***Publisher:*** National Wildlife Federation.

8.35 Zoobooks

Grade: Students, grades K-6+ *Zoobooks* examines wildlife and the animals' habitats. Each issue focuses on a single animal or a group of animals, and explores such subjects as body structure, behavior, and basic needs. Brief, factual text is accompanied by colorful photographs and drawings. Back issues are available.

Issues/price: 10 per year; $20.95 per year; $2.95 per issue. ***Publisher:*** Wildlife Education.

Investigating the characteristics of worms

PART 4

ANCILLARY RESOURCES FOR ELEMENTARY SCIENCE TEACHERS

OVERVIEW

CHAPTER 9
MUSEUMS AND OTHER PLACES TO VISIT

CHAPTER 10
PROFESSIONAL ASSOCIATIONS AND U.S. GOVERNMENT ORGANIZATIONS

Part 4 Overview

Part 4, "Ancillary Resources for Elementary Science Teachers," provides information about resources outside the classroom that can help enrich the experiences of teaching and learning science. Specifically, it focuses on facilities, associations, and federal organizations that have programs, services, and materials relevant to some aspect of hands-on, inquiry-based elementary school science education.

The first of the two chapters in this part of the guide, chapter 9, "Museums and Other Places to Visit," identifies facilities that teachers can take their elementary school science classes to visit—for example, museums, zoos, aquariums, science and technology centers, planetariums, and botanical gardens. These facilities are diverse in terms of size, areas of emphasis, and types of materials and support offered. They are places that not only can be visited by science classes but that often provide local outreach, kits, publications, teacher training, and other services.

They include, for example, a regional science discovery center with in-service education on science content and hands-on learning in Anchorage, Alaska; a dolphin research center with an education hotline in Grassy Key, Florida; a world-renowned museum in San Francisco, California, with more than 600 interactive exhibits; and a children's museum with a hands-on science bar in Portland, Maine. Such diverse resources can meet many different needs of individual teachers and their science classes across the country.

About 600 facilities throughout the United States and several in Canada are listed in chapter 9. Of those, half are annotated with information about their programs for students, the materials they can provide, and the types of education and support they offer for teachers.

The listing and the annotations are based on responses to a national survey conducted by the National Science Resources Center (NSRC).

Chapter 10, "Professional Associations and U.S. Government Organizations," highlights about 120 institutions engaged in active efforts to provide information, services, or materials for the enhancement of elementary science teaching. These listings represent many scientific fields—physics, biology, chemistry, geology, astronomy, entomology, and others. A teacher needing support in a certain scientific area will likely find a source of professional help through these annotations.

The annotations in chapter 10 present information in two categories: "Programs/services" and "Publications/materials." Within these categories there is wide variety, again reflecting the diversity of the organizations themselves.

In "Programs/services," readers will find, for example, mention of in-service workshops on space topics for teachers nationwide; databases of experts in various scientific fields who are available for teacher-scientist partnerships, classroom demonstrations, and student mentoring; information hotlines; and conferences and seminars for teachers. Also mentioned (and highlighted in boldface type) are formal programs such as the National Science Foundation's Teacher Enhancement Program, the Community Service Centers Project of the Quality Education for Minorities Network, and the Saturday Workshop Program of the Gifted Child Society. The "Publications/materials" category identifies such forms of assistance as periodicals, curriculum units and guidelines, catalogs, and audiovisual and computer-based materials.

Programs and organizations that serve as centralized sources of information—for example, clearinghouses and networks—are included in chapter 10. There are also annotations for groups of facilities, such as the U.S. Department of Energy's national laboratories and specialized facilities, that offer science education programs. Such listings can provide teachers with a starting point for a productive search for particular information or assistance.

The information on professional organizations in chapter 10 was gathered through a formal survey conducted by the NSRC. The material on federal organizations draws on information in the directory of federal resources in mathematics and science education, *Guidebook to Excellence,* produced by the Eisenhower National Clearinghouse for Mathematics and Science Education.

It was not possible to include every organization or facility that might provide assistance, materials, and information for hands-on, inquiry-centered science teaching. Readers are encouraged to utilize what is presented here and to seek out additional sources suitable to meeting their needs for professional development and for assistance in the classroom.

Because some of the detailed information presented in these annotations will inevitably change with time, chapters 9 and 10 should be treated as starting points for gathering further information. Teachers will want to contact the organizations listed to arrange for class visits and to obtain specific information, such as dates and duration of classes, workshops, and other programs; any costs involved; exact descriptions of items listed here in somewhat generic categories—"teacher's guide," "field trip," and so forth. By following up on information in chapters 9 and 10, individual teachers, schools, or school systems might significantly enhance the effectiveness of their science education efforts.

CHAPTER 9

Museums and Other Places to Visit

"Museums and Other Places to Visit" identifies and provides information about local facilities that can enrich hands-on science programs in elementary schools. The facilities were selected on the basis of the following criteria:

- They offer resources that can help elementary teachers teach science more effectively.
- They provide interactive science experiences that can complement students' classroom experiences.
- They are "visitable"—that is, they are sites to which teachers can take their science classes.

A glance through the chapter reveals the richness of the resources that meet these criteria. Besides museums, zoos, and science and technology centers, there are planetariums, aquariums, and botanical gardens, among many other types of facilities. Small local sites, moderate-sized organizations, and world-renowned institutions provide resources and assistance to support hands-on science teaching and learning.

Chapter 9 has two sections—the "Complete Regional Listing" and the "Select Annotated Listing." The former provides the names and locations (towns or cities) of almost 600 facilities in the United States and several in Canada. About half of the 600 names are in boldface type; annotations for those institutions appear in the "Select Annotated Listing."

The almost 300 facilities in the "Select Annotated Listing" are considered to be making a particularly significant effort to help teachers teach science more effectively. Each annotation provides the address and telephone number, a brief description of the facility, and information about the resources it offers in support of hands-on science teaching at the elementary school level. The annotations do not list every resource and program at an institution, but they provide a general sense of the facility and indicate types of support available. The annotations are based on information from the facilities themselves.

Readers are urged to scan the entire annotations listing for printed and other resources that might be available to them outside their own local area. For further information about particular programs or materials, or for information about costs or fees for any programs, publications, or materials, readers are encouraged to call the facilities directly.

The regional and annotated lists are arranged by geographical regions (see the map on page 170). Within each region the states are listed alphabetically. The name of each institution appears alphabetically within its state listing.

Touring the National Air and Space Museum

The nine geographical regions, arranged in a roughly west-to-east array, are as follows:

- **Pacific Region**
  Alaska, California, Hawaii, Oregon, Washington
- **Mountain Region**
  Arizona, Colorado, Idaho, Montana, Nevada, New Mexico, Utah, Wyoming
- **Great Plains/Midwest Region**
  Iowa, Kansas, Minnesota, Missouri, Nebraska, North Dakota, South Dakota
- **South Central Region**
  Arkansas, Louisiana, Oklahoma, Texas
- **Great Lakes Region**
  Illinois, Indiana, Michigan, Ohio, Wisconsin
- **Southeast Region**
  Alabama, Florida, Georgia, Kentucky, Mississippi, North Carolina, South Carolina, Tennessee, Virginia, West Virginia
- **Middle Atlantic Region**
  Delaware, District of Columbia, Maryland, New Jersey, New York, Pennsylvania
- **New England Region**
  Connecticut, Maine, Massachusetts, New Hampshire, Rhode Island, Vermont
- **Canada**
  Canadian Provinces

The addresses provided with the annotations are locational but are not necessarily mailing addresses. Inquiry should be made to verify them as mailing addresses before relying on them for that purpose.

Despite efforts to be as inclusive as possible, given constraints of time and space, the listings here are not exhaustive. Other facilities may exist or may be developing that would fit the criteria applied here. Teachers are encouraged to seek out and utilize those resources as well. The absence of any facility from these listings is not meant as a reflection on the quality of its programs and resources.

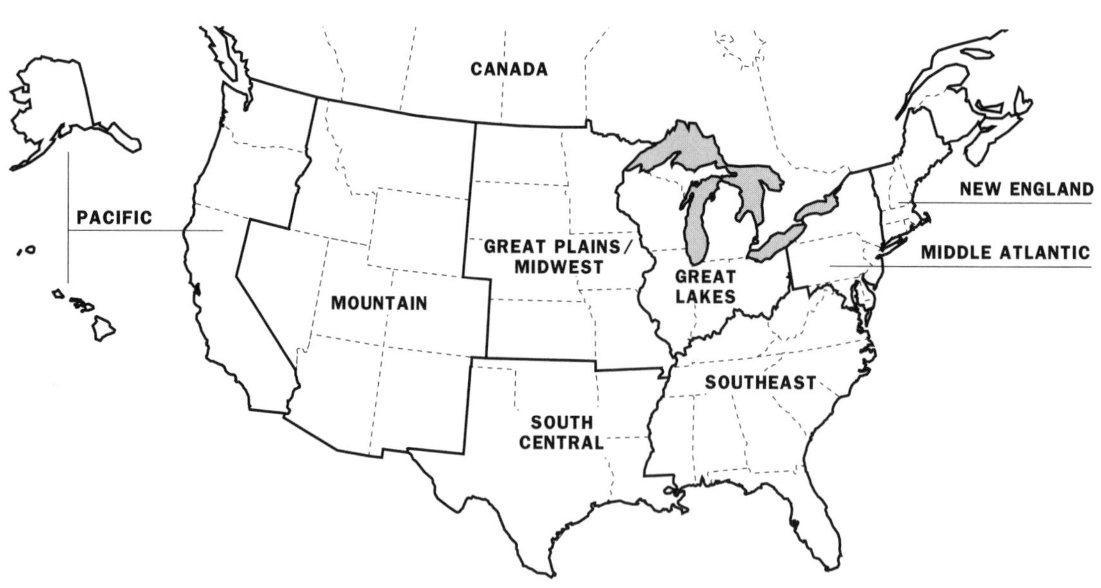

COMPLETE REGIONAL LISTING

ABOUT THE "COMPLETE REGIONAL LISTING"

The "Complete Regional Listing" provides the names and locations (towns or cities) of almost 600 facilities in the United States and several in Canada. About half of the 600 names are in boldface type; annotations for those institutions appear in the "Select Annotated Listing" on pages 179-221.

This list is arranged by geographical regions (see the map on page 170). Within each region the states are listed alphabetically. The name of each institution appears alphabetically within its state listing.

The nine geographical regions, arranged in a roughly west-to-east array, are as follows:

- **Pacific Region**
  Alaska, California, Hawaii, Oregon, Washington
- **Mountain Region**
  Arizona, Colorado, Idaho, Montana, Nevada, New Mexico, Utah, Wyoming
- **Great Plains/Midwest Region**
  Iowa, Kansas, Minnesota, Missouri, Nebraska, North Dakota, South Dakota
- **South Central Region**
  Arkansas, Louisiana, Oklahoma, Texas
- **Great Lakes Region**
  Illinois, Indiana, Michigan, Ohio, Wisconsin
- **Southeast Region**
  Alabama, Florida, Georgia, Kentucky, Mississippi, North Carolina, South Carolina, Tennessee, Virginia, West Virginia
- **Middle Atlantic Region**
  Delaware, District of Columbia, Maryland, New Jersey, New York, Pennsylvania
- **New England Region**
  Connecticut, Maine, Massachusetts, New Hampshire, Rhode Island, Vermont
- **Canada**
  Canadian Provinces

For easy reference, an "entry number" (for example—9.1 for Alaska) appears at each state's name in the "Complete Regional Listing." This series of entry numbers continues without interruption into the annotated listing, where each institution has its own entry number.

PACIFIC REGION

9.1 Alaska

The Imaginarium: A Science Discovery Center (Anchorage)
Pratt Museum (Homer)
University of Alaska Museum (Fairbanks)

9.2 California

Alum Rock Discovery Center (Youth Science Institute) (San Jose)
Bay Area Discovery Museum (Sausalito)
Cabrillo Marine Aquarium (San Pedro)
California Academy of Sciences (San Francisco)
California Museum of Science and Industry (Los Angeles)
Carter House Natural Science Museum (Redding)
Chabot Observatory and Science Center (Oakland)
Children's Discovery Museum of San Jose (San Jose)
Chula Vista Nature Center (Chula Vista)
Coyote Point Museum for Environmental Education (San Mateo)
Discovery Museum Learning Center (Sacramento)
Discovery Science Center—Launch Pad (Costa Mesa)
Elkhorn Slough National Estuarine Research Reserve (Watsonville)
The Exploratorium (San Francisco)
¡Explorit! Science Center (Davis)
Fresno Metropolitan Museum (Fresno)
Great Valley Museum of Natural History (Modesto)
Hall of Health (Berkeley)
Hi-Desert Nature Museum (Yucca Valley)
Lawrence Hall of Science, University of California (Berkeley)
Lawrence Livermore National Laboratory, Visitors Center (Livermore)
The Lindsay Museum (Walnut Creek)
The Living Desert (Palm Desert)

9.2 California (continued)

Lori Brock Children's Discovery Center (Bakersfield)
Los Angeles Zoo (Los Angeles)
Marine World-Africa USA (Vallejo)
Maturango Museum of the Indian Wells Valley (Ridgecrest)
Monterey Bay Aquarium (Monterey)
Natural History Museum of Los Angeles County (Los Angeles)
The Oakland Zoo in Knowland Park (Oakland)
Pacific Grove Museum of Natural History (Pacific Grove)
Palm Springs Desert Museum (Palm Springs)
Palo Alto Junior Museum (Palo Alto)
Rancho Santa Ana Botanic Garden, Claremont Colleges (Claremont)
Randall Museum (San Francisco)
Reuben H. Fleet Space Theater and Science Center (San Diego)
Sacramento Zoo (Sacramento)
Sanborn Discovery Center (Youth Science Institute) (Saratoga)
San Diego Aerospace Museum (San Diego)
San Diego Natural History Museum (San Diego)
San Diego Zoo (San Diego)
San Francisco Zoological Gardens (San Francisco)
Santa Ana Zoo (Santa Ana)
Santa Barbara Botanic Garden (Santa Barbara)
Santa Barbara Museum of Natural History (Santa Barbara)
Sea World (San Diego)
Shorebird Nature Center (Berkeley)
Stephen Birch Aquarium-Museum, Scripps Institution of Oceanography (La Jolla)
Strybing Arboretum and Botanical Gardens (San Francisco)
The Tech Museum of Innovation (San Jose)
University of California Museum of Paleontology (Berkeley)
Vasona Discovery Center (Youth Science Institute) (Los Gatos)

9.3 Hawaii

Bishop Museum (Honolulu)
Haleakala National Park (Makawao)
Harold L. Lyon Arboretum, University of Hawaii at Manoa (Honolulu)
Hawaii Volcanoes National Park (Hawaii Volcanoes National Park)
Honolulu Zoo (Honolulu)
National Tropical Botanical Garden (Lawai)
Sea Life Park Hawaii (Waimanalo)
Waikiki Aquarium, University of Hawaii at Manoa (Honolulu)

9.4 Oregon

Douglas County Museum of History and Natural History (Roseburg)
The High Desert Museum (Bend)
Metro Washington Park Zoo (Portland)
Mount Pisgah Arboretum (Eugene)
Oregon Museum of Science and Industry (Portland)
Pacific Northwest Museum of Natural History (Ashland)
Wildlife Safari (Winston)
Willamette Science and Technology Center (WISTEC) (Eugene)
Wonder Works, A Children's Museum (The Dalles)
World Forestry Center (Portland)

9.5 Washington

Hanford Museums of Science and History (Richland)
LifeTrek—Northwest Museum of Health and Science (Spokane)
Marine Science Society of the Pacific Northwest (Poulsbo)
Mt. Rainier National Park (Ashford)
Museum of Flight (Seattle)
North Cascades Institute (Sedro Woolley)
Northwest Trek Wildlife Park (Eatonville)
Pacific Science Center (Seattle)
The Seattle Aquarium (Seattle)
The Whale Museum (Friday Harbor)
Woodland Park Zoological Gardens (Seattle)

MOUNTAIN REGION

9.6 Arizona

Arizona Science Center (Phoenix)
Arizona-Sonora Desert Museum (Tucson)
Desert Botanical Garden (Phoenix)
Flandrau Science Center and Planetarium, University of Arizona (Tucson)
Kitt Peak Museum (Tucson)
Lowell Observatory (Flagstaff)
Pima Air and Space Museum (Tucson)
Tucson Children's Museum (Tucson)

9.7 Colorado

Cheyenne Mountain Zoological Park (Colorado Springs)
The Children's Museum of Denver (Denver)
Colorado School of Mines Geology Museum (Golden)
Denver Botanic Gardens (Denver)
Denver Museum of Natural History (Denver)
Denver Zoological Gardens (Denver)
Florissant Fossil Beds National Monument (Florissant)
Hall of Life (Denver)
May Natural History Museum and Museum of Space Exploration (Colorado Springs)
Museum of Western Colorado (Grand Junction)
National Center for Atmospheric Research (NCAR) (Boulder)
National Renewable Energy Laboratory (Golden)
Pueblo Zoo (Pueblo)
Rocky Mountain National Park (Estes Park)
University of Colorado Museum (Boulder)

9.8 Idaho

The Discovery Center of Idaho (Boise)
Idaho Museum of Natural History, Idaho State University (Pocatello)

9.9 Montana

Glacier National Park (West Glacier)
Museum of the Rockies, Montana State University (Bozeman)

9.10 Nevada

Lied Discovery Children's Museum (Las Vegas)

9.11 New Mexico

Bradbury Science Museum (Los Alamos)
¡Explora! Science Center (Albuquerque)
Las Cruces Museum of Natural History (Las Cruces)
New Mexico Bureau of Mines Mineral Museum (Socorro)
New Mexico Museum of Natural History and Science (Albuquerque)
Rio Grande Zoological Park (Albuquerque)
Santa Fe Children's Museum (Santa Fe)
The Space Center (Alamogordo)

9.12 Utah

Canyonlands Field Institute (Moab)
College of Eastern Utah Prehistoric Museum (Price)
Hansen Planetarium (Salt Lake City)
Hogle Zoological Garden (Salt Lake City)
Monte L. Bean Life Science Museum, Brigham Young University (Provo)
Utah Museum of Natural History, University of Utah (Salt Lake City)
Zion National Park Museum (Springdale)

9.13 Wyoming

Greybull Museum (Greybull)
Yellowstone National Park (Yellowstone Park)

GREAT PLAINS/MIDWEST REGION

9.14 Iowa

Blank Park Zoo of Des Moines (Des Moines)
Science Center of Iowa (Des Moines)
Science Station (Cedar Rapids)

9.15 Kansas

Children's Museum of Wichita/ Science Center (Wichita)
Kansas Cosmosphere and Space Center (Hutchinson)
Kansas Learning Center for Health (Halstead)
Kauffman Museum, Bethel College (North Newton)
KU Natural History Museum, University of Kansas (Lawrence)
Lake Afton Public Observatory, Wichita State University (Wichita)
Lee Richardson Zoo (Garden City)
Mid-America Air Museum (Liberal)
Pratt Wildlife Center and Aquarium (Pratt)
Topeka Zoological Park (Topeka)

9.16 Minnesota

The Bakken Museum and Library (Minneapolis)
Bell Museum of Natural History, University of Minnesota (Minneapolis)
Headwaters Science Center (Bemidji)
Minnesota Children's Museum (St. Paul)
Minnesota Landscape Arboretum, University of Minnesota (Chanhassen)
Minnesota Zoological Garden (Apple Valley)
Science Museum of Minnesota (St. Paul)

9.17 Missouri

Dickerson Park Zoo (Springfield)
The Discovery Center (Springfield)
Kansas City Museum (Kansas City)
Kansas City Zoological Gardens (Kansas City)
The Magic House, St. Louis Children's Museum (St. Louis)
Missouri Botanical Garden (St. Louis)
St. Louis Science Center (St. Louis)
St. Louis Zoological Park (St. Louis)

9.18 Nebraska

Folsom Children's Zoo and Botanical Garden (Lincoln)
Fontenelle Forest Nature Center (Bellevue)
Hastings Museum (Hastings)
Henry Doorly Zoo (Omaha)
Neale Woods Nature Center (Omaha)
Omaha Children's Museum (Omaha)
Pioneers Park Nature Center (Lincoln)
Riverside Park Zoo (Scottsbluff)
University of Nebraska State Museum (Lincoln)

9.19 North Dakota

Dakota Zoo (Bismarck)
Gateway to Science Center (Bismarck)
Roosevelt Park Zoo (Minot)

9.20 South Dakota

Badlands National Park (Interior)
South Dakota Discovery Center and Aquarium (Pierre)
Wind Cave National Park (Hot Springs)

SOUTH CENTRAL REGION

9.21 Arkansas

Arkansas Museum of Science and History (Little Rock)
Little Rock Zoological Gardens (Little Rock)
Logoly State Park (McNeil)
Mid-America Museum (Hot Springs)

9.22 Louisiana

Alexandria Zoological Park (Alexandria)
Aquarium of the Americas (New Orleans)
Audubon Zoological Garden (New Orleans)
The Children's Museum of Lake Charles (Lake Charles)
Greater Baton Rouge Zoo (Baton Rouge)
Lafayette Natural History Museum, Planetarium, and Nature Station (Lafayette)
Louisiana Arts and Science Center (Baton Rouge)
Louisiana Children's Museum (New Orleans)
Louisiana Nature and Science Center (New Orleans)
Sci-Port Discovery Center (Shreveport)
Walter B. Jacobs Memorial Nature Park (Shreveport)

9.23 Oklahoma

Harmon Science Center (Tulsa)
Oklahoma City Zoo (Oklahoma City)
Oklahoma Museum of Natural History, University of Oklahoma (Norman)
Omniplex Science Museum (Oklahoma City)
Tulsa Zoological Park (Tulsa)

9.24 Texas

Abilene Zoological Gardens (Abilene)
Armand Bayou Nature Center (Houston)
Austin Children's Museum (Austin)
Big Thicket National Preserve (Beaumont)
Caldwell Zoo (Tyler)
The Centennial Museum at the University of Texas at El Paso (El Paso)
The Children's Museum of Houston (Houston)
The Dallas Aquarium (Dallas)
Dallas Civic Garden Center (Dallas)
Dallas Museum of Natural History (Dallas)
The Dallas Zoo (Dallas)
Don Harrington Discovery Center (Amarillo)
El Paso Zoo (El Paso)
Environmental Science Center (Houston)
Fort Worth Museum of Science and History (Fort Worth)
Fort Worth Zoological Park (Fort Worth)
Fossil Rim Wildlife Center (Glen Rose)
Foundation for the Museum of Medical Science (Houston)
Heard Natural Science Museum and Wildlife Sanctuary (McKinney)
Houston Museum of Natural Science (Houston)
Houston Zoological Gardens (Houston)
Insights—El Paso Science Museum (El Paso)
McAllen International Museum (McAllen)
McDonald Observatory Visitors Center (Fort Davis)
National Wildflower Research Center (Austin)
San Antonio Botanical Center (San Antonio)
San Antonio Zoological Gardens and Aquarium (San Antonio)
Science Land—Denton's Discovery Museum (Denton)
The Science Place (Dallas)
Science Spectrum (Lubbock)
Sea World of Texas (San Antonio)
Space Center Houston (Houston)
Strecker Museum (Waco)
Welder Wildlife Foundation (Sinton)
Witte Museum (San Antonio)

GREAT LAKES REGION

9.25 Illinois

The Adler Planetarium (Chicago)
Brookfield Zoo (*See* Chicago Zoological Park)
Chicago Academy of Sciences (Chicago)
Chicago Botanic Garden (Glencoe)
Chicago Children's Museum (Chicago)
Chicago Zoological Park (Brookfield Zoo) (Brookfield)
Discovery Center Museum (Rockford)
Fermilab Lederman Science Education Center (Batavia)
Field Museum of Natural History (Chicago)
Illinois State Museum (Springfield)
John G. Shedd Aquarium (Chicago)
Kohl Children's Museum (Wilmette)
Lakeview Museum of Arts and Sciences (Peoria)
Lincoln Park Zoological Gardens (Chicago)
Museum of Science and Industry (Chicago)
Museum of the Chicago Academy of Sciences (Chicago)
The Science Center (Carbondale)
SciTech—Science and Technology Interactive Center (Aurora)
Shedd Aquarium (*See* John G. Shedd Aquarium)

9.26 Indiana

The Children's Museum of Indianapolis (Indianapolis)
Evansville Museum of Arts and Science (Evansville)
Fort Wayne Children's Zoo (Fort Wayne)
Indianapolis Zoo (Indianapolis)
Mesker Park Zoo (Evansville)
Muncie Children's Museum (Muncie)
Potawatomi Zoo (South Bend)

9.27 Michigan

Abrams Planetarium, Michigan State University (East Lansing)
Ann Arbor Hands-On Museum (Ann Arbor)
Belle Isle Nature Center (Detroit)
Binder Park Zoo (Battle Creek)
Chippewa Nature Center (Midland)
Cranbrook Institute of Science (Bloomfield Hills)
Detroit Zoo (Royal Oak)
Fernwood Botanic Garden (Niles)
Flint Children's Museum (Flint)
Hall of Ideas, Midland Center for the Arts (Midland)
Impression 5 Science Museum (Lansing)
John Ball Zoological Garden (Grand Rapids)
Kalamazoo Public Museum (Kalamazoo)
Kingman Museum of Natural History (Battle Creek)
Michigan Space Center, Jackson Community College (Jackson)
The Michigan State University Museum (East Lansing)
Muskegon County Museum (Muskegon)
Nichols Arboretum (Ann Arbor)
Oakwoods Metropark Nature Center (Flat Rock)
Potter Park Zoo (Lansing)
Robert T. Longway Planetarium (Flint)
Sarett Nature Center (Benton Harbor)
Sloan Museum (Flint)
Southwestern Michigan College Museum (Dowagiac)

9.28 Ohio

Akron Zoological Park (Akron)
Aullwood Audubon Center and Farm (Dayton)
Cincinnati Museum of Natural History and Planetarium (Cincinnati)
Cincinnati Zoo and Botanical Garden (Cincinnati)
Cleveland Botanical Garden (Cleveland)
Cleveland Children's Museum (Cleveland)
Cleveland Metroparks Zoo (Cleveland)
Cleveland Museum of Natural History (Cleveland)
Columbus Zoological Park (Powell)
COSI/Columbus—Ohio's Center Of Science and Industry (Columbus)
The Dayton Museum of Natural History (Dayton)
Great Lakes Museum of Science, Environment and Technology (Cleveland)
The Holden Arboretum (Kirtland)
Lake Erie Nature and Science Center (Bay Village)
McKinley Museum of History, Science and Industry (Canton)
Orton Geological Museum, Ohio State University (Columbus)
Sea World of Ohio (Aurora)
Shaker Lakes Regional Nature Center (Cleveland)
Trailside Nature Center and Museum (Cincinnati)
The Wilderness Center (Wilmot)

9.29 Wisconsin

Discovery World (Milwaukee)
Henry Vilas Park Zoo (Madison)
International Crane Foundation (Baraboo)
Madison Children's Museum (Madison)
Milwaukee Public Museum (Milwaukee)
The Museum of Natural History (Stevens Point)
Olbrich Botanical Gardens (Madison)
University of Wisconsin-Madison Arboretum (Madison)
Zoological Society—Milwaukee County Zoo (Milwaukee)

SOUTHEAST REGION

9.30 Alabama

Alabama Museum of Natural History (Tuscaloosa)
Anniston Museum of Natural History (Anniston)
Birmingham Botanical Gardens (Birmingham)
Birmingham Zoo (Birmingham)
Children's Hands-On Museum (Tuscaloosa)
The Exploreum Museum of Discovery (Mobile)
George Washington Carver Museum (Tuskegee Institute)
U.S. Space and Rocket Center (Huntsville)

9.31 Florida

Biscayne National Park (Homestead)
The Children's Science Center (Cape Coral)
Discovery Science Center (Ocala)
Dolphin Research Center (Grassy Key)
Florida Aquarium (Tampa)
Florida Museum of Natural History, University of Florida (Gainesville)
Imaginarium Hands-On Museum and Aquarium (Fort Myers)
Great Explorations, The Hands On Museum (St. Petersburg)
Gulf Islands National Seashore (Gulf Breeze)
Miami Museum of Science and Space Transit Planetarium (Miami)
Mote Marine Laboratory/Aquarium (Sarasota)
Museum of Arts and Science (Daytona Beach)
Museum of Discovery and Science (Fort Lauderdale)
Museum of Natural History of the Florida Keys (Marathon)
Museum of Science and History of Jacksonville (Jacksonville)
Museum of Science and Industry (Tampa)
Orlando Science Center (Orlando)
The Science Center of Pinellas County (St. Petersburg)
Sea World of Florida (Orlando)
Silver River Museum and Environmental Education Center (Ocala)
South Florida Science Museum (West Palm Beach)

9.32 Georgia

Fernbank Museum of Natural History (Atlanta)
Fernbank Science Center (Atlanta)
Georgia Southern University Museum (Statesboro)
The Museum of Arts and Sciences (Macon)
National Science Center (Fort Gordon)
Oatland Island Education Center (Savannah)
Savannah Science Museum (Savannah)
SciTrek—The Science and Technology Museum of Atlanta (Atlanta)
The State Botanical Garden of Georgia (Athens)
University of Georgia Museum of Natural History (Athens)
Zoo Atlanta (Atlanta)

9.33 Kentucky

Hardin Planetarium (Bowling Green)
John James Audubon Museum (Henderson)
The Living Arts and Science Center (Lexington)
Louisville Science Center (Louisville)
Louisville Zoological Garden (Louisville)

9.34 Mississippi

J. L. Scott Marine Education Center and Aquarium (Biloxi)
Maritime and Seafood Industry Museum (Biloxi)
Mississippi Museum of Natural Science (Jackson)
Russell C. Davis Planetarium (Jackson)
University Museums, The University of Mississippi (University)
William M. Colmer Visitor Center (Ocean Springs)

9.35 North Carolina

Adventures in Health Children's Museum (Greenville)
The Arts and Science Center (Statesville)
Cape Fear Museum (Wilmington)
Catawba Science Center (Hickory)
Colburn Gem and Mineral Museum (Asheville)
Discovery Place and Nature Museum (Charlotte)
Harris Visitors Center—Carolina Power and Light Company (New Hill)
The Health Adventure (Asheville)
Imagination Station Science Museum (Wilson)
Morehead Planetarium, University of North Carolina at Chapel Hill (Chapel Hill)
Natural Science Center of Greensboro (Greensboro)
North Carolina Aquarium at Fort Fisher (Kure Beach)
North Carolina Aquarium at Pine Knoll Shores (Atlantic Beach)
North Carolina Aquarium on Roanoke Island (Manteo)
North Carolina Botanical Garden (Chapel Hill)
North Carolina Maritime Museum (Beaufort)
North Carolina Museum of Life and Science (Durham)
North Carolina State Museum of Natural Sciences (Raleigh)
North Carolina Zoological Park (Asheboro)
Piedmont Environmental Center (High Point)
Rocky Mount Children's Museum (Rocky Mount)
Schiele Museum of Natural History and Planetarium (Gastonia)
SciWorks, the Science Center and Environmental Park of Forsyth County (Winston-Salem)
Western North Carolina Nature Center (Asheville)

9.36 South Carolina

Brookgreen Gardens (Murrells Inlet)
The Charleston Museum (Charleston)
Columbia Museum of Art and Gibbes Planetarium (Columbia)
Greenville Zoo (Greenville)
Museum of York County (Rock Hill)
Riverbanks Zoological Park (Columbia)
Roper Mountain Science Center (Greenville)
The South Carolina Botanical Garden (Clemson)
South Carolina State Museum (Columbia)
World of Energy at Keowee-Toxaway (Seneca)

9.37 Tennessee

American Museum of Science and Energy (Oak Ridge)
The Creative Discovery Museum (Chattanooga)
Cumberland Science Museum (Nashville)
East Tennessee Discovery Center (Knoxville)
Grassmere Wildlife Park (Nashville)
Hands On! Regional Museum (Johnson City)
Knoxville Zoological Gardens (Knoxville)
Lichterman Nature Center (Memphis)
Memphis Pink Palace Museum and Planetarium (Memphis)
Memphis Zoo and Aquarium (Memphis)

9.38 Virginia

D. Ralph Hostetter Museum of Natural History (Harrisonburg)
Leander J. McCormick Observatory (Charlottesville)
M. T. Brackbill Planetarium (Harrisonburg)
Norfolk Botanical Garden (Norfolk)
Orland E. White Arboretum (Boyce)
Richmond Children's Museum (Richmond)
Science Museum of Virginia (Richmond)
Science Museum of Western Virginia (Roanoke)
Shenandoah National Park (Luray)
Virginia Air and Space Center and Hampton Roads History Center (Hampton)
Virginia Living Museum (Newport News)
Virginia Marine Science Museum (Virginia Beach)
Virginia Museum of Natural History (Martinsville)
Virginia Museum of Transportation (Roanoke)
Virginia Zoological Park (Norfolk)
Watermen's Museum (Yorktown)

9.39 West Virginia

Good Children's Zoo (Wheeling)
Sunrise Museum (Charleston)

MIDDLE ATLANTIC REGION

9.40 Delaware

Brandywine Zoo (Wilmington)
Delaware Museum of Natural History (Wilmington)

9.41 District of Columbia

Capital Children's Museum (Washington, D.C.)
Explorers Hall—National Geographic Society (Washington, D.C.)
National Air and Space Museum, Smithsonian Institution (Washington, D.C.)
National Aquarium (Washington, D.C.)
National Museum of American History, Smithsonian Institution (Washington, D.C.)
National Museum of Natural History, Smithsonian Institution (Washington, D.C.)
National Zoological Park, Smithsonian Institution (Washington, D.C.)

9.42 Maryland

Baltimore Zoo (Baltimore)
Brookside Gardens (Wheaton)
Calvert Marine Museum (Solomons)
Carrie Weedon Natural Science Museum (Annapolis)
The Chesapeake Beach Railway Museum (Chesapeake Beach)
Columbus Center (under development) (Baltimore)
Cylburn Nature Museum (Baltimore)

Howard B. Owens Science Center (Lanham)
Jefferson Patterson Park and Museum (Saint Leonard)
Maryland Science Center (Baltimore)
National Aquarium in Baltimore (Baltimore)
Smithsonian Environmental Research Center (Edgewater)
30th Street Nature Center (Mt. Rainier)
Watkins Nature Center (Upper Marlboro)

9.43 New Jersey

Bergen County Zoological Park (Paramus)
Cape May County Park Zoo (Cape May)
The George C. Frelinghuysen Arboretum (Morris Township)
Liberty Science Center (Jersey City)
Monmouth Museum (Lincroft)
The Morris Museum (Morristown)
The Newark Museum (Newark)
The New Jersey State Aquarium at Camden (Camden)
New Jersey State Museum (Trenton)
Reeves-Reed Arboretum (Summit)
Trailside Nature and Science Center (Mountainside)
The Wetlands Institute (Stone Harbor)

9.44 New York

Alley Pond Environmental Center (Douglaston)
American Museum of Natural History (New York)
American Museum—Hayden Planetarium (New York)
Aquarium for Wildlife Conservation (Brooklyn)
Aquarium of Niagara Falls (Niagara Falls)
Brookhaven National Laboratory Science Museum (Upton)
Brooklyn Botanic Garden (Brooklyn)
The Brooklyn Children's Museum (Brooklyn)
Bronx Zoo (*See* New York Zoological Society—Bronx Zoo/Wildlife Conservation Park)
Buffalo Museum of Science (Buffalo)
Central Park Wildlife Center (New York)
Children's Museum of History, Natural History and Science (Utica)
Children's Museum of Manhattan (New York)
The Corning Museum of Glass (Corning)
George Landis Arboretum (Esperance)
The Greenburgh Nature Center (Scarsdale)
Hayden Planetarium (*See* American Museum—Hayden Planetarium)
The Hicksville Gregory Museum (Hicksville)
The Hudson River Museum of Westchester (Yonkers)
Institute of Ecosystem Studies (Millbrook)
Intrepid Sea-Air-Space Museum (New York)
Museum of Science and Technology (Syracuse)
Museum of the Hudson Highlands (Cornwall-on-Hudson)
The New York Botanical Garden (Bronx)
New York Hall of Science (Corona)
New York State Museum (Albany)
New York Zoological Society—Bronx Zoo/Wildlife Conservation Park (Bronx)
Pember Museum of Natural History (Granville)
Queens Botanical Garden (Queens)
Roberson Museum and Science Center (Binghamton) and Kopernick Space Education Center (Vestal)
Rochester Museum and Science Center (Rochester)
Ross Park Zoo (Binghamton)
Schenectady Museum and Planetarium (Schenectady)
Science Discovery Center of Oneonta (Oneonta)
Science Museum of Long Island (Manhasset)
Sciencenter (Ithaca)
Sci-Tech Center of Northern New York (Watertown)
Scotia-Glenville Children's Museum (Scotia)
Seneca Park Zoo (Rochester)
Staten Island Botanical Garden (Staten Island)
Staten Island Children's Museum (Staten Island)
Staten Island Institute of Arts and Sciences (Staten Island)
Staten Island Zoo (Staten Island)
Utica Zoo (Utica)
Vanderbilt Museum (Centerport)
Westmoreland Sanctuary (Mount Kisco)

9.45 Pennsylvania

The Academy of Natural Sciences of Philadelphia (Philadelphia)
Awbury Arboretum (Philadelphia)
The Carnegie Museum of Natural History (Pittsburgh)
The Carnegie Science Center (Pittsburgh)
Erie Zoo (Erie)
The Franklin Institute Science Museum (Philadelphia)
Hands-on House, Children's Museum of Lancaster (Lancaster)
Morris Arboretum of the University of Pennsylvania (Philadelphia)
The Museum of Scientific Discovery (Harrisburg)
National Aviary in Pittsburgh (Pittsburgh)
The North Museum of Natural History and Science, Franklin and Marshall College (Lancaster)
Philadelphia Zoological Garden (Philadelphia)
The Pittsburgh Children's Museum (Pittsburgh)
The Pittsburgh Zoo (Pittsburgh)
Please Touch Museum (Philadelphia)
Reading Public Museum and Art Gallery (Reading)
The Schuylkill Center for Environmental Education (Philadelphia)
SMART Discovery Center (Bethlehem)
Venango Museum of Art, Science and Industry (Oil City)
Wagner Free Institute of Science (Philadelphia)
ZOOAMERICA North American Wildlife Park (Hershey)

NEW ENGLAND REGION

9.46 Connecticut

Beardsley Zoo (Bridgeport)
The Bruce Museum (Greenwich)
Connecticut Audubon Society (Hartford)
Connecticut State Museum of Natural History (Storrs)
Dinosaur State Park (Rocky Hill)
The Discovery Museum (Bridgeport)
Eli Whitney Museum (Hamden)
Lutz Children's Museum (Manchester)
The Maritime Center at Norwalk (Norwalk)
Mystic Marinelife Aquarium (Mystic)
Science Center of Connecticut (West Hartford)

9.47 Maine

The Children's Museum of Maine (Portland)
L. C. Bates Museum (Hinckley)
Maine State Museum (Augusta)
Mount Desert Oceanarium (Southwest Harbor)
Owls Head Transportation Museum (Owls Head)

9.48 Massachusetts

Aquarium of the National Marine Fisheries Service (Woods Hole)
Berkshire Botanical Garden (Stockbridge)
The Berkshire Museum (Pittsfield)
Cape Cod Museum of Natural History (Brewster)
The Children's Museum (Boston)
Children's Museum at Holyoke (Holyoke)
The Computer Museum (Boston)
The Discovery Museums (Acton)
Harvard Museums of Cultural and Natural History, Harvard University (Cambridge)
Laughing Brook Education Center and Wildlife Sanctuary (Hampden)
Museum of Science, Boston (Boston)
National Plastics Center and Museum (Leominster)
New England Aquarium (Boston)
New England Science Center (Worcester)
South Shore Natural Science Center (Norwell)
Springfield Science Museum (Springfield)
Thornton W. Burgess Museum (East Sandwich)
Worcester County Horticultural Society/Tower Hill Botanic Garden (Boylston)

9.49 New Hampshire

Audubon Society of New Hampshire (Concord)
The Children's Museum of Portsmouth (Portsmouth)
Seacoast Science Center (Rye)

9.50 Rhode Island

Audubon Society of Rhode Island (Smithfield)
Museum of Natural History (Providence)
Roger Williams Park Zoo (Providence)

9.51 Vermont

The Discovery Museum (Essex Junction)
Fairbanks Museum and Planetarium (St. Johnsbury)
Montshire Museum of Science (Norwich)

CANADA

9.52 Canadian Provinces

Aitken Bicentennial Exhibition Centre (Saint John, New Brunswick)
Calgary Zoo, Botanical Garden and Prehistoric Park (Calgary, Alberta)
Canadian Museum of Nature (Ottawa, Ontario)
Discovery Centre (Halifax, Nova Scotia)
Metropolitan Toronto Zoo (Toronto, Ontario)
National Aviation Museum (Ottawa, Ontario)
National Museum of Science and Technology (Ottawa, Ontario)
Ontario Science Centre (Don Mills, Ontario)
Saskatchewan Science Centre (Regina, Saskatchewan)
The Science Centre (Calgary, Alberta)
Science North (Sudbury, Ontario)
SCIENCE WORLD British Columbia (Vancouver, British Columbia)
Vancouver Aquarium, Canada's Pacific National Aquarium (Vancouver, British Columbia)

SELECT ANNOTATED LISTING

ABOUT THE "SELECT ANNOTATED LISTING"

The "Select Annotated Listing" provides annotations for the almost 300 facilities that appear in boldface type in the "Complete Regional Listing," on pages 171-178.

The "Select Annotated Listing" is arranged by geographical regions (see the map on page 170). Within each region the states are listed alphabetically. The name of each institution appears alphabetically within its state listing.

The nine geographical regions, listed in a roughly west-to-east array, are as follows:

- **Pacific Region** Alaska, California, Hawaii, Oregon, Washington
- **Mountain Region** Arizona, Colorado, Idaho, Montana, Nevada, New Mexico, Utah, Wyoming
- **Great Plains/Midwest Region** Iowa, Kansas, Minnesota, Missouri, Nebraska, North Dakota, South Dakota
- **South Central Region** Arkansas, Louisiana, Oklahoma, Texas
- **Great Lakes Region** Illinois, Indiana, Michigan, Ohio, Wisconsin
- **Southeast Region** Alabama, Florida, Georgia, Kentucky, Mississippi, North Carolina, South Carolina, Tennessee, Virginia, West Virginia
- **Middle Atlantic Region** Delaware, District of Columbia, Maryland, New Jersey, New York, Pennsylvania
- **New England Region** Connecticut, Maine, Massachusetts, New Hampshire, Rhode Island, Vermont
- **Canada** Canadian Provinces

For easy reference, an "entry number" (for example—9.53 for The Imaginarium: A Science Discovery Center, in Anchorage, Alaska) appears with the name of each institution in the "Select Annotated Listing." This series of entry numbers continues without interruption from the "Complete Regional Listing," where each individual state has an entry number.

Each annotation provides the address and telephone number, a brief description of the facility, and information about the resources it offers in support of hands-on science teaching at the elementary school level. The annotations do not list every resource and program at an institution, but they provide a general sense of the facility and the types of support it offers.

To arrange class visits and for information about particular programs, materials, costs or fees, and publications, readers should contact the facilities directly.

The addresses provided with the annotations are locational but are not necessarily mailing addresses.

PACIFIC REGION

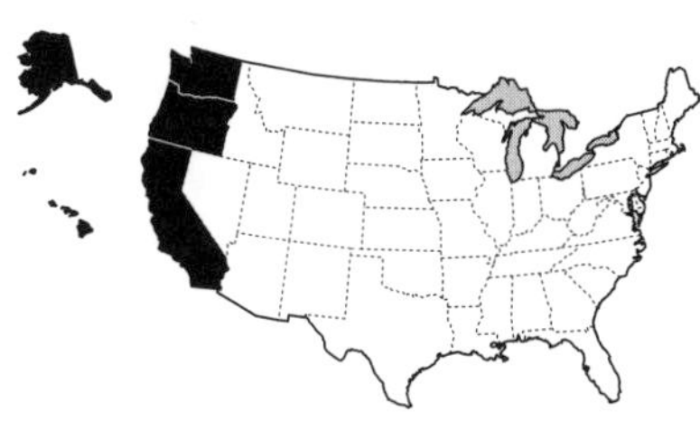

Alaska

9.53 **The Imaginarium: A Science Discovery Center,** 725 W. Fifth Ave., Anchorage, AK 99501
(907) 276-3179

Regional discovery center focusing on the life, earth, and physical sciences, with special emphasis on the animals and ecology of Alaska. ***Programs for students:*** At the Imaginarium: classes; guided tours; field trips. At schools: outreach programs; traveling exhibits. ***Materials:*** Loans of live animals and plants. ***Education and support for teachers:*** In-service education on science content and hands-on learning.

California

9.54 **Bay Area Discovery Museum,** 557 E. Fort Baker, Sausalito, CA 94965
(415) 487-4398

Children's museum with a science lab, a media center, and a discovery hall; emphasis on estuary ecology, biology, geology, and ethnobotany, especially as related to San Francisco Bay area ecosystems. ***Programs for students:*** At the museum: workshops; participatory exhibitions; field trip programs (grades K-1 and 2-5). At schools: outreach programs. ***Materials:*** Hands-on activity books;

pre-/postvisit materials. ***Education and support for teachers:*** In-service education to integrate natural sciences and the arts.

9.55 Cabrillo Marine Aquarium, 3720 Stephen White Dr., San Pedro, CA 90731
(310) 548-7562

Museum/aquarium, with 35 aquariums and exhibits, located on the shore adjacent to sandy beaches, salt marsh, and rocky shore habitats; focused on the marine life of southern California. ***Programs for students:*** At the aquarium: wetlab/field workshops; guided tours; hands-on exhibits; whalewatching boat trips. At schools: outreach programs. ***Materials:*** Teacher's guides. ***Education and support for teachers:*** In-service workshops on marine and environmental topics and on hands-on learning; resource library.

9.56 California Academy of Sciences, Golden Gate Park, San Francisco, CA 94118-4599
(415) 221-5100

Research-based institution that includes a natural history museum, aquarium, planetarium, and discovery room; focused on life sciences, natural history and evolution, astronomy, physics, and chemistry. ***Programs for students:*** At the academy: planetarium programs; guided tours; hands-on exhibits; after-school and Saturday classes. At schools: outreach vans. ***Materials:*** Activity books; kits with curriculum guides and audiocassettes; lending boxes of hands-on materials; teacher's guides. ***Education and support for teachers:*** In-service education on science content and hands-on learning; library resource center; newsletter.

9.57 California Museum of Science and Industry, 700 State Dr., Los Angeles, CA 90037
(213) 744-7444

Extensive science and technology museum, with an IMAX theater; focused on physical sciences, human biology and health, aerospace, technology, zoology, the environment, and the relationship of science to the arts and humanities. ***Programs for students:*** At the museum: participatory exhibits; guided tours; science workshops; parent-child programs. At schools: outreach programs. ***Materials:*** Teacher's guides; activity sheets: *Science Explorers*. ***Education and support for teachers:*** In-service workshops on science topics and hands-on learning; leadership conferences.

9.58 Chabot Observatory and Science Center, 4917 Mountain Blvd., Oakland, CA 94619-3014
(510) 530-3480

A 111-year-old observatory and planetarium and a science center scheduled to open in 1997; current focus on astronomy and related sciences to be extended to earth, life, and environmental sciences. ***Programs for students:*** At the observatory: observatory and telescope workshops; planetarium shows; hands-on exhibits. At schools: portable planetarium; traveling exhibits; environmental education programs. ***Materials:*** Hands-on activity books; curriculum units with hands-on materials; teacher's guides; audiovisual and computer-based materials; catalog of materials. ***Education and support for teachers:*** In-service education on science content and hands-on learning; information and resources online; newsletter.

9.59 Children's Discovery Museum of San Jose, 180 Woz Way, San Jose, CA 95110-2780
(408) 298-5437

Museum with a freshwater aquarium and more than 150 interactive exhibits. ***Programs for students:*** At the museum: hands-on exhibits; classes. At schools: outreach programs.

9.60 Coyote Point Museum for Environmental Education, 1651 Coyote Point Dr., San Mateo, CA 94401
(415) 342-7755

Nature center with an environmental hall, wildlife habitats, and a curriculum library; emphasis on life sciences and the environment. ***Programs for students:*** At the museum: hands-on exhibits; programs for school groups; after-school classes (grades 1-3); guided tours; field trips. At schools: outreach programs. ***Materials:*** Hands-on activity books; curriculum units and supplemental activities developed upon request; loans of "experience boxes" and mounted specimens; audiovisual materials. ***Education and support for teachers:*** In-service workshops on science content and hands-on learning; newsletter.

9.61 Discovery Museum Learning Center, 3615 Auburn Blvd., Sacramento, CA 95628
(916) 277-6181

Science center with a discovery trail and a planetarium; focused on astronomy, botany, earth sciences, life science and the human body, matter and energy, and robotics. ***Programs for students:*** At the center: docent-led tours; planetarium shows; programs with live animals. At schools: assembly programs, including a traveling Star Dome. ***Materials:*** Hands-on activity books; lending boxes of hands-on materials; teacher's guides.

Education and support for teachers: In-service education on science content and hands-on learning, including workshops on several national curriculum projects.

9.62 The Exploratorium, 3601 Lyon St., San Francisco, CA 94123
(415) 563-7337

One of the world's major hands-on museums, with a center for teaching and learning; focused on science, art, and human perception. ***Programs for students:*** At the museum: 650 interactive exhibits; field trips. At schools: outreach programs. ***Materials:*** Hands-on activity books; catalog of materials. ***Education and support for teachers:*** At the center: summer institute (has 2,000 graduates) for teachers of grades K-12, concentrating on science content, hands-on learning, and innovative approaches to teaching discovery-based science; quarterly magazine *Exploring.*

9.63 Lawrence Hall of Science, University of California, Centennial Drive, Berkeley, CA 94720
(510) 642-4193

Science museum and leading center for educational research; develops and disseminates model programs, such as the Full Option Science System (FOSS) and Great Explorations in Math and Science (GEMS) series of curriculum units; facilities include a participatory planetarium and discovery-oriented physics, biology, and computer labs. ***Programs for students:*** At Lawrence Hall: classes; hands-on exhibits; field trips. At schools: outreach programs; traveling exhibits. ***Materials:*** FOSS and GEMS units; catalogs of materials. ***Education and support for teachers:*** In-service education on science content and hands-on learning; extensive library of science education and curriculum materials; newsletter.

9.64 Lawrence Livermore National Laboratory, Visitors Center, 7000 East Ave., Livermore, CA 94550
(510) 424-0576

National laboratory with an active educational program, focusing on physics. ***Programs for students:*** At schools: science and technology presentations with about 20 scientific demonstrations, including light and laser experiments, by Science Presentation Volunteers. ***Materials:*** Teacher's guides. ***Education and support for teachers:*** In-service education on science content.

9.65 The Lindsay Museum, 1931 First Ave., Walnut Creek, CA 94596
(510) 935-1978

Wildlife and natural history museum, with wild animals and a Discovery Room, focused on life history, geology, ecology, and the environment. ***Programs for students:*** At the museum: hands-on exhibits; guided tours. At schools: outreach programs; traveling exhibits. ***Materials:*** Loans of taxidermal specimens. ***Education and support for teachers:*** In-service classes on science content and hands-on learning; letter-answering service; newsletter.

9.66 The Living Desert, 47-900 Portola Ave., Palm Desert, CA 92260
(619) 346-5694

Botanical garden and wildlife park, including 200 acres of gardens representing various desert ecosystems of the world, 1,000 acres of wilderness preserve and hiking trails, and a discovery room open on weekends. ***Programs for students:*** At the park: classes; guided tours; hands-on exhibits. At schools: outreach programs. ***Materials:*** Hands-on activity books; teacher's guides. ***Education and support for teachers:*** Workshops; newsletter.

9.67 Los Angeles Zoo, 5333 Zoo Dr., Los Angeles, CA 90027
(213) 666-4090

Zoo, with educational programs that emphasize an understanding of and appreciation for wildlife and conservation. ***Programs for students:*** At the zoo: workshops; guided tours. At schools: outreach programs. ***Materials:*** Curriculum materials and activities for school classes; Zoo Discovery Kits (grades PreK-2) for zoo visits led by teachers; slide sets. ***Education and support for teachers:*** Workshops on science content and hands-on learning, for the classroom and for zoo visits.

9.68 Monterey Bay Aquarium, 886 Cannery Row, Monterey, CA 93940
(408) 648-4850

Renowned aquarium and marine research institution, with hands-on discovery labs and a touch pool; focused on marine biology, ecology, geology, meteorology, oceanography, and on the methods and processes of science. ***Programs for students:*** At the aquarium: programs for school groups; self-guided tours. At schools: outreach programs (including aquaravan with live animals). ***Materials:*** Pre-/postvisit, curriculum, and audiovisual materials; a series of natural history books; catalog of materials. ***Education and support for teachers:*** In-service education on science content and hands-on learning, including field, exhibit, lab, and classroom experiences; leadership programs.

9.69 Natural History Museum of Los Angeles County, 900 Exposition Blvd., Los Angeles, CA 90007
(213) 744-3466

Museum comprising the original museum on Exposition Boulevard, Page Museum of La Brea Discoveries,

William S. Hart Museum in Newhall, Calif., and the Natural History Museum of Los Angeles County at Burbank; facilities include hands-on discovery centers and an insect zoo; emphasis on earth and life sciences and anthropology. ***Programs for students:*** At the museums: classes; workshops; field trips; tours for school groups; hands-on exhibits. At schools: outreach programs; traveling insect zoo; earthmobile. ***Materials:*** Lending boxes with science specimens; teacher's guides. ***Education and support for teachers:*** Courses in natural history; lectures; library.

9.70 Palm Springs Desert Museum, 101 Museum Dr., Palm Springs, CA 92263
(619) 325-7186

Museum of art, the performing arts, and natural science, with a nature trail; focused on the life sciences, geology, ethnobotany, and various interdisciplinary areas. ***Programs for students:*** At the museum: guided tours; hands-on exhibits; formal museum classes (grades 2-5); overnight field trips (grades 4-5). At schools: classes; traveling exhibits. ***Materials:*** Kits of desert species for loan; teacher's guides. ***Education and support for teachers:*** Science project workshops on science content and hands-on learning; lending library.

9.71 Rancho Santa Ana Botanic Garden, 1500 No. College Ave., Claremont, CA 91711
(909) 625-8767

Botanic garden, affiliated with the Claremont Colleges, featuring an 86-acre display of California native plants; focused on research and education in botany and on conservation and cultivation of native plants. ***Programs for students:*** At the garden: hands-on learning centers; guided tours. At schools: outreach programs. ***Materials:*** Hands-on activity books; loans of hands-on materials and live specimens; pre-/postvisit teacher's packets; curriculum and audiovisual materials. ***Education and support for teachers:*** Workshops to review national and California curricula in biological and environmental sciences.

9.72 Randall Museum, 199 Museum Way, San Francisco, CA 94114
(415) 554-9600

Children's museum on 16 acres, with live animals, a petting corral, and a hiking trail; emphasis on physical, life, earth, and environmental sciences. ***Programs for students:*** At the museum: hands-on exhibits; classes for school groups; after-school classes; vacation-time workshops; guided tours. At schools: outreach programs (limited). ***Materials:*** Discovery lending kits; curriculum materials. ***Education and support for teachers:*** In-service workshops on science content and hands-on learning, including national curriculum projects; newsletter.

9.73 Reuben H. Fleet Space Theater and Science Center, 1875 El Prado, Balboa Park, San Diego, CA 92101
(619) 238-1233

Science center, with a planetarium, Omnimax theater, and Challenger Learning Center, focused on physical and space sciences and astronomy. ***Programs for students:*** At the center: hands-on exhibits; self-guided tours; presentations; after-school classes. At the Challenger Center: programs and simulated space voyage for classes; tours to Palomar Observatory at the California Institute of Technology. At schools: outreach programs; traveling exhibits. ***Materials:*** Hands-on activity books; teacher materials and resource guides with many student activities; some lending boxes; audiovisual materials; catalog of materials. ***Education and support for teachers:*** In-service workshops on science content and hands-on learning.

9.74 San Diego Natural History Museum, 1788 El Prado, Balboa Park, San Diego, CA 92101
(619) 232-3821

Regional research and educational museum, with desert and earth science discovery labs, and (under development) an Environmental Science Education Center; focused on life and earth sciences and the environment, but also emphasizing interdisciplinary fields that combine science with society and the arts and humanities. ***Programs for students:*** At the museum: ecology field walks; guided/self-guided tours; workshops (grades K-3). At schools: outreach presentations. ***Materials:*** Specimens and videos for loan; curriculum materials (in English and Spanish) to accompany museum visits; teacher's guides. ***Education and support for teachers:*** In-service education including workshops, classes, field trips, and expeditions; resource lending library.

9.75 San Diego Zoo, 2920 Zoo Dr., San Diego, CA 92103
(619) 231-1515

World-renowned zoo on 100 acres, operated by the Zoological Society of San Diego. ***Programs for students:*** At the zoo: classes. At schools: outreach programs; traveling exhibits. ***Materials:*** Interdisciplinary curriculum packets on various topics (e.g., rain forests, dinosaurs); audiovisual materials; loans of live animals and plants; catalog of materials. ***Education and support for teachers:*** In-service workshops on science content and hands-on learning; newsletter.

9.76 Santa Barbara Botanic Garden, 1212 Mission Canyon Rd., Santa Barbara, CA 93105-2199
(805) 682-4726

Botanic garden and arboretum with a herbarium, focusing on horticultural research and the preservation of biological diversity, especially of California's native flora. ***Programs for students:*** At the garden: after-school and holiday classes; workshops; field trips. At the garden and at schools: garden tours and school outreach programs that complement one another and are designed for specific grades. ***Materials:*** Activity-based resource guides; nature kits for loan; flier describing materials. ***Education and support for teachers:*** In-service education on science content and hands-on learning in the environmental sciences; library; newsletter.

9.77 Santa Barbara Museum of Natural History, 2559 Puesta del Sol Rd., Santa Barbara, CA 93105
(805) 682-4711

Natural history museum, including a planetarium, with a satellite marine museum (The Sea Center) on Stearns Wharf featuring a touch tank; emphasis on natural history and marine science. ***Programs for students:*** At the museums: presentations and guided programs for school groups; hands-on exhibits. At schools: outreach programs; traveling exhibits. ***Materials:*** Hands-on activity books; curriculum units; natural objects and kits for loan; teacher's guides; catalog of materials. ***Education and support for teachers:*** Summer workshops on science content and hands-on learning.

9.78 Sea World, 1720 So. Shores Rd., San Diego, CA 92109-7995
(619) 226-3834

Aquarium, oceanarium, and marine museum; focused on marine science, with emphasis on ecology and conservation. ***Programs for students:*** At Sea World: classes; guided/self-guided tours; hands-on exhibits. At schools throughout the western United States: assembly programs; live, interactive television programs via satellite, cable, and Public Broadcasting System. ***Materials:*** Teacher's guides; audiovisual and computer-based materials; catalog of materials. ***Education and support for teachers:*** In-service education on science content and hands-on learning, including courses for college credit.

9.79 Stephen Birch Aquarium-Museum, Scripps Institution of Oceanography, 2300 Expedition Way, La Jolla, CA 92093-0207
(619) 534-FISH

Aquarium and museum of ocean science serving as the public education center for the Scripps Institution of Oceanography; focused on the oceans and global science. ***Programs for students:*** At the aquarium-museum: classes; guided tours; hands-on exhibits; field activities. At schools: outreach programs. ***Materials:*** Teacher's guides; curriculum materials; discovery kits. ***Education and support for teachers:*** In-service workshops on science content and hands-on learning.

9.80 The Tech Museum of Innovation, 145 W. San Carlos St., San Jose, CA 95113
(408) 279-7148

Interactive museum and learning center, with emphasis on learning about science and technology through active involvement. ***Programs for students:*** At the museum: classes and programs (grades 4-6); hands-on exhibits; guided tours. At schools: outreach programs (limited). ***Materials:*** Hands-on activity books; teacher's guides; audiovisual and computer-based materials; catalog of materials. ***Education and support for teachers:*** In-service workshops on science content and hands-on learning; newsletter.

Hawaii

9.81 Bishop Museum, 1525 Bernice St., Honolulu, HI 96817-0916
(808) 847-3511

Cultural and natural history museum, with a planetarium and an observatory; emphasizes zoology, botany, and archaeology. ***Programs for students:*** At the museum: classes; guided tours; hands-on exhibits; field trips. At schools: outreach programs. ***Materials:*** hands-on activity books; lending boxes of hands-on materials; teacher's guides; audiovisual and computer-based materials. ***Education and support for teachers:*** In-service workshops on science content and hands-on learning.

9.82 Sea Life Park Hawaii, Makapu'u Point, Waimanalo, HI 96795
(808) 259-7933

Oceanarium with an education center, on the island of Oahu, focused on marine science and marine conservation. ***Programs for students:*** At the oceanarium: programs; hands-on exhibits. At schools: outreach programs; traveling exhibits. ***Materials:*** Hands-on activity books; lending boxes of hands-on materials; teacher's guides; audiovisual materials. ***Education and support for teachers:*** In-service workshops on science content and hands-on learning; teacher resource library.

9.83 Waikiki Aquarium, 2777 Kalakaua Ave., Honolulu, HI 96815
(808) 923-9741

Research-based marine aquarium of the University of Hawaii at Manoa, emphasizing ecology, habitats, adaptations for survival, and conservation of Hawaiian and Pacific marine life. ***Programs for students:*** At the aquarium: classes; guided/self-guided tours; hands-on exhibits. At outer district schools: outreach programs (grades 3-6). ***Materials:*** Teacher's guides; audiovisual and pre-/postvisit materials; catalog of materials. ***Education and support for teachers:*** In-service workshops on science content; newsletter.

Oregon

9.84 The High Desert Museum, 59800 So. Hwy. 97, Bend, OR 97702-8933
(503) 382-4754

Regional, participation-oriented, "living" museum focused on the natural history of the arid Intermountain West. ***Programs for students:*** At the museum: classes on natural and cultural history; science-focused field trip programs; self-guided tours. At schools within 150-mile radius of the museum: outreach programs. ***Materials:*** Science resource kits for rural outreach. ***Education and support for teachers:*** In-service education on science content and hands-on learning in life and earth sciences; newsletter.

9.85 Metro Washington Park Zoo, 4001 S.W. Canyon Rd., Portland, OR 97221
(503) 226-1561

City zoo with special emphasis on endangered wildlife issues at the local, regional, and international levels. ***Programs for students:*** At the zoo: classes; hands-on exhibits. At schools: zoomobile with outreach programs. ***Materials:*** Hands-on activity books; field guides for nature trail; lending boxes of hands-on materials; teacher's guides; pre-/postvisit and audiovisual materials. ***Education and support for teachers:*** In-service workshops on science content and hands-on learning; newsletter.

9.86 Oregon Museum of Science and Industry, 1945 S.E. Water Ave., Portland, OR 97214-3354
(503) 797-4000

Science and technology museum, with a planetarium, Omnimax theater, botanical garden, environmental center, and education resource center. ***Programs for students:*** At the museum: many hands-on classes and exhibits; week-long day camps at sites from beach to desert; guided tours; field trips. At schools in Oregon, Alaska, California, Colorado, Idaho, and Washington: outreach assemblies and classroom programs with hands-on activities; interactive demonstrations (some with live animals); portable planetarium. ***Materials:*** Hands-on activity books; teacher's guides; audiovisual and computer-based materials; catalog of materials. ***Education and support for teachers:*** In-service workshops and courses on science content and hands-on learning, both at the museum and at schools anywhere in the Pacific Northwest; newsletter.

9.87 Pacific Northwest Museum of Natural History, 1500 E. Main St., Ashland, OR 97520
(503) 488-1084

Highly interactive natural history museum, with a discovery center and realistic, multisensory exhibits reflecting six ecosystems of the Northwest; focused on the physical, life, earth, and environmental sciences. ***Programs for students:*** At the museum: hands-on exhibits (many with computer interactions); classes; self-guided tours; presentations with live animals. ***Materials:*** Hands-on activity books; supplemental materials; magazine for students. ***Education and support for teachers:*** Workshops on science content and hands-on learning; newsletter.

9.88 World Forestry Center, 4033 S.W. Canyon Rd., Portland, OR 97221
(503) 228-1367

Forestry center with a museum, an information institute, and a 70-acre working tree farm and outdoor education site in Wilsonville, Oreg.; focused on the study and conservation of global forests and forest resources. ***Programs for students:*** At the museum and tree farm: guided tours; learning lab presentations. At the museum: hands-on activity stations. At schools: outreach programs. ***Materials:*** Hands-on activity kits; curriculum units with hands-on materials and teacher's guides. ***Education and support for teachers:*** International information network on forest resources; newsletter.

Washington

9.89 Marine Science Society of the Pacific Northwest, Marine Science Center, 18743 Front St., N.E., Poulsbo, WA 98370
(206) 779-5549

Small marine facility on the shore of Puget Sound, focusing on the marine environment. ***Programs for students:*** At the facility: hands-on instruction; guided tours; hands-on exhibits. At schools: outreach programs (including field studies). ***Materials:*** Hands-on activity books; science kits of hands-on materials and live animals for loan; teacher's guides; audiovisual and computer-based materials; catalog of materials. ***Education and support for teachers:*** In-service workshops on science content and hands-on learning.

9.90 North Cascades Institute, 2105 Hwy. 20, Sedro Woolley, WA 98284
(206) 856-5700

Institute focusing on field-based, experiential, environmental education in the Greater North Cascades ecosystem, including the North Cascades National Park, Puget Sound, and the Columbia River Basin. ***Programs for students:*** In North Cascades National Park: 3-day mountain school (grade 5, with teachers and parents); in the Skagit River watershed: field trips to local streams and habitats (grade 4). At schools: outreach programs on watershed education. ***Materials:*** Curriculum and resource materials; catalog of field seminars. ***Education and support for teachers:*** In-service workshops and field seminars focused on watersheds, natural history, and experiential teaching.

9.91 Pacific Science Center, 200 Second Ave., No., Seattle, WA 98109-4895
(206) 443-2001

Science and technology center with an IMAX theater, a planetarium, and an extensive science education program. ***Programs for students:*** At the center: more than 200 hands-on exhibits; classes; demonstrations; laser light shows; peer-teaching workshops; field-study programs at summer camps. At schools in a majority of school districts in Washington State: seven traveling vans bringing interactive assemblies, hands-on classes, and hands-on exhibits. ***Materials:*** Hands-on activity books; materials and, where appropriate, lesson plans for continuing various Science Center education programs; audiovisual and computer-based materials. ***Education and support for teachers:*** Hands-on workshops for teams (a teacher and five students); teacher institutes on science content and hands-on learning; newsletter.

9.92 The Seattle Aquarium, Pier 59, Waterfront Park, Seattle, WA 98101
(206) 386-4300

Regionally focused marine science institution, with a discovery lab and tide pool; provides outdoor environmental education programs for both students and teachers. ***Programs for students:*** At the aquarium: guided tours; hands-on exhibits; hands-on classes, with live animals; comprehensive early-childhood program. At schools: interactive programs; traveling exhibits, with live animals. ***Materials:*** Hands-on activity books; lending boxes of hands-on materials; teacher's guides; pre-/postvisit and audiovisual materials; catalog of materials. ***Education and support for teachers:*** In-service workshops on science content and hands-on learning.

9.93 Woodland Park Zoological Gardens, 5500 Phinney Ave. No., Seattle, WA 98103
(206) 684-4800

Zoo featuring naturalistic exhibits and an education center with a discovery room; focus includes major ecosystems of the world and wildlife conservation. ***Programs for students:*** At the zoo: hands-on exhibits; programs for school groups; guided tours. At schools: outreach programs. ***Materials:*** Hands-on activity books; curriculum packets; loan kits; videos; catalog of materials. ***Education and support for teachers:*** In-service workshops, lectures, and classes on science content and hands-on learning; newsletter.

MOUNTAIN REGION

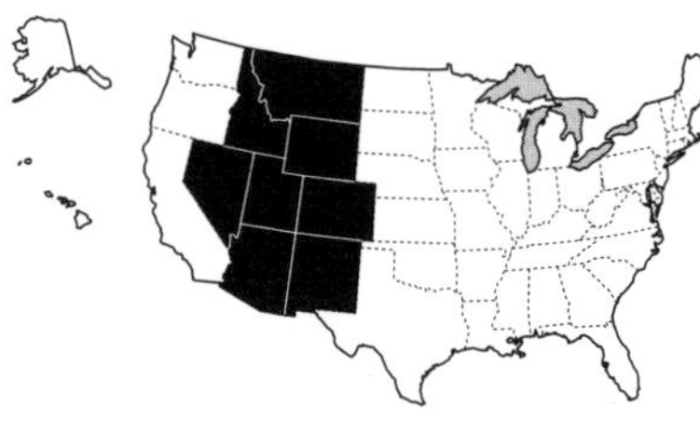

Arizona

9.94 Arizona Science Center, 147 E. Adams St., Phoenix, AZ 85004-2331
(602) 256-9388

Science and technology center, with a planetarium. ***Programs for students:*** At the center: classes; interactive exhibits. At schools: outreach programs, including family telescope nights. ***Materials:*** Field trip guides. ***Education and support for teachers:*** In-service workshops on science content and hands-on learning; newsletter.

9.95 Arizona-Sonora Desert Museum, 2021 No. Kinney Rd., Tucson, AZ 85743-9719
(602) 883-1380

Natural history museum focusing on the ecology of the Sonora Desert region; most exhibits outdoors, consisting of living representations of plant and animal communities; educational programs emphasize conservation. ***Programs for students:*** At the museum: programs for school groups, including docent-led tours. At schools: outreach programs. ***Materials:*** Hands-on activity books; kits on ecological subjects for loan. ***Education and support for teachers:*** In-service workshops on desert ecology; field trips; hikes.

9.96 Desert Botanical Garden, 1201 No. Galvin Pkwy., Papago Park, Phoenix, AZ 85008
(602) 941-1217

Botanical garden and research facility, with plants representing more than 4,000 species; focused on arid-land plants of the world, with special emphasis on succulents and native plants of the southwestern United States. ***Programs for students:*** At the garden: workshops; guided tours with hands-on demonstrations; interactive investigation stations. At schools: outreach programs. ***Materials:*** Hands-on activity books; curriculum units with hands-on materials; teacher's guides and information packets; teacher's checklist for self-guided tours; video; catalog of materials. ***Education and support for teachers:*** In-service education on science content and hands-on learning; field-test site for curriculum materials.

9.97 Flandrau Science Center and Planetarium, University of Arizona, Tucson, AZ 85721
(602) 621-4515

University-based science center, with a domed theater and interactive-exhibit halls; focused on astronomy, physics, and computers. ***Programs for students:*** At the center: programs; guided tours. At schools: outreach programs. ***Materials:*** Teacher's guides. ***Education and support for teachers:*** In-service education on science content and hands-on learning; newsletter.

9.98 Kitt Peak Museum, Tucson, AZ 85735-9734
(602) 322-3426

Education-oriented, astronomy-based museum located at Kitt Peak National Observatory, focused on astronomical research and the activities of the observatory; exhibits also emphasize aspects of the Native American culture and natural history of the surrounding desert. ***Programs for students:*** At the museum: guided tours and "star-party" activities featuring a hands-on approach to telescopes and sky-object identification. At schools: audiovisual and lecture-format outreach programs; traveling exhibits. ***Materials:*** Teacher's guides; audiovisual and computer-based materials. ***Education and support for teachers:*** In-service education on science content.

9.99 Lowell Observatory, 1400 W. Mars Hill Rd., Flagstaff, AZ 86001
(602) 774-2096

Research observatory, with a Visitor Center featuring many instruments modified for interactive display; emphasis on astronomy and physical and earth sciences. ***Programs for students:*** At the observatory: interactive displays; more than 20 programs and workshops on various astronomical topics; guided tours. ***Materials:*** Workshop materials; fact sheets. ***Education and support for teachers:*** Visitor Center and Clark telescope can be reserved for teacher workshops.

Colorado

9.100 Colorado School of Mines Geology Museum, 16th and Maple, Golden, CO 80401-1887
(303) 273-3815

Small, university museum in the geosciences, with considerable collections of minerals, rocks, fossils, gems, and mining artifacts. ***Programs for students:*** At the museum: guided tours (including local geology); hands-on exhibits. At schools: outreach programs. ***Materials:*** Teaching trunks and fossil kits of hands-on materials for loan; excess mineral and fossil material (not in the collection) available upon request.

9.101 Denver Museum of Natural History, 2001 Colorado Blvd., in City Park, Denver, CO 80205
(303) 370-6357

Museum with an IMAX theater and a planetarium, focused on earth, life, environmental, anthropological, and health sciences and planetarium studies. ***Programs for students:*** At the museum: classes; guided tours; hands-on exhibits; field studies/trips. At schools: outreach programs; traveling exhibits. ***Materials:*** hands-on activity books; lending boxes of hands-on materials; teacher's guides. ***Education and support for teachers:*** In-service education on science content and hands-on learning.

9.102 **Denver Zoological Gardens,** City Park, Denver, CO 80205
(303) 331-4100

Zoo with several naturalistic displays, including Bird World, Northern Shores (the Arctic), and Tropical Discovery. ***Programs for students:*** At the zoo: topical guided tours; self-guided tours. At schools: outreach van with school programs about the prairie (grades 3-4) and reptiles (grades 5-7); speakers bureau. ***Materials:*** Previsit teacher packets for zoo visits and outreach programs. ***Education and support for teachers:*** In-service workshops; newsletter.

Idaho

9.103 **The Discovery Center of Idaho,** 131 Myrtle St., Boise, ID 83702
(208) 343-9895

Participatory science museum, with a planetarium. ***Programs for students:*** At the center: grade-specific demonstrations; classes; hands-on exhibits. At schools: traveling exhibits. ***Materials:*** Teacher's guides; audiovisual and computer-based materials. ***Education and support for teachers:*** In-service workshops on science content and hands-on learning; extensive teacher training program in astronomy; teacher resource center.

9.104 **Idaho Museum of Natural History,** 1066 So. Fifth, Pocatello, ID 83209
(208) 236-3168

Natural history museum of Idaho State University; focused on several physical sciences in addition to natural history fields (paleontology, geology, botany, archaeology, and ethnography). ***Programs for students:*** At the museum: classes; guided tours. At schools: exhibits trailer; two mobile science-lab classrooms. ***Materials:*** Hands-on activity books and support materials; teacher's guides; discovery boxes and other educational resources for loan; audiovisual and pre-/postvisit materials; catalog of resource materials. ***Education and support for teachers:*** newsletter.

Montana

9.105 **Museum of the Rockies,** 600 W. Kagy Blvd., Bozeman, MT 59715
(406) 994-5283

Museum at Montana State University, focused on the natural and cultural history of the Northern Rocky Mountain region; emphasizes archaeology, geology, ethnology, paleontology, and astronomy. ***Programs for students:*** At the museum: hands-on exhibits; programs for school groups; guided tours; field studies. At schools: outreach programs, including a portable planetarium and traveling trunks. ***Materials:*** Dinologues (on dinosaurs): a series of educational videos, slide sets, activity kits, fossil casts, and teacher workbooks relating to biology, microbiology, astronomy, geology, chemistry, physics, and anatomy. ***Education and support for teachers:*** In-service workshops on science content and hands-on learning.

Nevada

9.106 **Lied Discovery Children's Museum,** 833 Las Vegas Blvd., No., Las Vegas, NV 89101
(702) 382-3445

Children's museum, with more than 100 hands-on exhibits and an in-house radio station. ***Programs for students:*** At the museum: educational programs; guided tours; field trips; quarterly newspaper (grades 4-5). At schools: outreach programs; traveling exhibits. ***Materials:*** Packets, provided before guided tours; audiovisual materials. ***Education and support for teachers:*** In-service workshops on science content and hands-on learning; newsletter.

New Mexico

9.107 **¡Explora! Science Center,** First Plaza Galeria at Second and Tijeras, Albuquerque, NM 87102
(Temporary quarters, until 1996)
(505) 842-6188

Recently opened science and technology center, with initial focus on physical science concepts (including air pressure, fluids, sound, motion, light, and electricity) and health; moving to permanent quarters in 1996. ***Programs for students:*** At the center: more than 30 interactive hands-on exhibits; demonstrations; classes. At schools: outreach program combining science and art; traveling exhibits. ***Materials:*** Teacher's guides; previsit materials. ***Education and support for teachers:*** Workshops.

9.108 **New Mexico Museum of Natural History and Science,** 1801 Mountain Rd., NW, Albuquerque, NM 87104-1375
(505) 841-8837

Natural history museum focusing on earth and life sciences, with special emphasis on strengthening science outreach programs for rural elementary

Mountain Region (continued)

schools. ***Programs for students:*** At the museum: classes; guided tours; hands-on exhibits; summer science camps. At schools: outreach programs; traveling exhibits. ***Materials:*** Hands-on activity books; lending boxes of hands-on materials; teacher's guides; audiovisual materials. ***Education and support for teachers:*** Statewide in-service education programs on science content and hands-on learning; newsletter.

9.109 Rio Grande Zoological Park, 903 Tenth St., S.W., Albuquerque, NM 87102
(505) 843-7413

Zoo with naturalistic exhibits and discovery stations. ***Programs for students:*** At the zoo: presentations; guided tours; hands-on exhibits. At schools: local outreach programs; zoomobile (travels statewide). ***Materials:*** Hands-on activity books; teacher's guide; educational packets for use on-site; video on animal communication (grades K-3), with teacher's manual. ***Education and support for teachers:*** Workshops on using the zoo and on Suitcase for Survival (contains endangered-animal artifacts).

9.110 Santa Fe Children's Museum, 1050 Old Pecos Trail, Santa Fe, NM 87501
(505) 989-8359

Children's museum, with live animals and an ongoing, hands-on outdoor ecology project; emphasis on physics, biology, botany, and the earth and environmental sciences. ***Programs for students:*** At the museum: participatory exhibits; classes; guided tours. At schools: outreach programs, with live animals and plants. ***Materials:*** Curriculum units with hands-on materials. ***Education and support for teachers:*** In-service workshops on hands-on learning; resource library; newsletter.

9.111 The Space Center, Top of New Mexico Highway 2001, Alamogordo, NM 88310
(505) 437-2840

Space center complex with a four-story museum, space theater (planetarium and Omnimax), and air and space park. ***Programs for students:*** At the center: guided/self-guided tours; numerous classes; planetarium shows. At schools in Arizona, Texas, and Colorado: outreach programs with grade-specific, hands-on learning experiences; traveling exhibits. ***Materials:*** Hands-on activity books; lending boxes of hands-on materials; teacher's guides; audiovisual and computer-based materials; catalog of materials. ***Education and support for teachers:*** In-service workshops at schools on science content and hands-on learning, using national curricular materials; resource library.

Utah

9.112 Canyonlands Field Institute, 1320 So. Hwy. 19, Moab, UT 84532
(800) 860-5262

Educational institute situated in and using as its classroom the canyons of southeastern Utah (including Arches National Park, Canyonlands National Park, and several Bureau of Land Management Wilderness Study Areas); focused on physical, earth, and life sciences; also emphasizes scientific, recreational, and social aspects of the environment. ***Programs for students:*** At the institute: multidiscipline program for school groups. ***Materials:*** Instructional materials for teachers. ***Education and support for teachers:*** Programs; workshops; teaching assistantships.

9.113 Hansen Planetarium, 15 So. State St., Salt Lake City, UT 84111
(801) 538-2104

Planetarium and space science museum, emphasizing astronomy and astrophysics, space science, physics, and chemistry. ***Programs for students:*** At the planetarium: planetarium shows; discussions on space topics; science demonstrations; hands-on exhibits; telescope observing sessions. At schools: assemblies; classroom visits; exhibits; portable planetarium. ***Materials:*** Lending boxes with hands-on materials; teacher's guides; computer-based materials.

9.114 Utah Museum of Natural History, University of Utah, President's Circle, 200 So. University St., Salt Lake City, UT 84112
(801) 581-4303

University-based natural history museum focusing on physical, life, and earth sciences. ***Programs for students:*** At the museum: classes; guided tours; field studies. At schools: outreach classes. ***Materials:*** Teaching kits with hands-on materials and lesson plans for loan. ***Education and support for teachers:*** In-service classes on science content and hands-on learning; field trips; letter-answering service.

Wyoming

9.115 Yellowstone National Park, Yellowstone Park, WY 82190
(307) 344-7381

National park, with five visitors centers and two museums focused on the natural and cultural history of Yellowstone National Park. ***Programs for students:*** Expedition: Yellowstone! (EY!), an interdisciplinary environmental education program (grades 4-6), designed either for classes at schools or as a several-day expedition with a Park Ranger. ***Materials:*** Catalog of materials; hands-on activity books; curriculum units with hands-on materials; audiovisual materials; teacher's guides on EY! ***Education and support for teachers:*** In-service education on science content and hands-on learning in connection with EY!

GREAT PLAINS/MIDWEST REGION

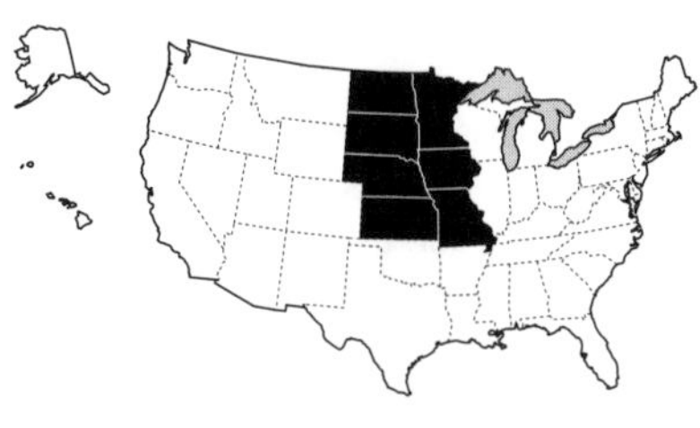

Iowa

9.116 Blank Park Zoo of Des Moines, 7401 S.W. 9th St., Des Moines, IA 50315
(515) 285-4722

Naturalistic zoo, all outdoors, with almost 1,000 animals of about 100 species; emphasis on informal education through observation of animals in settings similar to their native environments. ***Programs for students:*** At the zoo: programs for school groups; field studies. At schools: outreach programs. ***Materials:*** Under development.

9.117 Science Center of Iowa, 4500 Grand Ave., Greenwood-Ashworth Park, Des Moines, IA 50312
(515) 274-6868

Science center with a Challenger Learning Center and planetarium, emphasizing the life, physical, and space sciences, astronomy, and mathematics. ***Programs for students:*** At the center: classes; hands-on exhibits; field trips. At schools: outreach programs. ***Materials:*** Lending boxes of hands-on materials; teacher's guides. ***Education and support for teachers:*** In-service workshops on science content and hands-on learning.

9.118 Science Station, 427 First St., S.E., Cedar Rapids, IA 52401
(319) 366-0968

Science center, focused primarily on various areas of physics. ***Programs for students:*** At the center: classes; demonstrations; interactive exhibits; programs for school groups. At schools: outreach programs, including hands-on activities. ***Materials:*** Hands-on activity books; teacher's guides.

Kansas

9.119 Kansas Cosmosphere and Space Center, 1100 No. Plum, Hutchinson, KS 67501-1499
(316) 662-2305

Space center, with a planetarium, Omnimax theater, and Hall of Space Museum; focused on physical sciences, human biology, and earth and space sciences. ***Programs for students:*** At the center: Discovery workshops; classes; guided tours; field trips to Johnson Space Center. At schools: week-long traveling program (grades K-3); *Voyager* space science assembly program. ***Materials:*** Curriculum units with hands-on materials; teacher's guides; audiovisual and computer-based materials. ***Education and support for teachers:*** Teachers and Space in-service workshops on science content and hands-on learning, onsite/offsite; National Aeronautics and Space Administration (NASA) Regional Teacher Resource Center; newsletter.

9.120 Kauffman Museum, Bethel College, North Newton, KS 67117
(316) 283-1612

Cultural and natural history museum, providing prairie-centered science education for south central Kansas. ***Programs for students:*** At the museum: classes; guided tours. At schools: traveling exhibits. ***Materials:*** Curriculum units with hands-on materials; teacher's guides; loans of museum artifacts. ***Education and support for teachers:*** In-service workshops on prairie ecology and hands-on learning; newsletter.

9.121 KU Natural History Museum, 602 Dyche Hall, University of Kansas, Lawrence, KS 66045-2454
(913) 864-4540

Research-based natural history museum with collections of more than 5 million specimens; focused on vertebrate and invertebrate fossils, and modern insects, plants, and vertebrates, and astronomy. ***Programs for students:*** At the museum: exhibits; workshops; field trips. At schools: outreach programs. ***Materials:*** Traveling kits of museum specimens with curriculum materials; audiovisual materials. ***Education and support for teachers:*** In-service workshops on science content.

9.122 Lake Afton Public Observatory, MacArthur Rd. at 247th St., W., Wichita, KS 67260
(316) 794-8995

Small observatory and astronomy museum affiliated with Wichita State University. ***Programs for students:*** At the observatory: observatory programs; hands-on exhibits. At schools: classroom presentations; portable learning centers. ***Materials:*** Astronomy activity books; curriculum guidelines; videotape programs; instructional games. ***Education and support for teachers:*** In-service workshops on science content and hands-on learning.

Minnesota

9.123 Bell Museum of Natural History, University of Minnesota, 10 Church St., S.E., Minneapolis, MN 55455-0140
(612) 624-7083

University museum of natural history serving as a center for the JASON Project on oceanography curriculum, with a Touch and See Room; focused on life and earth sciences, life history, and the environment. ***Programs for students:*** At the museum: hands-on exhibits (especially in Touch and See Room); classes; guided tours; field trips. At schools: outreach programs (by special arrangement). ***Materials:*** Hands-on activity books; curriculum guides; Bell Museum Learning Kits with hands-on specimens and activity guides. ***Education and support for teachers:*** In-service workshops on science content and hands-on learning; wildlife information service; newsletter.

9.124 Headwaters Science Center, 413 Beltrami, Bemidji, MN 56601
(218) 751-1110

Science and environmental learning center; emphasis on the physical, life, earth, space, and environmental sciences. ***Programs for students:*** At the museum: programs; hands-on exhibits; guided tours; nature field trips. At schools: outreach programs, including a portable planetarium. ***Materials:*** Hands-on activity books; curriculum units with hands-on materials; supplemental activities; audiovisual and computer-based materials; magazines for students; catalog of materials. ***Education and support for teachers:*** In-service education on science content with visiting scientists, and workshops on hands-on learning; teacher resource room.

9.125 Minnesota Children's Museum, 1217 Bandana Blvd., No., St. Paul, MN 55108
(612) 644-5305

Children's museum, offering interactive experiences for children 6 months to 10 years old and their teachers and parents; uses an interdisciplinary approach in presenting science, arts, and culture in varied formats. ***Programs for students:*** At the museum: Discovery Workshops. At schools: outreach programs. ***Materials:*** Curriculum units with hands-on materials. ***Education and support for teachers:*** In-service education on science content and hands-on learning.

9.126 Minnesota Zoological Garden, 13000 Zoo Blvd., Apple Valley, MN 55124
(612) 432-9000

State zoological garden (480 acres, more than 2,000 animals), with a children's zoo and Zoolab; involves 200,000 students and teachers annually in its education programs on wildlife, environmental issues, and conservation. ***Programs for students:*** At the zoo: wildlife quest classes; guided tours; hands-on exhibits; field trips. At schools: zoomobile with programs; speakers bureau. ***Materials:*** Hands-on activity books; curriculum units; teacher's guides; catalog of materials. ***Education and support for teachers:*** In-service workshops on science content and hands-on learning.

9.127 Science Museum of Minnesota, 30 E. 10th St., St. Paul, MN 55101
(612) 221-9488

Renowned science museum with a nature center and an Omnitheater, operating a Museum Magnet School in partnership with the St. Paul Public Schools; emphasizes a broad range of sciences with varied object- and activity-centered programs. ***Programs for students:*** At the museum: hands-on exhibits; classes; demonstrations; field trips. At schools: assembly programs; week-long resident programs. ***Materials:*** Exhibit guides; lending boxes of hands-on materials; teacher's guides; catalog of materials. ***Education and support for teachers:*** In-service workshops on science content and hands-on learning; teacher conferences, field trips, and institutes; newsletter.

Missouri

9.128 Kansas City Museum, 3218 Gladstone Blvd., Kansas City, MO 64123
(816) 483-8300

Museum of history, science, technology, and natural history, with a planetarium and a Challenger Learning Center; emphasis on weather, paleontology, astronomy, and genetics, among other areas. ***Programs for students:*** At the museum: classes; guided tours; hands-on exhibits. At schools: outreach programs, including a portable planetarium. ***Materials:*** Hands-on activity books; lending boxes with hands-on materials; teacher's guides. ***Education and support for teachers:*** In-service education on science content and hands-on learning.

9.129 The Magic House, St. Louis Children's Museum, 516 So. Kirkwood Rd., St. Louis, MO 63122
(314) 822-8900

Children's museum devoted to providing hands-on learning experiences; emphasis in exhibits and outreach programs on water, magnets, air, simple machines, and much more; includes an area called

"A Little Bit of Magic" for 1- to 7-year-olds. ***Programs for students:*** At the museum: guided/self-guided tours; more than 50 curriculum-related hands-on exhibits; Piaget-based Expericenter (hands-on learning laboratory). At schools: assembly and hands-on learning programs. ***Materials:*** Activity books; child-oriented guide to each exhibit. ***Education and support for teachers:*** In-service workshops on science content and hands-on learning; preview of museum before class visits.

9.130 Missouri Botanical Garden, 4344 Shaw Ave., St. Louis, MO 63110
(314) 577-5141

Renowned and popular botanical garden, with numerous specialized gardens and greenhouses, 2,400-acre Shaw Arboretum, a nature preserve at Gray Summit, and Henry Shaw Academy. ***Programs for students:*** At the garden and arboretum: classes; guided/self-guided tours; interactive exhibits; field studies. At the academy: several more-intensive education programs. At schools: outreach programs. ***Materials:*** Hands-on activity books; Suitcase Science Kits for loan locally; teacher's guides; audiovisual materials. ***Education and support for teachers:*** In-service education on science content and hands-on learning, including summer workshops and travel-study programs; teacher resource center.

9.131 St. Louis Science Center, 5050 Oakland Ave., St. Louis, MO 63110
(314) 289-4444

Science center, including a planetarium, Omnimax theater, and a discovery room, and with more than 600 hands-on exhibits focusing on technology, human society, ecology and the environment, and space science. ***Programs for students:*** At the museum: classes; interactive demonstrations (grades 3-8); hands-on rooms; planetarium and laser light shows. At schools: Outreach Van, with demonstrations, dynamic activities; portable planetarium programs; science festivals. ***Materials:*** Teacher's guides; extensive pre-/postvisit materials. ***Education and support for teachers:*** In-service education on hands-on learning; previsit briefings; newsletter.

9.132 St. Louis Zoological Park, Forest Park, St. Louis, MO 63110
(314) 768-5466

Zoo with more than 4,300 animals, and featuring a Classroom of the Future. ***Programs for students:*** At the zoo: classes with live-animal demonstrations; docent-led tours; hands-on exhibits; self-guided scavenger hunts. At schools: outreach programs. ***Materials:*** Hands-on activity books; lending boxes of hands-on materials (Zoocase Science Kits); 6-week science curriculum units; teacher's guides; audiovisual and computer-based materials; catalog of materials. ***Education and support for teachers:*** In-service workshops on science content and hands-on learning; library and teacher resource center; newsletter.

Nebraska

9.133 Hastings Museum, 1330 No. Burlington, Hastings, NE 68902
(402) 461-4629

General and natural history museum, with a planetarium, an IMAX theater, and a Discovery Center; focused on astronomy, biology, zoology, geology, paleontology, archaeology, and space science. ***Programs for students:*** At the museum: hands-on exhibits; presentations for school groups; planetarium shows; IMAX films; orientation and self-guided tours. ***Materials:*** Information packets including suggested activities; teacher's manuals for films. ***Education and support for teachers:*** In-service workshops on hands-on learning; film previews.

9.134 Henry Doorly Zoo, 3701 So. 10th St., Omaha, NE 68107
(402) 733-8400

Zoological park featuring more than 2,000 animals, with emphasis on wildlife conservation. ***Programs for students:*** At the zoo: hands-on exhibits; guided/self-guided tours; classroom programs with live animals. At schools: zoomobile visits; speakers bureau. ***Materials:*** Lending boxes with hands-on materials; teacher's guides; activity guides; audiovisual materials. ***Education and support for teachers:*** In-service workshops on science content; newsletter.

9.135 University of Nebraska State Museum, Morrill Hall, 14th and U St., Lincoln, NE 68588-0332
(402) 472-2637

Natural science museum, with a planetarium and a discovery room; emphasizes life science, earth science and paleontology, and space science. ***Programs for students:*** At the museum: Encounter Center (discovery) programs; planetarium and laser light shows; guided tours; hands-on gallery programs; field trips. At schools: outreach programs; traveling exhibits. ***Materials:*** Lending boxes of hands-on materials; lesson plans; audiovisual and computer-based materials; catalog of materials. ***Education and support for teachers:*** In-service workshops and programs on science content and hands-on learning; NASA Teacher Resource Center; newsletter.

Great Plains/Midwest Region (continued)

North Dakota

9.136 **Gateway to Science Center,** 2700 State St., Gateway Mall, Bismarck, ND 58501
(701) 258-1975

Science center focused on the physical, life, earth, and atmospheric sciences and engineering. ***Programs for students:*** At the center: hands-on exhibits; programs for school groups; guided tours. ***Materials:*** Activity questionnaires; instructional materials. ***Education and support for teachers:*** In-service workshops on science content and hands-on learning; newsletter.

9.137 **Roosevelt Park Zoo,** 1219 Burdick Expressway, E., Minot, ND 58701
(701) 857-4166

Zoo and regional center for wildlife education, featuring approximately 200 mammals, birds, and reptiles, with a children's zoo and a zoo education center. ***Programs for students:*** At the zoo: classes; guided tours. At the center: exhibit area for hands-on, interactive activities. At schools: outreach programs; traveling exhibits. ***Materials:*** Lending boxes of hands-on materials; teacher's guides; audiovisual materials. ***Education and support for teachers:*** Workshops; reference center (at the zoo education center) with wildlife books and magazines.

South Dakota

9.138 **South Dakota Discovery Center and Aquarium,** 805 W. Sioux Ave., Pierre, SD 57501
(605) 224-8295

Discovery center and aquarium, with a planetarium, and (150 meters away in the Missouri River), Discovery Island. ***Programs for students:*** At the center: more than 60 hands-on exhibits; planetarium shows; laboratory activities. On Discovery Island: wetlands ecology field site. At schools in South Dakota, Nebraska, and North Dakota: outreach programs; traveling exhibits; portable planetarium. ***Materials:*** Lending kits.

SOUTH CENTRAL REGION

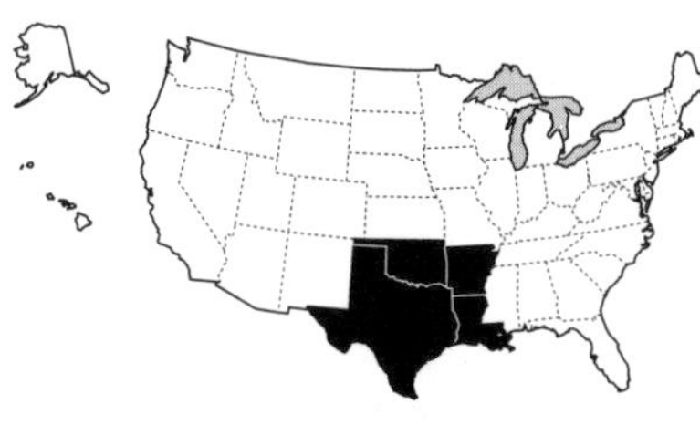

Arkansas

9.139 Arkansas Museum of Science and History, MacArthur Park, Little Rock, AR 72202
(501) 324-9231

Science museum concentrating on natural sciences, life sciences, and geology. ***Programs for students:*** At the museum: classes with live animals; hands-on exhibits. At schools: outreach programs with live animals; 6-week series of summer classes traveling the state to rural areas. ***Materials:*** Activity books; loans of kits; audiovisual materials; catalog of materials. ***Education and support for teachers:*** In-service education on science content and hands-on learning.

9.140 Little Rock Zoological Gardens, One Jonesboro Dr., Little Rock, AR 72205
(501) 663-4733

Zoo with more than 700 specimens from six continents. ***Programs for students:*** At the zoo: self-guided tours with materials; guided tours; hands-on exhibits in the spring. ***Materials:*** Teacher's guides; pre-/postvisit materials. ***Education and support for teachers:*** In-service education on hands-on learning.

9.141 Mid-America Museum, 500 Mid-America Blvd., Hot Springs, AR 71913
(501) 767-3461

Science museum with an aquarium, a laser theater, and interactive exhibits focused on human perception, energy, matter, and life. ***Programs for students:*** At the museum: Energy Scavenger Hunt and Museum Odyssey (students explore the museum to answer questions about interactive exhibits). At the museum and at schools: portable planetarium. At schools: outreach programs. ***Materials:*** Hands-on activity books; science activity boxes for loan in Arkansas; teacher's guides; museum guidebook for educators. ***Education and support for teachers:*** In-service workshops on hands-on learning, based on science activity boxes.

Louisiana

9.142 Aquarium of the Americas, Audubon Institute, One Canal St., New Orleans, LA 70178
(504) 565-3033

Internationally known aquarium; exhibits about 8,000 animals from the waters in and around North, Central, and South America in five galleries, each focused on a different habitat. ***Programs for students:*** At the aquarium: microlab and touch-pool hands-on exhibits; workshops; participatory shows; guided tours. At schools: outreach programs with an aquavan. ***Materials:*** Hands-on activity books; lending boxes of hands-on materials; teacher's guides; audiovisual materials. ***Education and support for teachers:*** In-service workshops on science content, hands-on learning, and regional and national curriculum projects.

9.143 Audubon Zoological Garden, Audubon Institute, 6500 Magazine St., New Orleans, LA 70118
(504) 861-2537

Zoological garden with more than 1,500 animals, and including a botanical garden and a nature and conservation center. ***Programs for students:*** At the zoo: workshops; presentations; hands-on exhibits. At schools: outreach programs with a zoomobile. ***Materials:*** Hands-on activity books; teacher's guides; audiovisual materials. ***Education and support for teachers:*** In-service workshops on science content and hands-on learning in several areas of natural history; some workshops on national curriculum projects.

9.144 The Children's Museum of Lake Charles, 925 Enterprise Blvd., Lake Charles, LA 70601
(318) 433-9420

Hands-on science museum for children of all ages. ***Programs for students:*** At the museum: programs and hands-on exhibits rotated every 2 months and presented in lesson-plan format. At schools: outreach programs. ***Materials:*** Hands-on activity books; teacher's guides. ***Education and support for teachers:*** In-service education on science content and hands-on learning; newsletter.

9.145 Greater Baton Rouge Zoo, 3601 Thomas Rd., Baton Rouge, LA 70806
(504) 775-3877

Municipal zoo; emphasis in educational programs on conservation, natural history and evolution, and environmental awareness. ***Programs for students:*** At the zoo: hands-on exhibits; programs for school groups; guided tours. At schools: outreach programs, with slide shows and live animals. ***Materials:*** Teacher's guides; audiovisual materials. ***Education and support for teachers:*** Workshops.

9.146 **Lafayette Natural History Museum, Planetarium, and Nature Station,** 637 Girard Park Dr., Lafayette, LA 70503
(318) 268-5544

Museum with a planetarium, a 33-acre nature trail, and a Nature Station; focused on areas of the physical and natural sciences, including astronomy, spectroscopy, model rocketry, archaeology, and the environmental sciences. ***Programs for students:*** At the museum: hands-on exhibits; guided tours. At the Nature Station: programs on environmental science; trail walks. At schools: outreach programs. ***Materials:*** Lending boxes of hands-on materials; teacher's guides on the exhibits.

9.147 **Louisiana Arts and Science Center,** 100 So. River Rd., Baton Rouge, LA 70802
(504) 344-5272

Arts and science center that includes Science Station—a hands-on physical science gallery primarily designed for grades 4-9; exhibits focus on light and color, sound, electricity and magnetism, and simple machines. ***Programs for students:*** At the center: space and planetarium shows; guided tours; field trips; weekend and summer workshops. At schools: outreach programs. ***Materials:*** Teacher's guides; audiovisual materials. ***Education and support for teachers:*** In-service workshops on science content and hands-on learning.

9.148 **Louisiana Children's Museum,** 428 Julia St., New Orleans, LA 70130
(504) 523-1357

Children's museum, with a separate exhibit area for children 3 years old and younger, and a main exhibit area for 8- to 12-year-olds. ***Programs for students:*** At the museum: programs; hands-on exhibits. ***Materials:*** Teacher's guides. ***Education and support for teachers:*** In-service workshops on science content and hands-on learning.

9.149 **Louisiana Nature and Science Center,** Joe W. Brown Memorial Park, New Orleans, LA 70127
(504) 246-5672

Nature center within the New Orleans metropolitan area, with direct access to an urban forest and wetlands area. ***Programs for students:*** At the center: classes, guided tours; hands-on exhibits; field trips. At schools: outreach programs; traveling exhibits. ***Materials:*** Hands-on activity books; teacher's guides. ***Education and support for teachers:*** In-service workshops on science content and hands-on learning.

9.150 **Sci-Port Discovery Center,** 101 Milam St., Shreveport, LA 71101
(318) 424-3466

Science center actively involved with the Louisiana Statewide Systemic Initiative (LSSI) in teacher training and support; emphasis on the physical, life, space, and some earth sciences. ***Programs for students:*** At the center: workshops; summer science series with activities and materials. At schools: outreach programs; traveling exhibits. ***Materials:*** Teacher packets, including hands-on experiments related to exhibits. ***Education and support for teachers:*** In-service summer workshops on traveling and permanent exhibits; LSSI training and follow-up with packets, demonstrations, activities, and support during the year for teachers of grades 3-5 in seven Louisiana parishes.

Oklahoma

9.151 **Oklahoma City Zoo,** 2101 N.E. 50th St., Oklahoma City, OK 73111
(405) 424-3344

Zoo with an aquarium and an exotic horticultural collection. ***Programs for students:*** At the zoo: guided tours; a wide variety of hands-on classes and labs on animals. At schools: outreach programs. ***Materials:*** Hands-on activity books; loan of Suitcase for Survival (containing endangered-animal artifacts). ***Education and support for teachers:*** In-service workshops on hands-on learning.

9.152 **Oklahoma Museum of Natural History,** University of Oklahoma, 1335 Asp Ave., Norman, OK 73019
(405) 325-4712

University museum of natural history and anthropology, with school programs focused on ecology, zoology, geology, and paleontology. ***Programs for students:*** At the museum: classes with hands-on activities; field trips; week-long summer workshops on natural history themes. ***Materials:*** Curriculum units with hands-on materials; loans of museum mounts and preserved specimens. ***Education and support for teachers:*** Instructional materials.

9.153 **Omniplex Science Museum,** 2100 N.E. 52nd St., Oklahoma City, OK 73111-7198
(405) 424-5545

Science and technology museum with a planetarium and botanical garden; part of the larger Kirkpatrick Center Museum Complex; focused on geology, astronomy, paleontology, and the physical and life sciences.

Programs for students: At the museum: 300 hands-on exhibits; more than 100 science and planetarium programs. ***Materials:*** Lending boxes of hands-on materials and equipment (grades 4-6); teacher's guides; catalog of materials. ***Education and support for teachers:*** In-service workshops on science content and hands-on learning.

Texas

9.154 **Abilene Zoological Gardens,** Hwy. 36 at Loop 322, Abilene, TX 79604
(915) 676-6085

Zoo with a habitat-oriented discovery center and related activities. ***Programs for students:*** At the zoo: classes; guided tours. At schools: outreach programs, with live animals. ***Education and support for teachers:*** In-service workshops on science content and hands-on learning.

9.155 **Austin Children's Museum,** 1501 W. Fifth St., Austin, TX 78703
(512) 472-2499

Children's museum with activities integrating three themes: How Different People Live, The Human Experience, and Everyday Science and Technology. ***Programs for students:*** At the museum: hands-on exhibits on applied sciences; classes; guided tours; field trips. At schools: classes; after-school science programs. ***Materials:*** Curriculum units with hands-on materials and curriculum guidelines; supplemental activities for many exhibits; hands-on learning kits. ***Education and support for teachers:*** In-service education on science content and hands-on learning.

9.156 **Dallas Museum of Natural History,** First Ave. and Grand in Fair Park, Dallas, TX 75315
(214) 670-8457

Museum with a discovery center, focusing on the native plants and animals of Texas, including fossils. ***Programs for students:*** At the museum: classes; guided tours; hands-on exhibits. At schools: outreach programs; traveling exhibits. ***Materials:*** Hands-on activity books; lending boxes of hands-on materials; teacher's guides; pre-/postvisit and audiovisual materials; catalog of materials. ***Education and support for teachers:*** In-service workshops on science content and hands-on learning, including Project Wild (environmental education program emphasizing wildlife); teacher resource center; newsletter.

9.157 **Don Harrington Discovery Center,** 1200 Streit Dr., Amarillo, TX 79106
(806) 355-9547

Discovery center with a planetarium, focused on the physical, life, earth, space, and environmental sciences. ***Programs for students:*** At the center: hands-on exhibits; classes on science and health; planetarium shows; guided tours. At schools: traveling exhibits. ***Materials:*** Previsit materials. ***Education and support for teachers:*** In-service workshops on hands-on learning; newsletter.

9.158 **Environmental Science Center,** 8856 Westview Dr., Houston, TX 77055
(713) 465-9628

Science center, with a 5-acre arboretum and bird sanctuary and an outdoor classroom; focused on wildlife, natural history, geology, and oceanography. ***Programs for students:*** At the center: hands-on programs for school classes. ***Materials:*** Hands-on activity books; districtwide Elementary Science Kit program; loans of specimens, kits, and audiovisual materials; catalog of materials. ***Education and support for teachers:*** In-service programs; newsletter.

9.159 **Fort Worth Museum of Science and History,** 1501 Montgomery St., Fort Worth, TX 76107-3079
(817) 732-1631

Museum founded in 1941 in an elementary school, with a planetarium, Omni theater, discovery gallery for children 6 years old and younger, and outdoor fossil-digging area. ***Programs for students:*** At the museum: participatory demonstrations; guided tours; hands-on exhibits. At the Museum School: after-school, intersession, and Saturday classes; field trips. ***Materials:*** Lending boxes of hands-on materials; teacher's guides; pre-/postvisit materials. ***Education and support for teachers:*** Workshops on science content, with field trips and hands-on activities; preview events for Omni films and planetarium programs.

9.160 **Houston Museum of Natural Science,** One Hermann Circle Dr., Hermann Park, Houston, TX 77030
(713) 639-4600

Natural science museum with a planetarium, IMAX theater, Challenger Space Science Center, and an observatory; emphasis on physical, space, earth, and life sciences. ***Programs for students:*** At the museum: exploratorium of hands-on exhibits; guided tours; classes; field trips. At schools: outreach programs; traveling exhibits. ***Materials:*** Hands-on activity books; lending boxes of hands-on materials and living things; teacher's guides; audiovisual and computer-based materials; catalog of materials. ***Education and support for teachers:*** In-service workshops on science content and hands-on learning; newsletter.

South Central Region (continued)

9.161 **Insights—El Paso Science Museum,** 505 No. Santa Fe, El Paso, TX 79901
(915) 542-2990

Participatory science museum serving large sections of Texas, New Mexico, and the Mexican state of Chihuahua. ***Programs for students:*** At the museum: classes; guided tours; more than 180 interactive exhibits. At schools: outreach programs; traveling exhibits. ***Materials:*** Hands-on activity books; teacher's guides; computer-based materials. ***Education and support for teachers:*** In-service workshops on science content and hands-on learning; field trips; newsletter.

9.162 **McAllen International Museum,** 1900 Nolana, McAllen, TX 78504
(210) 682-1564

Art and science museum, with a Science Hall for grades 2-5; focused on earth sciences and natural history. ***Programs for students:*** At the museum: classes; guided tours; hands-on exhibits. At schools: hands-on programs; traveling exhibits. ***Materials:*** Teacher's guides; pre-/postvisit materials. ***Education and support for teachers:*** Newsletter.

9.163 **The Science Place,** 1318 Second Ave., Dallas, TX 75315
(214) 428-7200

Science center, with a planetarium and Kids Place (for early-childhood learning); emphasizes physics, chemistry, biology, astronomy, health, dinosaurs, and mathematics. ***Programs for students:*** At the center: classes; guided tours; planetarium shows; hands-on exhibits; field trips. At schools: outreach programs; traveling exhibits. ***Materials:*** Lending boxes of hands-on materials; teacher's guides; audiovisual materials; catalog of materials. ***Education and support for teachers:*** In-service workshops on science content and hands-on learning; newsletter.

9.164 **Sea World of Texas,** 10500 Sea World Dr., San Antonio, TX 78251
(210) 523-3606

Marine zoological park with living learning centers; focused on marine and environmental science. ***Programs for students:*** At Sea World: guided/self-guided tours; presentations with animals; field trips; classes. At schools: outreach programs. ***Materials:*** Curriculum guides; audiovisual materials; catalog of materials. ***Education and support for teachers:*** Workshops.

9.165 **Space Center Houston,** 1601 NASA Road One, Houston, TX 77058
(713) 244-2105

Space center, designed for both education and entertainment, providing a variety of space experiences and serving as the visitor complex for NASA's Johnson Space Center. ***Programs for students:*** At the center: self-guided class visits; hands-on exhibits, including computer simulators. ***Materials:*** Classroom activities; hands-on activity books and accompanying teacher's guides on space exhibits and attractions at the center. ***Education and support for teachers:*** Briefings on space science topics; newsletter.

9.166 **Witte Museum,** 3801 Broadway, San Antonio, TX 78209-6396
(210) 820-2181

Museum and, under development and expected to open in 1997, a science education center with interactive elements such as waterwheels, sundials, pulley lifts, and live insects. ***Programs for students:*** At the museum: classes; demonstrations; hands-on exhibits. At schools: outreach programs. ***Materials:*** Teacher's guides; audiovisual materials. ***Education and support for teachers:*** In-service workshops on hands-on learning; newsletter.

GREAT LAKES REGION

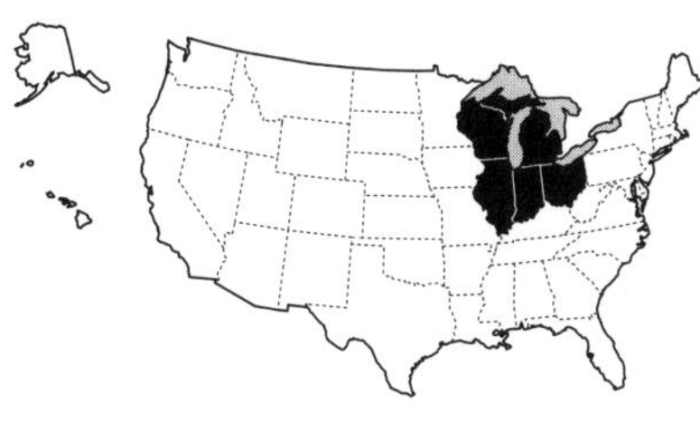

Illinois

9.167 The Adler Planetarium, 1300 So. Lake Shore Dr., Chicago, IL 60605
(312) 922-STAR

Planetarium and science museum focusing on astronomy, earth science, and the history of science; one of a constellation of three lakeside museums, along with the Field Museum of Natural History and the John G. Shedd Aquarium. ***Programs for students:*** At the planetarium: classes; hands-on exhibits; regional outreach with computer networking, becoming available nationally. At schools: outreach programs, including portable planetarium visits. ***Materials:*** Hands-on previsit materials; curriculum materials. ***Education and support for teachers:*** In-service workshops on science content; library with curriculum materials.

9.168 Chicago Botanic Garden, 1000 Lake-Cook Rd., Glencoe, IL 60022
(708) 835-5440

Living museum on 300 acres, with special emphasis on native plant communities—woodlands, prairies, and wetlands—and including an education center and a children's vegetable garden. ***Programs for students:*** At the garden: guided tours; hands-on exhibits; field trips; programs designed to complement school curriculum. At schools: outreach programs throughout the Chicago area. ***Materials:*** Hands-on activity books; lending boxes of hands-on materials; teacher's guides; catalogs of materials. ***Education and support for teachers:*** In-service workshops on science content and hands-on learning; newsletter.

9.169 Chicago Children's Museum, North Pier Chicago, 465 E. Illinois St., Chicago, IL 60611
(312) 527-1000

Children's museum and originator of numerous traveling exhibits; focused on the physical and life sciences, geology, meteorology, and environmental science. ***Programs for students:*** At the museum: hands-on exhibits; programs for school groups; guided tours. At schools: traveling trunk shows; programs. ***Materials:*** Hands-on activity books; curriculum units with hands-on materials; activity guides; pre-/postvisit, audiovisual, and computer-based materials. ***Education and support for teachers:*** In-service education on science content and hands-on learning; newsletter.

9.170 Chicago Zoological Park (Brookfield Zoo), 8400 W. 31st St., Brookfield, IL 60513
(708) 485-0263

Chicago's major zoo, with more than 2,000 animals representing more than 400 species, many in naturalistic habitats; emphasis on conservation. ***Programs for students:*** At the zoo: hands-on exhibits; classes; guided/self-guided tours. ***Materials:*** Hands-on activity books; teacher's guides; pre-/postvisit materials developed in collaboration with teachers to enhance classroom studies; catalog of materials. ***Education and support for teachers:*** In-service education on science content and hands-on learning; newsletter.

9.171 Fermilab Lederman Science Education Center, Batavia, IL 60510-0500
General information: (708) 840-8258
Teacher Resource Center:
(708) 840-8259

Fermilab, a world-famous high-energy physics laboratory that offers an extensive science education program; emphasizes physics and energy-related topics. ***Programs for students:*** At Fermilab: interactive teaching stations; informal classes emphasizing hands-on learning and process skills. At schools: outreach programs; hands-on exhibits. ***Materials:*** Curriculum units; catalog of materials. ***Education and support for teachers:*** In-service workshops on hands-on learning; teacher resource center for previewing collection of science education materials; directory of regional science resources; newsletter.

9.172 Field Museum of Natural History, Roosevelt Rd. at Lake Shore Dr., Chicago, IL 60605
(312) 922-9410

World-renowned research institution and museum focused on evolutionary biology and the environment and on cultural understanding and change, with more than 21 million specimens and artifacts in anthropology, botany, geology, and zoology; one of a constellation of three lakeside museums, along with the Adler Planetarium and the John G. Shedd Aquarium. ***Programs for students:*** At the museum: classes; guided tours; hands-on exhibits. At schools: traveling exhibits. ***Materials:*** Hands-on activity books; lending boxes/kits; teacher's guides; audiovisual materials; catalog of materials. ***Education and support for teachers:*** In-service workshops on science content and hands-on learning; training for teaching in urban neighborhoods; newsletter.

9.173 John G. Shedd Aquarium, 1200 So. Lake Shore Dr., Chicago, IL 60605
(312) 939-2426

Aquarium and oceanarium, including an aquatic science center, with more than 6,000 aquatic animals representing every region of the world; one of a constellation of three lakeside museums (along with the Field Museum of Natural History and Adler Planetarium). ***Programs for students:*** At the aquarium: specialized workshops and classes for student groups; hands-on exhibits; self-guided tours; local field trips. ***Materials:*** Lending boxes/kits; teacher's guides. ***Education and support for teachers:*** In-service education on science content and hands-on learning; teacher resource center; field trips.

9.174 Museum of Science and Industry, 57th St. and Lake Shore Dr., Chicago, IL 60637
(312) 684-1414

World-renowned, interactive museum, with more than 2,000 exhibits in 75 exhibit halls, discovery centers for grades PreK-K and K-4, and learning laboratories embedded within museum exhibits for grades 5-8; emphasis on physical sciences, technology, and industry. ***Programs for students:*** At the museum: programs for school groups; hands-on exhibits; guided tours. At schools: Science Club Network. ***Materials:*** Hands-on activity books; lending boxes/kits; teacher's guides; pre-/postvisit, audiovisual, and computer-based materials. ***Education and support for teachers:*** In-service education and teacher-parent workshops on science content and hands-on learning; newsletter.

9.175 Museum of the Chicago Academy of Sciences, 2001 No. Clark St., Chicago, IL 60614
(312) 549-0606

Natural science museum with a children's gallery, focusing on the natural sciences. ***Programs for students:*** At the museum: science lab activities; field studies; guided/self-guided tours; hands-on exhibits. At schools: outreach programs. ***Materials:*** Activity books; teacher's guides; audiovisual materials. ***Education and support for teachers:*** In-service workshops on science content and hands-on learning.

9.176 SciTech—Science and Technology Interactive Center, 18 W. Benton, Aurora, IL 60506
(708) 859-8112

Science and technology center, emphasizing the physical sciences, mathematics, and developing technologies, and featuring more than 200 hands-on exhibits, a solar telescope, and KIDSPACE (ages 4-6). ***Programs for students:*** At the center: classes; guided tours; hands-on exhibits. At schools: outreach classes with hands-on exhibits (grades 4-6). ***Materials:*** Hands-on materials for outreach programs. ***Education and support for teachers:*** In-service education on science content and hands-on learning linked to outreach programs.

Indiana

9.177 The Children's Museum of Indianapolis, 3000 No. Meridian St., Indianapolis, IN 46208
(317) 924-5431

Largest children's museum in the world, with a planetarium, computer discovery center, early-childhood education gallery, and nature preserve; focused on the natural and physical sciences, mathematics, history, art, and cultural studies. ***Programs for students:*** At the museum: classes; guided tours; hands-on exhibits. At the nature preserve: outdoor education. At schools: outreach programs; traveling exhibits. ***Materials:*** Hands-on activity books; loans of materials, including kits, science mounts and specimens, artifacts; pre-/postvisit, audiovisual, and computer-based materials; catalog of materials. ***Education and support for teachers:*** In-service workshops on science content; resource center; community resource database.

9.178 Fort Wayne Children's Zoo, 3411 Sherman Blvd., Fort Wayne, IN 46808
(219) 482-4610

Zoo on 40 acres, with more than 1,000 animals and three hands-on exhibit centers. ***Programs for students:*** At the zoo: miniclasses; hands-on exhibits. At schools: outreach programs. ***Materials:*** Hands-on activity books; lending boxes of hands-on materials; teacher's guides; audiovisual materials; grade-specific packets for teachers, with suggestions for pre-/postvisit activities; catalog of materials. ***Education and support for teachers:*** In-service workshops on science content and hands-on learning; newsletter.

9.179 Indianapolis Zoo, 1200 W. Washington St., Indianapolis, IN 46222
(317) 630-2040

Zoo designed around habitats, with animals in simulated natural environments; emphasis on preservation of species diversity. ***Programs for students:*** At the zoo: educational programs; hands-on exhibits; long-distance learning program. ***Materials:*** Lending boxes of hands-on materials; teacher's guides; audiovisual materials; link to IDEAnet. ***Education and support for teachers:*** In-service workshops on hands-on learning; newsletter.

9.180 Muncie Children's Museum, 306 So. Walnut Plz., Muncie, IN 47305
(317) 286-1660

Completely hands-on museum primarily for grades K-6, with a portable planetarium. ***Programs for students:*** At the museum: classes; guided tours; field trips. At schools: outreach programs; exhibits; traveling planetarium. ***Materials:*** Hands-on learning kits for loan; curriculum guides; audiovisual materials; catalog of materials. ***Education and support for teachers:*** In-service workshops on science content.

Michigan

9.181 **Ann Arbor Hands-On Museum,** 219 E. Huron St., Ann Arbor, MI 48104
(313) 995-5439

Science and technology center with about 200 interactive exhibits, a computer room (for 20 personal computers with educational programs and games), a discovery room, and a greenhouse; emphasis on physics, biology, human perception, and geology. ***Programs for students:*** At the museum: guided tours; weekend classes; field trips. At schools: outreach programs; traveling exhibits. ***Materials:*** Hands-on activity books; computer-based materials; catalog of materials. ***Education and support for teachers:*** Newsletter.

9.182 **Cranbrook Institute of Science,** 1221 No. Woodward Ave., Bloomfield Hills, MI 48303-0801
(313) 645-3230

Science center, with a planetarium, observatory, participatory physics hall, natural history exhibits, and a nature center with a discovery room and 315 acres of grounds. ***Programs for students:*** At the institute: multivisit, hands-on programs (grades K, 3, 5). At schools in southeast Michigan: outreach programs. ***Education and support for teachers:*** In-service workshops on science content and hands-on learning.

9.183 **Fernwood Botanic Garden,** 13988 Range Line Rd., Niles, MI 49120-9042
(616) 683-8653

Botanic garden and nature preserve, with emphasis on botany and horticulture; on ecological issues concerning water, wildlife, and endangered flora and fauna; and on the arts. ***Programs for students:*** At the garden: classes; hands-on exhibits; guided tours; field programs. At schools: programs with traveling naturalists. ***Materials:*** Hands-on activity books; curriculum units; teacher's guides; pre-/postvisit and audiovisual materials. ***Education and support for teachers:*** Newsletter.

9.184 **Impression 5 Science Museum,** 200 Museum Dr., Lansing, MI 48933-1922
(517) 485-8115

Science and technology center focused on chemistry, physics, and the environmental and biological sciences. ***Programs for students:*** At the museum: demonstrations; workshops; hands-on exhibits; field trips; newsletter for students. At schools: outreach programs. ***Education and support for teachers:*** In-service workshops on science content and hands-on learning.

9.185 **Kalamazoo Public Museum,** 315 So. Rose St., Kalamazoo, MI 49007
(616) 345-7092

Museum of history and technology, with a planetarium and a Challenger Learning Center. ***Programs for students:*** At the museum: hands-on exhibits (focused on natural history, human physiology, and technology); planetarium shows; space mission simulations. At schools: outreach programs. ***Materials:*** Lending boxes of hands-on materials. ***Education and support for teachers:*** In-service education on science content.

9.186 **Kingman Museum of Natural History,** W. Michigan Ave. at 20th St., Battle Creek, MI 49017
(616) 965-5117

Natural history museum with a planetarium; focused on earth science and natural history, astronomy, and the human body. ***Programs for students:*** At the museum: classes; guided tours; hands-on exhibits; field trips. At schools: outreach programs; traveling exhibits. ***Materials:*** Hands-on activity books; lending boxes of hands-on materials; loans of live animals and plants; teacher's guide; catalog of materials. ***Education and support for teachers:*** In-service workshops on science content and hands-on learning; library; newsletter.

9.187 **Michigan Space Center,** Jackson Community College, 2111 Emmons Rd., Jackson, MI 49201
(517) 787-4425

Space museum and educational center for the space sciences; exhibits focus on space exploration, astronomy, physics, geology, mathematics, electronics, and biology. ***Programs for students:*** At the center: demonstrations; guided tours; hands-on exhibits; films in Astro Theatre. At schools: outreach programs. ***Materials:*** Kits with materials and instructions; previsit and audiovisual materials. ***Education and support for teachers:*** In-service education on science content.

9.188 **Muskegon County Museum,** 430 W. Clay Ave., Muskegon, MI 49440
(616) 722-0278

Museum devoted to the preservation and interpretation of the natural and cultural history of Muskegon County, with programs in the life, physical, and earth sciences and astronomy. ***Programs for students:*** At the museum: science programs (an hour or less); guided tours; demonstrations; field trips. At schools: outreach programs. ***Materials:*** Hands-on activity books; lending kits with hands-on materials; teacher's guides; computer-based materials; catalog of materials. ***Education and support for teachers:*** In-service education on science content and hands-on learning; instructional materials; newsletter.

9.189 Sarett Nature Center, 2300 Benton Center Rd., Benton Harbor, MI 49022
(616) 927-4832

Nature center and environmental education facility on nearly 600 acres, with dry forest, meadow, wetland forest, and marsh along the Paw Paw River; also focuses on the natural history of the area. ***Programs for students:*** At the center: classes; interpretive nature walks; summer programs. At schools: outreach programs. ***Materials:*** Hands-on activity books; natural history videos and audiotapes. ***Education and support for teachers:*** In-service classes on science content and hands-on learning in natural history; interpretive trips led by naturalists.

9.190 Sloan Museum, 1221 E. Kearsley St., Flint, MI 48503
(810) 760-1169

General museum and science center that emphasizes transportation as well as earth, physical, and health sciences; part of the Flint Cultural Center, along with the Robert T. Longway Planetarium. ***Programs for students:*** At the museum: programs for school groups; field trips; hands-on exhibits; guided tours. At schools: outreach programs. ***Materials:*** Artifact kits; pre-/postvisit materials.

Ohio

9.191 Aullwood Audubon Center and Farm, 1000 Aullwood Rd., Dayton, OH 45414
(513) 890-7360

Regional environmental education center of the National Audubon Society for the seven-state Great Lakes region, with a 200-acre sanctuary including a working educational farm. ***Programs for students:*** At the center: classes; guided tours; hands-on exhibits. At schools: occasional programs. ***Materials:*** Hands-on activity books; curriculum units with hands-on materials; teacher's guides and instructional materials; previsit and audiovisual materials. ***Education and support for teachers:*** In-service workshops on science content and hands-on learning; newsletters.

9.192 Cincinnati Museum of Natural History and Planetarium, Museum Center at Union Terminal, 1301 Western Ave., Cincinnati, OH 45203
(513) 287-7020

Research-based museum and planetarium with a highly interactive children's discovery center. ***Programs for students:*** At the museum and planetarium: classes; hands-on exhibits. At schools: outreach programs; traveling exhibits. ***Materials:*** Lending boxes of hands-on materials; teacher's guides. ***Education and support for teachers:*** In-service workshops on science content and hands-on learning.

9.193 Cincinnati Zoo and Botanical Garden, 3400 Vine St., Cincinnati, OH 45220
(513) 281-4700

Zoo and botanical garden on 67 acres, with a children's zoo and an arboretum; focused on wildlife preservation and the environment. ***Programs for students:*** At the zoo: programs for school groups; guided tours; hands-on exhibits. At schools: outreach programs; traveling exhibits. ***Materials:*** Hands-on activity books; lending boxes of hands-on materials; teacher's guides; audiovisual materials. ***Education and support for teachers:*** In-service workshops on science content and hands-on learning; newsletter.

9.194 Cleveland Children's Museum, 10730 Euclid Ave., Cleveland, OH 44106
(216) 791-KIDS

Children's museum; produces interactive exhibits that travel to other museums. ***Programs for students:*** At the museum: science/mathematics programs for children and their families; guided tours; hands-on exhibits. ***Materials:*** Lending boxes of hands-on materials; teacher's guides; audiovisual materials. ***Education and support for teachers:*** In-service workshops on science content and hands-on learning; 4-week summer science institutes.

9.195 Cleveland Metroparks Zoo, 3900 Brookside Park Dr., Cleveland, OH 44109
(216) 661-6500

One of America's oldest zoos, on 165 acres in the heart of the city, with an education center and wide-ranging programs in conservation education. ***Programs for students:*** At the zoo: classes; programs; guided tours; hands-on exhibits; field studies. At schools: outreach programs. ***Materials:*** Lending boxes of hands-on materials; teacher's guides; videos; pre-/postvisit and computer-based materials. ***Education and support for teachers:*** In-service workshops on science content and hands-on learning; newsletters.

9.196 Cleveland Museum of Natural History, One Wade Oval Dr., University Circle, Cleveland, OH 44106-1767
(216) 231-4600

Major research-based natural history museum, with an observatory, a planetarium, a discovery room, and natural areas. ***Programs for students:*** At the museum: self-guided visits; presentations with live animals; hands-on programs; observatory/

planetarium programs; field studies. At schools: outreach programs, with live animals; portable planetarium. ***Materials:*** Extensive loan program (including portable dioramas, teaching kits, curriculum units, activity guides, slide sets, and videos); catalog of materials. ***Education and support for teachers:*** In-service workshops on science content and hands-on learning; extensive science resource center; travel/study trips; newsletter.

9.197 COSI/Columbus—Ohio's Center Of Science and Industry, 280 E. Broad St., Columbus, OH 43215-3773
(614) 228-2674

Science and technology center with a planetarium, emphasizing the physical, life, earth, and space sciences, technology, and many facets of the industrial and commercial worlds. ***Programs for students:*** At the center: hundreds of interactive exhibits; classes, shows, and demonstrations. At schools throughout Ohio and in parts of Kentucky, Michigan, Pennsylvania, and West Virginia: extensive outreach programs, with assemblies and hands-on classes. ***Materials:*** Catalog of Fun In Science kits.

9.198 The Dayton Museum of Natural History, 2600 DeWeese Pkwy., Dayton, OH 45414
(513) 275-9156

Museum consisting of Caryl D. Philips Space Theater (digistar planetarium), Dayton Science Center (physical sciences), Wild Ohio Exhibit (indoor zoo with animals native to Ohio), Bieser Discovery Center (hands-on science gallery), and exhibit galleries. ***Programs for students:*** At the museum: planetarium shows; hands-on natural and cultural history and physical science programs; guided/self-guided tours. Off-site: talks, with live animals. ***Materials:*** Geology loan kits; previsit activity packet for astronomy programs. ***Education and support for teachers:*** In-service workshops on hands-on learning.

9.199 The Holden Arboretum, 9500 Sperry Rd., Kirtland, OH 44094
(216) 256-1110

Largest U.S. arboretum, on 3,000 acres, with a horticultural science center. ***Programs for students:*** At the arboretum: extensive guided field trip programs and self-guided tours. At schools: outreach programs (limited). ***Materials:*** Materials for visits; audiovisual materials for loan. ***Education and support for teachers:*** In-service workshops and graduate classes on science content and hands-on learning; reference library; summer teacher-in-residence program for K-12 teachers to develop and test a science program; newsletter.

9.200 Sea World of Ohio, 1100 Sea World Dr., Aurora, OH 44202
(216) 562-8101

Marine-life park, focused on underwater and overwater animals in the park's varied marine environments and on marine ecology. ***Programs for students:*** At the park: programs for school groups; guided tours; hands-on exhibits; summer classes. At schools: hands-on, interactive assembly programs; traveling exhibits. ***Materials:*** Activity books; teacher's guides; catalog of materials. ***Education and support for teachers:*** In-service workshops on science content and hands-on learning.

Wisconsin

9.201 Olbrich Botanical Gardens, 3330 Atwood Ave., Madison, WI 53704
(608) 246-4550

Municipal botanical gardens, with a tropical conservatory, 14 acres of outdoor gardens, and a hands-on Explorer Space; program themes focus on plants, the environment, and tropical forests. ***Programs for students:*** At the gardens: classes for school groups (grades K-5); guided tours; hands-on exhibits. ***Materials:*** Curriculum packets with hands-on pre-/postvisit activities. ***Education and support for teachers:*** In-service classes on science content and hands-on learning and on using the gardens as a teaching resource.

9.202 University of Wisconsin-Madison Arboretum, 1207 Seminole Hwy., Madison, WI 53711
(608) 262-2746

Research-based, university arboretum, with an Earth Partnership Program (EPP) emphasizing prairie restoration. ***Programs for students:*** At the arboretum: guided tours of 1,100 acres of restored prairies, woodlands, and wetlands; EPP classes. At schools: presentations by naturalists; student-EPP research collaborations. ***Materials:*** Hands-on activity books; teacher's guides. ***Education and support for teachers:*** EPP workshops, meetings, and conferences, and EPP summer institutes sponsored by the National Science Foundation, all on prairie restoration and hands-on learning, with materials and a newsletter.

9.203 Zoological Society—Milwaukee County Zoo, 10005 W. Bluemound Rd., Milwaukee, WI 53226
(414) 771-3040

Zoo with an education center, focused on animal science and environmental issues. ***Programs for students:*** At the zoo: classes; workshops; presentations; guided/self-guided tours; hands-on exhibits. At schools: zoomobile programs. ***Materials:*** Activity books; pre-/postvisit activities; teacher's guides. ***Education and support for teachers:*** In-service workshops on science content.

SOUTHEAST REGION

Alabama

9.204 Anniston Museum of Natural History, 800 Museum Dr., Anniston, AL 36202
(205) 237-6766

Regional museum and nature center with nature trails and a wildlife garden, focused on biology, zoology, and the environment. ***Programs for students:*** At the museum: classes and workshops; programs with live animals; guided/self-guided tours; hands-on exhibits. At schools: outreach programs with live animals and hands-on objects. ***Materials:*** Traveling trunks for loan; teacher's guides; audiovisual materials. ***Education and support for teachers:*** In-service education in science content and hands-on learning; newsletter.

9.205 Birmingham Botanical Gardens, 2612 Lane Park Rd., Birmingham, AL 35223
(205) 879-1227

Botanical gardens and bird sanctuary on 67 acres, representing multiple ecosystems; focused on biology, botany, horticulture, and the environment. ***Programs for students:*** At the gardens: propagation workshop (grade 5); guided tours. ***Materials:*** Curriculum unit with hands-on materials for workshop; audiovisual materials; three Grow Labs for 1- to 2-year loan to schools; catalog of materials. ***Education and support for teachers:*** In-service education on propagation; workshops; horticultural library.

9.206 The Exploreum Museum of Discovery, 1906 Spring Hill Ave., Mobile, AL 36607
(205) 471-5923

Science museum dedicated to hands-on science learning, mainly in the physical and natural sciences; principal exhibitor of national traveling exhibits in the region. ***Programs for students:*** At the museum: classes; hands-on exhibits; guided tours; summer science enrichment classes; field trips. At schools: outreach programs and traveling exhibits. ***Materials:*** Loans of curriculum boxes; teacher's guides; audiovisual materials. ***Education and support for teachers:*** Lending library; newsletter.

9.207 U.S. Space and Rocket Center, One Tranquility Base, Huntsville, AL 35805
(800) 63SPACE

Space center with rocket and shuttle parks, a spacedome theater, and a space museum; offers bus tours of NASA's Marshall Space Flight Center. ***Programs for students:*** At the center: classes; hands-on exhibits; 5- to 8-day programs (including U.S. Space Camp, Academy, and Aviation Challenge programs) in aviation and space flight (grades 4-12); field trips. ***Materials:*** Field trip guide. ***Education and support for teachers:*** Graduate and in-service workshops on science content and hands-on learning; NASA Teacher Resource Center.

Florida

9.208 The Children's Science Center, 2915 N.E. Pine Island Rd., Cape Coral, FL 33909
(813) 997-0012

Children's science center, principally for grades K-6, with hands-on programs covering many aspects of science, including natural history, medicine, mathematics, and engineering. ***Programs for students:*** At the museum: programs for school groups; guided tours; field trips. At schools: outreach programs. ***Materials:*** Hands-on activity books; teacher's guides; pre-/postvisit, audiovisual, and computer-based materials. ***Education and support for teachers:*** In-service education on science content; newsletter.

9.209 Discovery Science Center of Central Florida, 50 So. Magnolia Ave., Ocala, FL 34474
(904) 620-2555

Science center and natural history museum, with special focus on physics, astronomy, and human physiology. ***Programs for students:*** At the center: more than 30 interactive exhibits and demonstrations. At schools in 14 surrounding counties: portable planetarium programs. ***Materials:*** Teacher's guides; pre-/postvisit materials. ***Education and support for teachers:*** In-service education on science content and hands-on learning; newsletter.

9.210 Dolphin Research Center, U.S. Hwy. 1 at Mile Marker 59, Grassy Key, FL 33052
(305) 289-1121

Research center (with about 15 dolphins) and educational organization focused on marine mammals and the environment. ***Programs for students:*** At the center: hour-long walking tours; week-long interactive Dolphinlab; and other programs. At schools: Adopt-a-Dolphin program; speakers; career counseling. ***Materials:*** Curriculum guidelines; career publications for students; dolphin slide show; computer-based CD-ROM dolphin program. ***Education and support for teachers:*** Education hotline; Dolphinlab scholarship; newsletter.

9.211 Florida Aquarium, 701 Channelside Dr., Tampa, FL 33602
(813) 273-4000

New aquarium (opened in 1995), with areas devoted to Florida's wetlands, bays and beaches, coral reefs, and offshore waters, and with staffed teaching wetlabs in three major galleries. ***Programs for students:*** At the aquarium: auditorium presentations; aqua-class teaching lab and customized wetlab programs; field trips; guided/self-guided tours; hands-on exhibits. At schools: outreach programs; traveling exhibits. ***Materials:*** Curriculum units with hands-on materials; teacher's guides; audiovisual materials; magazine for students. ***Education and support for teachers:*** In-service workshops on science content and hands-on learning; information hotline; newsletter.

9.212 Florida Museum of Natural History, University of Florida, Gainesville, FL 32611-2035
(904) 392-1721

Both a university research-and-teaching museum and the state museum of natural history; focused on the natural history, archaeology, and ethnography of the state and region. ***Programs for students:*** At the museum: classes; guided tours; hands-on discovery area; summer field trips. At schools: programs on requested topics; suitcase exhibits. ***Materials:*** Educational packets; curriculum guidelines on exhibit topics; teacher's guides; videocassettes; previsit materials. ***Education and support for teachers:*** Statewide teacher workshops on science content and hands-on learning; educational tours.

9.213 Great Explorations, The Hands On Museum, 1120 Fourth St., So., St. Petersburg, FL 33701
(813) 821-8992

Hands-on museum with five pavilions for permanent exhibits and one for changing exhibits; focused on arts, sciences, and health. ***Programs for students:*** At the museum: programs for school groups. At schools: auditorium and classroom programs; shows with a portable planetarium; traveling hands-on exhibits. ***Materials:*** Hands-on activity books; loans of live animals and plants; teacher's guide. ***Education and support for teachers:*** In-service workshops on science content and hands-on learning.

9.214 Miami Museum of Science and Space Transit Planetarium, 3280 So. Miami Ave., Miami, FL 33129
(305) 854-4247

Science museum, with a natural history collection, a wildlife center (with 150 live animals), an aviary, and Space Transit Planetarium. ***Programs for students:*** At the museum: classes; guided tours; demonstrations; more than 150 hands-on exhibits. At the planetarium: multimedia astronomy and laser shows. At schools: outreach programs. ***Materials:*** Hands-on activity books; lending boxes of hands-on materials; audiovisual and computer-based materials; catalog of materials. ***Education and support for teachers:*** In-service education on science content and hands-on learning; Technology Training Center for Florida Department of Education; teacher resource library; newsletter.

9.215 Museum of Arts and Science, 1040 Museum Blvd., Daytona Beach, FL 32114
(904) 255-0285

Museum featuring a planetarium, a hands-on section, and the use of adjacent Tuscawilla Park Preserve and 150-acre Spruce Creek Preserve/Environmental Education Center; emphasis on the arts, sciences, and history. ***Programs for students:*** At the museum: discovery drawers; classes; guided tours; Summer Science Institute in life and environmental sciences, marine biology, zoology, and archaeology. At the planetarium: curriculum-related, grade-specific programs; field trips. At the museum and education center: environmental programs. ***Materials:*** Lesson plans; catalog of materials. ***Education and support for teachers:*** In-service education on science content; newsletter.

9.216 Museum of Discovery and Science, 401 S.W. Second St., Fort Lauderdale, FL 33312-1707
(305) 467-6637

Museum with an IMAX theater and several science labs, focusing on science, technology, health, and mathematics. ***Programs for students:*** At the museum: hands-on exhibits, including six major thematic exhibits; programs; guided/self-guided tours. At schools: outreach programs; traveling exhibits. ***Materials:*** Teacher's guides. ***Education and support for teachers:*** In-service education on science content and hands-on learning.

9.217 Museum of Science and History of Jacksonville, 1025 Museum Circle, Jacksonville, FL 32207-9053
(904) 396-7062

Museum, with a planetarium and a live-animal area with an aviary, marine aquarium, and native plant garden; emphasizes the natural, physical, and medical sciences. ***Programs for students:*** At the museum: planetarium shows; demonstrations; guided tours; science camps. At schools: outreach programs; traveling exhibits. ***Materials:*** Hands-on activity books, lending boxes with teacher's guides; loans of live animals and plants; audiovisual materials;

catalog of materials. ***Education and support for teachers:*** In-service education on science content and hands-on learning; newsletter.

9.218 Museum of Science and Industry, 4801 E. Fowler Ave., Tampa, FL 33617-2099
(813) 987-6324

Science center, with a planetarium, an IMAX Theater, a Discovery Room, and a Challenger Learning Center; emphasizes physical, earth, space, life, and environmental sciences and archaeology. ***Programs for students:*** At the center: 400 exhibits; self-guided tours; hands-on classes; planetarium and IMAX shows; telescope viewing; half- and full-day camps; fossil and archaeological field trips. At schools: assembly programs; hands-on classes; portable planetarium. ***Materials:*** Curriculum units with hands-on materials to accompany program topics. ***Education and support for teachers:*** Workshops and seminars for teachers on science content and hands-on learning; newsletter; magazine.

9.219 Orlando Science Center, 810 E. Rollins St., Loch Haven Park, Orlando, FL 32803
(407) 896-7151

Science center, with a planetarium and an observatory; focused on science, technology, and mathematics through interaction, exploration, and experiential learning. ***Programs for students:*** At the center: classes; hands-on exhibits; field trips. At schools: outreach programs; traveling exhibits. ***Materials:*** Activity sheets; lending boxes of hands-on materials; teacher's guides; audiovisual materials; catalog of materials. ***Education and support for teachers:*** In-service education on hands-on learning; newsletter.

9.220 The Science Center of Pinellas County, 7701 22nd Ave., No., St. Petersburg, FL 33710
(813) 384-0027

Science center with a botanical garden, planetarium, computer center, discovery center, and nature trail; focused on the physical, life, earth, and space sciences. ***Programs for students:*** At the center: classes; guided tours; hands-on exhibits; extensive 8-week summer program of more than 130 1-week workshops; field trips. At schools: mobile outreach programs. ***Materials:*** Hands-on activity books; loans of science-related equipment and live animals; catalog of materials for loan. ***Education and support for teachers:*** In-service education on science content and hands-on learning; reference library; newsletter.

9.221 Sea World of Florida, 7007 World Dr., Orlando, FL 32821
(407) 351-3600

Marine park, focused on marine animals and the park's diverse marine environments. ***Programs for students:*** At the park: programs for school groups; guided tours; hands-on exhibits. At schools: outreach programs; traveling exhibits. ***Materials:*** Hands-on activity books; teacher's guides; audiovisual materials; catalog of materials. ***Education and support for teachers:*** In-service workshops on science content and hands-on learning.

Georgia

9.222 Fernbank Museum of Natural History, 767 Clifton Rd., N.E., Atlanta, GA 30307-1221
(404) 378-0127

Natural history museum, closely linked with the Fernbank Science Center, featuring an IMAX Theatre, a hands-on Naturalist Center, and two children's discovery rooms; emphasis on natural history, earth sciences, ecology, zoology, and chemistry. ***Programs for students:*** At the museum: classes; hands-on exhibits; guided tours. ***Materials:*** Supplemental materials for all programs and exhibits. ***Education and support for teachers:*** In-service education on science content and hands-on learning; newsletter.

9.223 Fernbank Science Center, 156 Heaton Park Dr., N.E., Atlanta, GA 30307-1398
(404) 378-4311

Science center of DeKalb County School System, closely linked with Fernbank Museum of Natural History; includes a planetarium, observatory, 65-acre forest, greenhouses, gardens, and laboratories. ***Programs for students:*** At the center: hands-on exhibits; planetarium shows; numerous classes and programs for school groups. At schools: outreach programs; traveling exhibits. ***Materials:*** Lending kits; children's newsletter; catalog of materials. ***Education and support for teachers:*** In-service workshops on science content; magazine.

9.224 National Science Center, Bldg. 25722 (Discovery Center 29727), Fort Gordon, GA 30905-5689
(706) 791-7680

Science center (authorized by act of Congress in 1985), operating a Preview Discovery Center with innovative and interactive exhibits, a Mobile Discovery Center, and a Discovery Center devoted to communications and electronic technology; focused on mathematics, science, electronics, and communications, with material and technical support from the U.S. Army Signal Corps at Fort Gordon. ***Programs for students:*** At the centers: classes; field trips. At schools: outreach programs with the mobile center; Science-by-Mail (national student/scientist pen pal program for grades 4-9). ***Materials:*** Demonstration and experiment kits; videocassettes; lesson plans; computer programs. ***Education and support for teachers:*** In-service education on science content and hands-on learning; Teacher Resource Center; newsletter.

9.225 Savannah Science Museum, 4405 Paulsen St., Savannah, GA 31405
(912) 355-6705

Science museum, with a nature preserve, planetarium, hands-on discovery room, and tower with a Foucault pendulum; emphasis on herpetology, geology, archaeology, and astronomy. ***Programs for students:*** At the museum: classes; guided tours; planetarium programs. At schools: outreach programs. ***Materials:*** Loans of live animals and plants. ***Education and support for teachers:*** Opportunity for involvement in summer-long research project on the loggerhead sea turtle.

9.226 SciTrek—The Science and Technology Museum of Atlanta, 395 Piedmont Ave., N.E., Atlanta, GA 30308
(404) 522-5500

Science and technology center, with live science demonstrations, hands-on science and mathematics activities in six permanent halls, KIDSPACE (ages 2-7), and a working research laboratory behind glass; focused principally on the physical sciences and technology. ***Programs for students:*** At the museum: workshops; hands-on exhibits. ***Materials:*** Hands-on activity books; lending boxes of hands-on materials; exhibit guides. ***Education and support for teachers:*** In-service education on science content and hands-on learning; newsletter.

9.227 Zoo Atlanta, 800 Cherokee Ave., S.E., Atlanta, GA 30315
(404) 624-5600

Zoo with extensive educational activities and a strong focus on wildlife conservation, featuring an Environmental Resource Center and a Conservation Action Resource Center with activities on four continents. ***Programs for students:*** At the zoo: guided tours; programs for school groups. At schools: zoomobile visits. ***Materials:*** Hands-on activity books; activity boxes; teacher's guides; videotapes and CDs for loan; curriculum supplements; pre-/postvisit activities. ***Education and support for teachers:*** Workshops on science content and hands-on learning; instructional materials; teacher resource center; newsletter.

Kentucky

9.228 The Living Arts and Science Center, 362 No. Martin Luther King Blvd., Lexington, KY 40508
(606) 255-2284

Center with art galleries and science exhibits; emphasis on science education outreach. ***Programs for students:*** At the center: classes; guided tours; hands-on exhibits. At schools: workshops; presentations; traveling exhibits. ***Materials:*** Traveling kits; teacher's guides; audiovisual and computer-based materials. ***Education and support for teachers:*** In-service workshops on science content and hands-on learning; newsletter.

9.229 Louisville Science Center, 727 W. Main St., Louisville, KY 40202
(502) 561-6103

Science center, with an IMAX theater, KIDSPACE (discovery room for children 7 years old and younger), six modern science classrooms, and numerous traveling exhibits. ***Programs for students:*** At the center: discovery lab; classes; assembly presentations; hands-on exhibits; weekend and week-long Science, Technology, and Recreation (STAR) summer camp. At schools: outreach programs, including a portable planetarium. ***Materials:*** Hands-on activity books; teacher's guides. ***Education and support for teachers:*** In-service education on science content and hands-on learning; summer institutes; newsletter.

9.230 Louisville Zoological Garden, 1100 Trevilian Way, Louisville, KY 40213
(502) 459-2181

Zoo on 73 acres in a park setting, with 1,500 animals in more than 60 environmental exhibits, and with Metazoo Education Center and a HerpAquarium with arid, water, and forest habitats. ***Programs for students:*** At the zoo: classes. At the center: live-animal exhibits; microscope stations; "biofact" exhibits. At the HerpAquarium: guided tours. At schools: outreach programs. ***Materials:*** Hands-on activity books; lending boxes of hands-on materials; teacher's guides; program kits for teacher-guided class visits. ***Education and support for teachers:*** In-service workshops on science content and hands-on learning; newsletter.

Mississippi

9.231 Mississippi Museum of Natural Science, 111 No. Jefferson St., Jackson, MS 39202
(601) 354-7303

State of Mississippi's biological and natural science museum, focusing on the state's natural history; massive aquarium system and indoor garden. ***Programs for students:*** At the museum: presentations and hands-on exhibits. At schools: exhibits and interactive programs. ***Materials:*** Object kits; teacher's guides; pre-/postvisit and audiovisual materials; museum artifact kits, some for loan (requiring teacher to attend hands-on workshop). ***Education and support for teachers:*** In-service workshops on hands-on learning; natural science library (available by appointment); newsletter.

9.232 University Museums, The University of Mississippi, University, MS 38677
(601) 232-7073

Two small university museums—the Mary Buie Museum and the Kate Skipwith Teaching Museum—with a children's hands-on room; science programs focused on physics and on life, space, and earth sciences, including ecology and natural history. ***Programs for students:*** At the museums: physics tours; summer science camp. At schools: outreach programs. ***Materials:*** Hands-on activity books; lending trunks of hands-on materials; teacher's guides; instructional materials on environmental education; audiovisual materials. ***Education and support for teachers:*** Newsletter.

North Carolina

9.233 Colburn Gem and Mineral Museum, Pack Place Education, Arts and Science Center, 2 So. Pack Sq., Asheville, NC 28801
(704) 254-7162

Museum focusing on earth sciences, mineralogy, gemology, and paleontology. ***Programs for students:*** At the museum: classes; guided tours; mineral shows; hands-on exhibits. At schools: outreach programs. ***Materials:*** Curriculum units with suggested activities; teacher's guides; audiovisual materials for loan; pre-/postvisit and computer-based materials. ***Education and support for teachers:*** In-service workshops on hands-on learning; newsletter.

9.234 Discovery Place, 301 No. Tryon St., Charlotte, NC 28202, **and Nature Museum,** 1658 Sterling Rd., Charlotte, NC 28209
(704) 372-6261

Two jointly run facilities, with programs on astronomy, on the physical, chemical, health, natural, environmental, and space sciences, and on computer science. Discovery Place—a science museum with a planetarium, aquarium, rain forest, OMNIMAX theater, Challenger Learning Center, and early-childhood education center. Nature Museum—a small museum with live animals, in a community park. ***Programs for students:*** At both museums: demonstrations; classes; hands-on exhibits. At schools: outreach programs. ***Materials:*** Lending boxes of hands-on materials. ***Education and support for teachers:*** In-service workshops in science content and hands-on learning.

9.235 Imagination Station Science Museum, 224 E. Nash St., Wilson, NC 27893
(919) 291-5113

Science and mathematics learning center, with 80 hands-on exhibits covering basic physical and life science principles, a computer lab, and a miniplanetarium. ***Programs for students:*** At the museum: live science programs (on chemistry, cryogenics, flight, electricity, and sound); planetarium shows; guided tours; workshops. At schools: science-on-wheels programs. ***Materials:*** Hands-on activity books; traveling science trunks; teacher's guides; audiovisual and resource materials; catalog of materials. ***Education and support for teachers:*** In-service workshops on science content and hands-on learning; newsletter.

9.236 Morehead Planetarium, E. Franklin St., Chapel Hill, NC 27599
(919) 549-6863

Planetarium of the University of North Carolina at Chapel Hill (UNC-CH), working closely with the Center for Mathematics and Science Education of UNC-CH School of Education, and drawing children from three states; emphasis on astronomy and space science education. ***Programs for students:*** At the planetarium: shows, tied, where possible, to state curricula; Saturday morning classes. At schools: outreach programs. ***Materials:*** Curriculum guides; catalogs of materials from other resource agencies. ***Education and support for teachers:*** In-service workshops on science content and hands-on learning; information service; newsletter.

9.237 The Natural Science Center of Greensboro, 4301 Lawndale Dr., Greensboro, NC 27408-1899
(919) 288-3769

Science education complex featuring a museum, zoo, and planetarium, with traditional natural history exhibits, modern interactive and technological exhibits, and discovery labs. ***Programs for students:*** At the center: demonstrations; classes; hands-on exhibits; field trips. At schools: outreach programs. ***Materials:*** Lending boxes of hands-on materials. ***Education and support for teachers:*** In-service education on science content and hands-on learning.

9.238 North Carolina Maritime Museum, 315 Front St., Beaufort, NC 28516-2125
(919) 728-7317

State museum with dual focus: (1) boats, boat building, and maritime history; and (2) marine sciences as part of coastal natural history. ***Programs for students:*** At the museum:

audiovisual programs; programs with live animals; guided/self-guided tours; hands-on exhibits; field trips to coastal habitats. At schools: outreach programs; traveling exhibits. ***Materials:*** Hands-on activity books; lending boxes of hands-on materials; audiovisual materials; staff-authored field guides to local habitats; catalog of materials. ***Education and support for teachers:*** In-service workshops on science content and hands-on learning; newsletter.

9.239 North Carolina Museum of Life and Science, 433 Murray Ave., Durham, NC 27704
(919) 220-5429

Regional science and technology center, with learning labs, and two discovery rooms; emphasis on aerospace, the human body, physical science, animals, geology, and weather. ***Programs for students:*** At the museum: hands-on indoor and outdoor exhibits; classes. At schools: outreach programs, including a portable planetarium, neighborhood ecology program, and programs with live animals. ***Materials:*** Science loan kits; Sharing Science with Children guides for teachers, parents, scientists, and engineers; postvisit activities. ***Education and support for teachers:*** In-service workshops on science content and hands-on learning; science resource center; newsletter.

9.240 North Carolina State Museum of Natural Sciences, 102 No. Salisbury St., Raleigh, NC 27603
(919) 733-7450

Research-based natural history museum, with a discovery room and fossil lab (a working laboratory of paleontology), concentrating on the state's biological diversity. ***Programs for students:*** At the museum: hands-on exhibits; classes; field trips; self-guided tours. At schools: statewide outreach programs. ***Materials:*** Lending boxes of hands-on materials; teacher's guides. ***Education and support for teachers:*** 1- and 3-day field trips led by a naturalist, emphasizing both science content and hands-on learning; newsletter.

9.241 North Carolina Zoological Park, 4401 Zoo Pkwy., Asheboro, NC 27203
(910) 879-7000

Zoo on 500 acres, with natural habitats for plant and animal species from Africa and North America, focusing on interpreting behavior and ecological relationships; also features a discovery room. ***Programs for students:*** At the zoo: classes; guided tours; informational scavenger hunts; hands-on exhibits. At schools: traveling exhibits. ***Materials:*** Lending boxes of hands-on materials; lesson plans; fact sheets. ***Education and support for teachers:*** 2-day summer workshops and a year-long program on using the zoo in science and mathematics instruction.

9.242 Piedmont Environmental Center, 1220 Penny Rd., High Point, NC 27265
(910) 883-8531

Environmental education center and wildlife refuge on 376 acres, with 11 miles of hiking/nature trails; focused on natural history, ecology, and environmental education. ***Programs for students:*** At the center: 18 hands-on classes emphasizing field studies and data manipulation; field trips. ***Education and support for teachers:*** Hands-on workshops; newsletter.

9.243 Schiele Museum of Natural History and Planetarium, 1500 E. Garrison Blvd., Gastonia, NC 28054
(704) 866-6900

Natural history museum and planetarium, with a theater, an arboretum, and an earth-space center; emphasis on natural history, earth and life sciences, ethnology, and environmental education. ***Programs for students:*** At the museum: hands-on exhibits; classes; guided/self-guided tours; field trips. At schools in more than 20 counties: outreach programs; traveling exhibits. ***Materials:*** Hands-on activity books; lending boxes of hands-on materials; teacher's guides; audiovisual and computer-based materials; catalog of materials. ***Education and support for teachers:*** In-service workshops on science content and hands-on learning; newsletter.

9.244 SciWorks, the Science Center and Environmental Park of Forsyth County, 400 Hanes Mill Rd., Winston-Salem, NC 27105
(919) 767-6730

Science center with a planetarium and a 15-acre environmental park; emphasizes life science, and physical, earth, space, and environmental sciences. ***Programs for students:*** At the center: hands-on exhibits; classes; programs for school groups; planetarium shows; guided tours. At schools in 22 regional districts: outreach programs. ***Materials:*** Pre-/postvisit materials; teacher's guides. ***Education and support for teachers:*** In-service workshops on science content and hands-on learning; newsletter.

South Carolina

9.245 Greenville Zoo, 150 Cleveland Park Dr., Greenville, SC 29601
(803) 467-4300

Regional zoo, promoting awareness of and appreciation for the animal kingdom. ***Programs for students:*** At the zoo: self-guided tours; hands-on classes on animals, conservation, and ecology. At schools in nine-county area: zoomobile visits; hands-on programs (grades 3 and above). ***Materials:*** Lending boxes of hands-on materials; teacher's guides; activity packets designed to augment the local school curriculum. ***Education and support for teachers:*** In-service workshops on science content and hands-on learning.

9.246 Museum of York County, 4621 Mount Gallant Rd., Rock Hill, SC 29732-9905
(803) 329-2121

General museum, with a nature trail and a planetarium; emphasizes natural history, astronomy, physical science, and archaeology. ***Programs for students:*** At the museum: classes; guided/self-guided tours; hands-on exhibits. At schools: outreach programs (including traveling trunks). ***Materials:*** Lending boxes of self-contained curriculum units with resource materials; videos as a previsit package. ***Education and support for teachers:*** In-service education on science content and hands-on learning, including Project Wild (environmental education program emphasizing wildlife); newsletter.

9.247 Roper Mountain Science Center, 504 Roper Mountain Rd., Greenville, SC 29615-4229
(803) 281-1188

Multifaceted science center, on 62 acres, operated by the local school system as a local resource and also for teachers statewide; features the following: a planetarium, observatory, living-history farm, arboretum, sea-life room with aquariums and a touch tank, health education center, chemistry and physics labs, and discovery room. ***Programs for students:*** At the center: classes; planetarium shows; guided tours; hands-on exhibits. At schools: outreach programs; traveling exhibits. ***Materials:*** Hands-on activity books; lending boxes of hands-on materials; teacher's guides; loans of live animals; audiovisual and computer-based materials; previsit activities; catalog of materials. ***Education and support for teachers:*** In-service courses and workshops on science content and hands-on learning; natural science institute.

9.248 South Carolina State Museum, 301 Gervais St., Columbia, SC 29201
(803) 737-4921

General museum, with a Science Discovery Theatre; emphasis on natural history, science, and technology. ***Programs for students:*** At the museum: hands-on classes; guided/self-guided tours; demonstration programs. ***Materials:*** Teacher's guides; previsit and audiovisual materials; lists of suggested postvisit activities. ***Education and support for teachers:*** In-service workshops on science content and hands-on learning.

Tennessee

9.249 The Creative Discovery Museum, 321 Chestnut St., Chattanooga, TN 37402
(615) 756-2738

Children's museum, primarily for the elementary grades, focused on science and the arts. ***Programs for students:*** At the museum: programs; hands-on exhibits; guided tours. At area schools: outreach workshops in collaboration with Oak Ridge National Laboratory's Science Education Center. ***Materials:*** Teacher's guides; pre-/postvisit, audiovisual, and computer-based materials. ***Education and support for teachers:*** In-service workshops on science content and hands-on learning; teacher resource center.

9.250 Hands On! Regional Museum, 315 E. Main St., Johnson City, TN 37601
(615) 928-6509

Children's museum with an aquarium, featuring programs and materials on the physical, life, earth, and environmental sciences. ***Programs for students:*** At the museum: guided tours; programs; hands-on exhibits. At schools: outreach classes; traveling exhibits. ***Materials:*** Lending boxes with hands-on materials; teacher's guides; audiovisual and computer-based materials. ***Education and support for teachers:*** In-service education on science content; newsletter.

9.251 Memphis Pink Palace Museum and Planetarium, 3050 Central Ave., Memphis, TN 38111
(901) 320-6320

Museum and planetarium; museum also operates the Coon Creek Science Center, at a renowned, upper-Cretaceous fossil site located in McNairy County; exhibits focus on natural and cultural history of the region. ***Programs for students:*** At the museum: laboratory, demonstration, and science theater experiences. At the planetarium: live presentations; recorded shows; field trips. At schools: outreach programs. ***Materials:*** Lending boxes of hands-on materials with teacher's guides. ***Education and support for teachers:*** In-service workshops on science content; newsletter.

Virginia

9.252 Science Museum of Virginia, 2500 W. Broad St., Richmond, VA 23220
(804) 367-1013

Science and technology museum and education center, with a planetarium and space theater, Omnimax theater, demonstration laboratories, 250 interactive exhibits in the areas of aerospace, electricity and power, physics, chemistry, astronomy, and crystallography, and other programs in the life sciences. ***Programs for students:*** At the museum: classes; guided tours; planetarium shows; hands-on exhibits. At schools: outreach programs; traveling exhibits. ***Materials:*** Hands-on activity books; loans of live animals; teacher's guides for all exhibits; audiovisual and computer-based materials. ***Education and support for teachers:*** In-service workshops on science content and hands-on learning; newsletter.

9.253 Science Museum of Western Virginia, One Market Square, Roanoke, VA 24011
(703) 342-5710

Science museum with a planetarium; emphasizes a wide range of sciences, including energy, natural history, and physical science. ***Programs for students:*** At the museum: classes; labs; guided tours; hands-on exhibits; early-childhood science education programs; planetarium shows. At schools: outreach programs, including portable planetarium and traveling exhibits. ***Materials:*** Lending boxes of hands-on activity materials; catalog of materials. ***Education and support for teachers:*** Workshops; teacher resource center; newsletter.

9.254 Virginia Air and Space Center and Hampton Roads History Center, 600 Settlers Landing Rd., Hampton, VA 23669
(804) 727-0800

Center for aerospace education with an IMAX theater, serving as the visitors center for the NASA Langley Research Center; focused primarily on the science, history, and technology of aviation and space. ***Programs for students:*** At the centers: guided tours; classroom experiences; hands-on exhibits; field activities. ***Materials:*** Hands-on activity books; teacher's guides; audiovisual and computer-based materials. ***Education and support for teachers:*** In-service education on science content and hands-on learning; NASA Teacher Resource Center.

9.255 Virginia Living Museum, 524 J. Clyde Morris Blvd., Newport News, VA 23601
(804) 595-1900

Living museum, featuring native animals and plants, an aviary, a nature trail, a planetarium and observatory, and a discovery center; focused on the life and earth sciences. ***Programs for students:*** At the museum: planetarium programs; science survey classes; environmental science laboratories; guided/self-guided tours; hands-on exhibits. At schools: participatory assembly programs; classes, with live animals. ***Materials:*** Discovery boxes with teacher resource packets for loan; catalog of materials. ***Education and support for teachers:*** In-service science seminars and field trips; courses on hands-on learning; reference library.

9.256 Virginia Marine Science Museum, 717 General Booth Blvd., Virginia Beach, VA 23451
(804) 437-4949

Marine museum with aquariums and a discovery room. ***Programs for students:*** At the museum: classes; hands-on exhibits; whale-watch, dolphin-watch, and ocean collection boat trips (grades 4 and above). At schools: outreach programs; traveling exhibits. ***Materials:*** Teacher's guides. ***Education and support for teachers:*** In-service workshops on science content and hands-on learning.

9.257 Virginia Museum of Natural History, 1001 Douglas Ave., Martinsville, VA 24112
(703) 666-8600

Center for statewide research and outreach on the natural history of Virginia. ***Programs for students:*** At the museum: classes; hands-on exhibits; guided tours. At schools throughout the state: inquiry-based, participatory programs; traveling exhibits. ***Materials:*** Hands-on activity books; educational resource kits for loan; teacher's manuals; audiovisual materials; catalog of materials. ***Education and support for teachers:*** In-service workshops on science content and hands-on learning throughout the state; newsletter; magazine.

West Virginia

9.258 Good Children's Zoo, Oglebay Park, Wheeling, WV 26003
(304) 243-4030

Zoo with an aquarium and a planetarium, on 65 acres, featuring native North American and some domestic animals; also emphasizes environmental education, astronomy, and space science. ***Programs for students:*** At the zoo: programs for school groups, including planetarium shows; animal-contact area. At schools: outreach programs, with live animals. ***Materials:*** Hands-on activity books; lesson plans; pre-/postvisit and audiovisual materials. ***Education and support for teachers:*** In-service workshops on science content and hands-on learning.

MIDDLE ATLANTIC REGION

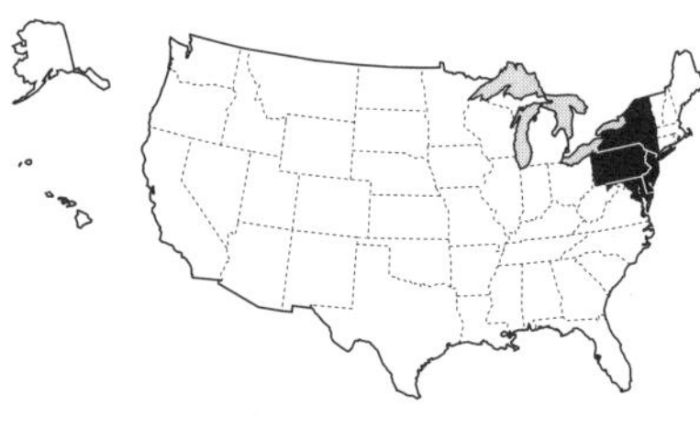

District of Columbia

9.259 National Air and Space Museum, Smithsonian Institution, 6th and Independence, S.W., Washington, DC 20560
(202) 357-1300

National museum, focusing on the technology, science, and history of aviation, rocketry, and space exploration, featuring many historic air- and spacecraft, an IMAX theater, and a planetarium. ***Programs for students:*** At the museum: school classes; guided tours; field trips. At schools: outreach programs; traveling exhibits. ***Materials:*** Hands-on activity books; curriculum packets; audiovisual and computer-based materials; catalog of materials. ***Education and support for teachers:*** In-service workshops on science content and hands-on learning; education resource center; newsletter.

9.260 National Museum of American History, Smithsonian Institution, 14th and Constitution, N.W., Washington, DC 20560
(202) 357-2700

National museum focusing on American culture, science, and technology; includes Science in American Life exhibition that examines the relationship between science and society from 1876 to the present, and features a Hands-On Science Center. ***Programs for students:*** At the museum: classes; guided tours; hands-on exhibits. ***Materials:*** Curriculum units on science-society issues. ***Education and support for teachers:*** Teacher resource area in Hands-On Science Center.

9.261 National Museum of Natural History, Smithsonian Institution, 10th and Constitution, N.W., Washington, DC 20560
(202) 357-2700

National museum with an insect zoo, discovery room, the Living Marine Ecosystem, and (for grades 6 and up) the Naturalist Center, where students can experience hands-on research. ***Programs for students:*** At the museum: lesson tours; hands-on exhibits; classroom programs. ***Materials:*** Hands-on activity books; teacher's guides; previsit materials; catalog of materials. ***Education and support for teachers:*** In-service education on science content and hands-on learning; workshops and summer institutes.

9.262 National Zoological Park, Smithsonian Institution, 3001 Connecticut Ave., N.W., Washington, DC 20008-2598
(202) 673-4717

National zoo, with focus extending beyond traditional zoology to botany, anthropology, ethology, ecology, and paleontology, and with numerous interactive learning opportunities such as Amazonia, the Reptile Discovery Center, Invertebrate Hall, and Zoo Lab. ***Programs for students:*** At the zoo: classes; guided tours; hands-on exhibits. At schools: outreach programs; traveling exhibits. ***Materials:*** Hands-on activity books; lending boxes/kits; teacher's guides; audiovisual materials; catalog of materials. ***Education and support for teachers:*** In-service workshops on science content and hands-on learning; newsletter.

Maryland

9.263 Baltimore Zoo, Druid Hill Park, Baltimore, MD 21217
(410) 396-7102

Zoo with state-of-the-art exhibits (e.g., Maryland Wilderness and African Watering Hole). ***Programs for students:*** At the zoo: guided tours; classroom programs featuring live animals. At schools: outreach programs with a zoomobile. ***Materials:*** Lending boxes of hands-on materials; teacher's guides; catalog of materials. ***Education and support for teachers:*** In-service workshops on science content and hands-on learning; newsletter.

9.264 Calvert Marine Museum, 14150 Solomons Island Rd., Rte. 2, Solomons, MD 20688
(410) 326-2042

Marine museum with a 15-tank estuarium, a discovery room, a touch tank, and various outdoor environments; focused on the paleontology of Calvert Cliffs, estuarine life of the Patuxent River and Chesapeake Bay, and local maritime history. ***Programs for students:*** At the museum: hands-on exhibits; guided tours; classes; nature walks; fossil field experience. ***Materials:*** Hands-on activity books; curriculum units with hands-on materials; audiovisual and supplemental materials. ***Education and support for teachers:*** In-service workshops on science content and hands-on learning.

9.265 Howard B. Owens Science Center, 9601 Greenbelt Rd., Lanham, MD 20706
(301) 918-8750

Science center that includes a planetarium and a Challenger Learning Center, serving a large county school system. ***Programs for students:*** At the center: classes; guided tours;

docent programs for sixth-graders to share science with younger students; field trips. At schools: outreach programs. ***Materials:*** Hands-on activity books; lending boxes of hands-on materials; teacher's guides; audiovisual and computer-based materials; catalog of materials. ***Education and support for teachers:*** In-service workshops on science content and hands-on learning; newsletter.

9.266 Maryland Science Center, 601 Light St., Baltimore, MD 21230
(410) 685-5225

Science center, with a planetarium and an IMAX theater; focused on the environmental, physical, life, and space sciences, and mathematics. ***Programs for students:*** At the museum: hands-on exhibits; planetarium and IMAX shows; field trips. At schools: participatory demonstration programs; portable planetarium classes. ***Materials:*** Teacher's guides. ***Education and support for teachers:*** In-service workshops on science content and hands-on learning.

9.267 National Aquarium in Baltimore, Pier 3, 501 E. Pratt St., Baltimore, MD 21202-3194
(301) 576-3800

State-of-the art aquatic institution with a diverse collection of more than 5,000 aquatic animals, dedicated to encouraging lifelong learning and participation in the conservation of the environment. ***Programs for students:*** At the aquarium: classes; hands-on exhibits; field trips. At schools: outreach programs. ***Materials:*** Hands-on activity books; curriculum and audiovisual materials; teacher's guide; catalog of materials. ***Education and support for teachers:*** In-service education on science content and hands-on learning.

9.268 Smithsonian Environmental Research Center, Contees Wharf Road, Edgewater, MD 21037
(410) 798-4424

Research-based environmental education center on 2,700 acres along the Chesapeake Bay and Rhode River, offering nature trails, canoeing through wetlands, and an opportunity to see the center's scientists at work. ***Programs for students:*** At the center: group outdoor activities involving marsh, forest, and river. At schools: outreach programs. ***Materials:*** Hands-on activity books; curriculum units with hands-on materials; supplementary activities; audiovisual and computer-based materials. ***Education and support for teachers:*** In-service workshops on science content and hands-on learning; teacher resource library; newsletter.

New Jersey

9.269 Liberty Science Center, Liberty State Park, 251 Phillip St., Jersey City, NJ 07305-4699
(201) 200-1000

Science center with more than 250 interactive exhibits in science and technology, a Kodak OMNI theater, and a science theater. ***Programs for students:*** At the center: films; presentations; educational programs, many under the Discovery Trails program (students use the center's exhibits to complete a challenge back in the classroom, the results of which may be incorporated into a presentation for display at the museum). ***Materials:*** Hands-on activity books; previsit materials; teacher's guides; catalog of materials. ***Education and support for teachers:*** In-service workshops on science content and hands-on learning.

9.270 The Newark Museum, 49 Washington St., Newark, NJ 07101
(201) 596-6550

General museum with a planetarium and a small zoo, emphasizing astronomy and the life and earth sciences. ***Programs for students:*** At the museum: hands-on exhibits; planetarium shows; guided tours. At schools: outreach programs, including a portable planetarium. ***Materials:*** Extensive lending collections of ence objects (charts, models, a plant, geological, and animal specimens); teacher's guides. ***Education and support for teachers:*** In-service workshops on science content and hands-on learning.

9.271 The New Jersey State Aquarium at Camden, One Riverside Dr., Camden, NJ 08103-1060
(609) 365-3300

Aquarium with an open-ocean tank and an outdoor sea pool; emphasis on marine life. ***Programs for students:*** At the aquarium: classroom, amphitheater, and auditorium programs; hands-on exhibits. At schools: classroom and auditorium programs with live animals. ***Materials:*** Teacher's guides. ***Education and support for teachers:*** In-service workshops on science content and hands-on learning; newsletter.

9.272 The Wetlands Institute, 1075 Stone Harbor Blvd., Stone Harbor, NJ 08247-1424
(609) 368-1211

Scientific research and public education institute, with an aquarium, a salt marsh trail, and a discovery room; concerned with environmental sciences, intertidal salt marshes, and coastal ecosystems. ***Programs for students:*** At the institute: classes; guided tours. At schools: outreach programs. ***Materials:*** Hands-on activity booklets complementing school programs at the institute; pre-/post-visit materials. ***Education and support for teachers:*** Workshops on marine sciences and estuarine ecosystems; teacher resource center; newsletter.

New York

9.273 American Museum of Natural History, Central Park West at 79th St., New York, NY 10024
(212) 769-5300

World-renowned, research-driven museum with an education department founded in 1884, a separate planetarium (Hayden Planetarium), Naturemax theater (IMAX), a discovery room, and a natural science center; emphasis on anthropology, astronomy, paleontology, many branches of zoology, and mineral sciences. ***Programs for students:*** At the museum: education programs; guided tours; field trips. At schools: outreach programs; traveling exhibits. ***Materials:*** Hands-on activity books; lending boxes of hands-on materials; teacher's guides; computer-based materials. ***Education and support for teachers:*** In-service workshops on science content and hands-on learning.

9.274 American Museum—Hayden Planetarium, 81st St. and Central Park West, New York, NY 10024
(212) 769-5920

Renowned planetarium, with a sky theater (for planetarium), a space theater (with 22 screens), and several museum halls, focused on astronomy, meteorology, and space science. ***Programs for students:*** At the planetarium: planetarium shows. ***Materials:*** Lists of recommended hands-on activity books and of audiovisual and computer-based materials. ***Education and support for teachers:*** In-service workshops in astronomy and space science; occasional student/teacher workshops; extensive course program in astronomy, meteorology, aviation, and celestial navigation.

9.275 Aquarium for Wildlife Conservation, Boardwalk and West 8th St., Brooklyn, NY 11224
(718) 265-3400

Indoor/outdoor facility on 13 acres, with more than 3,400 live specimens and featuring Discovery Cove, an award-winning building with a touch-it tank, devoted to hands-on science education. ***Programs for students:*** At the aquarium: classes; guided tours; interactive exhibits. At schools: outreach programs. ***Materials:*** Hands-on activity books and sheets; teacher's guides; kits with curriculum units, resources, and bibliographies. ***Education and support for teachers:*** In-service workshops on science content and hands-on learning.

9.276 Brooklyn Botanic Garden, 1000 Washington Ave., Brooklyn, NY 11225
(718) 622-4433

Research-based botanic garden with a museum, conservatory, herbarium, teaching greenhouses, and a children's discovery center and garden; leader in formal and informal science education for 80 years. ***Programs for students:*** At the garden: workshops; garden explorations; guided tours; field trips. At schools: indoor gardening facilities; hands-on science curricula. ***Materials:*** Hands-on activity books; teacher's guides; previsit and audiovisual materials; catalog of materials. ***Education and support for teachers:*** In-service workshops on science content and hands-on learning; newsletter.

9.277 The Brooklyn Children's Museum, 145 Brooklyn Ave., Brooklyn, NY 11213
(718) 735-4400

World's first children's museum, now housed in a modern, underground building, with a resource library and greenhouse; emphasizes natural science, culture, and history. ***Programs for students:*** At the museum: hands-on exhibits; guided tours; field trips providing interactive and entertaining learning experiences. At schools: outreach programs. ***Materials:*** Hands-on activity books; lending boxes of hands-on materials; teacher's guides; loans of objects from natural history collection. ***Education and support for teachers:*** In-service education on science content and hands-on learning.

9.278 Children's Museum of Manhattan, 212 W. 83rd St., New York, NY 10024
(212) 721-1234

Children's museum, with centers for environmental science, media, the performing arts, and early-childhood education; emphasizes environmental (especially urban) issues, as well as visual and performing arts activities. ***Programs for students:*** At the museum: interactive displays; hands-on activities; guided tours. At schools: outreach programs. ***Materials:*** Pre-/postvisit and curriculum materials. ***Education and support for teachers:*** In-service seminars on content and hands-on learning in environmental science, media, and the performing arts.

9.279 The Hicksville Gregory Museum, Heitz Pl. and Bay Ave., Hicksville, NY 11801
(516) 822-7505

Long Island's earth science center, with a primary collection of minerals and fossils, augmented by exhibits on local geology and water resources.

Programs for students: At the museum: classes; guided tours. At schools: outreach programs. ***Materials:*** Postvisit materials; rock and mineral kits and narrated slide sets for loan. ***Education and support for teachers:*** In-service education on earth science topics and the local environment; newsletter.

9.280 Institute of Ecosystem Studies, Rte. 44A, Millbrook, NY 12545
(914) 677-5359

Research and education institute, with an outdoor science center and indoor displays, focusing on ecology and environmental education. ***Programs for students:*** Indoors: hands-on exhibits. At the outdoor center: programs combining ecological research and nature appreciation. ***Materials:*** Hands-on activity books; curriculum units focused on converting the classroom into a center of ecological research; audiovisual and computer-based materials. ***Education and support for teachers:*** In-service education, including Schoolyard Ecology, a nationwide network of in-service institutes for elementary teachers in using hands-on, investigative approaches to teaching ecology in their schoolyards; newsletter.

9.281 Museum of Science and Technology, 500 So. Franklin St., Syracuse, NY 13202
(315) 425-9068

Discovery center with a planetarium and a teacher resource center. ***Programs for students:*** At the center: exhibits; interactive planetarium presentations; curriculum-related workshops. At schools: traveling science program; portable planetarium shows; ChemFair and PhysicsFair workshops. ***Materials:*** Hands-on activity books; loan kits; teacher's guides; audiovisual and computer-based materials. ***Education and support for teachers:*** In-service workshops on science content and hands-on learning.

9.282 The New York Botanical Garden, 200th St. and Southern Blvd., Bronx, NY 10458-5126
(718) 817-8700

Research-based, 250-acre botanical garden and arboretum with a conservatory and greenhouses focusing on plant development, plant/animal relationships, and ecology and habitat study. ***Programs for students:*** At the garden: workshops; guided/self-guided tours. At schools: outreach programs. ***Education and support for teachers:*** In-service workshops on science content and hands-on learning.

9.283 New York Hall of Science, 47-01 111th St., Flushing Meadows, Corona Park, Corona, NY 11368
(718) 699-0005

Science center, with more than 150 interactive exhibits emphasizing physical and life sciences. ***Programs for students:*** At the center: student workshops; guided tours; hands-on exhibits. At schools: outreach programs. ***Materials:*** Hands-on activity books; lending boxes of hands-on materials; teacher's guides; audiovisual and computer-based materials. ***Education and support for teachers:*** In-service workshops on science content and hands-on learning; multimedia reference library.

9.284 New York State Museum, Rm. 9B52, Cultural Education Center, Albany, NY 12230
(518) 474-5877

Oldest and largest state museum in the country, focusing on the geology, biology, anthropology, and history of New York State. ***Programs for students:*** At the museum: classes; hands-on exhibits; guided tours. At schools: outreach programs, including alliance with local magnet school. ***Materials:*** Lending boxes with hands-on materials; teacher's guides; pre-/postvisit suggestions. ***Education and support for teachers:*** In-service workshops on science content and hands-on learning; newsletter.

9.285 New York Zoological Society—Bronx Zoo/Wildlife Conservation Park, 185th St. and Southern Blvd., Bronx, NY 10460
(718) 220-5131

Zoo with a wide range of hands-on student programs and teacher-training programs focused on animals, habitats, adaptations, and conservation. ***Programs for students:*** At the zoo: hands-on exhibits; classes; guided tours. ***Materials:*** Hands-on activity books; lending boxes of hands-on materials; teacher's guides; curriculum and audiovisual materials; catalog of materials. ***Education and support for teachers:*** In-service workshops and seminars on science content and hands-on learning; magazine.

9.286 Roberson Museum and Science Center, 30 Front St., Binghamton, NY 13905, and **Kopernick Space Education Center,** Underwood Rd., Vestal, NY 13850
Roberson Museum: (607) 772-0660
Kopernick Center: (607) 748-3685

General and science museum with Link Planetarium (including 50 hands-on exhibits) and, nearby, Kopernick Center (Roberson's newly expanded public observatory, with three observatories and five science labs, designed for young people); focused on astronomy, earth and physical sciences, technology, and computers. ***Programs for students:*** At the museum and center: hands-on exhibits; classes; guided tours; field trips. At schools: outreach programs; traveling exhibits. ***Materials:*** Lending boxes of hands-on materials; teacher's guides; audiovisual and computer-based materials. ***Education and support for teachers:*** In-service workshops on science content and hands-on learning; newsletter.

9.287 Rochester Museum and Science Center, 657 East Ave., Rochester, NY 14607
(716) 271-4320

Large center, composed of the Rochester Museum, Strasenburgh Planetarium, Gannett School of Science and Man, and nearby Cumming Nature Center; focused on astronomy, chemistry, and botany, and the earth, space, and environmental sciences. ***Programs for students:*** At the museum and nature center: programs and classes for school groups; self-guided tours. At the Gannett School: classes; workshops; expeditions. At the planetarium: shows. At schools: outreach programs. ***Materials:*** Curriculum units with hands-on materials; audiovisual materials. ***Education and support for teachers:*** In-service workshops on science content and hands-on learning.

9.288 Schenectady Museum and Planetarium, Nott Terrace Heights, Schenectady, NY 12308
(518) 382-7890

General museum with a planetarium, and a 90-acre nature preserve in nearby Niskayuna, N.Y.; emphasis on physics, human perception, space, geology, health, animals, and plants. ***Programs for students:*** At the museum and nature center: hands-on exhibits; classes; planetarium programs. At schools: outreach programs. ***Materials:*** Lending boxes of hands-on materials; audiovisual materials. ***Education and support for teachers:*** Teacher workshops; newsletter.

9.289 Science Museum of Long Island, Leeds Pond Preserve, 1526 No. Plandome Rd., Manhasset, NY 11030
(516) 627-9400

Regional science activity center and nature center on a 36-acre wildlife preserve; focused on a broad range of life, physical, and earth sciences and on natural history, ecology, mathematics, and technology. ***Programs for students:*** At the center: hands-on classes and exhibits; demonstrations; guided tours; field trips; field studies. At schools: hands-on classes; demonstrations for large audiences; portable planetarium; science-on-wheels van. ***Materials:*** Loans of live animals and plants. ***Education and support for teachers:*** In-service workshops on science content and hands-on learning; newsletter.

9.290 Sci-Tech Center of Northern New York, 154 Stone St., Watertown, NY 13601
(315) 788-1340

Science and technology center with 35 hands-on exhibits, focused on the physical, life, and earth sciences and technology. ***Programs for students:*** At the center: hands-on exhibits; classes (grades K-3 and 4-6); guided tours. At schools: outreach programs. ***Materials:*** Hands-on activity books; curriculum units with hands-on materials; teacher's guides. ***Education and support for teachers:*** In-service workshops on science content and hands-on learning.

9.291 Staten Island Children's Museum, 1000 Richmond Terr., Staten Island, NY 10301
(718) 273-2060

General museum for children; emphasis on integrating the performing, visual, literary, and musical arts to teach science content. ***Programs for students:*** At the museum: classes; guided tours; hands-on exhibits. At schools: outreach programs; traveling exhibits. ***Materials:*** Hands-on activity books; lending boxes of hands-on materials; teacher's guides; pre-/postvisit materials. ***Education and support for teachers:*** In-service workshops on science content and hands-on learning.

9.292 Staten Island Institute of Arts and Sciences, 75 Stuyvesant Pl., Staten Island, NY 10301-1998
(718) 727-1135

General museum, with science focus on the life and earth sciences; Davis Education Center nearby. ***Programs for students:*** At the museum and center: classes; guided tours; field trips. At the center: environmental education field experiences as a follow-up to introductory lessons in the classroom. At Staten Island schools: outreach programs. ***Materials:*** Hands-on activity books; teacher's guides; pre-/postvisit materials. ***Education and support for teachers:*** Workshops on science content.

9.293 Staten Island Zoo, 614 Broadway, Staten Island, NY 10310
(718) 442-3100

Zoo, with a noted reptile collection, an aquarium, tropical forest and African savannah exhibits, and a children's center with domestic farm animals. ***Programs for students:*** At the zoo: programs for school groups. At schools: Traveling Zoo. ***Materials:*** Hands-on activity books; teacher's guides and instructional materials; catalog of materials. ***Education and support for teachers:*** In-service workshops on science content and hands-on learning.

Pennsylvania

9.294 The Academy of Natural Sciences of Philadelphia, 1900 Benjamin Franklin Pkwy., Philadelphia, PA 19103-1195
(215) 299-1100

Research-based natural history museum, focused on biology, zoology, earth science, geology, paleontology, natural history, and ecology. ***Programs for students:*** At the museum: classes; guided tours; museum safaris; hands-on exhibits. At schools: outreach programs; traveling exhibit (Dinosaur Day). ***Materials:*** Dinosaur resource guide; catalog of materials. ***Education and support for teachers:*** In-service workshops on science content and hands-on learning; newsletter.

9.295 The Carnegie Museum of Natural History, 4400 Forbes Ave., Pittsburgh, PA 15213
(412) 622-3131

Research-based natural history museum, with a discovery room and an educational loan collection of more than 4,000 specimens, artifacts, and thematic kits; emphasis on paleontology, geology, life sciences, archaeology, and anthropology. ***Programs for students:*** At the museum: classes; interpretive tours; hands-on learning opportunities. At schools: outreach programs; traveling exhibits. ***Materials:*** Hands-on activity books; thematic kits; curriculum materials; catalog of materials. ***Education and support for teachers:*** In-service courses on science content and hands-on learning.

9.296 The Carnegie Science Center, One Allegheny Ave., Pittsburgh, PA 15212-5850
(412) 237-3300

Science and technology center, with a planetarium, observatory, Omnimax theater, and computer learning lab. ***Programs for students:*** At the center: programs; hands-on exhibits. At schools: outreach programs. ***Materials:*** Hands-on activity books; teacher's guides. ***Education and support for teachers:*** In-service workshops on science content and hands-on learning.

9.297 Erie Zoo, Erie Zoological Society, 423 W. 38th St., Erie, PA 16508
(814) 864-4091

Zoo with more than 300 animals on 15 acres, with a children's zoo. ***Programs for students:*** At the zoo: guided tours; presentations; classes. At schools: hands-on outreach programs, with live animals. ***Materials:*** Hands-on activity books; lending boxes with thematic units, materials, and activities; audiovisual materials. ***Education and support for teachers:*** In-service workshops on science content and hands-on learning.

9.298 The Franklin Institute Science Museum, 20th St. & The Benjamin Franklin Pkwy., Philadelphia, PA 19103-1194
(215) 448-1200

World-renowned science and technology museum, with a planetarium, Omniverse theater, discovery theater, and children's museum; covers a broad range of sciences, technology, and mathematics. ***Programs for students:*** At the museum: interactive exhibits; self-guided tours; Omniverse films; theater presentations; demonstrations; workshops; long-distance learning linked to museum programming. At schools: assembly programs. ***Materials:*** Teacher's guides; hands-on science activity kits; materials for self-guided tours. ***Education and support for teachers:*** In-service workshops on science content and hands-on learning; leadership programs.

9.299 Hands-on House, Children's Museum of Lancaster, 2380 Kissel Hill Rd., Lancaster, PA 17601
(717) 569-KIDS

Museum for children ages 2-10, emphasizing learning by doing, with activities that allow children to explore concepts in the physical sciences, paleontology, and geology, and that promote environmental awareness and conservation. ***Programs for students:*** At the museum: eight interactive exhibits. At schools throughout south central Pennsylvania: outreach workshops (grades K-3). ***Materials:*** Pre-/post-workshop classroom activities.

9.300 The Museum of Scientific Discovery, Strawberry Square, Third and Walnut, Harrisburg, PA 17101-1819
(717) 233-7969

Science and technology center with discovery labs, a discovery bar for interactive demonstrations, and a tot spot (ages 2-6); emphasizes physics, earth sciences, biology, health, mathematics, and technology. ***Programs for students:*** At the center: discovery lab workshops (enhanced field trip workshops); more than 100 participatory presentations and demonstrations; more than 100 interactive exhibits. At schools: outreach assembly programs; hands-on workshops; portable planetarium; Pennsylvania chapter of Science-by-Mail (national student/scientist pen pal program for grades 4-9). ***Materials:*** Hands-on activity books; teacher's guides; pre-/postvisit materials. ***Education and support for teachers:*** In-service workshops on science content and hands-on learning; newsletter.

Middle Atlantic Region (continued)

9.301 National Aviary in Pittsburgh, Allegheny Commons West, Pittsburgh, PA 15212
(412) 323-7235

A zoo for birds—more than 450, representing 225 species—with five discovery stations and a botanical garden. ***Programs for students:*** At the aviary: guided/self-guided tours; classes; discovery workshops; bird shows. At schools: outreach programs. ***Materials:*** Hands-on activity books; curriculum units with hands-on materials; teacher's guides; pre-/postvisit and audiovisual materials. ***Education and support for teachers:*** Environmental discovery workshops and in-service workshops on science content and hands-on learning.

9.302 The North Museum of Natural History and Science, Franklin and Marshall College, College and Buchanan Ave., Lancaster, PA 17604-3003
(717) 291-3941

Museum of natural history and science, with a planetarium, herbarium, and hands-on discovery room. ***Programs for students:*** At the museum: interactive tours; hands-on exhibits; planetarium shows; field trips; 8-week, award-winning summer science program. At schools: outreach programs. ***Materials:*** Hands-on activity books; curriculum units with hands-on materials. ***Education and support for teachers:*** Adult education workshops; newsletter.

9.303 Philadelphia Zoological Garden, 3400 W. Girard Ave., Philadelphia, PA 19104-1196
(215) 243-1100

Zoo and botanical collection on 42 acres, with 1,600 animals representing 500 species, and including two areas designed especially for children—the Treehouse (with simulated animal habitats) and a children's zoo. ***Programs for students:*** At the zoo: classes; guided tours; animal demonstrations; hands-on exhibits. At schools: outreach programs. ***Materials:*** Hands-on activity books; teacher's guides; audiovisual materials. ***Education and support for teachers:*** In-service workshops on science content and hands-on learning; newsletter.

9.304 Please Touch Museum, 210 No. 21st St., Philadelphia, PA 19103
(215) 963-0667

Museum for children ages 1 to 7, integrating science, arts, and humanities, with science included in all exhibits. ***Programs for students:*** At the museum: hands-on exhibits; in-depth presentation of one exhibit with each class visit. At schools: regional outreach programs. ***Materials:*** Traveling trunks containing an extensive manual and 2 weeks' worth of books, artifacts, games, and other materials, for shipment anywhere in the United States; pre-/postvisit materials. ***Education and support for teachers:*** In-service training on hands-on learning and teaching science in early elementary grades.

9.305 Wagner Free Institute of Science, Montgomery Ave. and 17th St., Philadelphia, PA 19121
(215) 763-6529

Historic museum, focused primarily on natural history, geology, and paleontology. ***Programs for students:*** At the museum: hands-on classes; guided tours; lectures. At schools: outreach programs. ***Materials:*** Hands-on activity books; lending boxes of hands-on materials. ***Education and support for teachers:*** Courses, lectures, and workshops on science; in-service workshops on hands-on learning; newsletter.

NEW ENGLAND REGION

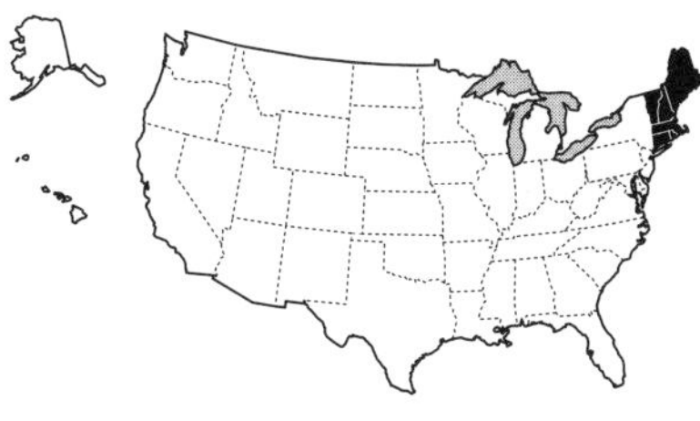

Connecticut

9.306 Connecticut Audubon Society, 118 Oak St., Hartford, CT 06106
(203) 527-8737

Statewide organization operating Hartford Environmental Center, an environmental education center; Fairfield Nature Center and Birdcraft Museum, both in Fairfield; Holland Brook Nature Center in Glastonbury; a seacoast facility in Milford; and 16 other sites for field-study activities; emphasis on environmental education. ***Programs for students:*** At the nature centers: classes; programs; field studies. At the museum: classes; guided tours. At schools: outreach programs; traveling exhibits. ***Materials:*** Hands-on activity books; curriculum units with hands-on materials; audiovisual materials (from the museum). ***Education and support for teachers:*** In-service workshops on science content and hands-on learning.

9.307 The Discovery Museum, 4450 Park Ave., Bridgeport, CT 06604
(203) 372-3521

Museum focusing on the physical sciences and the arts, with a planetarium and a Challenger Learning Center. ***Programs for students:*** At the museum: hands-on exhibits; classes for school groups. At schools: participatory programs. ***Materials:*** Hands-on activity books; lending boxes; teacher's guides; audiovisual and computer-based materials. ***Education and support for teachers:*** In-service workshops on science content and hands-on learning; newsletter.

9.308 Lutz Children's Museum, 247 So. Main St., Manchester, CT 06040
(203) 643-0949

Children's museum, primarily for the elementary grades, covering science and natural history, as well as art, history, and social studies. ***Programs for students:*** At the museum: hands-on exhibits; guided tours; field trips. At schools: outreach programs; traveling exhibits. ***Materials:*** For loan: more than 100 teacher kits on various science topics, many with teacher's guides and lesson plans; catalogs of materials. ***Education and support for teachers:*** In-service education on hands-on learning; workshops on national hands-on science programs; newsletter.

9.309 The Maritime Center at Norwalk, 10 No. Water St., Norwalk, CT 06854
(203) 852-0700

Aquarium and maritime history museum with an IMAX theater, a primary participant in the JASON Project and The Voyage of the *Mimi;* focused on marine and environmental sciences and ecology. ***Programs for students:*** At the center: hands-on exhibits; classes; JASON- and *Mimi*-related programs; guided/self-guided tours; ecology cruises; coastal field programs. At schools: outreach programs with hands-on activities. ***Materials:*** Curriculum units with hands-on materials; loans of live animals and plants; audiovisual and supplemental materials; teacher's guides. ***Education and support for teachers:*** In-service workshops on science content and hands-on learning; teacher resource room; newsletter.

9.310 Mystic Marinelife Aquarium, 55 Coogan Blvd., Mystic, CT 06355-1997
(203) 572-5955

Aquarium and marine-life museum with a marine theater. ***Programs for students:*** At the aquarium: hands-on exhibits; guided tours. At the aquarium and at schools within a 75-mile radius: 36 classes (grades PreK-6), also offered as outreach programs. At field sites (salt marshes and estuary): field study programs. ***Materials:*** Hands-on activity books; lending boxes/kits; teacher's guides; pre-/during-/postvisit activity kits; fact sheets and research updates; catalog of materials. ***Education and support for teachers:*** In-service education on science content and hands-on learning, at the aquarium, at schools, and in the field.

9.311 Science Center of Connecticut, 950 Trout Brook Dr., West Hartford, CT 06119
(203) 231-2824

Science and technology museum, with a planetarium, a center with live animals, and an affiliated nature center; focused on life, environmental, earth, and physical sciences and engineering. ***Programs for students:*** At the center: hands-on exhibits; classes; field studies; field trips. At schools: hands-on classes; assembly programs; traveling physics-discovery room. ***Materials:*** Hands-on activity books; teacher's guides; computer-based materials. ***Education and support for teachers:*** In-service workshops on science content and hands-on learning at the museum or at schools; newsletter.

Maine

9.312 The Children's Museum of Maine, 142 Free St., Portland, ME 04101
(207) 828-1234

Children's museum with a computer lab and a hands-on science bar, serving children ages 1-14, with an interdisciplinary approach to the sciences, arts, and humanities, placing special focus on science. ***Programs for students:*** At the museum: hands-on exhibits; demonstrations; after-school curriculum program; guided tours. At schools: outreach programs; traveling exhibits. ***Materials:*** Curriculum units with hands-on materials; supplemental activities. ***Education and support for teachers:*** In-service workshops on science content and hands-on learning; newsletter.

9.313 Maine State Museum, State House Station 83, Augusta, ME 04333
(207) 289-2301

Regional museum serving as a repository for the historic and prehistoric evidence of Maine's past, with science programs and exhibits emphasizing natural history, paleontology, engineering, and technology. ***Programs for students:*** At the museum: classes; guided tours. ***Materials:*** Loans of archaeological artifacts. ***Education and support for teachers:*** Upon request, additional information on science-related topics covered in museum exhibits.

9.314 Mount Desert Oceanarium, Clark Point Rd., Southwest Harbor, ME 04679
(207) 244-7330

Oceanarium, lobster museum, and lobster hatchery and marsh walk, located at three sites near one another, emphasizing marine life, natural history, aquaculture, and commercial fishing in Maine. ***Programs for students:*** At the sites: programs; guided tours; hands-on exhibits. At schools: outreach programs; traveling exhibits.

Massachusetts

9.315 Cape Cod Museum of Natural History, Rte. 6A, Brewster, MA 02631
(508) 896-3867

Museum with an aquarium, a nature and conservation center, and a trail system traversing woodlands, salt marsh, beach, and tidal estuaries; emphasis on natural history, with a strong Cape Cod focus. ***Programs for students:*** At the museum: classes; guided tours; field trips. At schools: school/after-school programs; hands-on exhibits. ***Materials:*** Loans of science-enrichment kits; teacher's guides; audiovisual materials. ***Education and support for teachers:*** In-service workshops on natural history topics and hands-on learning; instructional materials; newsletter.

9.316 The Children's Museum, Museum Wharf, 300 Congress St., Boston, MA 02210-1034
(617) 426-6500

Children's museum with strong physical and life science components; produces exhibits that travel to other science/discovery museums, demonstrating principles of physical science with everyday objects. ***Programs for students:*** At the museum: classes; hands-on exhibits. At schools: outreach programs. ***Materials:*** Hands-on activity books; multimedia kits on more than 25 topics in natural history and physical science; teacher's guides; audiovisual materials; catalog of materials. ***Education and support for teachers:*** In-service workshops on science content and hands-on learning; newsletter.

9.317 Children's Museum at Holyoke, 444 Dwight St., Holyoke, MA 01040
(413) 536-5437

Children's museum, integrating areas of science, art, and society, with science emphasis on physics, chemistry, botany, and zoology. ***Programs for students:*** At the museum: hands-on exhibits; self-guided tours; programs for school groups; after-school programs. At schools: outreach programs. ***Materials:*** Curriculum units with hands-on materials; audiovisual and supplemental materials. ***Education and support for teachers:*** Summer workshops on science content; in-service education on science activity kits; workshops on special exhibits; newsletter.

9.318 The Discovery Museums, 177 Main St., Acton, MA 01720
(508) 264-4200

Complex with two museums: the Children's Discovery Museum for preschoolers, devoted to "learning through play," and the Science Discovery Museum for school-age children, consisting of hands-on interactive exhibits focused on earth science, physics, nature, and mathematics. ***Programs for students:*** At the preschoolers' museum: parent/child workshops. At schools: inquiry-based science outreach programs. At both museums: classes and special programs. ***Materials:*** Hands-on activity books; teacher's guides. ***Education and support for teachers:*** In-service workshops on science content and hands-on learning.

9.319 **Harvard Museums of Cultural and Natural History,** Harvard University, 26 Oxford St., Cambridge, MA 02138
(617) 495-3045

Four university museums of international renown: Museum of Comparative Zoology, Peabody Museum of Archaeology and Ethnology, Botanical Museum, and Mineralogical Museum. ***Programs for students:*** At the museums: guided tours; hands-on exhibits; hour-long programs for school groups on themes suggested by exhibited materials. At schools: nationally broadcast educational telecom program. ***Education and support for teachers:*** At a school's request: in-service workshops on science content and hands-on learning.

9.320 **Museum of Science, Boston,** Science Park, Boston, MA 02114-1099
(617) 589-0100

Renowned museum, housing 400 permanent exhibits on the process of science and on natural history and the physical sciences, with three staffed discovery spaces, a planetarium, an OMNI theater, and the world's largest air-insulated Van de Graaf generator. ***Programs for students:*** At the museum: hands-on exhibits; demonstrations; more than 25 programs for school groups; science theater presentations; Science-by-Mail (national student/scientist pen pal program for grades 4-9). At schools: outreach programs. ***Materials:*** Science kits on 16 topics; computer-based materials; catalog of materials. ***Education and support for teachers:*** In-service workshops on science content and hands-on learning.

9.321 **New England Aquarium,** Central Wharf, Boston, MA 02110-3399
(617) 973-5200

Aquarium with an education center featuring two learning galleries, a wet lab, and an aquarium library; focused on aquatic education and conservation. ***Programs for students:*** At the aquarium: guided tours; demonstrations; whale-watch trips; exploration of local marine life by boat. At schools: assemblies; class programs. ***Materials:*** Hands-on activity books; curriculum units with hands-on materials; audiovisual and supplemental materials; teaching kits. ***Education and support for teachers:*** In-service education on science content and hands-on learning; information service; teacher resource center; newsletter.

9.322 **New England Science Center,** 222 Harrington Way, Worcester, MA 01604
(508) 791-9211

Museum and wildlife center focused on environmental science, earth systems, and global change, with an observatory, a planetarium/omnisphere, a telecommunications center, a children's discovery room, and more than 100 animals (27 species) and 60 acres that include nature trails, streams, ponds, and wetlands areas. ***Programs for students:*** At the center: classes; guided tours; hands-on exhibits. At schools: outreach programs, including semester or year-long collaborative programs. ***Materials:*** Teacher's guides. ***Education and support for teachers:*** In-service workshops on science content and hands-on learning; library.

9.323 **Springfield Science Museum,** 236 State St., Springfield, MA 01103
(413) 733-1194

Regional museum with 10 exhibit halls, including an exploration center; focused on natural history, physical science, and anthropology. ***Programs for students:*** At the museum: hands-on exhibits; participatory day-trip programs; guided tours. At schools: outreach programs, including a portable planetarium. ***Materials:*** 25 enrichment activity kits for rent; catalog of materials. ***Education and support for teachers:*** In-service seminars and workshops on science content and hands-on learning.

New Hampshire

9.324 **Audubon Society of New Hampshire,** 3 Silk Farm Rd., Concord, NH 03301-8200
(603) 224-9909

Organization that operates Audubon House in Concord, N.H., Paradise Point Nature Center in Hebron, N.H., dePierrefeu-Willard Pond Wildlife Sanctuary in Antrim, N.H., Seacoast Science Center in Rye, N.H., and more than 50 other wildlife sanctuaries, critical habitat areas, and easements throughout the state. ***Programs for students:*** At Audubon House: hands-on exhibits; classes; field trips. At schools: extensive, participatory, environmental education programs. ***Materials:*** Hands-on activity books; curriculum units with hands-on materials; teacher's guides; audiovisual materials for loan. ***Education and support for teachers:*** In-service workshops on science content and hands-on learning, some on national programs, some at teachers' schools, many in summer; instructional materials; newsletter.

New England Region (continued)

9.325 **Seacoast Science Center,** Rte. 1A, at Odiorne Point State Park, Rye, NH 03870
(603) 436-8043

Aquarium and environmental education center at a 300-acre park featuring seven distinct habitats; focused on marine and coastal biology, natural sciences, and cultural history. ***Programs for students:*** At the center: outdoor classes; guided tours. At schools: outreach programs, with live animals. ***Materials:*** Hands-on activity books; teacher's guides with activities for classes at the center; pre-/postvisit activities. ***Education and support for teachers:*** Seasonal workshops; newsletter.

Rhode Island

9.326 **Audubon Society of Rhode Island,** 12 Sanderson Rd., Smithfield, RI 02917
(401) 949-5454

Headquarters for a 78-acre habitat area and four wildlife refuges, and location of the Teacher Resource Center, a statewide lending library of environmental materials. ***Programs for students:*** At refuges and at schools: field trip programs led by Audubon educators. At schools: hands-on outreach programs. ***Materials:*** Lending boxes; hands-on activity books; curriculum units with hands-on materials; teacher's guides; audiovisual materials; magazine for students. ***Education and support for teachers:*** In-service workshops on science content and hands-on learning; magazine.

9.327 **Museum of Natural History,** Roger Williams Park, Providence, RI 02907-3600
(401) 785-9450

Natural history museum, with a planetarium, an education center, and a marine invertebrate touch tank; focused on environmental, life, earth, and space sciences, and astronomy. ***Programs for students:*** At the museum: planetarium programs; interactive gallery tours; auditorium presentations; hands-on exhibits. ***Materials:*** Gallery guide; natural history loan kits. ***Education and support for teachers:*** In-service education on astronomy and on hands-on learning.

9.328 **Roger Williams Park Zoo,** Elmwood Ave., Providence, RI 02905
(401) 785-3510

One of America's first zoos, with more than 700 live animals on 35 acres in naturalistic settings; emphasis on nature conservation, with an active research and breeding program. ***Programs for students:*** At the zoo: tours. At schools: zoomobile visits. ***Materials:*** Hands-on activity books; teacher's guides; pre-/postvisit activities for students and teachers. ***Education and support for teachers:*** In-service education on science content and hands-on learning; field trips.

Vermont

9.329 **The Discovery Museum,** 51 Park St., Essex Junction, VT 05452
(802) 878-8687

Science museum for grades K-12, with a planetarium and a 1950s-style diner in which students participate in hands-on experiments; emphasis on the physical, natural, and environmental sciences. ***Programs for students:*** At the museum: participatory exhibits; classes and workshops; guided tours; planetarium shows; field trips. At schools: classroom workshops and experiments. ***Materials:*** Lending kits with hands-on materials; supplemental activities; catalog of materials. ***Education and support for teachers:*** Teacher training sessions; newsletter.

9.330 **Fairbanks Museum and Planetarium,** Main and Prospect, St. Johnsbury, VT 05819
(802) 748-2372

General museum and planetarium, also including the Northern New England Weather Center, and offering instructional programs in biology, ecology, meteorology, astronomy, geology, and physics. ***Programs for students:*** At the museum: hands-on natural history exhibits; classes. At field study sites: programs. At schools: outreach programs. ***Materials:*** Lending boxes of hands-on materials. ***Education and support for teachers:*** In-service workshops on science content and hands-on learning; lending library of science materials.

9.331 **Montshire Museum of Science,** Montshire Rd., Norwich, VT 05055
(802) 649-2200

Science museum and education center, with 100 acres of woodland and trails along the Connecticut River; focused on the natural and physical sciences, ecology, and technology. ***Programs for students:*** At the museum: workshops; classes; self-guided tours; hands-on exhibits and demonstrations. At schools: hands-on exhibits; portable planetarium; rent-a-scientist programs. ***Materials:*** Teacher's guides; catalog of materials. ***Education and support for teachers:*** In-service workshops and courses on science content and hands-on learning.

CANADA

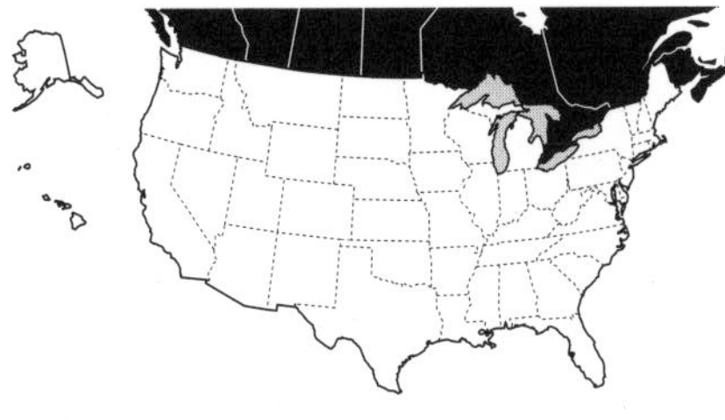

9.332 National Museum of Science and Technology, 1867 St. Laurent Blvd., Ottawa, Ontario, Canada K1G 5A3
(613) 991-3044

Science and technology museum, emphasizing physical and space sciences, computers, and technology. ***Programs for students:*** At the museum: hands-on exhibits; programs for school groups. ***Materials:*** Teacher's guides; audiovisual materials; pre-/postvisit materials and activity sheets available to program participants; catalog of materials. ***Education and support for teachers:*** In-service workshops on hands-on learning.

9.333 Ontario Science Centre, 770 Don Mills Rd., Don Mills, Ontario, Canada M3C 1T3
(416) 429-4100

Renowned science center, with a Challenger Learning Center and numerous hands-on exhibits focused on the life, physical, earth, and space sciences. ***Programs for students:*** At the center: hands-on participatory workshops; presentations to school groups; and hands-on exhibits. At schools: outreach programs. ***Materials:*** Hands-on activity books; teacher's guides; pre-/postvisit materials. ***Education and support for teachers:*** In-service workshops on science content and hands-on learning; newsletter.

9.334 Saskatchewan Science Centre, Winnipeg St. and Wascana Dr., Regina, Saskatchewan, Canada S4P 3M3
(306) 791-7900

Science center in two facilities: an IMAX theater and a Powerhouse of Discovery with more than 80 hands-on exhibits; emphasis on the physical, life, and environmental sciences. ***Programs for students:*** At the center: shows; demonstrations; programs for school groups; table-top science experiences; workshops. ***Materials:*** Hands-on activity books; teacher's guides. ***Education and support for teachers:*** In-service workshops on science content and hands-on learning; newsletter.

9.335 The Science Centre, 701 11th St., S.W., Calgary, Alberta, Canada T2P 2C4
(403) 221-3700

Science museum, including a multimedia science theater with Digistar projector, exhibit halls, and a science demonstration area. ***Programs for students:*** At the center: science demonstrations; hands-on exhibits; science theater presentations; multimedia shows; science/technology competitions. At schools: inflatable planetarium. ***Materials:*** Hands-on activity books; teacher's guides; pre-/postvisit materials. ***Education and support for teachers:*** Workshop on hands-on science associated with exhibits and multimedia shows.

9.336 Science North, 100 Ramsey Lake Rd., Sudbury, Ontario, Canada P3E 5S9
(705) 522-3701

Northern Ontario's original science center, with an IMAX theater, nickel mine, fossil lab, and solar telescope; focused on the physical, life, earth, space, environmental, and information sciences, and technology. ***Programs for students:*** At the center: classes; hands-on exhibits; field trips. At schools: outreach programs; traveling exhibits. ***Materials:*** Lending boxes of hands-on materials. ***Education and support for teachers:*** In-service workshops on science content and hands-on learning; newsletter.

9.337 SCIENCE WORLD British Columbia, 1455 Quebec St., Vancouver, British Columbia, Canada V6A 3Z7
(604) 687-8414

Science center with an Omnimax theater, emphasizing all the sciences, technology, and mathematics. ***Programs for students:*** At the center: interactive displays; shows; demonstrations; workshops. At schools throughout British Columbia: science presentations and hands-on displays. ***Materials:*** Hands-on activity books; teacher's guides; traveling discovery boxes; pre-/postvisit, audiovisual, and computer-based materials. ***Education and support for teachers:*** In-service education on science content and process skills; orientation evenings before class visits; lecture series; newsletter.

9.338 Vancouver Aquarium, Canada's Pacific National Aquarium, in Stanley Park, Vancouver, British Columbia, Canada V6B 3X8
(604) 685-3364

Canada's Pacific National Aquarium, focused on the conservation of aquatic life. ***Programs for students:*** At the aquarium: guided tours; hands-on exhibits; field trips; curriculum-based programs. At schools: aquavan; speakers bureau. ***Materials:*** Hands-on activity books; teacher resource manual and pre-/postvisit materials with each formal on-site program. ***Education and support for teachers:*** In-service workshops on marine biology and hands-on learning; newsletter.

CHAPTER 10

Professional Associations and U.S. Government Organizations

Many groups of professional scientists and educators engage in active efforts to improve precollege science education and offer assistance relevant to elementary science teaching. Chapter 10 provides information about such professional associations, societies, and U.S. government organizations and lists many of the programs, services, publications, and materials that are available to schools and teachers from these sources.

This listing is based on the results of a formal survey conducted by the National Science Resources Center and on information in the *Guidebook to Excellence,* a directory of federal resources in mathematics and science education produced by the Eisenhower National Clearinghouse for Mathematics and Science Education.

The chapter includes about 120 annotations, each to a specific association or organization. Several sources of assistance, such as field centers, regional resource centers, and networks of affiliated organizations, may be represented within one annotation. For example, the entry for the National Aeronautics and Space Administration, Education Division, refers to the nine NASA Teacher Resource Centers located at NASA Field Centers serving multistate areas.

Each annotation provides the organization name, address, and telephone number. (An officer or executive director is named only when the organization itself does not have a fixed address.) Brief descriptive phrases highlight relevant programs, services, publications, and materials. Program and project names are highlighted in boldface type.

This listing is not exhaustive, and the absence of any organization is not intended as a reflection on the quality of its programs or on their possible value for elementary hands-on science teaching. Readers are encouraged to identify additional sources of assistance.

10.1 American Association for the Advancement of Science, 1333 H St., NW, Washington, DC 20005 (202) 326-6400

U.S. science organization that embraces all the sciences, with membership of 140,000 individuals and nearly 300 science societies and organizations. ***Programs/services:***

- Extensive programs and materials produced by the association's Directorate for Education and Human Resources include the following: **Annual Forum for School Science; Collaboration for Equity in Science;** radio programs *Science Update* and *Kinetic City Super Crew* (the latter with teacher's guide, home activities, and call-in); senior scientists to collaborate with individual teachers; database of scientists who are available to help teachers; project **SLIC** (Science Linkages in the Community) to train people to teach science. ***Publications/ materials:*** Books in many fields of science and science education,

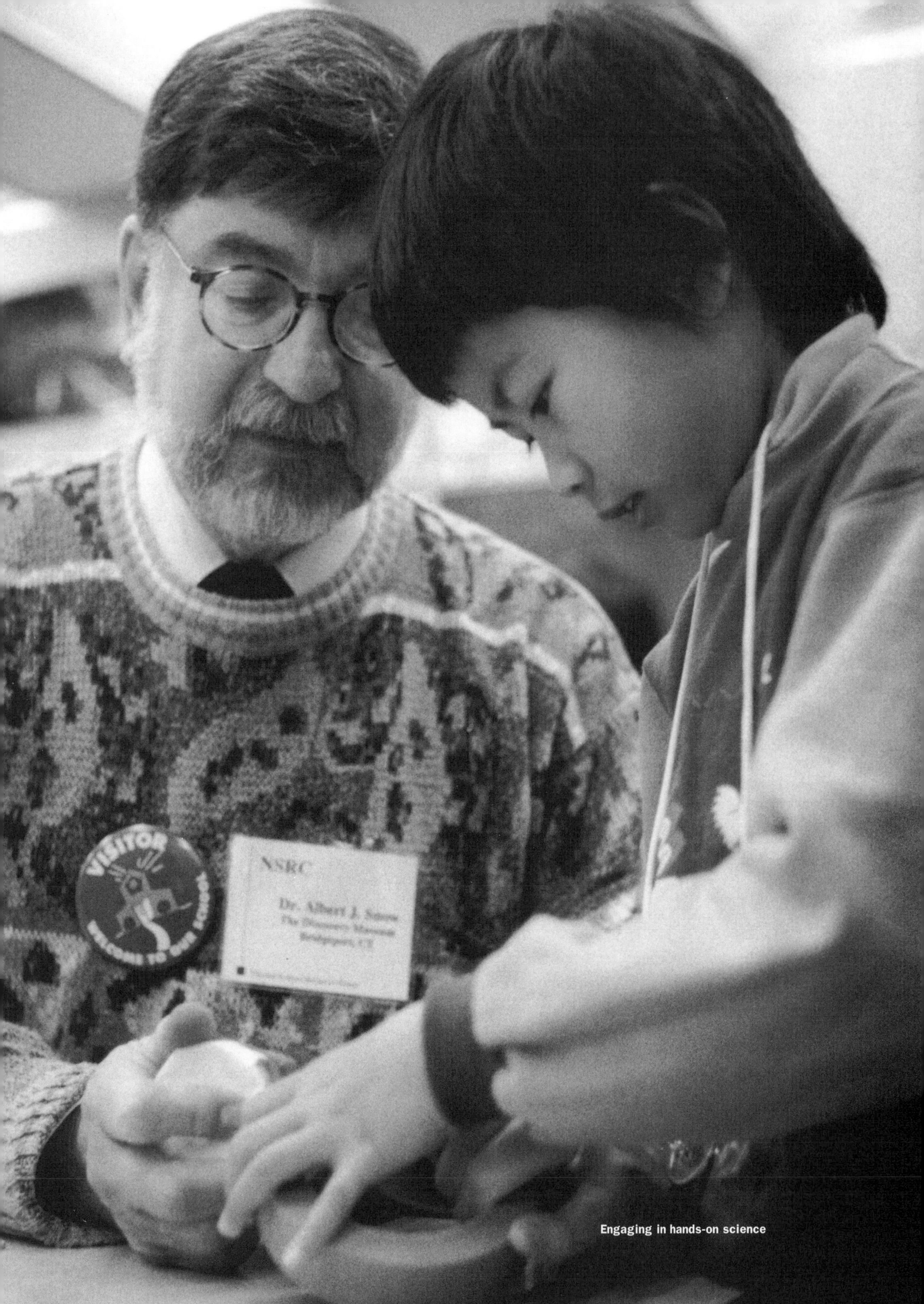

Engaging in hands-on science

including *IDEAAAS: Sourcebook for Science, Mathematics and Technology Education* (3rd ed.); *Science Education News; Science Books & Films* (review magazine); videos focused on out-of-school programs for minorities, girls, and disabled students; posters.

- **Project 2061:** a long-term science education reform initiative (grades K-12), seeking science literacy for all high school graduates. ***Publications/materials:*** *Science for All Americans,* on science literacy; *Benchmarks for Science Literacy,* a curriculum design tool defining expectations for science knowledge for grades 2, 5, 8, and 12; other books and computer-based materials on curriculum design, exemplary resources, and research.

10.2 American Association of Physics Teachers, American Center for Physics, One Physics Ellipse, College Park, MD 20740
(301) 209-3300

Professional association of more than 11,000 college-level physicists, high school physics teachers, and others interested in the quality of physics education. ***Programs/services:*** Cooperates with American Physical Society (*see* 10.15) in **Teacher-Scientist Alliance Institute** to mobilize scientists in support of systemic reform of elementary science education.

10.3 American Astronomical Society (AAS), 2000 Florida Ave., NW, Suite 400, Washington, DC 20009
(202) 328-2010

Professional society of more than 6,000 astronomers, physicists, and other scientists in related fields. ***Programs/services:*** **AAS Teacher Resource Agents,** a program funded by the National Science Foundation, providing 4-week summer institutes at three regional sites (in Arizona, Illinois, and Maryland); the program prepares teachers (grades K-12) to be resource agents who present workshops to other teachers.

10.4 American Ceramic Society, 735 Ceramic Pl., Westerville, OH 43081
(614) 794-5898

Professional society of 16,000 scientists, engineers, educators, and others interested in a wide range of ceramics, such as glasses, cements, and refractories. ***Programs/services:*** Links scientists to schools nationwide to serve as mentors, to make in-school presentations, and to invite students to the workplace; through these links, the society fosters scientist-teacher collaborations and partnerships that provide teachers and students access to the society's publications and materials. ***Publications/materials:*** *Science on Wheels* (experiment manual); ceramic sample kit; *Ceramics—Into the Future* (video).

10.5 American Cetacean Society, P.O. Box 2639, San Pedro, CA 90731
(310) 548-6279

Volunteer organization of more than 2,500 scientists, educators, and lay persons interested in education about and devoted to the protection of whales, dolphins, and porpoises. ***Programs/services:*** Information hotline; volunteer opportunities for teachers. ***Publications/materials:*** *Gray Whale Teaching Kit; Whalewatcher* (journal); newsletter; bibliography; information sheets available free of charge to children.

10.6 American Chemical Society, 1155 16th St., NW, Washington, DC 20036
(202) 452-2113

Principal professional society of chemists, with 145,000 members. ***Programs/services:*** **Operation Chemistry (OpChem),** funded by the National Science Foundation and involving 2-week workshops for teacher-training teams and subsequent workshops nationwide for thousands of teachers; **Community Science Grants** for children and adults to explore hands-on science as teams. ***Publications/materials:*** Curriculum guidelines; supplemental activities; audiovisual materials; *WonderScience* (activities magazine for upper-elementary students and adults working together; published jointly with the American Institute of Physics (*see* 10.12)); video and booklet supporting chemists who go into the classroom; newsletter; posters.

10.7 American Forest Foundation, 1111 19th St., NW, Suite 780, Washington, DC 20036
(202) 463-2462

A publicly supported conservation and education organization and a resource center on sustainable forestry. ***Programs/services:*** Cosponsored with the Western Regional Environmental Education Council: **Project Learning Tree (PLT)**—a comprehensive environmental education program for students (PreK through 12) in 50 states and 6 foreign countries, focused on a broad range of environmental issues and designed to develop critical thinking skills. Project Learning Tree is also a distribution network for PLT curriculum and other materials; workshops, with accompanying instructional materials, are provided for teaching PLT. ***Publications/materials:*** PLT curriculum units and teacher's guides; computer-based and other materials distributed mostly through the PLT network; newsletter.

10.8 American Geological Institute, 4220 King St., Alexandria, VA 22302-1507
(703) 379-2480

Federation of more than 25 professional, scientific, and technical associations in the earth sciences. ***Publications/materials:*** *Adventures in Geology,* a text-based approach to geology and science teaching (for grades K-3, 4-6); *Earth Science Content Guidelines,* a report, including activities, to guide the inclusion of earth science content in curriculum for grades K-12, with ideas and activities in the areas of solid earth, water, air, ice, life, and earth in space.

10.9 American Indian Science and Engineering Society, 1630 30th St., Suite 301, Boulder, CO 80301
(303) 492-8658

Society of American Indian and non-Indian students, scientific professionals, and interested corporations providing programs for American Indian students and their teachers to enhance student interest and abilities in science by linking hands-on, student-centered science to culture and community with uniquely Indian programs and curricula; science focus on biology, human biology, environmental sciences, and science/technology and society. ***Programs/services:*** Workshops at society meetings; institutes; surplus equipment; technical assistance; information hotline; National American Indian Science Fair. ***Publications/materials:*** Curriculum units; teacher's guides; audiovisual and computer-based materials; *Winds of Change Magazine* for students; newsletter; posters.

10.10 American Institute of Aeronautics and Astronautics, The Aerospace Center, 370 L'Enfant Promenade, SW, Washington, DC 20024
(202) 646-7444

Principal technical society for engineering and science in aviation and space, with 45,000 members. ***Programs/services:*** Volunteers, usually acting through local sections of the institute, provide teacher workshops, tutor and mentor students, judge science fairs, sponsor essay contests, hold paper airplane contests, and work with teachers and students.

10.11 American Institute of Biological Sciences, 730 11th St., NW, Washington, DC 20001-4521
(202) 628-1500

Umbrella organization of professional life science societies and institutions responsible for the Biological Sciences Curriculum Study (BSCS). ***Programs/services:*** Sessions at annual meetings; database of scientists who are available to help teachers. ***Publications/materials:*** *BioScience* (monthly magazine).

10.12 American Institute of Physics, American Center for Physics, One Physics Ellipse, College Park, MD 20740-3843
(301) 209-3100

Organization of 10 professional societies (totaling 75,000 members) and 19 affiliated societies in physics and related fields; concerned with collecting and disseminating information about physics, physics education, and the history of physics. ***Programs/services:*** **Science Education for Every Kid (SEEK); Students to Explore and Experience Science**—hands-on demonstrations for sixth-grade inner-city students. ***Publications/materials:*** *WonderScience* (activities magazine for upper-elementary students and adults working together; published jointly with American Chemical Society (*see* 10.6)); *Physics Education News* (semimonthly electronic newsletter).

10.13 American Meteorological Society, 1701 K St., NW, Suite 300, Washington, DC 20006
(202) 466-5728

Professional scientific society of more than 11,000 members; focused on meteorology, climatology, and oceanography. ***Programs/services:*** Two national projects—**Project ATMOSPHERE** (meteorology and climatology) and the newer **Maury Project** (oceanography)—to train teachers (grades K-12) in these areas: 1-week institutes for master teachers, and monitoring of subsequent workshops nationwide in which the master teachers train other teachers. ***Publications/materials:*** Teacher's guides, materials, hands-on activities solely for use in the two projects; audiovisual and computer-based materials; newsletter.

10.14 American Nuclear Society, 555 No. Kensington Ave., La Grange Park, IL 60525
(708) 579-8230

International scientific and educational organization composed of physicists, chemists, engineers, educators, and other professionals involved in nuclear science or engineering. ***Programs/services:*** Multifaceted **Public Education Program (PEP);** PEP Educational Outreach from local sections of the society, providing scientist collaborations, speaker resources, and information hotlines. ***Publications/materials:*** Instructional materials for teachers; newsletter.

10.15 American Physical Society, American Center for Physics, One Physics Ellipse, College Park, MD 20740
(301) 209-3263

Principal professional society for physicists and physics students, with more than 40,000 members; focused primarily on physics and also on physics education. ***Programs/services:*** **Teacher-Scientist Alliance Institute,** a national cooperative effort operated with the American Association of Physics Teachers (*see* 10.2) to mobilize scientists in support of efforts at systemic reform of elementary science education. Scientists from areas with school districts engaged in systemic reform are recruited, taught about reform issues, and expected to recruit and teach other scientists in their areas.

10.16 American Physiological Society, 9650 Rockville Pike, Bethesda, MD 20814-3991
(301) 530-7132

Professional society of about 7,000 scientists; focused on how the human body functions. ***Programs/services:*** Database of scientists who are available to help teachers; online information service on educational materials, programs, and activities. ***Publications/materials:*** Resource sheets (e.g., a list of resources, criteria for gender and race equity, and issues in animal research).

10.17 American School Health Association, P.O. Box 708, Kent, OH 44240
(216) 678-1601

Association committed to safeguarding the health of school-aged children, with 4,000 health professionals working in schools. ***Programs/services:*** Sessions and workshops at annual National School Health Conference. ***Publications/materials:*** Curriculum guidelines and units with hands-on materials; instructional materials in *Journal of School Health.*

10.18 American Society for Cell Biology, 9650 Rockville Pike, Bethesda, MD 20814
(301) 530-7153

Society of more than 7,000 scientists. ***Programs/services:*** Scientist collaborations with individual teachers; database of scientists who are available to help teachers; letter-answering service for students; speakers.

10.19 American Society for Microbiology, 1325 Massachusetts Ave., NW, Washington, DC 20005
(202) 942-9283

Oldest biological science society in the world, with 40,000 members. ***Programs/services:*** **Scientist-Educator Network** consisting of scientists who are available to provide assistance as presenters, resource people (for advice, supplies, and classroom visits), advisers to teachers on curriculum and projects, providers of laboratory tours, judges at science fairs, and, sometimes, mentors to students (to advise on projects and to be shadowed during the workday); database of members of this network is available to science teachers. ***Publications/materials:*** "How-to" manual for scientists involved in outreach efforts at schools.

10.20 American Society of Plant Physiologists, 15501 Monona Dr., Rockville, MD 20855-2768
(301) 251-0560

Society of more than 5,000 plant-science researchers and teachers. ***Programs/services:*** Encourages scientist collaborations with individual teachers and teacher-scientist partnerships, which it supports with a videotape for scientists on using fast-growing plants in the classroom.

10.21 American Zoo and Aquarium Association, 7970-D Old Georgetown Rd., Bethesda, MD 20814
(301) 907-7777

Association of more than 160 zoos, zoological parks, and aquariums, supporting membership excellence in conservation, education, science, and recreation. ***Programs/services:*** **Suitcase for Survival,** a national program that provides suitcases filled with confiscated wildlife products and accompanied by educational materials to educate youth about protected wildlife and how illegal trade threatens the extinction of certain species. Program cosponsors: U.S. Fish and Wildlife Service, World Wildlife Fund, National Fish and Wildlife Foundation, and American Zoo and Aquarium Association (AZA); AZA coordinates the program. Teacher-training workshops are held at selected zoological parks and aquariums nationwide; a complete list of zoos and aquariums that disseminate Suitcase for Survival is available from AZA.

10.22 Association for Supervision and Curriculum Development (ASCD), 1250 No. Pitt St., Alexandria, VA 22314-1453
(703) 549-9110

Educational association with more than 190,000 members. ***Programs/services:*** Dissemination of information on educational research and practice, and activities addressing teaching and learning in all fields; sessions at annual conference; **Professional Development Institutes** (of 1 to 3 days) in major U.S. cities; sponsorship of networks (usually with newsletters) that meet at annual conferences. ***Publications/materials:*** *ASCD Curriculum Handbook; Brown's Directories of Instructional Programs* (annual guide to commercial materials); *Only the Best* (annual guide to computer-based materials); *Curriculum Materials Directory* (annual guide to noncommercial materials); *Educational Leadership* (journal); ASCD books; *Hands-On Elementary Science* (materials for 20 workshops), from TERC (*see* 10.105), Cambridge; audio-/videotapes.

10.23 Association of Astronomy Educators, 5103 Burt St., Omaha, NE 68132
(402) 556-0082

Association dedicated to improving astronomy education at all levels from kindergarten through college by encouraging the development and exchange of information about effective curricula, materials, facilities, and groups. ***Programs/services:*** Workshops and sessions at National Science Teachers Association meetings. ***Publications/materials:*** Newsletter; occasional publications.

10.24 Association of Science-Technology Centers (ASTC), 1025 Vermont Ave., NW, Suite 500, Washington, DC 20005
(202) 783-7200

Worldwide organization of science centers and museums, planetariums, space theaters, nature centers, aquariums, natural history museums, children's museums, and other facilities, with more than 270 members in the United States and Canada. ***Programs/services:***

- Created and operates **YouthALIVE!**—a program for underserved adolescents (grades 5-12) delivered by nearly 50 museums that are members of either ASTC or the Association of Youth Museums (*see* 10.25). (Contact ASTC for current list of disseminating museums.) Newsletter, directory of programs, and "How-to" manual for YouthALIVE! are available. The program provides hands-on enrichment programs with structured opportunities (for grades 5-8), such as clubs, camps, classes, workshops, and field trips, to heighten interest and involvement of targeted adolescents in the physical sciences; museums design their individual programs, often working with community-based organizations, and seek minimum involvement of 120 hours per year for 2 or 3 years for each student; ASTC provides technical assistance and professional development for museum staff members.

Publications/materials: *The ASTC/CIMUSET Directory* of member institutions (CIMUSET is the International Committee of Science and Technology Museums, of the International Council of Museums); publications catalog.

10.25 Association of Youth Museums, 1775 K St., NW, Suite 595, Washington, DC 20006
(202) 466-4144

Professional service organization serving more than 330 member museums worldwide. ***Programs/services:*** Provides forum for interaction, a source for information and professional development, and a focus for collaboration among youth museums and traditional museums with a special interest in children and family audiences.

10.26 Astronomical Society of the Pacific, 390 Ashton Ave., San Francisco, CA 94112
(415) 337-1100

A 105-year-old scientific and educational society with members from 50 states and more than 60 countries. ***Programs/services:*** Program of workshops and other activities for teachers (grades 3-12) at society's summer annual meeting; program to link astronomers with classroom teachers; information hotline. ***Publications/materials:*** Instructional materials; information packets; resource guides; audiovisual and computer-based materials; posters; comprehensive mail-order catalog of these materials; free quarterly newsletter on teaching astronomy in grades 3-12.

10.27 Atlantic Center for the Environment, 39 So. Main St., Ipswich, MA 01938
(508) 356-0038

Organization of 5,000 educational professionals, university students, and others concerned with environmental issues involving marine biology, ornithology, climatology, and oceanography in northern New England, Atlantic Canada, and eastern Quebec. ***Programs/services:*** Workshops with instructional materials; scientist-teacher collaborations; lab visits and research opportunities for school students; speakers for classrooms. ***Publications/materials:*** Curriculum units with hands-on materials; teacher's guides; audiovisual and computer-based materials; posters.

10.28 Atlantic Salmon Federation, P.O. Box 429, St. Andrews, New Brunswick, Canada E0G 2X0
(506) 529-4581

International organization of more than 5,000 conservationists, scientists, government officials, and salmon fishermen; promotes conservation and wise management of Atlantic salmon and its environment. ***Programs/services:*** **Fish Friends,** a program for educating elementary school children about fish ecology, growth, and survival, that includes the following: in-class presentations, an egg-incubation aquarium for each classroom, field trips to release salmon reared in the classroom to local waterways, and in-service workshops for participating teachers. ***Publications/materials:*** Curriculum guide; curriculum supplements; audiovisual materials; magazine for students; posters.

10.29 Challenger Learning Centers, Challenger Center for Space Science Education, 1029 No. Royal St., Suite 300, Alexandria, VA 22314
(703) 683-9740

Network of more than 25 centers in the United States and Canada, about half at museums, focused on space science, and using simulation, teamwork, creative problem solving, and responsible decision making. ***Programs/services:*** Space flight simulators with hands-on learning experiences and classroom-based projects for students; workshops for teachers using hands-on activities and mission simulation models, with faculty drawn partly from NASA Teacher-in-Space finalists. ***Publications/materials:*** Hands-on instructional units on space topics.

10.30 The City College Workshop Center, NAC 4/220, City College of City University of New York, Convent Ave. and 138th St., New York, NY 10031
(212) 650-8436

Programs/services: Center provides a national model for in-service education of teachers (grades K-8), directly and through master teachers, in constructivist, inquiry-centered methods of teaching science and mathematics; primary focus is New York City schools; the model and technical assistance are also disseminated in other U.S. locations and in foreign countries. Center offers 4-week summer institutes followed by 20 intensive weekly follow-up sessions, many in actual classrooms, on how to teach children in this way; similar summer institute and weekly follow-up sessions on how to teach teachers to teach in this way.

10.31 Cornell Lab of Ornithology, 159 Sapsucker Woods Rd., Ithaca, NY 14850-1999
(607) 254-2440

International center for the study, appreciation, and conservation of birds and an authoritative source of information about birds. ***Programs/services:*** Provides up-to-date ornithological data to scientists and communications media worldwide; developed two projects allowing participation in hands-on, inquiry-based activities—**Project FeederWatch,** to help scientists track winter bird populations at feeders, and **Project PigeonWatch,** to help scientists answer questions about pigeon behavior. ***Publications/materials:*** Home course for adults on bird biology; bird sound recordings on cassettes and CDs; slide collection, with copies at nominal fee; newsletter.

10.32 Council for Elementary Science International, c/o Dr. Betty Burchett, CESI Membership Chair, 212 Townsend Hall, University of Missouri, Columbia, MO 65211
(314) 882-4831

Professional organization with 1,600 members and a Division Affiliate of the National Science Teachers Association (*see* 10.84), dedicated to stimulating, improving, and coordinating science teaching (grades pre-K through 8). ***Programs/services:*** Make-and-Take sessions. ***Publications/materials:*** Sourcebooks for teaching elementary science; research monographs on teaching science; file sheets; VHS video; *CESI Science.*

10.33 Council for Exceptional Children, 1920 Association Dr., Reston, VA 22091-1589
(703) 620-3660

Network of 59 state and provincial federations, 1,012 chapters, and 17 divisions make up this international professional organization dedicated to improving educational outcomes for individuals with disabilities and/or who are gifted. ***Programs/services:*** Annual convention; topical conferences; symposiums; workshops; conferences of state federations. ***Publications/materials:*** Extensive literature on special education, including curriculum materials, with semiannual catalog; *TEACHING Exceptional Children* and *Exceptional Children* (journals); newsletter; publications of the various divisions.

10.34 Council of State Science Supervisors, c/o Dr. Thomas Keller, Council President, Maine Department of Education, 23 State House Station, Augusta, ME 04333-0023
(207) 287-5920

Organization consisting of a science supervisor/specialist/consultant from each of the 50 states and other jurisdictions (e.g., the District of Columbia, Puerto Rico, Guam). ***Programs/services:*** Sessions at National Science Teachers Association conventions (regional and national); program of **Presidential Awards for Excellence in Science and Mathematics Teaching;** coordination of individual members' work in creating curriculum guidelines, frameworks, and standards within their respective areas; information dissemination, primarily to members.

10.35 Educational Equity Concepts, 114 E. 32nd St., Suite 701, New York, NY 10016
(212) 725-1803

National organization dedicated to producing educational programs and materials free from bias regarding gender, race and ethnicity, disability, and income; offers the following:

- *Playtime Is Science,* a physical science activity program (for PreK through 3), with hands-on curriculum materials, audiovisual materials, and facilitator notebook; staff development and parent training provided; sessions on this program held at meetings and workshops.
- *What Will Happen IF . . . Young Children and the Scientific Method,* physical science curriculum (for grades K-2 or K-3); curriculum guide and staff development guide; newsletter.

10.36 Education Development Center, 55 Chapel St., Newton, MA 02158-1060
(617) 969-7100

International education research and development firm founded in 1958, with a Center for Learning, Teaching, and Technology among its subdivisions. ***Programs/publications:*** **Insights,** a comprehensive K-6 science curriculum. ***Services:*** Workshops at meetings of National Science Teachers Association and other organizations; technical assistance to Statewide Systemic Initiatives (*see* 10.82) in 24 states and Puerto Rico; assistance to several school districts in implementing systemic reform.

10.37 Eisenhower National Clearinghouse for Mathematics and Science Education, The Ohio State University, 1929 Kenny Rd., Columbus, OH 43210-1079
(614) 292-7784; (800) 621-5785

Clearinghouse financed by U.S. Department of Education.***Services/materials:*** Science education information (grades K-12): comprehensive collection of curriculum resources in many formats (print, audio, multimedia, video, kits, games), for which a detailed catalog, *ENC Online,* is available via modem (1-800-362-4448); Telnet and Gopher (enc.org); and World Wide Web (http://www.enc.org). Many other products and services are available in print and electronic format, including a database of federal programs, electronic visits to particular schools, and a reference service. Information is also available via e-mail (info@enc.org).

10.38 Entomological Society of America, 9301 Annapolis Rd., Lanham, MD 20706-3115
(301) 731-4535

Professional scientific society with 9,200 members; focused on insects. ***Programs/Services:*** Insect Expo sessions at society meetings. ***Publications/materials:*** *Insect Appreciation Digest* for teachers; slide collection; newsletter; posters.

10.39 Environmental Action Coalition, 625 Broadway, 2nd Floor, New York, NY 10012
(212) 677-1601

Nonprofit organization concerned with education in the areas of household hazardous waste, recycling, waste prevention, and urban forestry. ***Programs/services:*** Environmental library with curriculum guides and lists of the guides; teacher-training workshops; speakers at career days. ***Publications/materials:*** Curriculum units with hands-on materials; supplemental activities; audiovisual materials.

10.40 EPIE Institute, 103-3 W. Montauk Hwy., Hampton Bays, NY 11946
(516) 728-9100

Consumer-oriented organization that evaluates educational products. ***Programs/services:*** Curriculum Analysis Services for Educators (CASE), a computer-based process whereby EPIE (Educational Products Information Exchange) determines the degree of alignment of a school's curricular goals and objectives with textbooks, other instructional materials, and tests. ***Publications/materials:*** TESS (The Educational Software Selector), a database with information on more than 3,000 educational software programs ranging over all the sciences and social sciences (including citations to reviews), available in MS-DOS, Macintosh, and CD-ROM versions; *The Latest and Best of TESS* (print directory based on TESS (*see* 7.18)); *EPIEgram* (newsletter).

10.41 ERIC Clearinghouse for Science, Mathematics, and Environmental Education, The Ohio State University, 1929 Kenny Rd., Columbus, OH 43210-1080
(614) 292-6717; (800) 276-0462; 800-LET-ERIC (for new users)

Clearinghouse and international information network, 1 of 16 in the ERIC (Educational Resources Information Center) system, which is supported by the U.S. Department of Education. ***Services/programs:*** Collects, catalogs, and provides access to educational materials; offers reference and referral services; produces bibliographic information; maintains extensive database of reports, curricular and instructional materials, evaluations, and information on programs, practices, and policies in science, mathematics, and environmental education; accessible and searchable on CD-ROM or over Internet: e-mail (ericse@osu.edu); Gopher (gopher.ericse.ohio-state.edu); World Wide Web (http://www.ericse.ohio-state.edu).

10.42 4-H SERIES Project Office, University of California at Davis, HCD, Davis, CA 95616-8523
(916) 752-8824

Office at the University of California, Davis, that created and operates the following 4-H-related programs funded by the National Science Foundation:

- **4-H SERIES (Science Experiences and Resources for Informal Education Settings)**—national program in which 9-to-12-year-olds are led by trained teens in science activities in out-of-school settings, then follow up with related community service projects.
- **4-H YES (Youth Experiences in Science)**—national after-school program in which 5-to-8-year-olds are led by trained teens in science activities at child care centers for school-age children.

Both programs are delivered at 4-H SERIES Regional Leadership Centers at the University of California, Davis; University of Missouri, Cooperative Extension of Lawrence County, Mount Vernon, Mo.; Cornell University, Cooperative Extension, Broome County, Binghamton, N.Y.; and Rock Eagle 4-H Center, Eatonton, Ga.; 4-H YES is also available at local 4-H offices.

10.43 Geological Society of America, P.O. Box 9140, Boulder, CO 80301-9140
(303) 447-2020

Professional scientific society with more than 16,000 members. ***Programs/services:*** **Partners for Excellence Program (PEP),** a national network of people committed to enhancing science education for children and fostering collaborations and partnerships between teachers and scientists; sessions for teachers at annual meeting; free PEP membership for teachers. Available through PEP: national database of scientist partners (for grades K-12); scientist mentors and tours for students of the society's facility. ***Publications/materials:*** Activity and resource packets; slide sets; video; regional field trip guidebooks.

10.44 Geothermal Education Office, 664 Hilary Dr., Tiburon, CA 94920
(800) 866-4436

Nonprofit educational office focused on K-12 education about geothermal energy. ***Programs/services:*** Free workshops for teachers; scientist collaborations and information from a scientist database; 24-hour 800 number for free materials; referrals for more technical information; classroom speakers; class visits to geothermal power plants; scientist mentors for students; poster and essay contests. ***Publications/materials:*** Curriculum unit (grades 4-6); curriculum guidelines and activity suggestions offered by phone; audiovisual materials; *Steam Press* (annual journal of geothermal education in newsletter format); newsletter; posters.

10.45 Gifted Child Society, 190 Rock Rd., Glen Rock, NJ 07452
(201) 444-6530

Society of 4,000 educators, parents, and gifted children that provides training for educators, assistance for parents, and support for gifted children. ***Programs/services:*** Conferences and seminars for teachers; scientist collaborations with teachers; equipment for loan; information hotline; semiannual newsletter; speakers; **Saturday Workshop** program, scientist mentors, scholarships, and competitive examinations for children. ***Publications:*** Newsletter.

10.46 The GLOBE Program, 744 Jackson Pl., NW, Washington, DC 20503
(202) 395-7600

Worldwide network of students (grades K-12) making environmental observations and sharing findings with one another and with the scientific community via Internet and World Wide Web; lead agency in this program—National Oceanic and Atmospheric Administration. For further information: e-mail (info@globe.gov) and World Wide Web (http://www.globe.gov).

10.47 Great Lakes Planetarium Association (GLPA), c/o Dr. D. David Batch, GLPA President, Abrams Planetarium, Michigan State University, East Lansing, MI 48824
(517) 355-4676

Regional association of professionals from planetariums (including many that are school-based) in Illinois,

Indiana, Michigan, Minnesota, Ohio, and Wisconsin; association focus is on astronomy and space science, but also includes geology, earth science, and meteorology. ***Programs/services:*** Workshops for teachers at annual conference; information about the region's planetariums and their programs. ***Publications/materials:*** Resource banks of slides; planetarium show scripts; booklets on teaching astronomy and on the use of a planetarium for astronomy education; member newsletter.

10.48 Great Plains Planetarium Association (GPPA), c/o Ms. April Whitten, GPPA President, Mallory-Kountze Planetarium, University of Nebraska, Omaha, NE 68182-0266
(402) 554-2510

Regional association of professionals from planetariums (including many that are school-based) in Iowa, Kansas, Missouri, Nebraska, North Dakota, Oklahoma, and South Dakota; association focus is on astronomy and space science, but also includes physics, earth and environmental sciences, and history of science. ***Programs/services:*** Workshops for teachers at annual conference; information about the region's planetariums and their programs. ***Publications/materials:*** Newsletter; surplus equipment (donated through newsletter); audiovisual materials.

10.49 Harvard-Smithsonian Center for Astrophysics, Science Education Department, 60 Garden St., MS-71, Cambridge, MA 02138
(617) 495-9798

Small department in a large astrophysical research center; focused on curriculum development, teacher enhancement, and applications of advanced technology; emphasis mostly but not solely on higher grades. ***Services:*** **Project SPICA**, a program providing teacher workshops in astronomy education (grades K-12), supported by a teacher manual of 37 activities, developed by teachers recruited nationwide; workshops at National Science Teachers Association meetings. ***Publications/materials:*** *Harvard-Smithsonian Case Studies in Science Education* (videos, with accompanying guide materials, giving visual models of science education reform, for in-service and pre-service teacher education programs).

10.50 High-Scope Educational Research Foundation, 600 No. River St., Ypsilanti, MI 48198-2898
(313) 485-2000

Research, development, training, and public advocacy organization focused on bringing active, hands-on science learning to grades K-3. ***Programs/services:*** K-3 workshop sessions at meetings; week-long K-3 science workshops. ***Publications/materials:*** Teacher's manual that includes K-3 student activities.

10.51 Institute for Chemical Education, University of Wisconsin, Department of Chemistry, 1101 University Ave., Madison, WI 53706
(608) 262-3033

National organization centered at the University of Wisconsin-Madison, with a network of field centers and affiliates across the country devoted to helping teachers at all grade levels (kindergarten through college) revitalize science in the schools. ***Programs/services:*** Two-week workshops at various regional sites; 4-week workshops in Madison; summer fellowships; **Chem Camps** for students (grades 5-8). ***Publications/materials:*** Supplemental activities; instructional materials for teachers; kits and devices; newsletter.

10.52 Institute for Earth Education, Cedar Cove, Greenville, WV 24945
(304) 832-6404

International educational organization consisting of a volunteer network of individuals and member organizations; fosters earth education programs. ***Programs/services:*** Earth Education interest sessions and workshops conducted by associates around the country; International Earth Education Conferences. ***Publications/materials:*** Develops and disseminates complete educational programs (Earthkeepers, Sunship Earth, SUNSHIP III, Earth Caretakers); *Talking Leaves* (journal); *Earth Education Sourcebook;* other books and program materials.

10.53 International Wildlife Coalition, 70 E. Falmouth Hwy., East Falmouth, MA 02536
(508) 548-8328

Worldwide coalition that researches and protects great whales, dolphins, porpoises, seals, and other marine mammals, and operates the Whale Adoption Project. ***Programs/services:*** In the **Whale Adoption Project** of the International Wildlife Coalition (IWC), individuals or classes pay to "adopt" a humpback whale; the project supports many IWC activities, including **Project SWIMS** (Studying Whales Integrated with Math and Science), in which educators (mostly of grades 6-9) receive direct experience in marine research techniques, whale biology, and related subjects in classroom settings aboard the research vessel *R/V Navaho*. ***Publications/materials:*** *Whales of the World* (biology curriculum, with 11 activities, developed and tested by teachers for grades 2-5); newsletter for children.

10.54 **JASON Project,** JASON Foundation for Education, 395 Totten Pond Rd., Waltham, MA 02154
(617) 487-9995

Annual 2-week interactive field trip, taking half a million students on remote scientific expedition via satellite; emphasis on wide range of earth science and environmental research topics; available at 27 Primary Interactive Network Sites (PINS), including 7 museums and 3 NASA Field Centers (*see* 10.59)—Ames, Goddard, Johnson. ***Services:*** Live TV programs from expeditions, with interactive features; simulation of expedition site at each PINS; participation in actual expedition by selected students and teachers; e-mail, Gopher, and World Wide Web homepage with expedition reports, data, and other educational electronic resources. ***Publications/materials:*** Curriculum units on expeditions available 6 months before each expedition. For further information: e-mail (info@JASON.org); Gopher (gopher.jason.bridgew.edu); World Wide Web (http://seawifs.gsfc.nasa.gov/JASON.html).

10.55 **Los Alamos National Laboratory,** P.O. Box 1663, MSP278, HR-SEO, Los Alamos, NM 87545
(505) 667-1919

One of 10 national laboratories of the U.S. Department of Energy (*see* 10.74), with an active program in science education. ***Programs/services:*** **Science at Home,** a program to promote scientific curiosity and improve scientific literacy, with workshops anywhere in the United States to train trainers and teachers on materials that partner teachers, parents, and students (grades K-8) in science activities; various other regional and local programs.

10.56 **Middle Atlantic Planetarium Society (MAPS),** c/o Ms. Laura Deines, MAPS President, Southworth Planetarium, 96 Falmouth St., University of Southern Maine, Portland, ME 04103
(207) 780-4249

Regional association of professionals from planetariums (including many that are school-based) in Delaware, the District of Columbia, Maryland, New Jersey, New York, Pennsylvania, Virginia, and West Virginia; association focus is on astronomy and space science. ***Programs/services:*** Workshops for teachers at society meetings; teacher-scientist partnerships; facilitation of loans of Starlab portable planetariums among member planetariums; information about the region's planetariums and their programs. ***Publications/materials:*** *Under Roof, Dome, and Sky* (collection of activities developed and used by member planetariums); newsletter.

10.57 **Mineral Information Institute,** 475 17th St., Suite 510, Denver, CO 80202
(303) 297-3226

Private organization supported by professional associations, private companies, and foundations. ***Programs/services:*** Disseminates information about metals, minerals, and energy resources. ***Publications/materials:*** Supplementary activities; audiovisual and computer-based materials; posters.

10.58 **National Aeronautics and Space Administration, Central Operation of Resources for Educators (CORE),** Lorain County Joint Vocational School, 15181 Rte. 58 So., Oberlin, OH 44074
(216) 774-1051, Ext. 293

Worldwide distribution center for NASA audiovisual educational materials. ***Publications/materials:*** Free catalog (send request on school letterhead).

10.59 **National Aeronautics and Space Administration, Education Division,** Code FEE, NASA Headquarters, Washington, DC 20546-0001

Programs/services: The following programs and services of the National Aeronautics and Space Administration (NASA) are delivered via 9 NASA Field Centers that serve multi-state areas. These Field Centers are located at NASA Marshall Space Flight Center, Ala.; NASA Ames Research Center, Moffett Field, Calif.; Jet Propulsion Laboratory, Pasadena, Calif.; NASA Kennedy Space Center, Kennedy Space Center, Fla.; NASA Goddard Space Flight Center, Greenbelt, Md.; NASA Stennis Space Center, Stennis Space Center, Miss.; NASA Lewis Research Center, Cleveland, Ohio; NASA Johnson Space Center, Houston, Tex.; and NASA Langley Research Center, Hampton, Va. Two other field centers serving only their own states are the NASA Dryden Flight Research Facility, Edwards Air Force Base, Calif.; and Wallops Flight Facility, Wallops Island, Va.

- [(202) 358-1518] The **Aerospace Education Services Program** consists of traveling aerospace-education units with classroom programs, teacher-enhancement workshops (1 hour to 2 weeks long) on integrating aerospace into the curriculum, and assembly programs (grades K-12).
- [(202) 358-1518] The **Community Involvement Program,** an intensive community program emphasizing aerospace, seeks to involve service clubs, government officials, and the private sector, in addition to schools: offers in-service workshops (1 week to 1 month long), assemblies, exhibits, public events.
- [(202) 358-1540] The **NASA Teacher Resource Center Network** comprises 9 Teacher Resource Centers, located at the 9 NASA Field Centers listed above in this

entry. The Teacher Resource Centers disseminate NASA educational materials (videotapes, slides, audiotapes, publications, lesson plans, and activities) emphasizing science, mathematics, and technology. These materials are also disseminated by 47 Regional Teacher Resource Centers in 36 states, and by NASA's Central Operation of Resources for Educators (*see* 10.58).

- [(202) 358-1518] NASA's **Urban Community Enrichment Program** trains lead-teacher teams to conduct interdisciplinary aerospace activities in schools and to train other teachers.

10.60 National Aeronautics and Space Administration, NASA Marshall Space Flight Center, Mail Code CL-01, Huntsville, AL 35812-0001
(205) 961-1225

Programs/services: **NASA Spacelink,** a computer information service providing a large variety of aeronautics and space information, including lesson plans and activities; access via modem [(205) 895-0028] or Internet [spacelink.msfc.nasa.gov for Gopher; Telnet; ftp; and World Wide Web—preceded by http://]. (For other programs and services at NASA Marshall Space Flight Center, *see* 10.59.)

10.61 National Association for Research in Science Teaching (NARST), c/o Dr. John R. Staver, NARST Executive Secretary, Center for Science Education, 219 Bluemont Hall, Kansas State University, Manhattan, KS 66506
(913) 532-6294

Professional association of more than 1,000 members worldwide, organized to improve science teaching through research. ***Programs/services:*** Annual convention, with more than 200 research papers. ***Publications/materials:*** *Journal of Research in Science Teaching;* newsletter.

10.62 National Association for the Education of Young Children, 1509 16th St., NW, Washington, DC 20036-1426
(800) 424-2460

Association of 75,000 professional educators and others involved with preschool and primary school education. ***Publications/materials:*** More than 100 books, monographs, and other materials (catalog available) on early childhood education; *Young Children* (journal); posters.

10.63 National Association of Biology Teachers, 11250 Roger Bacon Dr., No. 19, Reston, VA 22090
(703) 471-1134

Professional society of more than 7,000 biology educators and administrators, representing all grade levels. ***Programs/services:*** Annual convention; occasional 1- and 2-day regional summer workshops. ***Publications/materials:*** Monographs and special publications; *The American Biology Teacher* (magazine); newsletter; catalog of materials; posters.

10.64 National Association of Elementary School Principals, 1615 Duke St., Alexandria, VA 22314
(703) 684-3345

Organization serving 26,000 elementary and middle school principals in the United States and Canada, with an affiliate in every state. ***Programs/services:*** Annual convention, with some sessions on science. ***Publications/materials:*** *Principal* (magazine); newsletter; other publications.

10.65 National Audubon Society, 700 Broadway, New York, NY 10003
(212) 979-3000

Organization with 600,000 members and 40 state and 500 local groups (distinct from Audubon Societies of certain states, which are independent); concerned with ecology, natural resources, wildlife, and habitats. ***Programs/services:*** **Audubon Adventures** urban training program (grades 4-6), with teacher's guide; scholarships for educators to attend ecology workshops; **Youth Camp** in Maine (for 10-to-14-year-olds). ***Publications/materials:*** Curriculum units with hands-on materials; videos with accompanying teacher's guides; software on ecology topics.

10.66 National Center for Health Education, 72 Spring St., Suite 208, New York, NY 10012-4019
(212) 334-9470

Organization that promotes health education in schools, families, and communities. ***Programs/services:*** Development, management, and dissemination of **Growing Healthy,** a comprehensive school health program (grades K-6); teacher-training workshops for Growing Healthy. ***Publications/materials:*** Guide to the adoption of Growing Healthy program; curriculum units with hands-on materials; curriculum guidelines; supplemental activities; audiovisual materials.

10.67 National Center for Improving Science Education, 2000 L St., NW, Suite 603, Washington, DC 20036
(202) 467-0652

Division of The NETWORK of Andover, Mass., an organization dedicated to educational reform. ***Programs/services:*** Provides guidance for educational policymakers, curriculum developers, and practitioners by synthesizing findings in policy studies, research reports, and exemplary practices and by transforming them into practical resources, with one area of emphasis chosen for synthesis work each year; offers workshops by technical assistance teams. ***Publications/materials:*** Curriculum guidelines; guidelines for policymakers; information for parents in resource book and pamphlets; books and monographs (publications list available).

10.68 National Center for Research on Teacher Learning, Michigan State University, College of Education, 116 Erickson Hall, East Lansing, MI 48824-1034
(517) 355-9302

Research center supported by the U.S. Department of Education. ***Programs/services:*** Conducts research on how teachers learn to teach and engage students in active learning, with some projects specifically focused on science and mathematics.

10.69 National Center for Science Teaching and Learning, The Ohio State University, 1929 Kenny Rd., Columbus, OH 43210-1015
(614) 292-3339

Research center supported by the U.S. Department of Education. ***Programs/services:*** Conducts research on noncurricular factors (such as social/cultural, organizational, and technological) affecting science students and teachers (grades K-12).

10.70 National Consortium for Environmental Education and Training, University of Michigan, School of Natural Resources, Ann Arbor, MI 48109-1115
(313) 998-6726

Consortium (funded by the U.S. Environmental Protection Agency (*see* 10.119)) of academic institutions, corporations, and nonprofit organizations headed by the University of Michigan; operates national program for providers of in-service education to teachers (grades K-12), natural resource management professionals, and environmental educators. ***Programs/services:*** Workshops for in-service providers; dissemination of information; coordination of environmental information nationwide. ***Publications/materials:*** Environmental education toolbox for in-service providers.

10.71 National Earth Science Teachers Association, 2000 Florida Ave., NW, Washington, DC 20009
(202) 462-6910

Professional society of 1,500 earth science teachers. ***Programs/services:*** Workshops and rock swaps at national and regional National Science Teachers Association meetings; summer field trips and field conferences. ***Publications/materials:*** *The Earth Scientist* (membership journal); scripted slide sets.

10.72 National Energy Foundation, 5225 Wiley Post Way, Suite 170, Salt Lake City, UT 84116
(801) 539-1406

Nonprofit educational organization devoted to the development of instructional materials and the implementation of innovative teacher-training and student programs. ***Programs/services:*** Workshops for teachers on mining education; student-team energy patrols; student debate program. ***Publications/materials:*** Curriculum units with hands-on materials; curriculum guidelines; supplementary materials; posters; newsletter for teachers; catalog of materials.

10.73 National Geographic Society, 1145 17th St., NW, Washington, DC 20036
(800) 368-2728

World's largest nonprofit scientific and educational organization. ***Publications/materials:*** *National Geographic Kids Network,* a computer- and telecommunications-based science curriculum (grades 4-6), developed in cooperation with TERC (*see* 10.105) and focused on acid rain, weather, water quality, trash, nutrition, and solar energy, in which student-scientists investigate real-world scientific issues and exchange information with other students around the world, providing hands-on experience in scientific methods and computer technology; CD-ROMs; interactive videodiscs; films; books; *National Geographic Magazine.*

10.74 National Laboratories and Facilities of the U.S. Department of Energy (DOE), c/o U.S. Department of Energy, Office of Scientific and Technical Information, P.O. Box 62, Oak Ridge, TN 37831
(615) 576-8401

Programs/services: **Science education programs:** The U.S. Department of Energy's 10 national laboratories and 30 specialized facilities throughout the United States offer a wide variety of regional and local science education programs in their respective localities. The laboratories are Argonne National Laboratory, Argonne, Ill.; Brookhaven National Laboratory, Upton, N.Y.; Fermi National Accelerator Laboratory,

Batavia, Ill.; Idaho National Engineering Laboratory, Idaho Falls, Idaho; Lawrence Berkeley Laboratory, Berkeley, Calif.; Los Alamos National Laboratory, Los Alamos, N.Mex.; National Renewable Energy Laboratory, Golden, Colo.; Oak Ridge National Laboratory, Oak Ridge, Tenn.; Pacific Northwest Laboratory, Richland, Wash.; and Sandia National Laboratories, Albuquerque, N.Mex., and Livermore, Calif. Other leading DOE laboratories include Lawrence Livermore National Laboratory, Livermore, Calif.; Princeton Plasma Physics Laboratory, Princeton, N.J.; and Stanford Linear Accelerator Center, Stanford, Calif. For a description of all of DOE's science education programs, request the *Education Programs Catalog* from the U.S. Department of Energy's Office of Scientific and Technical Information at the address above.

10.75 National Marine Educators Association, P.O. Box 51215, Pacific Grove, CA 93950
(408) 648-4841

Association of professionals from education (kindergarten through graduate school), science, business, government, museums, aquariums, and marine research, with more than 1,200 members and 15 regional chapters; focused on marine, physical, earth, and life sciences, marine education, and marine history, literature, songs, and art. ***Programs/services:*** Teacher's workshops and opportunities for networking with scientists at annual conference and at conferences organized by regional chapters. ***Publications/materials:*** *The Journal of Marine Education,* with activities; newsletter, with reviews of curricular materials.

10.76 National Network for Science and Technology (NNST), 6H Berkey Hall, Michigan State University, East Lansing, MI 48824-1111
(517) 355-0180

Network of land grant universities, Cooperative Extension Systems, and other organizations in all 50 states, concerned with children, youth, and families at risk; promotes science and technology literacy. ***Programs/services:*** Technical and program assistance for extension faculty and collaborators to develop and implement effective programs; national and regional training and symposia; research and development; electronic clearinghouse. For further information: e-mail: (nnst@mes.umn.edu); Gopher and Telnet: (gopher-cyfernet.mes.umn.edu).

10.77 National Research Council; Center for Science, Mathematics, and Engineering Education, 2101 Constitution Ave., Washington, DC 20418
(202) 334-2353

The National Research Council (NRC) is the operating arm of three honorary academies: the National Academy of Sciences, the National Academy of Engineering, and the Institute of Medicine. NRC's primary concern is advising the federal government on matters of science and technology policy. It has become increasingly active in efforts to improve science education and has been a leader in the development of standards for precollege science education, completing the development of the National Science Education Standards (*see* 6.34) in 1995. NRC's Center for Science, Mathematics, and Engineering Education is concerned with curriculum development and review; educational policy, research, assessment, and evaluation; K-12 policy and practice; and postsecondary policy and practice. ***Programs/services:***

- [(202) 334-3628] The **National Science Education Standards project** has a comprehensive outreach strategy to support national, state, and local utilization of the Standards through leadership and resource development, partnerships and networks, and targeted symposia and workshops.
- [(202) 357-2555] **National Science Resources Center** (*see* 10.83), a joint program of the National Academy of Sciences and the Smithsonian Institution, is concerned with reforming science education and producing resources for teaching science.
- [(202 334-2110] **Project RISE** (Regional Initiatives in Science Education) provides scientists and engineers with information and resources to assist them in contributing effectively to K-12 science education partnerships ranging from classroom interactions to systemic reform programs.

10.78 National Science Education Leadership Association, P.O. Box 5556, Arlington, VA 22205
(703) 524-8646

A 1,200-member association of chairpersons, department heads, science supervisors, coordinators, and other leaders in science education; focused on improving science education through leadership development. ***Programs/services:*** Miniconferences; leadership institutes; other programs to develop leadership skills. ***Publications/materials:*** *Science Leadership Trend Notes*; *NSELA Handbook; Science Educator* (journal).

10.79 National Science Foundation, Directorate for Education and Human Resources, 4201 Wilson Blvd., Arlington, VA 22230
(703) 306-1600

The Directorate for Education and Human Resources of the National Science Foundation, an independent federal agency, is a major force for improving science education in the United States; it initiates and sponsors a wide variety of projects to improve education in science, mathematics, and engineering. ***Programs/services:*** The Directorate's work is carried out by three divisions and one office:

- Division of Elementary, Secondary, and Informal Education (*see* 10.80), concerned with curriculum and teacher enhancement in science, mathematics, and engineering.
- Division of Human Resource Development (*see* 10.81), concerned with broadening the participation in science, mathematics, and engineering of persons in underrepresented groups.
- Division of Undergraduate Education [(703) 306-1670], concerned with teacher preparation; included among its efforts—the new **Collaboratives for Excellence in Teacher Preparation Program.**
- Office of Systemic Reform (*see* 10.82), concerned with three large-scale reform programs: the **Rural Systemic Initiatives Program, Statewide Systemic Initiatives Program,** and **Urban Systemic Initiatives Program.**

Publications/materials: *Guide to Programs* (for current fiscal year); *Indicators of Science and Mathematics Education; Indicators of Science and Engineering Education*; other reports; fact sheets.

10.80 National Science Foundation; Directorate for Education and Human Resources; Division of Elementary, Secondary, and Informal Education, 4201 Wilson Blvd., Rm. 885, Arlington, VA 22230
(703) 306-1620

Programs/services: The Division of Elementary, Secondary, and Informal Education operates the following National Science Foundation (*see* 10.79) programs:

- [(703) 306-1615] The **Informal Science Education Program** supports nonschool projects (for example, by museums and youth organizations) to increase involvement with science, mathematics, and technology.
- [(703) 306-1614] The **Instructional Materials Development Program** supports development of innovative, comprehensive, and diverse materials implementing standards-based reform in science, mathematics, and technology.
- [(703) 306-1620] The **Local Systemic Change through Teacher Enhancement Program** supports comprehensive, systemic efforts at fundamental reform of science, mathematics, and technology education in grades K-12 in whole schools, targeting at least 200 teachers in each program and emphasizing teacher enhancement and instructional materials.
- [(703) 306-1613] The **Teacher Enhancement Program** supports projects to enhance the content knowledge and pedagogical skills of teachers of science, mathematics, and technology in grades K-12.

10.81 National Science Foundation, Directorate for Education and Human Resources, Division of Human Resource Development, 4201 Wilson Blvd., Rm. 815, Arlington, VA 22230
(703) 306-1640

Programs/services: The Division of Human Resource Development operates the following National Science Foundation (*see* 10.79) programs:

- [(703) 306-1633] The **Comprehensive Partnerships for Minority Student Achievement Program** supports programs for comprehensive pre-college education reform in school systems with significant minority populations.
- [(703) 306-1637] **Programs for Persons with Disabilities** supports programs to develop new teaching methods, increase recognition of needs and capabilities of students with disabilities, promote accessibility of appropriate instructional materials and technologies, and increase availability of mentoring resources.
- [(703) 306-1637] **Programs for Women and Girls** supports model projects, experimental projects, and information-dissemination activities to improve the science, mathematics, and technology education of women and to increase their numbers in these fields.

10.82 National Science Foundation, Directorate for Education and Human Resources, Office of Systemic Reform, 4201 Wilson Blvd., Rm. 875, Arlington, VA 22230
(703) 306-1690

Programs/services: The following National Science Foundation (*see* 10.79) programs support systemic improvements in science, mathematics, and technology education in grades K-12:

- [(703) 306-1684] The **Rural Systemic Initiatives Program** supports projects to make systemic improvements in science, mathematics, and technology education in rural, economically disadvantaged regions.
- [(703) 306-1682] The **Statewide Systemic Initiatives Program** supports comprehensive, systemic, statewide efforts to change educational systems and improve science, mathematics, and technology education.
- [(703) 306-1684] The **Urban Systemic Initiatives Program** supports comprehensive, systemic efforts at fundamental reform of science, mathematics, and technology education in large urban school systems.

10.83 **National Science Resources Center,** Smithsonian Institution, MRC-502, Arts and Industries Bldg., Rm. 1201, Washington, DC 20560
(202) 357-2555

Organization sponsored jointly by the National Academy of Sciences and Smithsonian Institution to contribute to the improvement of science education in the nation's schools. ***Programs/services:*** Workshops at National Science Teachers Association and other meetings; two annual **Leadership Institutes** to train teams from school districts across the country on science education reform issues and methods; annual **Scientists and Engineers Working Conferences** to increase involvement of participants in science education; technical support for school districts involved in science education reform; support of other organizations in reform efforts. ***Publications/materials:*** *Science and Technology for Children,* a series of 24 core curriculum units (grades 1-6) in the physical, life, and earth sciences; *Resources for Teaching Elementary School Science* and projected companion volumes for middle and high schools; *Science for All Children* (forthcoming), a comprehensive guide to systemic science education reform in the nation's schools; newsletter.

10.84 **National Science Teachers Association (NSTA),** 1840 Wilson Blvd., Arlington, VA 22201-3000
(703) 243-7100

Organization committed to improving science education at all levels, PreK through college, with membership of 52,000, including science teachers, supervisors, administrators, scientists, and business and industry representatives. ***Programs/services:*** One national and three regional conferences per year; certification of science teachers in eight teaching-level and discipline-area categories; computer bulletin board; employment registry; educational tours; nearly 20 award programs for teachers; award programs for students; **NASA Educational Workshops for Elementary School Teachers (NEWEST)** [(703) 312-9296]—2-week workshops for teachers (grades K-6) on aerospace topics and techniques for incorporating them in curricula, conducted by NASA scientists at various NASA Field Centers (*see* 10.59) using both NSTA and NASA materials. ***Publications/materials:*** *Science and Children* (magazine); *NSTA Reports!* (newspaper); curriculum units; supplementary activities; other instructional materials and publications; posters; complete catalog of titles.

10.85 **National Urban Coalition,** 1875 Connecticut Ave., NW, Suite 400, Washington, DC 20009
(202) 986-1460; (800) 328-6339

Urban action and advocacy organization, focused on ensuring that students of all races, cultures, and ethnic backgrounds are educated in mathematics, science, and technology for the workforce of tomorrow. ***Programs/services:*** Award-winning program, **Say YES to a Youngster's Future,** featuring Say YES 3- and 4-week summer institutes for teachers, in-service workshops at schools and other local sites for Say YES teachers during school year, and stipends for program activities. ***Publications/materials:*** Curriculum units and other materials for the Say YES and Family Math and Science programs; *Say YES Gazette* (newsletter); posters.

10.86 **National Wildlife Federation,** 8925 Leesburg Pike, Vienna, VA 22184-0001
(800) 245-5484

Federation of 6,500 state and territorial conservation organizations and associate members. ***Programs/services:*** 3-day **NatureQuest** workshops for educators and nature and science counselors at sites around the country; **Conservation Summits** for interested adults; **Wildlife Camps** (for students age 9-13). ***Publications/materials:*** *NatureScope* (series of curriculum units and supplemental activities); *Ranger Rick* (magazine for students age 6-12).

10.87 **Network for Portable Planetariums,** c/o Ms. Sue Reynolds, Planetarium Specialist, Onondaga-Cortlandt-Madison BOCES, P.O. Box 4774, Syracuse, NY 13221
(315) 433-2671

Nationwide network of users of portable and small stationary planetariums, established to help members deliver planetarium-based educational experiences; focused on astronomy and space science. ***Programs/services:*** Database of portable-planetarium experts throughout the world who are available for career and technical consultation and workshops; semiannual regional meetings for reviewing materials in the public domain file, demonstrating lessons and techniques, and discussing common problems. ***Publications/materials:*** Public domain file of curriculum materials and materials (pre- and post-) for planetarium visits.

10.88 **North American Association for Environmental Education,** 1255 23rd St., NW, Suite 400, Washington, DC 20037
(202) 884-8912

Professional organization of persons involved with environmental education; promotes environmental education programs and provides information about them. ***Programs/services:*** Operates **VINE (Volunteer-led Investigations of Neighborhood Ecology)** for 8-to-11-year-olds, involving urban community organizations and parents in backyard and schoolyard explorations; 1-hour to 2-day sessions at annual conference; summer and school-year institutes for VINE Follow Through, to link schoolyard investigations with constructivist learning in classrooms. ***Publications/materials:*** Supplies for VINE schoolyard programs; curriculum guidelines; *Volunteers Teaching Children: A Guide for Establishing VINE Ecology Education Programs;* VINE and other environmental education publications and catalog; newsletter.

10.89 Northwest EQUALS, FAMILY SCIENCE, Portland State University, P.O. Box 1491, Portland, OR 97201-1491
(503) 725-3045

Regional site for the EQUALS and FAMILY MATH programs produced by EQUALS of Berkeley, Calif., and the developer and national disseminator of FAMILY SCIENCE. ***Programs/services:*** **FAMILY SCIENCE,** a national outreach program designed to teach science by having children (grades K-8) and parents learn and enjoy science together; modeled after FAMILY MATH of EQUALS, FAMILY SCIENCE addresses the underrepresentation of women and ethnic and racial minorities in the sciences by demonstrating the role science plays in daily life, schooling, and future work; teacher-education workshops ranging from 1 hour to 2 days at schools and agencies, and through regional dissemination sites in 37 states; teacher-scientist partnerships. ***Publications/materials:*** *FAMILY SCIENCE* (book on implementing the program).

10.90 Pacific Planetarium Association (PPA), c/o Mr. Jon Elvert, PPA President, 2300 Leo Harris Pkwy., Eugene, OR 97401
(503) 687-STAR

Regional association of professionals from planetariums (including many that are school-based) in Alaska, California, Hawaii, Nevada, Oregon, Washington; focused primarily on astronomy and earth and space science for grades K-12. ***Programs/services:*** State in-service workshops; annual conference; scientist collaborations with individual teachers, and teacher-scientist partnerships supported by individual planetariums; information about the region's planetariums and their programs.

10.91 Project WET, Montana State University/The Watercourse, 201 Culbertson Hall, Bozeman, MT 59717
(406) 994-5392

Nonprofit supplementary education program for educators and students (grades K-12), focused on water resources and related issues; cosponsored by the Watercourse (which was created with funding from the U.S. Department of the Interior's Bureau of Reclamation) and by the Western Regional Environmental Education Council; available through Project WET coordinators in 33 states. ***Programs/services:*** Workshops and institutes for teachers; teacher-scientist collaborations; information hotline. ***Publications/materials:*** *Project WET Curriculum and Activity Guide*, with more than 90 hands-on water activities; *Science Activities* (magazine for teachers); *WETnet Newsletter; The Watershed Manager Teacher's Guide and Software; The Water Story* (magazine for students); other publications and modules.

10.92 Project WILD, 5430 Grosvenor Lane, Bethesda, MD 20814
(301) 493-5447

Nonprofit interdisciplinary, supplementary education program on conservation and environmental issues for educators (grades K-12), developed jointly by the Western Association of Fish and Wildlife Agencies and the Western Regional Environmental Education Council; available in 50 states, the District of Columbia, 10 Canadian provinces, and several foreign countries. ***Programs/services:*** Two-day workshops for educators, usually available statewide and sponsored jointly by a state's wildlife agency and department of education. ***Publications/materials:*** Available only through workshops: *Project WILD Activity Guide* (emphasizing wildlife and habitat); *Project WILD Aquatic Education Activity Guide* (emphasizing water and aquatic systems).

10.93 Quality Education for Minorities Network, 1818 N St., NW, Suite 350, Washington, DC 20036
(202) 659-1818

Programs/services: Operates the **Community Service Centers Project,** a pilot effort to establish community service centers on college and university campuses located near low-income public housing, and targeting groups underrepresented in science: Native Americans, African Americans, Mexican Americans, Native Alaskans, and Puerto Ricans. Various educational activities offered at the centers, including some to empower students and parents to become advocates for quality education.

10.94 Rocky Mountain Planetarium Association (RMPA), c/o Ms. Bess Amaral, RMPA President, Robert Goddard Planetarium, 11th and No. Main, Roswell, NM 88201
(505) 624-6744

Regional association of professionals from planetariums (including many that are school-based) in Colorado, Idaho, Montana, New Mexico, Texas, Utah, Wyoming; focused on astronomy and space science. ***Programs/services:*** Information about the region's planetariums and their programs. ***Publications/materials:*** Some supplemental activities and audiovisual materials produced by individual planetariums, available from the association.

10.95 School Science and Mathematics Association, Department of Curriculum and Foundations, Bloomsburg University, 400 E. Second St., Bloomsburg, PA 17815-1301
(717) 389-4915

Organization with 1,100 members—science and mathematics teachers (elementary school through college)—emphasizing integration of science and mathematics. ***Programs/services:*** Workshops at annual meetings. ***Publications/materials:*** Curriculum units emphasizing science-mathematics integration; *Topics for Teachers* (monograph series); *Classroom Activities* (monograph series); *School Science and Mathematics* (journal); newsletter.

10.96 Science-by-Mail, Museum of Science, Boston; Science Park, Boston, MA 02114-1099
(800)-729-3300

National NSF-supported program: students (grades 4-9), supported and mentored by a pen pal scientist, work in small teams on two thematic "challenge packets"and one Big Challenge in science and technology per year. ***Services:*** Organization of teams and recruitment and matching of scientists by 11 science and children's museums in different parts of the country. ***Publications/materials:*** Hands-on packets with 4 to 6 theme-oriented experiments and the Big Challenge, containing materials to do the experiments, solve the challenge, and correspond with scientist mentors; instructional guide for each unit.

10.97 Sigma Xi, The Scientific Research Society, 99 Alexander Dr., P.O. Box 13975, Research Triangle Park, NC 22709
(800) 243-6534

Interdisciplinary honor society of more than 90,000 research scientists and engineers affiliated with some 500 local Sigma Xi groups throughout North America. ***Programs/services:*** Available mostly through local Sigma Xi groups: teacher-scientist partnerships; speakers bureaus; classroom demonstrations; curriculum development with teachers; sponsorship of science fairs; lab visits for students; scientist mentors for students. ***Publications/materials:*** From Society headquarters: *Scientists and Science Education* (annual report on the activities of the local groups); brochures to promote scientist-teacher partnerships and scientist involvement in reform efforts; names and addresses of the officers of local Sigma Xi groups. From local groups: curriculum guidelines and units; audiovisual and computer-based materials; lab equipment/supplies for loan or as gift.

10.98 Smithsonian Institution, Office of Elementary and Secondary Education, Arts and Industries Bldg., Rm. 1163, Washington, DC 20560
(202) 357-2425

Smithsonian Institution's central office for precollege education, drawing on the entire Smithsonian complex of museums, exhibitions, collections, and staff expertise to create a range of materials and programs. ***Programs/services:*** Summer seminars for teachers; Smithsonian Online on Internet. ***Publications/materials:*** Supplemental curriculum materials; "Mystery at the Museum" (videogame); *Art-to-Zoo* (journal); newsletter.

10.99 Society for Advancement of Chicanos and Native Americans in Science (SACNAS), Applied Sciences, Trailer #5, University of California at Santa Cruz, Santa Cruz, CA 95064
(408) 459-4272

Society of 600 professionals in science and education seeking to increase the participation of Latinos and Native Americans in science. ***Programs/services:*** Teacher workshops at annual meeting. ***Publications/materials:*** Newsletter, with a section on K-12 programs.

10.100 Society of Automotive Engineers, International, 400 Commonwealth Dr., Warrendale, PA 15096-0001
(412) 776-4841

Society of 60,000 engineers and scientists concerned with self-propelled vehicles on land and sea and in air and space. ***Programs/services:*** **World in Motion** project to help educate elementary school children; database of engineers and scientists who are available to help teachers and for collaborations and partnerships with teachers. ***Publications/materials:*** Curriculum units with hands-on materials; supplementary activities; audiovisual materials; posters.

10.101 Soil and Water Conservation Society, 7515 Northeast Ankeny Rd., Ankeny, IA 50021
(800) THE-SOIL

Multidisciplinary educational and scientific organization for professionals in natural resource management, with many activities carried out by local chapters. ***Programs/services:*** Teacher workshops; database of scientists who are available to help teachers; teacher-scientist partnerships; response to teacher requests for scientific information; internships and summer fellowships for teachers. ***Publications/materials:*** Cartoon booklets on natural resource topics for students (ages 8-11), and related teacher's guides.

10.102 Southeast Planetarium Association (SPA), c/o Ms. Kris McCall, SPA President, Sudekum Planetarium, 800 Ridley Blvd., Nashville, TN 37203
(615) 401-5077

Regional association of professionals from planetariums (including many that are school-based) in Alabama, Florida, Georgia, Kentucky, Louisiana, Mississippi, North Carolina, South Carolina, Tennessee, Virginia, West Virginia, and Puerto Rico; focused primarily on astronomy and earth science, and also on the physical sciences and biology. ***Programs/services:*** Sessions at annual meeting; database of scientists who are available to help teachers; promotion of scientist collaboration with individual teachers; information about the region's planetariums and their programs. ***Publications/materials:*** Newsletter.

10.103 Southwest Association of Planetariums (SWAP), c/o Mr. Bow Walker, SWAP President, Hudnall Planetarium, Tyler Junior College, P.O. Box 9020, Tyler, TX 75711
(903) 510-2312

Regional association of professionals from planetariums (including many that are school-based) in Arkansas, New Mexico, Oklahoma, and Texas; focused on astronomy and space science. ***Programs/services:*** Annual conference; information about the region's planetariums and their programs. ***Publications/materials:*** Newsletter.

10.104 SWOOPE (Students Watching Over Our Planet Earth), Rte. 6, Box 211, Fairmont, WV 26554
(304) 363-4309

Environmental education program in more than 1,100 schools in 50 states, the District of Columbia, Puerto Rico, Guam, and several foreign countries; creates and coordinates science research projects on environmental topics for students (grades K-12), and promotes collaborations over the Internet [e-mail: kanawha@aol.com] among schools nationwide; enrolls only teachers. ***Services:*** Provides teacher support through newsletters, online discussions, and individual support; creates computer protocols and links schools; sets research problems for students; processes and disseminates research results. ***Publications/materials:*** Background materials; hands-on laboratory activities.

10.105 TERC, 2067 Massachusetts Ave., Cambridge, MA 02140
(617) 547-0430;
e-mail: communications@terc.edu

Nonprofit education research and development organization focused on science and mathematics learning and teaching. ***Programs/services:*** **The Hub** (electronic source of materials and information). ***Publications/materials:*** *National Geographic Kids Network* (*see* 10.73), developed with National Geographic Society; **LabNet,** an electronic community of elementary and secondary teachers that fosters science and mathematics teaching; **Tabletop Junior** software for visualization in data collection and analysis; *Hands On!* (periodical on science, math, and technology education); publications on telecommunications.

10.106 Triangle Coalition for Science and Technology Education, 5112 Berwyn Rd., College Park, MD 20740-4129
(301) 220-0870

Coalition with representation from more than 100 member organizations, including business, industry, and labor, scientific and engineering societies, education associations, and government agencies, working to link national efforts at science education reform with local schools and school districts. ***Programs/services:*** Promotes collaborations and partnerships between teachers and volunteer scientists through several hundred action groups or alliances. ***Publications/materials:*** *Guide for Building an Alliance* and *Guide for Planning a Volunteer Program,* both dealing with science, mathematics, and technology education; numerous reports on reform efforts, state and federal programs, and other issues in science education; newsletter.

10.107 United States Space Foundation, 2860 So. Circle Dr., Suite 2301, Colorado Springs, CO 80906-4184
(800) 691-4000

Nonprofit organization with more than 1,200 corporate and individual members; promotes awareness of and support for U.S. space endeavors and includes an active education department and a NASA Regional Teacher Resource Center (*see* 10.59). ***Programs/services:*** **Getting Comfortable Teaching with Space:** graduate course in several states and in-service teacher workshops nationwide; **Space Discovery Adventure Workshops** for Colorado Springs teachers. ***Publications/materials:*** *Teaching With Space: K-6 Aviation, Space and Technology Resource Guide;* newsletter.

10.108 **U.S. Department of Agriculture; Cooperative State, Research, Education, and Extension Service,** Rm. 3441, South Bldg., Washington, DC 20250-0904
(202) 720-2908

Several programs concerned in whole or in part with science education are related to the 4-H programs of the U.S. Department of Agriculture:

- **Families, 4-H, and Nutrition**—School enrichment programs to encourage interest in mathematics and science; coordinated by State 4-H Leaders through County Cooperative Extension Services of land grant universities.
- **4-H SERIES and 4-H YES Projects** (*see* 10.42).
- **National Network for Science and Technology** (*see* 10.76).

10.109 **U.S. Department of Education, Office of Educational Research and Improvement,** 555 New Jersey Ave., NW, Washington, DC 20208
(202) 219-2050

An office of the U.S. Department of Education that supports research and disseminates information. Among its many other activities, this office operates or supports the following:

- [(202) 219-2116] Ten **Eisenhower Regional Mathematics and Science Education Consortia,** which provide information, technical assistance, and training to states, schools, and teachers to help improve mathematics and science programs and adapt and use exemplary instructional materials, teaching methods, curricula, and assessment tools. Located in Andover, Mass.; Aurora, Colo.; Austin, Tex.; Charleston, W.Va.; Honolulu, Hawaii; Montpelier, Vt.; Oak Brook, Ill.; Philadelphia, Pa.; Portland, Oreg.; Tallahassee, Fla.
- **ERIC (Educational Resources Information Center) Clearinghouse** (*see* 10.41).
- **Eisenhower National Clearinghouse for Mathematics and Science Education** (*see* 10.37).
- [(202) 219-2116] **Javits Gifted and Talented Students Education Program,** which funds projects to help schools teach students who are gifted and talented, especially if they are disadvantaged, handicapped, or have limited English.
- [(202) 219-1761] **National Assessment of Educational Progress,** which measures educational achievement of students in grades 4, 8, and 12, and, for science, uses a hands-on task and portfolio.
- [(202) 219-2134] **National Diffusion Network (NDN),** a system for disseminating more than 70 programs, products, and processes in mathematics, science, and technology education. After evaluation of educational resources by the U.S. Department of Education's Program Effectiveness Panel, NDN helps schools introduce programs into classrooms with a person-to-person system, using state facilitators, program developers, and certified trainers.
- [(202) 219-2187] Ten **Regional Educational Laboratories** that do applied research and development on educational programs, materials, and professional development and that work with states and localities to implement systemic school improvement. Located in Andover, Mass.; Aurora, Colo.; Austin, Tex.; Charleston, W.Va.; Honolulu, Hawaii; Oak Brook, Ill.; Philadelphia, Pa.; Portland, Oreg.; San Francisco, Calif.; and Tallahassee, Fla.
- [(202) 219-2097] **Star Schools Program,** which funds partnerships using telecommunications and distant-learning technologies (for example, satellites, fiber optics, computer networks) to improve education.
- [(202) 219-2143] **Teacher Networking Project,** a national grants program to make electronic networks and online services tools for professional development of teachers.

10.110 **U.S. Department of Education, Office of Elementary and Secondary Education,** 400 Maryland Ave., SW, Washington, DC 20208
(202) 401-0113

Programs/services: An office of the U.S. Department of Education supporting elementary and secondary education through programs for compensatory education, school improvement, special student populations, the **Eisenhower Mathematics and Science Education State Formula Grants Program,** and the **Christa McAuliffe Fellowship Program** for outstanding teachers.

10.111 **U.S. Department of Education, Office of Elementary and Secondary Education, School Effectiveness Division,** 600 Independence Ave., SW, Portals 4500, Washington, DC 20202-6140
(202) 260-2666

Programs/services: Division in the Office of Elementary and Secondary Education that operates the **Eisen-**

hower Professional Development State Grants Program, which supports teacher enhancement programs through both in-service and preservice training, via state educational agencies to local school systems.

10.112 **U.S. Department of Energy, Office of Science Education and Technical Information,** 1000 Independence Ave., SW, Washington, DC 20585

Office in the U.S. Department of Energy (DOE) that operates the following:

- [(202) 586-5779] **National Geographic Kids Network** (*see* 10.73), a training program for teachers, offered at selected DOE research laboratories and facilities, on this program of the National Geographic Society.
- [(202) 586-8949] **PreFreshman Enrichment Program (PREP),** which supports summer enrichment institutes for students (grades 6-10) at many community colleges, colleges, and universities nationwide, with academic-year follow-up.

10.113 **U.S. Department of the Interior, Bureau of Land Management, Anasazi Heritage Center,** P.O. Box 758, 27501 Hwy. 184, Dolores, CO 81323
(970) 882-4811

Programs/services: The national **Heritage Education Program,** focused on archaeology, history, and paleontology, provides educational experiences and teaching resources for schools, museums, and outdoor classrooms (grades 4-7).

10.114 **U.S. Department of the Interior, Bureau of Reclamation Environmental Education Program,** P.O. Box 25007 (D-5100), Denver, CO 80225-0007
(303) 236-9336, Ext. 223

Programs/services: Presents indoor and outdoor programs for students and teachers (grades K-12) on many environmental subjects, especially water, at many locales in all states west of the Mississippi.

10.115 **U.S. Department of the Interior, Earth Science Information Centers,** 507 National Center, Reston, VA 22092
(800) USA-MAPS

Programs/services: Nationwide information and sales centers for U.S. Geological Survey's map products and earth science publications. Centers located in Anchorage, Alaska; Denver, Colo.; Menlo Park, Calif.; Reston, Va.; Rolla, Mo.; Salt Lake City, Utah; Sioux Falls, S.Dak.; Spokane, Wash.; Stennis Space Center, Miss.

10.116 **U.S. Department of the Interior, National Park Service,** P.O. Box 37127, Suite 560, Washington, DC 20013-7127
(202) 523-5270

Programs/services: The National Park Service's **Parks as Classrooms Program** arranges workshops for teachers at more than 270 sites of the National Park Service to encourage building curricula around National Park resources; many sites have workshops focused at least in part on science.

10.117 **U.S. Department of the Interior, Watchable Wildlife,** Western Fish and Wildlife Staff, 3380 Americana Terr., Boise, ID 83706
(208) 384-3088

Programs/services: Twenty-eight-state network of state wildlife coalitions, with more than 2,400 wildlife-viewing areas; coordinated by state wildlife agencies, and offering guidebooks to state Watchable Wildlife facilities.

10.118 **U.S. Department of Transportation, Federal Aviation Administration, Aviation Education Division (AHR-15),** 800 Independence Ave., SW, Washington, DC 20591

Programs/services: Programs and services through the Aviation Education Division of the Federal Aviation Administration (FAA) include the following:

- [(202) 366-7500] **Aviation Education Resource Centers,** a national network at colleges, museums, and state aviation offices targeting grades K-12; centers disseminate FAA educational materials (print materials, videotapes, educational software); center personnel provide general information, conduct workshops, make presentations.
- [(202) 366-7500] **Aviation Education Workshops for Teachers** are held annually at colleges and universities nationwide to prepare teachers to teach aviation; FAA provides materials, speakers, and information.

10.119 **U.S. Environmental Protection Agency,** 401 M St., SW, Washington, DC 20460

Programs and services of the Environmental Protection Agency (EPA) include the following:

- [(202) 260-8619; Mail Code 1707] **Environmental Education Grants Program,** operated by EPA's Environmental Education Division (at address above), supports projects of state and local agencies and nonprofit organizations that design, demonstrate, or disseminate new approaches in environmental education—projects with wide potential applicability and addressing high-priority issues.
- [(202) 260-0578; Mail Code H-8105] **EPA Research Laboratory-based Education Programs** offer teaching materials, workshops, lab visits, class presentations, and in-service events (grades K-12) in the localities of 13 EPA research laboratories (4 at Research Triangle Park, N.C.; 2 in Cincinnati, Ohio; and 1 each in Las Vegas, Nev.; Ada, Okla.; Athens, Ga.; Gulf Breeze, Fla.; Duluth, Minn.; Corvallis, Oreg.; and Narragansett, R.I.).
- [(202) 260-7751; Mail Code 3404] Ten **Public Information Centers (PICs)** offering environmental education materials (such as publications, data, and exhibits) for students and teachers (grades K-12); located at regional EPA offices in Atlanta, Boston, Chicago, Dallas, Denver, Kansas City, New York, Philadelphia, San Francisco, and Seattle.

10.120 Young Astronaut Council, 1308 19th St., NW, Washington, DC 20036
(202) 682-1984

Corporation formed by the White House in 1984 to administer the **Young Astronaut Program,** a national education program promoting the study of science, technology, and mathematics by building on the excitement of space; with more than 27,000 Young Astronaut Chapters in every state and in 42 foreign countries. ***Programs/services:*** **Space School,** a live, interactive satellite TV course (grades 4-6); annual student conference; multidisciplinary competitions. ***Publications/materials:*** Space School teacher kit with resource pages and activity sheets, tracking the Space School TV program; year-long curriculum for school-based Young Astronaut Chapters.

10.121 Young Entomologists' Society, 1915 Peggy Pl., Lansing, MI 48910-2553
(517) 887-0499

Educational organization of more than 700 youth and amateur adult entomology enthusiasts. ***Programs/services:*** Insect science workshops; "Buggy Bookstore" with mail-order catalog, offering a wide selection of entomological handbooks, manuals, resource guides, educational materials, and related products. ***Publications/materials:*** *Insect World* (semimonthly "bug-info-letter" for students ages 6-11); curriculum and supplementary materials; audiovisual materials; bimonthly newsletter for students; extensive bibliography; posters.

APPENDIX A: PUBLISHERS AND SUPPLIERS

Appendix A provides names, addresses, and phone and fax numbers for the publishers and suppliers of books and materials annotated in this guide. The list is arranged alphabetically.

Some companies distribute print publications and curriculum materials or science apparatus as well, and some only one or the other of these categories. Before placing an order, readers should contact the publishers or suppliers directly for current ordering information (including shipping charges).

In compiling the guide, every effort was made to provide accurate, up-to-date bibliographic information. Annually updated information can be found in directories such as *NSTA Science Education Suppliers* (see 7.21), or in standard references such as *Books in Print* at local libraries or bookstores.

The annotations in this guide provide International Standard Book Numbers (ISBNs), when those were assigned, to help readers obtain commercially distributed materials. Some publishers use their own catalog numbers, however, so publishers should be consulted before ordering an item.

Readers are urged to seek out local sources for commercial products and recycled materials. They may also want to contact the new suppliers that are continually opening their doors.

AAAS (American Association for the Advancement of Science)
Education Department
1333 H St., NW
Washington, DC 20005
(202) 326-6605
Fax: (202) 371-9849

AAAS (American Association for the Advancement of Science)
Project on Science, Technology, and Disability
1333 H St., NW
Washington, DC 20005
(202) 326-6630
Fax: (202) 371-9849

Acorn Naturalists
17300 E. 17th St.
Suite J-236
Tustin, CA 92680
(800) 422-8886
Fax: (800) 452-2802

Addison-Wesley Publishing Company
School Services
One Jacob Way
Reading, MA 01867
(800) 552-2259
Fax: (800) 333-3328

AIMS Education Foundation
P.O. Box 8120
Fresno, CA 93747-8120
(209) 255-4094
Fax: (209) 255-6396

Air and Waste Management Association
Public Education Programs
One Gateway Center
3rd Floor
Pittsburgh, PA 15222
(412) 232-3444
Fax: (412) 232-3450

Allyn and Bacon
(*See* Prentice Hall/Allyn and Bacon)

Alpha Publishing Company
1910 Hidden Point Rd.
Annapolis, MD 21401-9720
(800) 842-6696
Fax: (410) 757-7868

American Chemical Society
(To order periodicals)
P.O. Box 3337
Columbus, Ohio 43210
(800) 333-9511
Fax: (614) 447-3671

American Forest Foundation
1111 19th St., NW
Washington, DC 20036
(202) 463-2462
Fax: (202) 463-2461

American Water Works Association
Member Services
6666 W. Quincy Ave.
Denver, CO 80235
(800) 926-7337
Fax: (303) 347-0804

Association for Supervision and Curriculum Development
1259 No. Pitt St.
Alexandria, VA 22314-1403
(703) 549-9110
Fax: (703) 549-3891

Association of Science-Technology Centers
1025 Vermont Ave., NW
Washington, DC 20005
(202) 783-7200
Fax: (202) 783-7207

Beech Tree Books
William Morrow and Company
1350 Avenue of the Americas
New York, NY 10019
(800) 843-9389
Fax: (201) 227-6849

R. R. Bowker
P.O. Box 31
New Providence, NJ 07974
(800) 521-8110
Fax: (908) 665-6688

BP International
(*See* Chemical Industry Education Centre)

California Academy of Sciences
Department of Educational Media
Golden Gate Park
San Francisco, CA 94118
(415) 750-7114
Fax: (415) 750-7346

California Foundation for Agriculture in the Classroom
1601 Exposition Blvd., FB 16
Sacramento, CA 95815
(916) 942-4380
Fax: (916) 923-5318

Cambridge University Press
(Distribution Center for curriculum units from Cambridge University Press, Cambridge, England, and Melbourne, Australia)
110 Midland Ave.
Port Chester, NY 10573-4930
(914) 937-9600
Fax: (914) 937-4712

Carolina Biological Supply Company
2700 York Rd.
Burlington, NC 27215
(800) 334-5551
Fax: (800) 222-7112

Carson-Dellosa Publishing Company
P.O. Box 35665
Greensboro, NC 27425-5665
(800) 321-0943
Fax: (800) 535-2669

CESI
(*See* Council for Elementary Science International)

Chemical Industry Education Centre
University of York
Heslington, York YO1 5DD
United Kingdom
011-44-1904-432600
Fax: 011-44-1904-432605

Children's Book Council
568 Broadway
Suite 404
New York, NY 10012
(212) 966-1990
Fax: (212) 966-2073

Children's Television Workshop
(For *Kid City*)
P.O. Box 53349
Boulder, CO 80322-3349
(800) 678-0613

Children's Television Workshop
(For *3-2-1 Contact*)
P.O. Box 53051
Boulder, CO 80322-3051
(800) 678-0613

Cobblestone Publishing
7 School St.
Peterborough, NH 03458
(603) 924-7209
Fax: (603) 924-7380

College of William and Mary, Center for Gifted Education
232 Jamestown Rd.
Williamsburg, VA 23185
(804) 221-2362
Fax: (804) 221-2184

The Communication Project
(*See* Scholastic Canada)

Cornell University
Instructional Materials Service
Department of Education
420 Kennedy Hall
Ithaca, NY 14853
(607) 255-1837
Fax: (607) 255-7905

Corwin Press
2455 Teller Rd.
Thousand Oaks, CA 91320
(805) 499-0721
Fax: (805) 499-0871

Council for Elementary Science International (CESI)
c/o Dr. John Penick, Publications Coordinator
789 Van Allen
Iowa City, IA 52242
(319) 335-1183
Fax: (319) 335-1188

The Cousteau Society
870 Greenbrier Circle, Suite 402
Chesapeake, VA 23320
(804) 523-9335
Fax: (804) 523-2747

Creative Publications
5623 W. 115th St.
Worth, IL 60482
(800) 624-0822
Fax: (800) 624-0821

Creative Ventures
P.O. Box 2286
West Lafayette, IN 47906

Cuisenaire Company of America
10 Bank St.
P.O. Box 5026
White Plains, NY 10606
(800) 237-3142
Fax: (914) 997-2192

Curriculum Publications Clearinghouse
Western Illinois University
Horrabin Hall 46
Macomb, IL 61455
(309) 298-1411
Fax: (309) 298-2869

Dale Seymour Publications
P.O. Box 10888
Palo Alto, CA 94303
(800) 872-1100
(415) 324-3424

Dellasta
(*See* Mondo Publishing; Dellasta publications available in United States from Mondo.)

Delmar
(*See distributor:* International Thomson Publishing)

Delmarva Power
Manager, Consumer and Community Relations
800 King St.
P.O. Box 231
Wilmington, DE 19899
(302) 429-3250
Fax: (302) 429-3618

Delta Education
P.O. Box 915
Hudson, NH 03051-0915
(800) 258-1302
Fax: (800) 880-6520

Discover Science Program
105 Terry Dr.
Suite 120
Newtown, PA 18940-3425
(800) 523-5948
Fax: (215) 579-8589

Education Development Center
55 Chapel St.
Newton, MA 02158-1060
(617) 969-7100
Fax: (617) 332-4318

Educational Products Information Exchange (EPIE) Institute
103-3 W. Montauk Hwy.
Hampton Bays, NY 11946
(516) 728-9100
Fax: (516) 728-9228

Educators Progress Service
214 Center St.
Randolph, WI 53956
(414) 326-3126
Fax: (414) 326-3127

Eisenhower National Clearinghouse
1929 Kenny Rd.
Columbus, OH 43210-1079
(614) 292-7784
(800) 621-5785
Fax: (614) 292-2066

Encyclopaedia Britannica Educational Corporation
310 So. Michigan Ave.
Chicago, IL 60604-9839
(800) 554-9862
Fax: (312) 347-7903

Enslow Publishing
Bloy St. and Ramsey Ave.
Box 777
Hillside, NJ 07205
(800) 398-2504
Fax: (908) 964-4116

ERIC Clearinghouse for Science, Mathematics, and Environmental Education
The Ohio State University
1929 Kenny Rd.
Columbus, OH 43210-1080
(800) 276-0462
Fax: (614) 292-0263

Evans Brothers
(*See* Trafalgar Square; Evans Brothers publications available in United States from Trafalgar Square.)

The Exploratorium
Mail Order Dept.
3601 Lyon St.
San Francisco, CA 94123
(800) 359-9899
Fax: (415) 561-0307

Federal Emergency Management Agency
P.O. Box 70274
Washington, DC 20024
(202) 646-2812
Fax: (202) 646-3104

Follett Software Company
1391 Corporate Dr.
McHenry, IL 60050-7041
(800) 323-3397
(815) 344-8700
Fax: (815) 344-8774

4-H Youth Programs, Cooperative Extension Service, Michigan State University
(*See* 4-H Youth Programs, Michigan State University Extension)

4-H Youth Programs
Michigan State University Extension
6H Berkey Hall
East Lansing, MI 48824-1111
(517) 355-0180
Fax: (517) 355-6748

Franklin Institute Science Museum
20th & The Benjamin Franklin Pkwy.
Philadelphia, PA 19103
(215) 448-1200
Fax: (215) 448-1235

Franklin Watts
5440 No. Cumberland Ave.
Chicago, IL 60656
(800) 672-6672
Fax: (312) 374-4329

Fulcrum Publishing Company
350 Indiana St.
Suite 350
Golden, CO 80401
(800) 992-2908
Fax: (303) 279-7111

Geothermal Education Office
664 Hilary Dr.
Tiburon, CA 94920
(800) 866-4436
(415) 435-7737

Good Apple
1204 Buchanan St.
P.O. Box 299
Carthage, IL 62321-0299
(800) 435-7234
Fax: (217) 357-3987

Great Plains National (GPN)
P.O. Box 80669
Lincoln, NE 68501-0669
(800) 228-4630
Fax: (402) 472-4076

Harcourt Brace and Company, Australia
30-52 Smidmore St.
Locked Bag 16
Marrickville NSW 2204
Australia

Harcourt Brace Jovanovich (Australia)
(*See* Harcourt Brace and Company, Australia)

Harcourt Brace Publishers
6277 Sea Harbor Drive
Orlando, FL 32887
(800) 782-4479
(800) 433-0001 (FL)
Fax: (800) 874-6418

HarperCollins
1000 Keystone Industrial Park
Scranton, PA 18512-4621
(800) 982-4377
Fax: (800) 922-4090

Heinemann/Heinemann Educational Books
361 Hanover St.
Portsmouth, NH 03801
(800) 541-2086
(603) 431-7894
Fax: (800) 847-0938

Heldref Publications
1319 18th St., NW
Washington, DC 20036-1802
(800) 365-9753
(202) 296-6267
Fax: (202) 296-5149

Holt, Rinehart and Winston
(*See distributor:* Harcourt Brace Publishers, Orlando, FL)

How the Weatherworks
1522 Baylor Ave.
Rockville, MD 20850
(301) 762-7669

Idea Factory
10710 Dixon Dr.
Riverview, FL 33569
(800) 331-6204
Fax: (813) 677-0373

International Society for Technology in Education (ISTE)
1789 Agate St.
Eugene, OR 97403-1923
(503) 346-4414
Fax: (503) 346-5890

International Thomson Publishing
7625 Empire Dr.
Florence, KY 41042
(800) 347-7707
Fax: (800) 451-3661

Jossey-Bass Publishers
350 Sansome St.
San Francisco, CA 94104
(415) 433-1767
Fax: (800) 605-BOOK

Keep America Beautiful
Mill River Plaza
9 W. Broad St.
Stamford, CT 06902
(203) 323-8987
Fax: (203) 325-9199

Kendall/Hunt Publishing Company
4050 Westmark Dr.
Dubuque, IA 52002
(800) 700-3544
Fax: (800) 772-9165

Kids Can Press
29 Birch Ave.
Toronto, Ontario M4V 1E2
Canada

Kids Discover
170 Fifth Ave.
6th Floor
New York, NY 10010
(800) 284-8276

Klutz Press
2121 Staunton Ct.
Palo Alto, CA 94306
(415) 857-0888
Fax: (415) 857-9110

Kraus International Publications
358 Saw Mill River Rd.
Millwood, NY 10546-1035
(800) 223-8323
Fax: (914) 762-1195

LaMotte Company
P.O. Box 329
Chestertown, MD 21620
(800) 344-3100
Fax: (410) 778-6394

Lawrence Erlbaum Associates
365 Broadway
Hillsdale, NJ 07642
(800) 926-6579
Fax: (210) 236-0072

Lawrence Hall of Science
(*See* LHS GEMS or LHS GEMS/PEACHES)

Learning
P.O. Box 54294
Boulder, CO 80322
(800) 753-1843

Learning Spectrum
1390 Westridge Dr.
Portola Valley, CA 94028
(800) 873-7672
Fax: (415) 851-7871

The Learning Team
10 Long Pond Rd.
Armonk, NY 10504
(800) 793-TEAM
Fax: (914) 273-2227

LEGO Dacta
P.O. Box 1600
Enfield, CT 06083-1600
(800) 527-8339
Fax: (203) 763-2466

Let's Get Growing
1900 Commercial Way
Santa Cruz, CA 95065
(408) 464-1868

LHS GEMS
Lawrence Hall of Science
University of California
Berkeley, CA 94720
(510) 642-7771
Fax: (510) 643-0309

LHS GEMS/PEACHES
Lawrence Hall of Science
University of California
Berkeley, CA 94720
(510) 642-7771
Fax: (510) 643-0309

Linda Poore
1964 La France Ave.
South Pasadena, CA 91030
(818) 441-2048 (same for voice & fax)

Macmillan Publishing Company
(*See distributor:* Prentice Hall/Allyn and Bacon)

Massachusetts Audubon Society
Educational Resources
South Great Rd.
Lincoln, MA 01773
(617) 259-9500
Fax: (617) 259-8899

Michigan State University Bulletin Office
10B Agriculture Hall
Michigan State University
East Lansing, MI 48824-1039
(517) 353-6740
Fax: (517) 353-7168

The Mid-Atlantic Center for Race Equity
(*See* Mid-Atlantic Equity Consortium)

Mid-Atlantic Equity Center, American University
(*See* Mid-Atlantic Equity Consortium)

Mid-Atlantic Equity Consortium
5454 Wisconsin Ave.
Suite 655
Chevy Chase, MD 20815
(301) 657-7741
Fax: (301) 657-8782

Milliken Publishing Company
1100 Research Blvd.
St. Louis, MO 63132
(800) 325-4136
Fax: (314) 991-4807

Mondo Publishing
One Plaza Rd.
Greenvale, NY 11050
(800) 242-3650
Fax: (516) 484-7813

Montgomery County Public Schools
Division of Academic Programs
Office of Instruction and Program Development
Elementary Science Coordinator
850 Hungerford Dr.
CESC Rm. 258
Rockville, MD 20850
(301) 279-3421
Fax: (301) 279-3153

Morrow Junior Books
1350 Avenue of the Americas
New York, NY 10019
(800) 843-9389
Fax: (212) 261-6689

Museum of Science
Science Kit Rental Program
Science Park
Boston, MA 02114-1099
(800) 722-5487
Fax: (617) 589-0474

National Academy Press
2101 Constitution Ave., NW
Lockbox 285
Washington, DC 20055
(800) 624-6242
(202) 334-3313 (Washington, DC, metropolitan area)
Fax: (202) 334-2451

National Air and Space Museum
Office of Education
Smithsonian, MRC-305
Washington, DC 20560
(202) 786-2101

National Arbor Day Foundation
100 Arbor Ave.
Nebraska City, NE 68410
(402) 474-5655
Fax: (402) 474-0820

National Association of Biology Teachers
11250 Roger Bacon Dr.
Reston, VA 22090
(800) 406-0775
Fax: (703) 435-5582

National Center for Improving Science Education
(*See* The Network)
2000 L St., NW
Suite 603
Washington, DC 20036
(202) 467-0652
Fax: (202) 467-0659

National Consortium for Environmental Education and Training
University of Michigan
School of Natural Resources and Environment
Dana Building
430 East University Ave.
Ann Arbor, MI 48109-1195
(313) 998-6726
Fax: (313) 998-6580

National Energy Foundation
5225 Wiley Post Way
Suite 170
Salt Lake City, UT 84116
(801) 539-1406
Fax: (801) 539-1451

National Energy Information Center
U.S. Department of Energy
Forrestal Bldg. - EI-231
Room 1F-048
1000 Independence Ave., SW
Washington, DC 20585
(202) 586-8800
Fax: (202) 586-0727

National 4-H Council
(*See* National 4-H Supply Service)

National 4-H Council Environmental Stewardship Program
(*See* National 4-H Supply Service)

National 4-H Supply Service
7100 Connecticut Ave.
Chevy Chase, MD 20815
(301) 961-2934
Fax: (301) 961-2937

National Gardening Association
180 Flynn Ave.
Burlington, VT 05401
(800) LETSGRO
Fax: (800) 863-5962

National Geographic Society
Educational Services
1145 17th St., NW
Washington, DC 20036-4688
(800) 368-2728
Fax: (301) 921-1575

National Geographic Society
(To order periodicals)
P.O. Box 2330
Washington, DC 20078-9955
(800) NGS-LINE
Fax: (301) 921-1575

National Science Resources Center
Smithsonian Institution, MRC-403
Arts and Industries Bldg.
Room 1201
Washington, DC 20560
(202) 357-2555
Fax: (202) 786-2028

National Science Teachers Association
(Formerly located in Washington, DC; currently in Arlington, VA; see next entry.)

National Science Teachers Association
1840 Wilson Blvd.
Arlington, VA 22201-3000
(800) 722-NSTA
Fax: (703) 522-6091

National Wildlife Federation
(To order curriculum units)
8925 Leesburg Pike
Vienna, VA 22184
(800) 432-6564

National Wildlife Federation
(To order periodicals)
P.O. Box 777
Mount Morris, IL 61054-8276
(800) 588-1650
Fax: (815) 734-1223

The Network
300 Brickstone Sq.
Suite 900
Andover, MA 01810
(800) 877-5400
Fax: (508) 475-9220

Office of Elementary and Secondary Education
Smithsonian Institution, MRC-402
Arts and Industries Bldg.
Room 1163
Washington, DC 20560
(202) 357-2425
Fax: (202) 357-2116

Optical Data Corporation
30 Technology Dr.
Warren, NJ 07059
(800) 524-2481
Fax: (908) 755-0577

Owl Communications
25 Boxwood Lane
Buffalo, NY 14227
(800) 387-4379 (U.S.)
Fax: (416) 971-5294 (Canada)

Oxford University Press
2001 Evans Road
Cary, NC 27513
(800) 451-7556
Fax: (919) 677-1303

Prentice Hall/Allyn and Bacon
200 Old Tappan Rd.
Old Tappan, NJ 07675
(800) 233-1360
Fax: (800) 445-6991

Project WILD
5430 Grosvenor Lane
Bethesda, MD 20814
(301) 493-5447
Fax: (301) 493-5627

Reading Is Fundamental
600 Maryland Ave., SW
Suite 600
Washington, DC 20024
(202) 287-3220
Fax: (202) 287-3196

The Regional School Energy Extension Project, Energy Center, Sonoma State University
(*See* SSU Academic Foundation)

Santa Barbara Botanic Garden
1212 Mission Canyon Rd.
Santa Barbara, CA 93105
(805) 682-4726
Fax: (805) 563-0352

Santa Barbara County Education Office
(*See* Santa Barbara Botanic Garden)

Sargent-Welch Scientific Co.
911 Commerce Ct.
Buffalo Grove, IL 60089
(510) 642-8718
Fax: (800) 676-2540

Scholastic Canada
123 Newkirk Rd.
Richmond Hill, Ontario L4C 3G5
Canada
(416) 883-5300

Scholastic Canada and The Communication Project
164 Tomlinson Circle
Markham, Ontario L34 9K2
Canada
(416) 940-2973

Scholastic, Inc.
(To order curriculum units, reference books, and periodicals except *Electronic Learning*)
2931 E. McCarty St.
Jefferson City, MO 65102
(800) 325-6149
Fax: (314) 635-5881

Scholastic, Inc.
Instructional Publishing Group
(To order Scholastic publications, contact Scholastic, Inc., Jefferson City, MO.)
555 Broadway
New York, NY 10012
(212) 343-6100

Scholastic, Inc.
(To order *Electronic Learning*)
P.O. Box 53796
Boulder, CO 80306
(800) 544-2917
Fax: (303) 604-7455

Scholastic Professional Books
(*See* Scholastic, Inc., Jefferson City, MO)

Schuylkill Center for Environmental Education
8480 Hagy's Mill Rd.
Philadelphia, PA 19128-1998
(215) 482-7300
Fax: (215) 482-8185

Science Kit and Boreal Laboratories
Elementary Science Division
777 East Park Dr.
Tonawanda, NY 14150-6764
(800) 828-7777
Fax: (716) 874-9572

Scienceland, Inc.
501 Fifth Ave., Suite 2108
New York, NY 10017-6165
(212) 490-2180
Fax: (212) 490-2187

Science Service, Inc.
Subscription Dept.
P.O. Box 1925
Marion, OH 43305
(800) 347-6969
Fax: (614) 382-5866

Science Teachers' Association of Western Australia
Suite 9
25 Walters Dr.
Osborne Park 6017
Western Australia
011-61-9-244-1987
Fax: 011-61-9-244-2601

Science Weekly, Inc.
Subscription Dept.
P.O. Box 70638
Chevy Chase, MD 20813
(800) 493-3559
(301) 656-3777
Fax: (301) 680-9240

Sea World
(*See* Sea World of California)

Sea World of California
Educational Materials
1720 South Shores Rd.
San Diego, CA 92109-7995
(800) 23-SHAMU
Fax: (619) 226-3634

SEMPCO
99 Factory St.
P.O. Box 3263
Nashua, NH 03061
(603) 889-1830

Silver Burdett Ginn
Education School Group
P.O. Box 2649
Columbus, OH 43216
(800) 848-9500
Fax: (614) 771-7361

Smithsonian Institution
(*See* Office of Elementary and Secondary Education)

Solomon Publishing
5830 Sovereign Dr.
Cincinnati, OH 45241
(513) 489-3033

SSU Academic Foundation
c/o Sonoma State University
Environmental Studies and Planning
1800 E. Cotati Ave.
Ronnert Park, CA 94928
(707) 664-2306
Fax: (707) 664-2505

Sunburst Communications
101 Castleton St.
P.O. Box 100
Pleasantville, NY 10570-0100
(800) 321-7511
Fax: (914) 747-4109

Superintendent of Documents
U.S. Government Printing Office
P.O. Box 371954
Pittsburgh, PA 15240-7954
(202) 512-1800
Fax: (202) 512-2250

Teacher Ideas Press/Libraries Unlimited
Box 6633
Englewood, CO 80155-6633
(800) 237-6124
Fax: (303) 220-8843

Teachers College Press
c/o AIDC
P.O. Box 20
Williston, VT 05495
(800) 488-2665
Fax: (802) 864-7626

Teachers' Laboratory
P.O. Box 6480
Brattleboro, VT 05302-6480
(802) 254-3457
Fax: (802) 254-5233

Tennessee Valley Authority
P.O. Box 1010
Muscle Shoals, AL 35662-1010
(205) 386-2714
Fax: (205) 386-2513

Tom Snyder Productions
80 Coolidge Hill Rd.
Watertown, MA 02172-2817
(800) 342-0236

Trafalgar Square
P.O. Box 257
North Pomfret, VT 05053
(800) 423-4525
Fax: (802) 457-1913

University of Toronto Press
5201 Dufferin St.
Downsview, Ontario M3H 5T8 Canada
(800) 565-9523
Fax: (416) 667-7832

University of Wisconsin
Center for Biology Education
Department of Plant Pathology
1630 Linden Drive
495 Russell Labs
Madison, WI 53706
(608) 262-6496
Fax: (608) 263-2626

U.S. Department of Education
Office of Educational Research and Improvement (OERI)
555 New Jersey Ave., NW
Washington, D.C. 20208-5570
(202) 219-1385
Fax: (202) 219-1402

U.S. Forest Service, Intermountain Region
Public Affairs Office
324 25th Street
Ogden, UT 85501
(801) 625-5827
Fax: (801) 625-5240

U.S. Government Printing Office
(*See* Superintendent of Documents)

U.S. Patent and Trademark Office
Office of Public Affairs
Washington, DC 20231
(703) 305-8341
Fax: (703) 308-5258

Vermont Institute of Natural Science
Churchill Road
Rural Route #2
Box 532
Woodstock, VT 05091
(802) 457-2779 (Both voice and fax)

Videodiscovery
1700 Westlake Ave., No.
Suite 600
Seattle, WA 98109-3012
(800) 548-3472
(206) 285-5400
Fax: (206) 285-9245

Videodiscovery
4658 Clinton St.
Burnaby, B.C. V5J 2K7
Canada
(604) 430-6397
Fax: (604) 451-5534

Western Illinois University
(*See* Curriculum Publications Clearinghouse)

WGBH Boston
ATTN: Print and Outreach
125 Western Ave.
Boston, MA 02134
(617) 492-2777 X3848
Fax: (617) 787-1639

The Whale Museum
P.O. Box 954
Friday Harbor, WA 98250
(206) 378-4710
Fax: (206) 378-5790

Whitman Distribution Center
10 Water St.
4th Floor
Lebanon, NH 03748
(603) 448-0317
Fax: (603) 448-2576

PUBLISHERS AND SUPPLIERS

Wildlife Education
9820 Willow Creek Rd.
Suite 300
San Diego, CA 92131-1112
(800) 477-5034
Fax: (619) 578-9658

John Wiley
1 Wiley Dr.
Somerset, NJ 08875
(800) CALL-WILEY
Fax: (908) 302-2300

William Morrow Publishing Co.
39 Plymouth St.
Fairfield, NJ 07004
(800) 943-9389
Fax: (201) 227-6849

Wings for Learning
(*See* Sunburst Communications)

Young Entomologists' Society
1915 Peggy Place
Lansing, MI 48910-2553
(517) 887-0499
Fax: (517) 887-0499

Young Naturalist Company
1900 No. Main
Newton, KS 67114
(316) 283-4103
Fax: (316) 283-9108

Zephyr Press
P.O. Box 66006
Tucson, AZ 85728
(602) 322-5090
Fax: (520) 323-9402

APPENDIX B: NSRC EVALUATION CRITERIA FOR CURRICULUM MATERIALS

Consistent with the National Science Resources Center's (NSRC's) philosophy of science teaching and with the recently published *National Science Education Standards* of the National Research Council, the materials included in *Resources for Teaching Elementary School Science* are hands-on and inquiry-centered. Briefly described, such materials provide opportunities for children to learn through direct observation and experimentation; they engage students in experiences not simply to confirm the "right" answer but to investigate the nature of things and to arrive at explanations that are scientifically correct and satisfying to children; and they offer students opportunities to experiment productively, to ask questions and find their own answers, and to develop patience, persistence, and confidence in their ability to tackle and solve real problems.

To produce evaluation criteria for identifying the most effective print instructional materials available, the NSRC drew upon three primary sources:

- the experience of teachers, superintendents, principals, and science curriculum coordinators across the United States;
- the quality standards identified by the NSRC for evaluating units of science instruction in its ongoing review of science curriculum materials under the auspices of the National Academy of Sciences and the Smithsonian Institution; and
- the National Science Education Standards, which were under development at the same time as this resource guide.

The evaluation criteria that NSRC developed were applied in the structured review process of curriculum materials for this guide. These criteria consist of two sets of questions. The first focuses on pedagogical issues, the second on science issues.

The pedagogical criteria elaborate on the following key questions: (1) Do the materials address the important goals of elementary science teaching and learning? (2) Are inquiry and activity the basis of the learning experiences? (3) Are the topic of the unit and the modes of instruction developmentally appropriate? Additional issues related to presentation and format and to hands-on science materials are then considered.

The set of criteria on science issues expands upon the key questions of whether the science content is accurate, up to date, and effectively presented. It then focuses on aspects of the way science is presented in the materials—for example, whether the writing style is interesting and engaging while respecting scientific language.

Two major considerations should be kept in mind when one is using this document:

- The NSRC evaluation criteria provide two gauges for assessing curriculum materials: first, they enunciate specific goals and, second, taken as a whole, they represent the overall level of quality necessary for materials to be effective. Therefore, while materials may not meet each individual criterion completely, they can still reach the overall level of effectiveness defined in the evaluation instrument. That is, if they offer hands-on, inquiry-centered, pedagogically and scientifically sound learning experiences, they may be considered effective even though they do not meet each specific criterion within these categories. The NSRC evaluation criteria were designed as a standard to be met, as the ideal level of quality to be sought, and as a working tool that can help inform science curriculum as it is developed.
- The expectations for core materials are more comprehensive than for supplementary materials. For example, core materials would be expected to provide assessment strategies, whereas science activity books would not. Likewise, core materials would allow students to study a concept in depth, while supplementary materials might provide only a general introduction or isolated activities.

The NSRC evaluation criteria are reprinted in full in this appendix. Teachers, curriculum specialists, curriculum developers, principals, superintendents, and those involved in various aspects of science education reform may find the criteria not only instructive, but useful as an actual review instrument when the need arises to consider the strengths and weaknesses of particular curriculum materials.

NATIONAL SCIENCE RESOURCES CENTER
SMITHSONIAN INSTITUTION • NATIONAL ACADEMY OF SCIENCES
Resources for Teaching Elementary School Science

SCIENCE INSTRUCTIONAL MATERIALS REVIEW FORM

TITLE: *or name of resource*

SERIES TITLE: *if applicable*

AUTHOR(S): *if applicable*

CITY/STATE: *where published*

PUBLISHER/SOURCE:

COPYRIGHT DATE: ISBN NO: ADVERTISED GRADE LEVEL(S): *grade(s)*

SUPPLIES: *availability of materials and kits for core curriculum materials*

COST: *suggested list price*

RESOURCE TYPE: *student activity book, teacher's guide, books on teaching science, etc.*

SUBJECT: *selected from major content categories*

Please supply the following information:

REVIEWER: ______________________________ DATE: ______________________
(reviewer's name) *(date of review)*

RECOMMENDED USER:

(check each that applies) _____ stu _____ tchr _____ adm _____ other (__________)

GRADE LEVEL(S) RECOMMENDED BY REVIEWER IF DIFFERENT FROM THE ADVERTISED LEVEL(S) STATED ABOVE:

(Please circle the specific grade level(s) for which you *believe these materials are most appropriate.)*

K 1 2 3 4 5 6 7 8 9 10 11 12

Reviewer: ______________________________

1

NATIONAL SCIENCE RESOURCES CENTER
Smithsonian Institution • National Academy of Sciences

PEDAGOGY

Instructions: The following questions are designed to help you identify the important elements of each criterion. Please respond by selecting "yes" if the material meets this goal and "no" if it does not. If "no" is selected, please explain the reason in the space provided below the question. In some instances, the question may not be applicable; then mark "NA."

CRITERIA	RATING
I. ADDRESSING THE GOALS OF ELEMENTARY SCIENCE TEACHING AND LEARNING	
Does the material focus on concrete experiences by the children with science phenomena? Reason:	Yes No NA
Does the material enable children to investigate important science concept(s) in depth over an extended period of time (core materials only)? Reason:	Yes No NA
Does the material contribute to the development of scientific reasoning and problem-solving skills? Reason:	Yes No NA
Does the material stimulate student interest and relate to their daily lives? Reason:	Yes No NA
Does the material allow for or encourage the development of scientific attitudes and habits of mind, such as curiosity, respect for evidence, flexibility, and sensitivity to living things? Reason:	Yes No NA
Are assessment strategies aligned with the goals for instruction? Reason:	Yes No NA
Will the suggested assessment strategies provide an effective means of assessing student learning? Reason:	Yes No NA

Reviewer: ______________________________

NSRC EVALUATION CRITERIA FOR CURRICULUM MATERIALS

CRITERIA	RATING
II. FOCUSING ON INQUIRY AND ACTIVITY AS THE BASIS OF LEARNING EXPERIENCES	
Does the material engage students in the processes of science? Reason:	Yes No NA
Does the material provide opportunities for students to make and record their own observations? Reason:	Yes No NA
Does the material provide opportunities for students to gather and defend their own evidence? Reason:	Yes No NA
Does the material provide opportunities for students to express their results in a variety of ways? Reason:	Yes No NA
Does the material provide opportunities for students to work collaboratively with others? Reason:	Yes No NA
Does the material include a balance of student-directed and teacher-facilitated activities? Reason:	Yes No NA

Reviewer: ______________________________

CRITERIA	RATING
III. INSTRUCTIONAL APPROACH	
Does the material present a logical sequence of related activities that will help students build conceptual understanding over several lessons? Reason:	Yes No NA
Does the suggested instructional sequence take into account children's prior knowledge and experiences? Reason:	Yes No NA
Are opportunities included to assess children's prior knowledge and experiences? Reason:	Yes No NA
Do the suggested student activities develop critical thinking and problem-solving skills? Reason:	Yes No NA
Does the material incorporate effective strategies for the teacher and/or the students to use in assessing student learning? Reason:	Yes No NA
Does the material incorporate technological applications of science and the interactions among science, technology and society? Reason:	Yes No NA
Do the subject matter and methods of instruction provide suggestions for integrating science with other important learning experiences in the elementary curriculum, such as mathematics, language arts, and social studies? Reason:	Yes No NA

Reviewer: ______________________________

ASSESSMENT OF PEDAGOGICAL APPROPRIATENESS OF MATERIALS

Please provide a *brief* overview of the concepts taught and the activities suggested in this material. It is not necessary to use complete sentences; words and brief phrases are sufficient.

With the above criteria in mind, please comment on any particular strengths in this material.

With the above criteria in mind, please comment on any particular weaknesses in this material.

After reviewing this material with only the above criteria for pedagogical appropriateness in mind, I would:

_______ recommend this material for inclusion

_______ not recommend this material for inclusion

Reviewer: ____

5

PRESENTATION AND FORMAT, MATERIALS, AND EQUITY

Instructions: The following questions are designed to help you identify the important elements of criteria involving presentation and format, materials, and equity issues. Please respond by selecting "yes" if the material meets this goal and "no" if it does not. If "no" is selected, please explain the reason in the space provided below the question. In some instances, the question may not be applicable; then mark "NA."

CRITERIA	RATING
PRESENTATION AND FORMAT	
Teacher materials: Does the background material for the teacher provide sufficient information on the scientific content? Reason:	Yes No NA
Does the background material for the teacher provide sufficient information on common student misconceptions? Reason:	Yes No NA
Is the format easy for a teacher to follow? Reason:	Yes No NA
Are the directions on implementing activities clear? Reason:	Yes No NA
Are the suggestions for instructional delivery adequate? Reason:	Yes No NA
Are the suggested times for instruction reasonable? Reason:	Yes No NA
Student materials: Are the written materials for the students well-written, age-appropriate, and compelling in content? Reason:	Yes No NA

Reviewer: ______________________________

NSRC Evaluation Criteria for Curriculum Materials

CRITERIA	RATING
HANDS-ON SCIENCE MATERIALS	
Teacher materials: Is a master source list of materials provided? Reason:	Yes No NA
Is a list of materials included for each activity? Reason:	Yes No NA
Is a complete set of materials readily available at a reasonable cost? Reason:	Yes No NA
Are refurbishment materials easily obtained and affordable? Reason:	Yes No NA
Student materials: Are the materials recommended for use appropriate for the designated age levels? Reason:	Yes No NA
Are appropriate safety precautions included, where needed? Reason:	Yes No NA
Are instructions on manipulating laboratory equipment and materials clear and adequate? Reason:	Yes No NA
SCIENCE FOR ALL	
Is the material free of cultural, racial, ethnic, gender, and age bias? Reason:	Yes No NA
Are appropriate strategies included/used to meet the needs of special/diverse populations? Reason:	Yes No NA

Reviewer: ______________________________

ASSESSMENT OF PRESENTATION AND FORMAT, HANDS-ON SCIENCE MATERIALS, AND EQUITY

With the above criteria in mind, please comment on particular strengths or weaknesses in this material.

After reviewing this material with only the above criteria for presentation and format, hands-on science materials, and equity issues in mind, I would:

________ recommend this material for inclusion

________ not recommend this material for inclusion

Reviewer: ____

RECOMMENDATION

Based upon all aspects of my review of this material,

________ I highly recommend this material for inclusion in *Resources for Teaching Elementary School Science*.

________ I recommend this material for inclusion in *Resources for Teaching Elementary School Science*.

________ I recommend this material for inclusion in *Resources for Teaching Elementary School Science* **with reservations**.

Primary reason for reservations: ____

____

____

________ I do **not** recommend this material for inclusion in *Resources for Teaching Elementary School Science*.

Primary reason for rejection: ____

____

____

Reviewer: ____

NATIONAL SCIENCE RESOURCES CENTER
SMITHSONIAN INSTITUTION • NATIONAL ACADEMY OF SCIENCES
Resources for Teaching Elementary School Science

SCIENCE INSTRUCTIONAL MATERIALS REVIEW FORM

TITLE: *or name of resource*

SERIES TITLE: *if applicable*

AUTHOR(S): *if applicable*

CITY/STATE: *where published*

PUBLISHER/SOURCE:

COPYRIGHT DATE: ISBN NO: ADVERTISED GRADE LEVEL(S): *grade(s)*

SUPPLIES: *availability of materials and kits for core curriculum materials*

COST: *suggested list price*

RESOURCE TYPE: *student activity book, teacher's guide, books on teaching science, etc.*

SUBJECT: *selected from major content categories*

The material you are reviewing has already been identified by teacher and science curriculum specialists, in a comprehensive review process, to be pedagogically effective instructional material that would support a "hands-on, constructivist, inquiry-based" elementary-school science program. Your task is to review the material (including the background information for teachers) to evaluate the science content for its accuracy and currency, and the effectiveness of its presentation.

Please supply the following information:

REVIEWER: ______________________ *(reviewer's name)* DATE: ______________________ *(date of review)*

Reviewer: ______________________

SCIENCE CONTENT, PRESENTATION, AND EQUITY

Instructions: The following questions are designed to help you identify the important elements of each criterion. Please respond by selecting "yes" if the material meets this goal and "no" if it does not. If "no" is selected, please explain the reason in the space provided below the question. In some instances, the question may not be applicable; then mark "NA."

CRITERIA	RATING
SCIENCE CONTENT	
Is the science content incorporated in the materials accurately represented? Reason:	Yes No NA
Is the science content consistent with current scientific knowledge? Reason:	Yes No NA
Are important ideas included? Reason:	Yes No NA
Are generalizations adequately supported by facts? Reason:	Yes No NA
Are facts clearly distinguished from theories? Reason:	Yes No NA
Do the suggested investigations lead to an understanding of basic principles? Reason:	Yes No NA
Do experiments and activities promote student understanding of how scientists come to know what they know and how scientists test and revise their thinking? Reason:	Yes No NA

Reviewer: ______________________________

11

CRITERIA	RATING
SCIENCE PRESENTATION	
Is science shown to be open to inquiry and controversy and free of dogmatism? Reason:	Yes No NA
Are different scientific viewpoints presented when appropriate? Reason:	Yes No NA
Are personal biases avoided? Reason:	Yes No NA
Is the writing style interesting and engaging, while respecting scientific language? Reason:	Yes No NA
Is vocabulary used to facilitate understanding rather than as an end in itself? Reason:	Yes No NA
Is science represented as an enterprise connected to society? Reason:	Yes No NA

CRITERIA	RATING
SCIENCE FOR ALL	
Is material free of cultural, racial, ethnic, gender, and age bias? Reason:	Yes No NA

Reviewer: ______________________________

ASSESSMENT OF SCIENCE CONTENT, PRESENTATION, AND EQUITY

With the above criteria in mind, please comment on any particular strengths in this material.

With the above criteria in mind, please comment on any particular weaknesses in this material.

RECOMMENDATION

After reviewing this material with the above criteria for science content and presentation in mind, I would:

_______ highly recommend this material for inclusion in *Resources for Teaching Elementary School Science*.

_______ recommend this material for inclusion in *Resources for Teaching Elementary School Science*.

_______ recommend this material for inclusion in *Resources for Teaching Elementary School Science* **with reservations**.

Primary reason for reservations: ____

____

____

_______ **not** recommend this material for inclusion in *Resources for Teaching Elementary School Science*.

Primary reason for rejection: ____

____

____

Reviewer: ____

THE INDEXES

The seven indexes that follow are designed to allow easy access to the information, materials, and organizations annotated in this guide. For example, the curriculum annotations in chapters 1 through 4 are indexed by title, author/series, and topic. In addition, indexes on grade level and curriculum area by grade level enable readers to find materials appropriate to specific curriculum needs.

The titles of the indexes and their general focus and coverage are as follows:

- The Title Index covers curriculum and other book and periodical titles annotated in chapters 1-4 and 6-8.
- The Index of Names (Authors, Series, Curriculum Projects) covers chapters 1-8.
- The Index of Topics in Curriculum Materials covers chapters 1-4, giving major topics of each module and activity book.
- The Index of Grade Levels of Curriculum Materials by Scientific Area covers chapters 1-4.
- The Index of Scientific Areas of Curriculum Materials by Grade Level covers chapters 1-4.
- The Subject Index covers the content of annotations in chapters 6-8 (Teacher's References) as well as information on the structure and development of the guide presented in the Introduction, Overviews, and appendixes.
- The Index of Ancillary Resources (Places to Visit / Organizations) covers chapters 9-10.

Throughout the indexes, the locator numbers in italic refer to page numbers. All other references are to entry numbers.

TITLE INDEX

TITLE INDEX

The Title Index covers curriculum and other book and periodical titles annotated in chapters 1-4 and 6-8. The locator numbers used are the entry numbers of the annotations.

TITLE INDEX

INDEX OF NAMES (AUTHORS, SERIES, CURRICULUM PROJECTS)

INDEX OF NAMES (AUTHORS, SERIES, CURRICULUM PROJECTS)

The Index of Names (Authors, Series, Curriculum Projects) covers chapters 1-8 (Curriculum Materials and Teacher's References). (See the Index of Ancillary Resources to locate information in chapters 9-10.)

All references are to entry numbers.

Index of Names (Authors, Series, Curriculum Projects)

INDEX OF TOPICS IN CURRICULUM MATERIALS

INDEX OF TOPICS IN CURRICULUM MATERIALS

The Index of Topics in Curriculum Materials covers chapters 1-4. Major topics in each module and activity book are given. (See the Subject Index to locate information on Teacher's References in chapters 6-8, and in the Introduction, Overviews, and appendixes. See the Index of Ancillary Resources for information in chapters 9-10.)

Index of Topics in Curriculum Materials

INDEX OF GRADE LEVELS OF CURRICULUM MATERIALS BY SCIENTIFIC AREA

INDEX OF GRADE LEVELS OF CURRICULUM MATERIALS BY SCIENTIFIC AREA

Identical information is presented in the two grade-levels indexes. The information is simply arranged differently:

- In this index, the disciplines (Earth Science, Life Science, Multidisciplinary and Applied Science, and Physical Science) are arranged under the grades (PreK-6).
- In the Index of Scientific Areas of Curriculum Materials by Grade Level, the grades are arranged under the disciplines.

As in chapters 1-4 to which these two indexes refer, the curriculum materials for each discipline are divided in the categories core, supplementary, and science activity books.

INDEX OF GRADE LEVELS OF CURRICULUM MATERIALS BY SCIENTIFIC AREA

GRADE 5

GRADE 6

INDEX OF SCIENTIFIC AREAS OF CURRICULUM MATERIALS BY GRADE LEVEL

INDEX OF SCIENTIFIC AREAS OF CURRICULUM MATERIALS BY GRADE LEVEL

Identical information is presented in the two grade-levels indexes. The information is simply arranged differently:

- In this index, the grades (PreK-6) are arranged under the disciplines (Earth Science, Life Science, Multidisciplinary and Applied Science, and Physical Science).
- In the Index of Grade Levels of Curriculum Materials by Scientific Area, the disciplines are arranged under the grades.

As in chapters 1-4 to which these two indexes refer, the curriculum materials for each discipline are divided in the categories core, supplementary, and science activity books.

INDEX OF SCIENTIFIC AREAS OF CURRICULUM MATERIALS BY GRADE LEVEL

PHYSICAL SCIENCE

SUBJECT INDEX

SUBJECT INDEX

The Subject Index covers the content of the annotations in Teacher's References (chapters 6-8). This index also refers readers to general information on the structure and development of the volume contained in the Introduction, Overviews, and appendixes.

For references to the science content of the curriculum materials annotated in chapters 1-4, see the Index of Topics in Curriculum Materials.

The locator numbers in italic refer to page numbers. All other references are to entry numbers.

Subject Index

INDEX OF ANCILLARY RESOURCES (PLACES TO VISIT / ORGANIZATIONS)

INDEX OF ANCILLARY RESOURCES (PLACES TO VISIT / ORGANIZATIONS)

The Index of Ancillary Resources covers chapters 9-10. It refers to both the regional and the annotated listings in chapter 9, and helps readers locate information in chapter 10 on organizations.

The locator numbers in italic refer to page numbers. All other references are to entry numbers.

Index of Ancillary Resources (Places to Visit / Organizations)

CREDITS

Front cover: Design and photo illustration by Francesca Moghari; original photo by Chuck Savage, © 1994/TSM; line illustrations by Max-Karl Winkler.

Inside front cover: Rick Vargas, Smithsonian Institution/courtesy of National Science Resources Center, Washington, D.C.

Pages xvi-1: Eric Long, Smithsonian Institution/courtesy of National Science Resources Center, Washington, D.C.

Pages 8-9: Photo by Richard Hoyt, from *Involving Dissolving,* a teacher's guide in the Great Explorations in Math and Science (GEMS) series, © the Regents of the University of California and used with permission. (GEMS is a series of more than 50 activity-based guides and handbooks, available from the Lawrence Hall of Science, University of California, Berkeley, Calif. 94720.)

Page 15: Photo by Caroline Kopp, © 1993 California Academy of Sciences, San Francisco, Calif. Used with permission.

Page 49: Richard Strauss, Smithsonian Institution/courtesy of National Science Resources Center, Washington, D.C.

Page 69: Dane Penland, Smithsonian Institution/courtesy of National Science Resources Center, Washington, D.C.

Page 97: Rick Vargas, Smithsonian Institution/courtesy of National Science Resources Center, Washington, D.C.

Page 123: Rick Vargas, Smithsonian Institution/courtesy of National Science Resources Center, Washington, D.C.

Pages 130-131: Richard Strauss, Smithsonian Institution/courtesy of National Science Resources Center, Washington, D.C.

Page 135: Dane Penland, Smithsonian Institution/courtesy of National Science Resources Center, Washington, D.C.

Page 149: Rick Reinhard/© Reading Is Fundamental, Inc. Used with permission.

Page 157: Dane Penland, Smithsonian Institution/courtesy of National Science Resources Center, Washington, D.C.

Pages 164-165: National Science Center, Fort Gordon, Ga. Used with permission. (An Honor Roll Teacher nominated by the National Science Center for the Association of Science-Technology Centers award helps her students as part of a National Science and Technology Week activity for 1995.)

Page 169: National Air and Space Museum, Smithsonian Institution, Washington, D.C. Used with permission.

Page 223: Bruce Cook/courtesy of National Science Resources Center, Washington, D.C. (From NSRC Working Conference for Scientists and Engineers, San Francisco, Calif., 1993.)

NOTES

NOTES

NOTES

NOTES

EVALUATION FORM FOR USERS OF *RESOURCES FOR TEACHING ELEMENTARY SCHOOL SCIENCE*

Your evaluation of this volume will be helpful as the National Science Resources Center develops additional resource guides. Please take time after having reviewed or used *Resources for Teaching Elementary School Science* to answer the following questions. Then fold, seal, and mail the form. (Postage is required.)

1. Who, including yourself, will use this resource guide in your school or district?

_____ Curriculum specialist
_____ Department chairperson
_____ Classroom teacher
_____ Media specialist
_____ Librarian
_____ Scientist
_____ University science educator
_____ School board member
_____ Other (Please specify: ______________________________)

2. How is this resource guide to be used? Indicate your PRIMARY use with a "1" and check all others that apply:

_____ For developing curriculum
_____ For supplementing an existing curriculum
_____ For curriculum adoption
_____ For the NSRC Evaluation Criteria for Curriculum Materials
_____ For identifying enrichment opportunities
_____ As a general reference
_____ For information on publishers/suppliers
_____ Other (Please specify: ______________________________)

3. Which sections of the resource guide are most useful? Please circle the appropriate response for EACH section.

SECTION	MOST USEFUL				LEAST USEFUL	NO OPINION
Introduction	1	2	3	4	5	6
Curriculum materials	1	2	3	4	5	6
Projects past and present	1	2	3	4	5	6
Books on teaching science	1	2	3	4	5	6
Science book lists/resource guides	1	2	3	4	5	6
Periodicals	1	2	3	4	5	6
Regional list of museums	1	2	3	4	5	6
Museum program annotations	1	2	3	4	5	6
Professional associations and U.S. government organizations	1	2	3	4	5	6
List of publishers/suppliers	1	2	3	4	5	6
Evaluation criteria	1	2	3	4	5	6
Indexes	1	2	3	4	5	6

4. Any specific comments concerning the contents or format of *Resources for Teaching Elementary School Science* will be appreciated.

____

____

____

____

____

Tape here

Fold here last

PLACE
STAMP
HERE

NATIONAL SCIENCE RESOURCES CENTER
ATTN: INFORMATION DISSEMINATION DIRECTOR
CAPITAL GALLERY BUILDING, SUITE 880, MRC 502
SMITHSONIAN INSTITUTION
WASHINGTON, DC 20560

Fold here first

MAILING LIST REQUEST

If you would like to receive the biannual *NSRC Newsletter,* please provide the following information:

Name ______________________________

Title ______________________________

Address ______________________________

City, State, Zip ______________________________

Telephone __________________ Fax __________________

RESOURCES FOR TEACHING ELEMENTARY SCHOOL SCIENCE

A completely revised edition of the best-selling resource guide *Science for Children: Resources for Teachers,* **Resources for Teaching Elementary School Science** is an annotated guide to hands-on, inquiry-centered curriculum materials and sources of help for teaching elementary science. The guide annotates about 350 curriculum packages, describing the activities involved and what students learn. Each annotation also lists recommended grade levels, accompanying materials and kits or suggested equipment, and ordering information. A section of references lists books about science and teaching, directories and guides to science trade books, and magazines. The book also lists about 600 science centers, museums, and zoos; almost 300 facilities that help teachers; more than 100 organizations to obtain resources; and names and addresses of publishers and suppliers.
ISBN 0-309-05293-9; 1996, 312 pages, 8 1/2 x 11, index, paperbound, single copy, $17.95; 2-9 copies, $13.50 each; 10 or more copies, $11.95 each (no other discounts apply)

NATIONAL SCIENCE EDUCATION STANDARDS

The **National Science Education Standards** is a landmark development effort that reflects the contributions of thousands of teachers, scientists, science educators, and other experts across the country. It offers a coherent vision of what it means to be scientificalliy literate, describing what all students should understand and be able to do at different grade levels in various science categories. The book describes the exemplary teaching practices that provide students with experiences that enable them to achieve scientific literacy, criteria for assessing and analyzing students' attainments in science, and the learning opportunities that school science programs afford. In addition, it describes the nature and design of the school and district science program, and the support and resources needed for students to learn.
ISBN 0-309-05326-9; 1995, 272 pages, 8 1/4 x 10 1/2, index, paperbound, single copy, $19.95; 2-9 copies, $16.50 each; 10 or more copies, $13.95 each (no other discounts apply)

Use the form on the reverse of this card to order your copies today.

RESOURCES FOR TEACHING ELEMENTARY SCHOOL SCIENCE

(Customers in North America Only)

Use this card to order additional copies of RESOURCES FOR TEACHING ELEMENTARY SCHOOL SCIENCE and the book described on the reverse. All orders must be prepaid. Please add $4.00 for shipping and handling for the first copy ordered and $0.50 for each additional copy. If you live in CA, DC, FL, MD, MO, TX, or Canada add applicable sales tax or GST. Prices apply only in the United States, Canada, and Mexico and are subject to change without notice.

___ I am enclosing a U.S. check or money order.

___ Please charge my VISA/MasterCard/American Express account.

Number: ______________________

Expiration date: ______________________

Signature: ______________________

Quantity Discounts:

5-24 copies	15%
25-499 copies	25%

To be eligible for a discount, all copies must be shipped and billed to one address.

PLEASE SEND ME:

Qty.	Code	Title	PRICE
___	ELESCT	**Resources for Teaching, single copy**	**$17.95**
___		**Reesources for Teaching, 2-9 copies**	**$13.50ea***
___		**Resources for Teaching, 10+ copies**	**$11.95ea***
___	SCISTT	**National Science Education Standards**	**$19.95**
___		**National Science Education 2-9 copies**	**$16.50ea***
___		**National Science Education 10 + copies**	**$13.95ea***

***No other discounts apply.**

Please print.

Name ______________________

Address ______________________

City ______________ State ________ Zip Code ________

RESC

To order by phone using VISA/MasterCard/American Express, call toll-free 1-800-624-6242 or call 202-334-3313 in the Washington metropolitan area. Fax 202-334-2451.

Customers in North America Only: Return this card with your payment to NATIONAL ACADEMY PRESS, 2101 Constitution Avenue, NW, Lockbox 285, Washington, DC 20055. You may also order through your favorite bookstore, or electronically via Internet at http://www.nap.edu. All international customers please contact National Academy Press for export prices and ordering information.

RESOURCES FOR TEACHING ELEMENTARY SCHOOL SCIENCE

(Customers in North America Only)

Use this card to order additional copies of RESOURCES FOR TEACHING ELEMENTARY SCHOOL SCIENCE and the book described on the reverse. All orders must be prepaid. Please add $4.00 for shipping and handling for the first copy ordered and $0.50 for each additional copy. If you live in CA, DC, FL, MD, MO, TX, or Canada add applicable sales tax or GST. Prices apply only in the United States, Canada, and Mexico and are subject to change without notice.

___ I am enclosing a U.S. check or money order.

___ Please charge my VISA/MasterCard/American Express account.

Number: ______________________

Expiration date: ______________________

Signature: ______________________

Quantity Discounts:

5-24 copies	15%
25-499 copies	25%

To be eligible for a discount, all copies must be shipped and billed to one address.

PLEASE SEND ME:

Qty.	Code	Title	PRICE
___	ELESCT	**Resources for Teaching, single copy**	**$17.95**
___		**Reesources for Teaching, 2-9 copies**	**$13.50ea***
___		**Resources for Teaching, 10+ copies**	**$11.95ea***
___	SCISTT	**National Science Education Standards**	**$19.95**
___		**National Science Education 2-9 copies**	**$16.50ea***
___		**National Science Education 10 + copies**	**$13.95ea***

***No other discounts apply.**

Please print.

Name ______________________

Address ______________________

City ______________ State ________ Zip Code ________

RESC

To order by phone using VISA/MasterCard/American Express, call toll-free 1-800-624-6242 or call 202-334-3313 in the Washington metropolitan area. Fax 202-334-2451.

Customers in North America Only: Return this card with your payment to NATIONAL ACADEMY PRESS, 2101 Constitution Avenue, NW, Lockbox 285, Washington, DC 20055. You may also order through your favorite bookstore, or electronically via Internet at http://www.nap.edu. All international customers please contact National Academy Press for export prices and ordering information.